D0195782

Praise for *Failure*

"Vicki Alger's *Failure* is a timely and well-researched *tour de force* that should be read by anyone interested in promoting genuine educational reform in America. After delineating the long history of educational policy in America, Alger focuses on the ineluctable growth of federal intervention in education policy since the Civil War. This intervention has fallen far short of attaining pedagogical improvement. And the regulatory creep it has wrought has included political entanglements and policy mischief wrought by the U.S. Department of Education (ED), established in 1979—serving as yet another example of the classic regulatory triangle of politicians, bureaucracy, and interest groups (e.g., NEA and teachers' unions) that too often serves the self-interest of stakeholders rather than the public interest in educational attainment. Calling for the 'strategic dismantling' of ED, Alger provides constructive examples of decentralization in other developed countries and in U.S. history."

> —**Donald A. Downs**, Professor of Political Science,
> University of Wisconsin

"The strongest pro-choice arguments for school reform—more power to parents and students—can be found in the pages of *Failure*. There is indeed risk in Vicki Alger's prescriptions but no doubt about the deadly cost of inaction."

> —**Juan Williams**, Political Analyst, Fox News Channel; former
> Senior Correspondent, National Public Radio; author, *Eyes on the
> Prize: America's Civil Rights Years, 1954–1965* and *Thurgood Marshall:
> American Revolutionary*

"American schools are among the most costly in the world. Yet U.S. students are among the mediocre achievers in math, science, and other subjects. In *Failure*, Vicki Alger explains why and how substantial improvements can be made."

> —**Herbert J. Walberg**, University Scholar and Research Professor of
> Education and Psychology, University of Illinois at Chicago

"Failure offers a fresh, provocative perspective on how American policymakers abandoned the Constitution in pursuit of a misguided vision that the federal government could improve upon generations of local and state control of education. Full of revelations, *Failure* offers a comprehensive history of federal education policy together with a step-by-step blueprint to dismantle the Department of Education and move forward with school choice and competition—the two best indicators of success in Alger's informative, cross-national analysis. Nations that favor parental choice and school competition, rather than compulsion and coercion, are leading the world in student test scores. And unlike other critics of federal education policy, Alger stresses the ongoing debate—from the Founders to the 1970s—over whether the federal government had any constitutional role to play in education. The answer, for the most part, is 'NO!' but political expediency has led both Democrats and Republicans alike down the road of increasing federal control of education. Now packed with eye-opening statistics and interesting anecdotes, *Failure* couples a compelling narrative with dispiriting data on how poorly American students have performed despite increased spending. Money is not the answer, nor is central control. The real solution is choice and competition. After decades of failed 'reforms,' Alger will sway readers with her argument for abolishing the Department of Education and getting the federal government out of the education business."

—**Jonathan J. Bean**, Professor of History,
Southern Illinois University

"The analysis in *Failure* is thorough and its conclusions are supported by its documented facts. The recommendations are grounded in the reality of now, *not* yesterday, and if ignored, America's position as the world's leader in educational preparedness of its citizenry will never be reclaimed. This book is a must-read for all who still believe that politicians know more about educating children than the parents to whom they belong."

—**T. Willard Fair**, President and Chief Executive Officer,
Urban League of Greater Miami, Florida

"Back in the 1980s, Presidential candidate Ronald Reagan proposed rolling back federal control of education and sending control back to the states and the people. That effort was stillborn, but if the people who were serious about Reagan's proposal then had *Failure* as a guide they would have gotten far further. This important book digs into the facts about low-school performance and counter-productive federal aid. Anyone who cares about America's schoolchildren should read and consider *Failure* for its background information, critical analysis, and root-and-branch reforms."

—**Williamson M. Evers**, Research Fellow, Hoover Institution; former US Assistant Secretary of Education for Planning, Evaluation and Policy Development

"In *Failure,* Vicki Alger traces the history of the growth in the federal role in education in America, a role that can be seen today in the regulatory reach of the U.S. Department of Education (ED) into the entire K–12 school system and much of post-secondary education. The heart of her excellent book is a description of the major programs it currently manages, most of which she shows have been judged ineffective or duplicative of other programs or services, most of which could be eliminated, and most of whose functions she shows could probably be carried out more successfully by state or local governments. The point of *Failure* is the charge that ED has overstepped constitutional boundaries in its attempts to address the educational problems it has chosen or been given to solve, and that it has failed in its efforts. For example, despite 50 years of increased funding and layers of regulations in the Elementary and Secondary Education Act (ESEA), there has been little if any upward movement of the education needle for low-achieving, low-income students, to judge by their scores on the nation's 'report cards' since the inception of the National Assessment of Progress tests in the late 1960s and early 1970s. Yet, Congress piled on more layers of regulation for ED to administer after passing a 1,000-page bill of unknown authorship in its 2015 re-authorization of ESEA without asking ED what policies in its previous ESEA programs may have contributed to the long plateau in the quality of the education these children have received. Nor has ED done a long overdue self-analysis. Alger makes a much-needed and well-reasoned case that returning the federal role in education to state and local governments and privatizing its role may bear more success in improving public education, especially the academic achievement of these children, than the 30-year history of an unaccountable but still growing federal bureaucracy has been able to show."

—**Sandra L. Stotsky**, Professor Emerita of Education Reform, University of Arkansas; former Senior Associate Commissioner, Massachusetts Department of Education

the Republic (it was turned down). She provides persuasive evidence that more than 100 programs administered by the U.S. Department of Education should be eliminated or made private. Her book will be an invaluable source for those who want to demonstrate that the federal government has been a drag on the nation's efforts to teach children and young adults, not a boost to those efforts, as some still contend."

—**Jane Shaw Stroup**, Vice Chairman and former President, John W. Pope Center for Higher Education Policy; former Senior Fellow, Property and Environment Research Center; former Associate Economics Editor, *Business Week*

"The United States spends more per capita on education than any nation on the globe with the possible exception of Switzerland. Yet remarkably Americans have little to show for it. It often seems that more spending only yields a more profound, dumbing-down effect, and Americans should know that the history of federal policy has contributed to this dismal result. In her remarkable book *Failure*, Vicki Alger explains in graphic detail how government schools have failed the nation. Billions of dollars are spent each year to promote schools that are not teaching the young anything of value. In fact, after more than thirty years of the U.S. Department of Education, it is clear that government bureaucracies do not improve with age. The education bureaucracy is ossified through mandates, regulations and union rules. Albert Shanker, former president of the United Federation of Teachers and American Federation of Teachers, stated his belief quite bluntly: 'When students start paying union dues, I will be as concerned about them as union members.' Government schooling emerged from the belief that immigrant parents could not be entrusted with the education of their children. As Dr. Alger notes, it is time for parents to consider the obverse of this claim and take charge of the education of their children. Educational choice is the alternative to government-dominated schools and precisely the antidote to marginal schooling. In so many respects, Dr. Alger is leading the way with a book that diagnoses the bureaucratic sclerosis in education and the prescription for the appropriate reforms for the future."

—**Herbert I. London**, President, London Center for Policy Research; former President, Hudson Institute

"In *Failure*, Vicki Alger calls the Department of Education (ED) to the front of the class—and grades it a big fat F. From the very day it started impoverishing the American student's mind on 4 May 1980 (when Ronald Reagan accurately christened it 'President Carter's new bureaucratic boondoggle') people have been searching in vain to find the word 'education' in the Constitution. Three and a half decades later, Alger systematically marshals the evidence to make the irresistible case that it is time to correct this governmental overreach and abolish the ED. This landmark book should fundamentally change the landscape of education in America without ever being allowed near the curriculum."

> —**Benjamin Harnwell**, Honorary Secretary, Working Group on Human Dignity, European Parliament; Founder and Director, Dignitatis Humanae Institute

"In *Failure*, Vicki Alger provides a provocative look at the current condition of the American education system and why dramatic changes are needed immediately."

> —**Diane M. Douglas**, State Superintendent of Public Instruction, Arizona Department of Education

"I have never read such a thorough history and analysis of the evolution of federal education policy, where it started, where it went wrong, and why we find ourselves compromised by the tension between federal, state, and local these days—a tension that has created confusion in the political world and caused generations of educators to believe wrongly that only programs created and administered by the U.S. Department of Education have their best interest at heart. That our founders and intellectual ancestors, from Mill and Paine to Madison and Jefferson called for the provision of choice for parents long before there ever was a public education system is a little known but critical historical fact. Vicki Alger teaches us that a marketplace of schools dictated by parental choice and charitable support for those who had little was alive and well in our early days as a democratic republic. States varied greatly in their approaches, precisely as the Founders intended. The education system of the most recent centuries looks nothing like the original schools that were unique, rigorous, and designed to succeed. After a colorful and well-documented tour of the most important discussions surrounding education from our inception until today, we learn that the same paternalistic arguments used today against parents as the best and first decision makers for their children are also rooted in the past, among those responsible for the foundation of government schooling. The common, public-funded system of coerced education was based on the 'learned' assessment that parents were unfit to make decisions. Thus it will come as little surprise to the reader the NEA factors prominently in the evolution of the national, and later federal role that would be established, despite the Founders' intentions otherwise and only tepid support from Congressional leaders in both parties as it first began to grow. *Failure* is the definitive guide to what came before, what evolved, and what exists today in federal education policy, and offers a compelling plan for corrective action fitting for any enterprise truly interested in great education for all."

> —**Jeanne R. Allen**, Senior Fellow and President Emeritus, Center for Education Reform

"In *Failure*, Vicki Alger vividly shows and in careful detail how much damage has been done to American education—from grade school through college—by the U.S. Department of Education. Her superb work strengthens the case that this federal agency was a bad idea from the very beginning and ought to be abolished forthwith."

> —**George Leef**, Columnist, *Forbes*; Director of Research, John W. Pope Center for Higher Education Policy; former Vice President, John Locke Foundation

"*Failure*, Vicki Alger's well-documented history of federal education policy, shows that this history goes back further and is more complex than even most education experts realize. Sadly, the bulk of this federal involvement has contributed to the sclerotic education system that we have in America today. Dr. Alger's careful and painstaking chronicle shows how the road to perdition in our education system was surely paved with good intentions, but just because a policy sounds good does not mean it will be good. I hope the entire Congress, the next President, and all education policy experts read and take to heart Dr. Alger's meticulous history of the failure of federal education policy. *Failure* is a great read and shows, among its many insights, how many original opponents of federal involvement in education were eerily prescient about the failures that were to come."

> —**Benjamin Scafidi**, Director, Education Economics Center, Kennesaw State University

"More than ever before, Americans are expressing a deep mistrust in the role of the federal government in education. If you want to understand why, then read Vicki Alger's marvelous book, *Failure: The Federal Misedukation of America's Children*. From the origins of the U.S. Department of Education through an examination of the effectiveness of federal programs, *Failure* provides a sobering, in-depth, wake-up call for those concerned about the ever-increasing federal intervention in schooling."

—**Robert C. Enlow**, President and Chief Executive Officer,
Friedman Foundation for Educational Choice

"*Failure* is absolutely excellent! It successfully highlights the seminal problem we face as a free society—the education of youth. This fine book reviews historical failures of past efforts and prescribes appropriate 21st century solutions. *Failure* should be a 'must read' for anyone interested in education policy."

—**Kent Grusendorf**, Director, Center for Education Freedom,
Texas Public Policy Foundation; former Chairman, Public
Education Committee, Texas House of Representatives

"Alger's *Failure* is exceptional and provides a recipe for restoring success to American education at all levels by ending federal controls in all respects. *Hurrah* for this distinctive and eminently readable prescription of decentralization to states and localities and fostering academic competition among schools."

—**John W. Sommer**, Knight Distinguished Professor Emeritus,
University of North Carolina, Charlotte

"*Failure* takes an important look at the impact of decades of growing federal intervention in education. Alger provides one of the most in-depth assessments to date of what taxpayers and students have gotten for this outsized federal intervention in education and systematically details what we've all expected is the answer: not much. *Failure* is a thorough defense of why educational choice markets, not Washington, hold the most promise for improving American education."

—**Lindsey Burke**, Will Skillman Fellow in Education,
Institute for Family, Community, and Opportunity,
Heritage Foundation

failure

INDEPENDENT
I N S T I T U T E

INDEPENDENT INSTITUTE is a non-profit, non-partisan, public-policy research and educational organization that shapes ideas into profound and lasting impact. The mission of Independent is to boldly advance peaceful, prosperous, and free societies grounded in a commitment to human worth and dignity. Applying independent thinking to issues that matter, we create transformational ideas for today's most pressing social and economic challenges. The results of this work are published as books, our quarterly journal, *The Independent Review*, and other publications and form the basis for numerous conference and media programs. By connecting these ideas with organizations and networks, we seek to inspire action that can unleash an era of unparalleled human flourishing at home and around the globe.

100 Swan Way, Oakland, California 94621-1428, U.S.A.
Telephone: 510-632-1366 • Facsimile: 510-568-6040 • Email: info@independent.org • www.independent.org

failure

The Federal
Miseducation of
America's Children

Vicki E. Alger

INDEPENDENT
INSTITUTE

OAKLAND, CALIFORNIA

Independent Institute
100 Swan Way, Oakland, CA 94621-1428
Telephone: 510-632-1366
Fax: 510-568-6040
Email: info@independent.org
Website: www.independent.org

Cover Design: Denise Tsui
Cover Image: © iStockphoto

Library of Congress Cataloging-in-Publication Data

Names: Alger, Vicki E.
Title: Failure : the federal misedukation of America's children / Vicki E.
    Alger, Ph.D.
Description: Oakland, CA : Independent Insitute, 2016. | Includes biblio-
    graphical references.
Identifiers: LCCN 2014049002| ISBN 9781598132120 (hardback : alk.
    paper) | ISBN 9781598132137 (pbk. : alk. paper)
Subjects: LCSH: United States. Department of Education—History. |
    Education and state—United States—History. | Education—Aims
    and objectives—United States—History. | Federal aid to education—
    United States—History.
Classification: LCC LB2807 .A74 2016 | DDC 379.73—dc23
LC record available at http://lccn.loc.gov/2014049002

Contents

Acknowledgments   xv

United States Department of Education Chronology   xvii

Introduction   xxiii

PART I   The History of the US Department of Education

1   When the Constitution Was Respected:
Federal Hands Off Education   3

2   Early Steps Toward a Federal Role in Education   23

3   Twentieth-Century Proponents Make the Case for
Federal Involvement in Education   51

4   With the New Department, a Larger and Larger Federal
Role in Education   79

5   Federal Education Initiatives by Executive Order   111

PART II   Results to Date

6   Has the US Department of Education Kept Its Promises?   129

7   American Students on the International Stage:
A Mediocre Performance   163

8   How the Top Performers Do It:
Alternative Models from Across the Globe   193

PART III **Returning the Federal Government to Its Constitutional Role in Education**

9 Ending, Not Mending, Federal Involvement in Education   221

10 Dismantling the US Department of Education Brick by Brick   233

11 A Blueprint for the Next Thirty Years: Parental Choice   287

12 A Blueprint for the Next Thirty Years: Privatizing the Federal Role   317

Conclusion   329

Notes   335

References   415

Index   437

About the Author   466

Acknowledgments

OVER THE PAST several years researching and writing *Failure*, the support of my husband David was a constant inspiration that made possible its eventual completion.

Well before I began drafting the manuscript, several people provided immense insight into the scope and structure of *Failure*. I am very grateful to Carrie Lukas for her advice and guidance during the initial planning and outline stages. JuliAnna Jelinek provided indispensible suggestions and help in expanding the original manuscript outline. The many conversations we had helped make the manuscript far better than I thought possible.

I also wish to thank several colleagues and friends whose research assistance and recommendations have helped make *Failure* more comprehensive than I originally imagined. Christina Villegas's insights on the early history of American education, before the advent of government schooling, helped bring to light the overlooked and—especially from today's perspective—enviable successes of a diversified education marketplace unfettered by centralized government management. I am also grateful to Diana McKibben for her research assistance in identifying alternative models to an increasingly intrusive US Department of Education. Her suggestions helped reaffirm that our Framers were right to leave constitutional authority over education to parents and citizens in each state.

Evelyn Stacey Heil's assistance in exploring the education systems of top-performing countries helped underscore the fact that competition for students among schools, not the size or spending of any government education agency, is a leading factor in strong student and school performance. I thank her for our many conversations over the years on this subject.

During the editing stages of *Failure*, several people offered comments and suggestions for which I am very grateful. The anonymous reviewers helped strengthen the manuscript's style, organization, and historical content.

I am especially grateful to the Independent Institute and its President, David J. Theroux, for sponsoring and overseeing the entire project. In particular, I am indebted to Independent's Acquisitions Director Roy M. Carlisle and Research Director William F. Shughart II for their editorial guidance, to Shelby Sullivan for preparing the Department of Education Chronology, and to the late Publications Director Gail Saari and the rest of the talented staff at Independent for their masterly work at each stage of the book's development.

United States Department of Education Chronology

1642   The Massachusetts Bay Colony founds the first compulsory education law in the English-speaking world.

1785   Congress passes the Land Ordinance, mandating that newly created states in the Western Territory set aside land for the maintenance of public schools.

1787   The Constitutional Convention is held.

September 14   Government-controlled education is left out of the Constitution by a majority vote.

1789   The Massachusetts Education Act is adopted, requiring towns with a population over 200 to provide mandatory elementary schooling.

Boston passes its own Education Act, leading to the first city-wide system of public schools in the country.

1800s   Education reformers shift focus from trying to achieve universal education to uniform education in response to religious tensions and a rise in immigrants.

1837   The Massachusetts Board of Education is formed, the country's first state education board.

1857   The National Education Association is formed as the National Teachers Association.

1859   *February 24*   President Buchanan vetoes the original Morrill land-grant bill.

1862   *July 2* President Lincoln signs the Morrill Act into law, funding nearly 60 colleges through public land grants.

1866   *February 7* At its annual meeting the National Association of School Superintendents forms a committee to propose a national education bureau in Congress.

February 14 US Representative James A. Garfield introduces the proposal and a draft bill in the House of Representatives.

1867   The first national education department is created.

February 27 The bill establishing a national education department is passed.

March 2 President Andrew Johnson signs "An Act to Establish a Department of Education" into law.

1868   *July 20* Congress downgrades the Department of Education to an Office of Education within the Department of the Interior.

1870   *March 3* Congress again downgrades the Office of Education to a Bureau of Education within the Department of the Interior.

1914   The Smith-Lever Act of 1914 and the Smith-Hughes Act of 1917 extend the education office's reach into secondary education.

1939   The Office of Education is transferred to the newly-created Federal Security Agency.

1953   The Federal Security Agency is reorganized as the Department of Health, Education, and Welfare, which now includes the Office of Education.

1958   The National Defense Education Act is enacted. While primarily focused on higher education, this law marks the first significant federal effort directed at elementary education as well as secondary education.

1965   The Elementary and Secondary Education Act (ESEA) is signed into law, increasing federal control over education through tax-based grants. It requires regular program evaluations as a condition of funding, but this requirement is largely ignored.

1970   The ESEA is reauthorized in spite of ongoing evidence that funds are being misspent. Requirements are added that federal aid is to supplement, not supplant, state and local aid to schools. The ESEA is amended and expanded in 1972 and 1974.

1975   The Education for All Handicapped Children Act, now called the Individuals with Disabilities Education Act (IDEA), is enacted to ensure public schools provide a "free and appropriate" education to students with disabilities.

1978   College students had posted the lowest SAT scores in 20 years, yet the ESEA is reauthorized and expanded, in spite of additional evidence showing federal programs have been ineffective and costly.

1979   *October 17* The US Department of Education is established.

1980   *May 4* The US Department of Education begins operations. On the same day presidential candidate Ronald Reagan calls it "President Carter's new bureaucratic boondoggle."

1981   An ESEA reauthorization amendment is introduced, converting federal program funding into block grants, consolidating programs, and increasing flexibility in exchange for less federal aid.

1982   President Reagan unveils his plan to replace the Department of Education with a smaller Foundation for Education Assistance. Programs would be consolidated into distinct block grants. The plan was not taken up by Congress.

1983   *April 26* The Excellence Commission releases *A Nation at Risk*, documenting performance declines and deficiencies. It states, "The Federal Government has the primary responsibility to identify the national interest in education."

1984   Abolishing the Department of Education is dropped from the Republican Party Plank at the 1984 convention. The new strategy is advancing an excellence agenda through the department.

1988   The Hawkins-Stafford ESEA amendments eliminate block grants, and increase federal Title I appropriations by $500 million on the condition that schools document improvement on new state-level National Assessment of Educational Progress (NAEP) assessments. Most states set their annual improvement targets as low as possible.

1989 George H. W. Bush convenes state governors, including then Arkansas Governor Bill Clinton, for a national education summit in Charlottesville, Virginia. Participants commit to national academic performance goals to be achieved by the year 2000.

1990 Wisconsin enacts the first modern-day voucher scholarship program for low-income students in Milwaukee.

1991 Bush unveils America 2000. Under the plan American students will lead the world in math and science performance, and the high school graduation rate will reach 90 percent by the year 2000. It proposes national standards and voluntary national tests, but it is not passed.
The first charter school opens in Minnesota.

1994 The ESEA is reauthorized. President Clinton renames and expands America 2000 as Goals 2000: The Educate America Act, which links states' ESEA funding to having federally approved education plans, including annual testing and ensuring students make adequate yearly progress.

1997 Arizona enacts the first tax-credit scholarship program. Unlike voucher scholarships, which are publicly funded, these scholarships are funded by private donors who may claim credits for their contributions on their state income taxes.

1998 *April 3* US Department of Education releases *Achievement in the United States: Progress Since A Nation at Risk*. It finds 17-year-olds' math and reading performance is largely unchanged since the early 1970s. On international comparisons, American students' relative performance ranking declines as they progress to higher grades in school.

2000 Florida enacts the first voucher scholarship program for students with disabilities.

2001   *January 23* President George W. Bush introduces his first legislative proposal, a 25-page concept paper outlining the No Child Left Behind Act (NCLB). It expands Clinton's ESEA reauthorization.

2002   NCLB is enacted with strict mandates on teacher quality, testing, and demonstrating adequate yearly progress toward the goal of 100 percent student proficiency in reading and math by the year 2014.

2002   The US Supreme Court upholds the constitutionality of Cleveland's voucher scholarship program (launched in 1996) in *Zelman v. Simmons-Harris*.

2004   The D.C. Opportunity Scholarship Program is enacted by Congress, offering low-income students scholarships to local private schools.

2008   The US Department of Education releases another update to *A Nation at Risk* called *A Nation Accountable*. It calls student performance "a national shame" and concludes, "If we were 'at risk' in 1983, we are at even greater risk now."

2009   President Obama signs into law the American Recovery and Reinvestment Act (ARRA).

        July As part of the ARRA, Obama launches Race to the Top, a $4.25 billion competitive grant program. To be eligible, states must agree to join one of two multi-state consortia and adopt common K–12 standards, among other requirements.

2010   *January 7* California becomes the first state to enact parent trigger legislation, which empowers parents to convert failing district-run public schools into independently operated charter schools.

        March 30 The Student Aid and Fiscal Responsibility Act is enacted as part of the Health Care and Education Reconciliation Act, making the Department of Education the sole college student loan lender.

2011   *April 11* The US Supreme Court deems tax-credit scholarships constitutional in *Arizona Christian School Tuition Organization v. Winn*, stating that opponents' case "assumes that all income is government property, even if it has not come into the tax collector's hands. That premise finds no basis in standing jurisprudence."

April 12 Arizona becomes the first state to enact an education savings account (ESA) program. Parents of eligible students who do not prefer a public school disenroll their child, and the state deposits 90 percent of what it would have spent into the child's ESA for approved education expenses.

September 23 Without congressional approval, President Obama launches his ESEA flexibility package granting states exemptions from certain mandates, including the 100 percent student proficiency deadline, in exchange for accepting other mandates such as adopting Common Core standards.

2012 **October** Every state except four has adopted Common Core standards.

2014 Indiana, Oklahoma, and South Carolina vote to replace Common Core standards. Minnesota never adopted Common Core math standards.

2015 **December** President Obama reauthorizes the ESEA. The updated version, called Every Student Succeeds Act (ESSA), returns some power over the nation's public schools to the states. Although the ESSA would end the Adequate Yearly Progress (AYP) mandates under NCLB, which require that all students in all states make "adequate" annual progress or have the state risk federal sanctions, the proposal would keep the annual testing structure in place. Federally mandated annual testing would continue to have a real effect on local school policy, while continuing the trend of record-breaking federal education budgets.

Introduction

THE SPECTER OF federal intervention in education has been a contentious issue since the American founding and remains so today. Nowhere does the word *education* appear in the Constitution. In fact, "powers not delegated to the United States by the Constitution, nor prohibited by it to the States, are reserved to the States respectively, or to the people," according to the Tenth Amendment. Certainly, the Framers of the US Constitution never spoke of any traditional or historical partnership between the federal government and the states with regard to schooling—in fact, they were entirely silent on a federal role in education, placing it among those unenumerated powers. Speaking for his colleagues at the Constitutional Convention in Philadelphia, Gouverneur Morris of Pennsylvania argued that congressional action to advance education "is not necessary."[1]

More than 200 years later, however, the US Congress decided in 1979 to establish the US Department of Education, with considerable powers that interface with state and local policy-making. By institutionalizing the federal role in education, they seemingly validated the right of the US government to have a voice in how a student should be educated. In a time when the Constitution is under duress from many quarters, that role has been widely accepted and rarely challenged, but many opponents have spoken against the federal role over the two centuries that it has been steadily growing.

The first step took place in 1862, when President Abraham Lincoln signed the Morrill Land Grant Act, which provided federal land grants to the states for the support and expansion of agricultural colleges. When it was being debated in 1859, US Sen. James M. Mason of Virginia worried about the long-term effects of "substituting the wisdom of Congress and the discretion of

Congress in the management of domestic affairs of the States . . . All this to be done—for what? That the States may be bribed by Federal power to conform their domestic policy to Federal will."[2]

A century later Sen. Barry Goldwater objected to the National Defense Education Act of 1958, which included twelve federal mandates on the states— a regulatory pittance by twenty-first-century standards. Speaking in opposition, Senator Goldwater said that "the federal government has no funds except those it extracts from the taxpayers who reside in the various States. The money that the federal government pays to State X for education has been taken from the citizens of State X in federal taxes and comes back to them, minus the Washington brokerage fee."[3]

The legislation was adopted, foreshadowing the 1965 Elementary and Secondary Education Act, which distributed nearly $25 billion in federal dollars by 2010, each dollar laden with strings mandating state and local educational policy. Andrew J. Rotherham, a former education adviser to President Bill Clinton during the passage of Goals 2000, which mandated various student achievement outcomes, noted that "any reform you want to accomplish in Washington has to be accompanied by some sugar, some money, to buy people off . . . [it's] essentially a bribe to the states."[4]

On the heels of the ESEA came calls for a US Department of Education, intended to manage and streamline the increasing federal efforts—and investment—in education. Again, this was not without opposition. Some believed the advent of the Department of Education amounted to a swan song for constitutionally limited government. Others saw it as a necessary concentration of power to enforce and improve education nationwide. Both views are mistaken.

As citizens, we have a responsibility to scrutinize our government institutions—in this case, the US Department of Education—taking candid note of their successes and failures. How did proponents of federal intervention in education overcome the constitutional challenges? Has the Department of Education fulfilled its many promises? Is it worthy of continued existence? And if it were abolished, what would be the impact on the young people who are our future? This book hopes to answer those questions.

In the first five chapters, I chronicle the transformation in thinking and the actions that culminated in the establishment of the Department of Education, following the growth of federal involvement into the present day. Four major changes in thought about education and the role of government in providing it occurred first, and they help explain where we are now. Prior to the mid-1800s was a constitutional period marked by restraint with regard to federal involvement in education. While Congress and presidents made numerous attempts to extend the reach of the federal government into higher education, not even the most ardent advocates suggested proceeding without first amending the Constitution. That restraint dissipated by 1860, when calls intensified for federal subsidies to agricultural colleges through Morrill Land Grant Acts. When President Lincoln signed the act into law in 1862, he ushered in today's system of federally subsidized postsecondary institutions—and with barely a word of opposition.

During the foothold period that followed, a US Education Department was established in 1867, but it was downgraded and defunded within one year and reshuffled from one Cabinet-level department to another over the next century. The department may very well have languished in obscurity indefinitely absent the progressive period that followed. Progressive education theories, most notably those of John Dewey, gained ascendancy in schools of education nationwide beginning in the early nineteenth century. Thanks to those theories, schooling and teacher instruction were increasingly institutionalized and taken over by the certified teaching "experts." Progressive pedagogical theories amounted to thinly veiled socialist political agendas that viewed classrooms as laboratories—and students as revolutionary guinea pigs. Socialization—the creation of docile, tolerant creatures of the state—became the unofficial curriculum camouflaged behind a bevy of experimental reading, writing, and 'rithmetic courses.

As the influence of progressive education spread throughout the early to mid-twentieth century, it paved the way for the fourth and final major change, the education power-politics period typified by the rise of influential special interest groups, most notably the National Education Association, the country's largest teachers union. By the 1970s the NEA had abandoned its predecessors' idealistic view that education should not be polluted by politics. On the contrary, to advance its influence over education—not to mention the substantial sums funding it—the NEA became increasingly adept at flexing its political muscle to elect politicians who would push for making education a distinct Cabinet-level department. The federal government, for its part, had learned that the states seemed willing to trade federal involvement for federal dollars—so establishing such a department simply formalized more than a century's worth of practice. These two developments helped solidify the establishment of today's US Department of Education.

If the department's first thirty years of operation teach us anything, however, it's that government bureaucracies do not improve with age. On the contrary, as shown in Part II, the US Department of Education is a cautionary tale about letting government exceed its constitutional bounds and reach into children's classrooms. Chapter 6 illustrates that the US Department of Education did not fulfill its promises, despite the infusion of more and more taxpayer dollars and the intrusion of federal curricular agendas into local classrooms. At an administrative level, the federal education machine is more unwieldy than ever. Most important, American students have been performing at about the same levels since before the department was created. The proliferation of federal programs and federal funding has had no appreciable effect on how well they do in school.

Of most concern in an increasingly competitive global economy, American students are performing at mediocre levels compared to their international peers, as we see in Chapter 7. The following chapter examines educational policy and practice to shed light on what's working in top-performing countries around the world.

Based on this information, you can reach your own conclusions. In Part III, I lay out my own thoughts about what the evidence suggests. Modification—tried again and again as the twentieth century turned to the twenty-first—has made matters worse. This situation demands bold and critical evaluation, and in Chapters 9 and 10 I suggest some measures that are warranted. The analysis of the history of the US Department of Education and my perspective on the relevant politics is the core theme of this book.

What next? Chapter 11 isolates a key factor from the top-performing nations overseas: Parental choice promotes competition among schools. Having to compete for students and their associated funding introduces powerful incentives for schools to be more responsive and efficient and to focus on improving student learning because otherwise they will lose students to better schools. In Chapter 12, we see how privatizing the federal role in postsecondary education—mostly accomplished through student loans and grants—can help both the students and the institutions they attend.

Not insignificantly, this strategy also restores constitutional authority over education to citizens of the states, affirming the decision of the Founders. More than thirty years after the creation of the US Department of Education students, taxpayers, and the country are not better off—but they can be. After decades of abdicating our constitutional rights over education under the guise of partnering with the federal government, we should not be surprised that Washington continues to act as the senior managing partner. It's time to dissolve that partnership once and for all and abolish the US Department of Education.

PART I

The History of the US Department of Education

1

When the Constitution Was Respected

Federal Hands Off Education

THROUGHOUT THE COLONIAL era and the early Republic, a diversity of nongovernment schooling options existed, long before the rise of government-mandated schooling. In their efforts to encourage education during this period, presidents and members of Congress exercised a level of constitutional restraint that might seem surprising today. Even the most ardent supporters of benevolent federal involvement in education, including Presidents George Washington, Thomas Jefferson, and James Madison, insisted that the Constitution made no provision for a federal role in education and that, absent a constitutional amendment, the federal government had no authority whatsoever in this arena. That sentiment began shifting as immigration increased.

Government schooling proponents insisted that immigrant parents with foreign customs and faiths could not be entrusted with the education of their children. Only a government schooling system could educate their children with a view to preserving the public order. Such arguments were largely informed by the ideas of Horace Mann, who helped lay the foundation for free, homogenized, and institutionalized schooling managed by experts.

This chapter examines early American views of federal involvement in education and the form schooling took prior to the mid-1800s. It concludes that government-run schools failed to establish the basic order proponents promised; however, proponents did manage to establish the notion of a system of institutionalized schooling supported by government, and this notion would help pave the way for the first national education department.

Early Views on Federal Involvement in Education

Whether the federal government should have a role in furthering education had been debated since the Constitutional Convention of 1787. During those meetings, Charles Pinckney of South Carolina and James Madison proposed four distinct plans for granting Congress authority to establish a university. On September 14, days before the Constitution was ratified, such authority was denied by a majority vote of six opposed.[1] In fact, the only recorded words of objection were those of Gouverneur Morris of Pennsylvania, who stated such authority "is not necessary."

After the Constitution was ratified, proposals for establishing a national university and allowing federal funding for educational institutions were routinely debated by Congress but ultimately defeated in the absence of clear constitutional authority.[2] Plans for a national university supported in whole or in part with public funds had also been proposed by Presidents Washington, Jefferson, and Madison; however, none of their plans passed constitutional muster. Congressional authority concerning education was confined to Article I, Section 8, Clause 8 of the US Constitution, the power to "promote the Progress of Science and useful Arts, by securing for limited Times to Authors and Inventors the exclusive Right to their respective Writings and Discoveries."

In his second inaugural address on March 4, 1805, President Jefferson reported that federal costs were being contained, and progress was being made toward retiring the national debt. He looked forward to the time when a federal surplus could be divided among the states to "be applied *in time of peace*" (emphasis original) to "great objects" such as education, provided there was "a corresponding amendment of the Constitution." In other words, supporting education remained an ongoing consideration at the national level; however, the primary role of the federal government was viewed as ensuring funds to support the military, meeting its foreign obligations, and, insofar as possible, avoiding internal taxation of citizens.[3]

The importance of education in a free society is evident in President Madison's first inaugural address delivered on March 4, 1809—again with the proviso that it should be promoted within constitutional bounds. Only after affirming his support of the Constitution and his respect for the rights of the states and the people did President Madison include among his remaining guiding principles a desire "to promote by authorized means improvements friendly to agriculture, to manufactures, and to external as well as internal commerce; [and] to favor in like manner the advancement of science and the diffusion of information as the best aliment to true liberty."[4]

Thus, President Madison thought education relating to the trades and the liberal arts should be promoted in a free republic but only "by authorized means," namely, constitutional ones. In his second annual message to Congress on December 5, 1810, President Madison again urged consideration of a national university "instituted by the National Legislature" and paid for "out of the vacant grounds which have accrued to the nation within those limits." President Madison envisioned his proposed national university "superadding to the means of education provided by the several States" and asserted that "though local in its legal character, [it] would be universal in its beneficial effects." According to President Madison:

> By enlightening the opinions, by expanding the patriotism, and by assimilating the principles, the sentiments, and the manners of those who might resort to this temple of science, to be redistributed in due time through every part of the community, sources of jealousy and prejudice would be diminished, the features of national character would be multiplied, and greater extent given to social harmony. But, above all, a well-constituted seminary in the center of the nation is recommended by the consideration that the additional instruction emanating from it would contribute not less to strengthen the foundations than to adorn the structure of our free and happy system of government.[5]

On February 18, 1811, Representative Samuel L. Mitchill of New York delivered a committee report to the House on President Madison's proposal for a national university. It aptly summarizes the sentiments of the early Republic up to that time concerning the importance of education and the proper role of the federal government:

> To a free people it would seem that a seminary . . . would be one of their best guards of their privileges, and a leading object of their care. Under this conviction, the patriotic spirit of Washington led him more than once to recommend . . . an attention to such undertaking . . .

Two other Presidents have subsequently presented the subject to the Legislature as worthy of especial consideration. Authorities so respectable, in favor of a project so desirable, carry with them great weight. A central school at the seat of the General Government, darting the rays of intellectual light, or rolling the flood of useful information throughout the land, could not fail to make a strong impression. A noble and enlarged institution may be conceived to impart its pupils the most excellent instruction, and, by properly qualifying persons to be teachers and professors, to introduce a uniform system of education among the citizens. On weighing these and other advantages, it was necessary to consider whether Congress possessed the power to found and endow a national university. It is argued, from the total silence of the Constitution, that such a power has not been granted to Congress . . . . The Constitution, therefore, does not warrant the creation of such a corporation by any express provision.[6]

Congressman Mitchill goes on to note that a university located within the District of Columbia and fully funded through private means would not be unconstitutional; however, one supported even in part by public lands was not appropriate. In fact, the committee report proceeds from a finance principle that today seems foreign. Mitchill continues:

The endowment of a university is not ranked among the objects for which drafts ought to be made upon the Treasury. The money for the nation seems to be reserved for other uses. The incorporation of a university, without funds, appears a fruitless and inefficient exercise of the legislative power . . . The matter then stands thus: The erection of a university . . . is not among the powers confided by the Constitution to Congress.[7]

With that, President Madison's proposal is not taken up by the House of Representatives. Madison proposed a national university again in his seventh annual message to Congress on December 5, 1815, and was again rejected. It is significant to note that President Madison never urged Congress to act without constitutional authority. Yet President Madison persisted the following year in his eighth annual message to Congress on December 3, 1816, stating,

"The importance which I have attached to the establishment of a university within this District on a scale and for objects worthy of the American nation induces me to renew my recommendation of it to the favorable consideration of Congress."[8]

About a week later, Rep. Richard Henry Wilde of Georgia spoke for the House committee responsible for considering President Madison's proposal. He noted that in this session for the first time a bill would be introduced favoring the establishment of a national university, in part because peaceful conditions and a budget surplus made it an opportune time. He explained:

> If American invention, unassisted as it has been, already excites the astonishment of Europe, what may not be expected from it when aided and encouraged? And why should not aid and encouragement be endowed by institutions like the present, founded and endowed by the munificence of the State? . . . Under a conviction, therefore, that the means are ample, the ends are desirable, the object fairly within the legislative powers of Congress, and the time a favorable one, your committee recommend[s] the establishment of a National University, and have directed their chairman to submit a bill and estimates for that purpose.[9]

Conditions shifted dramatically over the next few months, and in March 1817, Congressman Wilde appeared before the House recommending that his committee's consideration of a bill to establish a national university be postponed indefinitely. He predicted that one day their successors would benefit "from meditating among the tombs of National Education and Internal Improvement. . . . They would learn to distinguish those things which were intended for Congress, from those, if any, intended only for the people."[10]

Schooling before the US Department of Education

While Congress was debating what—if any—constitutional role it had to play in advancing education, a variety of schools were already well established in the states. Compulsory education laws were few and far between during the American colonial period, yet a variety of schools flourished. There were common schools, supported primarily by private donations and some local taxes; schools run by churches; schools that prepared students for college; charity schools for the poor; and private tutors.[11]

Massachusetts is said to have paved the way for government-run schooling in the United States with its compulsory education laws passed in the seventeenth century.[12] Indeed, the first compulsory education law in the English-speaking world was the 1642 literacy law enacted by the Massachusetts Bay Colony.[13] Revised and expanded in 1648, it required every town's selectmen to "have a vigilant eye over their neighbors" because, it argued, too many parents are negligent in their duty to educate their children, and education is a singular "benefit to any commonwealth."[14] In 1647, Massachusetts enacted another compulsory education law, called the Old Deluder Satan Act.[15]

As the colony developed socially and economically, the government did not enforce the law, yet the number and kind of schools proliferated in tandem with the arrival of more immigrants. These schools included local schools teaching practical trades as well as private schools teaching religion and academics. In fact, by 1720, Boston had more private schools than taxpayer-funded schools. Private schools were so prevalent that by the end of the American Revolution, most Massachusetts towns had no taxpayer-funded schools.[16] Such was the case throughout colonial New England.[17] Even in Rhode Island, the most reticent of the New England colonies to adopt laws for the establishment of schools, a variety of common and private schools existed, including schools specifically for women.[18]

In the colonies outside of New England, various land grants and tax laws were passed for the establishment of common schools, but private religious schools were the norm. The Society for the Propagation of the Gospel would commonly send missionaries and ministers to teach the young throughout the colonies, and Catholic missionary schools for Indians and general parochial schools were established in Maryland as early as 1677. In fact, many of the nation's best schools were established during this early colonial period, including the Moravian schools in Bethlehem and Nazareth, Pennsylvania, and the William Penn Charter School in Philadelphia, which was open to girls as well as boys and was also free for those who were unable to pay tuition.[19]

The free, unregulated system of education that prevailed throughout the colonies was conducive to a spirit of independence and contributed to the high literacy rates that were crucial for the spread of revolutionary ideas. In fact, as education author Samuel L. Blumenfeld noted, "Out of such educational freedom and diversity came enough consensus and agreement to make possible not only the Declaration of Independence, but also the pursuit of a long difficult war against Great Britain, and the establishment of a national government based on an ingenious Constitution."[20]

Thus, in a continued spirit of educational freedom, the US Constitution made no mention of education and, by its silence on the issue, reserved such power for the people of each state. As former colonies began drafting their state constitutions during the revolutionary period, tax-supported government schools flourished alongside private schools.[21] Parents of all backgrounds—economic, social, and religious—could find a school that was right for their children, and schools, in turn, had to serve students or lose them to competing schools nearby.

Up until the early 1800s education advocates largely emphasized the importance of universal access to primary and secondary education and were less focused on controlling, much less preventing, voluntary educational efforts. Government funding for education was not considered essential to universal access. In 1776 Adam Smith explained in *The Wealth of Nations* that educational instruction benefits society as a whole and that general benefit could justify public funding for it. Smith noted, however, that an even more compelling case could be made that education and instruction should be privately financed, either by the immediate beneficiaries themselves or by private benefactors.[22]

Not long afterward, Thomas Paine appears to predict that compulsory schooling proponents would justify public subsidies for government schools by appealing to the plight of poor children. In 1791 in the section of his seminal work *The Rights of Man* entitled the "Ways and Means of improving the Conditions of Europe, etc.," Paine suggests that instead of subsidizing a schooling system, public funds should instead be provided to poor parents directly in the form of vouchers so they could send their children to schools of their choice.[23] Paine also believed the poor should not be compelled to attend schools far away from their homes: "Education, to be useful to the poor, should be on the spot; and the best method, I believe, to accomplish this, is to enable the parents to pay the expense themselves."[24]

Nearly seventy years later in 1859, John Stuart Mill elaborated on this idea in his seminal work *On Liberty*. Like Paine, Mill believed parents, not government, should be allowed to choose their children's schools—even if they are poor. As Mill explains, just because the government mandates and subsidizes universal education, it does not follow that government is the proper provider of education:

> If the government would make up its mind to require for every child a good education, it might save itself the trouble of providing one. It might leave to parents to obtain the education where and how they pleased, and content itself with helping to pay the school fees of the poorer classes of children, and defraying the entire school expenses of those who have no-one else to pay for them.[25]

Thus, for Mill, the government should be the education funder, not its provider, leaving this role to many competing educational providers.

Given the prevalence of schools and voluntary financing structures during the late eighteenth and early nineteenth centuries, few state constitutions even mentioned education. In fact, of the sixteen state constitutions that were adopted and revised between the signing of the Declaration of Independence and the close of the eighteenth century (1776–1800), only seven explicitly mentioned education.[26] They focused largely on the encouragement of learning generally—much like Article I, Section 8, Clause 8 of the US Constitution. For example, the constitutions of Delaware and Georgia briefly directed the establishment of schools for the promotion of the arts and sciences. Yet those laws were largely ignored before being formally repealed in Delaware, and Georgia's law was repealed within just three years.[27] The constitutions of Massachusetts and New Hampshire extolled the importance of knowledge, wisdom, and virtue and directed the protection and encouragement of school societies; the constitutions of North Carolina, Pennsylvania, and Vermont encouraged the establishment of pauper and low-cost private schools.[28]

This emphasis on universal access was also evident at the national level. Congress passed the Land Ordinance of 1785, which mandated that newly created states in the Western Territory set aside land for the maintenance of public schools.[29] Two years later in 1787, Congress passed the Northwest

Ordinance, which stated, "Religion, morality, and knowledge, being necessary to good government and the happiness of mankind, schools and the means of education shall forever be encouraged."[30] Massachusetts, however, was the first state to lay the foundation for government-financed elementary and secondary schools beginning with its 1780 Constitution, which stated:

> . . . it shall be the duty of legislatures and magistrates, in all future periods of this commonwealth, to cherish the interests of literature and the sciences, and all seminaries of them; especially the university at Cambridge, public schools, and grammar-schools in the towns; to encourage private societies and public institutions.[31]

Less than 10 years later, in 1789, the Massachusetts Education Act was adopted, requiring that in all communities of at least 200 people, both boys and girls should be educated in the same subjects through the elementary level at public expense.[32] While these schools were locally managed and financed, without any centralized authority mandating academic, textbook, or teacher standards, this law did help pave the way for the current system of government-run schools.[33] In compliance with the 1789 Massachusetts law, Boston passed its own Education Act that same year, which gave rise to the first citywide system of public schools in the country.[34] That Boston prototype, however, would be almost unrecognizable to modern Americans, accustomed to believing that government-run schools are more democratic than private schools. As education author Blumenfeld explains of the Boston public schooling system:

> All primary education was still private, and a child had to be able to read and write to be eligible for the public grammar school at age seven. In addition, the public grammar schools had to compete with a large number of private schools for the school-age population. Also, the crowning glory of the public system was not a school for the poor but the elitist Boston Latin School, which provided, at public expense, the classical preparatory training needed by those intent on pursuing higher studies at Harvard College. Some of its students came from the wealthiest families in Boston. Thus, the purpose of the city school system was not to insure literacy for all or to provide special educational opportunities for the poor.[35]

Furthermore, groups pushing for the perpetuation of a tax-supported common school system were often those with a vested interest, such as educators, textbook writers, publishers, and suppliers.[36]

Connecticut and New Hampshire adopted laws similar to the one in Massachusetts, while New York went a step further with generous appropriations for establishing and maintaining schools statewide.[37] Those funds, however, were intended to finance schools only in part, meaning localities continued their financial support of their schools. Likewise, private religious schools were eligible for state funding, but parents were also expected to pay tuition.[38] States at the time varied in their public school maintenance laws. Absent compulsory laws, many citizens refused to tax themselves for new public schools when private schools, including abundant charity schools, were already educating children.

Although the push for general and common school laws was strong in New England, this was not the only part of the country where nongovernment schools flourished. The six middle colony states of Pennsylvania, Delaware, Maryland, Virginia, New Jersey, and Georgia were more reticent to embrace government control of education and instead sought to encourage schools administered through church and charitable organizations.[39] Legislation in these states was more likely to make provisions only for the very poor. For example, between 1801 and 1817, Maryland passed legislation funding schools for the poor through lottery, bank, and property taxes. In 1796 Delaware created a state school fund from the profits generated by tavern and marriage licenses. This fund was appropriated in 1817, when three counties were each granted $1,000 per year to instruct poor children in reading, writing, and arithmetic.[40] Pennsylvania and other states also passed tuition grant laws so children from poor families could attend private schools.[41] In 1822, Georgia appropriated $250,000 in a fund initially created for free schools to pay private school tuition for poor children.[42]

Rhode Island, North and South Carolina, Kentucky, and Tennessee took little to no substantive legal action promoting education or the establishment of schools prior to the 1830s. Most legal proposals in these states were not approved because of a lack of interest in state-supported schools.[43] Rhode Island's constitution did not even mention education until 1842. In 1800 a group of citizens petitioned for a school law that provided state funding and required the establishment of a school in every town for instruction in read-ing, writing, and arithmetic. Opposition to this law was so great, however, that it was repealed in 1803. In 1825, a common school for poor children was permitted in Newport, and by 1828 the legislature had passed a permissive state school law, but the number of public schools remained minimal.[44] Along with schools for the poor, schools for girls and minorities were also prevalent, and not just in the North.

Although much of the South was slower to establish an organized system of public schools, a variety of schools and academies were available, and the South led the nation in founding seminaries for girls.[45] Jesuits seeking to edu-cate Indians founded the earliest schools in Arkansas. By the early nineteenth century, the territory contained a system of reputable private schools. The first school law, passed in 1829, made provisions for admitting the poor to these private schools free of charge and specified that, when funds would permit, the territory should provide free instruction for all.[46]

Because Louisiana was initially settled by French adventurers, very few schools were instituted prior to Spanish possession of the territory in 1761. Even those schools that the Spanish established were poorly attended.[47] In 1805, the University of New Orleans, modeled after the University of France, was set up to provide comprehensive education for all grades throughout the territory, but the plan was impractical and soon failed. About the same time several academies were founded throughout the territory, and legislative appropria-tions providing for tuition assistance and the establishment of new schools became common. In 1847 a free school act was passed to guarantee at least three years of schooling to all those under the age of twenty-one.[48] As early as 1714, the French and Spanish missionaries who settled Texas constructed buildings to be used for churches, forts, and schools, and the Spaniards who occupied the territory went to great lengths to educate and convert the In-dians. In 1829, the Mexican government organized a quasi-public system for the purpose of teaching reading, writing, arithmetic, and Catholic catechism, but free tuition was limited to five poor students per school. The Mexican government also granted over 17,000 acres of land to English-speaking settlers for the purpose of establishing primary schools, but only four such schools were in operation by 1834.[49] Immediately after winning independence from

Mexico, the Texas republic chartered an academy, a college, and a university. When Texas was admitted into the union in 1845, its constitution required the legislature to establish a system of public schools.[50]

In Mississippi and Alabama, early French and Spanish settlers did very little to establish or maintain schools, although private tutors were employed by wealthy planters. Toward the end of the eighteenth century, however, New England settlers established a number of private schools in both states.[51] Shortly after, the two territories began authorizing the establishment of academies funded by a mix of tuition fees, public land grants, and special legislative assistance.[52] In 1826 Mobile, Alabama, instituted a system of public schools under a special law enacted for the county. Under this law, the county school board and commissioners were authorized "to establish and regulate schools, and to devise, put in force, and execute such plans and devices for the increase of knowledge, educating youth, and promoting the cause of learning in said county, as to them may appear expedient."[53]

In Florida, there was virtually no interest in public education until 1831, when several citizens of Tallahassee founded the Florida Educational Society. Branches of the society were given the task of establishing schools in towns of the territory, but no further action was taken until legislation was passed in 1835 to authorize the register of the land office to select lands granted by Congress "for schools, seminaries, and other purposes" and required that three school trustees be chosen in each town. Each town was permitted to lease the allotted lands, and each township committee could apply the proceeds as it saw fit. In many instances this funding was handed over to a private school.[54]

Government support for public schools grew, through land grants and taxes, yet the demand for private education remained strong during this era. According to University of Colorado, Boulder, economics professor Barry Poulson,

> Private education was widely demanded in the late eighteenth and nineteenth centuries in Great Britain and America. The private supply of education was highly responsive to that demand, with the consequence that large numbers of children from all classes of society received several years of education.[55]

Such results were achieved through a highly competitive schooling climate. Private schools, including schools run for profit as well as charity schools, offered a diverse curricula ranging from vocational technical to classical college preparatory for students from all walks of life. Today Americans are debating the merits of a homogenized, Common Core national curriculum; the course offerings in American schools before the rise of government schooling were very different. According to education historian Robert Seybolt:

> In the hands of private schoolmasters the curriculum expanded rapidly. Their schools were commercial ventures, and, consequently, competition was keen. To succeed at all, they were obliged to keep pace with current educational needs, and to respond immediately to any expression of these needs. Popular demands, and the element of competition forced them not only to add new courses of instruction, but constantly to improve their methods and technique of instruction. Town schools, and others supported by public money continued their old accustomed ways. Their curricula resisted change. The public mind that conceived them could not react promptly to a developing environmental situation. . . . It did not allow the schoolmaster freedom to effect changes in a curriculum which it had designated.[56]

Still, some education advocates feared that absent a government schooling system, large numbers of disadvantaged children would not receive an education. In 1817, for example, members of the Boston School Committee wanted to phase out private schools in favor of government schools, insisting that poor parents could not afford private school tuition.

The movement in support of compulsory government-controlled schools first gained momentum in Boston as a result of the growing power and influence of the Unitarian movement.[57] Because previous common schools were run largely by Calvinist clergy members, Unitarians sought to eliminate Calvinist influence by bringing the schools under centralized state control. The Unitarians' support for public education was based primarily on their rejection of the Calvinist understanding of the nature of man and salvation.[58] They dismissed the Calvinist notion of original sin and believed instead that salvation through faith could be replaced by salvation through education. Like the philosopher Jean-Jacques Rousseau, Unitarians held that man is innately good and perfectible but is corrupted by civilization. Thus, they believed that evil is the result of poverty and ignorance and could be eliminated through education.

In formulating a plan for public education, the Unitarians were greatly influenced by the writings of the English social reformer and communist Robert Owen.[59] According to Owen, capitalism and religion create a competitive, divisive, and irrational environment. Consequently, the poor cannot be trusted to raise their own children correctly because they are the ones who are most affected and corrupted by this environment. Ultimately, Owen held that human beings can be collectively shaped into any character, but a new uniform and collective education would be necessary to achieve this goal. Blumenfeld explains that although the Unitarians rejected Owen's socialism, they were "greatly persuaded by the idea that a child could be molded into a rational, virtuous human being by education."[60] Thus, to establish a basis for a collective system of education, members of the Boston School Committee, which included several influential members of the Unitarian church, campaigned in May 1817 to establish a system of primary public education. Committee members declared that such a system was necessary because, absent a government schooling system, large numbers of disadvantaged children would not receive an education. Yet the committee's own survey results revealed that, on the contrary, 96 percent of the city's children already attended school. Further, its survey underscored that even without mandatory attendance laws, the overwhelming majority of parents willingly paid for private instruction, and private charity schools abounded, enrolling children from families who could not afford to pay anything toward their education.[61] In spite of such findings, the idea of government-run schooling became increasingly popular.

God, Mann, and the Rise of Government Schooling in the States

Public school advocates launched a vigorous press campaign that ultimately succeeded in convincing Boston city officials to create a new government-run schooling system instead of working with existing private schools. As Blumenfeld explains:

> The promoters of the public primary schools focused their attention on the several hundred poor and delinquent children who were not in school. What [are] these children doing, they asked. Who has charge

of them? Where do they live? Why are they not in school? They warned that unless these children were rescued from neglect, they would surely become the criminals of tomorrow, and their cost to society would be far greater than the cost of public primary schools. What is curious about this campaign is that the promoters never suggested that perhaps the city might subsidize the tuition of children whose parents could not afford to send them to the dames' schools, thereby saving the taxpayers the cost of an entire public primary system. What they insisted on was an expansion of the public system to include the primary grades, and they would not settle for anything less. Their persistence paid off.[62]

These arguments, of course, foreshadowed the ones national education department advocates successfully used fifty years later. As of 1820, only around one in five Boston school children attended public schools, indicating the prevalence of private schools. Yet around this time a small group of schooling reformers petitioned the city government to have government-funded public schools replace private schools, insisting that poor families couldn't afford the tuition. In response, the Boston School Committee was formed and conducted a survey that ultimately found 96 percent of the city's primary students were already enrolled in schools—even though the vast majority of the city's schools were private and there were no compulsory school attendance laws. The survey revealed that most Boston parents were willing to pay out-of-pocket tuition, and charity schools accepted students whose parents could not afford to pay tuition. Undeterred, reformers and the local press focused on the 4 percent of children not in school to pressure the city government to create a Primary School Board to oversee a newly created system of government-funded schools throughout the city rather than allow local governments to subsidize private-school tuition for students from poor families.[63] Yet Boston was not an isolated instance.

In eleven states, virtually all minor children were already receiving an education without a government schooling system. Support for government schools was strongest among the wealthy, not the middle- and low-income families who stood to gain from publicly subsidized free government schools.[64] Recognizing this, by the 1830s reformers shifted their focus from universal education to the provision of a uniform education. A universal and uniform

government schooling system was considered the most practical way to counteract the increasing diversity of students and schools, which many reformers
believed threatened social cohesion.[65] Thus the notion of school as a benefit for
the schooled began a 180-degree shift. Beginning around this time, schooling came to be viewed as less about enlightening children and more about
teaching compliance with national values and protecting society.[66] Preserving
democracy through a universal, uniform system of government-run schools
was therefore considered integral to preserving democracy itself. Across the
Atlantic in Europe, many countries had begun implementing state-run schooling systems starting in the early 1800s. While Holland was the first country
to do so, the Prussian model had the most influence in the United States.[67]
Early American government schooling advocates, influenced by the Prussian
model, had only limited success in implementing a similar system—at first.
That changed with Horace Mann, who is credited as the father of American
public education.

As president of the Massachusetts State Senate, Mann was a key figure in
creating the country's first state education board, in 1837. Later that year, he
was appointed board secretary and served until 1848.[68] Mann favored the centralized Prussian education model designed to provide instruction in religious
doctrine and maintain the social structure in Germany's Protestant states.[69] It
was popularized by French philosopher Victor Cousin in his 1833 work, *Report
on the Condition of Public Instruction in Germany, and Particularly Prussia.* According to Cousin, the Prussian system was entirely state-controlled from the
lower grades through university.[70] The state supervised the training of teachers,
made school attendance compulsory, punished parents for withholding their
children from school, and aimed to make curricula and instruction uniform.
In Cousin's opinion, this public schooling system was "a prime example of
the superiority of centralized authority."[71] Such centralization, however, was
incompatible with the republican principles of the American Founders. For
this reason, Mann sought to give the government primary authority in a decentralized system.[72]

In sharp contrast to contemporary opponents of parental choice in education, Mann and his fellow education reformers had an expressly religious
purpose for establishing government schools: to protect a secularized Protes-

tantism against the corrupting influence of the growing Catholic immigrant population.[73] Opponents countered that centralized government control of schooling violated the principles of republican government, which gave priority to the rights of parents to educate their children in their own beliefs and traditions. Yet Mann's predecessors had already begun laying the foundation of a universal, uniform government schooling system for the good of the public order.

In 1826 government schooling advocates such as Massachusetts Congressman James G. Carter insisted that government had to assume control over schools to assure its own preservation. "The ignorant must be allured to learn, by every motive which can be offered to them," according to Carter. "And if they will not thus be allured, they must be taken by the strong arm of government and brought out, willing or unwilling, and made to learn, at least, enough to make them peaceable and good citizens."[74] Samuel Harrison Smith, a prominent Philadelphia literary publisher, advanced a similar sentiment in his award-winning late eighteenth-century essay for the American Philosophical Society. It is a national "duty to superintend and even to coerce the education of children," he said. "High considerations of expediency not only justify but dictate the establishment of a system which shall place under a control, independent and superior to parental authority, the education of children."[75] Samuelson shared his award with former surgeon general of the Continental Army Benjamin Rush, who vigorously campaigned for public schooling in Pennsylvania. "Our schools of learning, by producing one general and uniform system of education, will render the mass of the people more homogeneous and thereby fit them more easily for uniform and peaceable government," he wrote in 1786.[76]

The poor were not the only targets for advocates of coerced government schooling. Immigrants, Irish Catholic immigrants in particular, were considered an ominous threat to the public order. Starting in 1820, Irish Catholic immigration increased rapidly, reaching 4 million by the early twentieth century.[77] Writing for *The Massachusetts Teacher* in 1851, editor William D. Swan likened immigrants to pollutants of America's once pure rivers. Absent a means of purification, it would have been better, according to Swan, "that when our fathers declared these United States free and independent, they had, at the same time, established a rigid non-intercourse with the rest of the world." Swan elaborated on the need for compulsory government schooling of immigrants, explaining:

> Our chief difficulty is with the Irish. . . .With the old not much can be done; but with their children, the great remedy is EDUCATION. The rising generation must be taught as our own grown children are taught. We say must be, because in many cases this can only be accomplished by coercion. In too many instances the parents are unfit guardians of their own children. If left to their direction the young will be brought up in idle, dissolute, vagrant habits, which will make them worse members of society than their parents are; instead of filling our public schools, they will find their way into our prisons, houses of correction and almshouses. Nothing can operate effectually here but stringent legislation, thoroughly carried out by an efficient police; the children must be gathered up and forced into school, and those who resist or impede this plan, whether parents or priests, must be held accountable and punished.[78]

Starting in the 1850s, proponents of government schooling exploited nativist sentiment—especially anti-Catholic sentiment—to hasten the adoption of state constitutional provisions against using public funds for private, religiously affiliated schools.[79] Such provisions were referred to as Blaine amendments, named for Speaker of the House James G. Blaine (R-Me.).[80] While Congress defeated a similar amendment to the US Constitution, states systematically adopted such laws. In fact, after 1857 all but four states admitted to the Union had Blaine amendments in their constitutions prohibiting public funds going directly to religious schools.[81]

Mann's public school vision of transforming immigrants' children into proper citizens was a perfect fit for the prevailing wisdom about government's role in education and was heavily influenced by Cousin. Mann's notion closely resembles the Prussian notion of *Schulpflichtigkeit*, literally the national "school duty" or "school obligation" of parents to send their children to government-run primary schools. Cousin explained that parents' national school duty closely resembles the Prussian idea of *Dienspflichtigkeit*, or military conscription. "Military conscription, instead of voluntary enlistment, at first found many adversaries among us: it is now considered as a condition and a means of civilization and public order," according to Cousin. "I am convinced the time will come when popular instruction will be equally recognized as a social duty imperative on all for the sake of all."[82] Yet peaceful transformation of students into citizens within the public schools was not the reality for either orthodox Protestants or non-Protestant immigrants.

Religious tensions erupted throughout the 1850s and 1860s between orthodox Protestants and Catholics, including conflicts over which version of the Bible should be used in public school classrooms and over the use of textbooks that denigrated immigrants. The Philadelphia Bible Riots of 1844 left thirteen people dead, and St. Augustine's Church was burned to the ground. A few years later Maine's Supreme Court declared it was legal for public schools to compel Catholic students to read the Protestant Bible. Elsewhere, teachers beat Catholic students who refused to read the Protestant Bible.[83] As Cato Institute education scholar Neal McCluskey has noted, "As industrialization grew during and after Mann's crusade, and as poor Irish Catholic and later southern and eastern European immigrants poured onto America's shores, public schooling's indoctrination mission became even more central."[84]

While the states were embarking on their own experiments with government-run primary and secondary schools, Congress was initiating its own experiment with a nationwide system of federally subsidized universities as it debated two Morrill Land Grant bills. They were largely advanced under the benign auspices of encouraging practical higher learning to aid commerce and industry. Within five years, Congress enlarged its experiment by approving the country's first national education department.

2

Early Steps Toward
a Federal Role in Education

THE FIRST NATIONAL education department was established in 1867, although it was treated for many years like a government stepchild. Two profound and related shifts had paved the way for greater government involvement in schooling.

At the national level, congressional lawmakers and presidents no longer confined themselves to their constitutional limits with regard to education. After decades of failing to get enough support for a constitutional amendment granting Congress express authority in higher education, proponents of federal involvement simply stopped trying. The turning point came in 1857, when Rep. Justin S. Morrill of Vermont introduced a bill to support agricultural colleges with public land grants. This bill forever changed the terms of the debate from *whether* the federal government should seek a constitutional role in education through the amendment process, to the *expediency* of such a role, regardless of its constitutionality. Congress simply acted, a shift that foreshadowed twentieth-century rhetoric about the states' constitutional authority in education as "traditionally" or "historically" primary.

Meanwhile in the states, elected officials and those with political influence were convinced that parents could not be trusted with the education of their children. What began as an impulse to ensure equal access to schooling for disadvantaged children evolved into a push toward compulsory and—in no small part thanks to Horace Mann—uniform government schooling for all children under the auspices of promoting peace and civil unity. Echoes of those arguments persisted among twentieth-century proponents of a refurbished, Cabinet-level Department of Education, who insisted that centralizing policy decisions in a US Department of Education would dramatically improve schooling for disadvantaged students, while making all students across the board better, more tolerant achievers.

This chapter focuses on the developments and debates in Congress and in the states surrounding the establishment of a national education department, examining the various incarnations the department took over the next several decades as it was de-funded, downgraded, and shuffled from one Cabinet-level department to another. By the mid-twentieth century, what was called the Office of Education had become part of the Department of Health, Education, and Welfare. There its budget, staff, and stature grew exponentially. That growth foreshadowed the restoration in 1979 of a distinct, Cabinet-level Department of Education. Paving the way, however, were the Morrill Land Grant Acts adopted more than a century before.

The Morrill Land Grant Acts of 1859 and 1862

By the middle of the nineteenth century, the idea of a single national university located in Washington, DC, had been significantly enlarged. Lacking direct constitutional authority to intervene in education, some members of Congress saw another constitutional provision as a way to advance the idea of a national system of federally funded universities.

The notion was first floated in 1841 by Captain Alden Partridge of Norwich, Vermont, who submitted a plan to Congress recommending a national system of technical colleges supported by the proceeds from sales of public lands.[1] Beginning in 1850, congressional records show it considered and rejected several related memorials, resolutions, and petitions from state legislatures as well as agricultural organizations and conventions.[2]

Jonathan Baldwin Turner is credited with promoting support for the education of farmers and mechanics as early as 1851 in a speech delivered at Granville, Putnam County, Illinois, calling for a "Plan for an Industrial University for the state of Illinois."[3] Turner expanded his Granville Plan in 1852 by recommending the establishment of a national system of agricultural and technical colleges supported by federal grants of public land.[4] This plan was proposed to the Illinois General Assembly later that year, and on February 8, 1853, the Illinois General Assembly adopted a formal resolution asking Congress for "the liberal endowment of a system of industrial universities, one in each state of the Union."[5]

By this time, the schooling debates had begun to focus on Article IV of the Constitution, Section 3, Clause 2: "The Congress shall have Power to dispose of and make all needful Rules and Regulations respecting the Territory or other Property belonging to the United States; and nothing in this Constitution shall be so construed as to Prejudice any Claims of the United States, or of any particular State."[6]

On December 14, 1857, Rep. Justin Smith Morrill introduced a bill donating these public lands to the states and territories to "provide colleges for the benefit of agriculture and the mechanic arts."[7] On April 20, 1858, he introduced a substitute bill, which called for the federal government to aid the states (not territories) in establishing or supporting agricultural and mechanical colleges with donations of public land located within their respective borders. The donations would amount to 20,000 acres for each senator and representative a state had in Congress. States with no public land within their borders were to receive land scrip equal to that amount, which they could sell to raise funds for the support or establishment of such colleges.[8] Whether, or to what extent, Morrill based his bill on Turner's Granville plan is uncertain. Nevertheless, the Morrill land-grant bills introduced in 1857 and 1861 were similar.

The original Morrill land-grant bill narrowly passed the House on April 22, 1858, by a vote of 105 to 100.[9] In the following session on February 7, 1859, it passed in the Senate by a slim margin, 25 senators in favor and 22 opposed.[10] On February 24, 1959, however, President James Buchanan vetoed the bill.[11] Far from being a modest proposal, Morrill's bill would have awarded more than six million acres of land worth nearly $7.6 million, according to official estimates at the time.[12] To put the sheer scope of his plan into perspective, Morrill's bill called for a federal donation of land roughly equivalent to the size of present-day Vermont, his home state, and costing about double that state's 2010 total annual higher education expenditures, $99 million.[13]

Two years later on December 16, 1861, Representative Morrill introduced a slightly modified federal land-grant bill for agricultural colleges.[14] It increased the land donations to the states from 20,000 acres to 30,000 acres for each senator and representative a state had in Congress. The colleges to be supported included those teaching "military tactics" as well as agriculture and mechanics. In addition, annual reports would be submitted by the states to the secretary of the interior instead of a new officer in the Patent Office.[15]

Unlike its predecessor, the bill encountered little resistance. By the time Representative Morrill introduced his new land grant bill, the Civil War had broken out, and thirteen states had seceded, which dramatically minimized opposition in Congress.[16] The second Morrill land-grant bill passed both houses of Congress by wide margins, even though the House Committee on Public Lands recommended that it should not pass.[17] The bill passed the Senate on June 10, 1862, by a vote of 32 in favor and 7 opposed.[18] One week later the House followed suit, with 90 votes in favor and 25 votes opposed.[19] President Lincoln signed the Morrill Act into law on July 2, 1862.[20] At that time, nearly sixty colleges were funded by these land grants.[21] Today, more than 100 colleges and universities are part of the country's land-grant university system.[22]

The Morrill land-grant bills generated extensive and heated debate about their constitutionality and helped establish an enduring precedent of federal involvement in education. In fact, nearly a century later, education historian Harry Kursh noted that the Morrill Act of 1862 has been called the "first real Federal role in education, the first divergence from Constitutional intent."[23] The reaction of Sen. James S. Green of Missouri to the land-grant bill supports that view.

> We have lived in this Government, under the original founders, under their immediate successors, and from step to step, from 1789 down to the present period of time, and this is the first time that a serious effort has been made to endow agricultural colleges by a donation from the Federal Treasury. We are now acting upon innovation, upon departure from the principles bequeathed to us by our fathers, and we ought to know well the ground we tread upon before we take the fatal step . . . if we have accomplished so much in the last half century without any such institutions as this, and without any such aid as this, how much may we still accomplish if we fail to give now? Is it not dangerous to tamper with a subject that has progressed so rapidly, more rapidly than any country where agricultural colleges have been established?[24]

Morrill's Precedents and the Constitution

Representative Morrill was convinced that "the power of Congress to dispose of the public lands at its discretion is plain, absolute, and unlimited."[25] Nearly a century of precedent undermined his claim, however—including the very authorities Morrill invoked on behalf of his land-grant bill.

A careful review of the precedents Representative Morrill cited to promote his land-grant bill reveals that none of them would have advanced education at the expense of the Constitution. Until this point, Congress had confined itself to Article I, Section 8, Clause 8 of the US Constitution, which limits its power over education to "securing for limited Times to Authors and Inventors the exclusive Right to their respective Writings and Discoveries." Likewise, presidents had urged Congress, unsuccessfully, to support a constitutional amendment granting broader federal authority concerning education. Yet no president up to this time had ever urged Congress to assume such authority absent an amendment to the Constitution.

During his first annual message to Congress on January 8, 1790, President George Washington devoted particular attention to the advancement of knowledge alongside "the many interesting objects which will engage your attention," including defense, foreign affairs, naturalization, and common currency.[26] "The advancement of agriculture, commerce, and manufactures, by all proper means will not, I trust, need recommendation." For President Washington, however, it was an open question what role, if any, Congress could play. Thus he concluded his first address stating only that the matter "will be well worthy of a place in the deliberations of the Legislature," especially since similar proposals calling for federal aid for established institutions and congressional authority to found a national university had been defeated during the Constitutional Convention of 1787.[27] Just a few months after his first address, the House of Representatives heard a motion by Rep. William L. Smith of South Carolina to refer President Washington's suggestion to a select committee. The debate that ensued is instructive.

Rep. Michael J. Stone of Maryland objected, wondering "what part of the Constitution authorized Congress to take any steps in a business of this kind." He noted that Congress already encourages learning through the powers authorized in Article I, Section 8, Clause 8, adding that "this is going as far as we have power to go by the Constitution." Rep. Roger Sherman of Connecticut concurred, recalling that Congress was denied the authority to found a national university in the Constitutional Convention and that "this power should be exercised by the States in their separate capacity." Rep. John Page of Virginia, however, disagreed stating his belief that Congress did, in fact, have the right to promote science and literature. A select committee would help settle the matter, and if it were determined that Congress did not have such authority, he "should consider the circumstance as a very essential defect in the Constitution, and should be for proposing an amendment." The House, however, adjourned without a decision on the motion.[28]

President Washington's final address in 1796 again prompted debate in the House of Representatives, along with a distinct plan proposed by James Madison just days afterward, to allow a privately financed Memorial from the Commissioners of the Federal City in support of a university there. Many members feared that plans proposed by President Washington and Madison would at some point require congressional funding of a national university. The remarks of Rep. John Nicholas of Virginia capture the tenor of those discussions. "Again: the President has recommended the measure. I would not be supposed to want a due respect either for those Commissioners or for the President; but, merely because recommended by them, we are not warrantable in adopting it."[29] The House delayed further action on both President Washington's plan for a congressionally funded national university and Madison's proposal for a privately funded university located within the District of Columbia, indicating that a majority of representatives—albeit a slim majority with 37 favoring postponement, 36 opposed—preferred to err on the side of caution with regard to federal involvement in education.[30]

In addition to President Washington, Representative Morrill also invoked the authority of President Thomas Jefferson to garner support for his federal land-grant plan, citing the following remarks from his sixth annual message to Congress on December 2, 1806:

> Education is here placed among the articles of public care, not that it would be proposed to take its ordinary branches out of the hands of private enterprise, which manages so much better all the concerns

to which it is equal; but a public institution can alone supply those sciences which, though rarely called for, are yet necessary to complete the circle, all the parts of which contribute to the improvement of the country, and some of them to its preservation. . . . The present consideration of a national establishment for education, particularly, is rendered proper by this circumstance also, that if Congress, approving the proposition, shall yet think it more eligible to found it on a donation of lands, they have it now in their power to endow it with those which will be among the earliest to produce the necessary income. This foundation would have the advantage of being independent on war, which may suspend other improvements by requiring for its own purposes the resources destined for them.[31]

There are several important distinctions, however, between President Jefferson's proposal and Morrill's land grant bill. First, President Jefferson's remarks about the desirability of supporting education through federal funding or land occurred within the context of how best to expend federal surpluses. In his 1859 veto message, President Buchanan was clear that the national treasury was struggling to meet government obligations at the time and that it simply could not afford to donate land that could generate fair-market revenue for expressly defined functions.[32] Second, President Jefferson did not let his passion for promoting education cloud his practical judgment. In his 1806 message to Congress, he warned that war with any number of European nations could erupt, and so funding national security was President Jefferson's stated top priority.[33] As Sen. Clement C. Clay, Jr., of Alabama objected, Representative Morrill made no mention of President Jefferson's caveat that "I suppose an amendment to the constitution, by consent of the States, necessary, because the objects now recommended are not among those enumerated in the constitution, and to which it permits the public moneys to be applied."[34]

In passing, Representative Morrill named Presidents Madison, James Monroe, and John Adams as additional authorities lending credibility to his federal land-grant scheme. In the interest of time, however, he omits referring to their remarks on the subject. Like President Jefferson, each of those presidents ardently supported the expansion of education. Yet Madison, Monroe, and Adams spoke even more forcefully than President Jefferson about preserving constitutionally limited government first and foremost. Like Jefferson, Madison was constitutionally circumspect when it came to congressional involvement in education. Such circumspection is especially admirable since Madison proposed more defeated or ignored educational proposals than any other authority Morrill named as precedents.

President Monroe did indeed recommend that Congress be granted the power to establish institutions of learning. However, Monroe was clear during his first annual message on December 2, 1817, that he did not believe Congress currently possessed such authority under the Constitution. He recommended instead that an amendment be referred to the states and was confident that given the chance, they would approve it.[35] The states, however, were never given such an opportunity. In fact, just two years later in 1819, Rep. Mark Hill of Massachusetts moved to refer a constitutional amendment to the people granting Congress express authority to establish a national university. That motion was defeated.[36]

While Representative Morrill referenced Madison, Monroe, and Adams only in passing as compelling authorities for his federal land-grant plan, he insisted that President Andrew Jackson "was the steadfast friend of agriculture" and claimed, "There can be no question that General Jackson . . . would have approved of grants of land to all the States for the benefit of agricultural colleges."[37] Morrill cites select instances in which President Jackson approved specific land grants, but those examples hardly erase doubts about his supposed support for a federal land-grant plan for agricultural colleges. In fact, Sen. George E. Pugh of Ohio made a compelling case to the contrary when he invoked the May 3, 1854, veto message of President Franklin Pierce on a similar federal land-grant bill for insane asylums.[38] In it President Pierce recalled President Jackson's veto message of July 10, 1832, where he affirmed, "Nor is our Government to be maintained or our Union preserved by invasions of the rights and powers of the several States. In thus attempting to make our General Government strong we make it weak. Its true strength consists in leaving individuals and States as much as possible to themselves . . . not in binding the States more closely to the center, but leaving each to move unobstructed in its proper orbit."[39]

The constitutionality of federal intervention in internal improvements, including education, is paramount—regardless of how worthwhile or expedient a particular improvement plan may seem. For this reason, President Jackson explained, "If it be the wish of the people that the construction of roads and canals should be conducted by the Federal Government, it is not only highly expedient, but indispensably necessary, that a previous amendment of the Constitution . . . should be made." Specifically, for President Jackson, such an amendment should define and restrict federal power "with reference to the sovereignty of the States." President Jackson went on to conclude, "When an honest observance of constitutional compacts can not be obtained from communities like ours . . . the degrading truth that man is unfit for self-government [must be] admitted. And this will be the case if *expediency* be made a rule of construction in interpreting the Constitution" (Emphasis original).⁴⁰

Thus the precedents and authorities Representative Morrill invokes in support of his federal land-grant bill all urge constitutional circumspection and recognition that Congress is limited to expressly enumerated powers. In contrast, Morrill concluded his remarks on the House floor by claiming, "If we have the power to make special grants, in particular and individual cases, it would be more just and expedient, in its general application."⁴¹

While Representative Morrill at least attempted to make his land-grant bill appear constitutional, his fellow proponent, Sen. Jacob Collamer of Vermont, dispensed with any such pretense altogether. "If Congress has the power to pass the law in question, the court says it is constitutional . . . that is a test by which we can ascertain whether a bill is constitutional for us to pass," as Collamer put it. "Everything else in this case is a question of expediency, of propriety."⁴² Such casual disregard represents a stark departure from the constitutional circumspection of the Framers and early American statesmen. It also foreshadows the more open disregard, and in some cases outright hostility, for constitutionally limited government expressed by proponents of a national education department just a few years later in 1867.

Representative Morrill prefaced his remarks on the constitutionality of his federal land-grant plan with an observation about its expediency. "Concerted effort is necessary to educate and elevate whole nations," he insisted. "We do not ask for constant and persistent outlay and guidance; but a recognizance for once, and in the most convenient mode, of the propriety of encouraging useful knowledge among farmers and mechanics, in order to enlarge our productive power."⁴³ Morrill also quoted Adam Smith on the importance of "solid improvements of agriculture" to minimize the "precarious and uncertain possession" of commercial and manufacturing capital.[44] Yet Morrill failed to mention Smith's more germane remarks in *The Wealth of Nations* concerning "Expenses of the Institutions for the Education of Youth." These remarks counter Morrill's claims that endowments of federal lands to the states are indeed "the most convenient mode" for "encouraging useful knowledge," much less educating and elevating "whole nations."

As Smith explained, "For a very small expense the public can facilitate, can encourage, and can even impose upon almost the whole body of the people, the necessity of acquiring the most essential parts of education." Even so, according to Smith, "it still is not necessary that it should be derived from that general revenue of society." Endowments in other countries, insisted Smith, "not only corrupted the diligence of public teachers, but have rendered it almost impossible to have any good private ones." Endowing colleges and universities also subverts scientific advancement and innovation, said Smith:

> In general, the richest and best endowed universities have been the slowest in adopting those improvements, and the most averse to permit any considerable change in the established plan of education. Those improvements were more readily introduced into some of the poorer universities, in which the teachers . . . were obliged to pay more attention to the current opinions of the world.

In brief, "Those parts of education, it is to be observed, for the teaching of which there are no public institutions, are generally the best taught."[45]

Education historian Robert Seybolt made a similar observation about publicly funded elementary and secondary schools in the preceding chapter. Moreover, President Buchanan echoed Smith's objections to Representative Morrill's land grant plan in his veto message of February 24, 1859.

> It is extremely doubtful, to say the least, whether this bill would contribute to the advancement of agriculture and the mechanic arts. . . . The Federal Government . . . has confessedly no constitutional power to follow [the land donation] into the States and enforce the application of the fund to the intended objects.[46]

Worst of all according to Buchanan, federal donations to the states "would remove the most wholesome of all restraints on legislative bodies—that of being obliged to raise money by taxation from their constituents—and would lead to extravagance, if not to corruption. What is obtained easily and without responsibility will be lavishly expended."[47]

The State-Federal Relationship

Beyond the constitutional issues, opponents of Morrill's federal land-grant bill challenged the implication that Congress, and the federal government in general, is superior to the states. Senator Clay objected that "this bill treats the States as agents instead of principals, as the creatures, instead of the creators of the Federal Government; [it] proposes to give them their own property, and to direct them how to use it . . . It thus transposes the relations of the Federal and State governments."[48] Clay concluded that "the powers asserted in this bill are hostile to the reserved rights and the true interests of the States."[49]

Senator Clay refers first to Madison's remarks in *Federalist* No. 39, stating that "the proposed government cannot be deemed a NATIONAL [sic] one; since its jurisdiction extends to certain enumerated objects only, and leaves to the several States a residuary and inviolable sovereignty over all other objects."[50] Further, according to Madison in *Federalist* No. 45, "The State governments may be regarded as constituent and essential parts of the federal government; whilst the latter is nowise essential to the operation or organization of the former."[51] Next, Clay highlighted Madison's remarks in *Federalist* No. 40: "We have seen that in the new government, as in the old, the general powers are limited; and that the States, in all unenumerated cases, are left in the enjoyment of their sovereign and independent jurisdiction."[52] Then Senator Clay combined remarks made by Madison in *Federalist* Nos. 14 and 46: "Its jurisdiction is limited to certain enumerated objects, which concern all the members of the republic, but which are not to be attained by the separate provisions of any. . . . The federal and State governments are in fact but different agents and trustees of the people, constituted with different powers, and designed for different purposes."[53] Next, Clay quoted Madison in *Federalist* No. 45: "The powers delegated by the proposed Constitution to the federal government are few and defined. Those which are to remain in the State governments are numerous and indefinite."[54] In conclusion, Senator Clay turned to Alexander Hamilton's remarks in *Federalist* Nos. 23 and 17: "The principal purposes to be answered by union are these: the common defense of the members; the preservation of the public peace as well against internal convulsions as external attacks; the regulation of commerce with other nations and between the States; the superintendence of our intercourse, political and commercial, with foreign countries." In other words, in Hamilton's view, establishing a national system of universities was not the proper role of the federal government. Moreover, federal "supervision of agriculture and of other concerns of a similar nature . . . which are proper to be provided for by local legislation . . . would be as trouble-some as it would be nugatory."[55]

Opponents of the Morrill bill attempted to follow those precedents. Sen. James M. Mason of Virginia objected that "the assent of the States is asked by this bill to become the recipients of the alms of the Federal Government . . . [and] if they do not adopt the policy of Congress for the promotion of agri-culture, then they are not allowed to become the recipient of the alms of the Government."[56] Far from being a modest proposal, Mason noted, the Morrill legislation would require the creation of an entirely new agency because it required annual reports from the states on their agricultural colleges—one of the stated functions of the soon-to-be enacted national education department. An early iteration of the bill assigned responsibility for reviewing the reports to "a department of the Patent Office, the existence of which, up to this day at least, I trust, is unknown to the law." Mason speculated:

> This, I suppose, is the beginning of it, shadowing forth an event which is yet to come—"The agricultural department of the Patent Office!" . . . for the purpose of substituting the wisdom of Congress and the discre-tion of Congress in the management of domestic affairs of the States . . . All this to be done—for what? That the States may be bribed by Federal power to conform their domestic policy to Federal will. This is unques-tionably the extent to which the bill goes . . . to substitute their wisdom and intelligence in the domestic policy of the States for the wisdom and intelligence of the States themselves.[57]

Senator Pugh and Sen. James A. Bayard of Delaware likewise took particular exception to the Morrill bill's provisions requiring the states to dispose of donated lands as the federal government proscribed. "If you choose to grant public lands to the States . . . do so," argued Pugh, "but leave it to the wisdom of the States how to apply it, and not undertake to fetter them by conditions imposed in this bill . . . this attempt by Congress to assume control over the legislation of the States . . . is altogether the worst feature of the bill."[58] Bayard concurred, noting that "if we are to violate the Constitution of the United States under a general grant of the power of disposing of the public lands, by appropriating them for purposes not within our jurisdiction . . . give it away unconditionally, and trust their wisdom in the disposition of it."[59] Indeed, similar presumption about superior federal wisdom would permeate appeals for a national education department just a few years later.

Opponents of Morrill's land-grant bill also objected to another strain of federalism. Senator Pugh predicted that if the bill were accepted by state legislatures, it would be akin to them making a treaty with the federal government "as forever to supersede them . . . it is just as atrocious a violation of the organic law as if it were the act of an armed usurper."[60] Similarly, Senator Clay likened the Morrill bill to a bribe, noting that it would represent "a long step towards the overthrow of this truly Federal and the establishment of a really National Government. If Congress may provide for and direct the education of the people of the State, why not supply all their physical as well as moral wants?"[61]

In vetoing the first land grant bill, President Buchanan had warned about the dangers it posed to relations between the federal and state governments. Specifically, according to President Buchanan:

> The Constitution is a grant to Congress of a few but most important enumerated powers. . . . All other powers are reserved to the States and to the people. For the harmonious and efficient working of both, it is necessary that their several spheres of action should be kept distinct from each other. This alone can prevent conflict and mutual injury. *Should the time ever arrive when the State governments shall look to the Federal Treasury for the means of supporting themselves and maintaining*

their systems of education and internal policy, the character of both Gov-
ernments will be greatly deteriorated (Emphasis added).[62]

Despite all these objections, Representative Morrill's argument ultimately
persuaded a majority in Congress that the federal government possessed authority enough to encourage a national system of land-grant colleges. Shortly
thereafter proponents would use similar arguments to establish a national education department to advance a uniform system of public elementary schools
throughout the country.

An Act to Establish a Department of Education, 1867

As these events unfolded in Congress, state governments were building
public school systems with a core mission of "Americanizing" foreign-born
students, during a period that coincided with Reconstruction, increasing industrialization, and growing immigration. In fact, the immigrant population
roughly doubled from 1.4 million to 2.8 million between 1840 and 1859. By
the turn of the century, the number of immigrants had swelled to more than
8 million.[63] Thus the goal of schooling expanded to include amalgamating
immigrants by putting them together with native-born students, all of whom
would emerge from the government-run schooling system with a trade and
the skills to become productive wage-earners.

Looking back on these developments in the early twentieth century, leading education authority and Stanford University Dean of Education Ellwood
Cubberley wrote that the primary mission of government-run schools was not
advancing individual talents or opportunity. "Our city schools will soon have
to give up the exceedingly democratic idea that all are equal, and that society
is devoid of classes . . . and to begin a specialization of educational effort along
many new lines."[64] Specifically, he believed individuals would remain in the
condition of their birth, with no real possibility of upward mobility or better-
ment. "The employee tends to remain an employee; the wage-earner tends to
remain a wage-earner. . . . The worker in every field of trade and industry tends
more and more to become a cog in the machine," according to Cubberley.[65]

As a result, he noted, "Our schools are, in a sense, factories, in which
the raw products (children) are to be shaped and fashioned into products to

meet the various demands of life. The specifications for manufacturing come from the demands of twentieth-century civilization, and it is the business of the school to build its pupils according to the specifications laid down."[66] If students were fated for one job and could not hope to improve their lot in life, government-run schools were also charged with averting class warfare. "The danger from class sub-divisions has been constantly increasing, and more and more has been thrown upon the school the task of instilling into all a social and political consciousness that will lead to unity among our great diversity, and to united action for the preservation and improvement of our democratic institutions,"[67] Cubberley concluded.

Improving our democratic institutions, according to this way of thinking, required the distinctly undemocratic means of coercing parents—especially poor and immigrant parents—to send their children to government-run schools that would instill the proper "social and political consciousness." Cubberley defined this as "the Anglo-Saxon conceptions of righteousness, liberty, law and order, public decency, and government," which would counteract the effects of immigration. The presence of immigrants, he asserted "has served to dilute tremendously our national stock and to weaken and to corrupt our political life."[68] Reversing this trend was to be achieved by any means necessary, based on the belief that, as the Wisconsin Teachers Association put it in 1865, "children are property of the state."[69]

Given the prevalence of such thinking, it was a relatively small step to decide that states could not be trusted to fulfill their constitutional responsibilities over education and that national oversight by the federal government was necessary to ensure public order through education. Remember that during Reconstruction, the federal government had already assumed significant control of government affairs in the defeated states. Meanwhile, government schooling advocates had been pushing for the creation of the first US Department of Education.[70]

The National Teachers' Association, the predecessor of the National Education Association, had been formed in 1857.[71] Beginning with its annual meeting in 1864, the association initiated efforts to promote a national education bureau. At that meeting S. H. White of Peoria, Illinois, presented a paper titled "A National Bureau of Education."[72] In it he recommended that education be nationalized and that states surrender their sovereignty over education to a national entity, which would be better equipped to perpetuate a republican form of government and the country's general welfare. Such a bureau, according to White, would promote best practices among the states, as well as possess the necessary power and influence to improve "the national mind."[73]

At the next annual meeting of the National Teachers' Association, in 1865, members devoted significant attention to advancing a national education bureau. Andrew Jackson Rickoff of Cincinnati delivered a paper also called "A National Bureau of Education,"[74] but unlike White's conceptual vision, Rickoff's plan resembled a blueprint. On its face, the plan was "no radical innovation," as Rickoff put it.[75] "We need to ask for no higher power for the Commissioner of Education," according to Rickoff.[76] Appointed by the president, his proposed commission would compile and report information about schools from the several states and abroad. Like the commissioner of agriculture, the education commissioner would acquire and diffuse useful information and make occasional special reports if necessary.

Yet the modest responsibilities Rickoff outlined did not match his grand rhetoric about nationalizing education, including the conviction that "it is the duty of this National Teachers' Association to labor for the extension of an opportunity to acquire a good Common School education to every boy and girl in the land, white and black. . . . They, today, depend upon and look to the President and Congress of the United States for the light and liberty of education."[77] To succeed, the National Teachers' Association had to flex its collective muscle. As Rickoff explained, "What possible avenue of influence can be established between this Association and the Government at Washington? There is only one. The Government must recognize the cause of education as a part of its care, not by direct management alone, but, so far as may be, by influences of every kind, which can induce a people to regard the matters that concern it as the highest interest. A Department of Education must be established along side of the Department of Agriculture."[78] He acknowledged the National Teachers' Association would be accused of making the federal government a "missionary to propagate" a common-school system "and to interfere with the family and social arrangements of the people." Rickoff simply responded, "Well, be it so."[79]

At this same meeting, National Teachers' Association president Samuel S. Greene of Providence, Rhode Island, delivered an address called "The Educational Duties of the Hour."[80] In it he amplified Rickoff's sentiments, endorsing a plan proposed by Rev. Charles Brooks of Massachusetts for a national system of education, saying now was the time "to introduce into our Constitution the angelic agency of education."[81] This had not already occurred, Rickoff had explained, because "educational men have not pressed the consideration of the matter on Congress."[82] Whether such a system was possible, President Greene could not say, but echoing Rickoff he resolved that "here is the work to be done. And who, if not this Association, shall express positive opinions upon the best means to be employed."[83]

E. E. White put forward a similar plan, calling for a national bureau that mostly compiled data from the states about their schools and made it publicly available. Unlike Rickoff, however, White rejected the idea of a congressionally mandated national education system. Instead, he advocated conditional federal appropriations through a National Bureau of Education to "induce each state to maintain an efficient school system," similar to the inducements already offered by the federal grants of public lands for colleges and universities. This, he said, would not require any "questionable power by the general government."[84] Specifically, White claimed a national education bureau would help establish school systems "where they do not now exist, and prove a potent means of improving and vitalizing existing systems." Such a bureau would be managed "as to well-nigh revolutionize school instruction in this country, and this too without its being invested with any official control of the school authorities in the several States."[85] Echoing the sentiments of others, White argued that such superior performance would result from the fact that educators are experts. "Instead of being made a burrow for seedy politicians," White explained, the national education bureau "must be made the center of the ripest experience, and the most eminent attainments to be found among the educators of the country."[86]

Additional steps toward a national department were made at the 1866 annual meeting of the National Association of School Superintendents, where a committee was formed to craft a congressional memorial based on White's proposal for a national education bureau. Just one week after the committee's formation on February 14, General James A. Garfield, Representative from Ohio (and later president), introduced the memorial and a draft bill in the House of Representatives.[87] The legislation had three broad goals: to promote the interest of education; to help establish school systems; and to improve and vitalize existing school systems. The national bureau was to accomplish those objectives in six ways, summarized here:

1. Securing greater uniformity and accuracy in school statistics to make them reliable educational tests and measures
2. Compiling school system results to determine their comparative value
3. Compiling and publicizing experimental results in school instruction and management
4. Diffusing information about school funding, organization, maintenance, and operations
5. Helping communities avoid school organization errors and implement tried-and-true improvements
6. Diffusing "correct ideas" about the value of education concerning intellectual, moral, economic, and civic development

The National Association of School Superintendents signatories stated that "the assistance and the encouragement of the General Government are needed to secure the adoption of school systems throughout the country. . . . Indeed, the highest value of [a national education bureau] would be its quickening and informing influence, rather than an authoritative and directive control." Elsewhere, however, the signatories suggest they had greater powers in mind. "It is an imperative necessity of the American Republic that the common school be planted on every square mile of its peopled territory," they said. "The creation of a bureau of education by Congress would be a practical recognition of this great truth."[88]

As proposed, a simple statistics-gathering agency would have little influence over the states. The signatories, however, went on to "beg permission to suggest one other special duty which should be intrusted to the national bureau," namely investigating the management of federal land grants, which at the time totaled some $500 million.[89] As history has shown, the department's authority to investigate grants grew into administration of grants, both land and later funding. That development would prove critical to the national education department's growth in size and influence over the next century.

Nearly two months later on April 3, 1866, the bill returned from a select committee, which changed the title of the proposed organization from bureau to department.[90] The debates that ensued in both the Senate and the House are instructive. They were not straightforward exchanges between advocates of limited or centralized government. Instead the congressional debates reveal the conflicting opinions among actual and would-be proponents about what, in fact, a national education department was ultimately supposed to accomplish. Improving education throughout the country through a national department responsible simply for compiling and disseminating information to the states seemed a useful and constitutionally innocuous goal. Yet grandiose claims about universal education and minimum standards made in the context of establishing an education bureau indicate that advocates always envisioned a nationalizing role in education for the new bureau.

On June 5, 1866, Representative Garfield read the substitute bill (H.R. 276), which largely echoed the National Association of School Superintendents' memorandum. Its four sections are summarized here:

1. A Department of Education shall be established in Washington, DC, to gather school statistics from the states and territories and diffuse information that will assist "the people of the United States" to establish "efficient school systems" and promote the cause of education.

2. With the advice and consent of the Senate, the president will appoint a commissioner of education, who shall be paid $5,000 annually, and have the authority to appoint six clerks, paid annual salaries ranging from $1,200 to $2,000.

3. The commissioner of education shall report annually to Congress on his work and investigations, including in the first annual report an accounting of how the states have managed their federal land grants for education.

4. The commissioner of public buildings is directed to furnish "proper offices" for the Department of Education.[91]

Rep. Ignatius Donnelly of Minnesota initiated the first heated debate in the House of Representatives over Garfield's plan for a national education department. "Education for the country itself, that the entire population may rise to the level and above the level of the most favored royalties . . . [that] we may become the most enlightened people upon the face of the earth" was Donnelly's stated purpose for supporting Garfield's bill. "Is it not a shame . . . that this nation . . . should thus far have done literally nothing either to recognize or enforce education? . . . We will be told that we have left [education] to the states. Yes; and we have had rebellion as a consequence . . . Pass this bill and give education a mouthpiece and a rallying point."[92]

Rep. Samuel W. Moulton of Illinois advocated for a national education department in a similar vein. The republic, he argued, rests on the pillars of universal liberty and universal education. A national education department, he said, would be "a pure fountain from which a pure stream can be poured upon all the States. We want a controlling head by which the conflicting systems in the different States can be harmonized by which there can be uniformity, by which all mischievous errors that have crept in may be pointed out and eradicated. . . . I take the high ground that every child of this land is, by natural right, entitled to an education at the hands of somebody, and that this ought not be left to the caprice of individuals or of States so far as we have any power to regulate it."[93] All this could be accomplished, as Moulton explained, with a "controlling head" limited to as few as two clerks, which "would be sufficient to start the bureau" and "take possession of those pregnant facts, those figures, when they are brought here by the census takers."[94]

Another proponent, Rep. Nathaniel P. Banks of Massachusetts, adopted a more moderate and practical tone, insisting that he did not want "unnecessarily to concentrate power of the country here" in Washington. Instead, for $13,000 annually an education commissioner and four clerks would simply gather statistics, "nothing more than that." It would, in Banks's view, "be but an extension of the census of the people." He explained further that the proposed education department "is but temporary in nature; it is not interwoven with the government of the country so far that it cannot be dispensed with at any moment . . . failure of the appropriation will lead to the discontinuance of the bureau."[95] Nevertheless, Banks made it clear that only education would restore the general government "in perfect peace" and "in a more perfect form, even, than it has before existed."[96]

Rep. Andrew J. Rogers of New Jersey expressed shock at the scope of the proposed education department, regardless of proponents' stated assurances to the contrary. "I did not know . . . a bill of this character was before the House," Rogers noted. He then shed light on what he believed was the larger agenda behind the seemingly modest proposal for a statistics-gathering educational bureau:

> To establish here at the head of our federal affairs in Washington a bureau for the purpose of giving the principles by which the children of the different States shall be educated would be something never before attempted in the history of this nation . . . at no time in the history of this government, from the time of its first organization down to the present hour, was there ever before an attempt to establish a bureau or an institution of any kind or character at the head of Federal affairs . . . there is no authority under the Constitution of the United States to authorize Congress to interfere with the education of children of the different States in any manner, directly or indirectly . . . [the bill] proposed to put under the supervision of a bureau established at Washington all the schools and educational institutions of the different States of the Union by collecting such facts and statistics as will warrant them by amendments hereafter to the law now attempted to be passed to control and regulate the educational system of the whole country.[97]

Representative Rogers proceeded to note that every state already gathered school statistics, so the national education bureau bill actually would amount to "a centralized power . . . to tell the people of the South and the people of all the States of this Union what their system of education shall be. . . . If Congress has the right to establish an Educational Bureau here . . . [it] has the right to establish a bureau to supervise the education of all the children . . . of this country. You will not stop at simply establishing a bureau for the purpose of paying officers to collect and diffuse statistics in reference to education . . . let us take hold of the matter most thoroughly, and educate all the children of the country at the expense of the Government."[98]

Rep. Samuel J. Randall of Pennsylvania questioned the proposed national education department on practical grounds. He noted that "a bureau at an extravagant rate of pay, and an undue number of clerks collecting statistics . . . does not propose to teach a single child . . . its a, b, c's." On that basis, Randall countered the claim of Representatives Moulton and Donnelly that the country needed a "controlling head" to oversee education, noting that "to have a head without any body . . . would not, it appears to me, be of much utility."[99] Further, Randall noted the inherent futility of perpetuating American republican institutions through a department informed by foreign mores. Quoting from the work of his acquaintance and noted education author Frederick A. Packard, Randall continued:

> It is very easy to sketch a magnificent scheme of national instruction; beginning with the infant school and terminating in a colossal university; assigning a fixed term of years and a corps of teachers and professors to each grade, and drawing on the Treasurer of the United States at the close of the year, for twenty or forty millions to cover the expense. And it may be shown, moreover, that such stupendous enterprises have been successful in Holland, in France, and in Prussia. But we must never forget that with them the people depend on the government, while with us, the government depends on the people.[100]

Although Representative Randall stopped there, author Packard continued, saying, "The idea of 'Americanizing European philosophies' is as preposterous as that of oaking a pine tree, or potato-izing a head of cabbage."[101] Although unconvinced that a national education department should exist at all, Randall did propose an amendment creating an education bureau within the Department of the Interior, which already oversaw the census, borrowing the analogy used by national education department proponent Representative Banks.[102] Randall's amendment was rejected by a vote of 67 opposed and 53 in favor, but his compromise would later become a reality through an appropriations act approved by Congress in 1868.[103]

Like Representative Randall, Rep. Frederick A. Pike of Maine strenuously objected to the cost of the proposed national education department, which he insisted could be nearly twenty times more expensive than the $10,000 to $15,000 annual price tag suggested by proponents.[104] For Pike, "these matters of education had better be left to the States where they are much more economically managed and where they properly belong."[105] At the time, only two federal officers, the US treasurer and the head of the banking department, earned annual salaries of $5,000; while the president of Harvard, "the wealthiest institution in this country," earned $2,500, according to Pike. Further, he noted that annual agriculture department reports cost $200,000 to print.[106] Economics aside, however, Pike flatly rejected Representative Banks's characterization of the national education department as an "initiatory measure." Pike explained that "I suppose that this measure, which commences in criticism upon the public schools of this country, shall end in making direct appropriations for that purpose . . . now we have the initiation of a system. At another time it will be more fully developed. The school houses of this country will go under the control of the General Government."[107]

After days of debate, Representative Garfield took the House floor on behalf of his bill.[108] He began by noting that to date Congress had awarded fourteen states 53 million acres of public land in support of schools, beginning with the Land Ordinance of 1785.[109] Of course, this ordinance, along with the Northwest Ordinance of 1787, which urged the encouragement of education and schools, were authorized prior to the Constitution, under the Articles of Confederation.[110] Acknowledging the constitutional limitations of his plan, Garfield noted that "the genius of our Government does not allow us to establish a compulsory system of education." He believed, however, that publishing school facts and statistics would "shame out of their delinquency all the delinquent States of this country."[111] In response to objections about the cost of such a department, Garfield offered a rationale that is still used by education spending advocates: "It is cheaper to reduce crime than build jails. School-houses are less expensive than rebellion."[112]

When his time expired and the vote was called on June 8, 1866, the act establishing a department of education was narrowly defeated by a vote of 61 opposed and 59 in favor.[113] On June 19, the bill was reconsidered. As Representative Garfield pleaded, "It is an interest that has no lobby to press its claims. It is the voice of children of the land, asking us to give them all the blessings of our civilization." When the vote was taken again, the bill passed handily by a vote of 80 in favor and 44 opposed.[114] This change of heart has been attributed to Garfield's "persistent zeal with which he argued the measure in private."[115] Others have said he "bamboozled the preceding House into passing a worthless bill."[116]

Regardless, Senate debate on establishing a national education department began in February 1867. Sen. Lyman Trumbull of Illinois insisted that if the

US had "had a department of education from the beginning, I believe it would have been one of the best bureaus or departments which the Government could have had."[117] It would serve, as Trumbull described it, as "a center for the dissemination of information . . . in the way of building school-houses, in methods of imparting education."[118] Another proponent, Sen. Richard Yates of Illinois, expressed his disdain for what he called "the old Calhoun doctrine of States rights," which in his opinion "has resulted in woes immeasurable to this Government." These remarks encapsulate a growing disdain for constitutionally limited government with clearly enumerated powers. As such disdain grew, so too did calls for the federal government to centralize control over education, even without a constitutional amendment expressly granting it such authority. From this point forward, concluded Yates, "we are a nation, not States merely, with powers and attributes of sovereignty as a nation." In this context the national education department would serve, as Yates put it, "as a central department," a clearinghouse of the "collective wisdom of all these State institutions, . . . which we may see at a glance."[119] Sen. James Dixon of Connecticut concurred, adding that the "New England system of common school education must reach the whole mass of our people, or this country . . . cannot be sustained."[120]

In opposition to Trumbull, Sen. James W. Grimes of Iowa was scathing, characterizing the national education department "as being the great central depot of information and influence and control for all the common schools throughout the land," gathering "merely second-hand information that is collected from the superintendents of the common schools of different States." Sen. Willard Saulsbury of Delaware concluded the Senate debate on the bill, stating that "leaving out all questions of expediency or propriety. . . . In my judgment, Congress has no constitutional authority to enact such as measure as this."[121] On February 27, 1867, the bill establishing a national education department was passed. A motion introduced by Sen. Charles R. Buckalew of Pennsylvania to reconsider was taken up a few days later on March 1, 1867, but it was soundly defeated by a vote of 7 in favor and 28 opposed. On March 2, 1867, President Andrew Johnson signed "An Act to establish a Department of Education" into law.[122]

Developments from 1867 to 1960

"You will not stop at simply establishing a bureau for the purpose of paying officers to collect and diffuse statistics in reference to education." That was the prediction of Congressman Rogers of New Jersey.[123] History proved him right, although just how right he was would not become clear for another century.

The original department was comprised of an education commissioner with an annual salary of $4,000, a chief clerk earning $2,000 annually, one clerk earning $1,800 a year, and another clerk earning $1,600 a year: a total operating budget of less than $25,000.[124] By 2009, however, the US Department of Education had swelled to 4,200 employees and a budget of $67.3 billion, plus an additional $100 billion in funding for the ensuing two years through the American Recovery and Reinvestment Act of 2009.[125] In the interval, the department underwent several iterations before it was ultimately elevated to a Cabinet-level department in 1979.

On July 20, 1868, a congressional appropriations act reduced department funding and stipulated that it would lose its independence and be subsumed as the Office of Education within the Department of the Interior.[126] The following year on March 3, 1869, Congress once again reclassified the agency as the Bureau of Education through an annual appropriations act.[127] Under subsequent appropriations acts, the Bureau of Education remained within the Department of the Interior until 1939. The name Office of Education was restored in 1930.[128]

Despite the efforts of early education commissioners, the Office of Education grew slowly compared to other federal agencies because it had few significant responsibilities.[129] Until the early twentieth century, the national education office was largely concerned with elementary school education statistics and oversight of federal land grants for postsecondary institutions.

That began to change with the Smith-Lever Act of 1914 and the Smith-Hughes Act of 1917, which continued the precedent of federal involvement in education set by the Morrill Act of 1862 and its expansion in 1890 through the Agricultural College Act of 1890. Smith-Lever and Smith-Hughes extended the education office's reach into secondary education,[130] establishing education and training programs for high school students and individuals not attending college. They were the first acts requiring the states to fund specific programs to be eligible for federal funds. Over the next two decades vocational and land-grant programs were expanded, increasing the role of the Office of Education,[131] and calls intensified for an independent, Cabinet-level department.[132]

1923   President Warren G. Harding proposed such a department.

1924   The Joint Committee on Reorganization made a similar recommendation.

1932   President Herbert Hoover called for a single executive department of health, education, and recreational activities.

1937   The President's Committee on Administrative Management (also known as the Brownlow Committee or Brownlow Commission) recommended that a Department of Social Welfare subsume health, education, and social security duties.[133]

1939   The Office of Education was transferred to the newly created Federal Security Agency.[134]

Over the next decade, nearly a dozen significant pieces of federal education legislation were passed, including the Servicemen's Readjustment Act, commonly known as the GI Bill (1944) and the National School Lunch Act (1946).[135] By 1950, the Office of Education budget exceeded $15 million, and it oversaw more than $760 million in federal grants and assistance.[136] Three years later the Federal Security Agency was reorganized as the Department of Health, Education, and Welfare. President Dwight D. Eisenhower noted that an Advisory Committee on Education should be established within the Department of Health, Education and Welfare to advise the secretary on the agency's education programs. "The creation of such a Committee as an advisory body to the Secretary," according to President Eisenhower, "will help ensure the maintenance of responsibility for the public educational system in State and local governments while preserving the national interest in education through appropriate Federal action."[137] Ultimately, Eisenhower said, "the improvement achieved in administration will in the future allow the performance of necessary services at greater savings."[138]

In reality, during the 1950–60 decade, the Office of Education staff grew from about 500 to 1,500. By the mid 1960s, education expenditures had exceeded $32 billion, having increased 300 percent since 1945, and education spending as a share of national income had almost tripled since World War II.[139] Still, improved administration remained elusive. As reported by *Science* magazine in 1962, critics charged that the Office of Education "performs its original duties of gathering public education statistics slowly and not too well; that it undertakes no research that is likely to create controversy; that it is overawed by Congress and is dominated by national education organizations to such an extent that it has abdicated its responsibility for making educational policy for the nation."[140]

As the move toward a Cabinet-level department built, advocates relied on any number of justifications, including superior centralized expertise, better program management, greater equity for disadvantaged students, and a compelling national interest in education. Only a relative handful of twentieth-century opponents in Congress insisted that they lacked any constitutional authority to proceed.

3

Twentieth-Century Proponents Make the Case for Federal Involvement in Education

GREATER GOVERNMENT EFFICIENCY was a dominant theme of public policy in the twentieth century, prompting presidents to introduce nearly 100 reorganization proposals affecting about 240 agencies and departments from 1939 to 1966 alone.[1] At the same time, government continued to grow, with the Cabinet providing one measure: It took 160 years for the Cabinet to increase from the original five to nine departments. In just twenty-five years beginning in the 1950s, another four departments were added. The belief that centralization is synonymous with streamlining accelerated such growth. When President Jimmy Carter took office in 1976, proposals were pending for two additional departments, including the Department of Education.

The desirability of centralization permeated the thinking of its proponents. Since the late 1800s they had insisted that centralizing education would improve student learning, strengthen workforce skills, and improve the general welfare of all citizens. Whatever the empirical evidence, their conviction about the federal government's superior capacity to oversee and improve education was unshaken. If results were disappointing, more government centralization, not less, was the answer.

This thinking was supported by the early twentieth-century growth of progressive ideas about education, which had taken root in schools of education. Perhaps the most influential thinker was John Dewey, who founded the University of Chicago's Laboratory School in 1896. He advanced the belief that schools were key tools for social progress. Priority belonged to the needs of the community, according to Dewey, not those of individual students or the preferences of their parents.

In this milieu, more than 130 bills were introduced between 1908 and 1975 to re-create a department of education.[2] In fact, more than eighty pieces of supporting legislation were introduced from the time the Department of Health, Education, and Welfare (HEW) was established in 1953 to 1978.[3] As the smallest division within HEW, education was left, as Yale University visiting fellow David Stevens wrote in 1983, "in the care of third- and fourth-rate bureaucrats who had little claim on the time of HEW secretaries, let alone presidents."[4] Efforts to create an independent, Cabinet-level education department continued.

They came to fruition on October 17, 1979, when President Carter signed into law the Department of Education Organization Act, making the US Department of Education the thirteenth Cabinet agency in the federal government. Writing in February 1980, leading proponent Senator Abraham Ribicoff (D-Ct.), Chairman of the Senate Governmental Affairs Committee, explained, "But of those 13 agencies, none has been more thoroughly debated than the Education Department. Its long legislative history includes thousands of pages of congressional testimony, reports, and floor debate."[5] Proponents, however, were silent about the Department of Education Act of 1867 and the ensuing history.[6]

In this section, we will look at the crucial period beginning in 1977 leading up to when the Cabinet-level department was established in 1979, pausing first to examine the influence Dewey had in shaping the American notion of education and, perhaps more important, education politics.

John Dewey and the Institutionalization of Schooling

Several key developments beginning in the mid-1800s help explain the popularity of a nationalized education department. As discussed previously, Horace Mann was pivotal in the establishment of school boards and a Prussian-style system of uniform, mandatory schooling. Although the United States did not adopt the level of centralized government control over schooling that flourished in European countries, Mann was remarkably successful in advancing his ideas of institutionalized schooling at a time when decentralized schooling was the norm.

Another influence was the establishment of schools of education, which had grown along with the spread of government-run common schools. The normal schools provided pedagogical training for teachers to staff these classrooms. The first normal school opened in 1839 in Lexington, Massachusetts, but in just seventy years the number of state normal schools had more than doubled to 180 and enrolled over 100,000 students.[7] By the 1960s, these schools, unable to attract enough students interested solely in teaching, had been absorbed as schools of education within larger universities.[8] Earlier in the twentieth century, however, they made an ideal vehicle for the spread of Dewey's ideas on progressive education.

Like his predecessor Mann, Dewey had a deep-seated mistrust of individuals—parents in particular—when it came to schooling. Both men favored centralization and planned economies, and both believed children had to have the "right kind" of education to mold them into peaceable members of the larger community. Although Dewey supported child-directed learning, he had little confidence in the intelligence of the average person. He believed individuals were incapable of exercising or enjoying liberty without "congruity" between their human wants and the environment. Real freedom, for Dewey, had to be socially "buttressed" to ensure "economic command of environment."[9] In other words, he thought government intervention was needed to keep individuals from becoming adrift in a sea of liberty.[10]

Dewey's ideas often put him at odds with the American Founders. He derided the "established mechanisms" of limited government as "idolatry to the Constitution" and dismissed the self-evident truths of the Declaration of Independence for being "out of vogue" in an industrial age.[11] Instead of what he called the "simpler faith" of the American Founders, he urged educators to follow the lead of "totalitarian countries," where education was used to revolutionize every aspect of society.[12] Writing in 1897, Dewey insisted, "Every teacher should realize he is a social servant set apart for the maintenance of the proper social order and the securing of the right social growth. In this way the teacher is always the prophet of the true God and the usherer in of the true kingdom of heaven."[13] Dewey found his god in science, and his heaven was right here on Earth in the form of the properly structured social order.[14]

Dewey's *Democracy and Education* was hailed upon its release in 1916 for being as seminal as Rousseau's *Emile* or Plato's *Republic*. It quickly became the bible at Columbia University Teacher's College, thanks in no small part to one of Dewey's leading progressive disciples William H. Kilpatrick, who taught thousands of teaching candidates over the years in Dewey's pedagogical methods. Prior to the ascendancy of education schools, teachers came from all walks of life. They were parents, ministers, town officials, private tutors, grammar and high school graduates, college instructors, and those skilled in various trades.[15] Dewey, however, saw teachers as an anointed priesthood skilled in the scientific method of classroom experimentation, socialization, and imitative play.

Such experimentation replaced traditional pedagogy, which could be measured objectively in terms of whether students had acquired specific knowledge or skills. Experimentation for its own sake was the goal of Dewey's pedagogy. Because Dewey's teaching method emphasized "a trial of ideas," even if one trial is "practically—or immediately unsuccessful—it is intellectual, fruitful," he thought. In fact, the "educative process" was its own end, with no need to seek other impacts.[16] According to this thinking, teachers were not so much educators as agents in charge of properly socializing students to have acceptable attitudes and behaviors. To achieve the proper community in an industrial world, Dewey said, children must be trained by experts. At an extreme, education is freed from notions of individual learning and becomes a group activity to give students greater insight into society at large.

The National Education Association (NEA) and the Progressive Education Association (PEA), founded in 1919, eagerly embraced Dewey's ideas. Throughout the initial decades of the twentieth century, those organizations advanced numerous political agendas in the name of progressive education that all involved greater centralization and government control. They envisioned schools as revolutionary incubators headed by expert educators,[17] which meant that neither parents nor local communities could be trusted with schooling. Dewey paved the way for schooling experiments that dominated much of the twentieth century, including open classrooms, new math, and whole language,[18] with outcomes that advocates and opponents assessed differently.

By the time debates over (re-)establishing a US Department of Education renewed in earnest in the 1970s, the progressive education movement had helped create a groundswell of support for more centralized government control over education. Leading the way was the NEA. Deliberations about forming a political action committee had begun in 1968, and in 1972 NEA-PAC was established.[19] Recognizing the association's growing influence, then-Governor Carter began working with its leadership in 1974, the same year he announced his intention to run for president. Establishing a distinct Department of Education emerged as one of his first campaign promises.[20] In 1976, the NEA endorsed Carter, its first-ever presidential endorsement.[21] So critical was its support to the ticket, that even Vice President Walter Mondale later joked, "I've learned that if you want to go somewhere in national politics these days, you better get the NEA behind you."[22]

Having won the popular vote by one of the smallest margins in history, 50.1 percent, Carter was beholden to the NEA and would have to make good on his promise of a Cabinet-level Department of Education if he wanted its continued support in the next election.[23]

The Political Stars Align for a Twentieth-Century US Department of Education

On February 21, 1977, Senator Ribicoff, chairman of the Senate Governmental Affairs Committee, introduced the Department of Education Act of 1977 (S. 991),[24] the first in a series of similar bills leading to passage. What American education needs, Ribicoff said, "is a unified direction. It needs a full-time Secretary of Education who can . . . devote the time for the national education leadership needed."[25] A report by Ribicoff's committee elaborated on this concern, noting that "education will never be a priority as long as it is smothered in layers of bureaucracy . . . and diminished by a severe lack of attention in our National Government."[26] Co-sponsor Sen. Sam Nunn (D-Ga.) spoke on the same theme: "For too long, our educational programs have failed to receive the attention and status that their importance demands," he began, echoing the sentiments of nineteenth-century advocates of an education department. "Education needs and deserves a single spokesman who can articulate educational priorities, plans, and programs at the highest levels of Government."[27]

Increasing education funding was another goal. As Senator Nunn explained, federal funding for education is a compelling national interest: "Investment in education is investment in the future productivity of our Nation through the advancement of skills of the workers of tomorrow. Our educational goals are important ones and we cannot gamble with their success." The proposed education department, therefore, was a sure bet, in Nunn's opinion, "guaranteeing that our educational dollars are efficiently and economically spent in this process. The establishment of a Department of Education would represent a giant step toward the genuine reform needed in our educational programs."[28]

Renamed the following year as the Department of Education Organization Act of 1978 (S. 991), the bill was debated in the Senate Governmental Operations Committee in the winter of 1977 and early 1978.[29] These were the first congressional hearings on an independent national education department in almost twenty-five years. More than 100 witnesses, including academics, education organization representatives, and six former US commissioners of education testified before the committee over the course of ten days during a period that began on October 12, 1977, and concluded on May 17, 1978.[30] The committee unanimously passed the legislation along for full Senate consideration.[31]

Meanwhile, Rep. Jack Brooks (D-Tex.), chairman of the House Committee on Government Operations, introduced a Department of Education Organization Act (H.R. 13343) on June 29, 1978, along with co-sponsors Reps. Frank Thompson, Jr. (D-N.J.) and Michael T. Blouin (D-Iowa). The committee's Subcommittee on Legislation and National Security held five days of hearings from July 17 through August 2, 1978. The bill was reported for full House consideration by a vote of 27 to 15.

While the House bill awaited floor action, the Senate conducted three days of debate on September 19, 20, and 28, 1978.[32] In spite of contentious debates, the measure handily passed the Senate, but the House adjourned on October 15, 1978, without voting on its version of the bill. Thus both the Senate and House versions died.[33] Nevertheless, President Carter and Vice President Mondale, together with Senate and House sponsors, vowed to continue their efforts to establish a Department of Education during the next congressional session.[34]

On January 18, 1979, Senator Ribicoff, along with forty-two co-sponsors, introduced the Department of Education Organization Act of 1979 (S. 210).[35]

In a special message to Congress on February 13, President Carter urged the House and the Senate to consider his proposed education department legislation.[36] In response Ribicoff introduced a bill by the same name (S. 510) on February 22, 1979, on behalf of President Carter.[37] The president's bill was referred to the Senate Committee on Governmental Affairs, but no further action was taken.[38] Days later on February 27, 1979, Representative Brooks introduced H.R. 2444 on behalf of the Carter Administration, which served as the companion bill to S. 510.[39] The House version (H.R. 2444) was ultimately superseded by the Senate version (S. 210).[40]

From 1977 to 1979 Department of Education proponents offered five basic arguments on behalf of an independent Cabinet-level education department. The proposed Department of Education would:

1. Supplement, not supplant, state and local governments

2. Secure education's status as a national activity

3. Provide better management of federal education programs

4. Consolidate federal education programs to improve efficiency, and

5. Improve educational quality.

The following sections consider these arguments and the opposition's response in greater detail.

Supplementing, Not Supplanting, State and Local Governments

With just a handful of notable exceptions, education department advocates were largely unchallenged about the express constitutionality of the proposed education department. The first notable difference between nineteenth- and twentieth-century department of education debates is that many early advocates were surprisingly straightforward about their belief that since education was in the national interest, the federal government could—and should—take a leading role regardless of the Tenth Amendment. Given the expansion of federal aid and other programs throughout the twentieth century, the American public had become accustomed to federal involvement in education.

Supporters consistently spoke of a federal role to "supplement and complement" the states.[41] Yet, in spite of their stated intention to preserve states' constitutional authority, as originally proposed on February 21, 1977, the education
department bill made no mention whatsoever of state or local control. It said
simply that Congress finds:

> (1) education is of fundamental importance to the Nation and it is ap-
> propriate to reassess the condition of education in our Nation to insure
> that all Americans have an equal opportunity for a quality education;
> (2) existing Federal programs in support of education are fragmented
> and often duplicative and should be better coordinated in order to
> promote quality education; (3) the role and importance of education
> increases as our society becomes more complex . . . ; (4) public policy
> toward education is vital to the present and long-range interests of the
> United States; (6 [sic]) education must be broadly conceived . . . ; and
> (7) it is essential therefore to establish a Department of Education to
> provide Federal leadership.[42]

Unconvinced that the federal government would restrict itself solely to
supplementing and complementing the states, the *Washington Post* criticized
the proposed education department for "breaking with the long tradition
of a limited federal involvement in education."[43] In response, Sens. William
Roth, Jr. (R-Dela.) and John C. Danforth (R-Mo.) introduced an amendment
specifically providing that the proper federal role in education is "to assist
and supplement, but never supplant" state and local governments.[44] Senator
Ribicoff was also quick to add that the proposed education department "does
not seek to change or enlarge the Federal Government's role in education in
any way or to erode State or local control."[45] Commenting on the amendment colloquy among Senators Danforth, Roth, and Ribicoff, Sen. Harrison
Schmitt (R-N.M.), warned, "I am afraid they are doomed to failure. . . . The
bill and the bureaucracy are just inconsistent with the kind of colloquy that
has just taken place. . . . I am seriously concerned that it will not come about
the way these Senators hope it will."[46]

Nevertheless, Senator Ribicoff's Governmental Affairs Committee report
was insistent. "While the responsibility for educational policies and curricula
must continue to reside with States, localities, and private institutions," the

report stated, "there is a legitimate Federal interest, and defined role, in education." That defined role, it argued, is ensuring equal access to education and providing financial assistance to the states to "insure the people are receiving a quality education."[47] By appealing to a "legitimate federal interest," supporters were alluding to the Spending Clause of the Constitution, which states, "The Congress shall have power to lay and collect taxes, duties, imposts and excises, to . . . provide for the common defense and general welfare of the United States."[48]

President James Madison had explicitly rejected as an "absurdity" the notion that the Spending Clause "amounts to an unlimited commission to exercise every power which may be alleged to be necessary for the common defense or general welfare."[49] Why bother to enumerate congressional powers at all, he wondered, "if these and all others were meant to be included in the preceding general power?"[50] The US Supreme Court, however, has applied what many consider weak limitations on Congress's spending power. First, it must be used to promote the general welfare. Second, Congress cannot induce the states to act unconstitutionally. Third, funding conditions must be clearly stated and actually related to the federal program interest. Finally, congressional funding cannot be so coercive as to compel the states to accept it.[51]

Within the context of the 1977–79 debates, however, a handful of senators raised objections to a federal education department reminiscent of those made by opponents more than a century before. Sen. Barry Goldwater (R-Ariz.) was the first member to speak out against the Department of Education Organization Act. Arguing against transferring oversight of Indian education to the proposed federal education department, Senator Goldwater began by reviewing the federal government's track record to date concerning improving education for all children. He started by noting, "I can recall when I first came to this body nearly 25 years ago, I wholeheartedly opposed Federal aid to education, and I grew to be known as an opponent of education. No. I was an opponent of the Federal Government having anything to do with the education of my children in the elementary schools."[52]

Senator Goldwater was referring to his early years in office, a time when his home state of "Arizona proudly turned down federal funds under the 1958 National Defense Education Act on the grounds that Arizonians, themselves, were quite capable of closing the [funding] gap."[53] Rejecting the notion that federal money is "free," Goldwater made the fundamental objection "that federal intervention in education is unconstitutional." He elaborated, saying:

> It is the fashion these days to say that responsibility for education "traditionally" rests with the local community—as a prelude to proposing an exception to the tradition in the form of federal aid. This "tradition," let us remember, is also the *law*. It is sanctioned by the Constitution of the United States, for education is one of the powers reserved to the States by the Tenth Amendment. Therefore, any federal aid program, however desirable it might appear, must be regarded as illegal until such time as the Constitution is amended. (Emphasis in the original)[54]

During those early years Senator Goldwater had also predicted that "federal aid *to* education invariably means federal control *of* education" [emphasis in original], based on the National Defense Education Act of 1958, which included twelve federal mandates on the states.[55] Looking at the state of education since it came under HEW's purview, Goldwater concluded, "I think it has gotten worse. I do not think there is a country in the world that has a worse system of education to educate their young people in the elementary levels than we have today. . . . Today what do we find in our colleges? Almost every college has a noncredit freshman class to teach students who graduated from high school how to read, write, and add. And yet we want to make a Department of Education. Frankly, I would like to do away with any Federal education."[56]

Senator Schmitt also offered a point-by-point refutation of the leading arguments made by department proponents, beginning with the claim that a separate department is merely a reorganization designed to achieve greater efficiency. "There is reason to question this view as to both the result and the motivation," began Schmitt. Far from promoting greater efficiency, he insisted, the true motivation for a department of education was the NEA's goal of nationalizing education. According to then-NEA President John Royer, "The Federal Government has a responsibility for education in and of itself." Based on that statement, Schmitt concluded,

> That is hardly just a reorganization. . . . the Federal government has become more and more involved in education. What started out as assis-

tance, primarily financial assistance . . . has emerged as de facto control through the threat of withholding funds upon which local systems had become dependent. The creation of a department of education obviously will strengthen this trend toward centralized decision-making in the field of education. . . . it is hoped that our efforts to improve Government will lead us to the realization that bureaucratic bigness is not bureaucratic goodness.[57]

Pointing to increasing federal education spending, Senator Schmitt said, "there is no reason to believe, nor is there any historical evidence to prove, that the quality of education will be improved by the increased Federal control that a new Department of Education would encourage."[58] In fact, continued Schmitt, "as we have been spending more money on education, as we have seen more and more Federal control and manipulation of education, the general quality of education has been declining. Obviously, more money and more bureaucratic control has not improved education overall. Money and lack of Federal control are clearly not the principal problems."[59] Schmitt concluded with a salient prediction of what the future would hold under the proposed education department:

It is not difficult to imagine this department establishing national "advisory" standards at some point in the future. Later, the department could require adherence to the compulsory standards, if Federal aid is to be continued. Next, standard tests, developed by the Federal Government, could be mandated to check whether the compulsory standards are being met. Last, State and local authorities will be coerced into acceptance of a standardized curriculum as the "only possible" guarantee of meeting compulsory standards. This is the classic bureaucratic process, one which we have seen again and again in recent decades, [and it] is the last thing that education in the United States needs and the last thing most Americans want.[60]

The third leading opponent of a federal education department was Sen. Samuel Hayakawa (R-Calif.), a distinguished academic. He began by taking issue with education department advocates' claims that the current bill had been studied in great depth. In fact, noted Hayakawa, such a department had existed in 1867 but "accomplished so little that within a short time, it was reduced to the status of a bureau in the Department of the Interior. The experiences of that time may not be relevant today, but this first failure is certainly not a good omen."[61] After reviewing the various related studies, commissions, and task force reports undertaken throughout the twentieth century, Hayakawa observed, "So far . . . I have not a single study that suggests the creation of a Department of Education at this time would be a desirable step."[62] Further, he added, "We have seen contradictory and politically motivated testimonies, but no systematic and disinterested analysis of the complex issues involved. . . . It seems to me that the creation of a Department of Education without such an inquiry would simply be a bureaucratic escape from reality."[63]

Along with Sens. Goldwater and Schmitt, Senator Hayakawa underscored the failure of national efforts thus far to improve education. "Federal outlays in the last 10 years have tripled," he observed, "while at the same time our educational standards have deteriorated even further. . . . We are spending, at the Federal level, about $20 billion annually for education, and Johnny still cannot read."[64] Hayakawa's main objection, however, concerned the constitutionality of a federal role in education. "I am obliged to point out that the drafters of S. 991 [the Department of Education Organization Act] sidestepped this issue," stated Hayakawa. Elaborating on this point, he insisted:

> Have the supporters of this bill given any thought to the significant fact that the United States has not a single Cabinet-level department which is responsible for an area that the Constitution has left to the States? . . . . the Federal Government has found a method of getting around this important provision in our Constitution by lavishly distributing money with categorical strings attached. In other words, the objections of the States to Federal involvement were usually silenced by increased funds. But let us not forget, the conflict remains.[65]

This conflict also has tangible effects. Senator Hayakawa reported that according to the American Council on Education, "The federal Government is perceived by various state officials as contributing some 8 percent of elementary and secondary school budgets and behaving as if it were the senior and managing partner of the educational enterprise."[66]

Education Is a National Activity, Deserving Greater Visibility and Status

Although the federal footprint in education had been increasing, along with its cost, proponents insisted that a Department of Education was critical to ensuring "that education receives the appropriate emphasis at the Federal level."[67] "The low status of education in the Federal Government," they claimed, "does not give rightful recognition to education as an important, fundamental national activity."[68] For President Carter, elevating the status of education at the federal level was a leading reason for creating the Department of Education. In his February 28, 1978, education message to Congress, he said a Department of Education will "let us focus on Federal educational policy, at the highest levels of our government."[69] A year later, in a message to Congress transmitting his proposed Department of Education legislation, President Carter again argued that such a department would "bring our Nation's educational challenges and the Federal Government's role in meeting them to the forefront of domestic policy discussion. . . . Establishing a Department of Education will create, for the first time, a Cabinet-level advocate for education with direct access to the President, the Congress, and the public."[70]

Introducing his own legislation, Senator Ribicoff shared the president's concern about education's low status at the federal level, arguing that it was "diminished by a severe lack of attention in our National Government."[71] Establishing a department, he concluded, "will help ensure that education issues receive proper attention at the Federal level and will enable the Federal Government to coordinate its education related activities more effectively."[72] Sen. Pete Domenici (R-N.M.) argued more forcefully, "A reorganization which recognizes the importance of education in our country is desperately needed if we are to ever make sense of the current unmanageable state of education."[73] Likewise, Sen. Carl Levin (D-Mich.) insisted that "the Federal Government has a vital and undeniable interest in the quality of our educational system at all levels, and in all parts of the country. . . . any national government that does not make the pursuit of highest quality education for its citizens a first-order priority is abdicating one of its most important responsibilities."[74]

The official Senate Committee on Governmental Affairs report concurred. "Democracy depends for its very existence on a highly educated citizenry.

Education is, perhaps, the single most pervasive function of American society."[75] The report continued, noting, "Establishment of a Department of Education would greatly increase the status and visibility of education in the Federal government and give it rightful recognition as a fundamental activity of American life."[76] In testimony before the Senate Committee on Governmental Affairs, US Commissioner of Education Ernest Boyer stated the case even more forcefully: "Education and democracy are inextricably interlocked, and it should have full partnership at the highest levels of government where the Nation's priorities are shaped."[77] In a similar vein during testimony before the Senate Committee on Governmental Affairs, the Rev. Jesse Jackson stated, "The elimination of ignorance, poverty, and disease requires increased emphasis on education. . . . everything worth doing and accomplishing has education as a foundation from which to start. . . . Education needs a full-time advocate."[78]

Department of Education opponents, however, seized upon proponents' inconsistencies. Rep. William S. Moorhead (D-Pa.) objected that,

> Education is already highly visible. It has enormous prestige. It is ingrained in the American fabric and psyche as a fundamental part of each American's birthright. . . . Not only does education have the prestige of being part of the American dream, but the Federal Government has already responded to the financial need of education. In the past 17 years, we have seen Federal education dollars expand from $1.237 billion in 1962 to $7.840 billion today (in constant 1972 dollars). Such growth was accomplished without a Department of Education.[79]

Similarly, in their joint statement opposing the creation of a Department of Education Reps. Benjamin S. Rosenthal (D-N.Y.), John Conyers, Jr. (D-Mich.), Henry Waxman (D-Calif.), Peter H. Kostmayer (D-Pa.), and Ted Weiss (D-N.Y.) said, "'Visibility' and 'status' are undefined catch phrases which hardly justify the creation of a Cabinet-level department of education. . . . It is also our view that Cabinet-level departments should be established only when there is a major national policy to carry out. There is no such major national policy with respect to Federal education efforts. . . . Greater concern with education does not require and is not assured by the creation of a separate department."[80] They concluded that "the proposal to create a separate Cabinet-level department of education lacks substance. Education already has Cabinet status and more than enough people to hold accountable for flaws in our educational efforts."[81]

A leading related concern among education department opponents was that education policy would become politicized. Brookings Institution Senior Fellow David W. Breneman asked: "Do we want to politicize education at the national level by creating an office that will become the focal point for partisan efforts, with the ideological course shifting with every change of Presidents? Regardless of the qualifying and limiting language built into the legislation, a vote for the Department is to answer each of those questions implicitly with a 'Yes.'"[82]

The NEA's central role in creating an education department amplified opponents' concerns about the politicization of education. "One important proponent is the National Education Association, which testified that 'the Federal Government ought to be paying as much as one-third the cost of public education,'" explained Rep. Lawrence Fountain (D-N.C.) in his opposition statement. Thus, Fountain concluded, "The NEA's goal . . . stands in sharp contrast with the approximately 8 percent the Federal Government presently contributes through all its programs to public education. What a field day the education interests could have in pressing for a large Federal percentage without having to compete with health and welfare advocates for a share of the HEW budget!"[83] Representative Kostmayer was also candid about the NEA's influence. "The National Education Association, which plays a role in all of our campaigns, and which strongly supports this department is a factor in these deliberations," he acknowledged, adding, "This seems to me to be another example of doing something largely at the behest of a special interest group."[84]

To be sure, other special interest groups besides the NEA lobbied Congress on behalf of a distinct US Department of Education, including the Council of Chief State School Officers, the National Schools Boards Association, the National PTA, the American Association of School Administrators, and the National Association of State Boards of Education. Yet the NEA was by far the most political, making itself a lightning rod for opponents of a US Department of Education.[85]

Twentieth-century opposition to the department echoed nineteenth-century concerns. In fact, Representative Fountain quoted extensively from his predecessors in his own opposition statement, including the observation of Rep. Samuel Moulton of Illinois about the 1867 education department. The urgency for an education department arose from a national meeting of "educational men," as Moulton put it, who concluded that "a Department of this kind was absolutely necessary for the benefit of the whole country and the promotion of educational interests of the country."[86] Fountain continued, recalling the 1867 remarks of Sen. Thomas Hendricks of Indiana: "I am not of the opinion that an establishment of this sort in this city through the General Government will really promote the cause of education in the country. It will be a benefit to a few persons; but that it will reach the masses of the people of the common schools of the country in any beneficial influence, I do not believe."[87] Representative Fountain's final assessment of the current education department mirrored that of Sen. Garrett Davis of Kentucky, who argued in 1867 that such a department "seems to be more of a device to create officers and patronage and to make drafts on the treasury than anything else."[88]

Better Management and Coordination of Federal Education Programs

Proponents devoted significant attention to the idea that the Department of Education was ultimately about better management. Opponents, however, were quick to point out the inconsistency of advocating that bigger government is needed to streamline, well, bigger government. At the time, HEW had 150,000 employees and oversaw more than 325 programs that "inevitably touch nearly every living American," according to Senator Ribicoff's Governmental Affairs Committee report.[89] To the detriment of education, he thought, all those programs were competing for attention—and funding. A separate department would go a long way toward minimizing competition and maximizing funding.

What American education needs, according to Senator Ribicoff, "is a unified direction. It needs a full-time Secretary of Education who can. . . . devote the time for the national education leadership needed."[90] Although the department would consolidate more than 170 education programs, another 100 programs would continue to be managed by other federal agencies, calling into question the prospects for a "unified direction" capable of minimizing duplication and maximizing efficiency.[91]

During the late 1970s there were more than 300 separate Federal education programs costing $25 billion. "The Federal presence in education is substantial. Over 40 Federal departments and agencies are involved in education grants, services, and regulations," according to the Committee on Governmental Affairs.[92] In response, Sen. Hubert Humphrey (DFL-Minn.) said, "It is necessary to have a more efficient mechanism for the coordination of these numerous programs in a sensible, workable, effective framework."[93] In fact, the express purpose of the Department of Education legislation was to "assist the Federal effort in coordinating education activities and programs."[94] HEW's "serious institutional weaknesses and deficiencies," Senator Ribicoff said, required a distinct education department.[95] That department, in turn, was supposed to improve "management of education and related programs by simplifying Federal procedures . . . and by eliminating unnecessary and duplicative burdens, including unnecessary paperwork, on the recipients of federal funds."[96]

Education department opponents, however, rejected such thinking outright. Representative Fountain thought it would be better to review existing programs and weed out ineffective ones, not "devote our energies to creating a new organizational structure which might well help to perpetuate many of these programs."[97] House Democrats argued against an education department along similar lines. In their joint opposition statement, Representatives Rosenthal, Conyers, Waxman, and Weiss countered,

It is our judgment that the proposed Department of Education . . . violates every good rule of management, good organization, and even good politics . . . reorganization has become a religion in Washington. It is deemed synonymous with reform, and reform with progress. It purifies bureaucratic blood and prevents stagnation and, for the true believer, reorganization can produce miracles, eliminate waste, save billions of dollars, and restore to health and vigor a chronically ill bureaucracy. We do not believe reorganization is a panacea, the magic elixir or the miracle drug it is claimed to be. In fact, it is not at all clear that any of the deficiencies in education today are even related to the organization chart.[98]

In a separate, bipartisan joint statement, eleven US Representatives concurred, noting that "a Department of Education is contrary to the recommendations of every Presidential Government reorganization commission under both Democratic and Republican presidents since and including the Hoover Commission, which issued its report in 1948."[99] In particular, they cited a stern admonition against the creation of a Department of Education from President Lyndon B. Johnson's Heineman Commission, which concluded that far from improving program management, such a department would "waste the President's major line deputies in the running of interference or errands for narrow groups. . . . To improve the management of domestic programs, we recommend that the President resist proposals to create additional departments likely to be dominated by narrow, specialized interests."[100]

Improved Efficiency, Cost Savings, and Accountability

According to President Carter in his February 28, 1978, education message to Congress, a Department of Education will "reduce Federal regulations and reporting requirements and cut duplication; [and] assist school districts, teachers, and parents to make better use of local resources and ingenuity."[101] A leading concern among proponents was that within HEW, "education officials cannot be held accountable because they are submerged under layers of bureaucracy and because they are not actually the individuals responsible for any decisions."[102] The Senate Committee on Governmental Affairs concluded, "Put simply, coordination fails when it is dropped in the hands of Federal officials below the policy-making level."[103] Moreover, the committee reported accounts from state education officials about growing regulatory burdens. One official told the committee that "he is forced to hire more than 20 staffers at average annual salaries of $20,000 just to keep up with Federal paperwork, rules, and regulations."[104] In 2010 inflation-adjusted dollars, that salary figure exceeds $63,000.

Senator Ribicoff promised this state of affairs would change: "The new Department will be the most streamlined department in the Federal Government."[105] A Department of Education that the committee envisioned would provide "a simple and clearly-ordered structure for Federal education programs. . . . The number of principal officers and offices would be reduced to just 11 [down from 22 in HEW's Education Division], all reporting directly to one individual—the Secretary of Education."[106]

Senator Levin recalled learning from Office of Management and Budget Director James T. McIntyre that getting new regulations through HEW took years in some cases:

> During 1978, the Office of Education published 21 final regulations. It took an average of 519 days from the first day of planning . . . to the day they were published. . . . The shortest time for this process was 220 days; the longest time was 1,296 days; 10 regulations took between 450 and 550 days. Under the Department of Education, we estimate the time devoted to the promulgation of regulations can be decreased by approximately three months.[107]

Proponents insisted that the Department of Education's "main purpose is to reorganize the Federal government to improve governmental efficiency, management, and coordination." Its creation, they insisted, would inspire "a new awareness and sensitivity" toward states and local school systems.[108] Senator Nunn was even more optimistic, arguing that establishing a Department of Education would lead to "a new era of cooperation, understanding, and excellence in our educational systems."[109]

One thing lacking in the debates was an assessment of the century-long record of federal engagement in schooling, which failed to show that federal intervention was correcting the lack of coordination, duplication, and waste throughout the states. Challenged to explain why increased federal intervention had not improved the overall quality of American education, Senator Ribicoff and other advocates insisted education had yet to be sufficiently federalized.

Many Republicans also appeared to believe an education department would give them an opportunity to make bigger government better. An amendment successfully introduced by Senator Roth attempted to improve government efficiency by putting an annual staff ceiling on the Department of Education. "One of the major criticisms of creating a new department of education has been the fear that in its authorization Congress is beefing up a bureaucracy, which is already bloated and straining an overtaxed budget. I feel we must be responsive to that concern," explained Roth.[110]

In terms of the Department of Education's costs, projections by the House Committee on Government Operations anticipated "no inflationary impact on prices and costs in the operation of the national economy."[111] Likewise, the Senate Committee on Governmental Affairs insisted that the department "will result in no additional cost, but will actually save millions of dollars. . . . The savings in dollars will be substantial."[112] Specifically, the Office of Management and Budget projected a long-term savings of more than $100 million by establishing the Department of Education.[113] Those savings were supposed to come from reducing staff from thirty officers to eleven principal officers, eliminating 350 to 450 positions, and hiring forty-two supergrade managers.[114]

Still, proponents could not avoid the stark reality that the proposed Department of Education, with a budget of $14.5 billion "will be larger than that of five existing Cabinet departments."[115] What's more, Congressional Budget Office estimates indicated that the near-term department costs would start at $5.2 million in FY 1980, then almost double, reaching $9.6 million in FY 1984.[116] Thus, in spite of assurances from proponent Sen. Jim Sasser (D-Tenn.) that "'bureaucratic creep' is not likely to infest the Department of Education,"[117] the committee recommended amending the enabling legislation to require annual personnel reports.[118]

Education department opponents were highly skeptical that a new bureaucracy would streamline old bureaucracies. Representative Fountain referred to 1867 education department opponent Rep. Andrew Rogers of New Jersey, who called the proposed nineteenth-century department a budget-busting "scheme of philanthropy." Rogers said: "In a short time this bureau will need more clerks and expenses for stationery . . . And where will it end? It will not stop until we run up a bill of expenses that will materially injure the finances of the Government."[119]

Using similar reasoning Rep. Leo J. Ryan (D-Calif.) said the proposed department "is more than a logical consolidation of Federal education programs housed in various federal agencies. . . . It is more, more, more. It is more money. . . . It is more personnel. . . . It is more advisory committees."[120] Senator

Hayakawa held that elected officials are ultimately responsible for allowing bureaucracies, regulations, and red tape to proliferate unchecked. "We in Congress should count ourselves among the problems endured by HEW," he explained. "We continue to throw program after program at HEW . . . we enact these laws, then throw caution to the wind, and we think no more about them until we get complaints from our constituents."[121]

Likening Congress's efforts to slow the expansion of government to Hercules's battle with the mythical Hydra, Sen. William Cohen (R-ME) concluded, "I have found no evidence which suggests the problems plaguing federal education programs—duplicative and conflicting regulations, burdensome and unnecessary paperwork, and unclear lines of authority—would disappear or even be significantly reduced were a separate Department of Education to be created." He added, "It is ironic that President Carter, who campaigned on the pledge to revamp the executive branch by reducing the number of federal agencies from 1,900 to 200, should be supporting legislation to create yet another Cabinet department."[122] He elaborated on just how big the proposed education department would be:

> As envisioned by the bill's sponsors, the Department of Education would include more than 150 programs and over 16,000 employees. . . . With a budget in excess of $14 billion, the Department of Education would be larger than five of the present Cabinet departments—State, Interior, Commerce, Justice, and Energy. And based on our experience with the self-perpetuating nature of federal agencies, it is safe to predict that the Department of Education would inevitably grow even larger. . . . One of the reasons advanced by those who favor creating a separate Department of Education is that greater efficiency would result from the consolidation of education programs now scattered throughout the federal bureaucracy in departments as diverse as Justice and Interior. This legislation, however, does very little to promote consolidation. Almost every non-HEW education program . . . would *not* [emphasis original] be transferred to the new department, and some disagreement still exists about those responsibilities that would be included under its jurisdiction. . . . Perhaps proponents hope that if

Congress would create a shell now, the President could use his reorganization authority in future years to transfer additional programs with only minimal congressional review or political opposition.[123]

Other opponents criticized the optimistic education department savings projections. Rep. Robert S. Walker (R-Pa.) noted that "the Department, from the outset, will contain ninety new supergrade and executive positions at an average salary of $50,000 each; in other words, $4.5 million of money 'for education' will go to pay many highly paid bureaucrats."[124] Senator Hayakawa added another constituency, noting that "the department would most likely respond to the National Education Association, school administrators and teachers rather than its obvious constituency—students and taxpaying parents. . . . It would be giving the NEA its own governmental department."[125]

Improve Educational Quality and Public Confidence

Senator Ribicoff also believed that a Cabinet-level Department of Education would "strengthen and improve American education."[126] According to the Senate Committee on Governmental Affairs, its creation would strengthen the federal commitment to ensuring equal educational opportunities, "supplement and complement" state and local governments "to improve the quality of education," promote improvements in basic skills, life-long learning, and "educational excellence" overall, and "substantially increase public confidence in our educational system" by encouraging the increased involvement of parents, students, and communities in the decision-making process."[127]

The committee report said the department would "assist promoting the quality and the relevance of education to individual needs"[128] amid growing concern about education quality. Reading skills among American students at this time had been in a decade-long decline. In 1977, college-bound students posted the lowest SAT scores in twenty years, and a leading university reported that half its freshman class had to enroll in remedial reading classes.[129]

Proponents' statistics, however, failed to make a case for an urgent need to expand educational options. For example, even without a distinct federal education department, one out of every three Americans was already enrolled at some level of public or private education by the late 1970s. Elementary and secondary enrollment among black students had increased 300 percent since 1969. Women were expected to earn more than half of the college degrees in 1978.[130] The number of 17-year-olds completing high school had also jumped to 80 percent from 50 percent in 1940.[131]

Nevertheless, the new department would "enable us to better serve 100 million men, mothers, fathers, parents, children, and teachers,"[132] Representative Brooks insisted. Likewise, Rep. Elliott Levitas (D-Ga.) believed the department would result in "better educational opportunity for the boys and girls and the young men and women in America. There is no question about that."[133] Speaker of the House Thomas "Tip" O'Neill (D-Mass.) agreed. "We need a special Department of Education . . . We are doing it in the best interests of ourselves, of our children, and of our Nation's educational future."[134]

Opponents did not accept that this debate was truly "about the children." In a joint statement opposing the creation of a Department of Education, Democratic Members of the House Committee on Government Operations said "we are convinced that the weaknesses in present Federal education efforts are totally unrelated to organizational deficiencies."[135] They continued, noting:

> The proposed legislation adds the words "new" and "improved" to the label of a product which would remain essentially the same. The quest for quality in education must continue. But it will not be advanced by the arbitrary isolation of educational programs from other social services. As members of the Committee on Government Operations, we strongly believe that major organizational shifts should not take place for cosmetic purposes.[136]

The statement continued:

> Those who stand to gain by this Department are the NEA and the other professionals representing education groups, and those in certain industries who profit from the programs. Children will not benefit. . . . This education-industrial complex need not answer to the American people who will complain about Federal domination of education policy, erosion of equal educational opportunities, and simply inefficient Government.[137]

Sen. Daniel Patrick Moynihan (D-N.Y.) stated his opposition even more strongly, arguing, "This is a bad proposal, not because its original purposes were bad. . . . This proposal is a backroom deal, born out of squalid politics."[138]

Rep. Bob Michel (R-Ill.) summed up his opposition to the Department of Education even more emphatically, "Once this silly idea is consigned to the oblivion it richly deserves, let us have the courage to admit that the Federal Government does not know what it is doing in education."[139] Representative Weiss highlighted the substantive deficiencies with the legislation. For all proponents' assurances of better administration, he noted, "there is no clear statement of what substantive changes or improvements in education the Department is intended to accomplish."[140] Representative Kostmayer concurred, stating that "the creation of a national education power structure serves no effective purpose. . . . I don't believe, nor do I think the American people are going to believe, that this new Department will improve the quality of education in the classroom."[141]

Senator Hayakawa aptly summed up the opposition to proponents' claims of improved education and public confidence by stating,

> Having this new department is rather like grasping at straws. We see there is a problem and attempt to solve it by creating a new department. I wish someone would tell me how this new department is going to make our children literate? Or how it will erase the violence that has erupted in our schools? Or how it will ensure that we get what we pay for with our tax dollars? Or how it will make our children better prepared for their futures?[142]

The Final Votes

Ultimately, Department of Education proponents prevailed. Yet as the previous sampling of debates suggests, the question of whether or not to enact the department was contentious and not settled along strictly partisan lines. On April 30, 1979, the Senate voted to pass the Department of Education Organization Act by a vote of 72 in favor and 21 opposed, with seven senators not voting.[143] Far from being a party-line vote, fully one-third of the votes in favor of establishing the Department of Education were cast by Republicans. Besides Roth, who was quoted here, they included Minority Leader and future Reagan White House Chief of Staff Howard Baker, Minority Whip Ted Stevens, and Sens. Thad Cochran, Orrin G. Hatch, Bob Packwood, and Strom Thurmond. The most prominent of the four Democrats who voted against the department was Senator Moynihan, while several other prominent Democrats did not vote, such as Sens. Daniel K. Inouye (D-Hawaii) and Birch Bayh (D-Ind.), who is considered the father of Title IX, implemented to promote greater equality for women in higher education.

Given the Democratic majority in Congress at the time, it would have been difficult to prevent passage of the Department of Education bill—but not impossible. For example, even if Senate Democrats' votes remained exactly as they were (48 in favor, 4 opposed, and 6 not voting), had the non-voting and affirmative-voting Republicans (1 and 24, respectively) joined Democrats voting against the department, the majority could have been whittled down to a mere two votes: 48 in favor and 46 opposed. As it stood, passing the Department of Education legislation in the House was already going to be an uphill battle. It could have been much steeper had the Senate vote been closer.

Beginning in June 1979, the House commenced weeks of debates on its Department of Education bill. Republicans opposed to it added several amendments, including reducing and capping overhead staff, barring abortions as part of the routine provision of medical care for employees, protecting school prayer, ending busing, and prohibiting racial quotas in college admissions. Whereas the Senate bill closely followed President Carter's priorities, the much-amended House version indicated just how controversial the proposed Department of Education was in the House.[144] On July 11, 1979, however, it narrowly passed with 210 representatives voting in favor, including 35 Republicans, and 206 opposed, including 89 Democrats.[145]

The House and Senate versions would have to be reconciled before the final vote in September 1979, and final passage was by no means assured. Such uncertainty could not have come at a worse time for Carter. We'll recall that at this time inflation was rising, energy shortages were erupting, and Americans were said to be confronting a "crisis of confidence."[146] The Carter administration sorely needed a domestic public policy victory, and establishing a Department of Education was considered critical—especially given the looming 1980 presidential election. Throughout the weeks and months leading up to the final vote, supporters and opponents shored up their ranks, and contrary to conventional wisdom, Republicans and Democrats filled both camps, albeit for different reasons.

While the relationship between President Carter and the NEA is well established, less well known was the association's bipartisan influence in Congress. More than 80 percent of NEA-endorsed congressional candidates had been elected in 1974, and with more than 1.7 million members, the NEA could claim that between 4,000 and 6,000 of them lived in every congressional district.[147] While it largely endorsed Democratic candidates, the NEA and its affiliates also endorsed and worked with Republicans during this time period, including Minority Leader Baker.[148] As noted previously, along with the NEA, several other influential education organizations, referred to at the time as the "Big Six," also supported the Department of Education. Council of Chief State School Officers, the National Association of State Boards of Education, the National School Boards Association, the Council of Great City Schools, the American Association of School Administrators, and the National PTA.[149]

Opposing the Department of Education was an unlikely coalition of Republicans and liberal Democrats.[150] Fueling democratic opposition was an alliance consisting of the American Federation of Teachers (AFT), the AFL-CIO, and the Catholic Conference. Not only were the NEA and the AFT bitter rivals, the latter had always been a labor organization, which worried that breaking up HEW to form a distinct Department of Education would distract Congress from adequately funding interconnected federal programs the AFT and its AFL-CIO allies favored.[151] The Catholic Conference, representing close to 50 million Catholics at the time, was concerned that the NEA-led public school lobby would take over the new department and impose federal control over private education.[152] Democratic leadership at the time also worried that the issue of a distinct Department of Education would fracture the party.[153]

In the end, the Department of Education was approved in the House on September 27, 1979, by just 14 votes, 219 in favor and 205 opposed.[154] Among those opposed were 81 Democrats, including John Conyers, Jim Dingell,

Geraldine Ferraro, and Richard Gephardt. The vast majority of Democrats voting against the department represented AFT, labor, and Catholic constituencies. Had less than half of the 30 Republicans voting in favor of the department, including future House Speaker Newt Gingrich (R-Ga.) and presidential candidate John B. Anderson (R-Ill.), voted against instead, the Department of Education likely would not have been established.[155]

4

With the New Department, a Larger and Larger Federal Role in Education

THE DEPARTMENT OF EDUCATION not only enshrined the federal government's role in American education, it served as a catalyst for expanding it throughout successive presidential administrations—Democratic and Republican alike. It also contributed to justification for an even more expansive (and expensive) federal role in education.

Even before the department was created, however, Congress had acted on a parallel track to increase the federal role in education via funding and the compliance with federal policy that dollars could extract from the states. This began in response to a competitive threat from overseas with the Soviet launch of the Sputnik satellite on October 4, 1957. Sputnik and the ensuing Space Race spawned the National Defense Education Act of 1958. Though the NDEA focused primarily on higher education, it was the first significant federal effort directed at elementary and secondary education.[1] Specifically, Title III provided federal matching grants to public schools and loans to private schools to improve the quality of math, science, and foreign language instruction. Schools could also use funds for capital projects, including construction of laboratories and equipment purchases. Within the first five years between 1959 and 1964, Title III federal funding reached $267 million; however, state and local agencies routinely overmatched the federal funding (a significant burden for localities since they funded 97 percent of the required matching funds), amounting to $12 million combined over this period. For all this additional spending, there was no way to reliably evaluate whether these programs were effective. Nevertheless, by 1964 every state was accepting Title III federal funding—except Arizona.[2]

Arizona's Senator Barry Goldwater was an outspoken opponent of the NDEA, taking particular issue with the premise animating federal involvement in education, namely, the notion that federal money is "free." He explained:

> The truth, of course, is that the federal government has no funds except those it extracts from the taxpayers who reside in the various States. The money that the federal government pays to State X for education has been taken from the citizens of State X in federal taxes and comes back to them, minus the Washington brokerage fee.[3]

As early as 1958, Goldwater predicted that "federal aid *to* education invariably means federal control *of* education."

Federal funding for Title III ceased in 1978.[4] The framework it established, however, endures today. The federal government uses its funding power to influence national education goals and policies. Although state participation remains voluntary, all states have demonstrated that the promise of "free" federal cash is inducement enough for them to enact federal education mandates. The pattern is at the core of the Elementary and Secondary Education Act of 1965 (ESEA), which is the legislation underlying the more contemporary No Child Left Behind Act (NCLB).

This chapter begins by examining the implementation and expansion of the Elementary and Secondary Education Act, which raises significant questions about the proper role of the federal government in American education. Should the federal government provide leadership, or should it instead be a supportive partner to the states? US Department of Education proponents believed the federal government could be both at once, even putting in what they considered to be strong parchment barriers preventing the federal government from usurping constitutional authority of the states and the people in education. Yet as a review of the ESEA's enactment and expansion over the last several decades reveals, the states routinely accepted federal authority, and members of Congress, as the Cato Institute's Neal McCluskey put it, made "bringing home the bacon—and getting reelected—job number one," rather than preventing the bacon from leaving their states in the first place. Happy to accept federal grants, states and school districts helped engender the ensuing ESEA regulatory burdens.

Although the ESEA preceded the creation of the US Department of Education, the new department had a multiplier effect on ESEA programs, and the two in tandem have vastly enlarged federal involvement in education over the last thirty-plus years. This chapter picks up the history of the Department of Education in 1980, when it opened for business under President Ronald Reagan. Although he had opposed the department when it was his predecessor's proposal, he failed to cut short its life, and federal activity in education flourished under succeeding presidents.

The Beginnings of the ESEA

The ESEA authorizes federal grants for elementary and secondary school programs for children of low-income families; school library resources, textbooks, and other instructional materials; supplementary educational centers and services; support for state education departments; and educational research and training.[5] It has been reauthorized eight times through 2001 and amended numerous times throughout its nearly fifty-year history.[6] Like the NDEA, the original ESEA contained an express prohibition against federal control over "curriculum, program of instruction, administration, or personnel of any educational institution or school system."[7] Nevertheless, the funding mechanism has opened the door to federal involvement in primary and secondary education.[8]

From the time the Constitution was ratified through the ESEA's enactment in 1965, just forty-one laws were passed related to federal education programs, according to McCluskey, compared to 117 such laws passed between 1965 and 2005.[9] From 2005 through 2010 alone, an additional five federal laws relating to elementary and secondary education have been passed.[10] Back in 1958, Senator Goldwater objected to the NDEA because it had twelve federal mandates.[11] Under the NCLB, federal mandates occupy more than 9,600 sections across ten titles filling some 670 pages.[12]

The ESEA was a cornerstone of President Lyndon Johnson's War on Poverty agenda. In 1964 he appointed Education Commissioner Francis "Frank" Keppel to head a secret presidential task force to develop a federal grant plan to improve educational achievement and opportunity for disadvantaged students. The challenge for Keppel was devising a plan that helped disadvantaged students, was not excessively burdensome to the states, and directed funds to schools based on total student enrollment, not just public school enrollment, to avoid controversy over aid to parochial schools. This was accomplished by making the ESEA an amendment to the federal impact aid law, which reimburses local school districts that cannot raise local property taxes because they are located on federal land.[13] Reflecting on the ESEA's passage, historian and former Johnson aide Eric F. Goldman noted in 1968, "In an astonishing piece of political artistry, the Congress had passed a billion-dollar law, deeply affecting a fundamental institution of the nation, in a breathtaking 87 days . . . The House had approved it with no amendments that mattered; the Senate had voted it through literally without a comma changed." Goldman credited the ESEA's swift passage to Johnson's political skill and his background as a former teacher.[14]

The original ESEA legislation enacted on April 11, 1965, included six titles:

Title I   Financial Assistance for Local Education Agencies for the Education of Children of Low-Income Families

Title II   School Library Resources, Textbooks, and other Instructional Materials

Title III   Supplementary Educational Centers and Services

Title IV   Educational Research and Training

Title V   Grants to Strengthen State Departments of Education

Title VI   General Provisions

At the insistence of Sen. Robert Kennedy (D-N.Y.), Title I recipient schools were required to put in place "effective procedures, including provision for appropriate objective measures of educational achievement, [that] will be adopted for evaluating at least annually the effectiveness of the programs in meeting the special educational needs of educationally deprived children." Further, those schools were to include this and other relevant information in annual reports to state education departments, which were responsible for verifying that schools used ESEA funds properly and effectively.[15] Other ESEA titles had reporting and verification requirements as well.[16] Almost immediately the ESEA did not work as planned.

School districts across the country began furiously spending available local and state funds to set up elaborate administrative bureaus. One reporter, referring to Milwaukee Public Schools' new Department of Federal Projects, quipped, "The beauty of federal aid . . . is that you can be paid for asking for it. School officials say that the cost of the proposed Department of Federal Projects to get federal aid will . . . be financed by, you guessed it, federal aid."[17] Affluent suburban school districts were also granted generous funding. The upscale Wisconsin suburb of Whitefish Bay, for example, sparked public outcry in 1967 when its public schools were awarded $25,000 in ESEA funds (more than $172,000 in 2010 dollars). To assure passage, the ESEA legislation had been written so that some 90 percent of school districts would be eligible for Title I funding. By 1967, Senator Kennedy expressed his doubts about Title I's effectiveness: "I . . . seriously question whether the people in the ghettos feel anything is really being done," he told colleagues.[18]

In 1969, his concern was the heart of a report by Ruby Martin of the Southern Center for Studies in Public Policy and Phyllis McClure of the NAACP Legal Defense and Education Fund called *Title I of ESEA: Is It Helping Poor Children?* Martin and McClure found Title I funds overwhelmingly flowed to affluent suburban school districts.[19] Investigations revealed that from 1965 through 1969 school districts had been spending much of the $4 billion in appropriated Title I funds on general education, not on low-income students. Worse, school districts were spending extravagant sums on lavish capital projects and salaries for staff who did not work with low-income students. One Fresno, California, school district built a countywide television station, costing nearly $1 million. A Detroit school district used $1.3 million in Title I funds to pay expenses it incurred for participating in the program. Districts were also using Title I funds for building swimming pools.[20] Memphis public schools, for example, spent $63,000 on eighteen portable pools. Textbook and commercial educational product companies, whose representatives were among the leading lobbyists for the ESEA's passage, also reaped millions of dollars when school officials used Title I funds to buy their products. Yet there was no evidence that those purchases actually helped low-income students.[21]

A separate study found that what little information they reported was "meaningless" and served "no conceivable evaluative purpose."[22]

ESEA Expansions Under Nixon, Ford, and Carter

In 1970, during Richard Nixon's administration, amendments clarified that federal aid was to supplement, not supplant, state and local aid to schools.[23] Federal studies through the late 1970s, however, continued to show that funds were not being used for the intended purposes.[24] Nevertheless, the ESEA was reauthorized and expanded in both 1972 and 1974.

By 1974 the ESEA was significantly expanded, including the addition of Title IX, barring gender discrimination in education programs, as well as the creation of the federal National Institute of Education and the National Center for Education Statistics to conduct research.[25] Compensatory programs were also expanded to include dozens of new public school categorical programs: dropout prevention projects, school health services, arts and career education, and women's equity and ethnic studies programs. In all, the 1974 Education Amendments directed more than $12 billion over four years to these programs. ESEA funding for special education also skyrocketed from $100 million in 1974 to $660 million in 1975, while Title VII allocations for non-English-speaking students amounted to $100 million.[26] Title I was and remains, however, the most expensive ESEA component. Fully 51 percent of the ESEA funds allocated in 1975, $1.8 billion, were for Title I programs.[27] The 1974 Education Amendments removed the poverty-level requirements for non-English-speaking students as well as disabled students.[28]

An interesting point is that the continuing expansion of the federal government into education took place during a politically conservative era. In 1965 most House Republicans had voted against the ESEA, but in 1974, their opposition was negligible.[29] Just fifteen days after taking office upon Nixon's resignation, President Gerald Ford signed the expanded ESEA, as well as the federal Education for All Handicapped Children Act, now called the Individuals with Disabilities Education Act (IDEA). The law protects the right of children with disabilities to a "free and appropriate" education. While certainly supportive of that goal, Ford had concerns that "this bill promises more than the Federal Government can deliver . . . falsely raising the expectations of the groups affected by claiming authorization levels which are excessive and unrealistic."[30] Specifically, the cost of the basic grants to the states under the original bill was estimated to grow from $100 million in 1978 to $3.1 billion in 1983.[31]

Today, IDEA is criticized as a bureaucracy-heavy and costly program, complete with perverse incentives to overidentify students with learning disabilities.

As the economy began to slow while federal education program costs continued to rise, a cash-strapped public was clamoring for accountability by the time President Jimmy Carter took office. SAT score declines and concerns over basic skills deficiencies garnered significant media attention by the late 1970s. A decade's worth of "open education" movement fads, emphasizing personal growth, encounter groups, and processes instead of actual academics, had resulted in classroom anarchy, poorly prepared students, and a fed-up public.[32]

In 1965 President Johnson had hailed education innovation as a core element of the ESEA. "Exciting experiments in education are under way," he explained. "Many of our children have studied the 'new' math. There are highly effective ways of teaching high school physics, biology, chemistry, and foreign languages. We need to take full advantage of these and other innovations. Specialists can spark the interest of disadvantaged students."[33] Research on such federally subsidized innovations suggested that this was not their impact. One extensive multiyear study conducted for the Office of Education released in 1978 by RAND found that in spite of a few isolated successes, overall the effect of federal policy with regard to innovation was "disappointing" and more federal funding did not necessarily allow schools to buy things that mattered.[34] RAND concluded:

> Our research adds to the growing body of literature that casts doubt on the effectiveness of federal education policy. It is now widely acknowledged . . . that federal reform efforts overestimated the extent to which schooling could serve as an effective agent for social reform. . . . Idealistic goals such as "eliminating illiteracy by 1984" (Right-to-Read Program) are patently unrealistic. . . . Most important, there is a growing belief that policymakers have overestimated the influence of federal incentives on local practices. They assumed that the incentives and disincentives associated with federal funds afforded considerable direct leverage, but the research evidence . . . strongly indicates that change in school district practice depends on local choices and factors little affected by federal incentives. In short, federal expectations need to be adjusted to the reality of limited federal influence.[35]

Another multiyear study commissioned by the Office of Education reached a similar conclusion. In 1977 the American Institutes for Research found "no clear evidence" that levels of innovation ensured reading gains. In fact, its study concluded that levels of innovation and "individualization" in instruction were "negatively rather than positively related to growth in arithmetic achievement." Those findings, according to the researchers, "should serve as a reminder to educators—as well as to parents and legislators—that educational innovation per se will not necessarily produce dramatic effects on student achievement."[36] Such findings prompted several states to adopt their own basic skills assessments. Thirty-eight states had basic skills assessments by 1978, jumping to all fifty states two years later.[37]

Reagan's New Federalism:
One Small Step for States, One Giant Leap for Bureaucracy

On the day it began operations on May 4, 1980, presidential candidate and California Gov. Ronald Reagan called the Department of Education "President Carter's new bureaucratic boondoggle" and insisted, "The answers to our problems are not still more federal agencies and federal spending." He vowed that if elected:

> I will use every resource at my command to eliminate programs, which serve no useful purpose . . . [One may find many programs that] are arguably well administered, but which spend money in a manner that is incomprehensible. Cutting such programs would be a high priority in my administration . . . I would work to transfer back to states and local—localities programs, which do not belong at the federal level. Welfare and education are two functions that should be primarily . . . carried out at the state and local levels. . . . The sources of revenue to fund these programs should also return to local government. Such a return would eliminate an unneeded level of bureaucracy and give the people more control over these important and expensive programs.[38]

Thanks to the ESEA, federal education funding had increased from $4 billion in 1965 to $25 billion in 1980.[39] The federal regulatory burden had also increased substantially. For instance, from 1964 to 1977 the number of federal laws affecting higher education increased 1,000 percent to more than 439. As of 1977, thirty-four congressional committees and about eighty subcommittees had jurisdiction over those laws.[40] By 1975 postsecondary institutions were reporting that their administrative costs associated with federally mandated higher education programs amounted to as much as one-quarter of their general administrative costs.[41] The Department of Education was supposed to improve this situation, but not everyone was convinced.

By the time Reagan assumed office, the tide of popular opinion had turned dramatically. Public distrust of the federal government was at an all-time high. Watergate had shaken Americans' faith in the federal government domestically, while the Iranian hostage crisis at the close of the 1970s reinforced a growing exasperation with federal ineptitude. Concerning education policy, "taxpayer revolts" had been erupting across the country in response to skyrocketing local property taxes, and outrage over forced busing continued. ESEA program funding was being diverted from low-income students and directed instead to more affluent districts and purposes unintended by the law.

The stage seemed to be set for scaling back the federal role in education by the time President Reagan took office in 1980. In fact, early on, Reagan appointed a fourteen-member task force to deliver education policy recommendations for accomplishing that goal.[42] Elimination of the Department of Education was a central pillar of his September 24, 1981, economic recovery plan. "By eliminating the Department of Education less than two years after it was created," said Reagan, "we can not only reduce the budget but ensure that local needs and preferences, rather than the wishes of Washington, determine the education of our children."[43]

Meanwhile, changes to the ESEA during President Reagan's first term were a microcosm of his broader policy objective to curb federal overreach in education, epitomized by the new Department of Education, which Reagan vowed to abolish. As part of the Omnibus Budget Reconciliation Act of 1981, the ESEA was reauthorized as the Educational Consolidation and Improvement Act, which went into effect in June 1982.[44] It consolidated twenty-nine smaller programs into state block grants and cut federal aid 15 percent, more than $1 million.[45] The purpose of the block grants was not revenue sharing but rather restoring local authority over education. The act's language indicated that the federal government was to assist states and localities to improve elementary and secondary education generally but not to direct those efforts. "At issue was the extent to which fifteen years of federal aid under the ESEA had actually 'built the capacity'—in terms of both ability and willingness—of state and local education agencies to run effective and equitable programs on their own," according to the States' Impact on Federal Education Policy Project. "If federal aid had in fact built local capacity, then block grants could perhaps advance 'federal goals' such as quality and excellence while, at the same time, decreasing federal oversight (and perhaps even cutting total federal aid)."[46] Since 1965, federal oversight had become increasingly costly yet had failed to produce compelling evidence of improved educational outcomes, as Reagan explained in his fiscal year 1983 budget:

> The responsibility for education rests primarily with parents and with State and local governments. In recent years, Federal intervention has imposed many burdensome requirements that have made the exercise of this responsibility both more costly and more difficult. To decrease the Federal Government's intervention gradually, the administration proposes to continue many of the existing programs in 1983, but at lower funding levels and with fewer regulatory and reporting requirements than in years past. In addition, this budget directs elementary, secondary, and higher education funds more toward those in greatest need. Most training and employment activities are and should be carried out by the private sector. Private businesses and employers are far more efficient than the Government at training workers for specific tasks that contribute to a productive economy. Government training in most cases has been expensive, often has been for people who would probably find work anyway, and too frequently has been for jobs that do not exist. The best contribution the Federal Government can make to the under-trained and unemployed is to encourage the steady expansion of the private economy and private employment.[47]

Against this backdrop, Reagan also worked to abolish the Department of Education during his first term.

President Reagan did not believe the parchment barriers erected in the Department of Education enabling legislation would actually preserve local control over education. Instead, he believed the very existence of a US Department of Education meant that the federal government would continue to expand and crowd out parents, along with local and state officials, when it came to setting education policy and practice. The steps he took against the department, however, were at odds with his stated goal of restoring local control over education by minimizing the role of the federal government—beginning with his choice for education secretary.

Given Reagan's insistence on eliminating the Department of Education, there were doubts about whether he would appoint anyone to replace Carter's appointee, Secretary of Education Shirley Hufstedler, who was widely considered a politically motivated appointee with no education experience and aspirations for a Supreme Court nomination.[48] In January 1981, however, Reagan appointed to that post Terrel H. Bell, Utah commissioner of higher education and US education commissioner in the Nixon and Ford administrations. Bell was also a member of the education community and did not draw resistance from the National Education Association (NEA). In fact, then-NEA Executive Director Terry Herndon praised Bell to *The Wall Street Journal* for being "a distinguished educator with wide experience who understands the problems and issues facing public education."[49] To others, Bell seemed a puzzling choice.

In October 1977, Bell had testified in favor of creating the Department of Education during one of Sen. Abraham Ribicoff's Governmental Affairs Committee hearings, saying "We need a US Department of Education. . . . I am thoroughly convinced that this legislation will be the most important event ever touching American education in the decade of the seventies."[50] During his own remarks the following year on the need for a Department of Education, Senator Ribicoff quoted Bell, who had testified earlier that in the current arrangement, "The Commissioner [of Education] is an executive level . . . in the government, and in HEW that is one of the lowest forms of human life."[51] Years later after resigning as secretary, Bell explained that it was always his intention "to preserve the traditional federal role in education. . . . To this day, I'm not certain why I was selected by the president, especially in view of the fact that I had once testified favorably on the bill that created the Department of Education."[52]

Once appointed secretary of education, however, Bell repeatedly insisted that he was not bothered by President Reagan's plan to dismantle the department he was supposed to run.[53] Shortly after Bell's appointment, the *Bangor*

Daily News seized upon this inconsistency, wondering on its editorial pages, "Has Mr. Bell had a change of heart? Or did Ronald Reagan in his campaign pledge to dismantle this unnecessary department merely pander for votes?"[54] Several weeks before Reagan delivered his September 1981 economic recovery plan, Secretary Bell forwarded the president his plan to dismantle the department.[55] Reaction to one version reported in the press sparked controversy. Sen. Daniel Patrick Moynihan (D-N.Y.) called the idea of abolishing the education department "mostly nonsense" because "no serious person" would ever suggest that "the Federal Government does not have responsibility for education."[56] In reality, Bell's abolition plan was anything but.

As noted previously, Secretary Bell favored preserving what he called a "traditional federal role in education." For him this meant supporting state and local education efforts though conducting and disseminating research, which officials could take or leave, and replacing narrow categorical or earmark program funding with block-grant funding to give states and localities wider latitude in financing their education priorities. Bell did oppose what by then had already become a standard practice of coercing states into compliance with federal mandates by threatening to withhold funding, what Bell considered "generally too drastic a response."[57] Still, Bell never suggested eliminating the Department of Education. Instead he recommended downgrading it to a sub-Cabinet entity along the lines of the National Science Foundation.

Most important, eliminating the Department of Education was not the policy course adopted by the Reagan Administration—in spite of the strong public rhetoric to the contrary. President Reagan's Department of Education Task Force delivered its decision memorandum in November 1981, which began by stating:

> The genius of American education is defined by local and popular control, diversity, open access, and pragmatic adaptation to problems. These principles, to which the American people are deeply attached, have served our country well. Nonetheless, the Federal Government, concerned about the Nation's research capabilities, the lack of equal educational opportunities and for other reasons, intruded into the educational arena. While this imposition started slowly with the providing

of aid and assistance and a distant involvement in curriculum, it soon grew into the intrusiveness of establishing educational requirements and supplanting local priorities. The establishment of the Department of Education in 1980 marked the zenith of the intrusiveness.[58]

In stark contrast, Reagan's task force concluded that the most "viable" option for "abolishing the Department of Education" was legislation replacing the department with a sub-Cabinet National Education Foundation to oversee school-based programs and assistance, and Reagan ultimately acquiesced.[59] The task force acknowledged two principal shortcomings with this plan. First, "It would continue a centralized Federal presence in the education field with potential for future expansion by statute;" and second, "Critics of the Department . . . might claim the Department has not really been eliminated only changed in name and dropped from Cabinet status."[60]

Thus the Reagan Administration's approach to the Department of Education was actually one of dismantling-by-downgrading, not outright abolition—although outright abolition is what Reagan emphasized in his January 26, 1982, State of the Union Address:

> The budget plan I submit to you on February 8th will realize major savings by dismantling the Departments of Energy and Education. . . . Our citizens feel they've lost control of even the most basic decisions made about the essential services of government, such as schools, welfare, roads, and even garbage collection. And they're right. . . . The main reason for this is the overpowering growth of Federal grants-in-aid programs during the past few decades. In 1960 the Federal Government had 132 categorical grant programs, costing $7 billion. When I took office, there were approximately 500, costing nearly a hundred billion dollars—13 programs for energy, 36 for pollution control, 66 for social services, 90 for education. And here in the Congress, it takes at least 166 committees just to try to keep track of them. You know and I know that neither the President nor the Congress can properly oversee this jungle of grants-in-aid.[61]

In his February 8, 1982, budget message to Congress, President Reagan emphasized revitalizing American federalism, which included reducing the growth of overall Federal spending by eliminating Federal activities that overstep the proper sphere of Federal Government responsibilities [and] reducing the Federal regulatory burden in areas where the Federal Government intrudes unnecessarily into our private lives or interferes unnecessarily with the efficient conduct of private business or of State or local government.[62]

Reagan's fiscal year 1983 budget proposed to "abolish the Department of Education and form a smaller Foundation for Education Assistance, transferring a number of programs to other agencies." Block grants to the states were also the subject of recommended education reform; however, Reagan did not, as commonly assumed, attempt to eliminate completely the federal role in education.[63] Instead, he noted the steady growth of federal influence over parental, state, and local education decisions, even though it provides only 10 percent of total education funding. He explained:

The creation of the Department of Education symbolized the progressive intrusion of the Federal Government into an educational system that has drawn its strength from diversity, adaptability, and local control. Legislation is being transmitted to abolish the Department of Education, form a Foundation for Education Assistance, and transfer several programs to other agencies whose missions are more appropriate for these activities. The Foundation and the other proposals in this budget would affirm that the primary responsibility for education rests with parents, the States, and local school systems. . . . The administration believes that Federal involvement should return to more traditional minimal levels.[64]

At the fiscal year 1983 budget signing ceremony, reporters did not question President Reagan about his plans to eliminate the Department of Education. Reagan, however, explained, "There has been no budget cut. There have been cuts in the rate of increase in spending. . . . What we are doing is reducing a rate of increase that, when I became President, was running at 17.4 percent, far ahead of any increase or any tax."[65] A few weeks later Reagan proposed his fiscal year 1984 budget, which documented that more than forty narrow categorical education programs had been combined into a single state block grant. Interestingly, only twenty-seven programs had been funded in recent years. In this budget, Reagan announced his plan to replace the Department of Education with a smaller Foundation for Education Assistance and to transfer numerous programs to other agencies. Targeted education and training programs were to be consolidated into distinct state block grants.[66]

In settling for this compromise, President Reagan opted for the worst of all possible worlds. His task force was initially divided.[67] It was reported that Secretary Bell threatened to resign if his foundation plan was not approved.[68] Meanwhile, other top advisers, including Reagan's domestic policy adviser Martin Anderson and Edwin Meese III, counselor to the president, favored actually eliminating the Department of Education.[69] Ultimately, Reagan and his task force agreed upon a modified education plan recommending that most education functions continue to be administered by a $10.7 billion national education foundation. The reasons for supporting this plan included that it would (1) be a palatable alternative for the twenty-one senators and 176 Representatives facing re-election who had voted to establish the department; (2) offer an acceptable alternative for other members of Congress and committee chairs who voted for the department; and (3) encounter less resistance from education special interest groups than eliminating the department outright.[70] Yet opting for Bell's plan did nothing to mollify education special interest groups, which pounced on the administration's "abolition" rhetoric.[71] Reagan also raised concerns among allies who noted, as Reagan's advisers predicted they would, that changing the department's status or name is not the same as eliminating it.[72]

While the president's task force was deciding what to do with the Department of Education, Secretary Bell was putting together an eighteen-member National Commission on Excellence in Schools.[73] Its purpose, according to Bell, was to "call attention to an alarmingly persistent decline in quality education."[74] Publicly, Bell insisted that the "success of this endeavor will not require the continued existence of the Department of Education, and the plans for dismantling of the department will go forward."[75] Yet in the same breath Bell also acknowledged that the federal government would continue to "play a useful coordination and advocacy role." Specifically, the federal government would use the commission's findings to highlight best practices and make them "contagious" through a federal "drive to persuade school boards and state education agencies to adopt policies that will raise the levels of expected achievement," including "changes in state and local standards."[76] As the *New York Times* reported, "Although the memorandum insists that the proposed action will 'fully support' the Reagan Administration's so-called New Federalism, in which it seeks to keep the Government from interfering in what it regards as functions of state and local governments, some critics may question that assertion."[77] That prediction proved accurate.

Just as President Reagan's task force was deeply divided over how exactly to abolish the Department of Education, members of Secretary Bell's Excellence Commission were also divided about what role, if any, the federal government should take in addressing its findings, which it released in April 1983 under the title, *A Nation at Risk*. It warned of the "rising tide of mediocrity" in American schools, which if imposed by an "unfriendly foreign power" would be considered "an act of war."[78] While "the average citizen today is better educated and more knowledgeable than the average citizen of a generation ago . . . *the average graduate* of our schools and colleges today is not as well-educated as the average graduate of 25 or 35 years ago, when a much smaller proportion of our population completed high school and college" [emphasis in original], the commission reported.[79]

Specifically, *A Nation at Risk* identified serious shortcomings in academic content, expectations, time, and teaching. International comparisons on nineteen assessments dating back to the 1970s revealed American students never ranked first or even second. Instead, they ranked last seven times.[80] Compared to the previous generation, American high school students of the late 1970s and early 1980s were subjected to a "cafeteria style curriculum in which the appetizers and desserts can easily be mistaken for the main courses." Fewer than one-third of students completed core courses in subjects such as math or foreign languages; while one-quarter of students' credits were earned in general track courses, including physical education, remedial English and math, and adult and marriage training classes. Compared to the American high school students who actually took four years of math and science courses, students in other developed countries had three times as many course hours. Courses in cooking and driving counted as much toward high school diplomas as chemistry, English, history, or math. In addition, teaching was drawing a large proportion of its new recruits from the bottom quarter of their high school and college classes; and about half of new math, science, and English teachers were not qualified to teach those subjects.[81]

Focusing on high school students, the Excellence Commission found performance declines and deficiencies across student subgroups. Close to 13 percent of all 17-year-olds were functionally illiterate. That rate jumped to nearly 40 percent for minority students. Performance on standardized tests for high school students overall as well as college-bound students had been steadily declining for nearly two decades. Meanwhile, college remediation rates steadily increased beginning in the mid-1970s so that by 1980, about one-quarter of all English and math courses offered at many four-year colleges and universities were remedial classes. Businesses and the military also complained that they struggled to find qualified applicants and had to devote significant time and resources remediating them.[82]

At the official White House *A Nation at Risk* release ceremony, some Excellence Commission members insisted that they had intentionally steered clear of controversial matters surrounding the federal role in education because "they were unable to agree on those issues."[83] That lack of consensus left room for partisans on both sides to claim victory for their favored policies—even though *A Nation at Risk* was silent on many of them. President Reagan believed that its findings were "consistent with our task of redefining the federal role in education" and supported his "call for an end to federal intrusion" in education. He pledged that he "would continue to work in the months ahead for passage of tuition tax credits, vouchers, educational savings accounts, voluntary school prayer, and abolishing the Department of Education."[84] Teachers union leaders and some elected officials, however, insisted the report supported more federal education spending. American Federation of Teachers President Albert Shanker responded to the report by saying that "state and local governments will not heed these recommendations without financial help." Along the same lines, Congressman Carl D. Perkins (D-Ky.), House Education and Labor Committee chairman, said, "I hope that as a result the President will recognize that we are going to have to put more resources and support into education."[85]

While Excellence Commission members carefully avoided what they considered the controversial issue of abolishing the Department of Education, *A Nation at Risk* contained many clear statements indicating they believed the federal government did indeed have a legitimate role in education. In its guidance on implementing its recommendations, the commission stated:

> The Federal Government, in cooperation with States and localities, should help meet the needs of key groups of students such as the gifted and talented, the socioeconomically disadvantaged, minority and language minority students, and the handicapped. . . . The Federal Government has the primary responsibility to identify the national interest in education. It should also help fund and support efforts to protect and promote that interest. It must provide the national leadership to ensure that the Nation's public and private resources are marshaled to address the issues discussed in this report.[86]

Thus, the Excellence Commission did not consider it controversial to state that the federal government has the "primary responsibility" in shaping national education policy. Further, the commission simply took for granted that the federal government has a constitutionally legitimate role in rectifying educational inequalities the states apparently cannot—a hallmark of old equity federalism.

> We believe the Federal Government's role includes several functions of national consequence that States and localities alone are unlikely to be able to meet: protecting constitutional and civil rights for students and school personnel; collecting data, statistics, and information about education generally; supporting curriculum improvement and research on teaching, learning, and the management of schools; supporting teacher training in areas of critical shortage or key national needs; and providing student financial assistance and research and graduate training.[87]

All this was to be accomplished, the commission continued, "with a minimum of administrative burden and intrusiveness."[88] Those conclusions reflected Secretary Bell's naïve vision of a "traditional" federal role in education: to have a leading, but supportive, relationship with the states and localities. That primary role would be bolstered by generous federal funding devoid of cumbersome categorical mandates on the states. Research, not restrictions, would solidify the states' recognition of the federal government's superiority in identifying best practices, and the states, in turn, would simply go along—if the price was right.

The release of *A Nation at Risk* is widely credited for derailing President Reagan's plan for eliminating the Department of Education. "We succeeded in drawing almost unprecedented attention from educators, parents, public and press," wrote Excellence Commission member Glenn T. Seaborg in 1991, a decade after the commission's formation. "Ironically, the overwhelmingly favorable reception of our report also doomed his plan to abolish the Department of Education."[89] Secretary Bell concurred in a commemorative article he wrote in 1993, saying, "Following the release of the report and this series of conferences, I heard no more about abolishing the Department of Education."[90] Preceded by Reagan's ill-advised appointment of Bell as education secretary and the weak final recommendation of his Department of Education task force, the release of *A Nation at Risk* turned out to be the final nail in the coffin of Reagan's stated goal to abolish the Department of Education.

The Reagan task force's tepid recommendation for downgrading the Department of Education did not win over supporters in Congress, which rejected the plan. Reagan referred to the abolition of the Department of Education just once more in his fiscal year 1984 budget.[91] In June of 1983, *Time* reported that

the President abandoned his promise to dismantle the Department of Education, which he was fond of describing during the 1980 campaign as "President Carter's new bureaucratic boondoggle." His strategists hope this change of heart will deprive the Democrats of a symbolic target. Instead, he is "redirecting" the department. Reagan has told Bell . . . to develop an "agenda for excellence" based on the [*Nation at Risk*] report's findings. The agenda, says Bell, will entail more federal lobbying rather than more federal money. The Secretary will encourage state legislatures to pass new taxes to support the public schools and impose stiffer high school graduation requirements. He will urge the states to draft master-teacher plans like the one pushed by Tennessee Governor Lamar Alexander, who wants to offer incentive payments to outstanding teachers. . . . White House aides concede that the impetus on the education issue will be hard to sustain, since the Administration is simply urging state and local action rather than offering a program of its own.[92]

Ultimately, abolishing the Department of Education was dropped from the Republican Party plank at its 1984 convention.[93]

Federal Education Involvement Resurfaces Under Reagan

In 1987, the ESEA reverted to its original premise that federal aid was essential for equalizing public school educational opportunities and achievement. That year Representatives Augustus Hawkins (D-Calif.) and Robert Stafford (R-Vt.) introduced the Hawkins-Stafford School Improvements, which increased federal Title I appropriations by $500 million on the condition that schools document measurable achievement gains, including gains among disadvantaged students. The Hawkins-Stafford amendments repealed the block-grant format of the Educational Consolidation and Improvement Act and restored the traditional categorical program funding framework of its predecessor, the ESEA. After two decades of the ESEA, not to mention the release of *A Nation at Risk*, the landmark 1983 report by Ronald Reagan's National Commission on Excellence in Education documenting the decades-long decline of American public school performance, members of Congress on both sides of the aisle wanted evidence that federal funds were closing achievement gaps.[94]

Thus it is interesting to note that the beginnings of the expansive federal testing regime in place today originate with the original ESEA of 1965 and Sen. Robert Kennedy's insistence that evaluation mandates be inserted into the enabling legislation.[95] Those requirements were amplified in 1987 by Representatives Hawkins and Stafford and the growing emphasis on schoolwide reform. In 1988, the National Assessment Governing Board was created to help make possible the reporting of state-level data from the National Assessment of Educational Progress (NAEP) through normal curve equivalents (NCEs). States defined their annual NCE improvements as low as possible to still be eligible for federal funding.[96] According to the States' Impact on Federal Education Policy Project, by 1988:

A majority of states set the lowest standard of improvement allowable under federal regulations: "normal curve equivalents" (NCEs) simply "greater than zero," which meant only the slightest measurable improvement from one school year to the next. (NCEs are not the same as grade levels, but they are analogous in that they compare progress made from year to year for students of the same age on a national scale; average students gain three NCEs per year on standardized tests.) Even states that set a standard of less than one NCE per year were found to need improvement. Some states set a more "ambitious" standard of one full NCE per year and, in those places, the proportion of schools found to need improvement was larger (despite the fact that "average students gained three NCEs per year"). A few states set a standard of negative NCEs—meaning that declining student achievement was deemed acceptable from year to year. Needless to say, giving states the freedom to set their own standards did not always lead to the kind of "accountability" for achievement that federal officials wanted.[97]

For the remainder of his administration, President Reagan pursued an excellence agenda in which the federal government outlined broad national education goals but left implementation to state and local officials. He continued to advocate, unsuccessfully at the national level, for several positive policies based on the idea of decentralization. While his block-grant approach was reversed, Reagan recommended other decentralized education polices, including locally developed tuition tax credit and voucher scholarship programs to maximize parental choice over their children's education. Reagan also wanted to empower families to save for college themselves through tax-exempt education savings accounts to reduce dependency on federal student loans and aid. At the same time, however, Reagan also supported ongoing federal aid for students from socioeconomically disadvantaged backgrounds, those with disabilities, and college students with financial need. He also supported federal legislation to address the shortage of math and science teachers.[98]

What President Reagan's new federalism did not do was tackle the centuries-old debate over what—if any—constitutional role the federal government has in education. Thus any difference between old-equity federalism and new-excellence federalism was ultimately a distinction more than a difference. Both versions granted that the federal government did indeed have a legitimate role in crafting national education policy. So understood, the only remaining question was how big of a role the federal government should have.

A "Kinder, Gentler" Federal Education Regime: The Bush Years

As the 1980s drew to a close, NAEP reading proficiency had declined slightly among 9- and 13-year-olds, along with SAT scores. Meanwhile, per-pupil expenditures increased 33 percent in real terms from $4,500 to more than $5,900. This increase came largely from the states and localities since the federal funding share dropped from nearly 10 percent to slightly more than 6 percent.[99] George H.W. Bush, who succeeded President Reagan, early on declared himself "the education president." The federal government under his watch would be a "kinder, gentler" force for education excellence by promoting national goals. The localities, in turn, would meet those goals as a "thousand points of light" with exemplars of successful schools.[100] Bush laid his federal education policy foundation in September 1989 when he convened the first national education summit between a president and state governors since the Depression, held in Charlottesville, Virginia. Bush's summit remarks clarified what role the federal government would play during his administration. "There are real problems right now in our educational system, but there is no one Federal solution," Bush said. "The Federal Government, of course, has a very important role to play... And we're going to work with you to help find answers, but I firmly believe that the key will be found at the State and local levels."[101]

Six national education goals emerged from the summit, largely shaped by then Arkansas Governor Bill Clinton. Bush presented those goals in his 1990 State of the Union address. By the year 2000:

1. All children in America will start school ready to learn.

2. The high school graduation rate will reach at least 90 percent.

3. American students will leave Grades 4, 8, and 12 having demonstrated competency in challenging subject matter including English, mathe-

matics, science, history, and geography; and every school in America will ensure that all students learn to use their minds well prepared for responsible citizenship, further learning, and productive employment in a modern economy.

4. US students will be first in the world in science and mathematics achievement.

5. Every adult American will be literate and possess the knowledge and skills necessary to compete in a global economy and exercise the rights and responsibilities of citizenship.

6. Every school in America will be free of drugs and violence and will offer a safe, disciplined environment conducive to learning.

Bush also created the National Education Goals Panel in July 1990 to report on progress toward those goals.[102] The following year Bush appointed former Tennessee Gov. Lamar Alexander as US secretary of education and presented their America 2000 program, the implementation plan for the National Goals Panel's education proposals. Key America 2000 components included the creation of national standards and voluntary national tests (American Achievement Tests) in English, math, science, history, and geography. Those tests would be administered to students in Grades 4, 8, and 12. Other components included direct federal grants to develop 535 New American Schools, which would serve as models for other schools. The program required every school and district to release report cards on their progress. America 2000 would also allow Title I funds to be used toward vouchers so low-income students could attend private schools. Congress defeated the America 2000 legislation in 1992, with Republicans objecting to national standards and Democrats opposing vouchers.[103]

Meanwhile, states began to take the lead in innovative education reforms that made parents, not politicians, agents of accountability. As a first step, Minnesota enacted the country's first charter school law, giving schools more autonomy over curriculum, hiring, and basic operations while holding them accountable for results. While no major federal education legislation was passed during President Bush's administration, spending increased markedly. Department of Education spending increased 41 percent between 1989 and

1992. Over this same period, federal education spending grew 25 percent. In all, federal education funding increased in constant 1995 dollars from $25.6 billion in 1965 to $66.0 billion in 1975. It then increased from $56.7 billion in 1985 to $71.7 billion in 1995.[104]

Clinton Links Goals 2000 to Title I Funding

Picking up and expanding the America 2000 program, President Bill Clinton advanced its goals in 1993 as Goals 2000: The Educate America Act. Although it closely resembled the earlier plan, it added provisions relating to teacher quality and parental responsibility. It also included a National Education Standards and Improvement Council, which would be responsible for reviewing states' voluntary standards against revised national standards. Passed in February 1994, the new program was linked to Title I funding. The 1994 ESEA reauthorization, called the Improving America's Schools Act (IASA), required states to develop education plans that coordinated with Goals 2000 and other federal acts to be eligible for Title I funding. Most of that funding during the last three out of the five reauthorization years was to be used developing state standards and the necessary assessments.

By linking Goals 2000 and IASA Title I funding, a new trajectory was set for an ever-increasing federal role in education. As the States' Impact on Federal Education Policy Project explained:

> IASA . . . marked one of the most significant uses of federal power in state and local education policy. By requiring that standards and accountability be the same for all children, it made Title I funding, the largest single federal funding stream for elementary and secondary education, contingent on state and local decisions around standards, testing, teacher training, curriculum, and accountability. . . . Though the federal contribution to education in 1994 remained low—about 7 percent of education funding in most states—the federal government was increasing its demands on state and local education agencies in exchange for federal dollars. This growing federal role in shaping education for all students provided the basis for increased federal funding in the years 1995–2000 and foreshadowed the even larger impact sought by Clinton's successor.[105]

As with previous iterations of the ESEA, the 1994 IASA preserved the express prohibition against federal control of schools' or states' educational curricula or assessments.[106] Goals 2000 funding alone was slated to increase from $94 million in 1994 to $490 million in 1999. Additional Title I funding, however, exceeded $6 billion.[107]

With that kind of funding at stake, states fell in line. By 1996, schools in forty-eight states were receiving Goals 2000 grants, and by 1998 more than one-third of the country's 15,000 school districts were receiving them.[108] Coinciding with this growth was the Republican revolution of 1994, including the Contract with America, which focused largely on Clinton's health care plan. Similarly, during the presidential election of 1996, abolition of the Department of Education reappeared only briefly as part of the Republican platform. In fact, Republican presidential candidate Bob Dole had given outspoken support to an early version of the legislation creating a Department of Education.

At the time, Senator Dole extolled the 1978 bill at some length saying, "Every day, millions and millions of children . . . sit in classrooms across America . . . I believe it is our responsibility to see that these young citizens receive the best education we can provide, and I feel that a new Department of Education is one way toward that goal. . . . I am hopeful that by a favorable vote on S. 991, we are taking a sizeable step toward improving the educational structure in our government."[109] Less than twenty years later as the Republican presidential candidate, Dole took a very different position, declaring, "We're going to eliminate the Department of Education. We don't need it in the first place. I didn't vote for it in 1979. . . . I didn't favor it. When it started, I voted against it. It was a tribute . . . after President Carter's election to the National Education Association."[110] The reappearance of the Department of Education abolition plank was short-lived, however, since the department had strong support from its affluent constituency, and Washington politicians knew it.[111]

During President Clinton's second term, Congress blocked his Voluntary National Tests plan. Bogged down with the Monica Lewinsky scandal, Clinton was not able to reauthorize the ESEA in 1999 with provisions ending social promotion of unprepared students and adding 100,000 more teachers. In spite of Republican opposition to this and other Clinton education plans, Republicans and Democrats in Congress now vied with one another over who supported the most generous federal education spending increases. In fact, between 1993 and 2001 discretionary federal education spending grew 53 percent in real terms, from $27.6 billion to $42.2 billion.[112]

If You Can't Beat 'Em, Join 'Em

Just three days after his inauguration on January 23, 2001, President George W. Bush introduced his first legislative proposal: a twenty-five-page concept paper outlining the No Child Left Behind Act (NCLB), which would supersede Clinton's IASA as the latest iteration of the ESEA. It built directly on the IASA and added exacting accountability metrics, including (1) All students must be proficient in reading, math, and science by 2014; (2) states must develop adequate yearly progress (AYP) proficiency targets that students must reach to achieve 100 percent proficiency by 2014; and (3) AYP targets must be disaggregated by student socioeconomic groups by income, race, gender, English language ability, and special education status. A school would be deemed failing and subject to sanctions if any student subgroup did not make AYP, including allowing students to transfer to better performing schools. Because that transfer option was limited to other public schools within a given district, in most instances better performing schools did not have room to take in additional students from surrounding failing schools.[113]

While its AYP requirements remained highly controversial, Congress passed NCLB with strong bipartisan support. The House passed it on May 23, 2001, by a vote of 384 to 45. The following month on June 14 the Senate passed NCLB by a vote of 91 to 8.[114] To achieve that support numerous provisions were eliminated that would have significantly increased parents' power over their children's education. Early on, Bush indicated that private school choice provisions, along with educational savings accounts, were expendable. Bush had also succeeded in excluding the abolition of the Department of Education from the Republican platform.

His reticence about parental choice in education, along with his seeming resignation to a perpetual federal presence in education in the interest of winning congressional support, was at odds with political reality. For the first time since 1952, Republicans controlled both houses of Congress.[115] Representative Mark Souder (R-Ind.), who voted against the NCLB legislation, aptly summed up the Republican about-face, saying, "We wouldn't have passed this bill under Bill Clinton . . . It's more money than we would have given to Bill Clinton, and we would never have given him a national test."[116]

Within its first year, the NCLB choice and standards provisions proved unworkable. The US Department of Education identified more than 8,600 Title I schools that would have to offer students transfer options because they failed to make AYP. Across the country, parents were either never notified of their children's transfer options or denied the option because better public schools nearby had no room. States tinkered with their proficiency definitions to help schools avoid a failing label, and they set their initial AYP improvement targets at laughably low rates. States also gamed the Unsafe School Choice Option, which required states to define and identify Persistently Dangerous Schools. Because states' definitions were so narrow and typically required three or more years of repeated disciplinary actions, in each year since NCLB's enactment, fewer than fifty schools nationwide have been designated persistently dangerous.[117]

Reflecting on NCLB's effectiveness after a decade of operation, the Cato Institute's Neal McCluskey recalled RAND's 1975 assessment that the ESEA was failing. No one in Washington would act, according to the report, because "the teachers, administrators, and others whose salaries are paid by Title I, or whose budgets are balanced by its funds, are . . . a more powerful constituency than those . . . disillusioned by its unfulfilled promise." NCLB is no better, according to McCluskey:

> Basically, the law was a victim of concentrated benefits and diffuse costs, a situation that hasn't changed in a decade of No Child Left Behind, the current version of the ESEA. The root problem is that the people with the most at stake in a policy are the most motivated to participate in the politics of it, giving them disproportionate power. In education, those people are the school employees whose very livelihoods depend on the system. And they want what everyone, ideally, wants: generous compensation and no accountability. This basic reality is why for decades Washington dumped money onto schools regardless of performance. It's why, once taxpayers got so fed up they demanded change, politicians created accountability regimes they never really

enforced. And it's why, when you dig into them, National Assessment of Educational Progress [NAEP] scores provide no meaningful evidence that NCLB has worked. Unfortunately, some people think that the solution is to double down on government power by imposing a federal curriculum. Not "voluntary, common standards," but standards forced onto states by the Race to the Top and NCLB waivers and accompanied by federally funded tests.[118]

As McCluskey notes, NCLB's impact on NAEP scores fails to provide support for its effectiveness. Comparing apparent gains based on state standards assessments to nationally representative NAEP reading and math performance data before and after NCLB's implementation, Harvard University's Jaekyung Lee found no appreciable improvement in reading or math performance and no sustained narrowing of the achievement gap. He estimated that by 2014, only about one-third of students would be proficient in reading, and at most about two-thirds of students would be proficient in math based on independent NAEP results. Lee predicted results for minority students would be far worse, with less than a quarter of low-income and minority students achieving NAEP reading proficiency and less than half achieving proficiency in NAEP math.[119] Actual results as of 2013 revealed that Lee had accurately predicted reading proficiency rates, but his math predictions were too rosy. Just over one-third of all students were proficient or better in math (35 percent), while around one in five low-income and minority students scored proficient or above (21 percent).

A University of California, Berkeley, research team led by Bruce Fuller also found that achievement gap improvements seen in the 1990s began fading away after NCLB.[120] "The slowing of achievement gains, even declines in reading, since 2002 suggests that state-led accountability efforts—well underway by the mid-1990s—packed more of a punch in raising student performance, compared with the flattening-out of scores during the 'No Child' era," said Fuller. At best NCLB may have sustained math gains already under way due to state-led initiatives, according to Fuller. "But we find no consistent evidence that federal reforms have rekindled the states' earlier gains."[121]

Other studies helped explain why. In response to federal NCLB mandates, states simply lowered their proficiency standards and passing scores, and they tinkered with annual performance gain percentages to appear as though students were making gains—just as they had done in the late 1980s in response to new mandates requiring higher student test scores in exchange for federal ESEA funding.[122] Numerous media investigations also revealed apparent student achievement gains were the result of cheating by school officials, including those in Atlanta, Baltimore, Dallas, Washington, DC, El Paso, Houston, and Philadelphia.[123] University researchers and journalists, however, were not the only critics of NCLB.

Among the most outspoken critics of NCLB and overreach by the US Department of Education was the NEA—an ironic twist considering it had been the driving force behind the department's creation in 1979. In 2005 the NEA and several school districts filed what was ultimately an unsuccessful lawsuit against the US Department of Education claiming NCLB amounted to an unfunded mandate. "At stake is a fundamental constitutional question regarding the power of Congress to shift costs for compliance with federal education mandates to states and local districts without making it clear from the outset that the federal government will not cover the costs of compliance," said NEA President Dennis Van Roekel.[124] Lawmakers in at least thirty states spoke out against NCLB, and officials from more than a half dozen states filed supportive amicus briefs, but no state formally joined the NEA suit. While NEA officials believed fear of reprisal from the US Department of Education was a contributing factor, Connecticut filed its own unsuccessful lawsuit, also claiming NCLB amounted to an unfunded mandate.[125]

Upping the ante, Utah threatened to adopt legislation opting out of NCLB entirely in 2004 on state sovereignty grounds. The White House and federal education officials responded with intensive lobbying that included warnings of the loss of tens of millions of dollars in federal funding if Utah enacted such a plan. While it did not enact a full opt-out, the following year Utah took what was called the strongest action of thirty-five states when it passed legislation establishing that state standards take precedence over federal ones.[126] That law passed one day after a letter arrived from then-Secretary of Education Margaret Spellings, noting that the move could threaten Utah's $76 million in federal funding. "I'd just as soon they take the stinking money and go back to Washington with it," said Republican state legislator Steve Mascaro in response. "Let us resolve our education problems by ourselves. I will not be threatened by Washington over $76 million."[127]

In addition to Connecticut and Utah, nine states adopted provisional opt-out laws, prohibitions against spending state funds on NCLB implementation, or had school districts that took legal action against NCLB: Colorado, Illinois, Louisiana, Maine, Michigan, New Jersey, Pennsylvania, Texas, and Vermont. Another thirteen states considered, but did not adopt, opt-out legislation: Arizona, Florida, Hawaii, Indiana, Maryland, Minnesota, New Hampshire, Nevada, New Mexico, North Dakota, Ohio, Oregon, and Wisconsin.[128] In response to the barrage of legislative and legal actions, the US Department of Education relented somewhat in 2005 by granting states more flexibility with waivers from certain achievement mandates, as long as they showed improvement. Yet under this arrangement, the US Department of Education, not the states, remained the final arbiter.[129] By the 2010–11 school year, close to half of the nearly 92,000 public schools nationwide (48 percent) did not make AYP—the highest percentage since 2002 when NCLB went into effect.[130]

In 1998 Pascal D. Forgione, Jr., then US commissioner of education statistics, reported on the country's progress since *A Nation at Risk*'s release. Seventeen-year-olds' average math and reading scores in 1996 were not appreciably different from those in the early 1970s. On international comparisons, American students' relative performance ranking showed declines as they progressed to higher grades in school. Specifically, the proportion of students ranking in the international top 10 percent in math declined from 9 percent in fourth grade to 5 percent in 12th grade and from 16 percent to 13 percent in science.[131]

Ten years later in April 2008, the US Department of Education released another update to *A Nation at Risk*. Nearly two-thirds (65 percent) of high school graduates were taking the recommended academic coursework, about four times the rate documented in 1983. Still, the report noted that not much had changed in terms of improved academic outcomes, constituting a "national shame":

> If we were "at risk" in 1983, we are at even greater risk now. The rising demands of our global economy, together with demographic shifts,

require that we educate more students to higher levels than ever before. Yet, our education system is not keeping pace with these growing
demands. Of 20 children born in 1983, six did not graduate from high
school on time in 2001. Of the 14 who did, 10 started college that fall,
but only five earned a bachelor's degree by spring 2007. . . . nearly a
third of our high school students still do not take the rigorous program
of study recommended in 1983 for all students. . . . Both easy courses
and this smorgasbord still remain, with diluted content now hiding
behind inflated course names. The educational achievement of 17-year-
old students has largely stagnated since then.[132]

Rather than prompt reconsideration of the federal government's role in
education, those findings served to strengthen the conviction shared by both
Democratic and Republican presidential administrations that the federal government and the department had a legitimate, "traditional" role in advancing
education policy. "Whatever else one might argue is the legacy of *A Nation
at Risk*, it clearly signaled the recognition of educational performance as a
national concern, an issue of national importance," concluded Education Statistics Commissioner Forgione in 1998 during the Clinton administration.[133]
A decade later in 2008, US Secretary of Education Spellings noted, "Over
the last eight years, the [George W. Bush] Administration and Congress have
worked together on education reform. . . . We have changed ourselves from
a nation at risk of complacency to a nation at work on its shortcomings and
accountable for results."[134]

5

Federal Education Initiatives by Executive Order

REAUTHORIZATION OF THE US Department of Education's single largest program was long delayed: The Elementary and Secondary Education Act (ESEA), reauthorized in 2001 as the No Child Left Behind Act (NCLB), was due for another renewal in 2007,[1] but took eight more years to achieve legislative approval with the 2015 passage of the Every Student Succeeds Act (ESSA). In the absence of legislation before the enactment of the 2015 act, Obama took executive action. Under the guise of increased flexibility for the states and in the absence of a congressionally reauthorized ESEA, President Obama authorized US Secretary of Education Arne Duncan to legislate federal education policy through issuing conditional waivers for the states in exchange for adopting his administration's education priorities, including implementing Common Core, a voluntary nationalized curriculum.

In 2009, President Obama directed billions of dollars in stabilization aid to the states under the American Recovery and Reinvestment Act, much of it dedicated to supporting education. That funding was intended as a short-term measure, but many states had not budgeted adequately to restore education funds once it expired. That same year, Secretary Duncan called for the ESEA reauthorization process to begin, urging education leaders to "join with us to build a transformative education law that guarantees every child the education they want and need—a law that recognizes and reinforces the proper role of the federal government to support and drive reform at the state and local level."[2] According to the States' Impact on Federal Education Policy Project:

> Traditionally in American history, education policy has been largely the province of the states, with the federal government providing some

financial support for various purposes at various times. In recent years, however, the federal government has taken on increasing leadership . . . asserting greater control over policy at the state and even local levels through legislation, regulations, and financial incentives. . . . From the 1950s through the 1970s, the primary goal of most federal aid to education was equity—attempting to redress the inequities in education that resulted from socioeconomic disadvantage, discrimination, and language background. In recent decades, however, the emphasis has shifted to closing achievement gaps by raising the effectiveness of education for all students.[3]

In 2011, Obama introduced an ESEA reauthorization, which ran into strong congressional opposition almost immediately and took another four years to become law. In the meantime, he reverted to implementing policy and administering education funds by executive action.

The following section details the history of federal education policy under Obama, showing the unprecedented level of federal centralization through the US Department of Education, and by implication, the Executive Branch. More and more, it seems that leaving a national education department intact cannot be reconciled with a constitutionally limited republican form of government.

Race to the Status Quo

Signed in February 2009, the American Recovery and Reinvestment Act earmarked some $70.3 billion of the $100 billion for elementary, secondary, and postsecondary education programs for three particular education programs: the State Fiscal Stabilization Fund; Title I, Part A of the Elementary and Secondary Education Act; and Individuals with Disabilities Education Act (IDEA), Part B. The result of those programs was to save or create jobs and advance education reforms.[4] As part of the initiative, in July 2009 Obama launched an additional education program: Race to the Top. Under this competitive grant program, states applied for a share of $4.35 billion in federal funding.[5] The program was "designed to encourage and reward States" for student achievement gains, focusing on four federal priority areas: adopting college- and career-ready standards and assessments; building data systems; recruiting and training effective teachers; and turning around failing schools.[6] "It's time to stop just talking about education reform and start actually doing it. It's time to make education America's national mission," Obama insisted in November 2009, just two weeks before states were invited to submit their Phase I applications for the program.[7] Forty states and the District of Columbia submitted applications, but just two states, Delaware and Tennessee, won grants totaling $600 million in March 2010.[8] The following August, forty-six states submitted applications, but just nine more states and the District of Columbia won Race to the Top Phase II grants totaling nearly $3.4 million.[9]

Many of those states' applications were hundreds of pages long, and some states sent representatives to Washington, DC, to give formal presentations of their applications.[10] The US Department of Education's first annual evaluation of those states' progress documented delays in implementation of promised teacher evaluation improvements and other reforms.[11] Within just a few months it was clear that federally induced education reforms in the states were largely "toothless."[12] The Government Accountability Office (GAO) reported in July 2009 that most of the states sampled had used federal funds simply to retain staff and status-quo education programs.[13] An American Association of School Administrators survey released the following month echoed those findings. Respondents also complained that added bureaucracy and inflexibility impeded any innovation efforts. As the association's President and Paw Paw, Michigan, Superintendent Mark Bielang put it, "The survey results echo a frustration my colleagues and I have long articulated: limited flexibility for the existing federal education funds cuts down on our ability to innovate, and the stimulus dollars come with limitations."[14] In the fall of 2011 the GAO again found that states had devoted funds largely to retaining current staff. School officials also reported anticipated reductions in the specified education services once the federal funding stopped flowing. Further, the GAO concluded that "as the deadline for obligating funds approaches, little is currently known nationally about the advancement of the four areas of educational reform."[15]

Nevertheless two additional Race to the Top phases were approved for 2011 and 2012, with budget requests exceeding $1 billion combined.[16] As of December 2011, seven more states were awarded $200 million combined in

Phase III grants.[17] Other targeted programs were also added. The Race to the Top-Early Learning Challenge was launched in 2011 and is jointly administered by the US Departments of Education and Health and Human Services. By the end of 2012, fully fourteen states had been awarded a share of more than $600 million in federal grants to expand access to early learning opportunities.[18] Districts became eligible to compete for a share of $400 million in federal Race to the Top-Districts funds in 2012 "to personalize education for students."[19] Thus, without the authorization of the expired ESEA, the US Department of Education convinced states to continue their participation.

Numerous opponents argued that the US Department of Education acted as the country's "super school board," just as opponents predicted it would decades ago.[20] According to the *New York Times*, "Mr. Duncan . . . has far more money to dole out than any previous secretary of education, and he is using it in ways that extend the federal government's reach into virtually every area of education, from pre-kindergarten to college."[21] Following the Race to the Top launched in 2009, the Student Aid and Fiscal Responsibility Act (SAFRA) was passed in 2010 as part of the Health Care and Education Reconciliation Act of 2010, also known as Obamacare.[22] SAFRA replaced federally subsidized guarantees to financial institutions that issue student loans with direct federal lending. In other words, the US Department of Education effectively became the sole lender to college students.[23]

Common Core Standards

Race to the Top became a vehicle for perhaps the most comprehensive expansion into American education to date: a curriculum referred to as the Common Core State Standards Initiative.[24] In the spring of 2009 the National Governors Association Center for Best Practices and the Council of Chief State School Officers announced that they would be developing common core standards and assessments.[25] Although the Common Core initiative has been presented by proponents as a grass-roots, state-led endeavor to promote college and career-ready academic standards, the US Department of Education was intimately involved from the start.[26] As early as January 2009 Secretary Duncan told *Education Week* that he would consider using Race to the Top funds to push for more uniform, national standards. "Sure, absolutely," he stated. "We want to reward rigor and challenge the status quo."[27] On February 9, 2009, at the annual meeting of the American Council on Education, Duncan insisted:

> If we accomplish one thing in the coming years—it should be to eliminate the extreme variation in standards across America. I know that talking about standards can make people nervous—but the notion that we have fifty different goalposts is absolutely ridiculous. . . . We are all part of one system of learning that begins at birth and never stops.[28]

On June 1, 2009, the National Governors Association announced that all but four states had joined the Common Core initiative.[29] The same day Duncan reiterated his earlier sentiment, telling the National Press Club, "We have 50 different standards, 50 different goal posts. And due to political pressure, those have been dumbed down. We want to fundamentally reverse that."[30] But how?

In an October 2009 address to the National Association of State Boards of Education, Secretary Duncan repeatedly emphasized federal cooperation with the states. Borrowing a phrase from Lyndon B. Johnson, Duncan explained that "the federal government is a 'partner not a boss' in education." Still, Duncan made clear, "For nearly 200 years, our federal government was a silent partner." Unlike his predecessors, "I'm not willing to be a silent partner . . . I plan to be an active partner," Duncan insisted.[31] Just weeks later, the US Department of Education required that states commit to adopting common standards to be eligible for Race to the Top grants, although not necessarily the Common Core initiative's set. The department defined those standards in the following way:

> Common set of K–12 standards means a set of content standards that define what students must know and be able to do and that are substantially identical across all States in a consortium. A State may supplement the common standards with additional standards, provided that the additional standards do not exceed 15 percent of the State's total standards for that content area.[32]

The department subsequently declined to quantify how many states are needed for a *consortium*, but it did state:

In this [Race to the Top] program, the phrase "common standards" does not refer to any specific set of common standards, such as the common core standards currently under development by members of the National Governors Association and the Council of Chief State School Officers. The Department declines to make changes in order to endorse any particular standards-development consortium.[33]

Nevertheless, the following year Obama reiterated in his March 10, 2010, reform blueprint that states must adopt college- and career-ready standards in exchange for federal dollars, stating:

Following the lead of the nation's governors, we're calling on all states to develop and adopt standards in English language arts and mathematics that build toward college- and career-readiness by the time students graduate from high school. States may choose to upgrade their existing standards or work together with other states to develop and adopt common, state-developed standards.[34]

As the Federalist Society's Robert S. Eitel and Kent D. Talbert noted, "While remaining facially neutral, the Department could rest easy in the knowledge that most states would come to the [Race to the Top] competition having already signaled intent to adopt or having adopted"[35] the Common Core standards. That was an accurate prediction. By October 2012, just four states had not adopted Common Core standards: Alaska, Nebraska, Texas, and Virginia.[36]

A growing number of experts agree that the standards set by the Common Core initiative are weak, costly, politicized, and ineffective.[37] Several leading experts, for example, argue that the standards are less rigorous than states' previous standards or the standards in top-performing countries. One proponent-turned-critic is Andrew C. Porter, dean of the University of Pennsylvania Graduate School of Education. "I was betting that a national curriculum would give us something like a fresh start in the standards-based-reform business," said Porter. His research, however, proved otherwise.

The common-core standards don't seem to build on what we've learned through decades of research and experience. The common core is not a new gold standard—it's firmly in the middle of the pack of current curricula. Even more surprising was what we found when we compared the common-core standards with the national curriculum standards of several countries whose students regularly beat the pants off US youngsters on international achievement tests like the Program for International Student Assessment, or PISA. . . . curricula in top-performing countries we studied—like Finland, Japan, and New Zealand—put . . . far more [emphasis] on basic skills, than does the common core. . . . Finally, I had hoped that along with a national curriculum, the common core would prompt us to develop better, more scientifically sound ways to assess student learning. . . . But what I know so far about the work of the two multi-state consortia developing the assessments isn't promising. It sounds as if the new assessments may ignore state-of-the-art research and technological advances, settling for tests that are much like the ones we already have. Meanwhile, innovative work on assessments that's been going on in the states has ground to a halt while everyone waits to see what the consortia come up with. If new standards don't bring us better curricula than what we already have, don't help us catch up with our international competitors, and don't lead to better assessments, then all the hoopla over the common core may turn out to be much ado about nothing.[38]

Secretary Duncan insisted that the Common Core initiative would put a stop to the politicization of academic standards. Yet a number of experts and academics involved with the standards validation process noted politics as usual—not quality standards—was job one.

Common Core proponent W. Stephen Wilson, a Johns Hopkins University mathematician who served on the National Governors Association Common Core advisory panel, acknowledged, "It turns out that nearly everyone was in favor of Common Core standards in mathematics if . . . they got to write them. As it turns out, no one got to write the standards. A committee wrote them." Moreover, because the states whose standards were being replaced were also in charge of hiring the committee, Wilson noted, "The pressures on the writing committee must have been enormous. The only reasonable expectation was that the result would resemble some sort of middle way between the states' various standards."[39] Stanford University mathematician James Milgram "shockingly, was the only math-content expert on the 25-member [validation] committee," noted Koret Foundation Senior Fellow Lance Izumi.[40] Testifying before the Texas State Legislature in May 2011, Milgram explained, "As a result of all the political pressure to make Core Standards acceptable to the special interest groups involved, there are a number of extremely problematic mathematical decisions that were made in writing them." These included standards set just high enough to avoid community college remedial classes but still so low that they do not cover topics required for admissions in most state universities nationwide. Moreover, the standards are so weak that compared to their global competitors, American fifth graders would be up to a year behind, and by seventh grade, they would trail their peers by nearly two years. In short, Milgram concluded that the Common Core standards are "in large measure a political document . . . written at a very low level and do not adequately reflect our current understanding of why the math programs in the high achieving countries give dramatically better results."[41]

Sandra Stotsky, Common Core Validation Committee member and University of Arkansas professor of education reform, concurred, noting that the college readiness standards are anything but. She concluded:

> At best, they point to little more than readiness for a high school diploma. . . . We face a possible decline in advanced mathematics coursetaking in high school by students in the broad middle third (or higher) of our high school-age population if Common Core's standards are adopted. Fewer students will enter high school with Algebra I under their belt. Students deemed "college-ready" will be encouraged to leave high school after grade 10 or 11 to enroll in a college degree program. We need to ask if it is wise to encourage students in the academic middle who have been deemed "college ready" to enroll in a public college (at their own expense) before they have completed their last year or two of high school (at public expense). . . . They will matriculate in a post-secondary institution with less mathematics knowledge than they would have had if they had first completed high school graduation requirements.[42]

That criticism applies to English language arts standards as well. Stotsky and coauthor Ze'ev Wurman, former US Department of Education senior policy adviser, noted that these standards largely emphasize "generic skills" meant for Grade 12, which indicates the influence not of experts grounded in "literary, rhetorical, and linguistic scholarship" but the "academically toxic influence of assessment experts and reading researchers."[43] Stotsky was among the early critics back in 2009 of the Common Core's emphasis on "informational texts."[44] By 2012, controversy erupted when it was revealed that examples of informational texts included a *New Yorker* article that was sympathetic to the Affordable Health Care for America Act, or Obamacare, and Executive Order 13423, "Strengthening Federal Environmental, Energy, and Transportation Management."[45] The practical consequence is that some district and school officials are now advising teachers that 70 percent of their courses must focus on such informational texts, rather than classic literature.

These examples raise serious questions about whether the federal government knows best when it comes to education or whether it is politically neutral. As Wurman aptly summed up:

> Analyses of the Common Core standards find them to be mediocre and not obviously better than many sets of state standards. . . . [or] those of high-achieving countries. . . . Moreover, their promise of college readiness rings hollow. Its college-readiness standards are below the admission requirement of most four-year state colleges. . . . I believe the Common Core marks the cessation of educational standards improvement in the United States. No state has any reason left to aspire for first-rate standards, as all states will be judged by the same mediocre national benchmark enforced by the federal government. Moreover, there are organizations that have reasons to work for lower and less-demanding standards, specifically teachers unions and professional teacher organizations. While they may not admit it, they have a vested interest in lowering the accountability bar for their members. With Common Core, they have a single target to aim for, rather than 50 distributed ones. So give it some time and, as sunset follows sunrise, we will see even those mediocre standards being made less demanding. This will be done in . . . faraway Washington D.C., well beyond the reach of parents and most states and employers.[46]

Race to the Waiver and "Re-envisioned" Federalism: Inflexible Flexibility

Although congressional reauthorization of the ESEA was not accomplished until late in Obama's second term, the largest expansion of the federal government into American education continued throughout his presidency. To be sure, Obama was not the first president to expand the federal role in education. George H.W. Bush set six national education goals. Bill Clinton pushed Goals 2000, which made adoption of specific standards a condition for federal funding. George W. Bush went further with NCLB in 2001. What set Obama apart from his predecessors, however, is that he long acted without the veneer of constitutionality provided by Congressional legislation. President and CEO of the National Center on Education and the Economy Marc Tucker put it more bluntly:

> More recently . . . the executive branch has acted independently to implement its agenda without the agreement of Congress. . . . The US Constitution leaves responsibility for education policy to the states. In recent years, however, the federal government has ignored the framers' intention. The changes have been instituted without any significant debate about the role of the federal government in elementary and secondary education. And now, the executive branch alone is setting education policy without the active participation of either the states or Congress.[47]

On March 13, 2010, Obama unveiled his blueprint for reauthorizing the ESEA (reverting to the original acronym instead of the more politically toxic Bush-era NCLB), proclaiming it "an outline for a re-envisioned federal role in education."[48] Secretary Duncan added that through the ESEA blueprint his department was "offering support, incentives and national leadership, but not at the expense of local control."[49] Yet the Obama Administration's re-envisioned federalism centralized government control over American education to an unprecedented extent. Obama's 2010 blueprint called for granting states flexibility from select ESEA mandates through US Department of Education-issued waivers.[50] Previous administrations had issued hundreds of such waivers over the years. What changed under Obama's re-envisioned federalism was that the Department of Education enacted his preferred reforms with or without Congress under the secretary's broad ESEA waiver authority.[51]

The showdown with Congress began in the spring of 2011 when Duncan began touting estimates crafted by his department claiming that, absent sweeping changes, some 82 percent of public schools nationwide would not meet federally mandated adequate yearly progress (AYP) mandates and would be deemed failing under the ESEA, more than double the percentage from the previous year.[52] In other words, the overwhelming majority of American schools would not meet the ESEA's goal of 100 percent student proficiency by the 2013–14 school year.

That estimate drew immediate criticism for being "misleading," "hype," and "way off base."[53] One of the chief critics was a former congressional aide who helped draft the 2001 NCLB law, Charles Barone, who went on to join Democrats for Education Reform, an organization that had usually been supportive of the Obama administration's education policies. According to Barone, Secretary Duncan's estimate was a "fiction." He also accused Duncan of "creating a bogeyman that doesn't exist. . . . Our fear is that they are taking it to a new level of actually manufacturing a new statistic—a 'Chicken Little' statistic that is not true—just to get a law passed. It severely threatens their credibility."[54] Duncan's projection was later discredited by the left-leaning Center on Education Policy, which found at most, 48 percent of public schools would be deemed failing under NCLB AYP benchmarks.[55] Throughout the summer and fall of 2011, the US Department of Education, under Obama's direction, continued its showdown with Congress. Secretary Duncan declared in June 2011 that his department would proceed with waivers from what he called the NCLB "train wreck."[56]

House Education and the Workforce Committee Chairman John Kline (R-Minn.) and House Early Childhood, Elementary and Secondary Education Subcommittee Chairman Duncan Hunter (R-Calif.) shot back that the department's plan "issuing new demands in exchange for relief . . . raises questions about the Department's legal authority to grant conditional waivers in exchange for reforms not authorized by Congress."[57] Education and the Workforce Committee Democrats echoed that belief in a separate report issued by Senior Democrat Rep. George Miller (D-Calif.). "Arbitrary flexibility policies that undermine equality of opportunity are not only morally repre-hensible," the committee insisted, "they are constitutionally suspect."[58] The Congressional Research Service concurred, stating that "a reviewing court could deem the conditional waiver to be arbitrary and capricious or in excess of the agency's statutory authority."[59]

Secretary Duncan disagreed. Duncan insisted using his statutory waiver authority was needed to raise instructional quality and student performance and that it was intended only as a temporary solution.[60] The stated purpose of granting flexibility waivers, according to Duncan, was that "we just want to be good partners there."[61] Duncan also insisted, "I'm frankly trying to get Wash-ington out of the way . . . Washington can never run public education. Educa-tion has always been and should be at the local level."[62] Yet it appeared to many that Duncan was trying to get Congress out of the way when he announced on August 8, 2011, during the congressional recess that the "President . . . has directed the Department of Education to move ahead in providing relief in return for reform."[63] Reaction was swift. Chairman Kline denounced the move as "a backdoor education agenda" intended to "micromanage American classrooms."[64] US Senator Marco Rubio (R-Fla.) derided it as a violation of separation of powers, and Senate Republicans introduced ESEA reauthoriza-tion bills that included prohibitions against conditional waivers.[65]

Just a few weeks later on September 23, 2011, President Obama launched his ESEA flexibility package declaring, "Given that Congress cannot act, I am acting."[66] That same day Secretary Duncan announced he would be exercising his authority under the ESEA to issue states flexibility waivers exempting them from the looming 100 percent proficiency deadline and other performance mandates.[67] The Obama administration's ESEA flexibility plan substituted new mandates for the old.[68] Specifically, among the department's flexibility requirements was that state education agencies adopt Common Core college-and career-ready standards in exchange for a waiver.[69] Ranking Member on the Senate Health, Education, Labor and Pensions Committee Sen. Mike Enzi (R-Wyo.) called the president's policy pronouncement "a fundamental and dramatic shift in authority from Congress to the Administration."[70]

While the Obama administration insisted that Congress was delaying acting, others across the political spectrum argued that the president was at fault. As early as 2010 former Democratic congressional aide Jack Jennings, who now heads the Center on Education Policy, blamed President Obama for campaigning on a pledge of "bringing sense to NCLB. We're 13 months into the administration, and there's no proposal to do that," he said.[71] House Education and the Workforce Committee Chairman Kline was even more direct:

> The president has indicated the failure to reauthorize current elementary and secondary education law rests squarely on the 112th Congress, which convened just nine short months ago. This assertion ignores the fact that for the entirety of 2009 and 2010, the Obama administration had a golden opportunity to advance policies to improve education through a Democrat-led House and Senate. Instead, the president and his allies in Congress chose to push failed stimulus and health care proposals.[72]

It is important to note that President Obama used stimulus and health care proposals to expand the reach of the education department and further its agenda. The American Recovery and Reinvestment Act, passed in 2009, made successive rounds of Race to the Top possible. The following year the Student Aid and Fiscal Responsibility Act, enacted as part of the Health Care and Education Reconciliation Act of 2010, ended the subsidy of financial institutions that make student loans through the Federal Family Education Loan Program and expanded the Federal Direct Student Loan Program administered by the Department of Education. The Health Care Act also funneled an additional $10 billion to states and school districts through an Education Jobs Fund, modeled after the State Fiscal Stabilization Fund created by the 2009 Recovery Act, to hire (or avoid laying off) teachers and other educators.[73] By the end of 2012, fully thirty-four states and the District of Columbia had been granted ESEA waivers under the auspices of what the Obama administration called a new federal partnership—one that did not require the approval of Congress or constitutional authority.[74]

Time to End the Tug-of-War

Within the first few years of NCLB's passage, several scholars could see where this new federal partnership with the states was going. One such scholar was Andrew Coulson, director of the Cato Institute's Center for Educational

Freedom, who asked at the time, "Should we have expected NCLB to have had a greater impact on achievement? And a related question: Should we imagine that if we give Congress another 5 years, or another 10, or another 15 years, that they will get the hang of this whole federal involvement in education thing and turn achievement around?"[75] Coulson continued with an apt analogy:

> We have doubled per pupil spending and yet we have flat achievement. We have had a precipitous, fantastic, staggering drop in the productivity of American education. To get a feel for how bad this period has been, you have to imagine buying something that you would have bought in 1969 but paying twice as much for it as people did then. Imagine buying a 1969 car today—no seatbelts, no airbags, no traction control, no antilock brakes—but having to pay twice what you would have paid if you bought it in 1969.We expect progress in every aspect of life except education, because we've been accustomed to this flat, stagnant achievement, despite rising costs. It's a terrible result, and it's a result that you only see in education. But fortunately, NCLB, federal involvement in education, more central planning, more spending from the central government—that is not the only policy option open to us. And after two full generations of that approach, and its complete ineffectiveness and wastefulness, it is about time we looked at some of the alternatives.[76]

Before we can recognize alternatives, however, we have to appreciate just how far down the wrong path we have traveled.

The federal government has no constitutional authority over education. The fact that since the earliest days of the Republic it appropriated funds—and the states were all too willing to accept them—does not change that reality. Over time, the notion of federal partnership became widespread in all areas, and specifically, the notion that the federal government was somehow better situated than parents and taxpayers, through their elected local and state representatives, to identify their most pressing educational needs.

In 2009 and 2010, a number of national opinion polls revealed that record levels of adults were dissatisfied with American elementary and secondary education, 54 percent, and nearly three-fourths believed the ESEA had made education no better or worse.[77] Nevertheless, 43 percent of Americans said they favored more federal involvement in education. Among parents of school-age children, support for greater federal involvement in education jumped to 56 percent.[78] It would seem that Americans have become so accustomed to federal involvement in education it is difficult to imagine something different, especially if such a change could adversely affect their children.

Yet, no one has held the department accountable for the outcomes it has fostered in its more than three decades of existence. That is the goal of the next chapter.

PART II

Results to Date

6

Has the US Department of Education Kept Its Promises?

WHEN THE ENABLING legislation creating the US Department of Education was passed and signed into law, proponents put forward five main purposes that the new department would serve:

1. Supplement, not supplant, state and local governments;
2. Secure education's status as a national activity;
3. Provide better management of federal education programs;
4. Consolidate federal education programs to improve efficiency; and
5. Improve educational quality.

It would seem the essence of fairness, then, to judge the department by whether it has met those goals. Only one seems on its face to be clearly achieved: Certainly, the department has secured education's status as a national activity.

Although the number of people employed by the Department of Education has actually declined from 7,400 people to about 4,500 (see Figure 6.1), its impact has grown substantially. During its first thirty years of operation alone, from 1980 through 2010, spending on elementary, secondary, and postsecondary programs increased more than 164 percent, or $57 billion in constant 2010 inflation-adjusted dollars,[1] reaching $92 billion.[2]

In early 2013, President Obama requested a $1.7 billion annual increase in Department of Education funding, the largest increase for any domestic agency, bringing the department's discretionary budget alone to nearly $70 billion.[3] That figure excludes more than $13 billion in mandatory department spending, as well as $60 billion for new Obama administration programs and $10 billion for the Education Jobs Fund approved in the summer of 2010.[4]

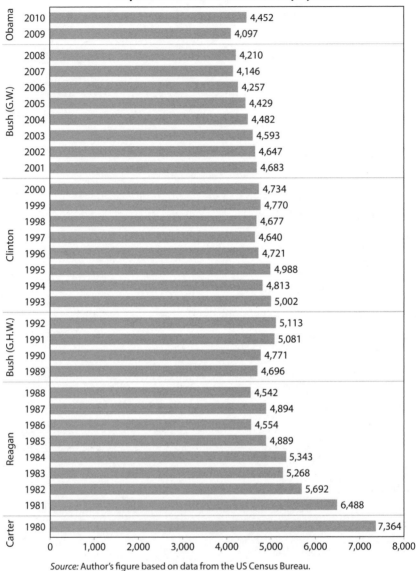

Department of Education Civilian Employment

President	Year	Employees
Obama	2010	4,452
Obama	2009	4,097
Bush (G.W.)	2008	4,210
Bush (G.W.)	2007	4,146
Bush (G.W.)	2006	4,257
Bush (G.W.)	2005	4,429
Bush (G.W.)	2004	4,482
Bush (G.W.)	2003	4,593
Bush (G.W.)	2002	4,647
Bush (G.W.)	2001	4,683
Clinton	2000	4,734
Clinton	1999	4,770
Clinton	1998	4,677
Clinton	1997	4,640
Clinton	1996	4,721
Clinton	1995	4,988
Clinton	1994	4,813
Clinton	1993	5,002
Bush (G.H.W.)	1992	5,113
Bush (G.H.W.)	1991	5,081
Bush (G.H.W.)	1990	4,771
Bush (G.H.W.)	1989	4,696
Reagan	1988	4,542
Reagan	1987	4,894
Reagan	1986	4,554
Reagan	1985	4,889
Reagan	1984	5,343
Reagan	1983	5,268
Reagan	1982	5,692
Reagan	1981	6,488
Carter	1980	7,364

Source: Author's figure based on data from the US Census Bureau.

Figure 6.1. Department of Education Employees, 1980–2010

Although the Department of Education is the smallest of the fifteen Cabinet-level departments today,[5] it ranks sixth in terms of its total gross obligations, which include not just program grants, subsidies, and contributions but also personnel salaries and benefits, contractual services and supplies, acquisitions of capital assets such as land, equipment, and structures, and fixed charges such as rent. Total obligations amounted to nearly $135 billion in 2010. This puts it ahead of the Departments of Veterans Affairs, Transportation, Homeland Security, Housing and Urban Development, Energy, Justice, State, Interior, and Commerce.[6]

Despite this large federal presence, however, the evidence is strong that the other goals have not been achieved. A Department of Education was supposed to supplement, not supplant, state efforts in education. It was supposed to provide better management and coordination of federal programs. It was supposed to consolidate and streamline those programs, improving efficiency and accountability. Above all, it was supposed to improve educational outcomes for America's children. This chapter examines each in turn, finding that none of the US Department of Education's other goals have been achieved.

Supplement, Not Supplant, State and Local Governments

The Founding Fathers never intended for the federal government to be a "partner" with the states in education. As we have seen, it was only by finding its way around the thorny question of constitutionality that Congress gradually enlarged the federal role the founders had not envisioned. Although the states largely accepted these intrusions in return for federal funds, the linkage was never without tension.

Twenty-five years after the creation of the US Department of Education, the tug of war between the states and the federal government seemed to reach a boiling point. States had been eager to accept the roughly $15 billion in annual federal funding under NCLB.[7] In exchange, states agreed to hire more highly qualified teachers, re-align or adopt yearly assessment systems, and measure students' adequate yearly progress (AYP)—all with a view toward achieving 100 percent proficiency across student subgroups in reading and math by the 2013–14 school year.[8] Well before that deadline, states began buckling under the weight of burdensome federal mandates, an ever-growing list of failing schools, and the reality that accepting federal funds amounting to no more than 40 percent of their ESEA program and compliance costs was not much of a bargain.

The administrative burden of a federal presence in education was well documented even prior to the creation of the Department of Education. As of 1977, the annual federal regulatory burden on school systems amounted to more than $2 million in Connecticut; nearly $8 million in Illinois; more than $3 million in Missouri; $2 million in Oklahoma; and nearly $1 million in New Mexico.

As time went on, the true cost to the states of federal funding had been growing more and more evident. Seven years before NCLB was enacted, the Government Accountability Office (GAO) reported that administrative and regulatory mandates imposed by federal education programs required, on average, 41 percent of state agencies' total education staffing and funding, even though the federal government contributed just 7 percent of that funding.[9] More specifically, just to keep up with federal education mandates and paperwork meant states had to hire nearly 13,400 full-time employees.[10] Once NCLB took effect, the administrative burden ballooned. After one year of operation in 2003, the added annual administrative burden to schools, districts, and state education agencies associated with overseeing Title I grants was 2.6 million hours.[11] After five years the NCLB administrative burden imposed to oversee Title I grants swelled two and half times to nearly 6.7 million hours at a cost of $141 million, according to the OMB.[12] By that point a majority of education agency employees in many states were hired just to oversee federal education programs.[13]

Since 2008, the annual Title I "burden hours" imposed on local and state education agencies have remained just under 8 million.[14] By 2011, however, the cost of those additional hours had grown to more than $235 million annually.[15]

ESEA requirements were so onerous one Virginia school district reported in 2005 that the costs of having to train its 14,000 teachers over the course of a single day were equivalent to hiring 72 additional teachers.[16] New ESEA regulations implemented in 2006 increased the administrative burden on states and localities by an estimated 6.7 million hours at a cost of $141 million.[17] More recently, state officials have reported that complying with the one-time American Recovery and Reinvestment Act funding requirements in 2009 was "time-consuming," particularly "in the face of shrinking staff."[18]

During a March 2011 Education and the Workforce Committee hearing on the paperwork burdens to schools imposed by the US Department of Education programs, Chairman Rep. Duncan Hunter (R-Calif.) observed:

> Here's what we know: too many schools and school districts are overwhelmed by unnecessary paperwork requirements. Currently, the paperwork burden imposed by the Department of Education is larger than that of the Department of Defense, the Department of Energy, the Department of Housing and Urban Development, the Department of the Interior, and the Department of Justice. From 2002 to 2009, the Department of Education's paperwork burden increased by an estimated 65 percent—an astounding number that continues to grow. . . . Recently, the administration proposed a 10.7 percent increase in the Department of Education's budget. As the federal role—and federal spending—in education has grown, so has the volume of regulations associated with education laws. It is important to note that, on average, only about 10 percent of a school's budget comes from federal funds, which is a disproportionately small amount when compared to the total cost of reporting requirements. During a recent hearing in this committee, we learned from school officials that the regulatory burden created by receiving federal funds often outweighs any potential benefits. . . . It is time to seriously reexamine the regulatory and paperwork burden the government has imposed on schools.[19]

Not only is the regulatory burden increasingly heavy, it is also increasingly complicated. As of January 2012, the US Department of Education listed 238 active "significant guidance documents" dating back as far as 1970. The lion's share of those guidance documents, 115 in all, related solely to various ESEA reporting requirements.[20] Similarly, in its latest review of federal program duplication and fragmentation, the GAO found that in the area of teacher quality, the "proliferation of programs complicates federal efforts to invest dollars effectively," including more than forty related ESEA programs.[21]

Presidential administrations have changed, but the imbalance of power between the states and the federal government concerning authority over education has not. If anything, the Obama Administration accelerated the trajectory set in motion under the George W. Bush Administration of more centralized government control over education.

Meanwhile, studies have begun to chronicle examples of how involvement by the US Department of Education has actually complicated educational advancement in the states and stifled innovation largely because of overlapping and contradictory mandates from one program to another.[22]

Provide Better Management of Federal Education Programs

When it opened in 1980, the Department of Education had ten major offices, an Intergovernmental Advisory Council on Education, and a Federal Interagency Committee on Education.[23] Education programs were transferred to the new department from the Department of Health, Education, and Welfare, as well as the Departments of Defense, Labor, Justice, and Housing and Urban Development, along with programs from the National Science Foundation. Had proponents succeeded in establishing the Department of Education as originally conceived, it would have also included personnel and programs transferred from the Department of Defense, with defense employees accounting for nearly 10,000 of the department's proposed 15,000 employees. The Education Department also would have taken over the operation of all overseas schools for military dependents, which at the time were the equivalent of the country's eleventh-largest school district.[24] Other estimates indicated the originally proposed Department of Education would have been even larger with more than 16,000 employees.[25] For the past twenty years, the Department of Education has had between 4,000 and 5,000 employees.[26]

Principal officers include the secretary of education and the undersecretary of education, along with six assistant secretaries of elementary and secondary education, postsecondary education, vocational and adult education, special education and rehabilitative services, educational research and improvement, and civil rights. A new education inspector general was added, along with four more officers appointed by the president to conduct congressional and public relations and policy development and an overseas dependents administrator.

Today, offices of the education secretary, deputy secretary, and undersecretary oversee more than two dozen major offices, centers, and White House initiatives (see Table 6.1).[27]

Table 6.1. Department of Education Coordinating Structure

Office of the Secretary
Office of Communications and Outreach
Office of the General Counsel
Office of Inspector General
Institute of Education Sciences
Office for Civil Rights
Office of Legislation and Congressional Affairs
Office of the Chief Financial Officer
Office of Management
Office of the Chief Information Officer
Office of Planning, Evaluation and Policy Development
Budget Service
Office of Educational Technology
Faith Based and Neighborhood Partnerships
International Affairs Office
Office of the Deputy Secretary
Office of Innovation and Improvement
Office of Special Education and Rehabilitative Services
Office of English Language Acquisition, Language Enhancement and Academic Achievement for Limited English Proficient Students
Office of Elementary and Secondary Education
Risk Management Service
Office of the Under Secretary
Federal Student Aid
Office of Vocational and Adult Education
Office of Postsecondary Education
White House Initiative on Asian Americans and Pacific Islanders
White House Initiative on Educational Excellence for Hispanic Americans
White House Initiative on Historically Black Colleges and Universities
White House Initiative on Tribal Colleges and Universities

Source: ED Coordinating Structure, updated May 2, 2012,
http://www2.ed.gov/about/offices/list/index.html

The Department of Education claims that it "delivers about 99 cents on the dollar in education assistance to States, school districts, postsecondary institutions, and students."[28] As of 2010, personnel compensation and benefits amounted to nearly $558 million of its $135 billion in total gross obligations, or less than 1 percent.[29] So understood, the department's 99 cents claim is accurate; however, it does not tell the whole story. A closer look at the kinds and amounts of expenditures, however, suggests the Department of Education may not be the bargain it purports to be.

Detailed obligations, or expenditures, are readily available from 1994 through 2010. They show that over this period the Department of Education's total gross obligations grew 170 percent or $85 billion in real, inflation-adjusted 2010 dollars. Proportionally, grants, subsidies, and contributions represented roughly 90 percent of the Department of Education's total obligations over this period, increasing in real terms from $45 billion in 1994 to $121 billion in 2010. Together, the remaining obligations represented about 10 percent of the department's total obligations over this period, increasing from $5.4 billion to $14.2 billion in real terms.

On its face, a 90 percent program ratio is impressive, but several other factors indicate that expenditures across the board should be much lower. As noted previously, from 1980 through 2010, spending for education programs increased 164 percent, while student enrollment grew 30 percent. This pattern holds true during the more recent 1994 through 2010 period, too. Elementary, secondary, and postsecondary enrollment increased by more than 11 million students during this time, or 18 percent. Meanwhile, Department of Education program grants, subsidies, and contributions grew nearly $76 billion in real, inflation-adjusted 2010 dollars, a 170 percent increase.

Comparing 1994 to 2010, Department of Education personnel declined by 361 employees, or 8 percent, but the cost of compensation and benefits increased 27 percent in real terms (see Figure 6.2A). Likewise, despite having fewer employees, obligations for acquisition of capital assets, which include land, equipment, and structures, increased 63 percent in real terms (see Figure 6.2A). Other expenditures categories increased even more. Contractual supplies and services increased 111 percent (see Figure 6.2A), while grants and fixed charges grew 173 percent (see Figure 6.2B). The increases suggest inefficiencies that the Department of Education was supposed to eliminate.[30]

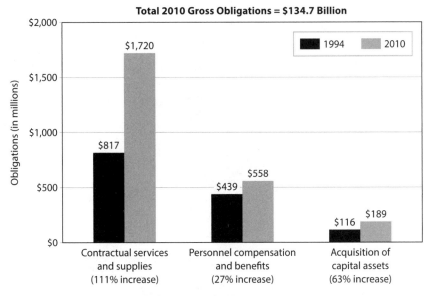

Total 2010 Gross Obligations = $134.7 Billion

Source: Author's figure based on respective years' data from the *Object*
Class Analysis of the *Budget of the United States Government.*

Notes:

1. Figures presented in inflation-adjusted 2010 dollars.

2. Contractual Services and Supplies includes travel and transportation of things and persons; rental payments to the Government Services Administration and others; communications, utilities, and miscellaneous charges; printing and reproduction; advisory, assistance, and other services; purchases of goods and services from government accounts; facilities and equipment operation and maintenance; other goods and services from non-federal sources; government-owned, contractor-operated (GOCO) operations; research and development contracts; and supplies and materials.

3. Personnel Compensation and Benefits includes permanent employees; other personnel compensation; special services payments; civilian personnel benefits; and benefits for former personnel.

4. Acquisition of Capital Assets includes equipment; land and structures; and investments and loans.

Figure 6.2A. Department of Education Obligations by Select Categories, 1994 and 2010 Compared

It is also worth noting that the $14.9 billion in 2010 non-program obligations is only slightly more than the Department of Education's entire originally proposed $14.5 billion budget thirty years ago.

Looking more closely at personnel expenditures, we find that from 2009 to 2010 the number of executive positions increased from ten to fifteen, with salaries averaging more than $160,000. The number of senior executive service

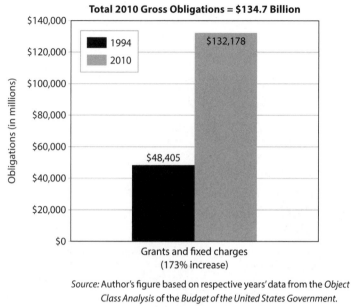

Figure 6.2B. Department of Education Grants and Fixed Charges Obligations, 1994 and 2010 Compared

employees stayed at seventy-nine, although in recent years the department had requested more than 100, with average annual salaries exceeding $170,000. The average compensation of general salary-schedule employees averaged more than $101,000 in 2010.[31]

Other illustrating examples come from contractual services. Research and statistics expenditures have remained a comparatively small program expenditure over the period from 1994 to 2010, while technological advances have reduced printing and reproduction expenditures from $24 million to $4 million. Offsetting these efficiencies are substantial increases in contracting costs, along with equipment purchases, which are distinct from maintenance expenditures. The GAO has documented long-standing concerns with the Department of Education's increasing reliance on contractors, as well as its oversight of them. As of 2010, the department's contract obligations totaled nearly $1.8 billion. Of the total, the GAO's investigation found about $130 mil-

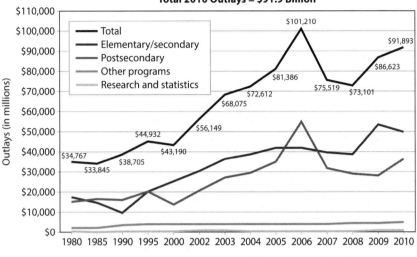

Total 2010 Outlays = $91.9 Billion

Source: Author's figure based on data from the US Department of Education.
Notes:
1. Amounts represent millions of constant 2010 dollars.
2. The increase in postsecondary expenditures in 2006 resulted primarily from an accounting adjustment.

Figure 6.3. Department of Education Program Outlays by Type and Level of Education, 1980–2010

lion in contracts did not have proper monitoring plans.[32] The department does not have a reliable method of projecting workload estimates, nor does it have a consistent performance management system, according to the GAO.[33] Since this review, costs have continued to rise.

Comparing student enrollments to the cost of Department of Education programs also raises questions. Major programs are divided into elementary and secondary education, postsecondary education, other programs, and education research statistics, which totaled nearly $92 billion in 2010 (see Figure 6.3).[34]

School districts, or local education agencies, receive the lion's share of the $92 billion Department of Education program funding (42 percent). Postsecondary students and institutions receive another 20 percent each of that funding. State education departments, or agencies, receive another 10 percent. The remainder goes to federal institutions as well as other education organizations, including funds for vocational education and federal programs at

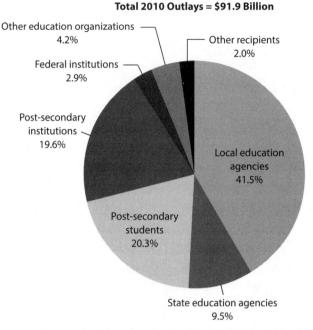

Total 2010 Outlays = $91.9 Billion

Other education organizations
4.2%

Other recipients
2.0%

Federal institutions
2.9%

Post-secondary
institutions
19.6%

Local education
agencies
41.5%

Post-secondary
students
20.3%

State education agencies
9.5%

Source: Author's figure based on data from the US Department of Education.
Notes:
1. Other recipients include American Indian tribes, private nonprofit agencies,
and banks.
2. Other education organizations include funds for vocational education and
for federal programs at libraries and museums.

Figure 6.4. Percentage of Department of Education Outlays
by Type of Recipient, 2010

libraries and museums, and other recipients such as American Indian tribes, private nonprofit agencies, and banks (see Figure 6.4).[35]

These spending increases seem unrelated to student enrollment growth over the same period (see Figure 6.5).[36] Elementary and secondary education spending increased 183 percent from 1980 through 2010, while enrollment increased only 18 percent, meaning spending increased ten times as much as student enrollment. Meanwhile, postsecondary spending over this period increased 143 percent, almost twice as much as the 74 percent enrollment increase. In all, total elementary, secondary, and postsecondary enrollment from 1980 through 2010 increased 30 percent, compared to a more than 164 percent increase in corresponding Department of Education program outlays.[37] Thus

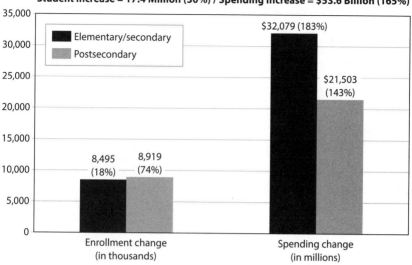

1980–2010
Student Increase = 17.4 Million (30%) / Spending Increase = $53.6 Billion (165%)

Source: Author's figure based on data from the US Department of Education.
Notes:
1. Enrollment figures are in thousands.
2. Spending figures are in millions of constant 2010 dollars.
3. Only elementary, secondary, and postsecondary outlays are included. Excluded are Department of Education outlays for other education programs as well as research and statistics.

Figure 6.5. Department of Education Program Outlays and Student Enrollment Changes, 1980–2010 Compared

the department's program spending increased more than five times as much as enrollment during its first thirty years. The sheer volume of programs it has administered may help to explain this discrepancy.

Consolidate Federal Education Programs to Improve Efficiency

Proponents during the 1970s had hoped the Department of Education would oversee all federal programs. They insisted that the department would reduce duplication and red tape, as well as streamline some 300 distinct federal education programs at the time, which were administered by more than forty agencies and departments.[38] That has never happened. The *Catalog of Federal Domestic Assistance*, which provides information about more than

2,200 federal assistance programs, indicates that the Department of Education, along with thirteen of its offices and institutes, oversees 153 education programs.

Since 1980, nearly 250 additional education programs have come and gone.[39] Back in 1979, just months before the Department of Education Organization Act was adopted, Sen. William Cohen (R-Me.) foresaw this likelihood and predicted that new programs would arise to replace every cancelled program.[40] At that time, Rep. Lawrence Fountain (D-N.C.) also rejected claims that the department would result in better management. He recommended instead a formal review of the 150 or so programs it was supposed to oversee to weed out programs "that have outlived their usefulness, that duplicate one another, of that simply don't work, [rather] than . . . devote our energies to creating a new organizational structure which might well help to perpetuate many of these programs."[41]

Another way to look at whether consolidation has worked is to follow the money. As of 2010, total federal on-budget or appropriated funding for education was $180 billion provided through all fifteen Cabinet-level departments, along with twenty-one additional federal agencies and programs.[42] Just more than half of that funding (51 percent), or $92 billion, went through the Department of Education, followed by the Departments of Health and Human Services (16 percent), Agriculture (11 percent), Veterans Affairs (5 percent), Defense (4 percent), and Labor (4 percent). Combined federal funding going through the other twenty-one federal agencies and programs accounted for slightly more than 5 percent of all on-budget 2010 federal education funding (see Figure 6.6).

In addition to the increase in federal on-budget education funding through the Department of Education, total federal on-budget funding for education has also grown, increasing 97 percent in real terms during this period, or $89 billion (see Figure 6.7).

In 2010 the GAO identified basic challenges concerning federal education programs. Its research into early education programs revealed several "complicating factors" that a Department of Education was supposed to address. Education programs were still dispersed throughout the federal government, the GAO found, and many programs continued to involve education yet serve

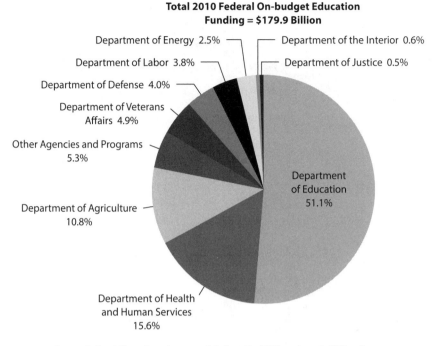

**Total 2010 Federal On-budget Education
Funding = $179.9 Billion**

Department of Energy 2.5%

Department of the Interior 0.6%

Department of Labor 3.8%

Department of Justice 0.5%

Department of Defense 4.0%

Department of Veterans
Affairs 4.9%

Other Agencies and Programs
5.3%

Department of Agriculture
10.8%

Department
of Education
51.1%

Department of Health
and Human Services
15.6%

Source: Author's figure based on 2010 data from the US Department of Education.

Notes:

1. "On-budget" refers to appropriated funds. Percentages do not include "off-budget" funds, which include both federal funding for education that is not tied to appropriations and non-federal funds generated by federal legislation such as private loans, grants, and aid.

2. The following Departments received less than 0.5 percent of on-budget funding for education in 2010, and are therefore excluded from the above figure: State, $729.5 million; Homeland Security, $538 million; Commerce, $192 million; Transportation, $178 million; Housing and Urban Development, $600,000; and Treasury, $100,000.

Figure 6.6. Percentage of Federal On-Budget Funds
for Education, by Agency, 2010

noneducational purposes. Finally, and more fundamentally, after interviewing representatives from all fifteen executive branch departments and ten independent federal agencies, the GAO concluded that no uniform definition of an education program exists.[43] In 2011 the GAO found that the Department of Education was one of a dozen or so agencies operating nearly 300 federal

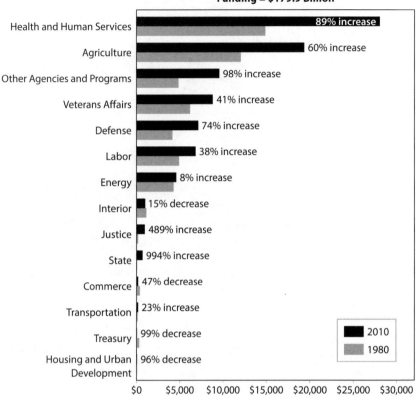

**Total 2010 Federal On-budget Education
Funding = $179.9 Billion**

Health and Human Services — 89% increase
Agriculture — 60% increase
Other Agencies and Programs — 98% increase
Veterans Affairs — 41% increase
Defense — 74% increase
Labor — 38% increase
Energy — 8% increase
Interior — 15% decrease
Justice — 489% increase
State — 994% increase
Commerce — 47% decrease
Transportation — 23% increase
Treasury — 99% decrease
Housing and Urban Development — 96% decrease

■ 2010
▨ 1980

$0 $5,000 $10,000 $15,000 $20,000 $25,000 $30,000

Federal education funding (in millions)

Source: Author's figure based on data from the US Department
 of Education.
Notes:
1. Figures presented in inflation-adjusted 2010 dollars.
2. The Department of Homeland Security was created in 2002 and is
 therefore excluded. In 2010, $539 billion in federal education fund-
 ing was appropriated through this department.

Figure 6.7. Federal On-Budget Education Funding by Department,
 1980 and 2010 Compared

social, education, and training programs, indicating a lack of coordination
and cost-containment, and inefficiency throughout the federal government.[44]

Consider just one education program area, teacher quality. Improving
teacher quality was a leading Obama administration priority, and in fiscal

year 2009, the federal government spent more than $4 billion to improve teaching among the country's 3 million educators. Yet the GAO concluded,

> Federal efforts to improve teacher quality have led to the creation and expansion of a variety of programs across the federal government; however, there is no government-wide strategy to minimize fragmentation, overlap, or duplication among these many programs. Specifically, GAO identified 82 distinct programs designed to help improve teacher quality, either as a primary purpose or as an allowable activity, administered across 10 federal agencies. . . . Further, in fiscal year 2010, the majority (53) of the programs GAO identified supporting teacher quality improvements received $50 million or less in funding and many have their own separate administrative processes. The proliferation of programs has resulted in fragmentation that can . . . limit the ability to determine which programs are most cost-effective, and ultimately increases program costs. For example in the Department of Education . . . eight different offices administer over 60 of the federal programs supporting teacher quality improvements. . . . Education officials believe that federal programs have failed . . . because, in part, federal programs that focus on teaching and learning of specific subjects are too fragmented to help state and district officials strengthen instruction and increase student achievement in a comprehensive manner.[45]

In addition, in spite of proponents' claims for greater savings through a streamlined Department of Education, the GAO discovered, "Reported estimated improper payments government-wide have steadily increased over the past decade from an estimated $20 billion in 2000 to approximately $125 billion in 2010. . . . GAO's work has demonstrated that improper payments continue to be a long-standing, widespread, and significant problem in the federal government."[46] Two of the worst-offending programs include the Department of Agriculture's National School Lunch Program and the Department of Education's Pell Grant Program, which made combined improper payments totaling an estimated $2.5 billion in fiscal 2010 alone.[47] Commenting on the GAO's findings, House Education and the Workforce Committee Chairman John Kline (R-Minn.) said, "When you have that many programs, none of them are going to work well." Kline concluded: "We need to look at this across agencies and really pare this thing down, change the way Washington works, change the way Washington spends taxpayer money, become more efficient, become more responsive."[48]

On-budget federal education appropriations do not include an additional $106 billion for various college student loan programs and work study programs supported by off-budget, nonappropriated federal funds and non-federal funds generated by legislation, including matching grants from institutions, employers, and states. Thus total federally directed support for education amounted to $289 billion in 2010 (see Figure 6.8).

In the past few years, several new, expansive Department of Education programs have been created, as described in Chapter 5. The GAO found in a 2011 report that the additional $100 billion for education allotted under the American Recovery and Reinvestment Act "added significantly to Education's responsibilities temporarily, but increases in program funds it administers and program activities have occurred for a decade, reflecting a longer-term trend of increasing responsibilities."[49] Specifically, the Office of Elementary and Secondary Education had to manage approximately $45 billion in additional grant funding and 700 more grants in fiscal year 2009 compared to 2008.[50] With regard to the Department of Education's Office of Federal Student Aid, the GAO explained that it "became the sole lender for all new federal student loans as of July 2010. The Department of Education projects that this new responsibility will increase the Direct Loan portfolio that it originates and services by approximately 127 percent between the end of FY 2009 and FY 2011."[51] Yet since 2006 the GAO has identified troubling security issues relating to personal information collected and used by the department, including student loan applications. In spite of attempts to bolster security, the GAO concluded that the Department of Education still cannot adequately ensure that departmental policies are followed.[52]

A look at programs administered under the ESEA suggests similar conclusions about an overall lack of streamlining and coordination. By the end of the George W. Bush Administration, the number of funded ESEA programs had swelled to sixty from just four in 1966. Total ESEA appropriations from 1966 through 2010 amounted to $642.3 billion in inflation-adjusted 2010 dollars.[53]

As shown in Figure 6.9, the number of funded ESEA programs remained fewer than ten until the late 1970s when the US Department of Education

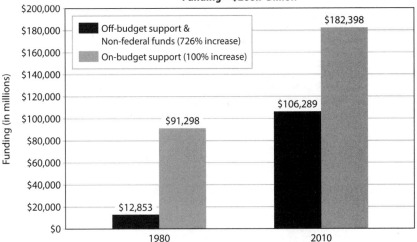

Source: Author's figures based on data from the US Department of Education.
Notes:
1. Figures represent 2010 inflation-adjusted dollars.
2. On-budget support refers to funding from federal appropriations for elementary, secondary, postsecondary, and other education, which includes libraries, museums, cultural activities, and miscellaneous research.
3. Off-budget support refers to non-appropriated federal funding for the William D. Ford Federal Direct Loan Program (commonly known as the Direct Loan Program), which provides student loans through federal funds rather than through private lenders.
4. Non-federal support refers to funds generated by federal legislation and includes the guaranteed Federal Family Education Loan Program (discontinued after 2010), Perkins Loans, Income Contingent Loans, Leveraging Educational Assistance Partnerships, Supplemental Educational Opportunity Grants, and Work-Study Aid. The latter four are supported by matching grants from institutions, states, and employers.

Figure 6.8. Federal Support for Education, 1980 and 2010 Compared

was created. In 1980, when the department began operations, the number of ESEA programs doubled to twenty-nine programs. During the Reagan Administration the number of ESEA programs declined sharply and remained at around twelve until the end of his term. Yet throughout the 1990s during both the Bush and Clinton administrations, the number of ESEA programs swelled again, increasing from thirty-three to forty-two. Throughout George W. Bush's administration, the number of ESEA programs proliferated even more, jumping from forty-nine programs in 2001 to a high of sixty programs. By 2010, the number had dropped to fifty-one.

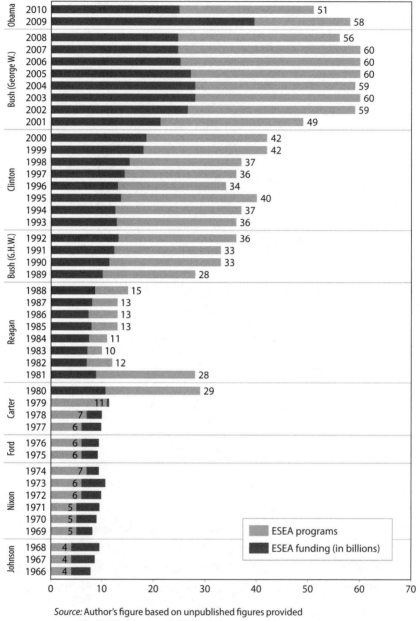

Figure 6.9. ESEA Programs and Appropriations, 1966–2010

Source: Author's figure based on unpublished figures provided
by the US Department of Education.
Notes:
1. Appropriation figures reflect inflation-adjusted 2010 dollar amounts.
2. Figure includes 2009 Recovery Act funding appropriated for various ESEA programs.

Since ESEA's inception in 1965, a total of 118 programs have been implemented. Just two programs from the late 1960s were still in existence as of 2010, Title I grants to local education agencies and English Language Acquisition. The average life span of an ESEA program is just under eleven years, suggesting that many programs are created during one administration, then eliminated or consolidated during the next. Even more compelling is the fact that only 15 percent of those programs have survived twenty or more years. Only 24 percent are ten to nineteen years old. The majority are less than ten years old. This indicates a concerning degree of politicization in which educational causes fall in and out of favor. The overall increase in ESEA programs, largely accelerated by the existence of a US Department of Education, seems to substantiate the prediction of Sen. William Cohen (R-Me). Back in 1979 he argued strenuously against the claim that an education department would streamline federal education programs. On the contrary, Sen. Cohen likened them to the heads of the mythical Hydra: cut one off, and two more grow back in its place. His analogy has proven apt.

From 1974 through 1981, when it was eliminated, the ESEA Ethnic Heritage program received more than $60 million. In 1980 and 1981 the Consumer's Education and Metric Education programs received more than $20 million combined. The Class Size Reduction program received a whopping $5.2 billion from 1999 through 2001, even though empirical evidence suggests that the effectiveness of reducing class sizes is heavily dependent upon teacher quality. More troubling than the abolition of politicized programs is their continuation. The Women's Educational Equity program, for instance, has received more than $188 million from 1980 through 2010, even though roughly the same proportion of women and men attain college and advanced degrees, and women outnumber men in the highest-growth doctoral fields. The Exchanges with Historic Whaling and Trading Partners program received more than $79 million from 2002 through 2010 "to develop culturally based educational activities, internships, apprentice programs, and exchanges to assist Alaska Natives, native Hawaiians, and children and families living in Massachusetts linked by history and tradition to Alaska and Hawaii, and members of any federally recognized Indian tribe in Mississippi." These examples illustrate that the ESEA is highly susceptible to politicization and diverting taxpayer funding away from its original purpose: improving the education outcomes of disadvantaged students.

Improve Educational Quality for American Children

Establishing a Department of Education was supposed to improve the organization and coordination of federal education programs, which would in turn result in better academic achievement and better education opportunities for all students, according to proponents. Opponents disagreed. "My yardstick for measuring the advisability and necessity for creation of a separate Department of Education is simple. I ask myself one question," stated Rep. Shirley Chisholm (D-N.Y.). "Will such a department significantly improve instruction and educational opportunities for this country's children? I can conclusively state that I know of no convincing evidence that leads me to believe that a Cabinet-level Department of Education or other structural changes will guarantee achievement of this most critical national objective."[54] The data suggest that she was right: American students—in particular elementary and secondary schoolchildren—are not better off in terms of academic performance.

The National Assessment of Educational Progress (NAEP), also referred to as the Nation's Report Card, is the largest ongoing nationally representative assessment of American students' subject-area knowledge and skills. Long-term trend (LTT) NAEP has measured performance of students ages nine, thirteen, and seventeen in reading (since 1971) and math (since 1973) at various intervals. The LTT NAEP science assessment was discontinued in 1999, but scores are available from 1969 for 17-year-olds and from 1970 for 9- and 13-year-olds.[55] National-level LTT NAEP performance is reported on a 0–500 score scale, and the descriptive performance levels used (150, 200, 250, 300, and 350) have the same meaning for all three age levels.[56] Because LTT NAEP has remained essentially the same since the early 1970s, it is a valuable yardstick for measuring student performance before and after the Department of Education's creation.[57]

Based on proponents' promises, one would expect student achievement gains to start materializing beginning in 1985, after the Department of Education had been operating for about five years. As Figures 6.10 through 6.12 show, across student ages, LTT NAEP performance has largely flat lined since the early 1970s through 1999 in science and through 2012 (the latest year data were available as of this writing) in reading and math.

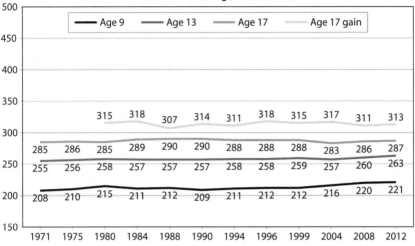

Source: Author's figure based on data from the US Department of Education, Digest of Education Statistics 2011, Table 125.

Figure 6.10. Long-Term Trend National Assessment of Educational Progress: Reading, 1971–2008

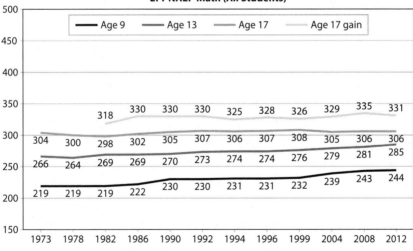

Source: Author's figure based on data from the US Department of Education, Digest of Education Statistics 2011, Table 141.

Figure 6.11. Long-Term Trend National Assessment of Educational Progress: Math, 1973–2008

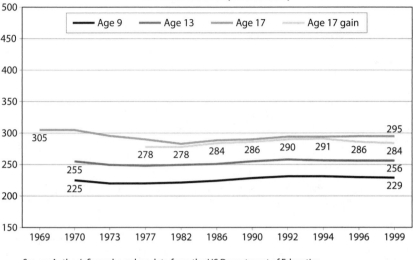

LTT NAEP Science (All Students)

Source: Author's figure based on data from the US Department of Education.
Notes:
1. NAEP long-term science assessments for 17-year-olds began in 1969; and assessments for 9- and 13-year-olds began in 1970.
2. NAEP long-term science assessments for students ages 9, 13, and 17 were discontinued in 1999.

Figure 6.12. Long-Term Trend National Assessment of Educational Progress: Science, 1969–1999

An interesting exercise is estimating what average 17-year-old scores would look like if the average 9-year-old performance trajectory simply held over the years—from age nine to age thirteen through age seventeen. That is why Figures 6.10 through 6.12 also include a distinct age seventeen gain trend line based on simple slope and gain calculations. Had average 17-year-old math scores improved commensurately with average 9- and 13-year-old gains, they would have been 25 scale score points higher in 2012, 331 compared to 306. Had average 17-year-old reading scores improved proportionately with average 9- and 13-year-old gains, they would have been 26 scale score points higher in 2012, 313 compared to 286. The situation is reversed for science. Given the average science score declines and plateaus among 9- and 13-year-olds over several years, that trajectory, combined with the declining trajectory in average science scores for 17-year-olds, would have actually resulted in a lower average scale score in 1999 for 17-year-olds, 284 compared to 295.

As it is, average LTT NAEP scores across subjects indicate that middle school students have remained at an intermediate skill level across subjects. They are capable of basic problem solving, interpreting simple tables, and making inferences and reaching generalizations (scores of 250–299). Over the past several decades, however, 17-year-olds have not moved beyond an intermediate level in reading and science (scores of 300–349), and in math they have barely done so, with average scores of 304 in 1973 inching upward to 306 in 2012. These performance levels indicate that students about to graduate high school have not progressed beyond doing computations using decimals, simple fractions, and common percentages. In nearly forty years (almost thirty years in the case of LTT NAEP science) the average American elementary, middle, and high school student has not progressed to more complex or advanced performance levels (scores of 350–500), including the ability to synthesize from specialized reading materials, solve multistep problems, or use detailed scientific knowledge.[58]

Thus LTT NAEP results indicate that the creation of a Cabinet-level Department of Education does not appear to have had a discernible effect on student achievement across subjects or age levels. This is especially apparent when comparing the average annual student performance percentage changes across ages and subjects with corresponding average annual Department of Education elementary and secondary spending percentage changes. What has been the return in student performance on our investment of federal education dollars?

As Figure 6.13 shows, average Department of Education spending changes based on inflation-adjusted dollars far exceeded corresponding student performance changes. Students made fractional average annual percentage gains in math and reading over a nearly thirty-year period, even though average spending increases amounted to 5 percent and 4 percent, respectively, for the years corresponding with those assessments. In science, annual spending increases averaged nearly 4 percent for the years corresponding with this assessment, yet corresponding annual student performance actually declined slightly. Department of Education spending has had no discernible impact on student performance. Figure 6.14 further illustrates this point.

Achievement of 17-year-olds is particularly important since they represent the end result of the American elementary and secondary public education

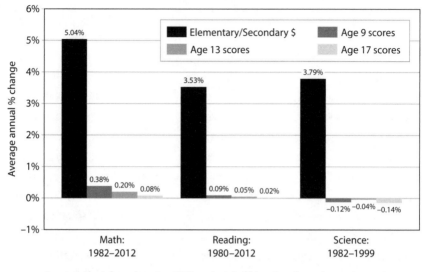

Notes:

1. Spending percentages are based on 2012, inflation-adjusted dollar amounts.

2. Annual percentage changes for spending and achievement scores correspond to subject assessment years, which vary by subject.

3. Long-term Trend NAEP science assessments for students ages 9, 13, and 17 were discontinued in 1999.

Figure 6.13. Average Annual Spending and Performance Changes, Select Years 1980–2012

system. That is why Figure 6.14 focuses on them. Tracking average 17-year-old performance changes and corresponding Department of Education spending changes over five-year periods beginning in 1970 through 2010 (the last year corresponding five-year data are available) shows that performance changes were flat while department spending changes were literally all over the map. During the early part of the Reagan administration, Department of Education spending declined, which is in keeping with President Reagan's early efforts to abolish the department. From that point on, Department of Education spending increased steadily every five years through 2000, then spiked upward about the time of President George W. Bush's No Child Left Behind Act. The seemingly sharp 2005–10 decline in education spending is actually not a decline. Education spending during this period simply increased at a

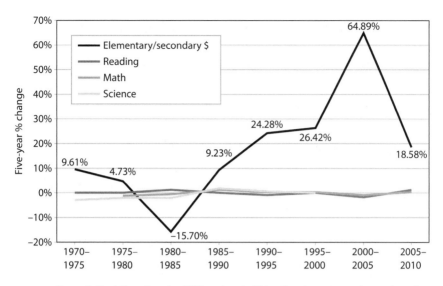

Source: Author's figure based on US Department of Education elementary and secondary education spending and long-term NAEP achievement scores for corresponding years.

Notes:

1. Spending percentages are based on 2010, inflation-adjusted dollar amounts.

2. Spending figures used prior to 1980 are Office of Education in the US Department of Health, Education, and Welfare on-budget funds for education and correspond with US Department of Education figures used from 1980 onward.

3. Percentage changes for spending and achievement scores correspond to subject assessment years, which vary by subject.

4. Long-term Trend NAEP science assessments were discontinued in 1999.

5. In cases where more than one assessment score was reported during a five-year period, an average was used.

Figure 6.14. 17-Year-Old Achievement and Education Spending, 1970–75 through 2005–10

lower rate by about 19 percent—compared to the previous five-year increase of almost 65 percent.

This analysis of student performance reveals that American students largely perform at average levels. Creation of a Department of Education has not had a discernible impact on this average student performance trend—in spite of spending increases that have grown ten times the rate of student enrollment.

Some may object that the performance of students with challenges, including those with disabilities or limited English, negatively affects average student scores and therefore they account for such little improvement over the past several decades. Prior to 2004, however, accommodations for special needs students were not allowed, and they were excluded from assessments.[59] Since average student achievement remained relatively flat before and after that period, special needs students do not appear to be responsible for artificially lowering average scores.[60]

Furthermore, LTT NAEP results are more likely to overstate average student achievement, rather than understate it. Participation in the NAEP assessment is largely voluntary, and there is no requirement for high schools to assess students in any NAEP subject.[61] It is reasonable to assume that low-performing students and schools would be more likely not to participate, which would inflate average results.[62]

A much more serious limitation of LTT NAEP data is that, at first, it did not report average scores for various student subgroups. In the early 1990s, however, the Department of Education began tracking NAEP results in certain subjects for various student subgroups: those identified as having disabilities, students from families whose incomes qualify them for the National School Lunch program, and students identified as English learners. It also gathered NAEP results by student ethnicity. This analysis looks at reading and math results for eighth-grade students across subgroups for all available assessment years from 1990 through 2013. Results disaggregated by race are available back to 1990, and results for other subgroups are available starting in 1996.

Main NAEP Reading assesses students' ability to read fiction, nonfiction, poetry, exposition, and documentary and procedural passages and measures their skills at identifying explicitly stated information, making inferences, and comparing multiple texts. Main NAEP Mathematics assesses students' ability with regard to numbers, measurement, geometry, probability and statistics, and algebra, as well as problem solving and reasoning.[63] While the mathematics framework has remained the same, the 2009 reading framework enhances the 1992 through 2007 framework by placing more emphasis on literary and informational texts, redefining reading cognitive processes, and adding a new vocabulary assessment.[64] Those changes should be kept in mind when reviewing reading results over time.

Main NAEP reading and mathematics results are reported on a 0–500 scale, corresponding to three achievement levels: basic, proficient, and advanced. In reading, eighth-grade students performing at the basic level (scores of 243–280) should be able to locate information; identify statements of main idea, theme, or author's purpose; and make simple inferences from texts. They should be able to interpret the meaning of a word as it is used in the text. At the proficient level (scores of 281–322) students should be able to provide relevant information and summarize main ideas and themes, as well as make supported inferences, connections, and analyze text features. Eighth-grade students performing at the advanced level (scores of 323–500) should be able to make connections within and across texts, and evaluate the strength of supporting evidence and the author's position.[65]

In mathematics, eighth-grade students performing at the basic level (scores of 262–298) should complete problems correctly, and they should be able to use fundamental algebraic and informal geometric concepts in problem solving. At the proficient level (scores of 299–332) students should understand the connections between fractions, percents, decimals, algebra, and functions. Eighth-grade students performing at the advanced level (scores of 333–500) should use number sense and geometric awareness to consider the reasonableness of an answer. They are expected to use abstract thinking to create unique problem-solving techniques and explain the reasoning processes underlying their conclusions.[66]

Eighth-grade students who are not low-income or English learners and do not have disabilities have performed at the basic level in reading since 1998. The average reading performance level of their counterparts identified as low-income is just above the basic level, while that of students with disabilities and English learners has averaged more than 10 scale score points below basic (see Figure 6.15).

Similarly, there are pronounced and chronic reading performance gaps among white, black, and Hispanic eighth graders in reading (see Figure 6.16). White eighth graders have performed at the basic reading level since 1992, whereas black and Hispanic students have started to perform at the basic reading level fairly consistently since 2002.

Eighth-grade students who are not low-income or English learners and do not have disabilities have also performed at the basic level in math since 1996 (see Figure 6.17). The average math performance level of their counterparts identified as low-income began rising just above the basic level in 2007, while that of students with disabilities and those identified as English learners has

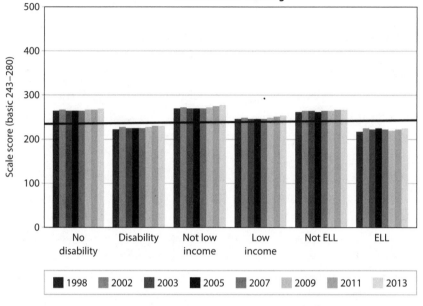

Figure 6.15. Eighth Grade Reading, Select Student Sub-Groups, 1998–2013

averaged more than 20 scale score points below basic since 1996. Math performance gaps also persist between white students, on the one hand, and black and Hispanic students on the other (see Figure 6.18). White eighth-graders have performed at basic math levels since 1990. Hispanic eighth-graders first starting performing at the basic math level in 2007, while black eighth-graders have performed below basic since 1990.

Average NAEP reading and math scores indicate that general education eighth-grade students have remained at basic performance levels for more than two decades. The reading and math performance of specific student subgroups that ESEA funding was supposed to help have also largely remained below or just at basic levels as well. Such performance indicates that on average, the targeted populations of students about to enter high school have barely the necessary rudimentary knowledge and skills in core academic subjects.

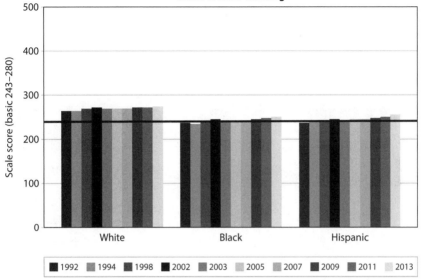

Grade 8: NAEP Reading

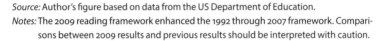

Source: Author's figure based on data from the US Department of Education.
Notes: The 2009 reading framework enhanced the 1992 through 2007 framework. Comparisons between 2009 results and previous results should be interpreted with caution.

Figure 6.16. NAEP Eighth Grade Reading, White, Black, and Hispanic Students 1992–2013

The performance of these students since 1990 contrasts with federal elementary and secondary funding increases over a corresponding period through 2012, the last year complete Department of Education spending data are available. Elementary and secondary spending, including ESEA expenditures for disadvantaged students, grew from $16.7 billion in 1990 to $38.6 billion in 2012 in inflation-adjusted dollars, representing a real expenditure increase of more than 130 percent.[67] Included in total elementary and secondary spending is ESEA funding that is supposed to help improve the academic performance of disadvantaged students. Over this same period, 1990 through 2012, ESEA appropriations increased from $12 billion to $23.4 billion, for a real funding increase of more than 93 percent. Meanwhile, from 1990 through 2013, the average increase in combined eighth-grade NAEP reading and math performance for ESEA targeted student populations was less than 10 percent. This means

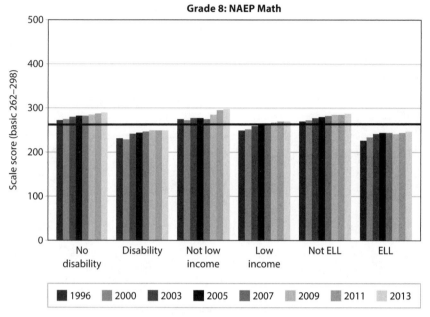

Source: Author's figure based on data from the US Department of Education.

Figure 6.17. NAEP Eighth Grade Math, Select Student Sub-Groups, 1996–2013

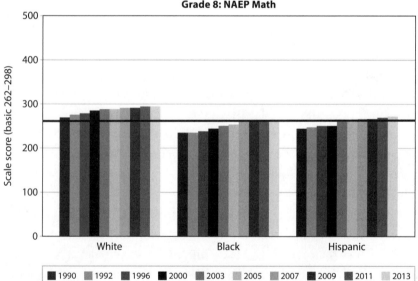

Source: Author's figure based on data from the US Department of Education.

Figure 6.18. NAEP Eighth Grade Math, White, Black,
and Hispanic Students, 1990–2013

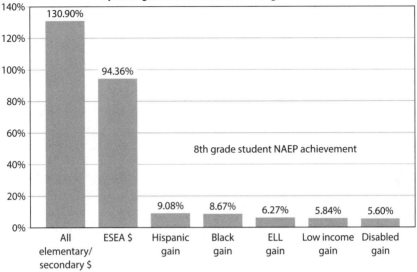

Source: Author's figure based on US Department of Education spending and NAEP performance data.

Notes:
1. Spending percentages based on real, inflation-adjusted 2012 dollars.
2. NAEP performance changes represent combined reading and math percentage changes for eighth grade students through 2013.

Figure 6.19. Elementary and Secondary Education Spending and Performance Changes, 1990–2013

the Department of Education's elementary and secondary education spending, including ESEA spending increases, grew at more than thirteen times the rate of the average corresponding performance increase, as shown in Figure 6.19.

Available performance results indicate that federal spending over the past two decades has far outpaced student performance gains, which still remain just at or below basic levels for disadvantaged student populations. Similarly, average student performance has remained constant. With no declines reported, you might ask, why the high level of attention being paid to student performance and efforts to improve it? The answer is foreign competition, and that is the subject we turn to next.

7

American Students on the International Stage
A Mediocre Performance

AN EXPRESS PURPOSE for establishing a US Department of Education was to improve American student achievement relative to their international peers. At stake, it was argued, was the country's global competitiveness. That goal has not been accomplished.

Recent headlines indicate that American student performance compared to other countries is declining. While that is true, the actuality is less alarming but nevertheless disturbing. Scores on various international assessments over the past several decades show instead that American student performance has just not substantially improved, much like long-term trends on the National Assessment of Educational Progress. Young Americans are losing ground comparatively because more countries are participating in the assessments, from a mere dozen about forty years ago to more than sixty countries and economies in 2012. As a greater number of participating countries exceed the international average, the US ranking is slipping because American student performance remains near the international average. In a competitive global economy, however, this is hardly good news.

Decades ago, the United States alone had achieved virtually universal elementary and secondary education and had a higher proportion of students graduating from high school compared to other countries.[1] Absent a competitive international climate, the comparative average performance of American students appeared stronger. Today developed and developing countries also have—or are approaching—near-universal education and secondary-school graduation rates that exceed our own. Thus, while schooling systems in other countries have emerged and evolved, the American schooling system has remained largely the same in terms of student performance. What has changed is that the United States is spending more for consistently average student performance. Important for this examination is the fact that the creation of a US Department of Education has not affected—much less improved—American student performance compared to students in other countries.

This chapter begins by looking at the performance of American students on international assessments over a period of several decades. Then it examines the data for possible explanations. A key finding is that the United States is producing remarkably consistent—and average—results despite spending that has increased over time and that substantially exceeds spending among competing countries, including the top performers. Narrowing the analysis, we look at the 2012 results for 15-year-olds to assess whether factors like a preponderance of immigrant or disadvantaged students in US schools may be skewing the results. Finally, we look for common factors among the top-performing countries and find a crucial one: competition.

An Overview of American Performance

International education assessments began in the late 1950s. The United States, in fact, participated in a pilot study conducted by the International Association for the Evaluation of Educational Achievement (IEA) assessing 13-year-old students from eleven other countries: Belgium, England, Finland, France, Germany (FRG), Israel, Poland, Scotland, Sweden, Switzerland, and Yugoslavia.[2] The results, released in 1962, showed that American students, together with German students, led in science but outperformed just three countries in math (Scotland, England, and Yugoslavia). In reading, American students performed near the middle of the pack.[3] IEA researchers acknowledged the sampling and test construction limitations of the pilot study, which was undertaken to see if international assessments could be reliably conducted.[4] While illustrative, this initial pilot study is not considered a conclusive barometer of international student performance.

After making necessary refinements and improvements the IEA conducted the First International Mathematics Study in 1964, followed by the First International Science Study begun in 1970–71.[5] Subsequent assessments were conducted in the 1980s, the Second International Mathematics Study and the Second International Science Study. These assessments are the precursors to today's Trends in International Mathematics and Science Study (TIMSS), which began collecting 9-year-old and 13-year-old student assessment data in 1995 and has done so every four years since.[6] The IEA conducted occasional reading literacy assessments in the decades since the 1960s but focused primarily on math and science assessments.[7] International reading literacy surveys began in 2000, when the Organization for Economic Cooperation and Development (OECD) first conducted its Program for International Student Assessment (PISA). Every three years PISA assesses 15-year-old literacy in reading, math, and science.[8] The IEA initiated its Progress in International Reading Literacy Study (PIRLS) of fourth-graders (9-year-olds) the following year in 2001, with recurring assessments every five years.[9]

Thus comparable international performance assessments prior to and since the creation of the Department of Education are not available to make possible a straightforward before-and-after comparison.[10] What available data do show is that similar to long-term NAEP results, American student performance is largely average. Figures 7.1 through 7.3B present American student performance on PISA in reading, math, and science for all years and age levels assessed. For consistency, student ages, not grades, are used. Age nine corresponds with fourth grade, and age thirteen corresponds with eighth grade. Unlike long-term NAEP, which assesses 17-year-olds, international assessments measure 15-year-old performance. Assessing this age group has the advantage of including students who may drop out by age seventeen if they are struggling. Thus international assessments can present a slightly clearer performance portrait of students near the end of their secondary schooling.

Figures 7.1 through 7.3B also present American student performance in terms of percentages above or below international averages. This is intended to reveal whether student performance is progressing beyond average levels, in this case averages relative to American students' international peers. Achieving such improvement was one reason for creating the Department of Education. While international rankings may make for eye-catching headlines, they are a poor gauge of student performance over time.[11] This is because fractional performance changes can significantly affect a country's relative standing—regardless of whether a country's student performance has improved or declined. A better measure for purposes of this analysis is how well American students perform relative to international averages.

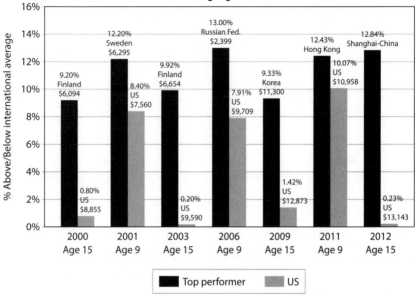

Figure 7.1. Percentages Above/Below the International Average, Reading: American and Top-Performing Students Globally, Ages Nine and Fifteen

Presenting American students in this way has several advantages. First, this method makes it possible to examine student performance changes in various subjects and age levels over time, regardless of the number of countries participating. Second, assessments of the same subjects and student age levels can measure different competencies. TIMSS, for example, focuses on math and science knowledge and skills students should have learned in school. PISA, in contrast, assesses literacy in those subjects with a view to the concepts students should be able to apply in the real world outside of the classroom.[12]

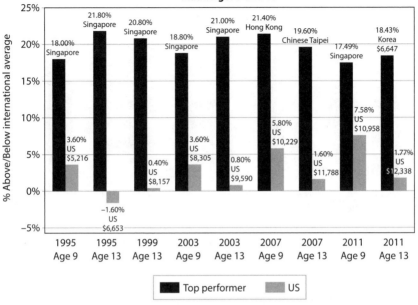

Math: Ages 9 and 13

Source: Author's figure based on IEA TIMSS results for ages nine and thirteen. Per-pupil expenditures are from the OECD in corresponding current year US dollar amounts.
Note: Per-pupil expenditures are not presented for countries with missing data.

Figure 7.2A. Percentages Above/Below the International Average, Math: American and Top-Performing Students Globally, Ages Nine and Thirteen

Both kinds of knowledge are important components of student achievement, and this method makes it possible to measure American students' relative performance taking both elements into account.

Finally, simply presenting numerical scale scores may seem the most straightforward approach, especially since the international assessments in this analysis all use 0–1,000 point scales, but the results would not be comparable. While the long-term NAEP assessment analysis did not materially change over time, this is not the case with international assessments. Even a single assessment series, such as PISA, can revise its frameworks, making it impossible to compare scores from previous years.[13] Comparability among several assessments is even more challenging. Even though various assessments use a 500 scale-point average, which may vary slightly from one assessment

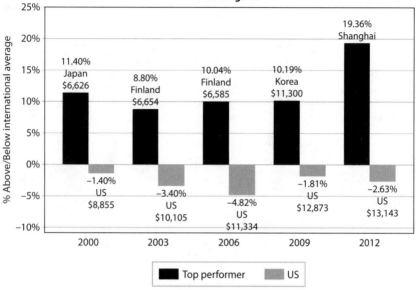

Math: Age 15

Source: Author's figure based on OECD PISA results for age fifteen. Per-pupil expenditures are from the OECD in corresponding current year US dollar amounts.

Notes:

1. Per-pupil expenditures are not presented for countries with missing data.

2. The 2012 US per-pupil expenditure amount is in 2011 dollars.

Figure 7.2B. Percentages Above/Below the International Average, Math: American and Top-Performing Students Globally, Age Fifteen

year to another, scale scores represent different achievement levels relative to the subjects and student ages assessed.[14] Presenting American student performance in terms of percentages above or below the international averages helps account for varying frameworks within and among different assessments. Ideally, American students would exceed international averages by greater percentages with each successive assessment year.

Figures 7.1 through 7.3B show that over the past two decades, American students across age levels and subjects have remained within a narrow band of average performance relative to their international peers. American 9-year-olds perform above the international averages in reading, math, and science by as much as 10 percent, 8 percent, and 8 percent higher, respectively. American 13-year-olds generally perform above the international averages as well, up to

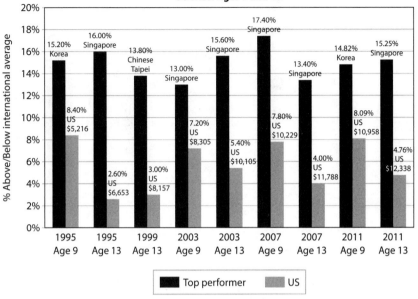

Science: Ages 9 and 13

Source: Author's figure based on IEA TIMSS results for ages nine and thirteen. Per-pupil
      expenditures are from the OECD in corresponding current year US dollar amounts.
Notes:
1. Per-pupil expenditures are not presented for countries with missing data.
2. The 2012 US per-pupil expenditure amount is in 2011 dollars.

Figure 7.3A. Percentages Above/Below the International Average,
        Science: American and Top-Performing Students Globally,
        Ages Nine and Thirteen

nearly 2 percent higher in math, and up to 5 percent higher in science. American 15-year-olds, however, generally perform at or below the international averages. While in reading, they score up to about 1 percent higher than the international average, they perform as much as 5 percent below the international math average, and as much as 2 percent below in science.

In isolation, such performance seems to run counter to dire predictions about the country's deteriorating international academic standing. In fact, according to *A Nation at Risk*, released in 1983, American students had placed last seven times on international assessments over the prior decade and were never first or second.[15] The reality is American students are and consistently

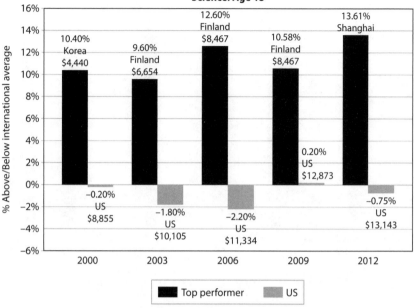

Source: Author's figure based on OECD PISA results for age fifteen. Per-pupil expenditures
are from the OECD in corresponding current year US dollar amounts.
Notes:
1. Per-pupil expenditures are not presented for countries with missing data.
2. The 2012 US per-pupil expenditure amount is in 2011 dollars.

Figure 7.3B. Percentages Above/Below the International Average, Science:
American and Top-Performing Students Globally, Age Fifteen

have been average performers on the whole. Nine-year-olds' performance is
stronger relative to their international peers, approaching 10 percent above
international averages, but at age thirteen American students perform squarely
within a 5 percent above-average performance band. At age fifteen, American
student performance is still within a +/- 5 percent average performance band;
however, that band shifts downward overall since in math and science they
typically perform below the international average. While some people may
be inclined to accept average student academic performance as good enough,
preferring to focus instead on children's well-roundedness or being socially
well adjusted, policymakers regularly equate American academic performance
with economic strength and global competitiveness. They might expect more
significant returns for their educational investment.

Is There a Payoff for Dollars Invested?

The United States spends more per pupil than both the international averages and top-performing countries in every given assessment year. If dollars matter more than other factors, American students should be exceeding international averages to a greater extent than their international peers. They are not. Besides comparing American student performance and performance of students from top-performing countries, Figures 7.1 through 7.3B also include corresponding average national per-pupil expenditures. Prepared by the OECD for primary and secondary school students, they are presented in current year US dollar amounts corresponding to the given assessment year. In this analysis, spending figures represent total funding amounts from all sources, which in the case of the United States means local, state, and federal expenditures, including but not limited to Department of Education spending. Historically, annual federal education spending has averaged around 10 percent of total education spending, and annual Department of Education spending amounts to roughly half of all federal education spending.[16] Thus, a general rule of thumb when reviewing the total US per-pupil expenditure amounts in Figures 7.1 through 7.3B is that US Department of Education spending represents about 5 percent.

A sobering picture begins to emerge when American students' internationally average performance is considered alongside the country's above-average per-pupil spending. As Figures 7.4A and B show, the United States spends far more per student than the OECD average at both the elementary and secondary levels. As of 2014 (the latest year data were available as of this writing), the United States spent nearly $11,000 per elementary student and more than $13,000 per secondary student. In contrast, the average OECD country spent about $3,000 less, at about $8,000 per elementary student and $9,000 per secondary student. In terms of percentage differences, the United States currently spends around 25 percent more at both the elementary and the secondary levels. Those percentages have narrowed over the past decade, largely because more countries that spend higher amounts are now participating in ongoing international assessments. Other countries that have regularly participated in ongoing assessments have also increased their spending, particularly at the elementary level.

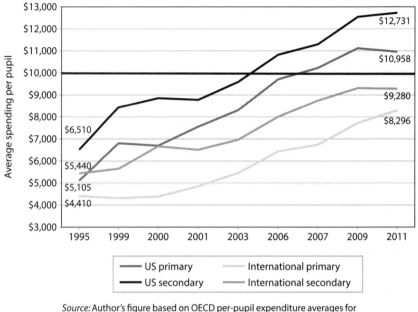

Source: Author's figure based on OECD per-pupil expenditure averages for corresponding years.

Note: All figures presented in current year US dollar amounts except 1995 figures, which were published as adjusted 1999 dollar amounts.

Figure 7.4A. Per-Pupil Spending Amounts: the United States and International Average Compared, 1995–2011

A handful of countries spend more than the United States. Faraway Luxembourg now spends the most of any OECD country, nearly $24,000 per elementary student and $16,000 per secondary student. Compared to the American elementary expenditure of $11,000, Norway spends more than $12,000, and Switzerland spends almost $13,000. At the secondary level, Austria spends slightly more than the United States at just over $13,000. Norway spends nearly $15,000, while Luxembourg and Switzerland are each top spenders at more than $16,000 each.[17] None of those countries, however, have been the top-performing country since 1995, as shown in Figures 7.1 through 7.3B. Focusing on the performance and expenditures of top performers underscores the discontinuity between elementary and secondary student expenditures and student performance in the United States by comparison.

In reading, 9-year-olds from Finland and the Russian Federation perform more than 12 percent higher than the international average and more

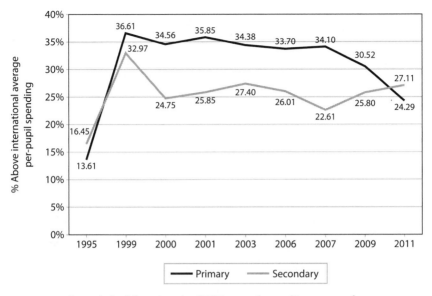

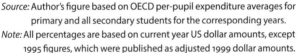

Source: Author's figure based on OECD per-pupil expenditure averages for primary and all secondary students for the corresponding years.
Note: All percentages are based on current year US dollar amounts, except 1995 figures, which were published as adjusted 1999 dollar amounts.

Figure 7.4B. American Per-Pupil Spending Percentages Above the International Averages, 1995–2011

than 2 percent higher on average than their American peers. Yet the United States outspends these top performers by an average of more than $4,600 per student. Similarly, in reading, 15-year-olds from Finland and the Republic of Korea perform more than 5 percent higher than the international average and their American peers. Yet the United States outspends these top performers by an average of more than $4,000 per secondary student. This pattern is even more pronounced for American elementary and secondary students in math and science.

In math, 9-year-olds from top performers Singapore and Hong Kong, along with 13-year-olds from Singapore and Chinese Taipei, score around 15 percent higher than the international average. On average those 9-year-olds perform 10 percent higher than their American peers, while top-performing 13-year-olds score more than 15 percent higher on average. Meanwhile, American elementary per-pupil expenditures average nearly $5,000 more than Korea's. At age fifteen, students from Japan and Korea perform around 10 percent higher than the international average and 12 percent better than their American peers. Yet the United States spends over $3,000 more per secondary student on average than those countries. A similar pattern emerges in science.

On average, 9-year-old students from the Republic of Korea, Finland, Japan, and the Russian Federation score 12 percent higher than the international science average. Those 9-year-olds perform more than 4 percent higher in science than their American counterparts, while 13-year-olds from those same countries perform 10 percent better than the international average and 5 percent higher than American 13-year-olds. Yet the United States spends nearly $4,000 more per elementary student on average than those countries. The performance/spending gap is even greater among older students. Along with 15-year-olds from these top-performing countries, students from many other countries outperform their American counterparts as well. Fifteen-year-olds from Estonia and Canada score approximately 6 percent higher than the international average and about 7 percent higher than their American peers. Yet the United States spends nearly $2,000 more per secondary student than Canada, and over $6,000 more than Estonia.

Overall, the United States is spending above-average amounts for average results compared to our international competitors. Specifically, compared to better performing countries, the United States spends nearly one-third more on average (32.2 percent) at the primary level, and close to one-quarter more (22.9 percent) at the secondary level. In particular, the United States also spends more than countries whose 15-year-olds outperform American students in reading, math, and science: on average close to 20 percent more in reading (19.2 percent), and fully one-quarter more in science (24.2 percent) and math (25.3 percent).

What are the economic consequences of paying more for average performance?

A recent analysis examined the potential effect on gross domestic product (GDP) of modest improvements among 15-year-olds on OECD PISA assessments. The analysis focused primarily on math and science performance, which is strongly correlated to economic growth.[18] The results showed a little could indeed go a long way. Increasing average PISA scores by 25 points over twenty years, a modest 1.25 points per year, for example, suggests US GDP would grow more than $40 trillion in real terms over the subsequent eighty years. Increasing average PISA scores by 56 points over that same period, almost 3 points per year for twenty-five years, indicates US GDP would grow more than $100 trillion over the subsequent eighty years.[19]

Why are American student scores failing to meet the marks that would stimulate this kind of economic growth? Seeking answers, we focus on the 2012 PISA results for 15-year-olds in reading, math, and science. PISA results give a solid indication of how well students about to enter postsecondary education or the workforce are prepared. Unlike other international assessments, PISA focuses specifically on subject-matter literacy related to applying what students have learned in school to real-world situations beyond school. We include in our analysis only countries whose 15-year-olds outperformed the United States on the PISA 2012 reading, math, and science assessments. For readability, those scores are presented as combined averages.

The Impact of Immigration and Economic Status

It is often assumed that other countries outperform the United States because their students are easier to educate, namely, these nations have fewer immigrants and students living in poverty. Actual statistics from across the globe, however, reveal that most top performers have more challenging student populations than the United States in terms of students' immigrant status and poverty levels. In reality, numerous social and health advances since 1970 have put American students far ahead of their international counterparts. These include advances in pediatrics and health care, child nutrition, access to early education options outside the government sector, and higher levels of parental education, along with diminishing rates of childhood poverty, low-birth weights, and other medical, social, and economic advances.[20] Meanwhile, actual international demographic and performance statistics show countries with higher levels of immigrant and impoverished students than the United States perform much better.[21]

As Figure 7.5A shows, fully twenty-one countries with available immigration data performed as well or better than the United States; however, the percentage of immigrant students does not appear to be a determining factor. Hong Kong has the highest overall PISA performance in reading, math, and science as well as the second highest immigrant student population, 35 percent.

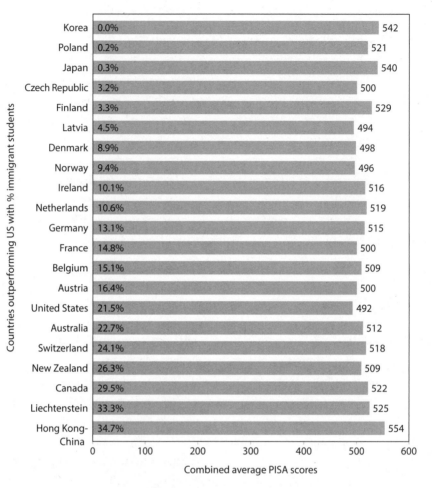

Source: Author's figure based on OECD, PISA Results 2012.
Note: PISA combined scores are author's average of 2012 reading, math, and science scores.

Figure 7.5A. PISA Average Scores and Percentage of Immigrant Students

In fact, of the countries with higher average PISA performance scores than the United States, six of them—or 30 percent—also have the same proportion of immigrant students or higher. Thus while slightly more than one in five American and Australian students are immigrants, Australian 15-year-olds score an average of 20 scale points higher in reading, math, and science. In Macao, China, where nearly two-thirds of students are immigrants, 15-year-olds score an average of more than 30 scale points higher. Fifteen-year-olds from Hong Kong, where 35 percent of students are immigrants, score over 60 scale score points higher than their American counterparts. In Canada, New Zealand, and Switzerland, where about one quarter of students are immigrants, 15-year-olds score 17 to 30 scale score points higher than American students.

A similar pattern is evident with regard to disadvantaged students, referred to as "resilient" students by the OECD because their PISA reading, math, and science performance is stronger than their socioeconomic backgrounds would suggest.[22] As Figure 7.5B shows, among the twenty-eight countries with statistics on resilient students that outperformed the United States, only Denmark had a similar proportion of resilient students, at around 5 percent. Much higher proportions of disadvantaged students demonstrate strong PISA performance, ranging from 15 to 20 percent, in such countries and economies as Shanghai, Hong Kong, Singapore, and newcomer Vietnam, which administered the PISA assessment for the first time in 2012. More than one dozen European countries, as well as Canada and Australia, also have higher proportions of resilient students that are excelling, including Switzerland and Estonia with around 10 percent each (Canada and Australia have more than 8 and 6 percent of resilient students, respectively).

These results suggest that having high proportions of immigrant and disadvantaged student populations does not destine countries to poor PISA performance rankings. Students with challenges can learn and can outperform their more advantaged peers.

So far, we've seen that neither spending nor demographic factors like immigration or socioeconomic disadvantage explain differences between top performers and the consistently average American students. President Barack Obama and many state elected officials have concluded from international assessments that longer school years are needed.[23] According to the PISA analysis, however, more is not better when it comes to schooling.[24] Top global performers prepare students in a fraction of the time compared to the United States.[25] Among thirty-six OECD member countries, the United States has the most teaching hours per public school year on average—1,097 compared to the international average of 710—across elementary, middle, and high school levels. Among the top international performers with available data, all sixteen countries that surpassed the United States on the 2012 PISA assessment

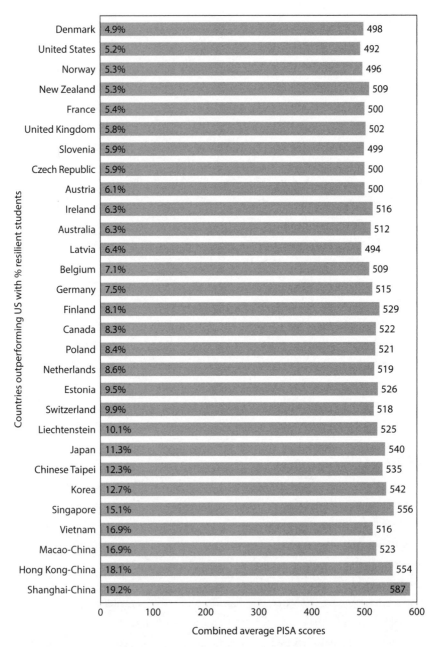

Source: Author's figure based on OECD, PISA Results 2012.
Note: PISA combined scores are author's average of 2012 reading, math, and science scores.

Figure 7.5B. PISA Average Scores and Resilient Students

had far fewer teaching hours per school year. Finland, Korea, and Japan had nearly the fewest teaching hours among leading PISA countries, with 603, 604, and 614 teaching hours, respectively. Meanwhile, with 562 and 584 teaching hours per school year, Denmark and Poland had the fewest teaching hours of all OECD assessment countries.[26]

What then makes the difference for top-performing students?

International Evidence on Competition and Student Performance

While many (although not all) of the top-performing countries have national education agencies and ministries, parents in a surprising number of countries have substantially more freedom to choose their children's schools. A common feature is an education finance system for a variety of schools that effectively blurs the distinction between *public* and *private*. The availability of public funding puts a variety of schools within financial reach of parents of all socioeconomic backgrounds, thereby leveling the playing field for students regardless of their circumstances. Many countries' funding schemes force schools to compete for students and their associated education dollars. A growing body of research shows such competition is the critical element for improving student performance. Unlike mandate-driven policies intending to raise student achievement, including nationalized course-content standards and testing, teacher certification requirements, and guaranteed school funding mandates, competition has real teeth. It introduces powerful incentives to perform and real consequences for failure. Those rewards and consequences are immediate because parents are empowered to act on behalf of their children rather than depend on politicians and special interests to devise the next great education reform scheme.

An OECD analysis by Ludger Woessmann, Elke Ludemann, Gabriela Schutz, and Martin R. West of PISA achievement for 265,000 students from thirty-seven countries found that competition for students accounts for up to two PISA grade-level equivalents.[27] Likewise, Jaap Dronkers of the European University Institute in Italy and Peter Robert of Hungary's Eötvös Loránd University found that school choice explains higher PISA math performance, even after controlling for differences across countries' educational systems and school choice approaches.[28]

Another examination of thirty-nine countries revealed that students in countries with higher private-school enrollments performed better. In fact, when private enrollment shares increase by 10 percent, students scored 6 points higher in math and 5 points higher in science on the IAE's TIMSS. Scores were even higher once nongovernment-funded independent private schools were included. "This suggests that student performance is higher in educational systems where private schools take over resource allocation from public decision-makers," concluded Woessmann of Germany's Kiel Institute of World Economics.[29]

OECD data also indicate that competition for students benefits children from disadvantaged socioeconomic backgrounds. Among the top five countries with above-average performance and a below-average impact of student socioeconomic background, competition for students was the most common characteristic.[30] In fact, OECD research has found that as the levels of public funding for privately managed schools rise, the socioeconomic gaps between publicly and privately managed schools fall. Thus in addition to improving student performance, competition for students also promotes equity.[31] An analysis by several scholars on the PISA math performance of 180,000 students from twenty-seven OECD countries found that students of every socioeconomic status benefit from school competition. In fact, lead researcher Gabriela Schutz observed that:

> There is not a single case where a policy designed to introduce accountability, autonomy, or choice into schooling benefits high-SES [socioeconomic status] students to the detriment of low-SES students. . . . This suggests that fears of equity-efficiency tradeoffs and cream-skimming in implementing market-oriented educational reforms are not merely exaggerated, but are largely mistaken. International evidence on the institutional determinants of efficiency and equity in schooling confirms that more efficient school systems can also be equitable if schools are induced to challenge all students to reach their full potential.[32]

Relying on a monopolistic schooling system hurts the global competitiveness of American students as well as the economy.

A Harvard University Program on Education Policy and Governance analysis showed that fewer American students are performing at advanced levels in PISA math. Specifically, the analysis found that thirty of the fifty-six participating countries had higher proportions of students scoring at the advanced level.[33] In a follow-up analysis, the Harvard authors wondered, "At a time of persistent unemployment, especially among the less skilled, many wonder whether schools are adequately preparing students for the 21st-century global economy." Their findings were sobering:

> Increasing the percentage of proficient students to the levels attained in Canada and Korea would increase the annual US growth rate by 0.9 percentage points and 1.3 percentage points, respectively. Since current average annual growth rates hover between 2 and 3 percentage points, that increment would lift growth rates by between 30 and 50 percent. When translated into dollar terms, these magnitudes become staggering. If one calculates these percentage increases as national income projections over an 80-year period (providing for a 20-year delay before any school reform is completed and the newly proficient students begin their working careers), a back-of-the-envelope calculation suggests gains of nothing less than $75 trillion over the period. That averages out to around a trillion dollars a year. Even if you tweak these numbers a bit in one direction or another to account for various uncertainties, you reach the same bottom line: Those who say that student math performance does not matter are clearly wrong.[34]

More than half of all OECD countries reported a reduction in restrictions on school choice among public schools over the past twenty-five years. Twelve OECD countries reported the creation of new autonomous public schools, and ten reported new funding mechanisms to promote school choice.[35] PISA officials have documented cases where schools that compete for student enrollment perform 15 points higher on average than schools that do not compete for enrollment.[36] Schools in 75 percent of the twenty-one countries with equal or better average PISA performance than the United States also reported having higher levels of competition for students.[37] More than one in five American schools (21 percent) reported having no competition for students, as shown in Figure 7.6. In contrast, more than 95 percent of schools in Macao, China,

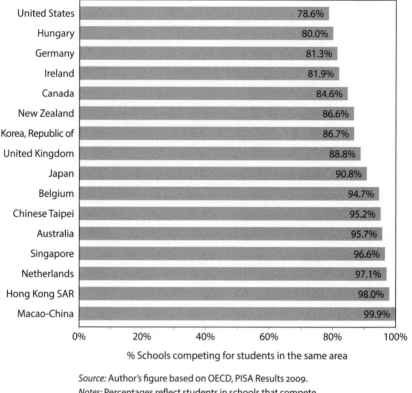

Figure 7.6. Percentage of Students in Schools Competing for Students

Hong Kong, the Netherlands, Singapore, Australia, and Chinese-Taipei report competing with other schools for students; while more than 90 percent of schools in Belgium and Japan report competing for students.[38]

Parental Choice and Student Performance

Competition for students through parental school choice was a more common characteristic among top global performers than selective school admissions (26 percent) or parental pressure on their children to do well in school (73 percent)—a common explanation for why students from Asian countries outperform their American counterparts. OECD countries have been expanding parental options over their children's schooling over the past several years. In many of these countries, both public and private schools are publicly funded, making them free of out-of-pocket costs to students from families of all socio-economic backgrounds.

In some eighteen OECD member countries, parents are free to choose their children's public schools.[39] The OECD reports seven public-school choice indicators for both the primary and secondary school levels: (1) whether initial school assignment is based on schools' geographical area; (2) whether families are given a general right to enroll in any traditional public school they wish; (3) whether choice of other public schools is restricted to the district or municipality; (4) whether choice of other public schools is restricted by region; (5) whether families must apply to enroll in a public school other than their assigned school; (6) whether there is free choice of other public schools if there are places available; and (7) whether there are other restrictions or conditions.[40] Figure 7.7 ranks countries according to how free parents are to choose their children's public schools based on a 0 to 14 point scale, with up to 2 points for each of the seven choice indicators if countries allow or do not restrict choice at both the primary and secondary level.

The United States ties with Norway and Chinese Taipei for offering parents the least freedom to choose public schools for their children. In these countries parents' choices are largely limited to schools where they can afford to live. If parents want another option, they must apply for schools outside their area, and the decision to accept students is left to districts or other school officials. In contrast, parents in Belgium, Macao, China, and Singapore have unfettered freedom to choose the public school they think is best for their children. Parents have nearly unfettered public school choice in New Zealand except for a single restriction at the secondary school level, which requires them to apply for a spot at schools outside their resident area. As becomes clear when compared to practices in other countries, American public schools are not equally open to all, nor do they have to take all comers as do government schools in nearly 70 percent of countries that performed as well or better than the United States on the 2009 PISA assessment.

All OECD countries provide direct government funding to public schools, and many provide it to private schools as well. In addition, many countries also provide public financial assistance to families to help offset the cost of

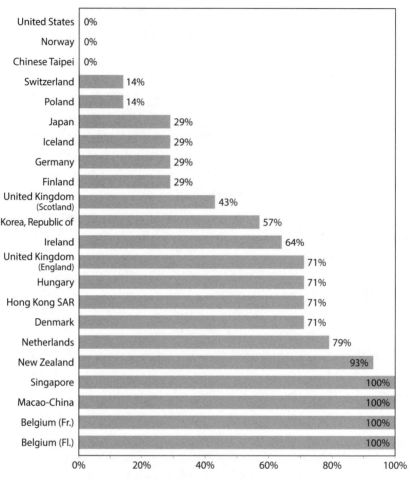

Freedom parents have to choose public schools

Source: Author's figure based on data from OECD,
Education at a Glance 2010, Table D.5.1.

Notes:

1. Information for Australia and Canada were not reported, so they are excluded from the figure.

2. The OECD does not report aggregate information for the United Kingdom and Belgium as PISA does. The figure therefore reports information for French and Flemish Belgium, as well as England and Scotland.

3. Percentages represent how free parents are to choose their children's public schools based on a 0 to 14 point scale, with up to 2 points for each of the seven choice indicators if countries allow choice at both the primary and secondary levels.

Figure 7.7. Comparative Freedom of Parents to Choose a Public School

tuition and other associated schooling costs. Fully eighteen OECD members offer parents nongovernment school options through vouchers or tax credits. Among the countries that performed as well or better than the United States, in thirteen countries publicly funded vouchers are available, including a pre-kindergarten voucher in Hong Kong; while tuition tax credits are available in six countries.[41] "Financial incentives are an important means of promoting school choice," according to the OECD. "Financial incentives such as publicly funded school vouchers/scholarships or tuition tax credits can help families choose a school other than the one assigned by helping to cover the cost of tuition."[42] The OECD reports across four financial incentives categories both the primary and secondary school levels: (1) vouchers; (2) tax credits; (3) funding immediately following students to schools of their choice; and (4) funding not directly following students but over time adjustments can be made. Within each of those categories, the OECD reports financial incentives available by school type, namely, public schools; government-dependent private schools, which receive more than half of their core funding from government agencies; and independent private schools.[43] Vouchers for government-dependent schools are available in about one-third of all OECD countries; dropping to one-fifth for independent private schools. Three out of four countries that permit vouchers limit scholarships to students from low-income families.[44] Tax credits or rebates for parents enrolling their children in government-dependent or independent private schools are available in ten OECD countries.[45]

Among the United States and the twenty-one countries that outperformed it, vouchers are available in 60 percent of them, while tax credits are available in 23 percent. Figure 7.8 ranks countries according to the financial incentives available affecting parents' ability to choose public or private schools based on a 0 to 21 point scale. Up to 2 points are for the availability of vouchers and tax credits for each school type at both the elementary and secondary levels (12 possible points); 2 points are awarded if funding immediately follows students regardless of the type of school they attend (6 possible points); and 1 point if delayed adjusted funding follows students regardless of school type (3 possible points).

New Zealand and Poland have about twice as many financial incentives for parental choice than the United States, around 60 percent compared to 29 percent. New Zealand and Poland both allow vouchers, and New Zealand

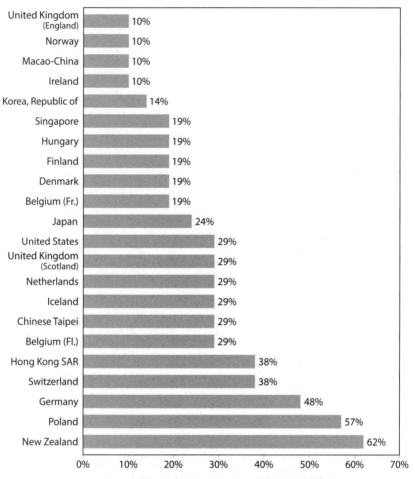

Financial incentives supporting parental choice

Source: Author's figure based on data from OECD, *Education at a Glance 2010*, Table D.5.3; and Annex 3, pp. 20–24.

Notes:

1. Information for Australia and Canada were not reported, so they are excluded from the figure.
2. The OECD does not report aggregate information for the United Kingdom and Belgium as PISA does. The figure therefore reports information for French and Flemish Belgium, as well as England and Scotland.
3. Percentages represent how free parents are to choose their children's public schools based on a 0 to 21 point scale, with up to 2 points for each of the seven choice indicators if countries allow choice at both the primary and secondary levels.

Figure 7.8. Financial Incentives Supporting Parental Choice

also allows tax credits for educational expenses, two options that help make a variety of education options more available. Funding also follows students to more school types than schools in the United States. Germany and Switzerland also permit funding to follow students to more schools, and both countries allow vouchers. Germany also allows tax credits for educational expenses.

It is important to note, however, that in the United States, the availability of K–12 vouchers and tax-credit scholarships is determined at the state level. Since the creation of the US Department of Education, dozens of voucher and tax-credit scholarship proposals have been introduced in Congress but never adopted. To be sure, those plans were not primarily voted down out of a concern for constitutionally limited government. Rather, those plans continue to be unpopular with advocates of government-controlled schooling. The one exception of a constitutionally permissible federal voucher program is the D.C. Opportunity Scholarship Program, limited as the name suggests to students in the Washington, DC, area. Thus when comparing freedom American parents have to choose schools compared to their international counterparts, it must be borne in mind that various state laws—not any US Department of Education policy—are responsible.

Table 7.1 provides more details about the financial incentives countries offer in support of parental freedom to choose their children's schools, as well as the percentage of students who attend schools where principals, teachers, or both have significant autonomy over resource allocation, curricula, and assessments.[46] Such autonomy matters because parents' freedom to choose their children's schools would not mean much if all schools were largely the same. In the United States, just 56 percent of students attend schools where principals or teachers, not local, regional, or national governments, largely control resource allocation, which includes hiring and firing teachers, determining teachers' salaries and raises, making school budgets, and determining school funding allocations. In contrast, in seven top-performing countries higher percentages of students attend schools where principals and teachers have considerable responsibility over school resource allocation: Macao, China, 91 percent; the Netherlands, 88 percent; Hungary, 78 percent; the United Kingdom, 72 percent; followed by New Zealand, Denmark, and Hong Kong, each with more than 62 percent. Who controls curricula and assessments is at least—if not more—important.

Table 7.1. Financial Incentives and School Autonomy

	PISA Reading, Math, and Science Average	% of students in schools competing for enrollment	% of students in schools where only principals/ teachers have considerable responsibility for resource allocation	% of students in schools where only principals/ teachers have considerable responsibility for curricula and assessment	Vouchers	Tax Credits
Australia	519	95.7%	48.3%	69.5%	–	–
Belgium	509	94.7%	46.2%	61.0%	x	–
Canada	527	84.6%	29.8%	31.0%	x	x
Chinese Taipei	519	95.2%	52.7%	78.8%	x	x
Denmark	499	77.8%	63.3%	66.0%	x	–
Finland	544	57.5%	31.8%	58.8%	–	–
Germany	510	81.3%	28.2%	64.0%	x	–
Hong Kong SAR	546	98.0%	61.7%	88.5%	x	–
Hungary	496	80.0%	77.7%	71.0%	–	–
Iceland	501	50.8%	55.3%	73.5%	–	–
Ireland	497	81.9%	41.2%	72.8%	–	–
Japan	529	90.8%	32.2%	93.5%	x	–
Korea, Republic of	541	86.7%	30.7%	89.0%	–	x
Macao, China	508	99.9%	90.5%	92.5%	x	–
Netherlands	519	97.1%	87.5%	93.8%	–	–
New Zealand	524	86.6%	67.8%	87.8%	x	x
Norway	500	40.1%	45.5%	47.0%	–	–
Poland	501	67.6%	37.2%	79.3%	x	–

	PISA Reading, Math, and Science Average	% of students in schools competing for enrollment	% of students in schools where only principals/ teachers have con- siderable responsi- bility for resource allocation	% of students in schools where only principals/ teachers have con- siderable responsi- bility for curricula and assessment	Vouchers	Tax Credits
Singapore	544	96.6%	29.8%	59.8%	x	—
Switzerland	517	37.9%	46.0%	35.5%	x	—
United Kingdom (England)	500	88.8%	71.8%	87.3%	—	—
United Kingdom (Scotland)	500	88.8%	71.8%	87.3%	—	x
United States	496	78.6%	55.8%	50.5%	x	x

Source: Author's table based on data from OECD, *PISA Results 2009: What Students Know and Can Do*; *PISA Results 2009: What Makes a School Successful*; *Education at a Glance 2010: OECD Indicators*; and *Education at a Glance 2010, Annex 3, Sources, methods, and notes.*

Notes:
1. Percentages reflect students in schools that compete with one or more schools for students in the same area.
2. PISA performance, school competition, and autonomy percentages are reported for the United Kingdom as a whole. The availability of vouchers and tax credits are reported for England and Scotland separately.
3. The availability of vouchers and tax credits was not reported for Australia.

Barely half of American students attend schools where principals and teachers take the lead in deciding curricula and assessments. In contrast, in 86 percent of the countries that outperformed the United States, large majorities of students attend schools where educators, not governments, largely determine education policies. More than 9 out of 10 students in the Netherlands,

Japan, and Macao, China, attend schools where educators make curricular and assessment decisions. Close to 9 of 10 students in Korea, Hong Kong, New Zealand, and the United Kingdom also attend such schools. In Poland, Chinese Taipei, Iceland, Ireland, Hungary, and Australia, more than 70 percent of students attend academically autonomous schools; while in Denmark, Germany, Belgium, Singapore, and Finland close to 60 percent of students attend schools where principals and/or teachers set curricula and assessment policies. This preponderance suggests that while other countries may have national education ministries, those ministries do not micromanage schools to the degree that the US Department of Education does its funding requirements. In addition, in other countries the notion of public education is not limited to government schools.

Because countries' educational systems and structures differ so much, another way to look at financial incentives supportive of parental choice is the extent to which government funding may be used at private schools, along the lines of what economist Milton Friedman has recommended. On average, 58 percent of the funding for privately managed schools in OECD countries comes from government sources, which include departments, local, regional, state, and national authorities.[47] Among the countries that outperformed the United States on the PISA assessment, in Finland, the Netherlands, and Hong Kong more than 90 percent of privately managed schools' funding comes from a government source (see Figure 7.9). Privately managed schools in Hungary, Ireland, Belgium, and Germany receive between 80 and 90 percent of their funding from the government. In contrast, privately managed school in the United States and the United Kingdom receive no government funding. What matters most, however, is that schools have autonomy and must compete for students—regardless of the sources of their funding.

Competition Makes the Grade

PISA officials have documented cases where schools that compete for students perform 15 points higher on average than schools that do not compete for students.[48] Fully 72 percent of the countries (fifteen) that performed as well or better than the United States had higher proportions of schools competing for students. Parents in 91 percent of those countries (nineteen) have more

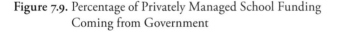

Source: Author's figure based on OECD, *Public and Private Schools: How Manage-ment and Funding Relate to Their Socio-economic Profile*, 2012, Table B1.4.
Notes:
1. Data were not reported for Iceland, Norway, Macao, China, or Singapore.
2. With the exception of Macao, China, where 96 percent of schools are privately managed, privately-managed schools in Iceland, Norway, and Singapore represent less than 2 percent of schools.

Figure 7.9. Percentage of Privately Managed School Funding
Coming from Government

freedom to choose their children's government schools than American parents. Financial incentives supporting parents' freedom to choose government or independent schools are also much more widely available in top-performing countries, including vouchers and tax credits. Finally, schools in 86 percent of countries that performed as well as or better than the United States had more autonomy over curricula and testing than American schools. Freedom for parents, competition for students, and autonomy for schools appear to be critical components to top-performers' success—not any centralized education ministry.

Other competitive practices are also common features among top-performing schooling systems, including performance pay for teachers. Outstanding teaching performance is rewarded in fourteen OECD countries. In nine of those countries schools, not state governments, determine performance-pay policies: the Czech Republic, Denmark, England, Finland, Hungary, the Netherlands, New Zealand, Sweden, and Slovenia. In two-thirds of OECD member countries, schools in disadvantaged areas offer teachers higher salaries, and ten countries offer higher pay for teachers in certain fields.[49]

The following chapter reviews in greater detail more than a dozen countries with more competition for students and higher performance compared to American students. Those countries provide valuable alternatives to a centralized, command-and-control model of nationwide schooling.

8

How the Top Performers Do It

Alternative Models from Across the Globe

FOCUSING ON PROGRAM for International Student Assessment (PISA) results from top-performing countries, the previous chapter revealed that contrary to claims that education policy is best when it is centralized, top-performing countries have high levels of competition for students. Given the performance of American 15-year-olds who are nearing the end of their secondary education, having a US Department of Education has not improved American student achievement relative to their international peers. Other countries with far greater socioeconomic challenges, including higher rates of poverty and immigration, have risen to the top of international performance rankings—all while spending far less than the United States. As the Cato Institute's Andrew Coulson put it, "If a particular approach to organizing and funding schools consistently outperforms other approaches across widely varying circumstances, we can be fairly confident that the observed pattern is the result of the system itself."[1] This chapter highlights several alternatives to a centralized, nationwide schooling system based on the practices used by fourteen countries that outperformed the United States.

This review reveals that student success has little—if anything—to do with having a national ministry or department of education. Neither Canada nor Macao, China, has ever had one. New Zealand downgraded its failing national education bureaucracy virtually overnight in 1989. Similarly, Korea divested the planning and administrative budget of its national education ministry to local entities in 1991. Meanwhile, countries with highly centralized education ministries, including Chinese Taipei, Hong Kong, Ireland, Japan, Korea, and Singapore, are actively pursuing policies to encourage more autonomy for schools and more options for students and parents; all of those countries have higher concentrations of students enrolled in nongovernment schools than the United States. Many European countries with well-established traditions of decentralization and freedom for parents to choose their children's schools, including Belgium and the Netherlands, are inspiring decentralization efforts throughout the European Union and as far away as Singapore. The United States is moving in the opposite direction, but it is not too late to reverse course based on the successes of other countries, starting with Australia.

Australia

Educational System. Australia has a decentralized educational system in which the eight states and territories are the primary authority instead of the federal Department of Education, Employment and Workplace Relations. Joint federal, state, and territorial councils collaborate on education policy, but state education departments recruit and appoint the teachers in government schools; provide buildings, equipment, and materials; and offer limited discretionary school funding for use by schools. Regional offices and schools in most jurisdictions take care of administration, staffing, and curriculum, although the extent of responsibility varies across jurisdictions.[2]

National Curriculum. While central authorities determine the curriculum and standards framework, schools have autonomy over curriculum details, textbooks, and teaching practices. State authorities specify curriculum for Grades 11 and 12 while also being responsible for examining and certifying student achievement for both government and nongovernment schools.[3] Yet Australia is moving toward a national curriculum and assessment system.[4] In 2008, state and federal authorities committed to the National Education Agreement, a national reform framework, and the Melbourne Declaration on the Educational Goals for Young Australians, which details the goals of Australian schooling.[5] The reform agenda includes several initiatives, including the creation of a national curriculum, the Australian Curriculum; national standards for teachers and school heads; and a national literacy and numeracy assessment for students in Grades 3, 5, 7, and 9. The Australian Curriculum, Assessment, and Reporting Authority and the Australian Institute of Teaching and School Leadership were established to help carry out these initiatives.[6]

This development is an outgrowth of efforts begun in 2003 by the Ministerial Council on Education, Employment, Training, and Youth Affairs to collect what are called national Statements of Learning for English, mathematics, science, and civics from the states and territories to help make curricula more consistent.[7] The Australian Curriculum is expected to be implemented by 2013.[8]

National Assessments. Federal and state authorities created the National Assessment Program for Australia in 2002. Since 2009, it has been managed by the Australian Curriculum, Assessment, and Reporting Authority. The National Assessment was introduced in 2009, and the national curriculum was adopted in 2011.[9] The National Assessment covers full-cohort assessments in literacy and numeracy for Grades 3, 5, 7, and 9; and sample assessments every three years in science, civics, and technology for Grades 6 and 10. Australian students also participate in the Trends in International Mathematics and Science Study (TIMSS) and PISA.[10] In addition to national assessments, states and territories conduct their own assessments at the end of Grade 12 to certify student achievement before graduation and preparation for higher education.[11]

School Autonomy. In spite of this recent trend toward nationalizing education, most Australian students attend highly autonomous schools, namely, those where principals or teachers have considerable responsibility over curricula and assessment policies. Currently 65 percent of Australian students attend schools with autonomy over assessment policies.[12] Fully 92 percent of students attend schools that have autonomy over textbook selection. Close to half of Australian students, 46 percent, attend schools that have autonomy over course content, while 75 percent of students attend schools with autonomy over which courses are offered.[13]

Parental Choice. Fully 96 percent of Australian students attend schools that must compete with one or more schools for enrollment.[14] Over the past several decades, the number of private schools in Australia has increased dramatically, resulting in changes within the public schools, creating distinctions among them. In fact, at 39 percent, Australia now has one of the highest private-school attendance rates of any country that outperformed the United States on the 2009 PISA assessment.[15] The Australian government encouraged the growth of private schools as part of its efforts dating back to the 1970s to equalize school funding. At that time, the Australian Schools Commission decided to give financial aid to poorer schools regardless of whether they were publicly or privately managed.[16] State governments have continued to increase government aid to the poorest schools, including private ones, because it expands educational opportunity and promotes equity.[17] As of 2010, just over one-third of students attended nongovernment schools.[18] Over the past decade the proportion of students in nongovernment schools has increased from 31 percent to 34 percent. Currently, 20 percent of Australian students attend Catholic private schools, while 14 percent attend independent private schools.[19] PISA reports that private-school students perform 44 points better in reading than public school students.[20]

Belgium

Educational System. Education in Belgium is largely a local matter, supported by the Dutch (Flemish)-, French-, and German-speaking communities. Federal Belgian authority is limited to determining the beginning and the end of compulsory education, minimum conditions for earning a diploma, and staff pensions.[21] The Belgian Constitution guarantees the right of all children to an education. It also guarantees freedom of education. By law, all citizens have the right to organize and establish schools. Parents are guaranteed the right to choose schools for their children, and government authorities cannot prohibit the establishment of private schools. In addition, all children are guaranteed that public schools supporting their parents' religious or philosophical beliefs will be accessible through public transportation.[22]

National Curriculum. In Belgium, education encompasses more than measurable knowledge and skills. Schools are expected to promote values and convictions according to their particular stated pedagogical frameworks. Thus while the Department for Educational Development in Flanders oversees general school quality, there is no uniform national curriculum. A government-funded Student Guidance Center exists as a consulting agency to assist students, parents, teachers, and school officials, but it does not manage curricula or assessments.[23] More than a decade ago, however, Flanders introduced a core curriculum for public and government-dependent private schools that emphasizes minimal grade-level academic and developmental targets.[24]

National Assessments. Beginning in the 2008–09 school year, the French-speaking community implemented a mandatory national primary school assessment.[25] Recently the Flemish government opted for a national system of voluntary surveys to assess students' mastery of core curriculum targets. The government, however, does not know the identity of individual students or schools, and there are no sanctions for schools or teachers.[26] Since Belgian schools determine their missions and teaching methodologies, they assess students against their own objectives and qualifications. At the pre-primary level there are only observation-based assessments that examine students' maturity, comparative advancement relative to their peers, and diagnostics if a student is deemed to be behind. At the primary level, teachers assess students annually to measure progress against their schools' objectives and to gauge teacher effectiveness. Students' grades are based on those annual assessments as well as regular course assessments administered throughout the school year. Those results are provided to parents, who then decide whether their child should repeat a grade or be placed in special education.[27]

School Autonomy. In virtually all cases (97 percent), assessment policies are made at the school or local level, along with textbook selection (98 percent). Course content and offerings are also, with few exceptions, made at the school and local level (74 percent and 86 percent, respectively).[28] These decisions and others, such as instructional philosophy and curriculum, are largely made by a school's governing body or board members. For schools without a school board, education networks are responsible for decision making. The networks have councils to create their own curricula.[29] The Organization for Economic Cooperation and Development (OECD) finds that, along with schools in the Netherlands, Belgian schools that "have more autonomy in defining their curricula and assessment practices also show higher performance."[30]

Parental Choice. School choice is a well-established policy in Belgium, and parents' freedom to choose their children's schools is constitutionally guaranteed. With very few exceptions schools cannot refuse to enroll students or refer them to another school.[31] Ninety-five percent of Belgium's students attend a school that competed for their enrollment against one or more schools. Specifically, 81 percent of students attend schools that compete with two or more schools for enrollment, while more than 12 percent compete against one other school.[32] To allow equal access for all students to attend schools that reflect their beliefs, Belgium offers low-income students vouchers to attend government-dependent, that is publicly subsidized, private schools.[33] It is important to note, however, that Belgium does not distinguish between *public* and *private* schools as the United States does. Virtually all schools are publicly subsidized; however, many public schools are privately managed by educational and religious organizations. Belgium has three overarching school types. Public community schools are overseen by the respective education departments of the Dutch, French, and German communities and must be philosophically and religiously neutral. Provinces and municipalities also run and fund public schools. Government-dependent private schools are abundant as well. These schools are privately run and publicly subsidized and may be denominational or nondenominational. Up to 95 percent of government-dependent private schools are religious.[34] The vast majority of privately run, publicly subsidized schools are Catholic, but there are also Islamic, Jewish, Orthodox, and Protestant schools, too. Nondenominational privately run, publicly subsidized schools include Montessori and Steiner method schools.[35] Independent private schools do not receive government funding. While such schools are free to open, the Flemish government does not recognize their certificates and diplomas. Students who wish to have them recognized must pass a test administered by the Flemish authorities.[36]

Canada

Educational System. Canada stands out among top global performers—along with Macao, China,—for not having a national education ministry or department.[37] Education is a strictly provincial or territorial matter, and over the past several years, authority over education has further decentralized. A number of deregulation and fiscal reforms during the 1990s were implemented to prevent an economic collapse. Those reforms are largely credited with saving Canada from the brink of bankruptcy and making it an economic leader among the G7 countries. The Ottawa government looked to constrain spending in a number of areas, which ultimately reduced government control and restructured how federal matters were managed. As a result, provinces were given a wider range of responsibilities—including both funding and implementing education policies.[38] Less federal involvement, overall, already allowed individuals, families, and business to be able to invest and be involved more in their community. Many of Canada's provinces continued the trend by further decentralizing their education structures and encouraging more school competition and growth in the nongovernment school sector.

In Alberta, specifically, the School Act states that parents have a right and responsibility to make decisions respecting the education of their children. Quebec created a law that required at least four parents on the Establishment Council, ensuring parents have a voice in the education system. Each province, such as Alberta, Ontario, and Quebec, has a completely different process for choosing curricula. Ontario's Ministry of Education takes up a rigorous evaluation of textbooks, whereas in Alberta, a group of teachers meet to review and analyze textbooks from various publishing companies. In Quebec, potential textbooks are distributed to various ministries.[39]

Provinces were given the ability to establish a variety of levels of school competition and autonomy. Some created competition through vouchers or payments directly to families to attend any school of their choice, including public, independent, and religious schools. Leveling the playing field for all students has improved public school education. Moreover, it has been found that "achievement scores are not only higher generally in the provinces that fund independent schools, but also higher particularly among students from less advantaged backgrounds," according to a study by the Vancouver-based Fraser Institute.[40]

National Curriculum and Assessment. Given Canada's localized approach to education, there is no national curriculum or assessment.

Parental Choice. Nationwide 85 percent of students attend schools that compete with at least one other school for enrollment.[41] While the availability of public funding for nongovernment schools varies across the country's ten provinces, 92 percent of Canadians live in areas where school choice is available.[42] Nongovernment schools in Quebec, Manitoba, Alberta, and British Columbia receive direct subsidies from the government, a policy that began to ensure Catholics had alternatives to once Protestant-controlled schools.[43] The value of private-school subsidies varies; they average about one-third of government school per-pupil spending.[44] In Alberta, Ontario, and Saskatchewan, full public funding is available for Catholic or Protestant private schools run by separate public school boards.[45] Alberta has had publicly funded private schools since the 1960s, and funding for them was increased in the early 1990s to encourage government-run schools to be more competitive. At 60 percent of public-school funding, Alberta now offers the most generous private-school subsidy; however, private schools must follow provincial governmental testing, curriculum, and hiring policies.[46] British Columbia has offered private-school subsidies since 1977 when the Independent Schools Support Act was adopted. Subsidies are currently tiered depending on the degree of government regulations private schools want to accept over curriculum and operating for profit. In general, subsidies average 35 percent of government school-operating costs.[47] Manitoba offers private-school subsidies worth 50 percent of per-pupil net operating public-school costs, and along with Quebec, is the only province that allows private schools to operate as for-profits. Yet private schools must adhere to provincial curriculum and teacher certification requirements.[48] Quebec has allowed private-school subsidies since 1968, and they are currently worth 35 percent of the total per-pupil public-school cost. To receive provincial funding private schools must adhere to curriculum and teacher certification requirements.[49] Ottawa's direct subsidy system was replaced in 2002 with a refundable tax credit.[50] However, after the 2003 election, the Liberal government rescinded it.[51] PISA reports that private school students perform 50 points better in reading than public school students.[52]

Chinese Taipei

Educational System. Taiwan has a three-tiered system including a central Ministry of Education, regional departments of education in the provinces, and local education bureaus at the county or city levels. Beginning in the 1990s, authority over education has decentralized with local bureaus having more authority over education policies.[53] Under the Educational Fundamental Act parents' rights to be involved in the children's education is assured, and schools must keep parents informed about regulations, course content, instructional methods, and assessment criteria.[54]

National Curriculum. Chinese Taipei has a partially standardized curriculum.[55] A compulsory education system for Grades 1 through 9 has existed since 1968, and the Ministry of Education extended compulsory education through Grade 12 in 2014. Prior to an array of educational reforms begun in the early 1990s, independent committees developed primary and junior high school curricula. Those curricular frameworks were subsequently integrated by 2004.[56] However, as National Taiwan Normal University Professor Shen-Keng Yang explains, the priorities of ongoing education reforms "are deregulating governmental control over education and exempting education from unnecessary constraints, safeguarding the children's and students' learning rights, protecting the parents' [right to choose] education patterns and paths for their immature children, and respect for the teachers' professional autonomy."[57]

National Assessment. No national assessment is required in Chinese Taipei.[58] In 2001 the previous entrance exam for senior high school was abolished and replaced with a more flexible Multi-route Promotion Program that allows junior high school students to enter senior high school by recommendation, application, or assignment. Regardless of the chosen path, all students must take the Basic Competency Test, which covers five subjects: Chinese, English, mathematics, natural science, and social science, and is linked to the integrated Grades 1 through 9 frameworks. Students may take the test multiple times and apply their best score toward admission. Junior high school students may also opt to take the Practical Technical Program offered by vocational schools instead.[59]

School Autonomy. As a result of ongoing deregulation in education, for 91 percent of schools in Chinese Taipei, student assessment policies are determined at the school and local level. All schools have autonomy over textbook selection. At virtually all schools (97 percent), course content is determined at the school and local level, while at nearly all schools (93 percent) course offerings are decided by school and local officials.[60]

Parental Choice. Recent revisions to the Private School Law and Elementary Education Law have reduced restrictions on private schools, and since 1985, twenty-three new independent private schools have opened.[61] Schools in Chinese Taipei face some of the strongest competition for students among top-performing PISA countries. More than 95 percent of schools report competing with at least one other school for students. In fact 85 percent of schools compete with two or more schools in the same area for students.[62] Tax credits are available for home-schooled students with special needs.[63] Vouchers are also available for students in government and private schools.[64] Compared to the United States, where private school enrollment represents less than 7 percent of all student enrollments, in Chinese Taipei one-third of students attend private schools, and all but one percent of those enrollments are in government-independent private schools, meaning the nation ranks first in independent private school enrollments among competitive countries that outperformed the United States.[65]

Germany

Educational System. Germany's sixteen *Laender*, or states, have legislative and administrative authority over education through their respective Ministries of Education and Cultural Affairs. Their powers include regulation over curricula, professional requirements, recruitment, and school quality matters. Some elements, such as defining grade scales, are standardized through treaties. Coordination of education, science, research, and culture is handled by the federal Standing Conference of the Ministers of Education and Cultural Affairs of the Laender, also referred to as the Standing Conference.[66]

National Curriculum. Germany has a partially standardized curriculum but no single national or common-core curriculum. The Standing Conference adopted a binding elementary school framework in pre-primary schools (ages three to six) in 2004 that makes language, reading and writing skills, and math and science explicit educational objectives. German, including spelling, writing, and literature, along with math, and natural and social science are mandatory in all Laender. Arts, physical education, foreign languages, and religious education are also taught in most primary schools.[67] According to the OECD, "At the secondary school level, eighth-grade mathematics education is currently regulated by more than 40 different curricula, which are all determined by the national educational standards. There are no common core-curricula across the Laender."[68] Curricula vary across grades in terms of detail and timing. In contrast, there are fourteen different science curricula that are not set by national standards. Three Laender have collaborated to develop their own science curriculum, while thirteen Laender each have individual curricula.[69]

National Assessments. Since 2007 cross-Laender assessments have been administered in Grade 3 for German and math, and in Grade 8 for German and students' first foreign language. The federal Standing Conference's Institute for Educational Progress developed the test items based on national education standards. Beginning in 2011 a similar assessment for math was administered across all sixteen Laender, and it will be administered again every five years.[70]

School Autonomy. Ninety-two percent of German students attend schools where assessment policies are set at the school and local level. Nearly all students, 97 percent, attend schools where textbook selection is determined at the school and local level. Fewer students attend schools where course content is determined at the school or local level, 69 percent, but virtually all students (98 percent) attend schools where course offerings are decided at the school and local levels.[71]

Parental Choice. Parental choice in education is constitutionally guaranteed in both Germany's Basic Law as well as in the various Laender Education Acts.[72] Restrictions on public schools have been relaxed in recent years, and more autonomous schools are being established with greater authority over their budgets and staff. Parents now have a greater variety of education options. The Laender have authorized the establishment of more focused schools at the primary level, including those with bilingual and mathematics emphasis. At the middle-school level parents may choose between full- or half-day options as well.[73] The right to establish private schools is also constitutionally guaranteed under Germany's Basic Law, as well as in the Laenders' constitutions. As the OECD explains, "This freedom to establish privately-maintained schools is combined with a guarantee of the privately-maintained school as an institution. Thus, constitutional law rules out a state monopoly of education."[74] However, privately managed schools must abide by federal health and safety regulations, and at the primary level, there are conditions for opening a privately managed school. To do so, the local education authorities must agree that the school would serve a pedagogical or denominational interest not currently being met by the public sector.[75] More than 81 percent of German students attend schools that compete with at least one other school in the area for enrollment.[76] Vouchers paid for by the Laender or local authorities are available to public school students to offset the cost of textbooks and other expensive teaching aids. The availability of vouchers for private schools varies from Land to Land.[77] Tax credits are also available to public and private school parents.[78]

Hong Kong

Educational System. Hong Kong has long had an established education system, known as the Education Bureau. This system was established independently of mainland China and was largely unaffected by Chinese policies over the twentieth century. Until the 1950s, education was largely reserved for the elite of Hong Kong. Starting in the early 1950s, however, the Hong Kong government partnered with churches, charities, and other agencies that had already been successful at establishing and financing local schools to make education more universally available. While educational opportunities were expanding, the reach of Hong Kong's government did not. On the contrary, the government has adhered to its historic noninterventionist approach in schooling.[79] In keeping with that philosophy, most schools are privately sponsored but publicly funded. A Code of Aid governs school operations, but it reflects the longstanding policy that government intervention in education should be minimal.[80]

National Curriculum and Assessment. The government issues curriculum guides and monitors the requirement of territory-wide exams in all schools except government-dependent private schools.[81] Hong Kong's Curriculum Development Council, a freestanding advisory body, advises the government on curriculum development for pre-primary to secondary schools. Supporting the Council is the Curriculum Development Institute, which provides professional leadership, coordinates curriculum development collaborations with local and international education providers, and supports school curriculum implementation.[82]

School Autonomy. "Independent private schools have always been very autonomous," according to the OECD.[83] In the mid-1990s Hong Kong launched its School-based Management Policy requiring all schools including government schools to establish Incorporated Management Committees. The intent is to give schools more flexibility in resource allocation and overall school management. Committee members are also supposed to be more broadly representative.[84] Hong Kong schools are among the most autonomous among top PISA performers. All students attend schools where assessment policies, textbook selections, and course offerings are determined at the school or local level. Moreover, virtually all students (98 percent) attend schools where course content is decided at the school or local level.[85]

Parental Choice. Hong Kong's education reforms place it highest among top-performing PISA countries, with 98 percent of students attending schools that compete with one or more schools for enrollment.[86] With the exception of a kindergarten voucher adopted in 2007, Hong Kong does not offer vouchers or tax credits, although it does offer a number of transportation subsidies.[87] Even so, parents have a wide variety of options. Hong Kong's commitment to minimal governmental interference in schooling is not surprising since there are a variety of privately managed, publicly subsidized schools. Independently operated schools are required to follow a Code of Aid, but it emphasizes procedures rather than operations.[88] In addition to government schools, there are also aided schools, Direct Subsidy Scheme schools, caput schools (local private schools), and international schools, such as those run by the English Schools Foundation.[89] Aided schools are publicly funded but privately managed by a sponsoring entity.[90] International schools teach a curriculum from their own country.[91] Direct-subsidy schools are private schools that receive some government funding in direct proportion to their enrollment and differ from aided schools in that they have much more autonomy, including exemptions from territory-wide testing.[92] An express purpose for allowing such schools is building a vibrant, high-quality private school sector, as the OECD explains, so "parents have greater choice in finding suitable schools for their children."[93] In fact, 93 percent of Hong Kong's students attend privately managed schools, ranking it second only to Macao, China, in terms of private school enrollment share.[94]

Hungary

Educational System. The fall of Communism in 1989 "gave a powerful impulse to the abolishment of the monopoly of the State, to the democratization, and modernization of the education and training systems across the board," according to the Hungarian Ministry of Education.[95] The 1993 Act on Public Education governed the Hungarian education system up through the administration of the 2009 PISA assessment. According to education officials, the Hungarian educational system had "produced an overdecentralized organization of public education that was unique in Europe, with a weak potential for quality enhancement, performance assessment and for the dissemination of innovation on a national scale."[96] Hungary's system of public administration was overhauled in 2010, when responsibility for education was taken over by the Ministry of National Resources.[97] Thus many decentralized and competitive practices in effect at the time of the PISA assessment described in this section are being replaced with greater government control over education.

National Curriculum. After it was adopted in 1995, Hungary began phasing in the National Core Curriculum, which set general standards concerning the volume and content of required subjects and identified basic skills along with learning objectives. Teachers and schools, however, retained autonomy over teaching methods and classroom practices so as not to stifle innovation.[98]

National Assessment. The Public Education Act required annual national assessments as part of schools' quality-control programs. Student performance in math and reading has been annually measured by the National Assessment of Basic Competencies since the 2001–02 school year. Since 2004, all students in Grades 6, 8, and 10 have been required to take the assessment of basic competencies. A separate national assessment for students in Grade 4, which began during the 2005–06 school year, covers reading, math, problem-solving, and writing.[99]

School Autonomy. As of the 2009 PISA assessment, virtually all students attended schools where principals and teachers were primarily responsible for setting assessment policies and selecting textbooks (98 percent). The majority of students also attended schools where course content (85 percent) and offerings (71 percent) were determined at the school or local level.[100]

Parental Choice. Eighty percent of students attend schools that compete with at least one other school for enrollment.[101] While Hungary does not offer vouchers or tax credits, the 1993 Act on Public Education enforces the right of a church, a legal entity, or an individual to found a school. The act also guarantees parents free choice in selecting their children's schools, as well as the right of students to choose a religious or other private school.[102] The state fully subsidizes public schools, while local governments partially subsidize privately managed schools up to 50 percent of their total costs.[103] Thus as with many other countries, private schools in Hungary are considered a part of the overall public education system. Since 1985 schooling options for parents have expanded, and the overall quality of schools has improved; however, to ensure equal access, authorities have restricted schools' selections processes.[104]

Ireland

Educational System. Ireland has a centralized education system overseen by the Minister for Education and Skills, who is a member of and responsible to the national parliament. The Department of Education and Skills runs the Irish education system. Virtually all primary and post-primary schools are state-funded and are required to operate under both the Education Act (1998) and the department's curriculum, assessment, and evaluation framework, based on the advice of the National Council for Curriculum and Assessment.[105]

National Curriculum. All public schools, including privately managed schools receiving public funding, must follow the standard national curriculum. Independent private schools, which receive no government funding and are not recognized under the Education Act 1998, may register their pupils under the Education (Welfare) Act 2000 as receiving a certain minimum education. Those that do almost always follow the national curriculum.[106]

National Assessments. National reading and math assessments are administered about every five years to a randomly selected cohort of students in publicly funded schools, but they are not mandatory.[107] Although not mandatory, state examinations are taken by virtually all students. Those not taking state examinations would be officially categorized as "early school leavers."[108]

School Autonomy. All Irish students attend schools where assessment policies and textbooks selection are carried out at the school or local level. Two-thirds of students attend schools where course content decisions are made at the school or local level, while nearly all students (99 percent) attend schools where course offerings are decided at the school or local level.[109]

Parental Choice. Ireland does not offer vouchers or tax credits since most schools are publicly subsidized. Nearly 82 percent of Irish students attend schools that must compete with at least one other school for enrollment.[110] All of Ireland's nearly 3,200 schools are publicly funded, but most are privately owned and managed by church authorities or religious orders. There are a variety of schools including religious schools, nondenominational schools, multidenominational schools, and Irish-medium schools, which offer instruction in the native Irish rather than English.[111] Multidenominational and Irish-language schools are the fastest-growing school subsectors.[112] In fact, private school enrollment surpasses government school enrollment, 57 percent compared to 43 percent.[113]

Japan

Educational System. The Fundamental Law of Education enacted in 1947 and amended in 2006 governs education practice in Japan. It stipulates that students are to have equal opportunities for a free, compulsory education for nine years. The Ministry of Education, Culture, Sports, Science, and Technology oversees education, along with local bodies that report to municipal boards of education. The federal government subsidizes national schools, while municipal schools are supported locally, with partial funding from the federal government. Private schools do not receive federal funding, but they do receive local government funding for maintenance and improvements. Private schools also receive donations from businesses. The 2006 amendment to the Law of Education, called "Zest for Living," devolved more control over education to local authorities and has given more authority over budgets and personnel to schools.[114]

National Curriculum. The national ministry officially sets the curriculum, with advice from the Central Council for Education. Unofficially, university professors and ministry staff play critical roles. The national curriculum is not strictly speaking mandatory; however, because the prefectures or municipalities are funded by the national ministry, they consider its curriculum policies as more than just guidance. Five subjects are emphasized—Japanese, social studies, mathematics, science, and foreign language—and the curriculum is highly demanding and detailed, being careful to ensure students progress as they should throughout the years.[115]

National Assessments. Until recently, Japan had no national tests. Concerned that the Koreans and the Chinese might outperform them, Japan implemented a national test of every student in Grades 6 and 9; however, they replaced that system with a targeted system assessing just a sample of students.[116] The test recordings are said to be similar to "statistics for popular sports teams" in other countries. The highly visible testing data give parents the information about which primary and middle school is getting their students into the best high schools and universities.[117]

School Autonomy. Virtually all Japanese students attend schools where principals and teachers decide on curricular and assessment policies. Fully 98 percent attend schools that determine assessment policies, 89 percent attend schools where principals and teachers select textbooks, 93 percent attend schools that determine course content, and 94 percent attend schools that determine course offerings.[118]

Parental Choice. With 91 percent of students attending schools that compete with at least one other school for enrollment and 85 percent attending schools that compete with two or more other schools, competition for students in Japan is fierce.[119] In terms of the proportion of students attending independent private schools, 27 percent, Japan ranks second only to Chinese Taipei, where 32 percent of students attend independent private schools.[120] Traditionally, Japan's education system was created to assign students to schools according to their location of residence. However, reforms over the past twenty-five years have expanded public and private school options. Reforms have reduced restrictions to school choice among public schools and promoted new independent private schools. Moreover, while Japan does not offer tax credits to attend private schools, public subsidies to independent private schools, akin to vouchers, are available.[121] More than 81 percent of kindergarten students attend private schools, compared to just 1 percent of primary students and 7 percent of junior high school students. Nearly 30 percent of high school students attend private schools.[122] Yet most Japanese students also receive additional instruction and tutoring after the formal school day from a variety of private providers called *juku*.[123] In fact, estimates from the national ministry, which is hostile to *juku*, suggest 39 percent of elementary students, 75 percent of middle school students, and 38 percent of high school students attend *juku*.[124] Other estimates suggest far more students attend *juku*. By Grade 5, one in three Japanese students is enrolled in a private, for-profit "after-school school." By Grade 8, close to half of all students are enrolled in such schools, increasing to 90 percent by Grade 9.[125] With recent reforms in Japan, new kinds of schools are encouraged to develop.[126] School corporations are allowed to open independent private schools, and since 2004, other entities such as businesses or nonprofit organizations may also open such schools.[127] As a result of those changes, 29 percent of Japanese students attend private schools, with 27 percent of students attending government-independent private schools.[128]

South Korea

Educational System. The Ministry of Education, Science, and Technology oversees education in Korea under Article 24 of the Act on Government Organization. In 1991, the Local Autonomy Law, as the name suggests, began devolving authority over education, with the ministry divesting much of its planning and administrative budget to local authorities.[129] The ministry outlined additional reform goals in its 2011 Major Policies and Plans document, including strengthening school autonomy.[130]

National Curriculum. Korea has a national curriculum as well as a set of operating guidelines for metropolitan and provincial education offices. Both the curriculum and the guidelines, however, are designed to preserve a great deal of flexibility for individual schools, each having its own particular characteristics and objectives.[131] The national curriculum is revised every five years, most recently in 2011.[132]

School Autonomy. There is, to a great extent, autonomy and freedom given to principals and teachers in making and implementing student assessment policies and textbooks. Specifically, more than 92 percent of students attend schools where principals and teachers set assessment policies, while 96 percent attend schools where they choose textbooks. In addition, virtually all Korean students attend schools where course content and offerings are decided at the school or local levels (96 and 97 percent, respectively).[133]

Parental Choice. Korea implemented vouchers in 2002 primarily for parents of 5-year-olds to ensure they have the option of attending kindergarten. These incentives have expanded private school development and improved public school education. As of 2009, more than 35 percent of Korean students attended private schools, with more than 17 percent attending government-independent private schools.[134] Tax credits are also available in Korea.[135] By 2011, at least twenty-three different types of high schools were offering a variety of programs in math, arts, and sciences. These high schools are overseen by the metropolitan and provincial offices of education.[136]

Macao, China

Educational System. Macao, China, like Hong Kong, is a special administrative region of China, following the "one country, two systems" model. In stark contrast to Hong Kong, however, the Macao government has no education ministry, and education is highly decentralized. Under Portugal's previous rule, churches, civic groups, individuals, and businesses in Macao established, funded, and ran schools.[137] Since its establishment in 1999 as a special administrative region of China, the Macao government has actively promoted the development of education through funding of schools, including fifteen years of subsidies, rather than management of them. "The Government encourages schools to develop their own characteristics and style in terms of mission, curriculum and teaching mode according to their backgrounds," according to the Macao Government Information Bureau. "The Government also supports the development of a diversified school system, to nurture more talent for society."[138] Macao's system of free schooling includes both public and private schools. Nonprofit private schools that follow a local education system of six years' primary education and three years each of lower and upper secondary education may apply for entry into the free schooling system. Macao's Education and Youth Affairs Bureau assists parents to enroll their children in public or private schools.[139] Yet recently there has been concern about the government's increasing interest in education. In fact, in February 2012 the Legislative Assembly passed the "Private School Teaching Staff System Framework," prompting private schools to transform their management. In response, the *Macau Daily Times* wondered, "Is Macau's Education System Changing?"[140]

National Curriculum and Assessment. The Education and Youth Affairs Bureau launched a second series of amendments to Macao's education system in 2004, including curricular changes; however, it focused on school-based curricular development to mitigate perceptions that Macao was reliant on mainland China, Hong Kong, or Taiwan.[141] Macao has no mandatory national assessment, but as of 2009 all 15-year-olds are required to take the PISA assessments.[142]

School Autonomy. Schools have high levels of autonomy in Macao, China. In fact, 95 percent of students attend schools where teachers and principals establish assessment policies. All students attend schools where principals and teachers choose textbooks; while 94 percent attend schools where they choose course content. A smaller percentage of students attend schools where course offerings are decided strictly at the school level, 81 percent, but another 14 percent attend schools where those decisions are shared with local officials.[143]

Parental Choice. Macao has the highest level of school competition for students. All students attend schools that compete with at least one other school for students, and 92 percent of students attend schools that compete with two or more schools for enrollment.[144] Both vouchers and tax credits are offered in Macao, China, and currently there are seventy-eight licensed schools in Macao, eleven public, and sixty-seven private.[145] In addition, among top-performing PISA countries with higher levels of school competition than the United States, Macao has the highest percentage of students enrolled in nongovernment schools, 96 percent.[146]

The Netherlands

Educational System. The Ministry of Education, Culture, and Science is primarily responsible for the educational system's structure, school funding, inspection, national examinations, and student support. Both publicly and privately managed schools receive government funding from the central government and to a lesser extent from municipal governments. Yet day-to-day school administration and management are decentralized, overseen by individual school boards. School boards implement curriculum, as well as personnel, student admissions, and budgetary policies. Boards can be responsible for a single school or several schools. Public school boards consist of municipality representatives, and private school boards are typically formed by associations or foundations.[147] The Dutch Inspectorate for Education visits schools at least once every four years to verify school performance and quality, more frequently if schools are performing poorly. Very low-performing schools can be sanctioned, even closed, by the Minister of Education, Culture, and Science. Findings from the inspectorate are reported back to the schools, the government, and the public.[148]

National Curriculum and Assessment. While the Dutch Ministry of Education, Culture, and Science sets subject-specific attainment targets, the Netherlands has no standardized curriculum or national assessment at the primary level.[149] The Netherlands does have primary school high-stakes exit exams developed by the government's National Institute for Educational Measurement. Although not mandatory, about 92 percent of Dutch students take them because most secondary schools require them.[150]

School Autonomy. Dutch schools traditionally are highly autonomous. Public, government-dependent private schools have been autonomous and highly decentralized since about 1920.[151] Every Dutch resident has the right under Article 23 of the Constitution to found a school, determine its missions and principles, and organize instruction. Public and private schools or their boards decide how and largely when to teach the core objectives of the Dutch curriculum based on their religious, philosophical, or pedagogical beliefs.[152] The Dutch government agreed in 2006 to an additional series of reforms in conjunction with the European Union's education goals for 2010, which included even greater autonomy for schools based on the practices of other top-performing PISA countries.[153] Specifically, the Dutch government is committed to giving schools "more opportunities to shape their programmes," showing "confidence in the professionals in the field, imposing fewer rules and less supervision," and "allowing more freedom for tailor-made solutions."[154] Consequently, individual schools decide how courses will be taught, but the Dutch Ministry of Education, Culture, and Science defines the courses that must be taught by setting subject-specific attainment targets.[155] Still, virtually all Dutch students attend schools that set their own assessment policies (99 percent) and choose textbooks (100 percent). Nearly all students also attend schools where course content (87 percent) and course offerings (89 percent) are decided by principals and teachers.[156]

Parental Choice. Freedom in education is the foundation of the Dutch educational system and is constitutionally guaranteed. In fact, the Dutch Constitution "places public and private schools on an equal financial footing."[157] Two-thirds of primary schools are privately run. The majority of private schools are Roman Catholic or Protestant, but other religious schools and schools based on pedagogical principles exist as well, such as Montessori schools.[158] Parents are therefore free to choose a school at the primary or secondary level.[159] Secondary schools, however, set their own admissions criteria, and students' acceptance depends on their primary school performance, results of the primary exit exam, and teachers' recommendations.[160] Almost all schools, 97 percent, compete with one or more schools for students.[161] While vouchers and tax credits are not available in the Netherlands, two-thirds of students attend privately run, publicly funded schools, compared to about one-third who attend public schools.[162] About 1,000 students attend government-independent private schools, which represent about 1 percent of all Dutch schools.[163] These schools do not receive government funding and include schools with a specific language focus.[164]

New Zealand

Educational System. The National Education Guidelines and the Education Act 1989 abolished the national Department of Education and replaced it with a much smaller Ministry of Education.[165] Authority over regular operations and management was decentralized to the school level, overseen by individual school boards of trustees, who are responsible for fulfilling the terms of their schools' charters. The ministry develops the national curriculum and operating guidelines for schools. It collects education statistics and monitors the education system's effectiveness. The ministry also allocates funds to education institutions and professional development programs. The Education Review Office evaluates school quality using a variety of indicators, including academic progress; student, staff, and community engagement; leadership and governance; and statutory compliance. The primary measure, however, is the effectiveness of the school's curriculum in promoting student learning. The New Zealand Qualifications Authority oversees and coordinates all national qualifications and manages the assessment and reporting systems for New Zealand's national high school qualifications.[166]

National Curriculum and Assessments. New Zealand has national curricula and assessments.[167] The national curricula include The New Zealand Curriculum for English-medium education introduced in 2007 and the Te Marautanga o Aotearoa curriculum for Māori-medium education introduced in 2008. While the two documents are distinct, they share similar goals.[168] New Zealand also implemented national standards for reading, writing, and math in 2010 for English-medium education and in 2011 for Māori-medium education. Those standards apply to students in Years 1 through 8.[169]

National Assessments. National testing is limited to students in Year 11. Until that point teachers use a range of assessment practices and professional judgment to monitor student progress and diagnose students' needs. Typically teachers develop their own assessments, although a variety of government and other resources are at their disposal to assist them.[170]

School Autonomy. The Ministry of Education develops national curriculum statements, but individual schools and teachers determine how they will be implemented, with oversight from their schools' boards of trustees. The Education Review Office monitors implementation and publishes findings.[171] Nearly all students (98 percent) in New Zealand attend schools where assessment policies are set at the school and local level, and virtually all students (99 percent) attend schools where textbooks are selected at the school level. Likewise, virtually all students attend schools where course content (99 percent) and course offerings (100 percent) are decided at the school and local levels.[172]

Parental Choice. Parents are free to choose their children's schools.[173] Nearly 95 percent of students attend public schools, and about 5 percent attend private schools.[174] Nearly 97 percent of students attend schools that must compete with at least one other school for enrollment, and both vouchers and tax credits are available in New Zealand.[175]

Singapore

Educational System. The Singapore Ministry of Education oversees the country's schooling system, but over the past several decades, authority over education has become more decentralized. Singapore's education system began moving away from a one-size-fits-all approach back in 1979. At that time multiple pathways for students were introduced to lower the dropout rate, improve educational quality, and develop a more technically skilled labor force.[176] Then in 1997 with the launch of Thinking Schools, Learning Nation, Singapore further reformed its educational system away from a centrally controlled model to a decentralized model that emphasizes individual ability, more choices for students, flexibility, and greater school autonomy.[177] With greater school autonomy and flexibility, the Ministry of Education had to re-envision accountability. School autonomy focused around geographic clusters, assisted by cluster superintendents who were successful former principals appointed to mentor school officials to promote academic excellence while maintaining the individual strengths of each school.

National Curriculum. While Singapore has devolved considerable authority to schools in recent years, it is still a centrally driven government system.[178] Schools in Singapore must follow the Ministry of Education's Desired Outcomes of Education, covering core skills and values ranging from literacy and numeracy to social and cooperative skills.[179] Officials from the Ministry of Education and its research division, the National Institute for Education, frequently visit schools and pay a great deal of attention to data schools report. Singapore has also made extensive use of international benchmarking and successful models. Thus, for all the remaining centralization, schools in Singapore are encouraged to innovate and incorporate a variety of teaching styles.[180] In fact, according to the Ministry of Education's Training and Development Division Director Winston Hodge:

> The national curriculum structures will be loosened through curriculum decentralization to allow schools to customize their curriculum to meet their students' needs. Certain subjects can be redesigned as a set of learning outcomes to allow schools room to innovate. . . . This allows schools greater autonomy and flexibility over curriculum time allocation. More time will be freed up from curriculum for students to develop skills and attitudes. MOE [Ministry of Education] will allow flexibility of integration of subjects to develop new understanding.[181]

National Assessment. At the end of Grade 6, Students take the Primary School Leaving Examination, which assesses students in English, native language, math, and science. Most students use their scores to inform their secondary school application decisions. Although secondary school attendance is not compulsory, virtually all students in Singapore enroll in secondary school.[182]

School Autonomy. With a growing emphasis on innovation, schools in Singapore are encouraged to pursue their own missions and goals, which schools themselves annually assess against nine functional areas that encompass academic and social benchmarks. External reviews occur every six years by the School Appraisal Branch of the Ministry of Education. Greater school autonomy has resulted in a clearer focus on developing effective leaders and practices.[183] Today most students attend schools where assessment policies (98 percent) and textbook selection (86 percent) are made at the school and local levels. Most students (84 percent) attend schools where course content is decided at the school and local level, while nearly all students (97 percent) attend schools where course offerings are determined at the school and local levels.[184]

Parental Choice. The state is the primary education provider in Singapore, and virtually all students (99 percent) are enrolled in government schools.[185] Compensatory private education is allowed, but it is heavily regulated.[186] Competition for students, however, is stiff, with more than 90 percent of schools reporting competing with two or more schools for students, plus an additional 6 percent competing with one other school.[187]

Competition in Education Trumps Centralization

Decreasing centralization and increasing competition have proven to be a winning strategy for top-performing countries across the globe. At a time when American political leaders insist we must prepare students for an increasingly competitive global economy, it makes little sense to preserve a status quo that shields schools from competition—and success. If the example of other countries teaches us anything, it is that so long as we maintain a US Department of Education, we are keeping the wrong people in charge of education. We are also perpetuating a structure that, as education scholar Matthew J. Brouillette puts it, "clashes with the political, economic, social, and cultural traditions of the United States to an extent unparalleled by any other institution in American society."[188] Even former American Federation of Teachers President Albert Shanker concluded:

> It's time to admit that public education operates like a planned economy, a bureaucratic system in which everybody's role is spelled out in advance and there are few incentives for innovation and productivity. It's no surprise that our school system doesn't improve: It more resembles the communist economy than our own market economy.[189]

The following chapter presents a blueprint for dismantling the US Department of Education, restoring program and operational funding to taxpayers in the states, and, most important, returning constitutional authority over education where it belongs—with parents.

PART III

Returning the Federal Government to Its Constitutional Role in Education

9

Ending, Not Mending,
Federal Involvement in Education

WHAT STEPS SHOULD we now take—and avoid—if equal and excellent educational opportunity for all American students is the goal? The first step is acknowledging that the educational performance of American students has not improved, in spite of massive spending increases. Second, we need to recognize that the US Department of Education has not achieved the promised administrative efficiencies, reduced paperwork, and better management of federal education programs. Third, we need to accept that the now commonplace notion that the federal government has some "traditional" or "historical" role in education has no constitutional basis. Likewise a stated purpose of the US Department of Education to "supplement and complement" states' educational efforts has no constitutional sanction.[1]

Failure to grasp these three realities results in proposed policy remedies that are doomed from the start. Chief among them is enhancing flexibility for states in setting education policy and attempting to promote excellence in education by having states compete for federal dollars based on performance promises. Other popular remedies are similarly flawed. States scrambling to make their accountability systems fit into a nationalized curriculum by adopting Common Core standards comes to mind immediately. National education tax credit or voucher programs crafted in Washington, DC, may also have tremendous superficial appeal, but like the nationalized Common Core curriculum, they too are misguided. The reason is that those and other policy remedies simply prolong a relationship between the states and federal government that has always been dysfunctional because they were never supposed to have an education relationship in the first place. As we have seen, there is no evidence for believing that officials in the federal government, including those in the US Department of Education, know best. Neither, for that matter, do state officials. The key difference is that state officials are closer to those who elect and hold them accountable. State citizens are best situated to keep state politicians away from interfering with the education decisions of parents.[2]

Efforts to fix the US Department of Education, to pass more effective federal legislation, to improve the targets for federal funds—none of these will provide an answer. To achieve the goal of improved student performance, only one remedy will work: an end to federal involvement in education.

In fact, efforts to abolish the US Department of Education began almost immediately after it was established—first in 1867 and again in 1979. Each time they failed because neither effort truly sought to abolish the department. Instead, beginning in 1868, it was downgraded, then shuffled around from one federal agency to the next, until it was restored to a full Cabinet-level federal department. The US Department of Education has not fulfilled any of the stated reasons for its existence—better, less expensive administration of federal education programs and the preservation of state and local control in education, much less improved student achievement. More than 140 years later, the US Department of Education has become the conduit for presidents to impose their education agendas on states, citizens, and students—with or without congressional authorization.

Restoring constitutional authority over education requires a genuine abolition plan. History has shown that half-measures such as departmental downgrades or block-grant schemes for redistributing taxpayer dollars will not prevent the US Department of Education from operating as a costly pass-through for the political agendas of Washington politicians and special interest groups—all at the expense of taxpayers and schoolchildren. That reality is the foundation of any blueprint to abolish the Department of Education.

A real opt-out plan eliminating the US Department of Education involves three basic steps. Step 1, eliminate all nineteen non-program offices and divisions. This step alone would save taxpayers more than $192 million in base salaries and awards associated with more than 1,800 department employees. On top of those savings would be another $13.9 billion in contractual services, supplies, and other overhead costs such as rent.[3] Step 2, return to taxpayers the funding currently diverted to Washington, DC, to maintain the Department of Education, its personnel, and programs. Conservative estimates suggest that Education Department programs and overhead represent close to 3 percent of the total federal budget.[4] That amount would correspond with a 3 percent across the board federal income tax reduction. Step 3, with their hard-earned money restored, taxpayers would decide which, if any, education programs to implement or expand in their own states.

This chapter provides an overview of a workable strategy, while the next chapter outlines how to do so office by office, program by program.

Strategic Dismantling of the US Department of Education

Under a functioning constitutional system, congressional failure to reauthorize the cornerstone $15 billion-a-year Elementary and Secondary Education Act (ESEA), dubbed No Child Left Behind when reauthorized in 2001, should have been a serious blow to the US Department of Education. Instead, Presidents George W. Bush and Barack Obama have used the Department of Education to set a preferred education agenda nationwide by attaching strings to federal funds. An opt-out plan begins by removing taxpayers' money from the control of the US Department of Education.

As summarized in Table 9.1, the US Department of Education oversees 125 programs that cost taxpayers nearly $216 billion combined in 2010. The department also employed nearly 4,600 people, who cost almost $468 million in total base salaries and awards.[5] Of the department's twenty-nine offices and divisions, ten oversee actual education programs. Granted that dismantling a bureaucracy of this size will not be easy or painless, there are some clear steps for moving forward, once the necessity of that action is recognized.

Step 1. Eliminate All Non-Program Offices and Divisions. Nineteen US Department of Education offices and divisions should be eliminated right away, including the immediate offices of the deputy and under secretaries. The four White House initiatives relating to targeted minority student populations should also be eliminated. If taxpayers want those programs restored, they can enact statewide programs through their respective legislatures. It has been suggested that the Office for Civil Rights be moved to the Department of Justice since it conducts constitutionally sanctioned work.[6] Yet its authority extends

Table 9.1. US Department of Education: Offices, Programs, and Costs

	Number of Employees	Base Salary and Awards	Number of Programs Adminis- tered	Annual Program Funding: 2010
Office of the Secretary				
Immediate Office of the Secretary	150	$11,185,521	5	$834,037,648
Office of Communications and Outreach	112	$12,299,933	0	$0
Office of the General Counsel	105	$13,820,321	0	$0
Office of Inspector General	328	$31,733,187	0	$0
Institute of Education Sciences	203	$23,091,865	4	$1,414,232,168
Office for Civil Rights	646	$62,737,900	0	$0
Office of Legislation and Congressional Affairs	20	$1,995,162	0	$0
Office of the Chief Financial Officer	197	$20,127,193	0	$0
Office of Management	194	$19,488,557	1	n/a
Office of the Chief Information Officer	134	$15,650,745	0	$0
Office of Planning, Evaluation and Policy Development	138	$14,920,926	0	$0
Budget Service	–	–	–	–
Office of Educational Technology	–	–	–	–
Faith Based and Neighborhood Partnerships	–	–	–	–
International Affairs Office	–	–	–	–
Sub-total	**2,227**	**$227,051,310**	**10**	**$2,248,269,816**
Office of the Deputy Secretary				
Immediate Office of the Deputy Secretary	17	$8,150,546	0	$0
Office of Innovation and Improvement	98	$9,080,261	12	$740,723,212

	Number of Employees	Base Salary and Awards	Number of Programs Adminis- tered	Annual Program Funding: 2010
Office of Special Education and Rehabilitative Services	284	$29,633,797	31	$16,030,177,646
Office of English Language Acquisition, Language Enhancement and Academic Achievement for Limited English Proficient Students	20	$2,186,358	1	$26,874,144
Office of Elementary and Secondary Education	266	$22,328,459	31	$22,163,839,280
Office of Elementary and Secondary Education—Office of Safe and Drug-Free Schools (Office of Safe and Healthy Schools)	48	$4,203,803	0	$0
Risk Management Service	–	–	–	–
Sub-total	**733**	**$75,583,224**	**75**	**$38,961,614,282**

Office of the Under Secretary

	Number of Employees	Base Salary and Awards	Number of Programs Adminis- tered	Annual Program Funding: 2010
Immediate Office of the Under Secretary	16	$3,887,063	0	$0
Federal Student Aid	1,224	$125,652,835	4	$170,517,470,000
Office of Vocational and Adult Education	90	$9,327,644	8	$1,734,399,747
Office of Vocational and Adult Education–National Institute for Literacy	2	$26,088	0	$0
Office of Postsecondary Education	247	$23,470,274	28	$2,230,999,207
White House Initiative on Asian Americans and Pacific Islanders	–	–	–	–
White House Initiative on Educational Excellence for Hispanic Americans	–	–	–	–
White House Initiative on Historically Black Colleges and Universities	–	–	–	–

Table 9.1. US Department of Education: Offices, Programs, and Costs, *continued*

	Number of Employees	Base Salary and Awards	Number of Programs Adminis- tered	Annual Program Funding: 2010
White House Initiative on American Indian and Alaskan Native Education	–	–	–	–
Sub-total	1,579	$162,363,904	40	$174,482,868,954
Advisory Councils and Committees	22	$567,713	0	$0
National Assessment Governing Board	33	$2,101,992	0	$0
Sub-total	55	$2,669,705	0	$0
Total	4,594	$467,668,143	125	$215,692,753,052

Sources: Author's table is based on data from the US Department of Education, the US Office of Personnel Management, and the *Catalog of Federal Domestic Assistance.*

Notes:

1. A "–" indicates data were not available.
2. The Office of Safe and Drug-Free Schools was moved to the Office of Safe and Healthy Schools within the Office of Elementary and Secondary Education effective September 26, 2011.

only to programs and activities that are federally funded, and under this plan US Department of Education programs will no longer receive such funding; the office would not have jurisdiction over education matters regardless of where it was relocated. In addition, seven Executive Branch agencies currently deal with the administration of justice.[7] A better approach would be for states to craft their own education-related antidiscrimination laws as needed and decide for themselves whether a distinct civil rights office is needed in their own justice departments.

Simply eliminating non-program offices and divisions within the US Education Department would save taxpayers more than $192 million in base

Table 9.2. US Department of Education Offices
and Divisions to Eliminate Immediately

	# Employees	Base Salary & Awards
Office of the Secretary		
Office of Communications and Outreach	112	$12,299,933
Office of the General Counsel	105	$13,820,321
Office of Inspector General	328	$31,733,187
Office for Civil Rights	646	$62,737,900
Office of Legislation and Congressional Affairs	20	$1,995,162
Office of the Chief Financial Officer	197	$20,127,193
Office of the Chief Information Officer	134	$15,650,745
Office of Planning, Evaluation and Policy Development	138	$14,920,926
Budget Service	–	–
Office of Educational Technology	–	–
Faith Based and Neighborhood Partnerships	–	–
International Affairs Office	–	–
Sub-total	**1,680**	**$173,285,367**
Office of the Deputy Secretary		
Immediate Office of the Deputy Secretary	17	$8,150,546
Office of Elementary and Secondary Education— Office of Safe and Drug-Free Schools (Office of Safe and Healthy Schools)	48	$4,203,803
Risk Management Service	–	–
Sub-total	**65**	**$12,354,349**
Office of the Under Secretary		
Immediate Office of the Under Secretary	16	$3,887,063
Office of Vocational and Adult Education— National Institute for Literacy	2	$26,088
White House Initiative on Asian Americans and Pacific Islanders	–	–

Table 9.2. US Department of Education Offices
and Divisions to Eliminate Immediately, *continued*

	# Employees	Base Salary & Awards
White House Initiative on Educational Excellence for Hispanic Americans	–	–
White House Initiative on Historically Black Colleges and Universities	–	–
White House Initiative on American Indian and Alaskan Native Education	–	–
Sub-total	18	$3,913,151
Advisory Councils and Committees	22	$567,713
National Assessment Governing Board	33	$2,101,992
Sub-total	55	$2,669,705
Total	1,818	$192,222,572

Sources: Author's table is based on data from the US Department of Education,
the US Office of Personnel Management, and the *Catalog of Federal Domestic Assistance.*

Notes:

1. A "–" indicates data were not available.
2. The Office of Safe and Drug-Free Schools was moved to the Office of Safe and Healthy
   Schools within the Office of Elementary and Secondary Education effective September
   26, 2011.

salaries and awards associated with more than 1,800 department employees.
Not shown in Table 9.2 are the additional benefits, contractual services, supplies, and other overhead costs contained in the US Department of Education's corresponding outlay reports, totaling some $13.9 billion in contractual
services, supplies, and other overhead costs such as rent. This elimination
could occur within a single fiscal year.

Step 2. Return Funding to Taxpayers. Rather than approve ongoing or
additional appropriations for the upcoming fiscal year, funding would instead
be returned to individual taxpayers as a federal income tax reduction. That tax
reduction should be expressly included as a line item in the corresponding fis-

cal year budget. With those funds in hand, it would be up to taxpayers in each state to decide whether they wanted to pay for education programs formerly under federal control and the related overhead. Funds formerly allocated to the US Department of Education's non-program offices and divisions should not be shifted to other federal programs and departments or used for deficit reduction or budget-balancing.

Along with funding formerly allocated to non-program offices and divisions of the US Department of Education, no more associated program funding would be appropriated in the forthcoming fiscal year federal budget. That funding would also be returned to federal taxpayers as an income tax reduction. Again, eliminating US Department of Education program and associated overhead funding to federal taxpayers could occur within a given fiscal year. Program funding allocated in previous fiscal years would be expended. Of course, the decision to end federal funding for the federal education programs currently administered by the US Department of Education does not necessarily mean those programs will not continue. The critical difference is that state citizens, not Washington politicians or special interest groups, will decide with their votes and their tax dollars.

Step 3. Taxpayers Determine Which, if Any, Programs to Preserve at the State Level. As US Department of Education program appropriations end, savings from the department's elimination would be returned to taxpayers, who in turn would determine whether they wish to preserve—and pay for—various programs in their states.

Following the Money

What happens to all the money that has been flowing through the US Department of Education on its way to states, school districts, and students? The details on this are available in the next chapter, but some general directions are clear.

Eliminate Duplicated Efforts. A primary benefit of the US Department of Education was supposed to be streamlining federal activity related to education, eliminating duplication and wasteful spending. This goal was never achieved, and doing so is an important part of the dismantling process. One example is US Department of Education spending on early childhood education, an area where the US Department of Health and Human Services has a long history of intervention via Head Start. In other cases, federal programs duplicate initiatives already under way in states and school districts, where they can be more carefully tailored to local needs.

Give the Reins to the States. Most federal grant programs are operated through designated officials in the states where grant recipients are located. These officials could take over the funding and oversight activities of existing grants for the rest of their term. Associated salary and administrative costs would be paid for out of funds previously paid to the respective Office of Innovation and Improvement grant officers, and their positions would expire with the grant. Through their state legislatures, state taxpayers would determine whether to initiate and support similar programs at the state level.

Privatize the Federal Role. Nongovernment agencies—private, philanthropic, nonprofit, and scholarly—are heavily invested in some areas where US Department of Education spending is high. A good example is the Institute of Educational Sciences, which has received uncommonly good marks from fiscal reviewers of the US Department of Education, like the Office of Management and Budget. Yet a plethora of scientific organizations, inside and outside universities, are conducting similar research and can move forward alone. Or look at teacher recruitment and training. The nonprofit Teach for America has been highly successful in recruiting high-quality students and placing them in the districts that most need bright, young teachers.

Return Money Directly to Taxpayers. As federal programs expire, state taxpayers should see a reduction in their federal taxes. They should be left to decide whether to reinvest these dollars in programs at the state level and to encourage their legislatures to pass the enabling laws.

It is worth considering that as things stand now under the prevailing relationship between the states and the federal government, roughly every decade or so as successive administrations assume office in Washington, DC, students, schools, teachers, and taxpayers are subjected to new nationwide education programs and mandates that require expensive replacement of the previous administration's programs with ones from the current administration.

Restoring authority and funding back to the states and the people would be far less disruptive and expensive than the status quo because as things stand now, federal funding is not guaranteed in perpetuity. On the contrary, most federal education funding has clear expiration or renewal dates. Thus state and school officials should already be anticipating the inevitable winding down of federal funding for various programs. What makes the strategic dismantling plan described in the following chapter different is that once control over education programs and funding is returned to the states, lawmakers, taxpayers, and educators can work more closely together at the local level to better ensure clear education policy priorities customized to meeting the specific needs of students in communities across the states—without all the chaos, cost, and upheaval of the previous several decades of federal leadership in education.

10

Dismantling the US Department of Education Brick by Brick

A LEADING ARGUMENT for creating the US Department of Education in the first place was that it would foster better management of federal education programs. Back in 1979 just months before its authorization, Rep. Lawrence Fountain (D-N.C.) proposed "another management option— namely, a critical review of . . . education programs to determine how many of them are really needed today." The critical program review that follows attempts to do just that. Absent any critical review, Fountain noted that "we have created a maze of programs. . . . It would be far more useful, in my judgment, to concentrate on weeding out programs that have outlived their usefulness, that duplicate one another, or that simply don't work, than to devote our energies to creating a new organizational structure which might well help to perpetuate many of these programs."[1]

More than thirty years of operations by the US Department of Education prove that Representative Fountain and his allies were right. According to the Office of Management and Budget (OMB), more than half of all Department of Education programs are not functioning (51 percent). Specifically, the OMB deems programs not performing if they earn a rating of "Results Not Demonstrated" (47 percent of programs), meaning "that a program has not been able to develop acceptable performance goals or collect data to determine whether it is performing." The OMB also rates programs "Ineffective" (4 percent of programs), meaning they "are not using your tax dollars effectively" and have not produced results "due to a lack of clarity regarding the program's purpose or goals, poor management, or some other significant weakness." About 33 percent of the Department of Education's programs are deemed "Adequate";

Table 10.1. US Department of Education Offices, Staff, and Programs Summary, 2010

Office Subdivisions	Number of Employees	Number of Programs Administered	Base Salary and Awards	Annual Program Funding: 2010	Total Salary, Awards, and Program Funding
1. Office of the Secretary					
1.1. Immediate Office of the Secretary	150	5	$11,185,521	$834,037,648	$845,223,169
1.2. Institute of Education Sciences	203	4	$23,091,865	$1,414,232,168	$1,437,324,033
1.3. Office of Management	194	1	$19,488,557	n/a	$19,488,557
Subtotal	**547**	**10**	**$53,765,943**	**$2,248,269,816**	**$2,302,035,759**
2. Office of the Deputy Secretary					
2.1. Office of Innovation and Improvement	98	12	$9,080,261	$740,723,212	$749,803,473
2.2. Office of Special Education and Rehabilitative Services	284	31	$29,633,797	$16,030,177,646	$16,059,811,443
2.3. Office of English Language Acquisition, Language Enhancement and Academic Achievement for Limited English Proficient Students	20	1	$2,186,358	$26,874,144	$29,060,502
2.4. Office of Elementary and Secondary Education	266	31	$22,328,459	$22,163,839,280	$22,186,167,739
Subtotal	**668**	**75**	**$63,228,875**	**$38,961,614,282**	**$39,024,843,157**
3. Office of the Under Secretary					
3.1. Federal Student Aid	1,224	4	$125,652,835	$170,517,470,000	$170,643,122,835
3.2. Office of Vocational and Adult Education	90	8	$9,327,644	$1,734,399,747	$1,743,727,391
3.3. Office of Postsecondary Education	247	28	$23,470,274	$2,230,999,207	$2,254,469,481
Subtotal	**1,561**	**40**	**$158,450,753**	**$174,482,868,954**	**$174,641,319,707**
Total	**2,776**	**125**	**$275,445,571**	**$215,692,753,052**	**$215,968,198,623**

Sources: Author's table is based on data from the US Department of Education, the US Office of Personnel Management, and the *Catalog of Federal Domestic Assistance.*

Note: Funding for the lone program administered by the Office of English Language Acquisition was eliminated in 2012 yet the office itself was still open as of April 2013.

9 percent are "Moderately Effective"; and just 6 percent receive the OMB's highest rating of "Effective."[2]

As the following program review reveals program duplication and ineffectiveness are rampant. In virtually all cases, US Department of Education programs can and should be eliminated, and funding should be returned to state taxpayers. This broad recommendation is in keeping with the conclusion of the Advisory Commission on Intergovernmental Relations more than thirty years ago, which, in the words of Rep. Fountain, is that "State governments assume 'substantially all' fiscal responsibility for supporting the public schools."[3]

This chapter details each program administered by the US Department of Education's Office of the Secretary, Office of the Deputy Secretary, and Office of the Under Secretary, with their corresponding subdivisions. As shown in Table 10.1, program and staff compensation funding amounted to nearly $216 billion annually as of 2010.

This section reviews the 125 programs administered by each US Department of Education subdivision within the Offices of the Secretary, Deputy Secretary, and Under Secretary.

1. The Office of the Secretary Programs

The Secretary of Education oversees the direction, supervision, and coordination of all department activities and is the principal adviser to the president on federal education policies, programs, and activities.[4] Through this office, ten programs are administered through three suboffices with 547 combined personnel. Altogether, associated program and staff funding amount to more than $2.3 billion annually.

1.1 The Immediate Office of the Secretary

1. Office of the Secretary				
1.1 Immediate Office of the Secretary	# Employees	Combined base salary & awards	Total # Programs administered	Combined annual program funding: 2010
	150	$11,185,521	5	$834,037,648

This subdivision provides advisory and logistical support to the secretary of education, including assuring his or her "specific interests, viewpoints, and policy are properly reflected" in all communications. This office within the overarching Office of the Secretary has 150 employees, whose combined base salaries and awards were nearly $11.2 million, including the US Secretary of Education Arne Duncan, whose base salary is $199,700. This office currently oversees five programs, four of which cost a combined $834 million annually. The Immediate Office of the Secretary also oversees a directed grants and awards program with an unspecified additional amount of funding. Three programs award one-year project grants or direct payments for specified purposes. Associated program funding and personnel spending with those programs should be eliminated altogether in one year. Associated program funding and personnel spending with an additional one-year grant program for veterans' dependents should be transferred to Veterans Affairs. The remaining Immediate Office of the Secretary program is the four-year, Race to the Top state project grants program.

Program title	**Race to the Top Early Learning Challenge**
Type of assistance	Project grants
Recipients	States
Length of assistance	Four years
Annual funding	$497,293,648
Authorization	American Recovery and Reinvestment Act of 2009, Executive Order Division A, Title XIV, Sections 14005, 14006 and 14013, Public Law 111-5, as amended, Department of Defense and Full-Year Continuing Appropriations Act, 2011, Consolidated Appropriations Act of 2012.
Description	To improve the quality of early childhood programs and to close the achievement gap for high-need children. The grant competition focuses on improving early learning and development programs for young children by supporting states' efforts to: (1) increase the number and percentage of low-income and disadvantaged children in each age group of infants, toddlers, and preschoolers who are enrolled in high-quality early learning programs; (2) design and implement an integrated system of high-quality early learning programs and services; and (3) ensure that any use of assessments conforms with the recommendations of the National Research Council's reports on early childhood.

Recommendation: The Race to the Top Early Learning Challenge should be suspended within one year. This program duplicates the Head Start program, enacted in 1965 and administered by the US Department of Health and Human Services, which also helps oversee the Race to the Top program.[5] Once a $96.4 million targeted government program for about a half million students, Head Start is now a nearly $8 billion program with 964,000 enrollees. The program originally cost around $172 per recipient, but today it costs about $7,839.[6] Departmental evaluations in 2010 and 2012 found that program impacts fade by the end of first grade; by the end of third grade there was virtually no distinction between participants and nonparticipants.[7] Instead, states should enact tax-free Early Education Savings Accounts so parents can set aside funds for early education options they think are best for their children. Allowing individual and corporate taxpayers to make tax-deductible contributions to nonprofit scholarship-granting organizations would help low- and moderate-income parents afford the early education options of their choice. States would realize savings from not having the additional administrative burden of federal grant applications and reporting. Encouraging the private sector to pay for schooling reduces reliance on states' general fund budgets and clears the way for innovative, effective early learning providers.[8]

• • •

Program title	Race to the Top
Type of assistance	Project grants
Recipients	States
Length of assistance	One year
Annual funding	$199,500,000
Authorization	American Recovery and Reinvestment Act of 2009, Division A, Title XIV, Sections 14005, 14006 and 14013, Public Law 111-5, as amended; Department of Defense and Full-Year Continuing Appropriations Act, 2011, Division B, Title VIII, Section 1832(b)(1), Public Law 112-10.
Description	To reward states that have made significant progress in achieving equity in teacher distribution; establishing a longitudinal data system; enhancing assessment for English language learners and students with disabilities; improving academic content and achievement standards; and providing effective support to schools identified for corrective action and restructuring.

Recommendation: After one year, the US Department of Education reported that states were behind in implementing promised reforms, and tracking how states actually spent grant money was a time-consuming, complex endeavor.[9] Dozens of school districts dropped out because the administrative costs exceeded the federal funding they would receive. No state had to return funding for failure to fulfill their grants. Rather than states competing to get back a share of their own taxpayers' funding (with federal strings attached), program funding should not be renewed after one year. Instead, states should encourage competition among all schools for students. Dozens of parental choice programs across the country assist parents in choosing the schools parents think are best for their children. Those programs have expanded options, increased school productivity, and kept administrative and operating costs to a minimum. Most important, such programs encourage innovation to an extent that no top-down government approach can.

• • •

Program title	**Directed Grants and Awards**
Type of assistance	Direct payments for a specified use
Recipients	Varies
Length of assistance	One year
Annual funding	Not separately identifiable.
Authorization	Act to Promote the Education of the Blind, 20 USC 101; Education for the Deaf Act; Higher Education Act.
Description	Objectives of the programs vary based on the directed grant award. Awards are made to specified institutions for purposes specified in the appropriations or authorization bills.

Recommendation: With the elimination of the Department of Education, no more funding will be authorized for various favored federal projects. Instead, funding is restored to taxpayers as part of an overall federal income tax reduction. Then they are free to fund any specified education programs they deem important.

• • •

Program title	**Teacher Education Assistance for College and Higher Education Grants (TEACH Grants)**
Type of assistance	Direct payments for a specified use
Recipients	Undergraduate and graduate students
Length of assistance	One year
Annual funding	$136,951,000
Authorization	Higher Education Act of 1965, as amended, Subpart 9, Title VI, Part A
Description	To provide annual grants of up to $4,000 to eligible undergraduate and graduate students who agree to teach specified high-need subjects at schools serving primarily disadvantaged populations for four years within eight years of graduation. For students who do not fulfill their service requirements, grants convert to Direct Unsubsidized Stafford Loans with interest accrued from the date of award.

Recommendation: Governments should not be in the businesses of manipulating market demand, and TEACH grants duplicate other efforts already under way.[10] Since 1990, for example, the nonprofit organization Teach for America has actively recruited high-quality teaching candidates and placed them in high-need schools nationwide. Currently, there are roughly ten applicants for every eligible place.[11] In addition, every state except Minnesota and New Jersey already has at least one program to encourage and assist students to complete teaching degrees, including scholarships, loan forgiveness programs, housing allowances, and tuition assistance.[12]

• • •

Program title	**Postsecondary Education Scholarships for Veteran's Dependents**
Type of assistance	Direct payments for specified use
Recipients	The student must be an eligible veteran's dependent whose parent or guardian was a member of the Armed Forces of the United States and died as a result of performing military service in Iraq or Afghanistan after September 11, 2001.
Length of assistance	One year
Annual funding	$293,000

Authorization	Higher Education Act of 1965, Executive Order Subpart 10, Title IV, Part A, Subpart 10, Section 420R
Description	To provide eligible veterans' dependent undergraduate postsecondary students with non-need based grant assistance to help meet educational expenses.

Recommendation: The US Department of Veterans Affairs is already set up to administer a variety of benefits and services, including financial and other assistance to dependents of service members and veterans.[13] This program is an earned benefit that properly belongs under the oversight of Veterans Affairs. All funding and necessary staff should be transferred.

• • •

Summary. Eliminating four programs and their associated staff would result in a savings of nearly $845 million, including $11.2 million in combined salaries and awards, as well as $834 million in program funding.

1. Office of the Secretary: Elimination Savings				
1.1. Immediate Office of the Secretary	# Employees	Combined base salary & awards	Combined annual program funding: 2010	Savings from Elimination
Race to the Top-Early Learning Challenge	89	$6,636,742	$497,293,648	$503,930,390
Race to the Top	36	$2,684,525	$199,500,000	$202,184,525
Teacher Education Assistance for College and Higher Education Grants (TEACH Grants)	25	$1,864,254	$136,951,000	$138,815,254
Directed Grants and Awards	–	–	–	–
Totals	150	$11,185,521	$833,744,648	$844,930,169

Notes:
1. The numbers of employees by program are estimates, assuming program staff size is relative to the total program funding.
2. Total average annual base salaries and awards by program are estimates derived by dividing the total annual base salary and awards amount by the number of employees.
3. No annual funding information was available for directed grants and awards. This

means the numbers of employees for other programs are likely overstated, while the total annual program savings are likely understated.

4. Program and staff costs for scholarships for veterans' dependents are excluded since that program should be transferred to Veterans Affairs. The program funding is less than 1 percent of the Immediate Office of the Secretary's total program funding, so an estimated one staff member earning an average annual salary of $75,000 would be moved.

1.2. The Institute of Education Sciences

1. Office of the Secretary				
1.2. Institute of Education Sciences	# Employees	Combined base salary & awards	Total # Programs administered	Combined annual program funding: 2010
	203	$23,091,865	4	$1,414,232,168

Also within the Immediate Office of the Secretary, the Institute of Education Sciences (formerly known as the Office of Educational Research and Improvement) was established within the US Department of Education by the Education Sciences Reform Act of 2002. Its mission is "to provide rigorous evidence on which to ground education practice and policy" through its four centers: Evaluation, Research, Statistics, and Special Education Research. This office within the overarching Office of the Secretary has more than 200 employees, whose combined base salaries and awards exceed $23 million. This office currently oversees four programs that altogether cost $1.4 billion annually.

Program title	Education Research, Development and Dissemination
Type of assistance	Project grants
Recipients	Colleges and universities
Length of assistance	Typically from one to five years
Annual funding	$165,000,000
Authorization	Education Sciences Reform Act of 2002, Title I, Parts A, B and D, Sections 133 and 172.
Description	To support the development and distribution of scientifically valid research, evaluation, and data collection that support learning and improve academic achievement.

Recommendation. This program is one of only a handful of Department of Education programs the OMB rates effective, its highest rating. Nevertheless, just because this government entity can do a job effectively does not mean it *should* do it. There is no shortage of scientific organizations outside of the federal government dedicated to conducting and disseminating education research to improve student learning and achievement. In terms of science grants, numerous other organizations within the federal government already disperse funding to postsecondary institutions as well. Postsecondary project grants currently overseen by the institute amount to less than 12 percent of its total program funding. These grants would not be renewed after existing grants expired, and no new grants would be issued. Project grants would be funded by state taxpayers if they opt to do so. States have long collected their own education statistics and could easily form voluntary consortia to perform the tasks currently performed by the institute.

• • •

Program title	**Research in Special Education**
Type of assistance	Project grants
Recipients	Colleges and universities
Length of assistance	Typically from one to five years
Annual funding	$53,213,000
Authorization	Education Sciences Reform Act of 2002, Part E
Description	To support scientifically rigorous research contributing to the solution of specific early intervention and education problems associated with children with disabilities.

Recommendation. The institute's special education research funding to colleges and universities for special education grants amounts to less than 4 percent of its total program funding. The OMB rated this program as "not performing" since it could not demonstrate results. Specifically, this program "does not have specific long-term outcome goals against which the impact of federal investments in special education and early intervention research can be measured." It also lacks "a comprehensive strategic plan" to guide research priorities and investments. Finally, the OMB noted, "No independent evaluation of the program has been conducted since the partial evaluation of program activities in 1991." Special education research funding should also be eliminated, leaving it to state taxpayers to decide what, if any, research they fund.

• • •

Program title	**Statewide Data Systems**
Type of assistance	Project grants
Recipients	State educational agencies
Length of assistance	Typically from one to three years
Annual funding	$42,165,500
Authorization	Educational Technical Assistance Act of 2002, Title II, Section 208, Public Law 107-79
Description	These grants are intended to enable state educational agencies to design, develop, and implement statewide longitudinal data systems to efficiently and accurately manage, analyze, disaggregate, and use individual student data, consistent with the Elementary and Secondary Education Act of 1965, and to facilitate analyses and research to improve student academic achievement and close achievement gaps.

Recommendation. Data system funding represents 3 percent of the institute's overall funding. Moreover, this program is largely an artifact of federal intervention in education. Freed from federal control, and with money restored to taxpayers, states could design data systems that better meet the needs of the parents, students, and taxpayers they represent—rather than inflexible mandates.

• • •

Program title	**Twenty-First Century Community Learning Centers**
Type of assistance	Formula grants
Recipients	State educational agencies
Length of assistance	One year
Annual funding	$1,153,853,668
Authorization	Elementary and Secondary Education Act of 1965 (ESEA), as amended, Title IV, Part B

Description	To create community learning centers that provide academic enrichment opportunities for children, particularly students who attend high-poverty and low-performing schools. The program is intended to help students meet state and local student standards in core academic subjects, such as reading and math; to offer students a broad array of enrichment activities that complement their regular academic programs; and to offer literacy and other educational services to the families of participating children.

Recommendation. Several other programs, including Head Start administered by Health and Human Services, already fund similar activities. According to its most recent review in 2003, the OMB gave this program its lowest "performing" rating of adequate for not collecting sufficient performance data. There is at best no difference between participants and nonparticipants and in some cases negative effects on participants.[14] No shortage of private and philanthropic organizations fund such community centers nationwide. State taxpayers would do better to fund the programs they believe work best for their communities without the interference and expense of the federal government. Current grants should expire and no new grants be issued.

• • •

Summary. A better approach to meeting local and community needs is returning more than $1.4 billion in annual institute program and staff funding to state taxpayers. They, in turn, would support the college and university research, data systems development, and community education efforts they prefer. More than 80 percent of institute funding would expire in one year with the elimination of the community learning center program. The remaining 20 percent of funding would be incrementally returned to taxpayers over the next four years as research and data systems grants expire.

1.2. Institute of Education Sciences: Elimination Savings				
1.2. Institute of Education Sciences	# Employees	Combined base salary & awards	Combined annual program funding: 2010	Savings from Elimination
Education Research, Development and Dissemination	24	$2,694,153	$165,000,000	$167,694,153

1.2. Institute of Education Sciences	# Employees	Combined base salary & awards	Combined annual program funding: 2010	Savings from Elimination
Research in Special Education	8	$868,872	$53,213,000	$54,081,872
Statewide Data Systems	6	$688,487	$42,165,500	$42,853,987
Twenty-First Century Community Learning Centers	166	$18,840,353	$1,153,853,668	$1,172,694,021
Totals	203	$23,091,865	$1,414,232,168	$1,437,324,033

Notes:

1. The numbers of employees by program are estimates, assuming program staff size is relative to the total program funding.
2. Total average annual base salaries and awards by program are estimates derived by dividing the total annual base salary and awards amount by the number of employees.

1.3. Office of Management

1. Office of the Secretary				
1.3. Office of Management	# Employees	Combined base salary & awards	Total # Programs administered	Combined annual program funding: 2010
	194	$19,488,557	1	—

"The mission of the Office of Management is to transform the Department of Education into a high-performance, customer-focused organization by providing services to our customers that help them do a better job of managing their people, processes, and overall strategy." The office has responsibility for the following program. The US Department of Education defines educational purpose broadly, including higher education, elementary and secondary education, libraries, administrative facilities, educational television and radio, rehabilitation and training, vocational education and research, and correctional education centers.

Program title	**Federal Real Property Assistance Program**
Type of assistance	Sale, exchange, or donation of property or goods

Recipients	Those groups, organizations, entities, or institutions providing educational programs including: states; their political subdivisions and instrumentalities; and tax-supported organizations or private nonprofit institutions held exempt from taxation under Section 501(C)(3) of the Internal Revenue Code of 1954 may apply.
Length of assistance	One to thirty years
Annual funding	Not separately identifiable.
Authorization	Department of Education Organization Act of 1979; Federal Property and Administrative Services Act of 1949, Section 203(k), as amended.
Description	Conveys surplus federal real property for broadly defined educational purposes at fair market value. The department notifies eligible institutions about available surplus federal real property, and interested institutions submit an application.

Recommendation. A recent Office of Inspector General audit determined that the US Department of Education's federal real property inventory consists of 261 properties valued at $86 million. That audit also revealed the department was not following its own procedures, compromising the effective disposal of its holdings.[15] Existing real property agreements pose no barrier to the department's elimination, however, since any pending agreements could be overseen by the US General Services Administration's Federal Real Property Council. Taxpayers would realize some $19.5 million in savings through the elimination of more than 190 positions.

2. Office of the Deputy Secretary Programs

The deputy secretary focuses on the development and implementation of policies, programs, and activities relating to elementary and secondary education matters. This mission addresses a wide spectrum of interests including safe and drug-free schools, special education and rehabilitative services to education of linguistically and culturally diverse students, and promotion of educational interventions and reforms. Three suboffices within the deputy secretary's office oversee seventy-five programs and employ 668 staff members. Together, annual program and compensation funding amount to more than $39 billion.

2. Office of the Deputy Secretary					
Office Subdivisions	# Employees	# Programs administered	Base Salary & Awards	Annual program funding: 2010	Total salary, awards, and program funding
2.1. Office of Innovation and Improvement	98	12	$9,080,261	$740,723,212	$749,803,473
2.2. Office of Special Education and Rehabilitative Services	284	31	$29,633,797	$16,010,417,869	$16,040,051,666
2.3. Office of English Language Acquisition, Language Enhancement and Academic Achievement for Limited English Proficient Students	20	1	$2,186,358	$26,874,144	$29,060,502
2.4. Office of Elementary and Secondary Education	266	31	$22,328,459	$22,163,839,280	$22,186,167,739
Subtotal	668	75	$63,228,875	$38,941,854,505	$39,005,083,380

2.1. *Office of Innovation and Improvement*

2. Office of the Deputy Secretary				
2.1. Office of Innovation and Improvement	# Employees	Combined base salary & awards	Total # Programs administered	Combined annual program funding: 2010
	98	$9,080,261	12	$740,723,212

Recommendation. The Office of Innovation and Improvement (OII) is the main adviser to the secretary and oversees competitive grant programs that support innovations in the education. In most cases, such grants may last up to five years. Funding and oversight of those multiyear grants should be transferred to designated officials in the states where grant recipients are located. The state-level positions responsible for overseeing active grants would be term-limited relative to the time period specified in the outstanding grants. Associated salary and administrative costs would be paid for out of funds previously paid to the respective federal grant officers. Through their state legislatures, state taxpayers would determine whether to continue supporting various programs.

The one exceptional program is the D.C. Opportunity Scholarship Program. Because of the constitutional relationship between Congress and the District of Columbia, funding for this program should be preserved; however, oversight of this program could be better handled as a direct appropriation to a private-sector philanthropic entity rather than through an entire Cabinet-level departmental office.

• • •

Program title	**Charter Schools**
Type of assistance	Project grants
Recipients	SEAs in States in which State law authorizes charter schools are eligible.
Length of assistance	One to three years
Annual funding	$255,518,938
Authorization	Elementary and Secondary Education Act of 1965, as amended, Title V Part B, Subpart 1.
Description	Supports the planning, development, and initial implementation of charter schools, as well as their replication and the dissemination of information about them. Charter schools increase educational options for parents and students and, in exchange for stricter academic accountability, are exempt from many statutory and regulatory requirements.

Program title	**Credit Enhancement for Charter School Facilities**
Type of assistance	Project grants
Recipients	A public entity, such as a state or local government entity, a private nonprofit entity, or a consortium of such entities may apply.

Length of assistance	One to five years
Annual funding	$10,035,836
Authorization	Elementary and Secondary Education Act of 1965 (ESEA), as amended, Title V, Part B, Subpart 2.
Description	Provides grants to eligible entities to leverage funds through credit enhancement initiatives in order to assist charter schools in using private-sector capital to acquire, construct, renovate, or lease academic facilities.

Recommendation: In its review of the charter schools grant program, the OMB assigned its lowest "performing" rating of adequate, in part because data collection and dissemination efforts needed improvement. Charter schools are highly localized by their very nature, since they are founded by parents, teachers, and other educators and managed on-site. Any replication, development, or planning is best handled at the local level, as are facilities-related activities. Numerous nongovernment public charter school organizations serve as clearinghouses for disseminating and conducting research and best practices. As of 2010, there were twenty charter school grants ranging from one to three years. There was one charter school facilities grant to provide enough credit to finance necessary construction. No new project grants should be channeled to charter schools. Facilities grants last up to five years, while charter school development and replication grants last up to three years. Details about the number and terms of such grants are not publicly available, so there is no way to know how many grants would be ongoing after the US Department of Education was eliminated. Based on the fiscal year 2011 annual funding amounts and average awards, there are an estimated twenty-one charter school grants, one of which is a facilities grant. No new charter school grants should be approved. Funding and oversight of active grants should be transferred to designated officials in the states where grant recipients are located. The state-level positions responsible for overseeing active grants would be term-limited relative to the time period specified in the outstanding grants. Associated salary and administrative costs would be paid for out of funds previously paid to the respective OII grant officers. Through their state legislatures, taxpayers would determine whether to continue supporting such programs after they expire.

• • •

Program title	**Investing in Innovation (i3) Fund**
Type of assistance	Project grants
Recipients	Local educational agencies
Length of assistance	Three to five years
Annual funding	$149,700,000
Authorization	American Recovery and Reinvestment Act of 2009 (ARRA), Title XIV, Public Law 111-5.
Description	Provides competitive grants to (a) local educational agencies or (b) partnerships between a nonprofit organization and one or more local agencies or a consortium of schools with a record of improving student achievement and attainment in order to expand the implementation of, and investment in, innovative practices that are demonstrated to have an impact on improving student achievement or student growth, closing achievement gaps, decreasing dropout rates, increasing high school graduation rates, or increasing college enrollment and completion rates.

Recommendation. The Investing in Innovation (i3) Fund was passed as part of the American Recovery and Reinvestment Act of 2009. Twenty percent of OII program funding is directed toward this program. Given stagnant student performance over the past several decades, there is no evidence for this program's effectiveness. As with OII charter school grants, i3 project grants can last up to five years. Based on the fiscal year 2011 annual funding amounts and average awards, there are an estimated nineteen i3 grants. Funding and oversight of active grants would be transferred to designated officials in the states where grant recipients are located. The state-level positions responsible for overseeing active grants would be term-limited relative to the time period specified in the outstanding grants. Associated salary and administrative costs would be paid for out of funds previously paid to the respective OII grant officers. Through their state legislatures, state taxpayers would determine whether to continue supporting such initiatives.

• • •

Program title	**Magnet Schools Assistance**
Type of assistance	Project grants
Recipients	Local education agencies that are implementing court-ordered, agency-ordered, or federally approved voluntary desegregation plans that include magnet schools are eligible to apply.
Length of assistance	One to three years
Annual funding	$99,800,000
Authorization	Elementary and Secondary Education Act of 1965, as amended, Title V, Part C
Description	Provides grants to eligible local educational agencies to establish and operate magnet schools that aim to eliminate, reduce, or prevent minority-group isolation in elementary and secondary schools while strengthening students' academic achievement.

Recommendation. At nearly $100 million annually, magnet schools assistance represents nearly 14 percent of all OII program funding. It received the OMB's lowest "performing" rating of adequate because it "needs to set more ambitious goals, achieve better results, improve accountability or strengthen its management practices." Funding and oversight of outstanding grants should be transferred to designated officials in the states where grant recipients are located. As with the previous OII grants, the state-level positions responsible for overseeing active grants would be term-limited relative to the time period specified in the outstanding grants. Associated salary and administrative costs would be paid for out of funds previously paid to the respective OII grant officers. Through their state legislatures, state taxpayers would determine whether to continue supporting such efforts.

• • •

Program title	**Teacher Quality Partnership Grants**
Type of assistance	Project grants
Recipients	States and partnerships that consist of at least one institution of higher education; a school, department, or program of education within the partner institution one school of arts and sciences within the partner institution; one high-need local educational agency and a high-need school or a consortium of high-need schools served by the high-need local educational agency.

Length of assistance	One to five years
Annual funding	$42,914,000
Authorization	Higher Education Act of 1965, as amended, Title II, Part A
Description	Improves student achievement; improves the quality of new and prospective teachers by improving the preparation of prospective teachers and enhancing professional development activities for new teachers; holds teacher preparation programs at institutions of higher education accountable for preparing highly qualified teachers; and recruits highly qualified individuals, including minorities and individuals from other occupations, into the teaching force.

Program title	**Transition to Teaching**
Type of assistance	Project grants
Recipients	State educational agencies; high-need local educational agencies; for-profit and nonprofit organizations with proven records
Length of assistance	Three years
Annual funding	$41,124,586
Authorization	Elementary and Secondary Education Act, as amended, Title II, Part C, Subpart 1, Chapter B.
Description	Recruits and retains highly qualified mid-career professionals (including highly qualified paraprofessionals) and recent graduates of institutions of higher education, as teachers in high-need schools, including by recruiting teachers through alternative routes to teacher certification and licensure; encourages the development and expansion of alternative routes to certification and licensure under state-approved programs that enable individuals to be eligible for teacher certification and licensure within a reduced period of time, relying on the experience, expertise, and academic qualifications of an individual or other factors in lieu of traditional course work in the field of education.

Recommendation. While the US Department of Education was intended to minimize program duplication, these two teaching-related project grants duplicate other programs within the department itself, including the Teacher Education Assistance for College and Higher Education Grants (TEACH grants) administered by the Immediate Office of the Secretary of Education. Combined, funding for Teacher Quality Partnership and Transition to Teaching project grants represents around 12 percent of the OII's total program funding. As with the TEACH program, these programs duplicate efforts already under way in the states. These project grants can last up to five years. Based on the fiscal year 2011 annual funding amounts and average awards, there are an estimated twenty-nine Teacher Quality Partnership grants and ninety-one Transition to Teaching project grants. Funding and oversight of active grants would be transferred to designated officials in the states where grant recipients are located. The state-level positions responsible for overseeing active grants would be term-limited relative to the time period specified in the outstanding grants. Associated salary and administrative costs would be paid for out of funds previously paid to the respective OII grant officers. Through their state legislatures, taxpayers would determine whether to continue supporting such initiatives after they expire.

• • •

Program title	**School Leadership**
Type of assistance	Project grants
Recipients	High-need local educational agencies and institutions of higher education.
Length of assistance	1 to 5 years
Annual funding	$29,161,560
Authorization	Elementary and Secondary Education Act, as amended, Title II, Part B, Subpart 5, Section 2151(b).
Description	Provides support to eligible entities in the development of innovative programs that recruit, develop, prepare, and mentor principals and assistant principals.

Recommendation. School leadership project grants represent about 4 percent of total OII program funding. As with efforts to recruit teachers, this program duplicates efforts already under way in the states. State and local initiatives are more likely to meet the specific needs of their schools and communities. Based on the fiscal year 2011 annual funding amounts and average awards, there are an estimated forty-three school leadership project grants, which can last up to five years. Funding and oversight of these grants should be transferred to designated state officials in the states where grant recipients are located. The state-level positions responsible for overseeing active grants would be term-limited relative to the time period specified in the outstanding grants. Associated salary and administrative costs would be paid for out of funds previously paid to the respective OII grant officers. Through their state legislatures, state taxpayers would determine whether to continue supporting such initiatives after they expire.

• • •

Program title	**Arts in Education**
Type of assistance	Project grants
Recipients	State educational agencies, local educational agencies, institutions of higher education
Length of assistance	One to four years
Annual funding	$27,446,996
Authorization	Elementary and Secondary Education Act (ESEA), as amended, Title V, Part D, Subpart 15
Description	Provides competitive grants that support the integration of the arts into the elementary and secondary school curriculum, with particular focus on improving the academic achievement of low-income students.

Program title	**Ready-To-Learn Television**
Type of assistance	Project grants
Recipients	Public telecommunications entity
Length of assistance	One to five years
Annual funding	$27,245,000
Authorization	Elementary and Secondary Education Act of 1965, as amended, Title II, Part D, Subpart 3
Description	Facilitates student academic achievement by developing educational programming and digital content, with accompanying educational support materials, for preschool and early elementary school children and their families.

Recommendation. Combined, Arts in Education and Ready-to-Learn Television project grants amount to nearly 8 percent of total OII funding. The Ready-to-Learn Television program was deemed as not performing by the OMB because it failed to measure results; evaluations did not address achievement or literacy outcomes, which are the focus of this program; and program outreach efforts did not have significant effects. With the technological advances of the past several decades, there is no shortage of high-quality, low-to-no-cost television or Internet arts and academic content available to children starting school. There is no compelling evidence that these enrichment programs have in fact raised student achievement. Based on the fiscal year 2011 annual funding amounts and average awards, there are an estimated eight Arts in Education grants, which can last up to four years. The estimated number of Ready-to-Learn Television grants cannot be determined, but they can last up to five years. Funding and oversight of active grants under both programs would be transferred to designated officials in the states where grant recipients are located. The state-level positions responsible for overseeing active grants would be term-limited relative to the time period specified in the outstanding grants. Associated salary and administrative costs would be paid for out of funds previously paid to the respective OII grant officers. Through their state legislatures, taxpayers would determine whether to continue supporting such initiatives.

· · ·

Program title	**Voluntary Public School Choice**
Type of assistance	Project grants
Recipients	State educational agencies; local educational agencies
Length of assistance	One to five years
Annual funding	$25,767,362
Authorization	Elementary and Secondary Education Act, as amended, Title V, Part B, Subpart 3
Description	Supports efforts to establish or expand public school choice programs to provide parents, particularly parents whose children attend low-performing public schools, with expanded education options for their children's education.

Recommendation. Funding for these grants amounts to nearly 4 percent of all OII program funding. The most expansive parental choice programs have been state-led initiatives that began without (in some cases, in spite of) federal involvement. All but three states, Alabama, Maryland, and North Carolina, along with the District of Columbia already have public school open enrollment policies. Three states require it only for low-performing students, while seventeen states require districts to accept out-of-district students regardless of performance.[16] Based on the fiscal year 2011 annual funding amounts and average awards, there are an estimated fifteen Voluntary Public School Choice grants. Funding and oversight of active grants, which can last up to five years, would be transferred to designated state officials in the states where grant recipients are located. The state-level positions responsible for overseeing active grants would be term-limited relative to the time period specified in the outstanding grants. Associated salary and administrative costs would be paid for out of funds previously paid to the respective OII grant officers. Through their state legislatures, state taxpayers would determine whether to continue supporting such initiatives.

• • •

Program title	**Fund for the Improvement of Education**
Type of assistance	Project grants
Recipients	State educational agencies, local educational agencies, institutions of higher education
Length of assistance	One year
Annual funding	$12,008,934
Authorization	Elementary and Secondary Education Act of 1965 (ESEA), as amended, Title V, Part D, Subpart 1
Description	Conducts nationally significant programs to improve the quality of education, assist all students to meet challenging state content standards, and contribute to the achievement of elementary and secondary students.

Recommendation. Funding for the Improvement of Education grants amounts to less than 2 percent of all OII program funding. Nationwide organizations and networks already exist that disseminate research and results of various state efforts to improve education. Program and associated salary funding should be returned to state taxpayers who would be free to support the programs they believe are the most effective at improving student performance.

• • •

Program title	**D.C. School Choice Incentive Program**
Type of assistance	Project grants
Recipients	An educational entity of the District of Columbia Government, a nonprofit organization
Length of assistance	One year
Annual funding	$20,000,000
Authorization	Scholarships for Opportunity and Results (SOAR) Act, (Division C of Public Law 112-10, the Department of Defense and Full-Year Continuing Appropriations Act, 2011).
Description	Provides low-income parents residing in the District of Columbia (District) with expanded options for the education of their children. This program is part of a broader school improvement effort in the District.

Recommendation. Because of the unique funding relationship between Congress and the District of Columbia, funding for this program does not violate the Constitution. From 2004 through 2010 the Opportunity Scholarship Program was administered by the nonprofit Washington Scholarship Fund.[17] In 2011 the D.C. Children and Youth Investment Trust Corporation took over administration. Involvement in this program by the Department of Education is at best unnecessary.

• • •

Office of Innovation and Improvement: Elimination Savings				
2. Office of the Deputy Secretary	# Employees	Combined base salary & awards	Combined annual program funding: 2010	Savings from Elimination
Charter Schools	34	$3,132,315	$255,518,938	$258,651,253
Investing in Innovation (i3) Fund	20	$1,835,119	$149,700,000	$151,535,119
Magnet Schools Assistance	13	$1,223,413	$99,800,000	$101,023,413
Teacher Quality Partnership Grants	6	$526,067	$42,914,000	$43,440,067
Transition to Teaching	5	$504,132	$41,124,586	$41,628,718

2. Office of the Deputy Secretary	# Employees	Combined base salary & awards	Combined annual program funding: 2010	Savings from Elimination
School Leadership	4	$357,481	$29,161,560	$29,519,041
Arts in Education	4	$336,463	$27,446,996	$27,783,459
Ready-To-Learn Television	4	$333,987	$27,245,000	$27,578,987
Voluntary Public School Choice	3	$315,873	$25,767,362	$26,083,235
Fund for the Improvement of Education	2	$147,213	$12,008,934	$12,156,147
Credit Enhancement for Charter School Facilities	1	$123,026	$10,035,836	$10,158,862
Totals	95	$8,835,088	$720,723,212	$729,558,300

Notes:

1. The numbers of employees by program are estimates, assuming program staff size is relative to the total program funding.
2. Total average annual base salaries and awards by program are estimates derived by dividing the total annual base salary and awards amount by the number of employees.
3. Program and staff costs for the D.C. Opportunity Scholarship Program are excluded.

Summary: Elimination of the Office of Innovation and Improvement would result in $730 million being returned to states and their resident taxpayers. There is no evidence that OII programs have accomplished their stated goals in spite of their hefty price tags.

• • •

2.2. *Office of Special Education and Rehabilitative Services*

2. Office of the Deputy Secretary				
2.2.Office of Special Education and Rehabilitative Services	# Employees	Combined base salary & awards	Total # Programs administered	Combined annual program funding: 2010
	284	$29,633,797	31	$16,010,417,869

This office supports people of all ages who have disabilities, primarily through special education, vocational rehabilitation, and research. It oversees thirty-one programs with a combined cost of more than $16 billion annually; however, two state grant programs account for 90 percent of the total Office of Special Education and Rehabilitative Services (OSERS) program budget: Special Education Grants ($11.5 billion) and Rehabilitation Services-Vocational Rehabilitation Grants ($3 billion). There are close to 300 staff members whose average salaries exceed $100,000. Other federal agencies already exist that oversaw such programs before the department's creation. Given that education is so broadly defined across the federal government, the department has expanded into a significant number of areas under the auspices of helping people with disabilities. The result is program duplication within OSERS itself, as well as across other federal agencies, including the Departments of Health and Human Services, Interior, Justice, and Labor, as well as the National Institutes of Health. As with the Office of Innovation and Improvement, a number of OSERS grants can last up to five years. Oversight of those outstanding grants should be returned to the states, along with the associated program and administrative funding.

• • •

Program title	**Special Education Grants to States**
Type of assistance	Formula grants
Recipients	State educational agencies
Length of assistance	One year
Annual funding	$11,465,960,974
Authorization	Individuals with Disabilities Education Act (IDEA), as amended, Part B, Sections 611-618, 20 USC 1411-1418.
Description	Provides grants to States to assist them in providing special education and related services to all children with disabilities.

Recommendation. The Individuals with Disabilities Education Act of 1975 (IDEA) authorizes several grants to states based on the age of the individuals being served. This Special Education state formula grant covers children ages three to twenty-one. The OMB rated this program as moderately effective but cautioned: "There is no independent evaluation to provide information on the relationship between outcomes for children with disabilities and the program. While performance on the Nation's Report Card has improved, drop-out rates have declined, and graduation rates have increased, there is limited information on the program's role in relation to these outcomes." In spite of various efforts over the past several decades to strengthen oversight in the Rehabilitation Act of 1973 and the IDEA (originally the Education for All Handicapped Children Act), the result has been weak enforcement, burdensome and costly regulations, few incentives for improvement, and perverse financial incentives to overidentify students with learning disabilities.[18]

• • •

Program title	**Rehabilitation Services-Vocational Rehabilitation Grants to States**
Type of assistance	Formula grants
Recipients	State agencies
Length of assistance	One to two years
Annual funding	$3,041,146,000
Authorization	Rehabilitation Act of 1973, Title I, Part A and B, Section 100-111
Description	Assists states in operating comprehensive, coordinated, effective, efficient, and accountable programs of vocational rehabilitation; helps them to assess, plan, develop, and provide vocational rehabilitation services for individuals with disabilities, consistent with their strengths, resources, priorities, concerns, abilities, capabilities, and informed choice so they may prepare for and engage in competitive employment.

Recommendation. Vocational Rehabilitation State Grants require states to match 21.3 percent of their award, unless the funded project involves construction. In that case the state share is 50 percent. The OMB gave this program its lowest "performing" rating of adequate, noting that the data collected did not make possible comparisons with other job training programs.[19] Several federal agencies already offer an array of rehabilitative programs. Based on the average awards for fiscal year 2011, there are an estimated seventy-one Vocational Rehabilitation State Grants, which can last up to two years. No new grants should be awarded under this program, and funding and oversight of active grants would be transferred to designated state officials. The state-level positions responsible for overseeing active grants would be term-limited relative to the time period specified in the outstanding grants. Associated salary and administrative costs would be paid for out of funds previously paid to the respective OSERS grant officers. Through their state legislatures, state taxpayers would determine whether to continue supporting such initiatives.

Funding for the remaining twenty-nine programs administered by OSERS amounts to $1.5 billion, 10 percent of its total program funding. The savings table below provides estimated numbers of staff and total salaries based on the corresponding program's share of total funding. In many cases, the estimated number of employees is less than one but still has a salary amount. This results from the estimation method used, but it is illustrative to approximate the associated staffing costs for each program, no matter how relatively small.

2.2. Office of Special Education and Rehabilitative Services: Elimination Savings				
Programs	# Employees	Combined base salary & awards	Combined annual program funding: 2010	Savings from Elimination
Special Education–Grants to States	203	$21,196,269	$11,465,960,974	$11,487,157,243
Rehabilitation Services–Vocational Rehabilitation Grants to States	54	$5,621,940	$3,041,146,000	$3,046,767,940
Special Education–Grants for Infants and Families	8	$810,711	$438,548,000	$439,358,711
Special Education–Preschool Grants	7	$690,186	$373,350,802	$374,040,988
National Institute on Disability and Rehabilitation Research	2	$201,542	$109,022,518	$109,224,060
Special Education–Personnel Development to Improve Services and Results for Children with Disabilities	2	$163,540	$88,465,714	$88,629,254
Centers for Independent Living	1	$148,085	$80,105,468	$80,253,553
Special Education–Technical Assistance and Dissemination to Improve Services and Results for Children with Disabilities	1	$90,224	$48,806,192	$48,896,416

Programs	# Employees	Combined base salary & awards	Combined annual program funding: 2010	Savings from Elimination
Special Education–State Personnel Development	I	$86,601	$46,846,000	$46,932,601
Rehabilitation Services–American Indians with Disabilities	I	$80,508	$43,550,117	$43,630,625
Rehabilitation Services–Independent Living Services for Older Individuals Who are Blind	I	$63,006	$34,082,698	$34,145,704
Supported Employment Services for Individuals with the Most Significant Disabilities	I	$53,837	$29,122,638	$29,176,475
Special Education–Technology and Media Services for Individuals with Disabilities	I	$52,951	$28,643,598	$28,696,549
Special Education–Parent Information Centers	<I	$51,710	$27,971,944	$28,023,654
Assistive Technology	<I	$47,341	$25,608,680	$25,656,021
Special Education–Technical Assistance on State Data Collection	<I	$46,216	$25,000,000	$25,046,216
Independent Living–State Grants	<I	$43,264	$23,403,100	$23,446,364
Rehabilitation Long-Term Training	<I	$36,528	$19,759,777	$19,796,305
Program of Protection and Advocacy of Individual Rights	<I	$33,395	$18,064,798	$18,098,193
Rehabilitation Services–Client Assistance Program	<I	$22,670	$12,263,424	$12,286,094
Special Education–Studies and Evaluations	<I	$21,143	$11,437,080	$11,458,223
Special Education–Olympic Education Programs	<I	$14,935	$8,078,810	$8,093,745

Programs	# Employees	Combined base salary & awards	Combined annual program funding: 2010	Savings from Elimination
Rehabilitation Training– Continuing Education	<1	$14,862	$8,039,244	$8,054,106
Rehabilitation Services Demonstration and Training Programs	<1	$11,940	$6,459,056	$6,470,996
Rehabilitation Training– State Vocational Rehabilitation Unit In-Service Training	<1	$9,867	$5,337,254	$5,347,121
Assistive Technology–State Grants for Protection and Advocacy	<1	$7,933	$4,291,400	$4,299,333
Capacity Building for Traditionally Underserved Populations	<1	$3,893	$2,106,110	$2,110,003
Training Interpreters for Individuals who are Deaf and Individuals who are Deaf-Blind	<1	$3,882	$2,099,977	$2,103,859
Rehabilitation Services– Service Projects	<1	$3,432	$1,856,280	$1,859,712
Rehabilitation Short-Term Training	<1	$832	$449,993	$450,825
Rehabilitation Training– General Training	<1	$555	$300,000	$300,555
Totals	**284**	**$29,633,797**	**$16,030,177,646**	**$16,059,811,443**

Notes:

1. The numbers of employees by program are estimates, assuming program staff size is relative to the total program funding.
2. Total average annual base salaries and awards by program are estimates derived by dividing the total annual base salary and awards amount by the number of employees.

Summary: Dozens of US Department of Education programs extend beyond education matters and are more appropriately handled at the state level and by philanthropic organizations. In addition to federal entities, there is no shortage of special education research organizations. No new OSERS grants should be awarded, while funding and oversight of active grants would be transferred to designated state officials. The state-level positions responsible for overseeing active grants would be term-limited relative to the time period specified in the outstanding grants. Associated salary and administrative costs would be paid for out of funds previously paid to the respective OSHER grant officers. Through their state legislatures, taxpayers would determine whether to continue supporting such initiatives.

2.3. Office of English Language Acquisition, Language Enhancement and Academic Achievement for Limited English Proficient Students

2. Office of the Deputy Secretary				
2.3. Office of English Language Acquisition, Language Enhancement and Academic Achievement for Limited English Proficient Students	# Employees	Combined base salary & awards	Total # Programs administered	Combined annual program funding: 2010
	20	$2,186,358	1	$26,874,144

The mission of the Office of English Language Acquisition, Language Enhancement, and Academic Achievement for Limited English Proficient Students is "providing national leadership" so English language learners attain proficiency and succeed academically.

Program title	**Foreign Language Assistance Program**
Type of assistance	Project grants
Recipients	State and local educational agencies
Length of assistance	Three to five years
Annual funding	$26,874,144
Authorization	Elementary and Secondary Education Act of 1965, as amended, Title V, Part D, Subpart 9
Description	Supports innovative model programs of foreign language study in public elementary and secondary schools.

Recommendation. In 2012 funding for this program was eliminated; however, the office itself remains open overseeing programs enacted since 2010. This office should be eliminated and staff compensation funding, nearly $2.2 million, should be returned to taxpayers.

2.4. Office of Elementary and Secondary Education

2. Office of the Deputy Secretary				
	# Employees	Combined base salary & awards	Total # Programs administered	Combined annual program funding: 2010
2.4. Office of Elementary and Secondary Education	266	$22,328,459	31	$22,163,839,280

According to the US Department of Education, "The mission of the Office of Elementary and Secondary Education is to promote academic excellence, enhance educational opportunities and equity for all of America's children and families, and to improve the quality of teaching and learning by providing leadership, technical assistance and financial support." The Office of Elementary and Secondary Education (OESE) has 266 employees and nearly $22.2 billion in annual funding for thirty-one programs. Far and away the largest program is Title I grants to schools, which account for nearly two-thirds, $14.4 billion, of the total program funding. A distant second is the Improving Teacher Quality State Grants, representing 11 percent, $2.5 billion, of total program funding. Like the Office of Special Education and Rehabilitative Services, the OESE focuses on special student populations, minority and low-income students in particular. Other federal agencies already exist that oversaw such programs before the Department of Education's creation. As it is, program duplication within OESE and other US Department of Education offices, not to mention across other federal agencies, is substantial.

Program title	**Title I Grants to Local Educational Agencies**
Type of assistance	Formula grants
Recipients	State educational agencies (SEAs). Local educational agencies (LEAs) and Indian tribal schools are sub-grantees.
Length of assistance	One to two years

Annual funding	$14,442,926,000
Authorization	Elementary and Secondary Education Act of 1965 (ESEA), as amended, Title I, Part A, 20 USC 6301
Description	Helps local educational agencies improve teaching and learning in high-poverty schools in particular for children failing, or most at-risk of failing, to meet challenging state academic achievement standards.

Recommendation. After decades of experience and numerous careful efforts to evaluate Title I performance, there is scant evidence that its programs have been systematically and significantly contributing to reducing disparities in achievement by improving the performance of disadvantaged student populations.[20] Creation of a US Department of Education has done little, if anything, to improve the quality of data collection.[21] On the contrary, official evaluations regularly find Title I funds are not being used as intended, while duplication, waste, and burdensome requirements abound.[22] Several reforms have been suggested over the years to improve flexibility and efficiency. These include allocating Title I funding as state block grants and, more recently, granting states waivers. A better approach would be to end Title I altogether and return funding to state taxpayers. Precisely whether or how to allocate education funding to disadvantaged students would be up to voters.

• • •

Program title	**Improving Teacher Quality State Grants**
Type of assistance	Formula grants
Recipients	State educational agencies and State agencies for higher education
Length of assistance	One to three years
Annual funding	$2,468,054,000
Authorization	Elementary and Secondary Education Act, as amended, Title II, Part A
Description	Provides grants to state educational agencies, local educational agencies, state agencies for higher education, and, through the latter, to eligible partnerships in order to increase student academic achievement through such strategies as improving teacher and principal quality and increasing the number of highly qualified teachers in the classroom.

Recommendation. Improving Teacher Quality State Grants are intended to raise student achievement by increasing teacher and school principal effectiveness. This program, however, has produced no results: Student achievement overall has remained flat for decades. In addition, five other teaching-related grant programs are administered by the US Department of Education alone, and the GAO has documented that the department is one of eight Executive Branch agencies that oversee general education, training, employment, and social services.[23] Specifically, it identified eighty-two distinct teacher quality programs administered across ten federal agencies.[24] The "proliferation of [teacher quality] programs complicates federal efforts to invest dollars effectively,"[25] the GAO concludes.

Funding for Improving Teacher Quality State Grants should be returned to state taxpayers, who could then urge state lawmakers to enact laws that make publicly funded teacher preparation entrance requirements, programs, and graduation requirements more rigorous.

• • •

Program title	Impact Aid
Type of assistance	Formula grants
Recipients	Local educational agencies
Length of assistance	Varies
Annual funding	$1,268,776,362
Authorization	Elementary and Secondary Education Act (OESE), as amended, Title VIII
Description	Provides financial assistance to local educational agencies where affected by federal activities, that is, where the tax base of a district is reduced through the federal acquisition of real property (Section 8002, ESEA), and where the presence of certain children living on federal property places a financial burden on the local agencies that educate them (Sections 8003 and 8007, ESEA).

Recommendation. The GAO has reported little meaningful data on how Impact Aid funds are used and whether those funds were benefiting students.[26] The OMB also rates this program as not performing since it has yet to demonstrate any results. These funds should be returned to state taxpayers. Schools in the respective states should file quarterly reports detailing how many federally connected students they enroll on a full-time basis, quantify the costs associated with those students that are not covered due to the absence of local property taxes, and submit those reports to a designated state agency for review. Like many public charter schools, government schools affected by federally connected students would be funded on a quarterly, current-year basis.

• • •

Funding for the remaining twenty-eight programs administered by the OESE amounts to $4 billion, 18 percent of its total program funding. Many of the programs listed in the table below are state project grants for highly targeted student populations. Other programs have to do with training and coordination relative to federal programs. Still other programs and project grants relate to the three largest OESE programs detailed above. It is also important to note that several programs overlap with programs run by other federal agencies. For example, the GAO notes that US Department of Education drug prevention programs are not technically prevention or treatment programs. Rather, they may engage in some related drug prevention/treatment activities. Moreover, the GAO noted that 80 percent of the federal drug prevention-related programs it reviewed, fifty-nine out of seventy-six, were overlapping and fragmented across fifteen federal agencies.[27] Funding associated with the OESE programs and overhead detailed in the table below should be returned to state taxpayers. There is no evidence that these government-run programs are effective, and if state taxpayers believe such programs are important to them, they can either support privately managed programs or vote to raise their taxes in support of state-run programs.

As with the previous savings summary table, the one below provides estimated numbers of staff and total salaries based on the corresponding program's share of total funding. In many cases, the estimated number of employees is less than one but still has an associated salary amount. This results from the estimation method used, but it is illustrative to approximate the associated staffing costs for each program, no matter how relatively small.

2.4. Office of Elementary and Secondary Education: Elimination Savings

Programs	# Employees	Combined base salary & awards	Combined annual program funding: 2010	Savings from Elimination
Title I Grants to Local Educational Agencies	173	$14,550,273	$14,442,926,000	$14,457,476,273
Improving Teacher Quality State Grants	30	$2,486,398	$2,468,054,000	$2,470,540,398
Impact Aid	15	$1,278,207	$1,268,776,362	$1,270,054,569
English Language Acquisition State Grants	8	$685,911	$680,850,550	$681,536,461
School Improvement Grants	6	$538,535	$534,561,734	$535,100,269
Teacher Incentive Fund	5	$402,167	$399,200,000	$399,602,167
Migrant Education State Grant Program	5	$396,910	$393,981,458	$394,378,368
Race to the Top–District Grants	5	$385,847	$383,000,000	$383,385,847
Grants for State Assessments and Related Activities	5	$382,795	$379,970,536	$380,353,331
Mathematics and Science Partnerships	2	$176,429	$175,127,044	$175,303,473
Rural Education	2	$175,829	$174,532,236	$174,708,065
Striving Readers	2	$160,885	$159,697,600	$159,858,485
Safe and Drug-Free Schools and Communities National Programs	1	$120,112	$119,226,070	$119,346,182
Indian Education Grants to Local Educational Agencies	1	$104,896	$104,122,338	$104,227,234
Consolidated Grant to the Outlying Areas	1	$66,583	$66,092,135	$66,158,718
Education for Homeless Children and Youth	1	$65,781	$65,296,146	$65,361,927
Comprehensive Centers	1	$51,591	$51,210,000	$51,261,591

Programs	# Employees	Combined base salary & awards	Combined annual program funding: 2010	Savings from Elimination
Title I State Agency Program for Neglected and Delinquent Children and Youth	1	$50,700	$50,326,146	$50,376,846
High School Graduation Initiative	1	$49,265	$48,902,000	$48,951,265
Advanced Placement Program (Advanced Placement Test Fee; Advanced Placement Incentive Program Grants)	1	$43,575	$43,253,320	$43,296,895
Native Hawaiian Education	<1	$34,501	$34,246,370	$34,280,871
Alaska Native Educational Programs	<1	$33,495	$33,248,370	$33,281,865
Migrant Education High School Equivalency Program	<1	$20,057	$19,908,535	$19,928,592
Indian Education– Special Programs for Indian Children	<1	$19,163	$19,021,880	$19,041,043
Migrant Education College Assistance Migrant Program	<1	$16,626	$16,503,156	$16,519,782
Grants for Enhanced Assessment Instruments	<1	$10,054	$9,980,000	$9,990,054
Civil Rights Training and Advisory Services	<1	$7,027	$6,975,022	$6,982,049
Territories and Freely Associated States Education Grant Program	<1	$5,037	$5,000,000	$5,005,037
Impact Aid Facilities Maintenance	<1	$4,890	$4,854,272	$4,859,162
Migrant Education Coordination Program	<1	$3,022	$3,000,000	$3,003,022
State Tribal Education Partnership (STEP)	<1	$1,898	$1,996,000	$1,997,898

Programs	# Employees	Combined base salary & awards	Combined annual program funding: 2010	Savings from Elimination
Totals	266	$22,328,459	$22,163,839,280	$22,186,167,739

Notes:

1. The numbers of employees by program are estimates, assuming program staff size is relative to the total program funding.
2. Total average annual base salaries and awards by program are estimates derived by dividing the total annual base salary and awards amount by the number of employees.

Summary: Elimination of the OESE would be a tremendous stride toward returning the federal government to its constitutionally limited bounds and restoring parental rights over their children's education—both directly and through their duly elected local and state representatives.

3. The Office of the Under Secretary Programs

The Office of the Under Secretary coordinates activities relating to post-secondary education, career-technical education, adult education, federal student aid, and White House initiatives, including the Initiative on Asian Americans and the Initiative on Pacific Islanders, Educational Excellence for Hispanics, Historically Black Colleges and Universities, and Tribal Colleges and Universities. It consists of three offices that oversee forty programs with combined funding of $175 billion.

3.1. *The Office of Federal Student Aid*

3. Office of the Under Secretary				
3.1. Office of Federal Student Aid	# Employees	Combined base salary & awards	Total # Programs administered	Combined annual program funding: 2010
	1,224	$125,652,835	4	$170,517,470,000

This office is the largest US Department of Education division with more than 1,200 employees who oversee an annual budget of $171 billion. For perspective, that amount exceeds the entire GDP of New Zealand. With those funds the Office of Federal Student Aid awards grants, work-study funds, and low-interest loans to more than 14 million students.

Program title	**Federal Direct Student Loans**
Type of assistance	Direct loans
Recipients	A US citizen, national, or person in the United States for other than a temporary purpose.
Length of assistance	Ten to thirty years
Annual funding	$132,731,924,000
Authorization	Higher Education Act of 1965, as amended, Title IV, Part D
Description	Provides loan capital directly from the federal government (rather than through private lenders) to vocational, undergraduate, and graduate postsecondary school students and their parents.

Recommendation. Government subsidies in the form of student loans—which are paid directly to the institutions—do not lower college prices. They chase them. Both public and private postsecondary institutions have been heavily subsidized by the federal government for decades. Compounding this situation are state and local subsidies for two- and four-year public institutions. Rather than contain college costs, government subsidies have helped fuel them.[28]

The postsecondary sector is in dire need of a student-centered, incentive-based, and results-oriented financing system if it is ever going to approach affordability again. A healthy dose of personal responsibility is needed as well. Simply ending the Federal Direct Student Loan program will not accomplish any of those goals—but it's a step in the right direction.

With the abolition of the US Department of Education, authority over issuing and managing student loans would be immediately restored to the private sector. Free-market opponents would likely object, noting the glaring abuses of the past, including private lender kickbacks to postsecondary institutions in exchange for preferred lender status, which resulted in less information and fewer solid lending options for students. Those abuses, however, occurred because of *a lack of* market competition, not because of it. Under a truly privatized system, a variety of lenders would have to compete for students' business directly rather than go through the financial aid offices at postsecondary institutions. The flow of loan cash would be reversed. Currently, federal loan funds go to postsecondary institutions. Students never touch a single dime.

• • •

Program title	**Federal Pell Grant Program**
Type of assistance	Direct payments for a specified use
Recipients	Undergraduate students and students pursuing a teaching certificate
Length of assistance	One year
Annual funding	$35,685,485,000
Authorization	Higher Education Act of 1965, Title IV, Part A, Subpart 1, as amended
Description	Provides eligible undergraduate postsecondary students who have demonstrated financial need with grant assistance to help meet educational expenses

Recommendation. Like the Federal Direct Student Loan program, the Pell Grant Program has grown tremendously over the past few decades, from 176,000 students and a cost to taxpayers of $48 million in 1973–74[29] to 8.1 million college students with grants worth $30 billion in 2009–10.[30] Fraud and waste have been rampant in the Pell Grant program for decades. Billions of dollars in Pell Grant funds have flowed to schools with inflated enrollment figures or entities setting up shell schools to pocket taxpayer funds—all because the US Department of Education never verified the paperwork.[31] The Pell Grant Program is one of thirteen federal programs designated "high error" by the OMB for making roughly $750 million or more in improper payments in a given year.[32] In fact, in each of the past several years, the Pell Grant program has wasted more than $1 billion due to verification and administrative errors related to the US Department of Education's lax oversight.[33] In addition, distinct investigations had to be conducted in 2010 because portions of Recovery Act funding intended for Pell Grant increases were used in fraudulent high school diploma and grant application scams.[34]

A more fundamental problem with the US Department of Education's approach is its effect on college affordability and access. Federal subsidies make college less affordable because, as Center for College Affordability and Productivity Director Richard Vedder explains, "When someone else is paying the bills, costs always rise."[35] Unfortunately, productivity does not rise along with those costs. Just over half of all four-year undergraduates (less than

55 percent) graduate in six years, while less than one quarter (23 percent) of two-year undergraduates complete a degree within three years.[36]

No politician wants to be accused of killing a program that is supposed to help the poor. "When it comes to higher education reform, war is Pell," is how Bellwether Education co-founder and *Eduwonk* writer Andrew Rotherham described his experience advising on reform a decade ago. Like federal direct student loans, the Pell Grant Program should be converted to privatized, performance-based lending, and lump-sum state appropriations to institutions should be replaced by per-student performance grants. These actions would begin to make postsecondary institutions more affordable. In addition, there would be powerful incentives for institutions to cut unnecessary costs and to direct savings to their own need-based aid programs.

• • •

Program title	**Federal Work-Study Program (ARRA)**
Type of assistance	Direct payments for a specified use
Recipients	Higher education institutions
Length of assistance	One year
Annual funding	$1,168,428,000
Authorization	Higher Education Act of 1965, as amended, Title IV, Part C; 42 USC. 2751-2756a
Description	Provides part-time employment to eligible postsecondary students to help meet educational expenses and encourages students receiving program assistance to participate in community service activities.

Recommendation. The Federal Work Study program provides funds for part-time employment to help financially needy students pay for their postsecondary education at about 3,400 participating institutions. Hourly wages cannot be less than the federal minimum wage, $7.25 per hour in 2010.[37] While most of the funds come from the federal government, postsecondary institutions and nonprofit employers pay up to 25 percent of students' earnings, and for-profit employers pay up to 50 percent.[38] Only about 1 percent of all undergraduate aid, which includes federal, institutional, and private-sector aid, is provided by this program.[39] Neither the federal government nor the US Department of Education creates jobs. At best they encourage busy work that dissipates once the public subsidies go away. Federal work study funds should be returned to taxpayers who run the businesses with the real jobs.

• • •

Program title	**Federal Supplemental Educational Opportunity Grants**
Type of assistance	Direct payments for a specified use
Recipients	Higher education institutions
Length of assistance	One year
Annual funding	$931,633,000
Authorization	Higher Education Act of 1965, as amended, Title IV, Part A, Subpart 3, 20 USC. 1070b-1070b-3
Description	Provides need-based grant aid to eligible undergraduate post-secondary students to help meet educational expenses.

Recommendation. The Federal Supplemental Educational Opportunity Grant program is intended to help financially needy students pay for their postsecondary education at about 3,800 participating institutions. Institutions must prioritize exceptionally needy students defined as having the lowest expected family contributions and Pell Grant recipients. They must also contribute 25 percent of the award amounts. New awards are worth up to $4,000 but average just over $700 for about 1.3 million recipients. There is no evidence that the opportunity grants are helping needy students complete college degrees. The funding should be returned to state taxpayers, who can found or expand privately managed entities to meet this need.

• • •

3.1. Office of Federal Student Aid: Elimination Savings

Programs	# Employees	Combined base salary & awards	Combined annual program funding: 2010	Savings from Elimination
Federal Direct Student Loans	953	$97,808,996	$132,731,924,000	$132,829,732,996
Federal Pell Grant Program (ARRA)	256	$26,296,322	$35,685,485,000	$35,711,781,322

Programs	# Employees	Combined base salary & awards	Combined annual program funding: 2010	Savings from Elimination
Federal Work-Study Program (ARRA)	8	$861,004	$1,168,428,000	$1,169,289,004
Federal Supplemental Educational Opportunity Grants	7	$686,512	$931,633,000	$932,319,512
Totals	1,224	$125,652,835	$170,517,470,000	$170,643,122,835

Notes: 1. The numbers of employees by program are estimates, assuming program staff size is relative to the total program funding.

2. Total average annual base salaries and awards by program are estimates derived by dividing the total annual base salary and awards amount by the number of employees.

Summary: The annual savings to taxpayers by eliminating US Department of Education higher education programs would be nearly $171 billion. That savings estimate is likely conservative because it does not include the additional costs associated with fraud investigations, waste, and other poor management practices. In addition, the profits made by the US Department of Education from student lending, totaling nearly $51 billion in 2012 alone, should also be returned to taxpayers rather than funneled back into other government programs.[40]

3.2. Office of Vocational and Adult Education

3. Office of the Under Secretary				
3.2. Office of Vocational and Adult Education	# Employees	Combined base salary & awards	Total # Programs administered	Combined annual program funding: 2010
	90	$9,327,644	8	$1,734,399,747

The Office of Vocational and Adult Education oversees and coordinates programs relating to adult education and literacy, career and technical education, and community colleges. It employs ninety staff members who run eight programs that cost more than $1.7 billion annually. Two programs, Career Technical Education and Adult Education state grants, account for virtually all of that funding (98 percent). The remaining programs are highly targeted programs for select populations. Beginning with the Vocational Rehabilitation Act of 1918, along with the Smith-Bankhead Act of 1920, these services traditionally focused on war veterans.[41] Currently, the US Department of Education is one of eight federal agencies providing related vocational and adult education services.[42] The GAO found forty-seven programs throughout the federal government, but only five have completed impact studies since 2004, so little is known about program effectiveness. Moreover, virtually all forty-seven programs throughout the federal government overlap both in terms of services and targeted beneficiaries, most of whom are Native Americans, veterans, and youth.[43]

Program title	**Career and Technical Education–Basic Grants to States**
Type of assistance	Formula grants
Recipients	State boards for career and technical education
Length of assistance	One year
Annual funding	$1,105,434,533
Authorization	Carl D. Perkins Career and Technical Education Act of 2006 (Perkins IV), Title I, 20 USC 2321
Description	Develops more fully the academic, career, and technical skills of secondary and postsecondary students who elect to enroll in career and technical education programs.

Recommendation. Career and Technical Education grants support programs run by local government schools, community colleges, four-year postsecondary institutions, and postsecondary education institutions run by the Department of the Interior's Bureau of Indian Education. Programs should be implemented by the states directly. Formula grant funds should be restored to taxpayers who are better situated than another Washington bureaucracy to gauge the needs in their communities and states.

• • •

Program title	**Adult Education—Basic Grants to States**
Type of assistance	Formula Grants
Recipients	Eligible state agencies
Length of assistance	Two-plus years

Annual funding	$596,120,370
Authorization	Adult Education and Family Literacy Act, (AEFLA), (Title II of the Workforce Investment Act of 1998), 20 USC. 9201 et seq
Description	Funds local programs of adult education and literacy services, including workplace literacy services, family literacy services, and English literacy and integrated English literacy-civics education programs. Participation in these programs is limited to adults and out-of-school youths age sixteen and older who do not have a high school diploma or equivalent and who are not enrolled or required to be enrolled in a secondary school under state law. See 20 USC 9202(1).

Recommendation. Using Adult Education state grants, more than 3,000 programs nationwide deliver instruction services to more than 2.4 million adults through government schools, community colleges, libraries, community-based organizations, and other providers. There is no shortage of private providers who offer these services without having to funnel taxpayer dollars through the US Department of Education. Funding for this program, along with the remaining programs in the Office of Vocational and Adult Education, should be returned to state taxpayers, who can decide which programs, if any, to implement or expand. The savings table below provides estimated numbers of staff and total salaries based on the corresponding program's share of total funding. In many cases, the estimated number of employees is less than one but has a salary amount. This results from the estimation method used, but it is illustrative to approximate the associated staffing costs for each program, no matter how relatively small.

• • •

3.2. Office of Vocational and Adult Education: Elimination Savings

Programs	# Employees	Combined base salary & awards	Combined annual program funding: 2010	Savings from Elimination
Career and Technical Education—Basic Grants to States	57	$5,945,054	$1,105,434,533	$1,111,379,587
Adult Education—Basic Grants to States	31	$3,205,950	$596,120,370	$599,326,320

Programs	# Employees	Combined base salary & awards	Combined annual program funding: 2010	Savings from Elimination
Career and Technical Education—Grants to Native Americans and Alaska Natives	1	$75,538	$14,045,740	$14,121,278
Adult Education National Leadership Activities	1	$60,900	$11,323,808	$11,384,708
Tribally Controlled Postsecondary Career and Technical Institutions	<1	$36,597	$8,145,676	$8,189,484
Career and Technical Education–National Programs	<1	$3,605	$7,844,280	$7,886,467
Native Hawaiian Career and Technical Education	0	$0	$2,809,148	$2,824,256
Grants to States for Workplace and Community Transition Training for Incarcerated Individuals	0	$0	$0	$0
Totals	90	$9,327,644	$1,745,723,555	$1,755,112,099

3.3. *Office of Postsecondary Education*

3. Office of the Under Secretary				
3.3. Office of Postsecondary Education	# Employees	Combined base salary & awards	Total # Programs administered	Combined annual program funding: 2010
	247	$23,470,274	28	$2,230,999,207

The US Department of Education's Office of Postsecondary Education oversees federal postsecondary education policy and programs that increase access to higher education. The two programs described below represent half of the total program funding, $1.1 billion.

Program title	**Higher Education Institutional Aid**
Type of assistance	Project grants
Recipients	Higher education institutions
Length of assistance	One to five years
Annual funding	$744,740,610
Authorization	Higher Education Act of 1965, as amended (HEA). Title III, Part A and Part F, HEA, Title V
Description	Helps eligible colleges and universities to strengthen their management and fiscal operations and to plan, develop, or implement activities including endowment building to strengthen the academic quality of their institutions.

Recommendation. The Higher Education Institutional Aid program provides grants to postsecondary institutions for capacity building. The US Department of Education provides a great deal of information on program inputs but little to no information on program results. The GAO has also documented that "federal assistance for higher education is fragmented across four departments," Education, the Department of the Treasury, Veteran's Affairs, and the Department of Defense.[44] There is no evidence that the US Department of Education has meaningfully improved management at higher education institutions in terms of administration or improved college access and completion. Funds for this program should be returned to state taxpayers who can then vote on programs that direct their tax dollars to deserving students.

• • •

Program title	**TRIO Upward Bound**
Type of assistance	Project grants
Recipients	Higher education institutions
Length of assistance	Five years
Annual funding	$352,832,000
Authorization	Higher Education Act of 1965, as amended, Subpart 2, Title IV, Part A, Section 402C, 20 USC 1070a-13

Description	Generates skills and motivation necessary for success in education beyond high school among low-income and potential first-generation college students and veterans. The goal of the program is to increase the academic performance and motivational levels of eligible enrollees so that such persons may complete secondary school and successfully pursue and complete a postsecondary educational program.

Recommendation. TRIO programs are funded through Title IV of the Higher Education Act of 1965 to help low-income individuals get a college degree and improve their economic opportunities. TRIO Upward Bound was created in 1964 under the Economic Opportunity Act. The Higher Education Act of 1965 established the Educational Talent Search program, while the Special Services for Disadvantaged Students (now the Student Support Services Program) was added through the Higher Education Amendments of 1968. The term *TRIO* originally referred to these three programs, but the acronym remains even though several more TRIO programs have subsequently been created, including the Educational Opportunity Centers created through the Higher Education Act Amendments of 1972; the Training Program for Special Programs Staff and Leadership Personnel established under the Education Amendments of 1976; and the Dr. Ronald E. McNair Post-Baccalaureate Achievement Program authorized by the Higher Education Amendments of 1986.

Upward Bound consists of three programs: regular Upward Bound, Veterans Upward Bound, and Upward Bound Math-Science. It is intended to impart the skills and motivation necessary for postsecondary education for disadvantaged students and those with poor high school preparation. More than 900 grants fund over 770 programs nationwide enrolling about 65,000 students. In general, participating students enroll in Grades 9 or 10 and remain in the program for twenty months. Through Upward Bound programs, students receive additional instruction in reading, writing, math, and science on college campuses after school, on Saturdays, and throughout the summer. The stated goal of the Upward Bound program is "to increase the rate at which participants complete secondary education and enroll in and graduate from institutions of postsecondary education." Commissioned evaluations of the program reveal that the program has had no detectable effect on college enrollment or degree acquisition. While the program was shown to increase the likelihood of earning vocational certificates, evaluators noted that the program largely attracts students who are already motivated and capable of pursuing postsecondary education.[45]

As with so many other US Department of Education programs dating back to the War on Poverty era, there is scant evidence that TRIO programs work. Even if these programs were successful, that would not justify the unconstitutional overreach by the federal government into education. As with the remaining twenty-six postsecondary programs, many of which focus on highly targeted student populations, funding for TRIO Upward Bound should be returned to state taxpayers who can decide which programs, if any, to implement or expand. The savings table below provides estimated numbers of staff and total salaries based on the corresponding program's share of total funding. In many cases, the estimated number of employees is less than one but has a salary amount. This results from the estimation method used, but it is illustrative to approximate the associated staffing costs for each program, no matter how relatively small.

• • •

3.3. Office of Postsecondary Education: Elimination Savings				
Programs	# Employees	Combined base salary & awards	Combined annual program funding: 2010	Savings from Elimination
Higher Education Institutional Aid	82	$7,834,725	$744,740,610	$752,575,335
TRIO Upward Bound	39	$3,711,805	$352,832,000	$356,543,805
Gaining Early Awareness and Readiness for Undergraduate Programs	33	$3,164,247	$300,783,000	$303,947,247
TRIO Student Support Services	32	$3,059,594	$290,835,000	$293,894,594
College Access Challenge Grant Program	17	$1,578,005	$150,000,000	$151,578,005
TRIO Talent Search	15	$1,430,398	$135,969,000	$137,399,398

Programs	# Employees	Combined base salary & awards	Combined annual program funding: 2010	Savings from Elimination
TRIO Educational Opportunity Centers	5	$501,564	$47,677,000	$48,178,564
TRIO McNair Post-Baccalaureate Achievement	5	$486,268	$46,223,000	$46,709,268
Strengthening Minority-Serving Institutions	4	$383,981	$36,500,000	$36,883,981
Graduate Assistance in Areas of National Need	3	$325,784	$30,967,940	$31,293,724
National Resource Centers Program for Foreign Language and Area Studies or Foreign Language and International Studies Program and Foreign Language and Area Studies Fellowship Program	2	$189,874	$18,048,762	$18,238,636
Child Care Access Means Parents in School	2	$168,341	$16,001,932	$16,170,273
Transition Programs for Students with Intellectual Disabilities into Higher Education	1	$115,489	$10,978,000	$11,093,489
Javits Fellowships	1	$101,908	$9,687,000	$9,788,908
Minority Science and Engineering Improvement	1	$99,772	$9,483,994	$9,583,766
Centers for International Business Education	1	$60,299	$5,731,864	$5,792,163
Overseas Programs–Group Projects Abroad	1	$51,457	$4,891,373	$4,942,830
TRIO Staff Training Program	<1	$37,125	$3,529,000	$3,566,125
Language Resource Centers	<1	$26,811	$2,548,528	$2,575,339

Programs	# Employees	Combined base salary & awards	Combined annual program funding: 2010	Savings from Elimination
Overseas Programs Special Bilateral Projects	<1	$25,945	$2,466,272	$2,492,217
Overseas Programs— Doctoral Dissertation Research Abroad	<1	$25,945	$2,466,272	$2,492,217
International Research and Studies	<1	$25,485	$2,422,500	$2,447,985
Fund for the Improvement of Postsecondary Education	<1	$16,906	$1,607,000	$1,623,906
Institute for International Public Policy	<1	$16,326	$1,551,890	$1,568,216
Undergraduate International Studies and Foreign Language Programs	<1	$10,968	$1,042,562	$1,053,530
Business and International Education Projects	<1	$9,297	$883,708	$893,005
American Overseas Research Centers	<1	$6,838	$650,000	$656,838
Graduate Research Opportunities for Minority Students (Minorities and Retirement Security Program)	<1	$5,118	$481,000	$486,118
Totals	247	$23,470,274	$2,230,999,207	$2,254,469,481

Notes:

1. The numbers of employees by program are estimates, assuming program staff size is relative to the total program funding.
2. Total average annual base salaries and awards by program are estimates derived by dividing the total annual base salary and awards amount by the number of employees.

Life Without the US Department of Education

This chapter detailed how nearly all US Department of Education programs could readily be handled at the state level, with funding coming directly from state taxpayers rather than being funneled through a Washington bureaucracy. After a review of 125 US Department of Education programs, one had already been slated for elimination as of this writing (the Office of Vocational and Adult Education's National Institute for Literacy). The D.C. Opportunity Scholarship Program does not violate the US Constitution, which reserves some district oversight to Congress, and should be preserved. The second program to be preserved is the Postsecondary Education Scholarships for Veteran's Dependents, which is an earned benefit, not an entitlement, that should be administered by Veteran's Affairs. Federal student loans should be privatized, and the remaining 121 programs currently overseen by the US Department of Education should be eliminated. The savings from the elimination/privatization of these programs, including associated salary costs, is $216 billion. Those savings do not include the roughly $50 billion in annual profit the US Department of Education has been making in recent years from student loans.[46] These funds should be returned to taxpayers as well rather than funneled into another federal government bureaucracy.

More than thirty years after the creation of the US Department of Education students, taxpayers, and the country are not better off—but they can be. After decades of waiving the constitutional barrier to a federal role in education under the guise of "partnering" with state governments, it's time to dissolve that partnership and abolish the US Department of Education.

11

A Blueprint for the Next Thirty Years
Parental Choice

WE HAVE SEEN the significant role that parental choice has played in the success of top-performing students on international tests. Shining examples of parental choice programs exist across the United States and in its capital, Washington, DC, where students largely from socioeconomically disadvantaged backgrounds are succeeding in high-quality schools at a fraction of what it would cost if they attended traditional public schools. Parental choice in education existed long before the Department of Education was established, and today's parental school choice programs have flourished apart from, and in the case of the D.C. Opportunity Scholarship Program, even in spite of the department. This chapter begins with an overview of the origins of contemporary parental choice programs. Next it reviews such programs and their contribution to improving educational quality.

The Rise of Vouchers

Vouchers are publicly funded scholarships that allow eligible students to attend private schools of their parents' choice. Instead of paying government-appropriated funds to school districts, elementary and secondary school voucher programs allocate those funds to scholarships that parents can use to pay partial or full tuition at participating private schools. Voucher programs currently provide greater access to quality programs and schools for students who have special needs, are from low-income families, or are attending a failing school.

The first twentieth-century voucher program was founded in 1990 in Milwaukee, Wisconsin. Currently, fourteen voucher programs in twenty-two states and Washington, DC, are assisting nearly 140,000 students to attend the schools of their parents' choice.[1] Town tuitioning voucher programs have existed in Maine and Vermont since 1873 and 1869, respectively, for students in towns without public schools.[2] The vast majority of voucher programs, however, serve students who are from low-income families or have special needs.

Nobel Prize-winning economist Milton Friedman is credited as the originator of the modern parental school choice movement. In 1955 he recommended that instead of assigning students to schools based on where their families can afford to live, government should instead "give each child, through his parents, a specified sum to be used solely in paying for his general education."[3] Government would continue to fund education, but it would not oversee any schooling system or interfere with parents' choices about where their children are educated. Public funds would be dispersed to parents in the form of vouchers, or scholarships, much like federal Pell Grants, food stamps, and housing vouchers.

Yet Friedman was hardly the first to suggest such a system. As Herbert J. Wahlberg and Joseph L. Bast explain:

> The value of universal education is undisputed and not all parents can afford to finance their children's education—but this does not justify government subsidies of only certain types of schooling. Vouchers would allow parents to choose schooling offered by private profit or non-profit enterprises. Friedman was not the first to suggest vouchers as a way to restore proper balance of capitalism and government in schooling.[4]

In 1776, philosopher Adam Smith argued against government administration of education because he believed it would be arbitrary; government officials "are seldom capable of exercising it with judgment," he said.[5] Likewise, founder Thomas Jefferson scoffed at the idea of a government-run schooling system in 1779 when he was governor of Virginia. "If it is believed that these elementary schools will be better managed by the governor and council . . . than by the parents within each ward," he observed, "it is a belief against all experiences."[6] Political economist John Stuart Mill argued against a homogenized, one-size-fits-all approach to schooling a few decades later. "A general

State education is a mere contrivance for molding people to be exactly like one another," he explained. "An education established and controlled by the state should only exist, if it exists at all, as one among many competing experiments."[7] Instead, Mill recommended that government "leave to parents to obtain the education where and how they pleased, and content itself with helping to pay the school fees of the poorer classes of children, and defraying the entire school expenses of those who have no one else to pay for them."[8]

It is also frequently assumed that parental choice in education is the brainchild of right-wing, free-market advocates. On the contrary, advocacy for parental choice and equal educational opportunity has garnered strong support from across the political spectrum for decades.[9] To be sure, many parental choice proponents share a limited-government philosophy. Like Friedman and Mill, Marquette University Professor Father Virgil C. Blum, S.J., argued in 1958:

> Government control over the processes of education is infinitely more objectionable than government control of businesses which supply the physical needs of life. . . . Freedom can survive, to a considerable degree, even if government tells the citizen what brand of food he must eat and what fashion of clothes he must wear. But freedom cannot long survive when government tells him what thoughts he must think.[10]

The business community has advocated for a more competitive educational system since 1966. That year, a US Chamber of Commerce Task Force of 100 national business leaders led by *Christian Science Monitor* Editor Erwin D. Canham recommended vouchers to help make the public education system more competitive.[11] The Council on Foreign Relations echoed the theme of greater competition through choice in 2012. "Educational failure puts the United States' future economic prosperity, global position, and physical safety at risk," warned the council's task force, co-chaired by Joel Klein, former head of New York City public schools, and Condoleezza Rice, former US secretary of state. The country "will not be able to keep pace—much less lead—globally unless it moves to fix the problems it has allowed to fester for too long."[12] Among the task force's recommendations was making structural changes to provide students with good choices. "Enhanced choice and competition, in an environment of equitable resource allocation, will fuel the innovation necessary to transform results."[13] In response the *Wall Street Journal* editorialized that "the real story is how much progress the reform movement has made when pillars of the establishment are willing to endorse a choice movement that would have been too controversial even a few years ago."[14]

Other advocates emphasized that parental choice in education would help mitigate the social injustice of limited educational opportunities for economically disadvantaged students. In 1968 Theodore Sizer and Philip Whitten published *A Proposal for a Poor Children's Bill of Rights* because in their opinion, "A system of public schools which destroys rather than develops positive human potential now exists. It is not in the public interest."[15] California was poised to become a national trailblazer that same year when a state legislative commission recommended education vouchers for low-income students. The commission concluded that "the sorry state of education in ghetto schools probably results from the monopolistic hold that the public schools have on poor and minority children."[16] The commission introduced the Self-Determination in Education Act of 1968, which would have let low-income parents use vouchers for their own children or pool them to form new schools or districts. The University of California Los Angeles Survey Research Center found that nearly 8 out of 10 Watts neighborhood parents supported the Self-Determination in Education Act, while two-thirds of them thought parental choice would improve Watts public schools.[17] The California State Legislature, however, never chose to consider the legislation.

Across the country, momentum for educational vouchers continued to build during the late 1960s and early 1970s. John E. Coons, William H. Clune III, and Stephen D. Sugarman, University of California, Berkeley, law professors, initiated the landmark school finance equity *Serrano v. Priest* lawsuits in 1968. They argued then that vouchers would rectify the disparities in existing school systems "that dispense public education by wealth." In his foreword to their 1970 book, *Private Wealth and Public Education,* the late James S. Coleman wrote that restoring equal educational opportunity for all students requires "a return of resources to each family, in the form of tuition vouchers."[18] Meanwhile, in 1969 the US Office of Economic Opportunity contracted with sociologist Christopher Jencks and his colleagues from Harvard University's Center for the Study of Public Policy to produce an education vouchers feasibility study for nonassigned, or voluntary, public school districts nationwide.[19] Jencks explained the rationale for their experimental voucher plan in the following way:

> Conservatives, liberals, and radicals all have complained at one time or another that the political mechanisms which supposedly make public schools accountable to their clients work clumsily and ineffectively . . . mounting an effective campaign to change local public schools takes an enormous investment of time, energy, and money. Dissatisfied though they may be, few parents have the political skill or commitment to solve their problems this way. As a result, effective control over the character of the public schools is largely vested in legislators, school boards, and educators—not parents. If parents are to take genuine responsibility for their children's education, they cannot rely exclusively on political processes. They must also be able to take individual action on behalf of their own children. At present, only relatively affluent parents retain any effective control over the education of their children. Only they are free to move to areas with "good" public schools, where housing is usually expensive. . . . The average parent has no alternative to his local public school. . . . Not only does today's public school have a captive clientele, but it in turn has become the captive of a political process designed to protect the interests of its clientele.[20]

The following year in 1970 the National Educational Finance Project concluded, "As long as the near-monopoly of the public school system exists intact, substantial technical changes are unlikely to be forthcoming." A finance system that "subsidizes the student rather than the school might indeed set off drastic changes in the organization of the whole industry."[21] Then in 1971 the White House Conference on Youth recommended that education vouchers "should be adopted initially on a pilot experimental basis to determine how best it might be run and what its likely impact is. We propose an annual appropriation of $50 million for this purpose," nearly $270 million in 2010 dollars.[22] In addition, the conference report recommended education vouchers be funded at both the local and state levels.[23] Then-Executive Director of the National Committee for Support of the Public Schools Gerald E. Stroufe endorsed this proposal.

The bipartisan policy support for educational vouchers during this time was remarkable. Economist Henry M. Levin, now at Columbia University Teachers College, observed in 1968 that the "fact that the new left . . . and the old right . . . can concur on the same educational palliative is reason enough to consider [parental choice] as a serious alternative to the present system."[24] Stephen Arons, University of Massachusetts at Amherst legal studies professor, concurred in 1972, stating, "When all these people are reported to agree with a political scheme, one wonders whether we have reached the millennium."[25]

Yet one political segment remained stalwart in their opposition: teachers unions. "While the [White House Conference on Youth] voucher plan has offered despairing parents hope," Stroufe observed, "the educator organizations have chosen to attack the source of hope rather than the causes of despair."[26] A leading reason for opposition from union leaders was their insistence that more funding, not more choice, would improve education. Even when assured of additional funding, however, union leadership still opposed the program because ultimately they wanted control over schools and associated policies that affect their membership and budget. Jencks predicted that teachers union opposition would largely subvert the program, saying that if "the National Education Association (NEA) and the American Federation of Teachers (AFT) have their way, we shall have no test at all."[27] He was correct. The NEA condemned the voucher experiment at its national convention in July 1970—six months before Jencks and his colleagues released the results of their feasibility study. Union delegates also demanded that Congress prevent any voucher experiment from taking place, and they discouraged local educators from participating.[28] Then-AFT President David Selden tried to have Congress stop the project.

Alum Rock Project Pilots Rough Seas

In spite of guaranteed additional funding from the federal government, teachers unions were successful in dissuading all but one public school district from participating in the voucher pilot program: California's Alum Rock School District in San Jose.[29] As California governor, Ronald Reagan urged experimentation. During his 1971 State of the State address Reagan recalled the findings of widespread functional illiteracy among California high school graduates by the Governor's Commission on Educational Reform. "It is not enough to say they have failed; it is more pertinent to ask, 'has the system failed?' and if so how can it be corrected?" He continued:

> There is always need for innovation in any system; education must be no exception. There are those who see the "voucher plan" as the answer to making schools more responsive. There are others who see it as a threat of unutterable evil. No one on either side seems to have facts upon which to base his often emotional stand. Why shouldn't we undertake some pilot tests in selected districts and thus introduce some facts into the debate?[30]

To pacify local affiliates of the NEA and the AFT, local private schools in Alum Rock were barred from participating.[31] Under the scaled-back pilot program, each of Alum Rock's twenty-four schools had to offer at least two distinct educational programs called "mini-schools" developed by teachers with community input. Parents could send their children to any of those schools; students were accepted on a first-come, first-served basis; and transportation was also included for students attending schools outside their neighborhoods.

By the Alum Rock program's third year, three out of five Alum Rock students were using vouchers to attend mini-schools of their parents' choice. Alum Rock teachers also favored the program, so much that in 1974 they amended their contracts to prevent the program from being dismantled without their approval.[32] Yet diminishing federal commitment combined with intensifying opposition from teacher unions ultimately led to the voucher experiment's demise.[33] After stepping down as AFT president, however, Selden had a change of heart about the pilot program in 1975, when he admitted, "Kids like them, teachers like them, parents like them—even I've come to like the vouchers in Alum Rock."[34] The *New York Times* reported that the program "rates an 'A' on several counts," including "less absenteeism and vandalism, more variety in educational offerings, and more enthusiasm for school on all sides . . ."[35]

Vouchers after Alum Rock

Voucher momentum continued to build throughout the 1970s. The Teachers National Field Task Force on the Improvement and Reform of American Education issued a final report in 1974 recommending trial vouchers "to offer alternative styles of education to students and parents. . . . If this should provide a better education and more satisfactory working conditions, it is worthy of further investigation."[36] Two years later the California Supreme Court issued its second decision in the *Serrano v. Priest* student equity funding lawsuit. It instructed the state legislature that tuition vouchers would be an acceptable remedy to inequitable funding.[37] More than twenty-five years later, one of the attorneys who initiated the case, John Coons, explained that he and his colleagues "were accused by the other side of supporting vouchers, and I said, 'You're absolutely right.'"[38]

Vouchers remained a leading public policy debate throughout the 1980s. In 1986 the National Governor's Association formed the Task Force on Parent Involvement and Choice, which recommended a public school voucher program, noting, "We can choose among 100 breakfast cereals, 200 makes of automobiles, 300 different religious denominations. Thus it is ironic that in this land of choice there is so little choice within the public school system."[39] A few years later in 1989 the City Club of Chicago urged voucherizing the state school finance system so parents could choose excellent public or private schools for their children.[40] During the Reagan presidential administration, an Advisory Panel on Financing Elementary and Secondary Education found that "the theory of voucherized education [is] in harmony with our objectives of returning educational control to the most local levels and even to the homes of America's school children." In 1988 the President's Commission on Privatization urged Congress to increase

> choice in education at elementary and secondary levels, just as it now fosters choice for adults through GI Bill payments and Pell Grants. The federal government should foster choice options (including vouchers) within national programs, encourage experimentation in education choice through the Secretary of Education's leadership, and increase research efforts to collect and disseminate information about choice programs conducted by state and local education agencies.[41]

President Reagan reiterated his commitment to vouchers in his 1988 annual address to Congress, when he instructed the Department of Education to draft model legislation for states to adopt the Elementary and Secondary Education Act's (ESEA) Title I voucher programs.[42] By the time his second term was coming to a close, Reagan had abandoned hope that Congress would include parental choice in federal education programs, even though 71 percent of American voters favored parental choice, according to a 1987 Gallup Poll.[43] Reagan's assessment about the viability of vouchers at the national level was based on nearly a decade of disappointment in trying to advance federal tuition tax credits for parents of elementary and secondary private school students.

The D.C. Opportunity Scholarship Program

Almost twenty years later Congress finally enacted a voucher program. The D.C. Opportunity Scholarship Program is the only federally funded school choice program in the nation. Enacted by Congress in 2004 as part of the District of Colombia School Choice Incentive Act, the opportunity program has enabled over 5,200 low-income students to escape one of the country's most expensive, dysfunctional, and dangerous schooling systems by providing scholarships for them to attend local private schools instead.[44] The program is part of the district's three-sector funding structure established under the School Choice Incentive Act, which provides funding in equal parts for DC public schools, the district's charter schools, and the Opportunity Scholarship Program.[45] The three-sector plan's funding for public and charter schools is in addition to their regular annual appropriations.[46] To be eligible for the opportunity scholarships, which can be used for tuition, fees, and transportation, applicants' families must either receive food stamps or earn less than 185 percent of the federal poverty line (which was about $42,600 for a family of four in 2012).[47]

Since its inception, the D.C. Opportunity Scholarship Program has provided its participants with a greater chance of success. According to a formal evaluation conducted by the Department of Education in 2010, fully 91 percent of participating students graduate from high school, compared to the average of just 56 percent for DC public school students and the 70 percent average among nonparticipating students from similar backgrounds.[48] In addition, 89 percent of program graduates go on to enroll at a two- or four-year college.[49] Parental satisfaction is another measure of success. Over 90 percent of parents participating in the program for the 2011–12 school year reported satisfaction with their child's school and academic progress, and 98 percent of participating families were planning to renew their scholarships for the 2012–13 school year.[50] These impressive results also come at a significantly lower cost than the D.C. Public Schools' per-pupil spending. Whereas scholarships for the 2011–12 school year were valued up to $12,000 for a high school student and $8,000 for a K–8 student, the D.C. Public School system spends nearly $30,000 a year per student.[51]

In spite of the D.C. Opportunity Scholarship Program's success rates and lower cost, the Obama administration and some in Congress, under pressure from teachers unions, attempted to end the program. In 2009, because of teacher opposition, Obama proposed phasing out the program by cutting funding for new scholarships. Moreover, when the program was up for re-authorization in June of 2009, Democrats in Congress authorized funding only through the 2009–10 school year instead of approving a typical five-year period.[52] In an effective attempt to phase out the program entirely, Sen. Dick Durbin (D-Ill.) also inserted language into the same spending bill that limited participation to current scholarship students, meaning no new scholarship students would be accepted, and added several expensive and onerous mandates on participating private schools.[53] In response to the program's uncertain future, Secretary of Education Arne Duncan decided not to admit any new students into the program and rescinded the scholarships of over 200 students in 2009.[54]

Duncan's decision was challenged in a petition signed by a majority of the D.C. City Council, including those members representing the city's poorest districts.[55] In 2011, a bipartisan, bicameral panel led by House Speaker John Boehner (R-Ohio), and Sens. Joseph Lieberman (Independent-Conn.), Susan Collins (R-Me.), and Dianne Feinstein (D-Calif.) worked to ensure continuation and expansion of the program by including reauthorization language in a congressional resolution funding the national government for the remainder of 2011. On April 15, 2011, Obama signed a five-year reauthorization of the D.C. Opportunity Scholarship Program as part of a broader budget deal. This reauthorization expanded the number of potential scholarship recipients, increased scholarship amounts, and mandated federal evaluation of the program's effectiveness.[56] Following reauthorization, more than 1,600 students enrolled in the program for the 2011–12 school year, a 60 percent increase over the previous year.[57] In addition, the D.C. Children and Youth Investment Trust Corporation, the nonprofit organization that took over administration of the program in 2010, received more than 1,200 new applications from parents seeking to enroll their children in the program for the 2012–13 school year.[58]

In spite of signing legislation to reauthorize and fully fund the D.C. Opportunity Scholarship Program, President Obama eliminated future funding in his fiscal year 2013 budget.[59] Although Speaker Boehner made clear that Congress would appropriate funds for the program, the Department of Education effectively refused to implement the law by imposing a cap on enrollment far below the number of students previously accommodated by the program.[60] As a result of this arbitrary enrollment cap, the D.C. Children and Youth Investment Trust Corp was forced to rescind scholarship offers to more than thirty children.[61]

In June of 2012, after working to restore funding, Speaker Boehner and Senator Lieberman announced that they had finally reached an agreement with the White House to remove the enrollment cap and fully implement the reauthorized and expanded program.[62] Following this agreement, the D.C. Children and Youth Investment Trust Corporation completed its lottery for the 2012–13 school year and announced that it would be extending scholarships of up to $12,205 for high school students and $8,136 for K–8 students to 1,489 returning students and 299 new students, for a total of 1,788 scholarships.[63]

Congress came last to supporting vouchers. For more than a decade, successful voucher programs had been enacted in the states (including programs in Milwaukee, Wisconsin; Cleveland, Ohio; and Florida). Likewise, states, not Congress, took the lead on enacting tuition tax-credit scholarship programs for private elementary and secondary school students.

Tuition Tax Credits for Private School Parents: The Failure of the Feds

Federal aid for nonpublic school parents was not always a partisan idea. In fact, attempts dating back to the 1960s at offering tax relief to parents of private school students were strongly bipartisan—as were counterefforts to squelch them. Sen. Daniel Patrick Moynihan (D-N.Y.) was a strong supporter of federal education aid for public and private schools alike. In 1981 he recalled his early efforts to equalize aid for private school students. Moynihan wrote the 1964 Democratic National Platform plank that later became part of the ESEA of 1965, in which federal aid was supposed to support both public and private school students. Yet federal aid disproportionately flowed to public schools, and that is when Moynihan began supporting federal tax credits to private school parents as a second-best approach to equitable federal education policy.[64] Such credits would enable private school parents to claim deductions for their out-of-pocket education expenses, such as tuition, fees, uniforms, and textbooks, on their federal income tax returns. Unlike vouchers, which are publicly funded scholarships paid for by direct government appropriations up front, tax credits do not require any direct government funding. Moynihan was not the only Democrat who supported federal assistance to private schools.

As the 1976 Democratic Party presidential candidate, Jimmy Carter garnered 57 percent of the Catholic vote at least in part for his assurance that he was "firmly committed to conducting a systematic and continuing search for constitutionally acceptable methods of providing aid to parents whose children attend non-segregated private schools."[65] Not two years later, however, it was widely reported that the "Carter administration is opposed to tuition tax credits in any form," including an amendment to the Tuition Tax Relief Act of 1978 introduced by Senators Moynihan, Robert Packwood (R-Or.), Abraham Ribicoff (D-Conn.), and William Roth (R-Dela.) that would have extended a version of college tuition tax-credit relief to parents of elementary and secondary private school students.[66] The amendment was defeated in the Senate, by a vote of 57–41.[67] During the following presidential election Reagan highlighted Carter's broken promise and efforts to defeat the tuition tax-credit measure. "Next year, a Republican White House will assist, not sabotage, congressional efforts to enact tuition tax relief into law," Reagan pledged.[68]

In 1981 Senators Moynihan, Packwood, and Roth reintroduced their unsuccessful 1978 tuition tax-credit amendment. With a Republican majority in the Senate, it was believed that there had never been a better time for passage of federal tax credits.[69] That belief was misplaced. During the summer of 1981 Assistant Treasury Secretary John Chapoton told the Senate Finance

Subcommittee on Taxation and Debt Management that tuition tax credits would have to wait until Reagan's economic recovery plan was completed, and Senate Finance Committee Chairman Bob Dole eliminated the tuition tax-credit amendment from the Economic Recovery Act of 1981, which President Reagan signed in August.[70] The following year, Dole reiterated his opposition to federal tuition tax credits. Yet Reagan included tuition tax credits of up to $500 per child as part of his Educational Opportunity and Equity Act of 1982. He also fired Undersecretary of Education William Clohan, who opposed tuition tax credits. That summer Assistant Treasury Secretary Chapoton again testified against them to the Senate Finance Committee, but with Reagan's ongoing support the committee passed the Educational Opportunity and Equity Act by a vote of 16 to 7 on September 16. Because the Senate recessed the following month for mid-term election campaigns, the bill never went to a full floor vote.[71]

Beginning in early 1983, President Reagan called for adoption of federal tuition tax credits in both his State of the Union address as well as his budget message. He also proposed another bill to Congress, the Educational Opportunity and Equity Act of 1983, which was the first piece of legislation, besides the budget, that he introduced that year.[72] Senate Majority Leader Howard Baker (R-Tenn.) assured the president that the tax credit bill would receive the highest priority, aside from the budget, and Reagan again met with Senator Dole and other key members of Congress to assure the legislation would be acted upon as quickly as possible.[73] The bill passed out of the Senate Finance Committee with bipartisan support; however, it encountered fierce resistance in Congress. The AFT and the NEA were urging members to oppose it, and Sen. David Boren (D-Okla.) vowed to lead a filibuster against what he called the "single most damaging legislative program I have ever viewed."[74] Opponents were also questioning the constitutionality of federal tax credits, even though the US Supreme Court had upheld Minnesota's state income tax deduction for education expenses.[75]

President Reagan worked with supporters throughout the summer and fall of 1983 to attach the Educational Opportunity and Equity Act to various bills, including tax repeal, railroad, mathematics and science education, and women's pension equity bills. In November supporters succeeded in attaching it to an Olympic funding bill at Majority Leader Baker's suggestion. Senator

Boren filibustered for one day before relenting. After an hour of debate, the Senate tabled the tuition tax-credit rider legislation by a vote of 59 to 38. Nine Democrats voted against federal tuition tax credits, and twenty-four Republicans voted to table the bill, including Baker.[76] His action is not altogether surprising given that just five years earlier, he was among the more than three out of four voting Republicans, including Senator Dole, who supported the Department of Education Organization Act of 1978 (S. 991).[77] At that time, Baker declared that the bill "marks a new and exciting day for education in the United States. I believe it will help usher in an era of improved coordination and cooperation in education programs across the country."[78]

During the 1984 presidential campaign, education remained a leading issue, but tuition tax credits did not. The 1980 Republican Party platform hailed tax credits as "a matter of fairness, especially for low-income families, most of whom would be free for the first time to choose for their children those schools which best correspond to their own cultural and moral values."[79] In stark contrast, they were dropped from President Reagan's 1984 six steps "to turn our schools around and return excellence to American education."[80] Reagan referred to federal tuition tax credits in his February 1985 State of the Union address and again in his February 1986 "America's Agenda for the Future" message.[81] By 1987, however, Reagan realized that Congress would likely not advance parental choice in education, neither vouchers nor tuition tax credits. He therefore began urging the states, along with Congress, "to enact proposals that will protect the rights of parents to guide their children and select from a broad array of educational options that emphasize excellence, character, and values."[82]

While Reagan was unsuccessful in advancing elementary and secondary tuition tax credits for private school parents, Senator Moynihan credited him for his efforts.

> The President has committed himself to providing tax credits to the parents of children in nonpublic schools. It is not new for persons aspiring to the Presidency to propose such aid. George S. McGovern did. Hubert H. Humphrey did. But President Reagan is the first such person to do so in office, a very different thing. Moreover, this advocacy comes at a time when a major study of nonpublic secondary schools by a group

headed by James S. Coleman has concluded they are quite good schools indeed, and that: "The factual premises of underlying policies that would facilitate use of private schools are much better supported on the whole than those underlying policies that would constrain their use."[83]

While focus in Washington may have been shifting away from parental choice in education, elsewhere it was taking center stage of intensifying education public policy debates—debates that once again transcended partisan lines.

Tuition Tax Credits Take Off in the States

Federal tax credits and deductions for parents of private school children do not exist, but several states have enacted them. Under state tax credit and deduction programs, parents receive a state income tax credit or deduction for approved educational expenses. The types of deductible expenses vary by the state, but approved expenses often include private school tuition, books, school supplies, computers, tutoring or educational assistance programs, and transportation. As of 2015, eight states allowed for individual tax credits or deductions: Alabama, Illinois, Indiana, Iowa, Louisiana, Minnesota, South Carolina, and Wisconsin. Also as of 2015, about 890,000 filers claimed those education tax credits or deductions.[84] Minnesota's educational tax deduction dating back to 1955 is the country's oldest and is capped at $2,000 per child. The program was deemed constitutional by the US Supreme Court in their 1983 *Mueller v. Allen* decision. In 1997 Minnesota also enacted an educational tax credit that is phased out for families earning more than $33,500, depending on family size.[85] Iowa has allowed an educational tax credit worth up to $250 since 1987.[86] Illinois enacted a $500 educational expense tax credit in 1999, followed by Louisiana a decade later in 2009, when it began allowing an educational tax deduction currently capped at 80 or 90 percent of state public school funding, depending on students' grade levels.[87] Two years later in 2011, Indiana enacted an educational tax deduction worth up to $1,000.[88] That same year South Carolina enacted the most generous tax credit in the country, which allows families with special needs children to take a credit worth up to $10,000.[89]

Tax credits and deductions help relieve the financial burden on private school parents who must pay out-of-pocket tuition as well as taxes for public schools their children do not attend. Tax credit scholarships accomplish this goal by awarding eligible students scholarships so their parents can attend the private school of their choice, and they offer scholarship donors tax credits—thereby directly benefitting students and taxpayers alike. Under tax-credit scholarship programs, individuals or businesses may contribute to nonprofit scholarship-granting organizations and receive state income tax credits. Tax credit scholarships are similar to voucher scholarships in that they enable eligible elementary and secondary students to attend public or private schools of their parents' choice; however, unlike voucher programs, which are publicly funded through government appropriations, tax credit scholarships are funded with private dollars through donations to nonprofit charitable scholarship-granting organizations. This private funding makes the administration of tax credit scholarships less susceptible to state and federal challenge.[90]

The country's first tax credit scholarship program was enacted in Arizona in April 1997.[91] As of the 2014–15 school year, twenty programs in sixteen states awarded about 195,000 scholarships.[92] Both publicly funded voucher scholarships and privately funded tax-credit scholarships have raised constitutional concerns over the years. Yet the US Supreme Court upheld the constitutionality of vouchers in 2002 in *Zelman v. Simmons-Harris*, ruling that public funds may support individual private-education choices when parents, not government, are doing the choosing. Because parents are making an educational, not a religious choice, there is no constitutional violation. The constitutionality of tax-credit scholarship programs is even clearer. In April 2011 the US Supreme Court settled the nearly fifteen-year battle over Arizona's—and the country's—oldest tax-credit scholarship program. Opponents of the Arizona program insisted that private donations are actually government funds. So understood, scholarship donors were paying their state taxes to nonprofit scholarship-granting organizations instead of the state government. The US Supreme Court's decision in *Arizona Christian School Tuition Organization v. Winn* stated that opponents' position "assumes that all income is government property, even if it has not come into the tax collector's hands. That premise finds no basis in standing jurisprudence."[93]

Schools by Charter:
Privately Operated Public Charter Schools

Another parental choice concept has also become popularized. The charter school concept originated in 1974 with a conference paper, "Education by Charter," by the late Ray Budde, a professor of educational administration at the University of Massachusetts Graduate School of Education. Budde used the phrase *charter school* to describe a district contract model that would allow teachers be more innovative in the classroom and manage schools.[94] In 1985 the president of the AFT, Albert Shanker, began advocating for greater public school choice to improve the likelihood of a good match between the interests of teachers and their students. Unlike Budde, however, Shanker envisioned charter schools as distinct from districts and created by teachers, or parents with teachers, who wanted new curricula or teaching strategies to improve instruction and student learning. In 1991, Shanker's vision became a reality when Minnesota passed legislation allowing the country's first charter school to open. Within just five years, more than 250 charter schools were operating in ten states. Commenting on this phenomenon, Shanker concluded, "As far as I'm concerned every school should be a charter school."[95]

Charter schools are public schools founded by teachers, parents, or community organizations that operate under a written contract with a state, school district, or other entity. Because they are public schools, charter schools are open to all students, they cannot charge tuition, they have no religious affiliation, and they abide by the same state and federal testing, financial, antidiscrimination, health, and safety regulations as traditional, district-run public schools. Unlike traditional public schools, however, charter schools operate with more autonomy and flexibility. Freed from district control, charter schools have more freedom to innovate, which has given rise to a wide variety of educational strategies, including back-to-basics, vocational, college preparatory, and Montessori.[96]

In exchange for more autonomy, charter schools are held strictly accountable for meeting the terms of their performance contracts, which detail each charter school's mission, program, goals, students served, financial plan, and assessment methods. The duration of charter schools' contracts varies from state to state, but contracts typically range from three to five years. At the end of the contract, the chartering agency determines whether to renew or end a school's contract based on academic results and fiscal management, as well as any other stipulated terms. Currently, nearly 3 million students nationwide attend more than 6,700 public charter schools in forty-three states and Washington, DC, representing more than 6 percent of all public schools nationwide.[97]

Public charter schools receive up to 36 percent less per-pupil funding than district public schools receive.[98] Unlike public school districts, charter schools have no taxing authority.[99] Therefore they have to live within their operating and capital budgets. Most important, if charter schools do not fulfill the terms of their charter contracts, they can be shut down rather than struggling along for years or decades at a time receiving additional taxpayer funding to turn their performance around. Besides providing students and their families with more educational options at a fraction of the cost to taxpayers, charter schools are also serving as incubators for more recent parental choice programs, including virtual or online learning opportunities. Charter schools are also important reform models under emerging "parent trigger" laws that empower parents to convert failing district-run public schools into independently operated charter schools.

Parental Choice Programs: Results Without the Red Tape

While overall student performance has remained about the same over several decades, available research on the eleven voucher scholarship programs and nine tax-credit scholarship programs in existence through 2010 shows positive results. These programs typically serve students from low-income families, students from failing public schools, and a higher proportion of students with disabilities compared to the public school population, 14 percent compared to 12 percent.[100] Likewise, they disproportionately serve low-income, minority, and academically struggling students. More than 54 percent of charter school students are classified as low-income, compared to 41 percent of district public school students. More than 52 percent of charter school students are also minorities, compared to 44 percent of district public school students.[101]

Achievement is also higher among parental choice program participants. For example, Florida charter schools have high school graduation rates 7 to

15 percentage points higher than district public schools. College attendance rates are also 8 to 10 percentage points higher. Graduation rates among D.C. Opportunity Scholarship recipients are also 21 percentage points higher than their public school counterparts.[102]

Overall, academic achievement gains have been documented among parental choice program participants in twelve of the thirteen existing "gold standard" scientific studies conducted as of 2015. No negative effects have been documented, and the average learning gains among parental choice students work out to nearly an extra month per year.[103] In fact, the sole gold standard study that failed to document student achievement gains was subsequently discredited when more than 120 scientific re-analyses of the data using rigorous methods found positive effects on the academic performance of the participating parental choice program students in all cases, 90 percent of which (108) were statistically significant.[104]

Contrary to concerns from opponents, parental choice programs also introduce healthy competition that puts powerful pressure on public schools to improve, which benefits nonparticipating students. Specifically, of the fourteen studies conducted on the competitive effects of parental choice programs in Florida, Arizona, Milwaukee, and the District of Columbia, eleven documented all positive effects from competition. The remaining three found no effects. Meta-analyses of hundreds of scientific studies spanning decades also show beneficial effects of competition on public schools "across all outcomes," including higher student achievement, graduation rates, efficiency, teacher salaries, and smaller class sizes, according to Columbia University Teachers College researchers.[105] States and taxpayers also benefit from better results at much lower costs. For example, tax-credit scholarship programs save taxpayer dollars because every student who uses a scholarship to attend a participating private school, which generally charges tuition that is lower than the public school per-pupil funding average, conserves state general funds. Depending on the state program, it takes only a small participation rate for tax-credit scholarship program savings to offset the up-front tax credit revenue loss to the general fund. As of 2006, operating tax-credit scholarship programs saved a combined $204 million in state and school district budgets in Arizona, Florida, and Pennsylvania. Existing voucher programs saved an additional $240 million from 1990 through 2006, and since that time the cumulative savings have been estimated to be at least $1.7 billion.[106]

Voucher and tax-credit scholarship programs, along with public charter schools, are not static parental choice reforms. On the contrary, they are inspiring a rich array of emerging dynamic reforms with great potential to restore parental control over their children's education.

Revolutionizing Learning Through Virtual Schools

Virtual schools provide students online learning opportunities as a supplement to or in place of traditional classroom learning. State virtual schools are usually created by legislation, a state-level agency, or a governor's office. Typically a state education agency administers virtual schools. Notable exceptions are Colorado's state virtual school, Colorado Online Learning, an independent nonprofit organization; the Michigan Virtual School, a division of a 501(c)(3) nonprofit organization, the Michigan Virtual University; and the Idaho Digital Learning Academy, a distinct government entity that by law exists apart from the state education agency.[107] Most state virtual schools are funded by state appropriations or grants, as well as the federal government, private foundation grants, and course fees.[108]

Just sixteen states had established virtual schools as of the 2002–03 school year.[109] As of the 2013–14 school year, thirty states had fully online schools enrolling 315,000 students, and 760,000 students in 26 states were taking supplemental courses through virtual schools.[110] State-led online initiatives differ from state virtual schools because they provide online tools and resources for schools statewide, but they do not have a centralized student enrollment or registration system for students in online courses. State-led online-learning initiatives are also funded mostly by separate legislative appropriations.[111]

Actual costs of providing online education include expert teachers, curriculum licensing and development, computers, course-delivery and data systems, special services, and physical materials. Virtual schools have upfront technological costs such as hardware, and bandwidth. Teachers also travel for in-person training and technical support. Yet overall virtual schools and programs are highly cost-effective. Available research finds that a state virtual school needs $4 million in start-up and operational funding to serve 5,000 one-semester enrollments.[112] Experts believe that the cost of serving full-time students in virtual schools ranges from $7,200 to $8,300 per student.[113] The operating costs at Kansas virtual schools were between $300 and $5,000 lower than the per-student costs at traditional public schools.[114] After reviewing the available audits and cost estimates, researchers at Indiana University concluded that the "operating costs of virtual schools fluctuate from program to program, but are generally lower or equal to the costs of traditional education."[115]

John Watson and Butch Gemin of Evergreen Consulting Associates, an online-learning consulting and research firm in Evergreen, Colorado, explain, "States that fund based on successful completion find that having defined benchmarks or milestones for incremental completion (for example, 50 percent and 100 percent complete) provides a more rational and predictable approach than 'all or nothing.'"[116] Student-centered, results-based financing is a cornerstone of the Florida Virtual School. "The funding includes an innovative twist in that it is based on student performance or successful completion of virtual programs or courses rather than seat time. Florida's virtual education options are not merely reforming education; they are transforming education," state education officials say.[117]

A results- or outputs-based financing structure represents a profound but necessary public policy shift if virtual schools are to succeed. This finance structure will require policymakers to revise "seat-time" mandates, which organize students by age-determined groupings, and mandatory attendance laws governed by school-day and school-year regulations.[118] As Florida Virtual School CEO Julie Young explains:

> In our early days of development, we were highly influenced by a 1992 SCANS report [Secretary's Commission on Achieving Necessary Skills]. One quote we've returned to over and again says, 'In our current system, time is the constant and achievement the variable. We have it backwards. Achievement should be the constant and time the variable.' As we continue to evolve, we keep this central focus on achievement as our guidepost for development.[119]

Holly Sagues, the chief strategist and policy officer for the Florida Virtual School, explained that before 2003 when legislation was passed changing the funding model from an appropriations-based system to a per-pupil, performance-based model, "We would figure out how many students we would be able to serve. . . . It really does hurt kids, because we had a waiting list a mile long, but we weren't funded appropriately. There was no way for us to grow our enrollment base with that model."[120] Once the funding model was changed, enrollment at the Florida Virtual School more than doubled, from 14,000 to 31,000 in one school year.[121]

Virtual schools also offer many areas for cost savings. Virtual schools, including virtual charter schools, have no taxing authority, which encourages sticking to budgets because they cannot make up for any shortfalls by raising property taxes as traditional public school districts do. For example, the Arkansas Virtual Academy serves grades K–8 across the state and operates as its own school district. It is funded through the same formula as a brick-and-mortar school, $5,905 per student, but it does not receive additional money from property taxes.[122] Thus such schools must operate within given annual budgets because they cannot tap local taxpayers for funding overrides. Virtual schools also do not have the facilities, cafeteria, and transportation costs traditional public school districts do. In fact, developing countries are turning to virtual education because they simply cannot afford the high construction and operations costs of traditional schools. In Singapore, for example, all secondary schools use online learning, and all teachers are trained to teach online. Each year it holds E-Learning Week when bricks-and-mortar schools are closed down to ensure virtual schooling is used to provide continuity in learning and enhance disaster preparedness. In fact, Singapore is also working to train its teachers to use *Second Life* (an online virtual world) for educating students.[123]

In addition to construction and maintenance savings, virtual schools achieve efficiency in other ways as well. Open education resources are helping make online courses more cost-efficient because online courses can be reused by multiple teachers.[124] Virtual education is also cost-effective because it offers students courses that meet their needs but that their school districts cannot afford to provide. It also does not require new construction to do so.[125] For states with large rural communities, online education makes it affordable for schools to hire high-quality, high-demand, and specialized teachers; under brick-and-mortar class size mandates, they would not have enough students the justify the teachers' salaries.[126] As the Alliance for Excellent Education concludes, "Whatever the configuration, innovative technologies offer the potential to improve productivity in schools just as it has in other sectors."[127] With a results-oriented focus and financing structure, virtual schools have strong incentives to promote attendance, curb truancy, and engage students better.[128] Research has shown that compared to traditional curricular and instructional approaches available to teachers, online teachers have more flexibility in engaging students and their colleagues and presenting content in innovative ways. Emerging, interactive technologies help students develop in-depth, higher-level thinking and extract significant meaning from the content.[129]

Enhancing educational access to a more diverse student population is another benefit of virtual schooling. Students want access to a greater variety of course offerings than their schools provide.[130] Students "need learning tools and processes that are not tethered to time, place and geographic boundaries."[131] Utah's state virtual school, the Electronic High School, provides supplemental courses and grants diplomas to students who are home-schooled exclusively, those who have dropped out of school and their class has graduated, and students with district referrals.[132]

Empirical research about the academic achievement of K–12 students participating in online education is sparse. A recent analysis sponsored by the US Department of Education, however, reviewed more than 1,000 studies comparing online learning with traditional learning. Online classes, whether completely online or hybrid (a blend of traditional classroom and online instruction), produce stronger average student achievement than traditional classes and promote more time-on-task.[133]

Evidence from specific state-based online education programs suggests they can improve student achievement at a lower cost that traditional classroom instruction.[134] Research also shows access to online courses increases on-time graduation rates and college/workforce readiness.[135] For example, 2009 passing rates of Georgia Virtual School students exceeded the state average for almost all courses that require an end-of-course test. The Georgia Virtual School plans to expand on this success by implementing proficiency-based advancement rules so students can move on to more advanced work when they are ready, rather than be held back by arbitrary seat-time regulations.[136] Likewise, legislation passed in 2009 in Missouri removed seat-time requirements so school districts offering virtual classes can be funded at 90 percent of the full-time amount for online students, once they complete their courses.[137] Ohio is enhancing online learning options by increasing advanced-placement course options to underserved students and abandoning rigid seat-time requirements. "Oftentimes, credit flexibility engages students in real-world learning experiences which better prepares them for college and careers," according to Ohio education officials.[138] Online education in Ohio empowers students to earn high school credits based on demonstrated subject area competency instead of, or in combination with, completing hours of classroom instruction. They can earn credits by completing coursework or even testing out of courses.[139]

Empowering Parents through Parent Trigger Laws

In January 2010 California became the first state to enact parent trigger legislation, which allows parents to petition to intervene and require failing schools take steps toward improving. If enough parents petition, failing schools can be converted to charter schools, staff can be replaced, or schools can be closed down. Parents with students in Compton's McKinley Elementary became the first group to succeed in using the law. In spite of repeated efforts by the Compton Unified School District to invalidate signatures and intimidate parents, on December 7, 2010, a group of fifty McKinley parents submitted their parent trigger petition to district officials with enough signatures to require them to convert the failing school to a charter school.[140] Like the Compton group, parents with children in chronically failing public schools consider parent trigger a lifeline. In contrast, the California Federation of Teachers has likened the parent trigger rule to a "lynch mob provision," while others in the education world, such as Bruce Baker, professor at Rutgers University Graduate School of Education, have equated parental control of public schools with "mob rule."[141]

The events leading up to the enactment of California's landmark parent trigger legislation are instructive. They serve as a glimpse into life without government operation of schools and represent a microcosm of how restoration of parental control over their children's education would work. After the demise of the Alum Rock pilot voucher program, numerous pieces of parental choice legislation were stymied in the California legislature. As K–12 education voucher and tax-credit scholarship programs proliferated in other states, the California legislature defeated close to a dozen pieces of similar legislation starting in the mid-1990s, including an Opportunity Scholarship Program for low-income students in April 1997.[142] In 2001, a tax credit plan to provide low-income students with private school scholarships was introduced but was killed in committee. It met the same fate when reintroduced the following year.[143] At the urging of parents and the Coalition on Urban Renewal and Education, a voucher program modeled after the Cal Grant higher education program was introduced in 2003 for the Compton Unified School District. It died in 2004 because the legislature failed to act on it.[144]

In 2008, a record-breaking five parental choice bills were introduced in the California Assembly. Three bills would have freed students from schools shown to be unsafe or failing by allowing them to transfer to other schools. Another bill would have provided tax credits to parents of private school students and home-schooled children, and the fifth bill would have let parents of special needs children use scholarships to choose other schools without having to hire attorneys and sue their school districts for private placements. The Assembly Education Committee heard the safe schools, special education, and one of the failing schools scholarships bills, while the Assembly Revenue and Taxation Committee heard the failing schools and tax-credit scholarship bills. Neither committee took action on any of those parental choice bills.

While this opposition continued, supported by the California Teachers Association and other public-schooling special interest groups, local education leaders and parents were laying the foundation for the country's first parent trigger law. In 2007 a high-profile showdown took place between a reform-minded, inner-city school principal and the California Teachers Association affiliate, the United Teachers of Los Angeles. Alain Leroy Locke Senior High School in the Los Angeles neighborhood of Watts was founded in response to the 1967 riots. The school was supposed to provide the neighborhood's minority students a high-quality education. It didn't. By 2006 just 5 percent of Locke High graduates went on to college, while 51 percent of the student body dropped out before graduating. Reform-minded principal Frank Wells was determined to turn things around. First he took back control of the school from rival gangs that had been terrorizing students. Shortly thereafter Wells began requiring teachers to submit weekly lesson plans, and that's when he began to face opposition from the teachers union. Wells also bucked prevailing orthodoxy that says school failure is the result of insufficient funding. "The more you fail, the more money they throw at you," Wells told the *Los Angeles Times.* "We're filthy rich; I don't want any more of your money. Send me quality teachers."[145] The final straw, however, came when Wells devised a plan to turn the failing school into a charter school, which would free it from onerous district and teachers union regulations standing in the way of improvement.

Wells had the support of Locke High parents, who likened their children's classrooms to a zoo, with students running amok while teachers sat idly by. Wells explained that it would take up to 100 years or more to get rid of all the bad teachers at his school given the union contract rules.[146] The charter school provided a quicker resolution, but his efforts to convert the failing district school into a charter school resulted in allegations that he allowed teachers to leave their classrooms to sign the necessary petition. In May 2007 the Los Angeles Unified School District had Wells removed from his office by three police officers and reassigned him to a district office where he was paid $600 a day to do nothing. Reports from signature gatherers later confirmed that none of the alleged petition improprieties had occurred, and Wells was exonerated. So, too, were Locke High students. In September 2007 the Los Angeles Board of Education voted 5 to 2 to hand over operations of Locke High School to Green Dot, a successful charter school operator. As of 2012, the Locke High School graduation rate had grown to 68 percent, and 56 percent of graduates—not 5 percent—were heading off to college.[147]

Not long thereafter in January 2009, a group of Los Angeles parents formed their own union, Parent Revolution, to advocate for the educational rights of their children. Working with community activists and California state legislators, they succeeded in enacting the country's first parent trigger legislation in 2010.[148] As of 2012, twenty states have considered parent trigger legislation, and six states besides California have adopted such a law: Connecticut, Indiana, Louisiana, Mississippi, Ohio, and Texas.[149] A national poll commissioned by StudentsFirst in 2012 found 70 percent of likely voters support parent trigger laws. These results were identical to those in a separate 2012 PDK/Gallup Poll.[150]

Education Savings Accounts: Decoupling
Government Financing and Management of Schools

Education savings accounts provide parents who withdraw their child from a public district or charter school with access to a government-authorized private savings account funded by a percentage of the child's state education dollars. Such accounts provide parents with more choice than vouchers because the account funds can be used for a variety of authorized educational expenses including private school tuition, textbooks, fees, tutoring, and college savings. In 2011 Arizona became the first state to enact enabling legislation, called the Empowerment Scholarship Accounts Program. Originally limited to students with special needs, this program served about 142 students in the 2011–12 school year.[151] Under the rules of the program, 90 percent of the funding the state would have sent to the public school district as base support calculated under state statute is placed in savings accounts for participating students instead. Parents simply inform the state education agency of their preference for a nonpublic school option and sign a form promising not to enroll their child in a public school during the corresponding school year. Any unspent money left in the account after the child graduates high school can be used for college expenses.[152]

In September 2011 the Arizona School Board Association, the Arizona Education Association, and others challenged the Empowerment Scholarship Accounts Program on the grounds that it violates Arizona's constitutional aid and religions clauses. The Maricopa County Superior Court rejected those arguments in January 2012, and the following May Arizona Governor Jan Brewer signed legislation expanding program eligibility for the 2013–14 school year to three new groups of students: students enrolled in a school or school district that receives a letter grade of D or F from the state; children of active-duty military parents; and children who have been adopted or are in the process of being adopted out of Arizona's foster care system.[153] In 2014 the Arizona Supreme Court reaffirmed the constitutionality of the program.[154] Also in 2014 Florida became the second state to enact an educational savings program, called the Personal Learning Scholarship Account program, which operates very similarly to Arizona's original program for special needs students.[155] As of this writing, three more states adopted ESA programs in 2015: Mississippi, Tennessee, and Nevada, whose programs stands out for making all public school students eligible regardless of special needs or circumstances.[156]

Parental Choice Succeeds
Where Federal Intervention Has Failed

While the release in 1983 of *A Nation at Risk* generated significant federal activity in education and has even been credited with saving the US Department of Education from elimination, none of the reforms it inspired included parental choice in education. In 1990 another wave of school reform was inspired by the Brookings Institution publication, *Politics, Markets, and America's Schools* by John Chubb and Terry Moe. Using the best available empirical data from the US Department of Education, Chubb and Moe showed that private schools outperformed public schools. The reason: Public schools were smothered by bureaucracy. Despite the thousands of reforms ushered in as a result of *A Nation at Risk*, including increasing teacher salaries, reducing class sizes, decentralizing consolidated school districts, and mandating teacher certification, public school performance had not improved. Chubb and Moe explained why:

> Reformers believe the source of [educational] problems is to be found in and around the schools, and that schools can be "made" better by relying on existing institutions to impose the proper reforms. We believe existing institutions cannot solve the problem, because they are the problem—and that the key to better schools is institutional reform.[157]

Thus the empirical evidence makes clear that government cannot solve the problem because government *is* the problem. Accountability must come from the private, not public sector, through parents choosing their children's schools. Schools must be immediately accountable to parents, instead of politicians, bureaucrats, or vested special interest groups. Absent parents' freedom to choose, there are no incentives to reform.

Another important work was published in 2003 by Stanford University's Hoover Institution, *Education and Capitalism: How Overcoming Our Fear of Markets Can Improve America's Schools*, by Herbert J. Walberg and Joseph L. Bast. While Chubb and Moe used political science to explain the failure of government schools, Walberg and Bast relied on the emerging field of education economics. Their work was possible in large part because of the significant number of parental choice programs enacted, beginning shortly after publication of *Politics, Markets, and America's Schools*. In 1990 Milwaukee became the first city to enact a voucher program along the lines of economist Milton Friedman's recommendations. Shortly thereafter, Cleveland followed suit, then Florida in 1999 with a statewide voucher program. In 1991 Minnesota enacted the first charter school law. In 1997 Arizona became the first state to enact a tuition tax-credit scholarship program. For Walberg and Bast, "The failure to understand economics leads to romanticism about the ability of government to finance and operate schools."[158] Parental choice helps put to rest such romanticism and awaken instead some much-needed reality.

Since the publication of *Education and Capitalism*, the number of parental school choice programs nationwide has nearly quadrupled, from seven in 2003 to fifty-seven in 2015.[159] Over the same period, the number of charter schools more than doubled from 2,959 in 2003 to 6,440 in 2014.[160] The expansion of parental choice is increasingly bipartisan; for example, almost half of all parental choice programs enacted in the states since 2007 were either approved by Democratic legislatures or signed by Democratic governors.[161]

In almost six decades since Friedman and others proposed education vouchers, parental choice options have expanded significantly. Currently, more than 300,000 students nationwide are participating in private-school parental choice programs using publicly funded voucher scholarships, privately financed tax-credit scholarships, and education savings accounts.[162] Charter schools enrolled more than 2.5 million students as of the 2013–14 school year.[163] Charter schools are also serving as incubators for additional parent-driven education reforms, including the conversion of failing district-run public schools to privately operated charter schools through parent trigger laws. Virtual schools, often operated as charter schools, are an increasingly popular education option that decouples geography from learning opportunities and offers highly individualized, student-centered instruction.[164] More than 1.8 million students were enrolled in online, or distance, education courses during the 2009–2010 school year.[165] These and other education reforms have advanced without—and in some cases in spite—of the US Department of Education.

Most important, the continuing proliferation of parental choice programs constitutes a needed restoration of the primacy of parents in their children's education. For all the legislative assurances and platitudes from government education officials about their importance, parents are largely relegated to the status of glorified bake sale boosters under a government schooling system. Government schooling defenders frequently cite the lack of parental involvement to justify school failures. Yet when such involvement matters most, namely, when it is time to pick their children's schools, parents' choices are largely constrained to where they can afford to live. It is no accident that the establishment of the first US Department of Education back in 1867 was preceded by a growing centralization and homogenization of education away from parents, localities, and state governments. Animating such centralization was the belief, in the words of the Wisconsin Teachers Association in 1865, that "children are property of the state."[166] That view was formerly repudiated in 1925 when the US Supreme Court ruled in *Pierce v. Society of Sisters* that:

> The fundamental theory of liberty upon which all governments in this Union repose excluded any general power of the state to standardize its children by forcing them to accept instruction from public teachers only. The child is not the mere creature of the state; those who nurture him and direct his destiny have the right and the high duty, to recognize and prepare him for additional obligations.[167]

Parental choice programs—more so than any assurances from politicians and government bureaucracies—ensure that fundamental liberty against standardization in principle and practice.

12

A Blueprint for the Next Thirty Years

Privatizing the Federal Role

WHILE MANY HIGHLY successful parental choice programs advancing education are already being initiated by state and local governments, another source of significant activity removing federal control is support for schools and their students from nonprofit or philanthropic organizations and private enterprise.

One area where privatization would have particularly positive effects is grants for postsecondary education. Admittedly, this thinking will buck the tide of current opinion on who should pay for a student's college or university degree. The Obama administration, along with postsecondary representatives and others, advanced a college-for-all agenda. It is no surprise, then, that a growing number of students believe that a college education is an entitlement that should be publicly funded, not a private good that they should pay for. More surprisingly, a recent survey of American CEOs revealed that close to half of them (47 percent) think the federal government has the greatest responsibility for improving postsecondary completion rates. Less than one in five of American business leaders (19 percent) believe they should take the lead instead.[1]

Understanding a few basics about postsecondary finance illustrates how privatization would produce benefits. On average, public, four-year institutions received $38,500 in revenue per undergraduate in the 2009–10 academic year, consisting of roughly $10,900 in self-generated income and gifts; $6,300 in government grants and contracts; and about $6,100 in other revenue. Most of that revenue is designated for specific purposes, such as ongoing capital projects or research. Rounding out the remaining postsecondary revenue is $7,300 in tuition and $7,900 in general local, state, and federal appropriations.[2]

Thus federal support for *students* actually goes to colleges and universities, where it has a negative impact.

In 1955 economist Milton Friedman suggested that postsecondary institutions would become more efficient if they competed for students and their education dollars.[3] In the decades that followed, several other leading economists from across the political spectrum concurred that directing public funds to students as grants would be more effective in promoting equal educational opportunity and improved access among low-income students.[4] Hong Kong University researchers Ben Jongbloed and Jos Koelman summarized the consensus in their extensive review of the related literature, stating that "the lack of competition in the [higher education] public sector has an ossifying effect. . . . The only way for schools to perform better is . . . a subjugation of schools to more competitive pressure."[5] Nearly forty years after Friedman first advocated against government subsidies for higher education, and after seeing the results of federal financial aid and other programs, Friedman explained, "I am much more dubious than I was when I wrote *Capitalism and Freedom* that there is any justification at all for government subsidy of higher education. The spread of PC [political correctness] right now would seem to be a very strong negative externality." In fact, Friedman suggested that "higher education should be taxed to offset its negative externalities."[6]

In this chapter, we look at the history of federally funded student loans and the benefits that would flow from putting student loans in the hands of private lending institutions. This strategy would do more than help students to achieve the education that matches their career goals. It would also tighten the reins on wasteful spending by postsecondary institutions and thus move to reduce the cost of higher education.

Student Direct Loans: Historical Analysis

The federal government first authorized $48 million in higher education loans back in 1958 under the National Defense Education Act. At that time eligibility was limited to low-income students as well as students who excelled in math, science, and foreign languages—skills deemed critical to the national interest for competing with the former Soviet Union. While good grades were subsequently eliminated as an eligibility requirement, the National Defense

Education Act gave rise to what are now need-based Federal Perkins Loans. A few years later, the Higher Education Act of 1965 created new federal loan programs for middle-income students and their families, Stafford Loans and Federal Family Education Loans.[7]

Over the next several decades federal student loan programs have continued to expand.[8] A sweeping change was made as part of the Health Care and Education Reconciliation Act of 2010, or Obamacare. Included in that act was the Student Aid and Fiscal Responsibility Act, or SAFRA, which expanded the Federal Direct Student Loan Program by ending federally guaranteed loans issued through Federal Family Education Loans. In other words, the federal government ended the practice of backing student loans issued by private lenders with taxpayer dollars and instead requires all new loans to originate directly from the US Department of Education. Thus direct federal lending has replaced federally guaranteed lending. This change has been criticized as a federal takeover of education and characterized as instituting a federal monopoly over student lending. The reality is that private-sector, free-market forces have had only a nominal (at best) influence on federal student loans for decades.

Under the guise of college affordability and access, Congress routinely modifies interest rates. As part of the College Cost Reduction and Access Act of 2007, for example, Congress progressively cut student loan interest rates from the 2006 rate of 6.8 percent down to 3.4 percent in 2011.[9] When that rate was set to expire, Congress froze the 3.4 rate for an additional year as part of the highway funding reauthorization bill, the Moving Ahead for Progress in the 21st Century Act.[10]

The US Department of Education also has an abysmal oversight record. Fraud and abuse have permeated this single-largest program since the department's inception. A 1991 Senate investigation concluded that between 1983 and 1990, fraud and mismanagement of the federal student loan program cost taxpayers a staggering $13 billion. The US Department of Education was vilified for its "gross mismanagement, ineptitude, and neglect," as well as its "dismal record" of handling loan abuses. Just three years later in 1994, the department admitted to losing as much as 10 percent of its entire budget annually—around $3 billion—because of defaults, fraud, and waste, prompting Secretary of Education Richard Riley to blast the department's administration and oversight as "worse than lax."[11] In 2002, the Government Accountability Office (GAO) set up a sting in which it created a fake school that enrolled phantom students who were awarded $55,000 in federal student loans.[12] The US Department of Education's incompetent management of federal student loans remained the subject of congressional hearings for the next several years.

The department's Inspector General John P. Higgins, Jr., testified before the House Committee on Government Reform in 2005 that federal student aid programs had been on the GAO's annual "high-risk" list since 1990. Only after promising to improve internal controls was it removed in early 2005. Nevertheless, Higgins noted, "The Department's student loan programs are large, complex, and inherently risky due to their design, reliance on numerous entities, and the nature of the borrower population. The loan programs rely on over 6,000 postsecondary institutions, more than 3,000 lenders, 35 guaranty agencies, and many contractors to assist in the administration of the programs."[13] During a May 10, 2007, House Committee on Education and Labor hearing, Chairman Rep. George Miller (D-Calif.) blasted the US Department of Education, saying its "oversight failures have been monumental. . . . Was this simply laziness? Was it incompetence? Was it a deliberate decision to look the other way while these things happened? Or was it a failing more sinister than that?" In response Education Secretary Margaret Spellings testified that "federal student aid is crying out for reform. The system is redundant, it's Byzantine, and it's broken. In fact, it's often more difficult for students to get aid than it is for bad actors to game the system."[14]

Not only had numerous defaults and instances of fraud come to light, financial institutions were also gaming the system. The 9.5 percent interest rate on student loans had been eliminated in the 1990s, yet many lenders used a loophole to collect federal subsidies at this higher rate, costing taxpayers billions of dollars.[15] This and other abuses continued despite oversight of the private loan market by the Federal Trade Commission, Securities and Exchange Commission, Federal Deposit Insurance Corporation, and the Federal Reserve.[16] The US Department of Education, however, was no innocent bystander.

In 2007 the GAO documented the widespread practice of lenders giving kickbacks to higher education institutions in exchange for preferred lender recommendations. Meanwhile, the department had not issued guidance on improper inducements since 1989, a situation that was not rectified until 2008.[17] Investigations revealed that a sole lender made 80 percent of all student loans at between 900 and 1,400 higher education institutions nationwide. More than 500 of those institutions recommended only one lender.[18] The US Department of Education responded by sending clarifications letters to 900 of those higher education institutions, but it issued no sanctions.[19] Such inaction is not surprising given that as of 2007, the US Department of Education had used its sanctioning authority only twice in twenty years to enforce prohibitions against improper inducements and limitations on borrower choice.[20]

The private sector is more accountable that the public sector when it comes to delivering goods and services because providers are motivated by the prospect of making a profit, yet restrained by lasting consequences if they break the law. Thus, powerful incentives keep the profit motive from running amok without extinguishing the drive to innovate and reach new clientele. The previous guaranteed federal lending system represented the worst of all possible worlds by dangling hundreds of billions of taxpayer dollars in front of lenders who had little to fear in the way of consequences. Specifically, not only did the federal government subsidize banks to compensate them for lower student loan interest rates along with administrative costs, it also used taxpayer dollars to insulate private-sector banks from poor lending decisions by subsidizing them up to 97 percent of the principal if students defaulted.[21] Making matters worse, student loan funds pass through institutions of higher education that also have little incentive to reduce the prospect of cash flow with rigorous oversight—particularly in the absence of any real consequences.

Yet direct federal lending is even worse. Under the current direct lending system, student loans originate with the US Department of Education, which has no incentive to make solid loans because there are no consequences for making bad ones. One way or another, taxpayers foot the bill. As for claims by Secretary of Education Arne Duncan about eliminating the "middle man," and in spite of all the rhetoric about the evils of private-sector profits preceding the switch, under the current direct federal lending scheme the US Department of Education still pays private-sector lenders to manage the student loans it issues.[22] With no incentive to make good loans—and lots of political pressure simply to make more loans—taxpayers will likely pay significantly more on defaults.

As it is, the three-year cohort default rate as of September 2011 was 13.4 percent, or 489,000 students.[23] What's more, a 2013 Office of Inspector General audit found that the US Department of Education's oversight of some $5.3 billion in active related contracts was weak, resulting in contracts that are overpriced and underperforming. Collecting on bad loans is a prime example. The OIG reported that since the department's system for handling defaulted student loans was implemented in October 2011 by a contractor, the "entities that service Federal student aid loans," namely private lenders, "have accumulated more than $1.1 billion in defaulted student loans that should be transferred to the Department for management and collection." Those bad debts have been accumulating because the updated collection system "has been unable to accept transfer of these loans." Consequently, "the Department is not pursuing collection remedies and borrowers are unable to take steps to remove their loans from default status."[24] Overpayments, along with bad debt, are also piling up because of flaws in the department's oversight of both the Direct Loan program and the Pell Grant program.[25]

Meanwhile, the Obama administration stayed mum about the fact that the US Department of Education has made a $120 billion profit over the past five fiscal years, largely due to low borrowing costs for the government and fixed interest rates on student loans.[26] Federal financial aid was intended to make college more affordable, not to enhance government balance sheets.

In addition, a growing body of evidence indicates government subsidies actually contribute to higher postsecondary costs.[27] The reason is that taxpayer-subsidized federal lending removes pressure on postsecondary institutions to keep costs down, while introducing perverse incentives to raise prices. In fact, college tuition prices alone have been increasing about twice the general inflation rate since 1958 when federal lending first started.[28] Robert E. Martin and Andrew Gillen of the Center for College Affordability and Productivity explain:

> Despite vast increases in financial aid over the years, the cost of attending college has continued to soar. It appears that colleges often delib-

erately raise their prices when aid is available, in essence "capturing" the aid. The end result is that higher financial aid does not produce an improvement in college affordability but rather an increased ability on the parts of colleges to fund other programs which are not related to fulfilling their educational missions. . . . The growth in colleges' costs and associated spending is the main obstacle for improving college affordability and . . . while external factors do contribute to the increase in costs for colleges, it is the decisions of colleges themselves that are the main driver of higher costs, particularly the desire to increase prestige.

Martin and Gillen found that if colleges actually used financial aid to lower costs for students, a typical four-year college degree would cost about $3,500 less, and overall higher education spending would be $59 billion lower each year.[29]

Student Direct Loans: A Privatizing Strategy

A privatized student loan system would work much like mortgage lending works now, except students would be approved for specified funding based on the strength of their loan application, which would include future employment prospects.

Students would detail their intended course of study, degree plans, and future employment goals. They would also narrow down their preferred postsecondary institutions based on the quality of their programs, prices, and graduation and employment rates. This simple exercise would restore a much-needed dose of reality among the growing college-is-an-entitlement generation, many of whom do not seem to appreciate that borrowing $100,000 or more for a degree to get a job that will pay at most $30,000 annually is not a smart investment. This simple exercise would make students savvier consumers, increasingly sensitive to college pricing; with loan cash in hand; they could more readily demand value or go elsewhere. Smart for-profit lenders (like sensible philanthropic scholarship organizations) would require end-of-semester progress reports and adjust students' qualified loans according to a mutually agreed upon set of criteria.

Over time this process would restore a sense of reality to postsecondary institutions as well, which, as *US News & World Report*'s Brian Kelly observed:

> If colleges were businesses, they would be ripe for hostile takeovers, complete with serious cost-cutting and painful reorganizations. You can be sure those business analysts would ask: Is the consumer getting the product we promised? What do you actually learn here? Can you guarantee a job? . . . On average, more than 40 percent of college students drop out. . . . some of the highest-ranked schools also have the most scholarship money, allowing them to "meet full need"—that is, offering low-to-no tuition to qualified, needy students. And maybe this chaos points to the start of a revolution. Maybe one day we will see actual price competition, with schools across the spectrum advertising their lower costs. It's hard to believe that higher education will be able to defy the laws of economics forever.[30]

Under a privatized lending system governed by the laws of economics, postsecondary institutions would have to focus on quality academics, affordable prices, and strong results such as on-time graduation and job placement rates, rather than attracting students with costly extras, such as swanky dorms, gyms, and winning sports teams. Serious institutions would scale back (or eliminate altogether) tenure policies that pay professors more to teach less. They would differentiate tuition prices based on real costs associated with different types of degrees. For example, science-related degrees requiring more expensive facilities would cost more, while liberal arts programs with lower overhead would cost less. Tuition could be further differentiated depending upon students' preferences for classes taught by full professors or teaching assistants. Institutions would likely weed out degree programs that rely on cross-subsidization from other programs (such as gender, ethnic, and other politicized fields) and begin implementing competency-based and online courses to help ensure students get the courses they need, when they need them, so they can complete their degrees on time and on budget. Nonacademic extras such as sports teams should be financially self-sufficient through self-generated funds, alumni gifts, and other donations. Conversely, institutions that opted to focus on frills instead of quality would see declining enrollments over time because students would become increasingly price-sensitive. Moreover, private lenders would be less willing to loan funds—or at least not as much—knowing students intended to use them at schools that are not focused on results.

Such private-sector lending practices have huge potential to transform higher education by expanding access and improving overall quality. As direct lending proponents have noted, subsidizing the college loan industry makes little sense with such a large and growing market.[31] Undergraduate enrollment has soared from 3.6 million in 1959 to more than 21 million in 2010.[32] About 60 percent of students borrow annually to help pay for a college education, and in spite of the current direct federal lending scheme, private student lending is on the rise.[33] American businesses also have an important role to play—particularly since a majority of employers (53 percent) report that finding employees with the necessary skills, training, and education is a major challenge.[34] Businesses should actively promote their willingness to enter into human capital contracts with undergraduate students. Under such contracts, business would assume responsibility for repaying loans in exchange for a specified number of work years, once students complete their degrees.

Instead of governments directing lump-sum appropriations to institutions, those funds should be directed to undergraduates in the form of annual performance grants. Students who complete their programs in four years would not have to pay back their grants; those who don't, would. Directing what amounts to $7,900 worth of government appropriations to individual undergraduates would incentivize them to find the best programs at the best prices since they would still be responsible for paying tuition and fees. The onus would be on institutions to keep other costs and their tuition prices down over the long term—without Congress tinkering with interest rates on loans or state governments imposing tuition price controls. Just as college prices did not balloon overnight, neither will they deflate right away; however, research suggests that postsecondary institutions would become much more tuition- and grant-driven—rather than subsidy-driven—within just three years under such a system.

Pell Grants: Historical Analysis

College-for-all, particularly among low-income and minority students, has been a cornerstone education policy of the Obama administration. During recent congressional testimony, Education Secretary Duncan announced that "overall, the number of Pell Grant scholarship recipients has increased more than 50 percent, from 6.2 million in 2008 to more than 9 million three years later. That is the biggest expansion of educational opportunity in higher education since the GI Bill."[35] A growing number of experts, however, note that the Pell Grant program has been long on promises and short on results measured by actual college completions. Commenting on the Obama administration's college-for-all agenda, the *Washington Post*'s Robert Samuelson concluded, "Like the crusade to make all Americans homeowners, it's now doing more harm than good. It looms as the largest mistake in educational policy since World War II."[36]

Elaborating on Samuelson's point, Richard Vedder, Ohio University economist and Center for College Affordability and Productivity director, explains:

> Emulating European social democracies with regards to social spending is not necessarily good. Europeans subsidize higher education even more than we do from the student perspective (low or zero tuition fees in many countries). To what end? Rates of economic growth that for the last three decades have been consistently, on average, lower than in the US? . . . Having more kids going to college is now probably increasing, not decreasing income inequality in the US. Too many kids, disproportionately from lower-income backgrounds, are going to college and, if they are fortunate to graduate (a big "if"), end up getting janitorial jobs that they could have obtained with a high-school diploma—and without running up huge college debts.[37]

Things were supposed to be different with Pell Grants. This program was established in the 1972 reauthorization of the Higher Education Act as the Basic Educational Opportunity Grant Program. In 1980 it was renamed after US Senator Claiborne Pell (D-R.I.).[38] This program provides need-based grants worth a maximum of $5,500 to low-income college and some graduate students, which can be used at any one of about 5,400 participating postsecondary institutions.[39]

Amid the rush to increase Pell funding amounts and expand student eligibility in recent years, little has been done to tighten oversight. An investigation in 2013 found that thousands of Michigan residents were enrolling in community colleges statewide, then not showing up for class. Pell jumpers or runners, as they are called, simply paid a few hundred dollars to enroll and pocketed the rest of their Pell Grant for the semester (about $2,750).[40]

Today "Pell grants are being scrutinized because taxpayers now spend more money on them . . . than on entire federal agencies."[41] Because they are grants rather than Federal Direct Student Loans, Pell recipients do not have to repay them. Yet Pell Grants have the same perverse effects on college pricing. As the Cato Institute's Neal McCluskey explains:

> Pell Grants are, at best, of limited value. Yes, they are needed by some people to go to college, but that's because they are largely built into college prices. Basically, give me a dollar more to pay for school and my college will charge me another buck. Of course it's not just Pell that influences prices—there are lots of other sources of aid, and colleges confront numerous variables that affect their costs—but subsidize something and prices will go up. And boy, do they go up in higher education![42]

McCluskey also correctly notes the problem with the federal government's involvement in matters that under the Constitution should be handled by the states.

> Government is an ineffective—and expensive—pass-through vehicle. Better to let taxpayers keep their hard-earned income, save it for their own or their children's education, or make donations to private scholarship organizations. That way, colleges and universities would have to compete for students and their cold, hard cash instead of lump-sum government appropriations. After all, it's harder to compete for tens of millions of undergraduates than it is to compete for politicians' appropriations votes.[43]

Pell Grants: A Privatizing Strategy

Since most students with Pell Grants also take out student loans, an important quality assurance measure that lenders could implement is the amount of available institutional need-based aid. Building institutions' need-based aid into lending decisions introduces powerful incentives for institutions to maintain and enhance their commitment to educating—and graduating—students with true financial need. In return, they are likely to attract more students. Under such a system the relative handful of postsecondary institutions that already meet full financial need or do not charge any tuition (most require students work on campus in lieu of tuition) would likely grow exponentially.[44]

Any need-based program should be carried out at the state and local levels, and there are plenty of models. State lawmakers could expand existing college savings plans. Privately managed trusts and philanthropic organizations could provide much more efficient needs-based aid to college students, without the fraud and waste of taxpayer dollars. Innovative education savings account programs like the ones Arizona and Florida have enacted are additional models.

Building on this idea, contributions from students themselves, family members, employers, and philanthropists should also be allowed to help promote personal responsibility when it comes to paying for college.

Conclusion

THE US DEPARTMENT of Education has not fulfilled any of the stated reasons for its existence—better, less expensive administration of federal education programs, the preservation of state and local control in education, and improved student achievement. As nineteenth-century opponent Rep. Samuel J. Randall of Pennsylvania predicted in 1866, a national education department would amount to "a bureau at an extravagant rate of pay, and an undue number of clerks collecting statistics . . . [that] does not propose to teach a single child . . . its a, b, c's."[1] More than a century later in 1979, opponents on opposite sides of the political spectrum shared Randall's skepticism.

Rep. Peter H. Kostmayer (D-Penn.) dismissed assurances of streamlined administration and improved education, arguing that

> the creation of a national education power structure serves no effective purpose. This is simply a cosmetic action—a response to the politics of the problem, not the problem itself. I don't believe, nor do I think the American people are going to believe, that this new Department will improve the quality of education in the classroom.[2]

Sen. Samuel Hayakawa (R-Calif.) echoed that sentiment:

> I wish someone would tell me how this new department is going to make our children literate? Or how it will erase the violence that has erupted in our schools? Or how it will ensure that we get what we pay for with our tax dollars? Or how it will make our children better prepared for their futures?[3]

The simple answer is it cannot and has not. From 1980 through 2010, US Department of Education spending outpaced student enrollment by a rate of more than five to one. For all that spending, American students are no better off in terms of academic performance. Results from the long-term National Assessment of Educational Progress, also known as the Nation's Report Card, show that student performance across subjects and grades has remained stuck at squarely average levels since the late 1960s and early 1970s. Creation of the US Department of Education has not had a discernible impact, in spite of assurances from proponents such as Rep. Elliott Levitas (D-Ga.) that the department would result in "better educational opportunity for the boys and girls and the young men and women in America. There is no question about that."

Students from other countries with greater socioeconomic challenges, including higher rates of poverty and immigration, have risen to the top of international performance rankings while their countries spend far less than the United States. Moreover, student success has little—if anything—to do with having a national ministry or department of education. Neither Canada nor Macao, China, has ever had one. New Zealand downgraded its failing national education bureaucracy virtually overnight in 1989. Similarly, Korea divested the planning and administrative budget of its national education ministry to local entities in 1991. Meanwhile, countries with highly centralized education ministries, including Chinese Taipei, Hong Kong, Ireland, Japan, Korea, and Singapore, are actively implementing more autonomy for schools and more education options for students and parents. Many European countries with well-established traditions of decentralization and freedom for parents to choose their children's schools, including Belgium and the Netherlands, are inspiring decentralization efforts throughout the European Union and as far away as Singapore. The reason is schools that compete for students perform better than schools that do not.

Close to three-fourths (72 percent) of the countries that performed as well or better than the United States on international assessments have higher proportions of schools competing for students. Parents in 91 percent of those countries have more freedom to choose their children's schools—both public and private—than American parents. Financial incentives supporting parents' freedom to choose the schools their children attend, including vouchers and tax credits, are also much more widely available in top-performing countries.

Schools in 86 percent of countries that performed as well or better than the United States also had more autonomy over curricula and testing than American schools. Freedom for parents, competition for students, and autonomy for schools appear to be critical components to top performers' success—not any centralized education ministry. Yet the United States has been moving in the opposite direction with one failed top-down education scheme after another emanating from Washington.

In spite of President Ronald Reagan's tough rhetoric about abolishing the US Department of Education, during his administration the department laid the foundation for an excellence agenda that foreshadowed the No Child Left Behind Era nearly two decades later. In 1990 George H.W. Bush assured Americans that by the year 2000 high school graduation rates would reach at least 90 percent, every school would be safe and drug-free, and American students would lead the world in math and science performance. President Bill Clinton subsequently transformed Bush's America 2000 agenda into the Goals 2000 agenda, including efforts to link US Department of Education funding to federal review of states' voluntary standards, reminiscent of today's Common Core voluntary standards. The millennium came and went without realizing the promises of Goals 2000. Yet the first legislative proposal by President George W. Bush was a concept paper outlining the No Child Left Behind Act, which guaranteed among other things that by the 2013–14 school year, all schoolchildren would be proficient in reading and math. Well before that deadline, it was clear no state was even close to meeting the 100 percent proficiency benchmark. Instead of admitting defeat, the Obama administration forged ahead issuing states waivers under the guise of flexibility, while making adoption of common core standards a condition for receiving federal education funds.

Back in 1980 President Reagan described the US Department of Education as "President Carter's bureaucratic boondoggle."[4] History has shown that this department continues to operate as every successive president's boondoggle. The cost and chaos inflicted on a national scale by the US Department of Education have been staggering, with new agendas, mandates, and administrative burdens imposed by each passing administration on students, schools, and states. By 2011 the burden to states and localities of complying with Title I mandates alone was estimated to be 7.8 million hours annually at a cost of $235 million. This is hardly indicative of, as US Department of Education proponent Sen. Sam Nunn (D-Ga.) put it back in 1979, "a new era of cooperation, understanding, and excellence in our educational systems."[5] On the contrary, the department has become a conduit for presidents and special interest groups to further their preferred education agendas—with or without congressional authorization. US Department of Education critics on both sides of the aisle saw this coming.

Sen. Daniel Patrick Moynihan (D-N.Y.) described the creation of the department as "a backroom deal, born out of squalid politics."[6] In a bipartisan statement against establishing a US Department of Education, House members argued:

> Those who stand to gain by this Department are the NEA and the other professionals representing education groups, and those in certain industries who profit from the programs. Children will not benefit. . . . This education-industrial complex need not answer to the American people who will complain about Federal domination of education policy, erosion of equal educational opportunities, and simply inefficient Government.[7]

Rep. Bob Michel (R-Ill.) summed up his opposition to the Department of Education even more emphatically, "Once this silly idea is consigned to the oblivion it richly deserves, let us have the courage to admit that the Federal Government does not know what it is doing in education."[8] Thomas Jefferson likewise scoffed at the idea of a government-run schooling system 200 years earlier in 1779 when he was governor of Virginia. "If it is believed that these elementary schools will be better managed by the governor and council . . . than by the parents within each ward," he observed, "it is a belief against all experiences."[9] Jefferson's observation is as true today as it was centuries ago. As recently as 2011 the Government Accountability Office confirmed that no uniform definition of *education program* even exists at the federal level.

Our Framers knew better and did have the courage to leave education in the capable hands of parents and local citizens. Nowhere does the word education appear in the Constitution. In fact, "powers not delegated to the United States by the Constitution, nor prohibited by it to the States, are reserved to the States respectively, or to the people," according to the Tenth

Amendment. A review of the prevalence and diversity of nongovernment schooling options throughout the colonial era and the early Republic reveals a quality education was available long before the rise of mandatory government schooling. In fact, support for government schools was strongest among the wealthy, not middle- and low-income families who would stand to gain from publicly subsidized free government schools if there were a desire or need for them. Meanwhile, presidents and members of Congress exercised a level of constitutional restraint in their efforts to encourage education that seems almost unrecognizable today. In fact, even the most ardent supporters of isolated federal involvement in education, including Presidents George Washington, Jefferson, and James Madison, insisted that absent a constitutional amendment, neither they nor Congress had any authority over education whatsoever.

Restoring constitutional authority over education requires a genuine abolition plan for the US Department of Education. History has shown that half measures such as departmental downgrades or block-grant schemes for redistributing funding will not prevent the US Department of Education from operating as an expensive pass-through for taxpayer dollars funding politicized agendas that at best have no demonstrable positive impact on student learning or expanded educational opportunities. Eliminating all US Department of Education non-program offices and divisions would save taxpayers more than $192 million, just in base salaries and awards associated with more than 1,800 department employees, plus another $13.9 billion in contractual services, supplies, and other overhead costs such as rent. Simply returning the funding currently diverted to Washington, DC, to maintain the US Department of Education, its personnel, and programs to taxpayers would correspond with a 3 percent across-the-board federal income tax reduction. With those funds in hand, taxpayers would be free to decide which, if any, education programs to implement or expand in their own states.

The savings from the elimination/privatization of more than 120 US Department of Education programs, including associated salary costs, is $216 billion. Those savings do not include the roughly $50 billion in annual profit the US Department of Education has been making in recent years from student loans. These funds should be returned to taxpayers as well, rather than funneled into another federal bureaucracy. Alternatives abound. Today shining examples of various parental choice programs exist across the country, including Washington, DC, where students largely from socioeconomically disadvantaged backgrounds are succeeding in high-quality schools at a fraction of what it would cost if they attended traditional government-run public schools.

Private school parental-choice programs serve students from low-income families and students from failing public schools; a higher proportion of participating students have disabilities compared to the public school population. Likewise, public charter schools disproportionately serve low-income, minority, and academically struggling students. Achievement is also higher among parental-choice program participants, as well as high school graduation and college attendance rates. In addition, parental-choice programs introduce healthy competition that puts powerful pressure on all schools to improve, which benefits both participating and nonparticipating students. Virtual and online schools are proliferating across the country, expanding individualized learning opportunities for students regardless of their geographical locations or circumstances. Educational savings account programs are another innovation that puts parents directly in charge of their children's education funding. Parents who do not prefer a public school simply inform their state education agency, and 90 percent of the funding that would have been spent on that child is instead deposited into a designated savings account. Parents can use those funds for private school tuition, tutoring, online courses, and any leftover funds can be used for future education expenses such as college.

Years before the US Department of Education was established, Sen. Barry Goldwater (R-Ariz.) concluded that "federal aid *to* education invariably means federal control *of* education."[10] We are witnessing that fact in stark relief today as states scramble to ditch their Bush-era No Child Left Behind standards and tests for the current Obama-era Common Core version—all for what has historically amounted to mere pennies on the dollar in terms of federal aid. More than thirty years after the creation of the US Department of Education, students, taxpayers, and the country are not better off—but we can be.

Notes

Introduction

1. Gouverneur Morris of Pennsylvania, quoted in "XI. Early Views and Plans Relating to a National University" in *The Executive Documents of the House of Representatives for the Second Session of the Fifty-third Congress 1893-94* (Washington, DC: Government Printing Office, 1895), 1293.
2. Remarks made by Sen. James M. Mason of Virginia on February 1, 1859, contained in the *Congressional Globe, 2nd Session, 35th Congress* (Washington, DC: John C. Rives), part of *A Century of Lawmaking for a New Nation: U.S. Congressional Documents and Debates, 1774–1875*, 719.
3. Sen. Barry Goldwater of Arizona, referring to the National Defense Education Act of 1958 in "Some Notes on Education," in *Conscience of a Conservative*, ed. CC Goldwater (Princeton, NJ: Princeton University Press, 2007), 75.
4. Andrew J. Rotherham, referring to President Clinton's Goals 2000 plan proposed in 1994. Quoted in Patrick J. McGuinn, *No Child Left Behind and the Transformation of Federal Education Policy, 1965–2005* (Lawrence, KS: University of Kansas Press, 2006), 91.

Chapter 1

1. *Documents Illustrative of the Formation of the Union of the American States, 69th Congress, 1st Session—House Document No. 398*, Selected, Arranged, and Indexed by Charles C. Tansill, (Washington, DC: Government Printing Office, 1927), 725 and 950; "XI. Early Views and Plans Relating to a National University" in *The Executive Documents of the House of Representatives for the Second Session of the Fifty-third Congress 1893-94* (Washington, DC: Government Printing Office, 1895), 1293.
2. For an excellent summary of these early debates, see Kerry L. Morgan, "Historical and Constitutional Limitations," Section II of *The Constitution and Federal Jurisdiction in American Education*, (Livonia, MI: Lonang Institute, 1985, 2006): 2–13.
3. Thomas Jefferson, Second Inaugural Address, March 4, 1805.
4. James Madison, First Inaugural Address, March 4, 1809.
5. James Madison, Second Annual Message, December 5, 1810.

6. Remarks made on February 18, 1811, contained in *The Debates and Proceedings of the Congress of the United States* [formerly known as *The Annals of the Congress of the United States*], 42 vols. (Washington: Gales and Seaton, 1834), 22: 976.

7. Ibid., 22: 976–77.

8. James Madison, Eighth Annual Message, December 3, 1816.

9. Remarks made on December 11, 1816, contained in *The Debates and Proceedings of the Congress of the United States* [formerly known as *The Annals of the Congress of the United States*], 42 vols. (Washington: Gales and Seaton, 1834), 30: 257–59, quotation from p. 259.

10. Remarks made on March 3, 1817, contained in *The Debates and Proceedings of the Congress of the United States* [formerly known as *The Annals of the Congress of the United States*], 42 vols. (Washington: Gales and Seaton, 1834), 30: 1063–64.

11. Matthew J. Brouillette, "The 1850s and Beyond: States Strengthen Government's Role in Education and Restrict Parental Choice," in *School Choice in Michigan: A Primer for Freedom in Education; A Guide for Exercising Parents' Rights and Responsibilities to Direct the Education of Their Children*, Mackinac Center for Public Policy, 1999, 5-6.

12. Samuel L. Blumenfeld, *Is Public Education Necessary?* (Old Greenwich, CT: Devin-Adair: 1981), 18–19.

13. Eric R. Eberling, "Massachusetts Education Laws of 1642, 1647, and 1648," in *Historical Dictionary of American Education*, ed. Richard J. Altenbaugh (Westport, CT: Greenwood Press, 1999), 225–26.

14. Quoted in Murray Rothbard, "Education: Free and Compulsory," reproduced by the Ludwig von Mises Institute, September 9, 2006; cf. Blumenfeld, *Is Public Education Necessary?* (Old Greenwich, CT: Devin-Adair, 1981), 16.

15. Edwin Grant Dexter, *A History of Education in the United States* (London: Macmillan & Co., LTD., 1904), 24–37; Blumenfeld, *Is Public Education Necessary?* (Old Greenwich, CT: Devin-Adair, 1981), 17–18; Ellwood P. Cubberley, *Public Education in the United States: A Study and Interpretation of American Educational History* (New York: Houghton Mifflin Co., 1919), 23–24, 28–32.

16. Brouillette, "The 1850s and Beyond," 4–10, quotation from p. 6. See also, Blumenfeld, *Is Public Education Necessary?* (Old Greenwich, CT: The Devin-Adair Company, 1981), 19–20.

17. Dexter, *A History of Education in the United*, 24–88.

18. Ibid., 51–52.

19. Ibid., 58, 60, 61, and 65.

20. Blumenfeld, *Is Public Education Necessary?*, 21.

21. James Mulhern, *A History of Education: A Social Interpretation*, 2nd ed. (New York: Ronald Press Co, 1959), 592–594; Blumenfeld, *Is Public Education Necessary?*, 20, 23–24, 43.

22. See the conclusion to Chapter 1 of *An Inquiry Into the Nature and Causes of the Wealth of Nations*, 1776. See also, Book 5, Chapter 1, Article 2.

23. Thomas Paine, *The Rights of Man*, ed. Henry Collins (New York: Penguin, 1984), Chapter 5, Part II.

24. Ibid.

25. John Stuart Mill, Chapter 5 of *On Liberty* in *'On Liberty' and Other Writings*, ed. Stefan Collini (Cambridge: Cambridge University Press, 1989).

26. Cubberley, *Public Education in the United States*, 61, 65–66.

27. Ibid., 68–69.

28. Ibid., 65–68.

29. "An Ordinance for Ascertaining the Mode of Disposing of Lands in the Western Territory," Library of Congress, *A Century of Lawmaking for a New Nation: U.S. Congressional Documents and Debates, 1774–1875, Journals of the Continental Congress*, Vol. 28, Friday, May 20, 1785, 375–81. The Tenth Amendment was proposed on September 25, 1789, and ratified on December 15, 1789.

30. See Article 3 of "An Ordinance for the Government of the Territory of the United States Northwest of the River Ohio." See Transcript of Northwest Ordinance (1787) cf. "Chronology of Federal Education Legislation" in Thomas D. Snyder and Sally A. Dillow, *Digest of Education Statistics 2011*, National Center for Education Statistics, Institute of Education Sciences, US Department of Education, 544.

31. See Chapter 5, Section 2 of the Constitution of Massachusetts, 1780.

32. William H. Jeynes, *American Educational History: School, Society, and the Common Good* (Thousand Oaks, CA: Sage Publications: 2007), 36–37.

33. Brouillette, Matthew J. "The 1850s and Beyond," 5–6.

34. Blumenfeld, *Is Public Education Necessary?*, 23.

35. Ibid., 24.

36. Ibid., 24.

37. By 1823 New York's common school fund had reached nearly $1 million: nearly $183,000 from the state fund, and $850,000 from private contributions, more than $1 million in all (about $22.5 million in 2012 dollars). See Blumenfeld, *Is Public Education Necessary?*, 57.

38. Brouillette, *School Choice in Michigan*, 6.

39. Cubberley, *Public Education in the United States*, 71–72.

40. Ibid., 72–73.

41. Blumenfeld, *Is Public Education Necessary?*, 25; Cubberley, *Public Education in the United States*, 247.

42. Cubberley, *Public Education in the United States*, 69.

43. Ibid., 69–70.

44. Ibid.

45. Dexter, *A History of Education in the United States*, 124.

46. Ibid., 130.

47. Ibid., 131.

48. Ibid., 132.

49. Ibid., 133.

50. Ibid., 134.

51. Ibid., 134, 136.

52. Ibid., 135–137.

53. Ibid., 137.

54. Ibid., 138.

55. Barry W. Poulson, "Education and the Family During the Industrial Revolution," in *The American Family and the State*, eds. Joseph R. Peden and Fred R. Glahe (San Francisco: Pacific Research Institute, 1986), 138.

56. Robert Seybolt, *Sources and Studies in American Colonial Education: The Private School* (New York: Arno Press, 1925), 102.

57. Blumenfeld, *Is Public Education Necessary?*, 28.

58. Ibid., 30.

59. Ibid., 37–42.

60. Ibid., 42.

61. Henry J. Perkinson, *The Imperfect Panacea: American Faith in Education*, 4th ed. (New York: McGraw-Hill, 1995), 14–16, 27–32; Blumenfeld, *Is Public Education Necessary?*, 43–44; Jeynes, *American Educational History*, 37–42.

62. Blumenfeld, *Is Public Education Necessary?* , 45–46.

63. Matthew J. Brouillette, *School Choice in Michigan*, 56 and 66.

64. See the remarks of Charles Ingersoll and James G. Cater in *Is Public Education Necessary?*, 57 and 62.

65. Matthew J. Brouillette, "The 1850s and Beyond," 4–10, quotation from p. 9. See also Gerald L. Gutek, *An Historical Introduction to American Education*, 2nd ed. (Prospect Heights, IL: Waveland Press, Inc., 1991), 63–67.

66. Robert B. Everhart, "From Universalism to Usurpation: An Essay on the Antecedents to Compulsory School Attendance Legislation," *Review of Educational Research*, Vol. 47, No. 3, (Summer 1977): 499–530, 522–24.

67. Blumenfeld, *Is Public Education Necessary?*, 36.

68. Brouillette, "The 1850s and Beyond," 8–10. Blumenfeld, *Is Public Education Necessary?* 162–83; Andrew J. Coulson, *Market Education: The Unknown History*, (New Brunswick, NJ: Social Philosophy and Policy Center and Transaction Publishers, 1999), 81–82.

69. Mulhern, *A History of Education*, 505; Blumenfeld, *Is Public Education Necessary?*, 11; Richman, *Separating School & State*, 40–41.

70. M. Victor Cousin, *Report on the Condition of Public Instruction in Germany, and Particularly Prussia*, trans. Sarah Austin (London: Effingham Wilson, Royal Exchange, 1834). This work was originally submitted to the French government in 1831 and published in New York City in the winter of 1834–35; op cit. Floyd R. Dain, *Education in the Wilderness* (Lansing, MI: Michigan Historical Society, 1968), 204.

71. Quoted in Dain, *Education in the Wilderness*, 204; Perkinson, *The Imperfect Panacea*, 22–27; cf. M. Victor Cousin, *Report on the Condition of Public Instruction in Germany, and Particularly Prussia*, trans. Sarah Austin (London: Effingham Wilson, Royal Exchange, 1834), 16, 20–21; Dexter, *A History of Education in the United*, 97–102; Blumenfeld, *Is Public Education Necessary?*, 140, 184; Cubberley, *Public Education in the United States*, 161.

72. Dexter, *A History of Education in the United States*, 100–101.

73. Perkinson, *The Imperfect Panacea*, 27–32.

74. James G. Carter, *Essays Upon Popular Education Containing a Particular Examination of the Schools of Massachusetts and an Outline of an Institution for the Education of Teachers* (Boston: Bowles & Dearborn, 1826), 48–49.

75. "Essays in Education," published in 1799. Quoted in Coulson, *Market Education*, 78.

76. Neal McCluskey, "As American as Bavarian Pie," *Cato Policy Report*, Vol. 30, No. 4 (July/August 2008): 11.

77. Cubberley, *Public Education in the United States*, 334–37.

78. William D. Swan, "Immigration," *The Massachusetts Teacher*, Vol. 4, No. 10 (October 1851): 2–3. With regard to the education of blacks, however, Swan advocated coerced exodus rather than coerced government schooling. See pp. 3–5.

79. Matthew J. Brouillette, "The 1850s and Beyond," 4–10. Quotation from p. 10.

80. "Republican James G. Blaine, who narrowly lost the 1884 Presidential election, did not invent the amendments identified with his name. One of the first was passed in Massachusetts in 1854 when the Know Nothings captured the governorship and both houses of the legislature. But Blaine tapped into this anti-immigrant and anti-Catholic sentiment with a proposal to correct a 'defect' in the federal Constitution. Though his Constitutional amendment failed by a handful of votes in Congress, parallel efforts at the state level were highly successful." See "The Blaine Game: The ACLU and Its Allies Pick Up the Banner of the Know Nothings," *Wall Street Journal*, Opinionjournal.com, December 7, 2003, http://www.opinionjournal.com/editorial/feature.html?id=110004393.

81. The exceptions are: Kansas (1859), West Virginia (1863), Nebraska (1866), and Hawaii (1959). See Matthew J. Brouillette, "The 1850s and Beyond," 4–10. Quotation from p. 10. See also David Kirkpatrick, "The Bigotry of Blaine Amendments," *Crisis in Education*, February 1998, 12.

82. M. Victor Cousin, *Report on the Condition of Public Instruction in Germany, and particularly Prussia*, Trans. Sarah Austin (London: Effingham Wilson, Royal Exchange, 1834), 24.

83. Coulson, *Market*, 81–82; Neal McCluskey, "As American as Bavarian Pie," 11–12.

84. McCluskey, "As American as Bavarian Pie," quotation from p. 11.

Chapter 2

1. Donald R. Brown, "Jonathan Baldwin Turner and the Land-Grant Idea," *Journal of the Illinois State Historical Society (1908–1984)*, Vol. 55, No. 4 (Winter 1962): 377.

2. See "VII. Congressional Grants of Land and Money for Colleges of Agriculture and the Mechanic Arts, 1862–1890" in *The Executive Documents of the House of Representatives for the Second Session of the Fifty-third Congress 1893–94* (Washington, DC: Government Printing Office, 1895), 1275.

3. Brown, "Jonathan Baldwin Turner and the Land-Grant Idea," 375–78.

4. Ibid., 376–77.

5. Ibid., 378–79.

6. For an excellent summary of these early debates, see Kerry L. Morgan, "Historical and Constitutional Limitations," Section II of *The Constitution and Federal Jurisdiction in American Education* (Livonia, MI: Lonang Institute, 1985, 2006), 2–13.

7. The following day it was referred to the Committee on Public Lands over Morrill's objection that the bill instead be referred to the Committee on Agriculture, where he believed it would get a more favorable hearing. See December 14 and 15, 1857, contained in the *Congressional Globe, 1st Session, 35th Congress* (Washington, DC: John C. Rives), part of *A Century of Lawmaking for a New Nation: U.S. Congressional Documents and Debates, 1774–1875*, 32–33 and 36–37.

8. See "VII. Congressional Grants of Land and Money for Colleges of Agriculture and the Mechanic Arts, 1862–1890" in *The Executive Documents of the House of Representatives for the Second Session of the Fifty-third Congress 1893–94* (Washington, DC: Government Printing Office, 1895), 1275.

9. Remarks made April 22, 1858, contained in the *Congressional Globe, 1st Session, 35th Congress* (Washington, DC: John C. Rives), part of *A Century of Lawmaking for a New Nation: U.S. Congressional Documents and Debates, 1774–1875*, 1742.

10. Sen. Alfred Iverson of Georgia was not present for the vote, and he later noted he would have voted against it, making the vote 25 in favor, 23 opposed. See the *Congressional Globe, 2nd Session, 35th Congress* (Washington, DC: John C. Rives), part of *A Century of Lawmaking for a New Nation: U.S. Congressional Documents and Debates, 1774–1875*, 857. Ten days later on February 17, 1859, the House informed the Senate that its amendments to the bill were approved, and H.R. No. 2, the agricultural land-grant bill was enrolled. See the *Congressional Globe, 2nd Session, 35th Congress* (Washington, DC: John C. Rives), part of *A Century of Lawmaking for a New Nation: U.S. Congressional Documents and Debates, 1774–1875*, 1073 and 1079.

11. James D. Richardson, ed., *Compilation of the Messages and Papers of the Presidents, 1789–1897*, 10 vols., (Washington, DC: Government Printing Office, 1896), 5:543–50.

12. Ibid., 5:543.

13. Six million acres is equivalent to about 9,700 square miles, slightly larger than the 2010 land area of Vermont according to the US Census Bureau, http://quickfacts .census.gov/qfd/states/50000.html. The value of $7.6 million in 1860 would be nearly $200 million in 2010 dollars. See Samuel H. Williamson, "Seven Ways to Compute the Relative Value of a U.S. Dollar Amount, 1774 to present," Measuring Worth, 2011, www.measuringworth.com/uscompare/. Vermont's estimated fiscal 2011 higher education spending includes state general funds, other state funds, and bonds. See Table 12 of the National Association of State Budget Officers, *State Expenditure Fund Report, 2010: Examining Fiscal 2009–2011 State Spending*, 23.

14. *Congressional Globe, 2nd Session, 37th Congress* (Washington, DC: John C. Rives), part of *A Century of Lawmaking for a New Nation: U.S. Congressional Documents and Debates, 1774–1875*, 99, http://memory.loc.gov/cgi-bin/ampage?collId=llcg&fileName =058/llcg058.db&recNum=64.

15. *Congressional Globe, 2nd Session, 37th Congress* (Washington, DC: John C. Rives), part of *A Century of Lawmaking for a New Nation: U.S. Congressional Documents and Debates, 1774–1875*, 2770. See "VII. Congressional Grants of Land and Money for Colleges of Agriculture and the Mechanic Arts, 1862–1890" in *The Executive Documents of the House of Representatives for the Second Session of the Fifty-third Congress 1893–94* (Washington, DC: Government Printing Office, 1895), 1275.

16. Ordinances of Secession of the 13 Confederate States of America, The Civil War Homepage, http://www.civil-war.net/pages/ordinances_secession.asp; Christopher P. Loss, "Why the Morrill Land-Grant Colleges Act Still Matters," *Chronicle of Higher Education*, July 16, 2012, http://chronicle.com/article/Why-the-Morrill-Act-Still/ 132877/.

17. As reported by Rep. John F. Potter of Wisconsin on May 29, 1862, in the *Congressional Globe, 2nd Session, 37th Congress* (Washington, DC: John C. Rives), part of *A Century of Lawmaking for a New Nation: U.S. Congressional Documents and Debates, 1774–1875*, 99.

18. Vote taken on June 10, 1862, contained in the *Congressional Globe, 2nd Session, 37th Congress* (Washington, DC: John C. Rives), part of *A Century of Lawmaking for a New Nation: U.S. Congressional Documents and Debates, 1774–1875*, 2441.

19. Vote taken on June 17, 1862, contained in the *Congressional Globe, 2nd Session, 37th Congress* (Washington, DC: John C. Rives), part of *A Century of Lawmaking for a New Nation: U.S. Congressional Documents and Debates, 1774–1875,* 2770.

20. *Congressional Globe, 2nd Session, 37th Congress* (Washington, DC: John C. Rives), part of *A Century of Lawmaking for a New Nation: U.S. Congressional Documents and Debates, 1774–1875,* 3062. http://memory.loc.gov/cgi-bin/ampage?collId=llcg&file Name=061/llcg061.db&recNum=2. See also Morrill Land Grant Act, 12 Stat. at Large 503 (1862); Library of Congress, "Primary Documents in American History: Morrill Act," http://www.loc.gov/rr/program/bib/ourdocs/Morrill.html.

21. For a map of land grant colleges and universities in 1862, see United States Department of Agriculture, "NIFA Land-Grant Colleges and Universities, 1862," updated January 30, 2015, http://nifa.usda.gov/resource/land-grant-colleges-and-universities -map-1862; See also *Public Acts of the Thirty-Seventh Congress of the United States, 2nd Session,* Ch. 130, "An Act Donating Public Lands to the Several States and Territories Which May Provide Colleges for the Benefit of Agriculture and the Mechanic Arts," signed into law July 2, 1862, by President Abraham Lincoln, 503–505; Morrill Act of 1862 (7 U.S.C. § 301 et seq.), http://us-code.vlex.com/vid/sec-land-grant-aid-colleges -19268404.

22. United States Department of Agriculture, "State and National Partners," updated August 24, 2011, http://www.csrees.usda.gov/qlinks/partners/state_partners.html.

23. Harry Kursh, *The United States Office of Education,* (Philadelphia: Chilton Company, 1965), 27. Even the limited purpose of the Act, to provide funds for colleges and universities from the sale of federal lands, has been expanded beyond its original purpose. By 1965, every state had "at least one college or university which received direct cash grants from the Federal Government, in lieu of land sales." *Id.* Quoted in Kerry L. Morgan, "Historical and Constitutional Limitations (cont'd)," Section II of *The Constitution and Federal Jurisdiction in American Education* (Livonia, MI: Lonang Institute, 1985, 2006), 2–13.

24. Remarks made on February 1, 1859, contained in the *Congressional Globe, 2nd Session, 35th Congress* (Washington, DC: John C. Rives), part of *A Century of Lawmaking for a New Nation: U.S. Congressional Documents and Debates, 1774–1875,* 720.

25. Remarks made April 20, 1858, contained in the *Congressional Globe, 1st Session, 35th Congress* (Washington, DC: John C. Rives), part of *A Century of Lawmaking for a New Nation: U.S. Congressional Documents and Debates, 1774–1875,* 1696.

26. George Washington, First Annual Message to Congress, January 8, 1790.

27. *Documents Illustrative of the Formation of the Union of the American States, 69th Congress, 1st Session—House Document No. 398,* Selected, Arranged, and Indexed by Charles C. Tansill (Washington, DC: Government Printing Office, 1927), 725. See also "XI. Early Views and Plans Relating to a National University" in *The Executive Documents of the House of Representatives for the Second Session of the Fifty-third Congress 1893–94* (Washington, DC: Government Printing Office, 1895), 1294.

28. Remarks made on May 3, 1790, contained in *The Debates and Proceedings of the Congress of the United States* [formerly known as *The Annals of the Congress of the United States*], 42 vols. (Washington: Gales and Seaton, 1834), 2:1603–04.

29. Remarks made on December 27, 1796, contained in *The Debates and Proceedings of the Congress of the United States* [formerly known as *The Annals of the Congress of the United States*], 42 vols. (Washington: Gales and Seaton, 1834), 6:1709.

30. Remarks made on December 21, 22, 26–27, 1796, contained in *The Debates and Proceedings of the Congress of the United States* [formerly known as *The Annals of the Congress of the United States*], 42 vols. (Washington: Gales and Seaton, 1834), 6:1694–1711.

31. Thomas Jefferson, Sixth Annual Message, December 2, 1806.

32. Richardson, ed., *Compilation of the Messages and Papers of the Presidents, 1789–1897*, 5:544.

33. Jefferson, Sixth Annual Message.

34. Ibid.

35. James Monroe, First Annual Message, December 2, 1817.

36. Remarks made on December 23, 1819, contained in *The Debates and Proceedings of the Congress of the United States* [formerly known as *The Annals of the Congress of the United States*], 42 vols. (Washington: Gales and Seaton, 1834), 35:780–81.

37. Remarks made April 20, 1858, contained in the *Congressional Globe, 1st Session, 35th Congress* (Washington, DC: John C. Rives), part of *A Century of Lawmaking for a New Nation: U.S. Congressional Documents and Debates, 1774–1875*, 1696.

38. Remarks made on February 1, 1859, contained in the *Congressional Globe, 2nd Session, 35th Congress* (Washington, DC: John C. Rives), part of *A Century of Lawmaking for a New Nation: U.S. Congressional Documents and Debates, 1774–1875*, 714–15; cf. Richardson, *Compilation of the Messages and Papers of the Presidents, 1789–1897*, 5:247–56.

39. Richardson, ed., *Compilation of the Messages and Papers of the Presidents, 1789–1897*, 5:251–252; cf. Andrew Jackson, "Bank Veto (July 10, 1832)," http://millercenter.org/president/speeches/detail/3636.

40. See veto message of May 27, 1830 in Richardson, *Compilation of the Messages and Papers of the Presidents, 1789–1897*, 2:491–92.

41. Remarks made April 20, 1858, contained in the *Congressional Globe, 1st Session, 35th Congress* (Washington, DC: John C. Rives), part of *A Century of Lawmaking for a New Nation: U.S. Congressional Documents and Debates, 1774–1875*, 1696.

42. Remarks made on February 1, 1859, contained in the *Congressional Globe, 2nd Session, 35th Congress* (Washington, DC: John C. Rives), part of *A Century of Lawmaking for a New Nation: U.S. Congressional Documents and Debates, 1774–1875*, 722.

43. Remarks made April 20, 1858, contained in the *Congressional Globe, 1st Session, 35th Congress* (Washington, DC: John C. Rives), part of *A Century of Lawmaking for a New Nation: U.S. Congressional Documents and Debates, 1774–1875*, 1693.

44. Remarks made April 20, 1858, contained in the *Congressional Globe, 1st Session, 35th Congress* (Washington, DC: John C. Rives), part of *A Century of Lawmaking for a New Nation: U.S. Congressional Documents and Debates, 1774–1875*, 1694; cf. Adam Smith, *An Inquiry Into the Nature and Causes of the Wealth of Nations*, ed. Edwin Cannan (Chicago: University of Chicago Press, 1976), Vol. 1, Book 3, Chapter 4, Article 2, "How the Commerce of Towns Contributed to the Improvement of the Country," 432–445.

45. Adam Smith, *An Inquiry Into the Nature and Causes of the Wealth of Nations*, ed. Edwin Cannan (Chicago: University of Chicago Press, 1976), Vol. 2, Book 5, Chapter 1, Article 2, "Of the Expenses of the Institutions for the Education of Youth," 282–309. Quotations are from pp. 305, 282, 301, 294–95, and 287.

46. Richardson, 5:546.

47. Ibid.

48. Remarks made on February 7, 1859, contained in the *Congressional Globe, 2nd Session, 35th Congress* (Washington, DC: John C. Rives), part of *A Century of Lawmaking for a New Nation: U.S. Congressional Documents and Debates, 1774–1875*, 852.

49. Ibid., 854; cf. James Madison, Seventh Annual Message, December 5, 1815.

50. Remarks made on February 7, 1859, contained in the *Congressional Globe, 2nd Session, 35th Congress* (Washington, DC: John C. Rives), part of *A Century of Lawmaking for a New Nation: U.S. Congressional Documents and Debates, 1774–1875*, 853; cf. Madison's remarks in *The Federalist Papers*, No. 39.

51. Ibid., 853; cf. Madison's remarks in *The Federalist Papers*, No. 45. In his remarks, Sen. Clay mistakenly quotes Madison as saying, "The State governments may be regarded as essential constituent parts of the federal government..."

52. Ibid., 853; cf. Madison's remarks in The Federalist Papers, No. 40.

53. Ibid., 853; cf. Madison's remarks in *The Federalist Papers*, Nos. 14 and 46.

54. Ibid., 853. See James Madison, *The Federalist Papers*, No. 45. Sen. Clay mistakenly quotes Madison as saying, "The powers reserved to the several States will extend to all the objects which, in the ordinary course of affairs, concern the lives, liberties, and properties of the people, and the internal order, improvement, and prosperity of the States."

55. Ibid., 853; cf. Hamilton's remarks in *The Federalist Papers*, Nos. 17 and 23.

56. Remarks made on February 1, 1859, contained in the *Congressional Globe, 2nd Session, 35th Congress* (Washington, DC: John C. Rives), part of *A Century of Lawmaking for a New Nation: U.S. Congressional Documents and Debates, 1774–1875*, 718.

57. Ibid., 719.

58. Remarks made on February 3, 1859, contained in the *Congressional Globe, 2nd Session, 35th Congress* (Washington, DC: John C. Rives), part of *A Century of Lawmaking for a New Nation: U.S. Congressional Documents and Debates, 1774–1875*, 785.

59. Ibid., 785.

60. Ibid., 715.

61. Remarks made on February 7, 1859, contained in the *Congressional Globe, 2nd Session, 35th Congress* (Washington, DC: John C. Rives), part of *A Century of Lawmaking for a New Nation: U.S. Congressional Documents and Debates, 1774–1875*, 852. Sen. Clay also quotes President Jackson in his December 4, 1833, veto message regarding "An act to appropriate for a limited time the proceeds of the sales of the public lands of the United States and for granting lands to certain States." (Sen. Pugh mistakenly states the veto message occurred in December 1834.) The portion cited by Clay is highlighted, but a fuller quotation is provided for context: "But this bill assumes a new principle...once admitted, it is not difficult to perceive to what consequences it might lead. . . the State governments shall derive all the funds necessary for their support from the Treasury of the United States. . . Congress . . . need *go but one step further and put the salaries of all the State Governors, judges, and other officers, with a sufficient sum for other expenses, in their general appropriation bill.*" See President Jackson's December 4, 1833, veto message in Richardson, *Compilation of the Messages and Papers of the Presidents, 1789–1879*, 3:56–69. Jackson's quotation cited by Sen. Clay appears on pp. 66–67.

62. Richardson, ed., *Compilation of the Messages and Papers of the Presidents, 1789–1897*, 5:545.

63. Department of Homeland Security, "Persons Obtaining Lawful Permanent Resident Status by Region and Selected Country of Last Residence: Fiscal Years 1820 to 2013," Table 2 of *2013 Yearbook of Immigration Statistics*.

64. Ellwood P. Cubberley, *Changing Conceptions of Education* (New York: Houghton Mifflin Co., 1909), 56–57.

65. Cubberley, *Public Education in the United States*, 349.

66. Ellwood P. Cubberley, *Public School Administration* (New York: Houghton Mifflin Co., 1916), 338.

67. Cubberley, *Public Education in the United States*, 357.

68. Ibid., 338.

69. Quoted in Coulson, *Market Education,* 83. See also McCluskey, "As American as Bavarian Pie," 11–12.

70. For a summary of those efforts, see "The Bureau of Education" in B. A. Hinsdale, comp., *U.S. Office of Education, Documents Illustrative of American Educational History*, 53d Cong., 2d sess., 1892–93, 2 vols. (Washington, DC: Government Printing Office, 1895, Library of American Civilization 10588), 2:1288–1292.

71. National Education Association, "Our History," http://www.nea.org/home/1704 .htm. For additional details see Part 1: The Birth of NEA (1857–1865), http://www .nea.org/home/11608.htm; Part 2: NEA after the Civil War through the Turn of the Century (1865–1910), http://www.nea.org/home/12172.htm, in Sabrina Holcomb, *NEA Today* series, *Answering the Call: A History of the National Education Association*.

72. "National Bureau of Education," Read before the National Teachers' Association by S.H. White in *The American Journal of Education*, Henry Baynard, ed., Vol. 15, No. 38 [New Series 13] (March 1865): 180–84.

73. Ibid., 182–84.

74. "National Bureau of Education," Address by Andrew Jackson Rickoff delivered before the National Teachers' Association, August 18, 1864 [should be 1865], in *The American Journal of Education*, Henry Baynard, ed., Vol. 16, No. 43 [New Series 18] (June 1866): 299–310.

75. Ibid., 305.

76. Ibid., 309–10.

77. Ibid., 301.

78. Ibid., 303.

79. Ibid.

80. "Educational Duties of the Hour," Introductory Discourse before the National Teachers' Association at Harrisburg, Penn., in August 1865 by Samuel S. Greene, President of the Association, in *The American Journal of Education*, Henry Baynard, ed., Vol. 16 [New Series Vol. 6], No. 42 [New Series 17] (March 1866): 229–243.

81. Ibid., 242.

82. "National Bureau of Education," Address by Andrew Jackson Rickoff delivered before the National Teachers' Association, August 18, 1864 [should be 1865], in *The American Journal of Education*, Henry Baynard, ed., Vol. 16, No. 43 [New Series 18] (June 1866): 308.

83. "Educational Duties of the Hour," 243.

84. "National Bureau of Education," Read before the National Association of School Superintendents by E.E. White in Washington, DC, on February 7, 1866, in *The*

American Journal of Education, Henry Baynard, ed., Vol. 16, No. 42 [New Series 17] (March 1866): 180.

85. Ibid., 184.

86. Ibid., 185.

87. Remarks made on February 14, 1866, contained in the *Congressional Globe, 1st Session, 39th Congress* (Washington, DC: John C. Rives), part of *A Century of Lawmaking for a New Nation: U.S. Congressional Documents and Debates, 1774–1875*, 835 and 846. For the full text of the "Memorial of the National Association of State and City School Superintendents to the Senate and the House of Representatives of the United States, February 10, 1866," see "VIII. Bureau of Education," part of "Education Report" in *The Executive Documents of the House of Representatives for the Second Session of the Fifty-third Congress 1893–94* (Washington, DC: Government Printing Office, 1895), 1290–91.

88. See "VIII. Bureau of Education," part of "Education Report" in *The Executive Documents of the House of Representatives for the Second Session of the Fifty-third Congress 1893–94* (Washington, DC: Government Printing Office, 1895), 1291.

89. Ibid.

90. Remarks made on April 3, 1866, contained in the *Congressional Globe, 1st Session, 39th Congress* (Washington, DC: John C. Rives), part of *A Century of Lawmaking for a New Nation: U.S. Congressional Documents and Debates, 1774–1875*, 1751; cf. "VIII. Bureau of Education," part of "Education Report" in *The Executive Documents of the House of Representatives for the Second Session of the Fifty-third Congress 1893–94* (Washington, DC: Government Printing Office, 1895), 1288–89.

91. See Rep. Garfield's remarks on June 5, 1866, contained in the *Congressional Globe, 1st Session, 39th Congress* (Washington, DC: John C. Rives), part of *A Century of Lawmaking for a New Nation: U.S. Congressional Documents and Debates, 1774–1875*, 2966.

92. Remarks made on June 8, 1866, contained in the *Congressional Globe, 1st Session, 39th Congress* (Washington, DC: John C. Rives), part of *A Century of Lawmaking for a New Nation: U.S. Congressional Documents and Debates, 1774–1875*, 2968.

93. Ibid., 3044–45.

94. Ibid.

95. Ibid., 3046.

96. Ibid.

97. Ibid., 2966–68.

98. Ibid., 2969.

99. Remarks made on June 8, 1866., 3048.

100. Ibid., 3047; cf. Frederick Adolphus Packard, *The Daily Public School in the United States* (Philadelphia: J. B. Lippincott & Co., 1866), 9.

101. Ibid.

102. Remarks made on June 8, 1866, contained in the *Congressional Globe, 1st Session, 39th Congress* (Washington, DC: John C. Rives), part of *A Century of Lawmaking for a New Nation: U.S. Congressional Documents and Debates, 1774–1875*, 3047; cf. Frederick Adolphus Packard, *The Daily Public School in the United States* (Philadelphia: J. B. Lippincott & Co., 1866), 9.

103. Ibid., 3051. The national education department's funding was reduced by Congress on July 20, 1868, through an appropriations act, which stipulated that after June 30,

1869, it would lose its independence and be subsumed as the Office of Education within the Department of the Interior. The agency remained within the Department of the Interior until 1939, but its title went through several iterations. It was renamed the Bureau of Education in 1870 until 1929, when the title Office of Education was restored. See the National Library of Education, "Office of Education Library—Early Years," http://www2.ed.gov/NLE/histearly.html. Sometime after October 15, 2012, the website was no longer available.

104. See the remarks concerning the education department's cost made by Rep. Moulton ($10,000 to $15,000 annually), Rep. Beaman ($13,000 annually), and Rep. Banks ($13,000 annually) on June 8, 1866, contained in the *Congressional Globe*, 1st Session, 39th Congress (Washington, DC: John C. Rives), part of *A Century of Lawmaking for a New Nation: U.S. Congressional Documents and Debates, 1774–1875*, 3044, 3046.

105. Ibid., 3047.

106. Ibid.

107. Ibid.

108. For Garfield's complete intended remarks, see "Education—A National Interest," Speech of James A. Garfield of Ohio in the House of Representatives, June 8, 1866, on a Bill "To Establish a National Bureau of Education," Reported by the Select Committee on the Memorial of the National Association of School Superintendents in *American Journal of Education*, Henry Baynard, ed., Vol. 1 [Entire Series Vol. XVI I], No. 1 (September 1867): 49–63.

109. Remarks made on June 8, 1866, contained in the *Congressional Globe, 1st Session, 39th Congress* (Washington, DC: John C. Rives), part of *A Century of Lawmaking for a New Nation: U.S. Congressional Documents and Debates, 1774–1875*, 3049.

110. Neil McCluskey, *Feds in the Classroom: How Big Government Corrupts, Cripples, and Compromises American Education* (Lanham, MD: Rowman & Littlefield: 2007), 12–13; "Why We Fight: How Public Schools Cause Social Conflict," Cato Institute, Policy Analysis No. 587, January 23, 2007; remarks at the American Action Forum on the Federal Government's Role in Education, April 13, 2011, http://american actionforum.org/testimony/excerpt-of-remarks-by-neal-mccluskey-on-the-federal -governments-role-in-edu.

111. Remarks made on June 8, 1866, contained in the *Congressional Globe, 1st Session, 39th Congress* (Washington, DC: John C. Rives), part of *A Century of Lawmaking for a New Nation: U.S. Congressional Documents and Debates, 1774–1875*, 3050.

112. Ibid.

113. Ibid., 3051.

114. Remarks made on June 19, 1866. Ibid., 3270.

115. Burke Aaron Hinsdale, *President Garfield and Education* (Boston: Osgood & Co., 1881), 165.

116. Theodore C. Smith, *The Life and Letters of James Abram Garfield*, 2 vols. (New Haven: Yale Univ. Press, 1925, Library of American Civilization 23799-800), 2:781, http:// books.google.com/books/about/The_Life_and_Letters_of_James_Abram_Garf .html?id=rXchAAAAMAAJ.

117. Remarks made February 26, 1867, contained in the *Congressional Globe, 2nd Session, 39th Congress* (Washington, DC: John C. Rives), part of *A Century of Lawmaking for a New Nation: U.S. Congressional Documents and Debates, 1774–1875*, 1842.

118. Ibid., 1844.

119. Ibid.
120. Ibid., 1843.
121. Ibid., 1893.
122. An Act to Establish a Department of Education (14 Stat. 434).
123. Remarks made on June 5, 1866, contained in the *Congressional Globe, 1st Session, 39th Congress* (Washington, DC: John C. Rives), part of *A Century of Lawmaking for a New Nation: U.S. Congressional Documents and Debates, 1774–1875*, 2969.
124. Kursh, *The United States Office of Education*, 15; cf. US Department of Education, "An Overview of the U.S. Department of Education," November 2009, http://www2 .ed.gov/about/overview/focus/what.html.
125. US Department of Education, "An Overview of the U.S. Department of Education," November 2009, http://www2.ed.gov/about/overview/focus/what.html.
126. The education department was abolished and superseded by the Office of Education in the Department of the Interior by the general appropriation act for Fiscal Year 1869 (15 Stat. 106), July 20, 1868. See 12.2 Records of the Office of the Commissioner of Education, 1870–1979, Records of the Office of Education (Record Group 12), 1870–1983, http://www.archives.gov/research/guide-fed-records/groups/012.html.
127. The Bureau of Education reclassification was part of the general appropriation act for fiscal year 1870 (15 Stat. 291), adopted March 3, 1869. See 12.2 Records of the Office of the Commissioner of Education, 1870–1979, Records of the Office of Education (Record Group 12), 1870–1983, http://www.archives.gov/research/guide-fed-records/ groups/012.html.
128. See 12.1 Administrative History and 12.2 Records of the Office of the Commissioner of Education, 1870–1979, Records of the Office of Education (Record Group 12), 1870–1983, http://www.archives.gov/research/guide-fed-records/groups/012.html; Kursh, *The United States Office of Education*, 13.
129. Ibid., 19.
130. Smith-Lever Act of 1914 (P.L. 95); Smith-Hughes Act of 1917, also known as the Vocational Education Act of 1917 (P.L. 64-347; 39 Stat. 929).
131. Kursh, *The United States Office of Education*, 143–44.
132. Ibid., 13.
133. Dwight D. Eisenhower, "Special Message to the Congress Transmitting Reorganization Plan of 1953 Creating the Department of Health, Education, and Welfare," March 12, 1953. Online by Gerhard Peters and John T. Woolley, The American Presidency Project. http://www.presidency.ucsb.edu/ws/?pid=9794.
134. Reorganization Plan No. I of 1939, July 1, 1939. See 12.1 Administrative History, Records of the Office of Education (Record Group 12), 1870–1983, http://www .archives.gov/research/guide-fed-records/groups/012.html.
135. Thomas D. Snyder and Sally A. Dillow, *Digest of Education Statistics 2010 (NCES 2011-015)* (Washington, DC: National Center for Education Statistics, Institute of Education Sciences, US Department of Education, April 5, 2011), 538–39.
136. Kursh, 39.
137. Dwight D. Eisenhower, "Special Message to the Congress Transmitting Reorganization Plan of 1953 Creating the Department of Health, Education, and Welfare," March 12, 1953. Online by Gerhard Peters and John T. Woolley, The American Presidency Project. http://www.presidency.ucsb.edu/ws/?pid=9794.

138. Ibid.
139. Kursh, *The United States Office of Education*, 37.
140. Ibid., 133.

Chapter 3

1. Remarks of Sen. Bob Dole (R-KS) in the *Congressional Record, Proceedings of the 95th Congress, Second Session*, Vol. 124, No. 147, September 20, 1978 (for legislative day of August 16, 1978), in *Legislative History of Public Law 96-88, Department of Education Organization Act Part 1 and Part 2*, 96th Congress, 2nd Session, Committee Print, US Congress, Washington, DC, Senate Committee on Government Operations, 1980, 285.
2. D. T. Stallings, "A Brief History of the U.S. Department of Education, 1979–2002," *Phi Delta Kappan*, Vol. 83, No. 9 (May 2002): 677–683: 678; Barbara Stahura, "The NEA and the U.S. Department of Education," in *National Education Association: 1857–2007: 150 Years of Advancing Great Public Schools* (Washington, DC: NEA, 2007), 86–91: 87, http://issuu.com/faircountmedia/docs/nea150/1?mode=a_p.
3. See "History of the Legislation" part of Department of Education Organization Act of 1978 (S. 991), Mr. Ribicoff, from the Committee on Governmental Affairs, submitting the following Report together with Additional Views (To accompany S. 991), August 9 (legislative day May 17), 1978, in *Legislative History of Public Law 96-88, Department of Education Organization Act Part 1 and Part 2*, 96th Congress, 2nd Session, Committee Print, US Congress, Washington, DC, Senate Committee on Government Operations, 1980, 77.
4. Quoted in Barbara Stahura, "The NEA and the U.S. Department of Education," in *National Education Association: 1857–2007: 150 Years of Advancing Great Public Schools*, 86–91: 87cf. David Stevens, "President Carter, the Congress, and NEA: Creating the Department of Education," *Political Science Quarterly*, Vol. 98, No. 4 (Winter 1983–84): 641–63.
5. See Preface to *Legislative History of Public Law 96-88, Department of Education Organization Act Part 1 and Part 2*, 96th Congress, 2nd Session, Committee Print, US Congress, Washington, DC, Senate Committee on Government Operations, 1980.
6. See "History of the Legislation," 75–78.
7. David F. Labaree, "An Uneasy Relationship: The History of Teacher Education in the University," Chapter 18 of *Handbook of Research on Teacher Education: Enduring Issues in Changing Contexts*, eds. Marilyn Cochran-Smith, Sharon Feiman Nemser, D. John McIntyre, and Kelly E. Demer, 3rd ed. (New York: Routledge/Taylor & Francis Group and the Association of Teacher Educators, 2008), 293.
8. Ibid., 294–96.
9. John Dewey, *Human Nature and Conduct: An Introduction to Social Psychology* (New York: Henry Holt, 1922), 305–06.
10. Henry T. Edmondson III, *John Dewey & Decline of American Education: How Patron Saint of Schools Has Corrupted Teaching & Learning* (Wilmington, DE: ISI Books, 2006), 5.
11. John Dewey, *Freedom and Culture* (New York: G. P. Putnam's Sons, 1939), 41–42, 156, 158; John Dewey, *The Public and its Problems* (New York: Henry Holt, 1927), 133; cf. Edmondson III, *John Dewey & Decline of American Education*, 68–72.

12. Dewey, *Freedom and Culture*, 9 and 13.

13. John Dewey, *My Pedagogic Creed* (New York: E.L. Kellogg & Company: 1897), 18.

14. Edmondson III, *John Dewey & Decline of American Education*, 74–75.

15. Labaree, "An Uneasy Relationship: The History of Teacher Education in the University," 291.

16. John Dewey, *Democracy and Education: An Introduction to the Philosophy of Education* (New York: Macmillan, 1916), 59, 117, and 362.

17. Coulson, *Market Education*, 288–89; Diane Ravitch, *Left Back: A Century of Battles Over School Reform* (New York: Simon & Schuster, 2000), 57–61; Edmondson III, *John Dewey & Decline of American Education*; Louis Menand, *The Metaphysical Club: A Story of Ideas in America* (New York: Macmillan, 2001), 333–48.

18. Edmondson III, *John Dewey & Decline of American Education*, 28–32.

19. NEA-PAC was changed to NEA Fund for Children and Public Education in 1998. See Craig Collins, "The Politics of Education," in *National Education Association: 1857–2007: 150 Years of Advancing Great Public Schools*, 66–71: 68 and 70; Stallings, "A Brief History of the U.S. Department of Education," 677–683: 678; Stahura, "The NEA and the U.S. Department of Education," 86–91: 87 and 89; Dale McFeatters, "Union Force Behind Carter to Disband," *Pittsburgh Press*, July 12, 1776.

20. Robert V. Heffernan, *Cabinetmakers: Story of the Three-Year Battle to Establish the U.S. Department of Education* (Lincoln, NE: iUniverse, 2001), 24–25.

21. Craig Collins, "The Politics of Education," in *National Education Association: 1857–2007: 150 Years of Advancing Great Public Schools*, 66–71: 67.

22. Stahura, "The NEA and the U.S. Department of Education," 86–91: 89–90; Allan M. West, *The National Education Association: The Power Base for Education* (New York: The Free Press, 1980), 201.

23. Even though Carter fulfilled his campaign promise to the National Education Association, just 52 percent of its members supported him in the 1980 election. Jennifer L. Fisher, "A Hermeneutics Approach to Studying Agenda-setting: The Postwar Education Agenda (1945–1998)," (PhD diss., University of West Virginia, 2000), 63.

24. See the remarks of Sen. Ribicoff in the *Congressional Record, Proceedings of the 95th Congress, First Session*, Vol. 123, No. 44, March 14, 1977 (for legislative day of February 21, 1977), part of "Introduction of S. 991 in 1977" in *Legislative History of Public Law 96-88, Department of Education Organization Act Part 1 and Part 2*, 96th Congress, 2nd Session, Committee Print, US Congress, Washington, DC, Senate Committee on Government Operations, 1980, 30.

25. Ibid., 31.

26. "The Need for a Department of Education," part of Department of Education Organization Act of 1978 (S. 991), Mr. Ribicoff, from the Committee on Governmental Affairs, submitting the following Report together with Additional Views (To accompany S. 991), August 9 (legislative day May 17), 1978, in *Legislative History of Public Law 96-88, Department of Education Organization Act Part 1 and Part 2*, 96th Congress, 2nd Session, Committee Print, US Congress, Washington, DC, Senate Committee on Government Operations, 1980, 70.

27. Remarks of Sen. Nunn in the *Congressional Record, Proceedings of the 95th Congress, First Session*, Vol. 123, No. 44, March 14, 1977 (for legislative day of February 21, 1977), part of "Introduction of S. 991 in 1977" in *Legislative History of Public Law*

96-88, Department of Education Organization Act Part 1 and Part 2, 96th Congress, 2nd Session, Committee Print, US Congress, Washington, DC, Senate Committee on Government Operations, 1980, 32–33.

28. Ibid.

29. Stallings, "A Brief History of the U.S. Department of Education," 677–683: 678; Benjamin D. Stickney and Laurence R. Marcus, *The Great Education Debate: Washington and the Schools* (Springfield, IL: Charles C. Thomas, 1984), 44.

30. The ten days of hearings were held on October 12 and 13, 1977; March 20 and 21, 1978; April 14, 18, and 27, 1978; May 8, 16, and 17, 1978. See "Summary of Hearings" part of Department of Education Organization Act of 1978 (S. 991), Mr. Ribicoff, from the Committee on Governmental Affairs, submitting the following Report together with Additional Views (To accompany S. 991), August 9 (legislative day May 17), 1978, in *Legislative History of Public Law 96-88, Department of Education Organization Act Part 1 and Part 2*, 96th Congress, 2nd Session, Committee Print, US Congress, Washington, DC, Senate Committee on Government Operations, 1980, 82–90.

31. See "History of the Legislation" part of Department of Education Organization Act of 1978 (S. 991), Mr. Ribicoff, from the Committee on Governmental Affairs, submitting the following Report together with Additional Views (To accompany S. 991), August 9 (legislative day May 17), 1978, in *Legislative History of Public Law 96-88, Department of Education Organization Act Part 1 and Part 2*, 96th Congress, 2nd Session, Committee Print, US Congress, Washington, DC, Senate Committee on Government Operations, 1980, 78, 142. See also "Text of S. 991 as Reported," 175–219.

32. See "History of the Legislation" part of Department of Education Organization Act of 1979, Report of the Committee on Governmental Affairs, US Senate, to Accompany S. 210 to Establish a Department of Education Together with Additional and Minority Views, March 27 (legislative day February 22), 1979, in *Legislative History of Public Law 96-88, Department of Education Organization Act Part 1 and Part 2*, 96th Congress, 2nd Session, Committee Print, US Congress, Washington, DC, Senate Committee on Government Operations, 1980, 539–40; Department of Education Organization Act, Mr. Brooks, from the Committee on Government Operations, submitted the following Report together with Additional and Dissenting Views (to accompany H.R. 13778), August 25, 1978, in ibid., 1007–1009.

33. Stallings, "A Brief History of the U.S. Department of Education," 677–683: 678; Maurice R. Berube, *American Presidents and Education* (Westport, CT: Greenwich Press, 1991), 52; and Stahura, "The NEA and the U.S. Department of Education," 86–91: 91.

34. See "History of the Legislation" part of *Department of Education Organization Act of 1979, Report of the Committee on Governmental Affairs, U.S. Senate, to Accompany S. 210 to Establish a Department of Education Together with Additional and Minority Views,* March 27 (legislative day February 22), 1979, in *Legislative History of Public Law 96-88, Department of Education Organization Act Part 1 and Part 2*, 96th Congress, 2nd Session, Committee Print, US Congress, Washington, DC, Senate Committee on Government Operations, 1980, 540.

35. See remarks of Sen. Ribicoff in the *Congressional Record, Proceedings of the 95th Congress, Second Session*, Vol. 125, No. 6, January 24, 1979 (for legislative day of January 18, 1979), in *Legislative History of Public Law 96-88, Department of Education Organization*

Act Part 1 and Part 2, 96th Congress, 2nd Session, Committee Print, US Congress, Washington, DC, Senate Committee on Government Operations, 1980, 423–27. See text of S. 210 on pp. 428–45. See also S. 210: Department of Education Organization Act of 1979, http://www.govtrack.us/congress/bill.xpd?bill=s96-210; Related Legislation, http://www.govtrack.us/congress/bill.xpd?bill=s96-210&tab=related.

36. See "Establishment of a Department of Education: Message from the President of the United States transmitting a Draft of Proposed Legislation to Establish a Department of Education and for Other Purposes," February 13, 1979, in *Legislative History of Public Law 96-88, Department of Education Organization Act Part 1 and Part 2*, 96th Congress, 2nd Session, Committee Print, US Congress, Washington, DC, Senate Committee on Government Operations, 1980, 1826–1851.

37. See the Carter administration's bill, S. 510, Department of Education Organization Act of 1979, in the *Congressional Record, Proceedings of the 95th Congress, Second Session*, Vol. 125, No. 24, March 1, 1979 (for legislative day of February 22, 1979), in *Legislative History of Public Law 96-88, Department of Education Organization Act Z Part 1 and Part 2*, 96th Congress, 2nd Session, Committee Print, US Congress, Washington, DC, Senate Committee on Government Operations, 1980, 488–514.

38. The Department of Education Organization Act (S. 510), THOMAS, the Library of Congress, http://thomas.loc.gov/cgi-bin/bdquery/D?d096:8:./temp/~bdtq67:@@@L&summ2=m&.

39. See "History of the Legislation" part of Department of Education Organization Act of 1979, Report of the Committee on Governmental Affairs, US Senate, to Accompany S. 210 to Establish a Department of Education Together with Additional and Minority Views, March 27 (legislative day February22), 1979, in *Legislative History of Public Law 96-88, Department of Education Organization Act Part 1 and Part 2*, 96th Congress, 2nd Session, Committee Print, US Congress, Washington, DC, Senate Committee on Government Operations, 1980, 540.

40. The Department of Education Organization Act (H.R. 2444), was introduced on February 27, 1979, by Congressman (Jack Brooks (D-TX). On July 11, 1979, H.R. 2444 was tabled and S. 210 passed instead. See THOMAS, the Library of Congress, http://thomas.loc.gov/cgi-bin/bdquery/?&Db=d096&querybd=@FIELD(FLD001+@4(Rural+schools)); http://thomas.loc.gov/cgi-bin/bdquery/D?d096:1:./temp/~bdpVLg:@@@L&summ2=m&. See also H.R. 2444: Department of Education Organization Act of 1979, http://www.govtrack.us/congress/bill.xpd?bill=h96-2444&tab=votes; Related Legislation, http://www.govtrack.us/congress/bill.xpd?bill=h96-2444&tab=related.

41. See, for example, the colloquy among Sen. Danforth, Sen. Ribicoff, and Sen. Roth, in the *Congressional Record, Proceedings of the 95th Congress, Second Session,* Vol. 124, No. 154, September 28, 1978 (for legislative day of September 26, 1978), in *Legislative History of Public Law 96-88, Department of Education Organization Act Part 1 and Part 2*, 96th Congress, 2nd Session, Committee Print, US Congress, Washington, DC, Senate Committee on Government Operations, 1980, 350–53.

42. The six findings are numbered incorrectly in the original February 21, 1977, bill text. See "Findings and Purposes," Sec. 2 of the Department of Education Act of 1977 (S. 991) as introduced, in the *Congressional Record, Proceedings of the 95th Congress, First Session*, Vol. 123, No. 44, March 14, 1977 (for legislative day of February 21,

1977), part of "Introduction of S. 991 in 1977" in *Legislative History of Public Law 96-88, Department of Education Organization Act Part 1 and Part 2*, 96th Congress, 2nd Session, Committee Print, US Congress, Washington, DC, Senate Committee on Government Operations, 1980, 32–33.

43. David W. Breneman and Noel Epstein, "Uncle Sam's Growing Clout in Education," *Washington Post*, August 6, 1978, quoted by Sen. Danforth in the *Congressional Record, Proceedings of the 95th Congress, Second Session,* Vol. 124, No. 154, September 28, 1978 (for legislative day of September 26, 1978), in *Legislative History of Public Law 96-88, Department of Education Organization Act Part 1 and Part 2*, 96th Congress, 2nd Session, Committee Print, US Congress, Washington, DC, Senate Committee on Government Operations, 1980, 351.

44. Remarks of Sen. Danforth in the *Congressional Record, Proceedings of the 95th Congress, Second Session,* Vol. 124, No. 154, September 28, 1978 (for legislative day of September 26, 1978), in *Legislative History of Public Law 96-88, Department of Education Organization Act Part 1 and Part 2*, 96th Congress, 2nd Session, Committee Print, US Congress, Washington, DC, Senate Committee on Government Operations, 1980, 351. See also "Areas of Discussion: Intergovernmental Relations," part of Department of Education Organization Act of 1978 (S. 991), Mr. Ribicoff, from the Committee on Governmental Affairs, submitting the following Report together with Additional Views (To accompany S. 991), August 9 (legislative day May 17), 1978, in *Legislative History of Public Law 96-88, Department of Education Organization Act Part 1 and Part 2*, 96th Congress, 2nd Session, Committee Print, US Congress, Washington, DC, Senate Committee on Government Operations, 1980, 140.

45. Remarks of Sen. Ribicoff in the *Congressional Record, Proceedings of the 95th Congress, Second Session,* Vol. 124, No. 154, September 28, 1978 (for legislative day of September 26, 1978), in *Legislative History of Public Law 96-88, Department of Education Organization Act Part 1 and Part 2*, 96th Congress, 2nd Session, Committee Print, US Congress, Washington, DC, Senate Committee on Government Operations, 1980, 353.

46. Remarks of Sen. Schmitt in the *Congressional Record, Proceedings of the 95th Congress, Second Session,* Vol. 124, No. 154, September 28, 1978 (for legislative day of September 26, 1978), in *Legislative History of Public Law 96-88, Department of Education Organization Act Part 1 and Part 2*, 96th Congress, 2nd Session, Committee Print, US Congress, Washington, DC, Senate Committee on Government Operations, 1980, 353–54.

47. "The Need for a Department of Education," part of Department of Education Organization Act of 1978 (S. 991), Mr. Ribicoff, from the Committee on Governmental Affairs, submitting the following Report together with Additional Views (To accompany S. 991), August 9 (legislative day May 17), 1978, in *Legislative History of Public Law 96-88, Department of Education Organization Act Part 1 and Part 2*, 96th Congress, 2nd Session, Committee Print, US Congress, Washington, DC, Senate Committee on Government Operations, 1980, 70.

48. US Constitution, Article I, Section 8, Clause 1. Based on Congressional power to regulate commerce among the states and the Necessary and Proper Clause granting Congress the power "to make all laws which shall be necessary and proper for carrying into execution the foregoing powers," twentieth century education department supporters believed, as their predecessors did, that they stood on sufficiently solid Constitutional footing.; cf. US Constitution, Article I, Section 8, Clauses 3 and 18.

49. James Madison, *Federalist* No. 41.

50. Ibid. See also James E. Ryan, "The Tenth Amendment and Other Paper Tigers: The Legal Boundaries of Education Governance," in *Who's In Charge Here? The Tangled Web of School Governance and Policy,* ed. Noel Epstein, (Denver: Education Commission of the States; Washington, DC: Brookings Institution Press, 2004), 49–50.

51. Ryan, "The Tenth Amendment and Other Paper Tigers," 49–50.

52. Remarks of Sen. Goldwater in the *Congressional Record, Proceedings of the 95th Congress, Second Session,* Vol. 124, No. 146, September 19, 1978 (for legislative day of August 16, 1978), in *Legislative History of Public Law 96-88, Department of Education Organization Act Part 1 and Part 2,* 96th Congress, 2nd Session, Committee Print, US Congress, Washington, DC, Senate Committee on Government Operations, 1980, 240–41.

53. Barry Goldwater, "Some Notes on Education," in *Conscience of a Conservative,* ed. CC Goldwater, (Princeton, NJ: Princeton University Press, 2007), 74.

54. Ibid., 72.

55. Ibid., 77–81. Quotation from p. 80.

56. Remarks of Sen. Goldwater in the *Congressional Record, Proceedings of the 95th Congress, Second Session,* Vol. 124, No. 154, September 28, 1978 (for legislative day of September 26, 1978), in *Legislative History of Public Law 96-88, Department of Education Organization Act Part 1 and Part 2,* 96th Congress, 2nd Session, Committee Print, US Congress, Washington, DC, Senate Committee on Government Operations, 1980, 295–385. See text of S. 991, 330–31.

57. Remarks of Sen. Schmitt in the *Congressional Record, Proceedings of the 95th Congress, Second Session,* Vol. 124, No. 154, September 28, 1978 (for legislative day of September 26, 1978), in *Legislative History of Public Law 96-88, Department of Education Organization Act Part 1 and Part 2,* 96th Congress, 2nd Session, Committee Print, US Congress, Washington, DC, Senate Committee on Government Operations, 1980, 295–385. See text of S. 991, 298–99 and 300.

58. Ibid., 300.

59. Ibid., 299.

60. Ibid., 298–99.

61. Remarks of Sen. Hayakawa in ibid., 359.

62. Ibid.

63. Ibid, 361.

64. Ibid, 360–61.

65. Ibid.

66. Quoted by Sen. Hayakawa, ibid., 361.

67. "Purpose of the Legislation" part of Department of Education Organization Act of 1978 (S. 991), Mr. Ribicoff, from the Committee on Governmental Affairs, submitting the following Report together with Additional Views (To accompany S. 991), August 9 (legislative day May 17), 1978, in *Legislative History of Public Law 96-88, Department of Education Organization Act Part 1 and Part 2,* 96th Congress, 2nd Session, Committee Print, US Congress, Washington, DC, Senate Committee on Government Operations, 1980, 65; "Purpose of the Legislation," part of *Department of Education Organization Act of 1979, Report of the Committee on Governmental Affairs, U.S. Senate, to Accompany S. 210 to Establish a Department of Education Together with Additional and Minority Views,* March 27 (legislative day February 22), 1979,

in Legislative History of Public Law 96-88, Department of Education Organization Act Part 1 and Part 2, 96th Congress, 2nd Session, Committee Print, US Congress, Washington, DC, Senate Committee on Government Operations, 1980, 528.

68. "The Need for a Department of Education" part of Department of Education Organization Act of 1978 (S. 991), Mr. Ribicoff, from the Committee on Governmental Affairs, submitting the following Report together with Additional Views (To accompany S. 991), August 9 (legislative day May 17), 1978, in *Legislative History of Public Law 96-88, Department of Education Organization Act Part 1 and Part 2*, 96th Congress, 2nd Session, Committee Print, US Congress, Washington, DC, Senate Committee on Government Operations, 1980, 69.

69. President Jimmy Carter, "Elementary and Secondary Education Message to the Congress," February 28, 1978, The American Presidency Project, http://www.presidency.ucsb.edu/ws/index.php?pid=30429&st=&st1=#axzz10enzLnS1.

70. President Jimmy Carter, "Department of Education Message to the Congress Transmitting Proposed Legislation," February 13, 1979, The American Presidency Project, http://www.presidency.ucsb.edu/ws/index.php?pid=31906&st=&st1=#axzz1pIx2WQSb.

71. "The Need for a Department of Education" part of Department of Education Organization Act of 1978 (S. 991), Mr. Ribicoff, from the Committee on Governmental Affairs, submitting the following Report together with Additional Views (To accompany S. 991), August 9 (legislative day May 17), 1978, in *Legislative History of Public Law 96-88, Department of Education Organization Act Part 1 and Part 2*, 96th Congress, 2nd Session, Committee Print, US Congress, Washington, DC, Senate Committee on Government Operations, 1980, 70.

72. "Summary and Purpose" in Department of Education Organization Act, Mr. Brooks, from the Committee on Government Operations, submitted the following Report together with Additional and Dissenting Views (to accompany H.R. 13778), August 25, 1978, in *Legislative History of Public Law 96-88, Department of Education Organization Act Part 1 and Part 2*, 96th Congress, 2nd Session, Committee Print, US Congress, Washington, DC, Senate Committee on Government Operations, 1980, 1006.

73. Remarks of Sen. Domenici in the *Congressional Record, Proceedings and Debates of the 96th Congress, First Session*, Vol. 125, No. 44, April 5, 1979, part of *Legislative History of Public Law 96-88, Department of Education Organization Act Part 1 and Part 2*, 96th Congress, 2nd Session, Committee Print, US Congress, Washington, DC, Senate Committee on Government Operations, 1980, 715.

74. Remarks of Sen. Levin in the *Congressional Record, Proceedings and Debates of the 96th Congress, First Session*, Vol. 125, No. 44, April 5, 1979, part of *Legislative History of Public Law 96-88, Department of Education Organization Act Part 1 and Part 2*, 96th Congress, 2nd Session, Committee Print, US Congress, Washington, DC, Senate Committee on Government Operations, 1980, 721.

75. "The Need for a Department of Education," part of Department of Education Organization Act of 1979, Report of the Committee on Governmental Affairs, US Senate, to Accompany S. 210 to Establish a Department of Education Together with Additional and Minority Views, March 27 (legislative day February 22), 1979, in *Legislative History of Public Law 96-88, Department of Education Organization Act Part 1 and Part 2*, 96th Congress, 2nd Session, Committee Print, US Congress, Washington, DC, Senate Committee on Government Operations, 1980, 519.

76. Ibid., 518.

77. Ibid., 519.

78. Ibid.

79. "Dissenting Views of Hon. William S. Moorhead" in Department of Education Organization Act, Mr. Brooks, from the Committee on Government Operations, submitted the following Report together with Separate, Additional, Supplementary, and Dissenting Views (to accompany H.R. 2444), May 14, 1979, in *Legislative History of Public Law 96-88, Department of Education Organization Act Part 1 and Part 2*, 96th Congress, 2nd Session, Committee Print, US Congress, Washington, DC, Senate Committee on Government Operations, 1980, 1161.

80. "Dissenting Views of Hon. Benjamin S. Rosenthal, Hon. John Conyers, Jr., Hon. Henry Waxman, Hon. Peter H. Kostmayer, and Hon. Ted Weiss," in Department of Education Organization Act, Mr. Brooks, from the Committee on Government Operations, submitted the following Report together with Additional and Dissenting Views (to accompany H.R. 13778), August 25, 1978, in *Legislative History of Public Law 96-88, Department of Education Organization Act Part 1 and Part 2*, 96th Congress, 2nd Session, Committee Print, US Congress, Washington, DC, Senate Committee on Government Operations, 1980, 1042.

81. Ibid., 1043.

82. Quoted in "Dissenting Views of Hon. John N. Erlenborn, Hon. Benjamin S. Rosenthal, Hon. Peter H. Kostmayer, Hon. John H. Wydler, Hon. Clarence J. Brown, Hon. Paul N. McCloskey, Hon. Thomas N. Kindness, Hon. Robert S. Walker, Hon. Arlan Stangeland, Hon. M. Caldwell Butler, Hon. Jim Jeffries, Hon. Olympia Snowe, and Hon. Wayne Grisham" in Department of Education Organization Act, Mr. Brooks, from the Committee on Government Operations, submitted the following Report together with Separate, Additional, Supplementary, and Dissenting Views (to accompany H.R. 2444), May 14, 1979, in *Legislative History of Public Law 96-88, Department of Education Organization Act Part 1 and Part 2*, 96th Congress, 2nd Session, Committee Print, US Congress, Washington, DC, Senate Committee on Government Operations, 1980, 1169–70.

83. "Additional Views of Hon. L. H. Fountain" in Department of Education Organization Act, Mr. Brooks, from the Committee on Government Operations, submitted the following Report together with Separate, Additional, Supplementary, and Dissenting Views (to accompany H.R. 2444), May 14, 1979, in *Legislative History of Public Law 96-88, Department of Education Organization Act Part 1 and Part 2*, 96th Congress, 2nd Session, Committee Print, US Congress, Washington, DC, Senate Committee on Government Operations, 1980, 1151.

84. "Dissenting Views of Hon. Peter H. Kostmayer," in Department of Education Organization Act, Mr. Brooks, from the Committee on Government Operations, submitted the following Report together with Additional and Dissenting Views (to accompany H.R. 13778), August 25, 1978, in *Legislative History of Public Law 96-88, Department of Education Organization Act Part 1 and Part 2*, 96th Congress, 2nd Session, Committee Print, US Congress, Washington, DC, Senate Committee on Government Operations, 1980, 1047.

85. Robert V. Hefferman, *Cabinetmakers: Story of the Three-Year Battle to Establish the U.S. Department of Education* (Lincoln, NE: iUniverse.com Inc., 2001), 75–76, and 118.

86. Quoted by Rep. Lawrence Fountain in "Additional Views of Hon. L. H. Fountain" in Department of Education Organization Act, Mr. Brooks, from the Committee on Government Operations, submitted the following Report together with Separate, Additional, Supplementary, and Dissenting Views (to accompany H.R. 2444), May 14, 1979, in *Legislative History of Public Law 96-88, Department of Education Organization Act Part 1 and Part 2*, 96th Congress, 2nd Session, Committee Print, US Congress, Washington, DC, Senate Committee on Government Operations, 1980, 1153.

87. Quoted by Rep. Lawrence Fountain in "Additional Views of Hon. L. H. Fountain" in Department of Education Organization Act, Mr. Brooks, from the Committee on Government Operations, submitted the following Report together with Separate, Additional, Supplementary, and Dissenting Views (to accompany H.R. 2444), May 14, 1979, in *Legislative History of Public Law 96-88, Department of Education Organization Act Part 1 and Part 2*, 96th Congress, 2nd Session, Committee Print, US Congress, Washington, DC, Senate Committee on Government Operations, 1980, 1152–53.

88. Ibid., p. 1153.

89. "The Need for a Department of Education" part of Department of Education Organization Act of 1978 (S. 991), Mr. Ribicoff, from the Committee on Governmental Affairs, submitting the following Report together with Additional Views (To accompany S. 991), August 9 (legislative day May 17), 1978, in *Legislative History of Public Law 96-88, Department of Education Organization Act Part 1 and Part 2*, 96th Congress, 2nd Session, Committee Print, US Congress, Washington, DC, Senate Committee on Government Operations, 1980, 71–72. See also "The Need for a Department of Education," part of Department of Education Organization Act of 1979, Report of the Committee on Governmental Affairs, U.S. Senate, to Accompany S. 210 to Establish a Department of Education Together with Additional and Minority Views, March 27 (legislative day February 22), 1979, in *Legislative History of Public Law 96-88, Department of Education Organization Act Part 1 and Part 2*, 96th Congress, 2nd Session, Committee Print, US Congress, Washington, DC, Senate Committee on Government Operations, 1980, 520–522.

90. Remarks of Sen. Ribicoff in the *Congressional Record, Proceedings of the 95th Congress, First Session*, Vol. 123, No. 44, March 14, 1977 (for legislative day of February 21, 1977), part of "Introduction of S. 991 in 1977" in *Legislative History of Public Law 96-88, Department of Education Organization Act Part 1 and Part 2*, 96th Congress, 2nd Session, Committee Print, US Congress, Washington, DC, Senate Committee on Government Operations, 1980, 31.

91. "The Need for a Department of Education" part of Department of Education Organization Act of 1978 (S. 991), Mr. Ribicoff, from the Committee on Governmental Affairs, submitting the following Report together with Additional Views (To accompany S. 991), August 9 (legislative day May 17), 1978, in *Legislative History of Public Law 96-88, Department of Education Organization Act Part 1 and Part 2*, 96th Congress, 2nd Session, Committee Print, U.S. Congress, Washington, DC, Senate Committee on Government Operations, 1980, 74.

92. "Purpose of the Legislation" part of Department of Education Organization Act of 1978 (S. 991), Mr. Ribicoff, from the Committee on Governmental Affairs, submitting the following Report together with Additional Views (To accompany S. 991), August 9 (legislative day May 17), 1978, in *Legislative History of Public Law 96-88,*

Department of Education Organization Act Part 1 and Part 2, 96th Congress, 2nd Session, Committee Print, US Congress, Washington, DC, Senate Committee on Government Operations, 1980, 64.

93. Quotation in ibid.

94. Ibid., 65; "Purpose of the Legislation," part of *Department of Education Organization Act of 1979, Report of the Committee on Governmental Affairs, U.S. Senate, to Accompany S. 210 to Establish a Department of Education Together with Additional and Minority Views,* March 27 (legislative day February 22), 1979, in *Legislative History of Public Law 96-88, Department of Education Organization Act Part 1 and Part 2,* 96th Congress, 2nd Session, Committee Print, US Congress, Washington, DC, Senate Committee on Government Operations, 1980, 530.

95. "The Need for a Department of Education" part of Department of Education Organization Act of 1978 (S. 991), Mr. Ribicoff, from the Committee on Governmental Affairs, submitting the following Report together with Additional Views (To accompany S. 991), August 9 (legislative day May 17), 1978, in *Legislative History of Public Law 96-88, Department of Education Organization Act Part 1 and Part 2,* 96th Congress, 2nd Session, Committee Print, US Congress, Washington, DC, Senate Committee on Government Operations, 1980, 69.

96. "Purpose of the Legislation," part of Department of Education Organization Act of 1978 (S. 991), Mr. Ribicoff, from the Committee on Governmental Affairs, submitting the following Report together with Additional Views (To accompany S. 991), August 9 (legislative day May 17), 1978, in *Legislative History of Public Law 96-88, Department of Education Organization Act Part 1 and Part 2,* 96th Congress, 2nd Session, Committee Print, US Congress, Washington, DC, Senate Committee on Government Operations, 1980, 68.

97. "Additional Views of Hon. L. H. Fountain" in Department of Education Organization Act, Mr. Brooks, from the Committee on Government Operations, submitted the following Report together with Separate, Additional, Supplementary, and Dissenting Views (to accompany H.R. 2444), May 14, 1979, in *Legislative History of Public Law 96-88, Department of Education Organization Act Part 1 and Part 2,* 96th Congress, 2nd Session, Committee Print, US Congress, Washington, DC, Senate Committee on Government Operations, 1980, 1150 and 1152.

98. "Dissenting Views of Hon. Benjamin S. Rosenthal, Hon. John Conyers, Hon. Henry A. Waxman, and Hon. Ted Weiss" in Department of Education Organization Act, Mr. Brooks, from the Committee on Government Operations, submitted the following Report together with Separate, Additional, Supplementary, and Dissenting Views (to accompany H.R. 2444), May 14, 1979, in *Legislative History of Public Law 96-88, Department of Education Organization Act Part 1 and Part 2,* 96th Congress, 2nd Session, Committee Print, US Congress, Washington, DC, Senate Committee on Government Operations, 1980, 1163.

99. "Dissenting Views of Hon. John N. Erlenborn, Hon. Benjamin S. Rosenthal, Hon. Peter H. Kostmayer, Hon. John H. Wydler, Hon. Clarence J. Brown, Hon. Paul N. McCloskey, Hon. Thomas N. Kindness, Hon. Robert S. Walker, Hon. Arlan Stangeland, Hon. M. Caldwell Butler, Hon. Jim Jeffries, Hon. Olympia Snowe, and Hon. Wayne Grisham" in Department of Education Organization Act, Mr. Brooks, from the Committee on Government Operations, submitted the following Report

together with Separate, Additional, Supplementary, and Dissenting Views (to accompany H.R. 2444), May 14, 1979, in *Legislative History of Public Law 96-88, Department of Education Organization Act Part 1 and Part 2*, 96th Congress, 2nd Session, Committee Print, US Congress, Washington, DC, Senate Committee on Government Operations, 1980, 1171–72.

100. Quoted in ibid., 1172.

101. President Jimmy Carter, "Elementary and Secondary Education Message to the Congress," February 28, 1978, The American Presidency Project, http://www.presidency .ucsb.edu/ws/index.php?pid=30429&st=&st1=#axzz10enzLnS1.

102. "The Need for a Department of Education," part of Department of Education Organization Act of 1979, Report of the Committee on Governmental Affairs, US Senate, to Accompany S. 210 to Establish a Department of Education Together with Additional and Minority Views, March 27 (legislative day February 22), 1979, in *Legislative History of Public Law 96-88, Department of Education Organization Act Part 1 and Part 2*, 96th Congress, 2nd Session, Committee Print, US Congress, Washington, DC, Senate Committee on Government Operations, 1980, 522–23.

103. "Improving the Federal Government's Responsibilities in Education: Better Interagency Coordination," part of Department of Education Organization Act of 1979, Report of the Committee on Governmental Affairs, US Senate, to Accompany S. 210 to Establish a Department of Education Together with Additional and Minority Views, March 27 (legislative day February 22), 1979, in *Legislative History of Public Law 96-88, Department of Education Organization Act Part 1 and Part 2*, 96th Congress, 2nd Session, Committee Print, US Congress, Washington, DC, Senate Committee on Government Operations, 1980, 535.

104. "The Need for a Department of Education," part of Department of Education Organization Act of 1979, Report of the Committee on Governmental Affairs, US Senate, to Accompany S. 210 to Establish a Department of Education Together with Additional and Minority Views, March 27 (legislative day February 22), 1979, in *Legislative History of Public Law 96-88, Department of Education Organization Act Part 1 and Part 2*, 96th Congress, 2nd Session, Committee Print, US Congress, Washington, DC, Senate Committee on Government Operations, 1980, 524.

105. Remarks of Sen. Ribicoff in the *Congressional Record, Proceedings and Debates of the 96th Congress, First Session*, Vol. 125, No. 44, April 5, 1979, part of *Legislative History of Public Law 96-88, Department of Education Organization Act Part 1 and Part 2*, 96th Congress, 2nd Session, Committee Print, US Congress, Washington, DC, Senate Committee on Government Operations, 1980, 683.

106. "The Need for a Department of Education," part of Department of Education Organization Act of 1979, Report of the Committee on Governmental Affairs, US Senate, to Accompany S. 210 to Establish a Department of Education Together with Additional and Minority Views, March 27 (legislative day February 22), 1979, in *Legislative History of Public Law 96-88, Department of Education Organization Act Part 1 and Part 2, 96th Congress, 2nd Session*, Committee Print, US Congress, Washington, DC, Senate Committee on Government Operations, 1980, 523–24.

107. See the remarks of Sen. Levin in the *Congressional Record, Proceedings and Debates of the 96th Congress, First Session*, Vol. 125, No. 44, April 5, 1979, part of *Legislative History of Public Law 96-88, Department of Education Organization Act Part 1 and Part 2*,

96th Congress, 2nd Session, Committee Print, US Congress, Washington, DC, Senate Committee on Government Operations, 1980, 722.

108. "Evaluation of Regulatory Impact," part of Department of Education Organization Act of 1979, Report of the Committee on Governmental Affairs, U.S. Senate, to Accompany S. 210 to Establish a Department of Education Together with Additional and Minority Views, March 27 (legislative day February 22), 1979, in *Legislative History of Public Law 96-88, Department of Education Organization Act Part 1 and Part 2*, 96th Congress, 2nd Session, Committee Print, US Congress, Washington, DC, Senate Committee on Government Operations, 1980, 607–608.

109. Remarks of Sen. Nunn in the *Congressional Record, Proceedings and Debates of the 96th Congress, First Session*, Vol. 125, No. 44, April 5, 1979, part of *Legislative History of Public Law 96-88, Department of Education Organization Act Part 1 and Part 2*, 96th Congress, 2nd Session, Committee Print, US Congress, Washington, DC, Senate Committee on Government Operations, 1980, 704.

110. See Amendment 1855 proposed by Sen. Roth, in the *Congressional Record, Proceedings of the 95th Congress, Second Session, Vol.* 124, No. 147, September 20, 1978 (for legislative day of August 16, 1978), in *Legislative History of Public Law 96-88, Department of Education Organization Act Part 1 and Part 2*, 96th Congress, 2nd Session, Committee Print, US Congress, Washington, DC, Senate Committee on Government Operations, 1980, 288–91; quotation on p. 290. Sen. Roth's amendment was included in the final version of Department of Education Organization Act of 1978 (S. 991), Title IV, Sec. 403 (a) Annual Authorization of Personnel, as passed by the Senate, see the *Congressional Record, Proceedings of the 95th Congress, Second Session, Vol.* 124, No. 154, September 28, 1978 (for legislative day of September 26, 1978), in *Legislative History of Public Law 96-88, Department of Education Organization Act Part 1 and Part 2*, 96th Congress, 2nd Session, Committee Print, US Congress, Washington, DC, Senate Committee on Government Operations, 1980, 406.

111. "Inflationary Impact" in Department of Education Organization Act, Mr. Brooks, from the Committee on Government Operations, submitted the following Report together with Additional and Dissenting Views (to accompany H.R. 13778), August 25, 1978, in *Legislative History of Public Law 96-88, Department of Education Organization Act Part 1 and Part 2*, 96th Congress, 2nd Session, Committee Print, US Congress, Washington, DC, Senate Committee on Government Operations, 1980, 1017.

112. "The Need for a Department of Education," part of Department of Education Organization Act of 1979, Report of the Committee on Governmental Affairs, US Senate, to Accompany S. 210 to Establish a Department of Education Together with Additional and Minority Views, March 27 (legislative day February 22), 1979, in *Legislative History of Public Law 96-88, Department of Education Organization Act Part 1 and Part 2*, 96th Congress, 2nd Session, Committee Print, US Congress, Washington, DC, Senate Committee on Government Operations, 1980, 525.

113. Ibid., 526; "Estimated Cost of the Legislation," 608.

114. Ibid., 525.

115. Ibid.

116. "Estimated Cost of the Legislation," part of *Department of Education Organization Act of 1979, Report of the Committee on Governmental Affairs, U.S. Senate, to Accompany S. 210 to Establish a Department of Education Together with Additional and*

Minority Views, March 27 (legislative day February 22), 1979, in *Legislative History of Public Law 96-88, Department of Education Organization Act Part 1 and Part 2,* 96th Congress, 2nd Session, Committee Print, US Congress, Washington, DC, Senate Committee on Government Operations, 1980, 608.

117. Remarks of Sen. Sasser in the *Congressional Record, Proceedings and Debates of the 96th Congress, First Session,* Vol. 125, No. 44, April 5, 1979, part of *Legislative History of Public Law 96-88, Department of Education Organization Act Part 1 and Part 2,* 96th Congress, 2nd Session, Committee Print, US Congress, Washington, DC, Senate Committee on Government Operations, 1980, 712.

118. "The Need for a Department of Education," part of Department of Education Organization Act of 1979, Report of the Committee on Governmental Affairs, US Senate, to Accompany S. 210 to Establish a Department of Education Together with Additional and Minority Views, March 27 (legislative day February 22), 1979, in *Legislative History of Public Law 96-88, Department of Education Organization Act Part 1 and Part 2,* 96th Congress, 2nd Session, Committee Print, US Congress, Washington, DC, Senate Committee on Government Operations, 1980, 526.

119. Quoted by Rep. Lawrence Fountain in "Additional Views of Hon. L. H. Fountain" in Department of Education Organization Act, Mr. Brooks, from the Committee on Government Operations, submitted the following Report together with Separate, Additional, Supplementary, and Dissenting Views (to accompany H.R. 2444), May 14, 1979, in *Legislative History of Public Law 96-88, Department of Education Organization Act Part 1 and Part 2,* 96th Congress, 2nd Session, Committee Print, US Congress, Washington, DC, Senate Committee on Government Operations, 1980, 1153.

120. "Dissenting Views of Hon. Leo J. Ryan," in Department of Education Organization Act, Mr. Brooks, from the Committee on Government Operations, submitted the following Report together with Additional and Dissenting Views (to accompany H.R. 13778), August 25, 1978, in *Legislative History of Public Law 96-88, Department of Education Organization Act Part 1 and Part 2,* 96th Congress, 2nd Session, Committee Print, US Congress, Washington, DC, Senate Committee on Government Operations, 1980, 1044.

121. Remarks of Sen. Hayakawa in the *Congressional Record, Proceedings and Debates of the 96th Congress, First Session,* Vol. 125, No. 44, April 5, 1979, part of *Legislative History of Public Law 96-88, Department of Education Organization Act Part 1 and Part 2,* 96th Congress, 2nd Session, Committee Print, US Congress, Washington, DC, Senate Committee on Government Operations, 1980, 709.

122. "Minority Views of Mr. Cohen," part of Department of Education Organization Act of 1979, Report of the Committee on Governmental Affairs, US Senate, to Accompany S. 210 to Establish a Department of Education Together with Additional and Minority Views, March 27 (legislative day February 22), 1979, in *Legislative History of Public Law 96-88, Department of Education Organization Act Part 1 and Part 2,* 96th Congress, 2nd Session, Committee Print, US Congress, Washington, DC, Senate Committee on Government Operations, 1980, 614; Remarks of Sen. Cohen in the *Congressional Record, Proceedings and Debates of the 96th Congress, First Session,* Vol. 125, No. 44, April 5, 1979, part of *Legislative History of Public Law 96-88, Department of Education Organization Act Part 1 and Part 2,* 96th Congress, 2nd Session, Committee Print, US Congress, Washington, DC, Senate Committee on Government Operations, 1980, 698–99.

123. Ibid.

124. "Dissenting Views of Hon. Robert S. Walker" in Department of Education Organization Act, Mr. Brooks, from the Committee on Government Operations, submitted the following Report together with Separate, Additional, Supplementary, and Dissenting Views (to accompany H.R. 2444), May 14, 1979, in *Legislative History of Public Law 96-88, Department of Education Organization Act Part 1 and Part 2*, 96th Congress, 2nd Session, Committee Print, US Congress, Washington, DC, Senate Committee on Government Operations, 1980, 1175.

125. Remarks of Sen. Hayakawa in the *Congressional Record, Proceedings and Debates of the 96th Congress, First Session*, Vol. 125, No. 44, April 5, 1979, part of *Legislative History of Public Law 96-88, Department of Education Organization Act Part 1 and Part 2*, 96th Congress, 2nd Session, Committee Print, US Congress, Washington, DC, Senate Committee on Government Operations, 1980, 708–709.

126. Remarks of Sen. Ribicoff in the *Congressional Record, Proceedings of the 95th Congress, First Session*, Vol. 123, No. 44, March 14, 1977 (for legislative day of February 21, 1977), part of "Introduction of S. 991 in 1977" in *Legislative History of Public Law 96-88, Department of Education Organization Act Part 1 and Part 2*, 96th Congress, 2nd Session, Committee Print, US Congress, Washington, DC, Senate Committee on Government Operations, 1980, 33.

127. "Purpose of the Legislation" part of Department of Education Organization Act of 1978 (S. 991), Mr. Ribicoff, from the Committee on Governmental Affairs, submitting the following Report together with Additional Views (To accompany S. 991), August 9 (legislative day May 17), 1978, in *Legislative History of Public Law 96-88, Department of Education Organization Act Part 1 and Part 2*, 96th Congress, 2nd Session, Committee Print, US Congress, Washington, DC, Senate Committee on Government Operations, 1980, 65–67.

128. "Purpose of the Legislation," part of Department of Education Organization Act of 1979, Report of the Committee on Governmental Affairs, US Senate, to Accompany S. 210 to Establish a Department of Education Together with Additional and Minority Views, March 27 (legislative day February 22), 1979, in *Legislative History of Public Law 96-88, Department of Education Organization Act Part 1 and Part 2*, 96th Congress, 2nd Session, Committee Print, US Congress, Washington, DC, Senate Committee on Government Operations, 1980, 530.

129. Remarks of Sen. Ribicoff in the *Congressional Record, Proceedings of the 95th Congress, First Session*, Vol. 123, No. 44, March 14, 1977 (for legislative day of February 21, 1977), part of "Introduction of S. 991 in 1977" in *Legislative History of Public Law 96-88, Department of Education Organization Act Part 1 and Part 2*, 96th Congress, 2nd Session, Committee Print, US Congress, Washington, DC, Senate Committee on Government Operations, 1980, 30–31; "The Need for a Department of Education" part of Department of Education Organization Act of 1978 (S. 991), Mr. Ribicoff, from the Committee on Governmental Affairs, submitting the following Report together with Additional Views (To accompany S. 991), August 9 (legislative day May 17), 1978, in *Legislative History of Public Law 96-88, Department of Education Organization Act Part 1 and Part 2*, 96th Congress, 2nd Session, Committee Print, US Congress, Washington, DC, Senate Committee on Government Operations, 1980, 71.

130. Remarks of Sen. Ribicoff in the *Congressional Record, Proceedings of the 95th Congress, First Session*, Vol. 123, No. 44, March 14, 1977 (for legislative day of February 21,

1977), part of "Introduction of S. 991 in 1977" in *Legislative History of Public Law 96-88, Department of Education Organization Act Part 1 and Part 2*, 96th Congress, 2nd Session, Committee Print, US Congress, Washington, DC, Senate Committee on Government Operations, 1980, 30–31.

131. "The Need for a Department of Education" part of Department of Education Organization Act of 1978 (S. 991), Mr. Ribicoff, from the Committee on Governmental Affairs, submitting the following Report together with Additional Views (To accompany S. 991), August 9 (legislative day May 17), 1978, in *Legislative History of Public Law 96-88, Department of Education Organization Act Part 1 and Part 2*, 96th Congress, 2nd Session, Committee Print, US Congress, Washington, DC, Senate Committee on Government Operations, 1980, 70.

132. Remarks of Rep. Brooks in the *Congressional Record, Proceedings and Debates of the 96th Congress, First Session*, July 11, 1979, part of Legislative History of Public Law 96-88, Department of Education Organization Act Part 1 and Part 2, 96th Congress, 2nd Session, Committee Print, US Congress, Washington, DC, Senate Committee on Government Operations, 1980, 1543.

133. Remarks of Rep. Levitas in the *Congressional Record, Proceedings and Debates of the 96th Congress, First Session,* July 11, 1979, part *of Legislative History of Public Law 96-88, Department of Education Organization Act Part 1 and Part 2*, 96th Congress, 2nd Session, Committee Print, US Congress, Washington, DC, Senate Committee on Government Operations, 1980, 1543.

134. Remarks of House Speaker O'Neil in the *Congressional Record, Proceedings and Debates of the 96th Congress, First Session*, September 27, 1979, part of *Legislative History of Public Law 96-88, Department of Education Organization Act Part 1 and Part 2*, 96th Congress, 2nd Session, Committee Print, US Congress, Washington, DC, Senate Committee on Government Operations, 1980, 1828.

135. "Dissenting Views of Hon. Benjamin S. Rosenthal, Hon. John Conyers, Jr., Hon. Henry Waxman, Hon. Peter H. Kostmayer, and Hon. Ted Weiss," in Department of Education Organization Act, Mr. Brooks, from the Committee on Government Operations, submitted the following Report together with Additional and Dissenting Views (to accompany H.R. 13778), August 25, 1978, in *Legislative History of Public Law 96-88, Department of Education Organization Act Part 1 and Part 2*, 96th Congress, 2nd Session, Committee Print, US Congress, Washington, DC, Senate Committee on Government Operations, 1980, 1042.

136. "Dissenting Views of Hon. Benjamin S. Rosenthal, Hon. John Conyers, Jr., Hon. Henry Waxman, Hon. Peter H. Kostmayer, and Hon. Ted Weiss," in Department of Education Organization Act, Mr. Brooks, from the Committee on Government Operations, submitted the following Report together with Additional and Dissenting Views (to accompany H.R. 13778), August 25, 1978, in *Legislative History of Public Law 96-88, Department of Education Organization Act Part 1 and Part 2*, 96th Congress, 2nd Session, Committee Print, US Congress, Washington, DC, Senate Committee on Government Operations, 1980, 1043.

137. "Dissenting Views of Hon. John N. Erlenborn, Hon. Benjamin S. Rosenthal, Hon. Peter H. Kostmayer, Hon. John H. Wydler, Hon. Clarence J. Brown, Hon. Paul N. McCloskey, Hon. Thomas N. Kindness, Hon. Robert S. Walker, Hon. Arlan Stangeland, Hon. M. Caldwell Butler, Hon. Jim Jeffries, Hon. Olympia Snowe, and Hon.

Wayne Grisham" in Department of Education Organization Act, Mr. Brooks, from the Committee on Government Operations, submitted the following Report together with Separate, Additional, Supplementary, and Dissenting Views (to accompany H.R. 2444), May 14, 1979, in *Legislative History of Public Law 96-88, Department of Education Organization Act Part 1 and Part 2*, 96th Congress, 2nd Session, Committee Print, US Congress, Washington, DC, Senate Committee on Government Operations, 1980, 1173.

138. Remarks of Sen. Moynihan in the *Congressional Record, Proceedings and Debates of the 96th Congress, First Session*, April 26, 1979, part of *Legislative History of Public Law 96-88, Department of Education Organization Act Part 1 and Part 2*, 96th Congress, 2nd Session, Committee Print, US Congress, Washington, DC, Senate Committee on Government Operations, 1980, 784–85.

139. Remarks of Rep. Bob Michel in the *Congressional Record, Proceedings and Debates of the 96th Congress, First Session*, September 27, 1979, part of *Legislative History of Public Law 96-88, Department of Education Organization Act Part 1 and Part 2*, 96th Congress, 2nd Session, Committee Print, US Congress, Washington, DC, Senate Committee on Government Operations, 1980, 1809.

140. "Dissenting Views of Hon. Ted Weiss" in Department of Education Organization Act, Mr. Brooks, from the Committee on Government Operations, submitted the following Report together with Separate, Additional, Supplementary, and Dissenting Views (to accompany H.R. 2444), May 14, 1979, in *Legislative History of Public Law 96-88, Department of Education Organization Act Part 1 and Part 2*, 96th Congress, 2nd Session, Committee Print, US Congress, Washington, DC, Senate Committee on Government Operations, 1980, 1167.

141. "Dissenting Views of Hon. Peter H. Kostmayer" in Department of Education Organization Act, Mr. Brooks, from the Committee on Government Operations, submitted the following Report together with Separate, Additional, Supplementary, and Dissenting Views (to accompany H.R. 2444), May 14, 1979, in *Legislative History of Public Law 96-88, Department of Education Organization Act Part 1 and Part 2*, 96th Congress, 2nd Session, Committee Print, US Congress, Washington, DC, Senate Committee on Government Operations, 1980, 1168.

142. *Congressional Record*, September 24, 1979, 25826.

143. *Congressional Record, Proceedings and Debates of the 96th Congress, First Session*, September 24, 1979, part of *Legislative History of Public Law 96-88, Department of Education Organization Act Part 1 and Part 2*, 96th Congress, 2nd Session, Committee Print, US Congress, Washington, DC, Senate Committee on Government Operations, 1980, 938.

144. See the remarks of Rep. James T. Broyhill (R-NC) in the *Congressional Record, Proceedings and Debates of the 96th Congress, First Session*, July 11 1979, part of *Legislative History of Public Law 96-88, Department of Education Organization Act Part 1 and Part 2*, 96th Congress, 2nd Session, Committee Print, US Congress, Washington, DC, Senate Committee on Government Operations, 1980, 1555–56.

145. See the motion to recommit by Rep. Erlenborn (R-IL) in the *Congressional Record, Proceedings and Debates of the 96th Congress, First Session*, July 11 1979, part of *Legislative History of Public Law 96-88, Department of Education Organization Act Part 1 and Part 2*, 96th Congress, 2nd Session, Committee Print, US Congress, Washington, DC, Senate Committee on Government Operations, 1980, 1558.

146. "Carter's 'Crisis of Confidence' Speech," *The American Experience*, PBS, http://www
.pbs.org/wgbh/americanexperience/features/general-article/carter-crisis-speech/.
147. Craig Collins, "The Politics of Education," in *National Education Association:
1857–2007: 150 Years of Advancing Great Public Schools*, 66-71: 67;and Heffernan,
Cabinetmakers, 25 and 28.
148. James Lee Annis, *Howard Baker: Conciliator in an Age of Crisis* (Knoxville: University
of Tennessee Press, 2007): 147; Heffernan, *Cabinetmakers*, 115–16.
149. Heffernan, *Cabinetmakers,* 18, 36–37, and 70–76ff; Jennifer L. Fisher, "A Hermeneutics Approach to Studying Agenda-setting: The Postwar Education Agenda (1945–
1998)," (PhD Diss. University of West Virginia, 2000): 62; States Impact on Federal
Education Policy, "Federal Education Policy and the States, 1945–2009. The Carter
Years: Department of Education," http://www.archives.nysed.gov/edpolicy/research/
res_essay_carter_dept_ed.shtml.
150. "House Narrowly Passes Department of Education Bill," *New York Times* via *The
Spokesman Review*, July 12, 1979.
151. Heffernan, *Cabinetmakers*, 36–37, 68, and 81.
152. Ibid., 114 ff.
153. Ibid., 82.
154. *Congressional Record, Proceedings and Debates of the 96th Congress, First Session*,
September 24, 1979, part of *Legislative History of Public Law 96-88, Department of
Education Organization Act Part 1 and Part 2*, 96th Congress, 2nd Session, Committee Print, US Congress, Washington, DC, Senate Committee on Government
Operations, 1980, 1829–1830. Updated figures from Govtrack.us House Vote #468,
96th Congress, September 27, 1979.
155. Ray Henry, "Newt Gingrich Ran as Moderate in Early Campaigns," *Huffington Post*,
February 26, 2012, http://www.huffingtonpost.com/2012/02/26/newt-gingrich
-moderate_n_1302205.html; Sheryl Gay Stolberg, "For Gingrich in Power, Prag-
matism, Not Purity," *New York Times*, December 20, 2011; John Anderson for
President 1980 Campaign Brochure, "Most polls show that if people believe John
Anderson can win, he will win. Your support will make Anderson President,"
http://www.4president.org/brochures/andersonlucey1980brochure.htm.

Chapter 4

1. Federal Education Policy History, National Defense Education Act of 1958, http://
federaleducationpolicy.wordpress.com/2011/06/03/national-defense-education-act
-of-1958-2/. The Smith-Hughes Act of 1917 awarded federal matching grants to the
states to support elementary and secondary agriculture-related vocational education
and to address concerns in the wake of World War I that a significant number of con-
scripts lacked basic skills. Today it is called the Perkins Act. Given its narrow scope, it
is not considered as far-reaching as the NDEA or the ESEA of 1965. See Christopher
Cross, "The Evolving Role of the Federal Government in Education," in "After Student Standards: Alignment" (Online: Pearson Assessments, 2005), 2, http://images
.pearsonassessments.com/images/NES_Publications/2005_02Cross_513_1.pdf; the
US Department of Education, Carl D. Perkins Career and Technical Education Act
of 2006, http://www2.ed.gov/policy/sectech/leg/perkins/index.html; Federal Educa-

tion Policy History, Vocational Education Act of 1917, or Smith-Hughes Act of 1917, http://federaleducationpolicy.wordpress.com/2011/02/19/1917-vocational-education -act-or-smith-hughes-act/.

2. Pamela Ebert Flattua et al., *National Defense Education Act of 1958: Selected Outcomes*, IDA, Science and Technology Policy Institute, March 2006, III-1-6.

3. Goldwater, *Conscience of a Conservative*, 76.

4. Pamela Ebert Flattua et al., *National Defense Education Act of 1958: Selected Outcomes*, IDA, Science and Technology Policy Institute, March 2006, III-3.

5. "Chronology of Federal Education Legislation," Chapter 4 of Thomas D. Snyder and Sally A. Dillow, *Digest of Education Statistics 2011*, National Center for Education Statistics, Institute of Education Sciences, US Department of Education, June 13, 2012, 545; US Department of Education, Elementary and Secondary Education: Table of Contents, http://www2.ed.gov/policy/elsec/leg/esea02/index.html.

6. The ESEA was reauthorized in 1968, 1972, 1978, 1983, 1989, 1994, 1999, and 2001. See the National Clearinghouse for English Language Acquisition (NCELA), ESEA Reauthorization, http://www.ncela.gwu.edu/content/2_esea_reauthorization; cf. Digitized Documents: 1965–2001 Elementary and Secondary Education Act (ESEA), States' Impact on Federal Education Policy Project (SIFEPP), New York State Archives, Albany, http://nysa32.nysed.gov/edpolicy/research/res_digitized.shtml.

7. Sec. 604 in Copy of the Original Elementary and Secondary Education Act of 1965 (P.L. 89-10; 79 Stat. 27), Federal Education Policy History, 57, http://federaleducation policy.wordpress.com/2011/02/19/1965-elementary-and-secondary-education-act/.

8. McCluskey, *Feds in the Classroom*, 42.

9. Ibid., 36.

10. Synder et al.,"Chronology of Federal Education Legislation," 550–51.

11. Goldwater, *Conscience of a Conservative*, 76.

12. Public Law 107-110 107th Congress, "No Child Left Behind Act of 2001," January 28, 2002, www2.ed.gov/legislation/esea02/107-110.pdf; cf. Public Law 107-110— US Government Printing Office. It is commonly said that the original bill had 1,100 pages. See *Federal Education Policy and the States, 1945–2009: A Brief Synopsis*, States' Impact on Federal Education Policy Project (SIFEPP), New York State Archives, Albany, January 2006, revised November 2009, 73–74.

13. *Federal Education Policy and the States, 1945–2009: A Brief Synopsis*, 16–17.

14. Quoted in Erik Robelen, "The Evolving Federal Role," *Education Week*, November 17, 1999. On March 26, 1965, the ESEA legislation passed the House by a margin of 263 to 153. Just 57 Democrats and 95 Republicans opposed it. On April 9, 1965, The Senate passed the ESEA legislation by an even larger majority, 73 to 18. Just three Democrats and 14 Republicans opposed it. See "To Pass H.R. 2362, The Elementary and Secondary Education Act of 1965," House Vote #26, 89th Congress, http://www .govtrack.us/congress/votes/89-1965/h26; "To Pass H.R. 2362, The Elementary and Secondary Education Act of 1965," Senate Vote #48, April 9, 1965, http://www .govtrack.us/congress/votes/89-1965/s48.

15. Title I, Sections 205 (5) and (6) and Section 206 (3)A. See Copy of the Original Elementary and Secondary Education Act of 1965, (P.L. 89-10; 79 Stat. 27), Federal Education Policy History, 31–32, http://federaleducationpolicy.wordpress.com/2011/ 02/19/1965-elementary-and-secondary-education-act/.

16. See, for example, Title II, Section 203; Title IV, Section 401, Sec. 2 (a) (2)(d); Title V, Sec. 510 (a) in Copy of the Original Elementary and Secondary Education Act of 1965, (P.L. 89-10; 79 Stat. 27), Federal Education Policy History, 37–38, 45, 54–55, http://federaleducationpolicy.wordpress.com/2011/02/19/1965-elementary-and-secondary-education-act/.

17. Quoted in *Federal Education Policy and the States, 1945–2009: A Brief Synopsis*, 18.

18. Ibid., 19.

19. Ruby Martin and Phyllis McClure, *Title I of ESEA: Is It Helping Poor Children?*, US Department of Health Education, and Welfare, December 1969.See also *Federal Education Policy and the States, 1945–2009: A Brief Synopsis*, 24–25.

20. Garvin Hudgins, "Title I of ESEA Plundered by Blunder," *Gettysburg Times*, December 15, 1969.

21. Martin and McClure, 27–28.

22. Quoted in *Federal Education Policy and the States, 1945–2009: A Brief Synopsis*, 24.

23. Erik Robelen, "40 Years After ESEA, Federal Role in Schools is Broader than Ever," *Education Week*, April 13, 2005.

24. See, for example, Donald H. McLaughlin, *Title I, 1965–1975: Synthesis of the Findings of Federal Studies*, American Institutes for Research in the Behavioral Sciences (Palo Alto, CA: 1977).

25. McCluskey, *Feds in the Classroom*, 41; *Federal Education Policy and the States, 1945–2009: A Brief Synopsis*, States' Impact on Federal Education Policy Project (SIFEPP), New York State Archives, Albany, January 2006, revised November 2009, 52; cf. Elementary and Secondary Education Amendment of 1974 (P.L. 93-380) in United States Statues at Large, Vol. 88, 93rd Congress, 2nd Session, US Government Printing Office, 488–514; Public Law 93-380, 93rd Congress, H.R. 69, August 21, 1974: An Act to Extend and Amend the Elementary and Secondary Act of 1965, and for Other Purposes, THOMAS, http://thomas.loc.gov/cgi-bin/bdquery/z?d093:H.R.69:.

26. *Federal Education Policy and the States, 1945–2009: A Brief Synopsis*, States' Impact on Federal Education Policy Project (SIFEPP), New York State Archives, Albany, January 2006, revised November 2009, 29 and 36.

27. Quoted in *Federal Education Policy and the States, 1945–2009: A Brief Synopsis*, States' Impact on Federal Education Policy Project (SIFEPP), New York State Archives, Albany, January 2006, revised November 2009, 29.

28. Quoted in *Federal Education Policy and the States, 1945–2009: A Brief Synopsis*, States' Impact on Federal Education Policy Project (SIFEPP), New York State Archives, Albany, January 2006, revised November 2009, 29; cf. McCluskey, *Feds in the Classroom,* 44.

29. Gareth Davies, See *Government Grow: Education Politics from Johnson to Reagan* (Lawrence: University of Kansas Press, 2007).

30. Gerald R. Ford, "Education for all Handicapped Children Act, Signing Statement," December 2, 1975. Ford Library and Museum, Ann Arbor, Michigan; cf. "Education for all Handicapped Children Act," *Human and Civil Rights: Essential Primary Sources*, eds. Adrienne Lerner, Brenda Lerner, and K. Lee Lerner (Detroit: Gale, 2006) 459–462, online via Global Issues in Context. Web. September 21, 2012.

31. Jim Cannon Memorandum, "Enrolled Bill S. 6 – Education for All Handicapped Children Act of 1975," presented to Gerald Ford, November 28, 1975, Library of Congress, National Archives.

32. Diane Ravitch, "The Sixties," Chapter 10 of *Left Back: A Century of Battles Over School Reform* (New York: Simon and Schuster, 2000), 366–407.

33. Lyndon B. Johnson, "Message from the President of the United States Transmitting Education Program," House of Representatives, Committee on Education and Labor, January 12, 1965, 88th Congress, 1st Session, Document #45, p. 16 of Copy of the Original Elementary and Secondary Education Act of 1965, (P.L. 89-10; 79 Stat. 27), Federal Education Policy History, 37–38, 45, 54–55, http://federaleducationpolicy .wordpress.com/2011/02/19/1965-elementary-and-secondary-education-act/.

34. Paul Berman and Milbrey Wallin McLaughlin, *Federal Programs Supporting Educational Change, Vol. III: Implementing and Sustaining Innovations*, prepared for the US Office of Education, Department of Health, Education and Welfare, RAND Corporation, May 1978, vi–vii, and 10–11.

35. Paul Berman and Milbrey Wallin McLaughlin, *Federal Programs Supporting Educational Change, Vol. III: Implementing and Sustaining Innovations*, Prepared for the US Office of Education, Department of Health, Education and Welfare, RAND Corporation, May 1978, 35.

36. Quoted in *Federal Education Policy and the States, 1945–2009: A Brief Synopsis*, States' Impact on Federal Education Policy Project (SIFEPP), New York State Archives, Albany, January 2006, revised November 2009, 43; cf. Noel Epstein, "Study Shows Innovation Education Makes Little Difference in Student Achievement," *The Modesto Bee*, January 4, 1977.

37. *Federal Education Policy and the States, 1945–2009: A Brief Synopsis*, States' Impact on Federal Education Policy Project (SIFEPP), New York State Archives, Albany, January 2006, revised November 2009, 43.

38. "Reagan Calls Department of Education 'Bureaucratic Boondoggle'," NBC News, New York, NY: NBC Universal, May 4, 1980, NBC Learns archives.

39. "The Bell Memorandum," *Education Week*, September 7, 1981.

40. Remarks of Sen. Hayakawa in the *Congressional Record, Proceedings of the 95th Congress, Second Session*, Vol. 124, No. 154, April 26, 1979 (for legislative day of September 26, 1978), in *Legislative History of Public Law 96-88, Department of Education Organization Act Part 1 and Part 2*, 96th Congress, 2nd Session, Committee Print, US Congress, Washington, DC, Senate Committee on Government Operations, 1980, 815–16.

41. Carol Herrnstadt Shulman, *Compliance with Federal Regulations: At What Cost?*, American Association for Higher Education-ERIC/ Higher Education Research Report No. 6, 1978, 35. Separately, Reagan had established a Presidential Task Force on Regulatory Relief. See Ronald Reagan, "Remarks Announcing the Establishment of the Presidential Task Force on Regulatory Relief," January 22, 1981. Online by Gerhard Peters and John T. Woolley, The American Presidency Project, http://www .presidency.ucsb.edu/ws/?pid=43635; Ronald Reagan, "White House Report on the Program for Economic Recovery," February 18, 1981. Online by Gerhard Peters and John T. Woolley, The American Presidency Project, http://www.presidency.ucsb.edu/ ws/?pid=43427; "Executive Order 12498 — Regulatory Planning Process," *Federal Register*, National Archives, http://www.archives.gov/federal-register/codification/ executive-order/12498.html. See also, US Advisory Commission on Intergovernmental Relations, *Federal Regulation of State & Local Governments: The Mixed Record of the 1980s* (Washington, DC: DIANE Publishing Company, 1993), 17–30.

42. "Department of Education Under Fire: Reagan's Task Force's Report Due," *School Library Journal*, Vol. 27, Issue 4 (December 1980): 8.

43. Ronald Reagan, "Address to the Nation on the Program for Economic Recovery," September 24, 1981. Online by Gerhard Peters and John T. Woolley, The American Presidency Project, http://www.presidency.ucsb.edu/ws/?pid=44296. Polling done during this time indicated popular opposition to federal intrusion in education as well as uncertainty about abolishing the Department of Education. Prior to Reagan's economic recovery plan address, just 27 percent of Americans favored abolishing the Department of Education, increasing to 32 percent afterward. See the Harris Survey taken September 19–24, 1981, and an ABC poll conducted September 25–26, 1981, quoted in Brandice Canes-Wrone, *Who Leads Whom? Presidents, Policy, and the Public* (Chicago: University of Chicago Press, 2006), 44–45. Yet other polls conducted over the next year showed that more than 80 percent of respondents did not believe education should be a federal function. See "Reagan Revolution Stalled in Education Department," *Education Update*, Vol. 6, No. 2, The Heritage Foundation, April 1982, Onalee McGraw, ed.; Onalee McGraw, "For Whom Does Terrel Bell Toil," *The Rock Hill Herald*, June 3, 1982.

44. Omnibus Budget Reconciliation Act of 1981 (P.L. 97-35), Bill Summary & Status, 97th Congress (1981–1982) H.R.3982, Library of Congress, http://thomas.loc.gov/cgi-bin/bdquery/z?d097:H.R.3982:; H.R. 3982 (97th): Omnibus Budget Reconciliation Act of 1981, http://www.govtrack.us/congress/bills/97/hr3982.

45. *Federal Education Policy and the States, 1945–2009: A Brief Synopsis*, States' Impact on Federal Education Policy Project (SIFEPP), New York State Archives, Albany, January 2006, revised November 2009, 45.

46. *Federal Education Policy and the States, 1945–2009: A Brief Synopsis*, States' Impact on Federal Education Policy Project (SIFEPP), New York State Archives, Albany, January 2006, revised November 2009, 48.

47. Federal Reserve Bank of St. Louis, *Budget of the United States Government, Fiscal Year 1983*, 97th Congress, 1st Session, FRASER Federal Reserve Archive, 5–104.

48. "Reagan names Terrel Bell Secretary of Education," *School Library Journal*, Vol. 106, Issue 3 (February 1, 1981): 286; Jack High, "DOE: Mixing Politics and Education," *Cato Institute Policy Report*, Vol. 2, No. 3 (March 1980): 3; David C. Savage, "Education of a New Department," *Educational Leadership*, Vol. 38, Issue 2 (November 1, 1980): 117–19; Washington AP, "Hufstedler Interested in High Court," *Herald-Journal*, November 1, 1979; "What's to Celebrate?," *Youngstown Vindicator*, May 7, 1980.

49. Quoted in "Reagan Names Terrel Bell Secretary of Education," *School Library Journal*, Vol. 106, Issue 3 (February 1, 1981): 286.

50. Quoted in "Bell's Testimony," *Bangor Daily News*, January 19, 1981. The article incorrectly cites the date of Bell's testimony as October 13, 1977. He actually testified the previous day, according to legislative records (however, those records say 1978 instead of 1977). See *Legislative History of Public Law 96-88, Department of Education Organization Act Part 1 and Part 2*, 96th Congress, 2nd Session, Committee Print, US Congress, Washington, DC, Senate Committee on Government Operations, 1980, 87 and 101.

51. Quoted by Sen. Ribicoff in the *Congressional Record, Proceedings of the 95th Congress, Second Session*, Vol. 124, No. 154, September 28, 1978 (for legislative day of Septem-

ber 26, 1978), in *Legislative History of Public Law 96-88, Department of Education Organization Act Part 1 and Part 2*, 96th Congress, 2nd Session, Committee Print, US Congress, Washington, DC, Senate Committee on Government Operations, 1980, 376–77.

52. Quoted in Christopher Connell, "Former Education Secretary Recounts Struggle with Radical Right," Associated Press, March 12, 1986. Referring to Terrel H. Bell, "Education Policy Development in the Reagan Administration," *Phi Delta Kappan*, Vol. 67, No. 7 (March 1986): 487–493.

53. See, for example, Judy Gibbs, "Terrel Bell: Education Secretary," *Nashua Telegraph*, January 8, 1981; Robert Parry, "Reagan Names Terrel Bell as Secretary of Education," *Schenectady Gazette*, January 8, 1981.

54. "Bell's Testimony," *Bangor Daily News*, January 19, 1981.

55. Bell forwarded his recommendation to the Task Force on August 6, 1981. See "Bell Proposes Options for Dept. of Education," *School Library Journal*, Vol. 28, Issue 1 (September 1, 1981): 18; "Decision Imminent on Agency's Fate," *Education Week*, Vol. 1, Issue 3, September 21, 1981. One month later *Education Week* published what it dubbed "The Bell Memorandum" summarizing his proposal for abolishing the Department of Education. See "The Bell Memorandum," *Education Week*, September 7, 1981.

56. Remarks of Sen. Moynihan in the *Congressional Record, Proceedings and Debates of the 96th Congress, First Session*, April 26, 1979, part of *Legislative History of Public Law 96-88, Department of Education Organization Act Part 1 and Part 2*, 96th Congress, 2nd Session, Committee Print, US Congress, Washington, DC, Senate Committee on Government Operations, 1980, 784–85; "Federal News Roundup: Bell's Views on E.D. Mostly Nonsense, Sen. Moynihan Says," *Education Week*, Vol. 1, Issue 8, October 26, 1981. Sen. Moynihan was referring to "The Bell Memorandum," *Education Week*, September 7, 1981.

57. "The Bell Memorandum," *Education Week*, September 7, 1981.

58. "Material for Review by the Cabinet Council on Human Resources: Dismantling the Department of Education," Friday, November 13, 1981, reproduced in "The Decision Memorandum to the President from the Task Force on the Education Department," *Education Week*, November 16, 1981.

59. Ibid. The task force, however, had been divided on this plan. Reagan's policy development assistant Martin Anderson and Edwin Meese III, counselor to the President, favored eliminating the Department of Education. See Eileen White, "Reagan Task Force Divided on Fate of US Agency," *Education Week*, November 2, 1981.

60. "Material for Review by the Cabinet Council on Human Resources: Dismantling the Department of Education."

61. Ronald Reagan, "Address Before a Joint Session of the Congress Reporting on the State of the Union," January 26, 1982. Online by Gerhard Peters and John T. Woolley, The American Presidency Project. http://www.presidency.ucsb.edu/ws/?pid=42687; cf. Veronique de Rugy and Marie Gryphon, "Elimination Lost: What Happened to Dismantling the Department of Education?," Cato Institute, February 11, 2004, http://www.cato.org/publications/commentary/elimination-lost-what-happened -abolishing-department-education.

62. Ronald Reagan, "Message to the Congress Transmitting the Fiscal Year 1983 Budget," Budget of the United States Government, Fiscal Year 1983—Executive Office

of the President, Office of Management and Budget, http://www.reagan.utexas.edu/ archives/speeches/1982/20882b.htm.

63. Federal Reserve Bank of St. Louis, Budget of the United States Government: Fiscal Year 1983, 97th Congress, 2nd Session, House Document No. 97-124, FRASER Federal Reserve Archives, 5–106.

64. Ibid., 5–109 and 110.

65. Ronald Reagan, "Remarks and a Question-and-Answer Session with Reporters at the Fiscal Year 1983 Budget Signing Ceremony," February 8, 1982. Online by Gerhard Peters and John T. Woolley, The American Presidency Project, http://www.presidency .ucsb.edu/ws/?pid=41965. See also, Ronald Reagan, "Message to the Congress Transmitting the Fiscal Year 1983 Budget," February 8, 1982. Online by Gerhard Peters and John T. Woolley, The American Presidency Project. http://www.presidency.ucsb .edu/ws/?pid=41977.

66. See Part 5 in *97th Congress, 2nd Session, House Document No. 97-124, Budget of the United States Government, Fiscal Year 1983*, Executive Office of the President, Office of Management and Budget, 5-105-106. Available at the Federal Reserve Bank of St. Louis, FRASER Archive.

67. Eileen White, "Reagan Task Force Divided on Fate of US Agency," *Education Week*, November 2, 1981.

68. "Reagan Revolution Stalled in Education Department," *Education Update*, Vol. 6, No. 2, The Heritage Foundation, April 1982, Onalee McGraw, ed.; McGraw, "For Whom Does Terrel Bell Toil," *The Rock Hill Herald*, June 3, 1982.

69. Eileen White, "Reagan Task Force Divided on Fate of US Agency," *Education Week*, November 2, 1981.

70. Ibid.; cf. "Material for Review by the Cabinet Council on Human Resources: Dismantling the Department of Education," Friday, November 13, 1981, reproduced in "The Decision Memorandum to the President from the Task Force on the Education Department," *Education Week*, November 16, 1981.

71. "Reagan Revolution Stalled in Education Department," *Education Update*, Vol. 6, No. 2, The Heritage Foundation, April 1982, Onalee McGraw, ed.; McGraw, "For Whom Does Terrel Bell Toil," *The Rock Hill Herald*, June 3, 1982.

72. Christopher Connell, "Former Education Secretary Recounts Struggle with Radical Right," Associated Press, March 12, 1986.

73. "Bell Sets up Commission to Study School Issues," *School Library Journal*, Vol. 28, Issue 2 (October 1981): 68–69.

74. Fred M. Hechinger, "About Education; New U.S. Approach: A Forum of Ideas," *New York Times*, August 25, 1981.

75. Quoted in ibid.

76. Quoted in ibid.

77. Ibid.

78. *A Nation at Risk: The Imperative for Educational Reform*, A Report to the Nation and the Secretary of Education, United States Department of Education, National Commission on Excellence in Education, April 26, 1983, 8.

79. "Indicators of the Risk" in *A Nation at Risk: The Imperative for Educational Reform*, A Report to the Nation and the Secretary of Education United States Department of Education, National Commission on Excellence in Education, April 26, 1983, 13.

80. Ibid., 10.

81. "Findings" in *A Nation at Risk: The Imperative for Educational Reform*, A Report to the Nation and the Secretary of Education, United States Department of Education, National Commission on Excellence in Education, April 26, 1983, 22–23.

82. Ibid., 11.

83. Quoted in Eileen White, "Bell Commission's 'Excellence' Study Acclaimed," *Education Week*, May 4, 1983.

84. Quoted in ibid.

85. Quoted in ibid.

86. "Implementing Recommendations" in *A Nation at Risk: The Imperative for Educational Reform*, A Report to the Nation and the Secretary of Education, United States Department of Education, The National Commission on Excellence in Education, April 26, 1983, 31–32. See Numbers 3, and 5.

87. Ibid., 32. See Number 4.

88. Ibid.

89. Glenn T. Seaborg, "Part 1: *A Nation at Risk* Revisited," August 1991, http://www.lbl .gov/Publications/Seaborg/risk.htm.

90. Terrel H. Bell, "Reflections One Decade after *A Nation at Risk*," *Phi Delta Kappan*, Vol. 74, Issue 8 (1993): 592 ff.

91. Christopher Connell, "Former Education Secretary Recounts Struggle with Radical Right," Associated Press, March 12, 1986; Federal Reserve Bank of St. Louis, Budget of the United States Government: Fiscal Year 1984, 98th Congress, 1st Session, No. 98-3, FRASER Archive, 5–88. See also Chris Edwards, "Department of Education: Timeline of Growth," Cato Institute, http://www.downsizinggovernment. org/education/timeline; Sheldon L. Richman, "The Sad Legacy of Ronald Reagan," *The Free Market*, Vol. 6, No. 10, Mises Institute, October 1988, http://mises.org/ freemarket_detail.aspx?control=488.

92. Anne Constable, Douglas Brew, and Maureen Dowd, "A Course in Politics," *Time*, June 20, 1983. See also "President Reagan's Education Plan, from Speech," *Education Week*, February 2, 1983.

93. Christopher Connell, "Former Education Secretary Recounts Struggle with Radical Right," Associated Press, March 12, 1986. See also Veronique de Rugy and Marie Gryphon, "Elimination Lost: What Happened to Dismantling the Department of Education?," Cato Institute, February 11, 2004, http://www.cato.org/research/ articles/gryphon-040211.html.

94. *Federal Education Policy and the States, 1945–2009: A Brief Synopsis*, States' Impact on Federal Education Policy Project (SIFEPP), New York State Archives, Albany, January 2006, revised November 2009, 52–53.

95. Ibid., 18.

96. Ibid., 52–54, www.archives.nysed.gov/.../ed_background_overview_essay.pdf. See also Deborah Adkins, G. Gage Kingsbury, Michael Dahlin, and John Cronin, *The Proficiency Illusion*, Fordham Institute, October 4, 2007; Eugene Hickok and Matthew Ladner, "Reauthorization of No Child Left Behind: Federal Management or Citizen Ownership of K–12 Education?," Heritage Foundation Backgrounder, June 27, 2007.

97. *Federal Education Policy and the States, 1945–2009: A Brief Synopsis*, States' Impact on Federal Education Policy Project (SIFEPP), New York State Archives, Albany, January 2006, revised November 2009, 54.

98. Christopher Connell, "Former Education Secretary Recounts Struggle with Radical Right," Associated Press, March 12, 1986.

99. *Federal Education Policy and the States, 1945–2009: A Brief Synopsis*, States' Impact on Federal Education Policy Project (SIFEPP), New York State Archives, Albany, January 2006, revised November 2009, 55.

100. Ibid., 54–55, www.archives.nysed.gov/.../ed_background_overview_essay.pdf; McCluskey, *Feds in the Classroom*, 55–56.

101. Quoted in *Federal Education Policy and the States, 1945–2009: A Brief Synopsis*, States' Impact on Federal Education Policy Project (SIFEPP), New York State Archives, Albany, January 2006, revised November 2009, 55–56.

102. High turnover, dwindling interest, and reduced funding led to elimination of the National Education Goals Panel in 2002. See *Federal Education Policy and the States, 1945–2009: A Brief Synopsis*, States' Impact on Federal Education Policy Project (SIFEPP), New York State Archives, Albany, January 2006, revised November 2009, 57.

103. Ibid., 57–59; McCluskey, *Feds in the Classroom*, 56–58.

104. Author's inflation-adjusted amounts based on unadjusted figures from *Federal Education Policy and the States, 1945–2009: A Brief Synopsis*, States' Impact on Federal Education Policy Project (SIFEPP), New York State Archives, Albany, January 2006, revised November 2009, 64.

105. *Federal Education Policy and the States, 1945–2009: A Brief Synopsis*, States' Impact on Federal Education Policy Project (SIFEPP), New York State Archives, Albany, January 2006, revised November 2009, 67–68.

106. *Federal Education Policy and the States, 1945–2009*, 64–66; McCluskey, *Feds in the Classroom*, 57–59.

107. *Federal Education Policy and the States, 1945–2009*, 65; McCluskey, *Feds in the Classroom*, 59.

108. *Federal Education Policy and the States, 1945–2009*, 65.

109. Remarks of Sen. Dole in the *Congressional Record, Proceedings of the 95th Congress, Second Session*, Vol. 124, No. 154, September 28, 1978 (for legislative day of September 26, 1978), in *Legislative History of Public Law 96-88, Department of Education Organization Act Part 1 and Part 2*, 96th Congress, 2nd Session, Committee Print, US Congress, Washington, DC, Senate Committee on Government Operations, 1980, 378–79.

110. PBS News Hour, "Issue and Debate: Education Reform," October 14, 1996, http://www.pbs.org/newshour/bb/politics/july-dec96/education_10-14a.html.

111. Neal McCluskey, *Feds in the Classroom*, 59–60.

112. Ibid., 60–62; *Federal Education Policy and the States, 1945–2009*, 72.

113. *Federal Education Policy and the States, 1945–2009*, 74–76.

114. "Final Vote Results for Roll-Call 145," *clerk.house.gov*, May 23, 2001, http://clerk.house.gov/evs/2001/roll145.xml; "On Passage of the Bill (H.R. 1, as amended)," http://www.senate.gov/legislative/LIS/roll_call_lists/roll_call_vote_cfm.cfm?congress=107&session=1&vote=00192.

115. McCluskey, *Feds in the Classroom*, 78–81.

116. Quoted in ibid., 80–81.

117. Ibid., 84–88.

118. Neal McCluskey, "NCLB: Perspectives on the Law," part of "NCLB Turns 10: Perspectives on the No Child Left Behind Act," *Education Week*, January 5, 2012.

119. Jaekyung Lee, *Tracking Achievement Gaps and Assessing the Impact of NCLB on the Gaps: An In-depth Look into National and State Reading and Math Outcome Trends*, Civil Rights Project at Harvard University, June 2006.

120. Bruce Fuller, Joseph Wright, Kathryn Gesicki, and Erin Kang, "Gauging Growth: How to Judge No Child Left Behind?," *Educational Researcher*, Vol. 36, No. 5 (June 2007): 268–278.

121. Quoted in "Test Scores Slow Under No Child Left Behind Reforms," American Educational Research Association, Newswise Press Release, July 27, 2007; cf. Fuller et al. "Gauging Growth."

122. Deborah Adkins, G. Gage Kingsbury, Michael Dahlin, John Cronin, *The Proficiency Illusion*, The Thomas B. Fordham Institute and the Northwest Evaluation Association, October 4, 2007. See also Yun Xiang, Michael Dahlin, John Cronin, Donna McCahon, *The Accountability Illusion*, The Thomas B. Fordham Institute and the Northwest Evaluation Association, February 19, 2009.

123. Ben Wolfgang, "Duncan: No Link between Cheating, NCLB," *Washington Times*, August 24, 2011; "Cheating," *District Dossier* (blog), *Education Week*, various dates, http://blogs.edweek.org/edweek/District_Dossier/cheating/; Associated Press, "Texas Education Agency Names Supervising District Board after Cheating Scandal in El Paso," *Washington Post*, December 6, 2012.

124. The case was *School District of the City of Pontiac, Mich., et al. v. Spellings*. "NEA Disappointed in Supreme Court's Decision to Deny Review of Unfunded Mandate Case," June 7, 2010, NEA Press Release. See also John R. Munich and Rocco E. Testani, "NEA Sues over NCLB," *Education Next*, Vol. 5, No. 4 (Fall 2005): 10.

125. "Teachers Union Still Plans NCLB Lawsuit," FoxNews.com, June 27, 2004, http://www.foxnews.com/story/0,2933,123858,00.html; "AASA [American Association of School Administrators] Supports NEA NCLB Lawsuit," National Association of State Boards of Education EDU Weblog, April 4, 2006, http://nasbe.blogspot.com/2006/04/aasa-supports-nea-nclb-lawsuit.html; Bess Keller, "NEA Files 'No Child Left Behind' Lawsuit," *Education Week*, April 20, 2005; Eddy Ramirez, "Connecticut's NCLB Lawsuit Is Dismissed," *U.S. News & World Report*, April 29, 2008, http://www.usnews.com/education/blogs/on-education/2008/04/29/connecticuts-nclb-lawsuit-is-dismissed. In May 2005 the New Jersey Assembly adopted a resolution urging joining Connecticut's lawsuit. See Education Commission of the States (ECS) State Policy Database, No Child Left Behind, http://www.ecs.org/ecs/ecscat.nsf/WebTopicView?OpenView&count=-1&RestrictToCategory=No+Child+Left+Behind.

126. Associated Press, "Utah GOP Lawmakers Rebel Against Bush Law," *NewsMax.com* Wires, February 17, 2005, http://archive.newsmax.com/archives/articles/2005/2/17/103007.shtml; Marie Gryphon, "Utah Stands Up for the Children," *Reason Online*, May 6, 2005, http://www.cato.org/publications/commentary/utah-stands-children.

127. Quoted in Ronnie Lynn, "Utah Bucks Feds on Schools," *Salt Lake Tribune*, April 20, 2005. See also Marie Gryphon, "Utah Stands Up for the Children," *Reason Online*, May 6, 2005.

128. Tom Loveless, *The Peculiar Politics of No Child Left Behind*, Brown Center on Education Policy, The Brookings Institution, August 2006, 12 and 27. See also Education Commission of the States (ECS) State Policy Database, No Child Left Behind, http://www.ecs.org/ecs/ecscat.nsf/WebTopicView?OpenView&count=-1&Restrict ToCategory=No+Child+Left+Behind; the National Conference on State Legislatures (NCSL), Education Legislation Database: 2001–2007, http://www.ncsl.org/issues -research/educ/education-legislation-enactments-2001-2007.aspx.

129. David J. Hoff, "States to Get New Options on NCLB Law," *Education Week*, April 12, 2005; "The U.S. Department of Education's Report to Congress on Waivers Granted Under Section 9401 of the Elementary and Secondary Education Act," April 2007.

130. Alexandra Usher, "AYP Results for 2010–11 — November 2012 Update," Center on Education Policy, November 1, 2012.

131. Pascal D. Forgione, Jr., *Achievement in the United States: Progress Since "A Nation at Risk,"* Center for Education Reform and Empower America, April 3, 1998, 3–4 and Figure G, 19.

132. *A Nation Accountable: Twenty-five Years After "A Nation at Risk,"* US Department of Education, April 2008, 1, 3–4.

133. Pascal D. Forgione, Jr., *Achievement in the United States: Progress Since "A Nation at Risk,"* Center for Education Reform and Empower America, April 3, 1998, 19.

134. *A Nation Accountable: Twenty-five Years After "A Nation at Risk,"* US Department of Education, April 2008, 15.

Chapter 5

1. Alyson Klein, "Post-election, Kline Talks ESEA Renewal, Fiscal Cliff, and Bipartisanship," *Politics K–12* (blog), *Education Week*, November 7, 2012, http://blogs.edweek .org/edweek/campaign-k-12/search.html?blog_id=49&tag=ESEA.

2. Quoted in *Federal Education Policy and the States, 1945–2009: A Brief Synopsis*, States' Impact on Federal Education Policy Project (SIFEPP), New York State Archives, Albany, January 2006, revised November 2009, 82.

3. Ibid.

4. US Government Accountability Office, *Funding Retained Teachers, but Education Could More Consistently Communicate Stabilization Monitoring Issues (GAO-11-804)*, September 22, 2011.

5. US Department of Education, "President Obama, U.S. Secretary of Education Duncan Announce National Competition to Advance School Reform," July 24, 2009, Press Release; U.S. Department of Education, Race to the Top Fund, http:// www2.ed.gov/programs/racetothetop/index.html; US Department of Education, "The American Recovery and Reinvestment Act of 2009: Saving and Creating Jobs and Reforming Education," March 7, 2009, Press Release; US Department of Education, "Nine States and the District of Columbia Win Second Round Race to the Top Grants," August 24, 2010, Press Release; Michele McNeil, "Race to Top Winners Push to Fulfill Promises, *Education Week*, September 19, 2012. See also Recovery.gov, http://www.recovery.gov/Pages/default.aspx.

6. US Department of Education, "Race to the Top Program Executive Summary," November 2009, 2.

7. The White House Office of the Press Secretary, "Remarks by the President on Strengthening America's Education System," November 4, 2009.

8. US Department of Education, "Delaware and Tennessee Win First Race to The Top Grants," March 29, 2010, Press Release; "16 Finalists Announced in Phase 1 of Race to the Top Competition Finalists to Present in Mid-March; Winners Announced in Early April," March 4, 2010, Press Release.

9. US Department of Education, "Nine States and the District of Columbia Win Second Round Race to the Top Grants," August 24, 2010, Press Release.

10. Jennifer A. Marshall, testimony before the Education Subcommittee on Early Childhood, Elementary, and Secondary Education, Committee on Education and the Workforce, United States House of Representatives, March 15, 2011, The Heritage Foundation, 4–5. See also US Department of Education, Race to the Top Fund: States' Applications, Scores and Comments for Phase 1, http://www2.ed.gov/programs/racetothetop/phase1-applications/index.html; States' Applications for Phase 2, http://www2.ed.gov/programs/racetothetop/phase2-applications/index.html.

11. US Department of Education, About the Annual Performance Report, https://www.rtt-apr.us/about-apr; Race to the Top Annual Performance Report, http://www.rtt-apr.us/. See also United States Government Accountability Office, *Race to the Top: Reform Efforts Are Under Way and Information Sharing Could Be Improved*, June 2011.

12. Andy Smarick, "Toothless Reform," *Education Next*, Vol. 10, No. 2 (Spring 2010): 15–22, http://educationnext.org/toothless-reform/; "Race to the Top Offers Last Chance to Salvage Stimulus Spending," *Education Next* News Alert, January 19, 2010.

13. US Government Accountability Office, *States' and Localities' Current and Planned Uses of Funds While Facing Fiscal Stresses (GAO-09-829)*, July 8, 2009.

14. Quotation from American Association of School Administrators, "Stimulus Helps Schools, but Not As Much As Hoped, According to National Survey," August 25, 2009, Press Release; Noelle M. Ellerson, "Schools and the Stimulus: How America's Public School Districts Are Using ARRA Funds," American Association of School Administrators, August 25, 2009, 4. See also Michael Alison Chandler, "Survey Finds Stimulus Funds Going to Help Schools Stay Afloat, Not Innovate," *Washington Post*, August 26, 2009.

15. US Government Accountability Office, *Report to Congress: Recovery Act Education Programs—Funding Retained Teachers, but Education Could More Consistently Communicate Stabilization Monitoring Issues (GAO-11-804)*, September 22, 2011, 46.

16. U. S. Department of Education, Race to the Top Fund, http://www2.ed.gov/programs/racetothetop/index.html; cf. Phase 1 Resources, http://www2.ed.gov/programs/racetothetop/phase1-resources.html; Phase 2 Resources, http://www2.ed.gov/programs/racetothetop/phase2-resources.html; $200 million was awarded to seven states in 2012. See Phase Three Resources, http://www2.ed.gov/programs/racetothetop/phase3-resources.html.

17. US Department of Education, "Department of Education Awards $200 Million to Seven States to Advance K–12 Reform," December 23, 2011, Press Release; US Department of Education, Race to the Top Fund: States' Applications for Phase 3, http://www2.ed.gov/programs/racetothetop/phase3-applications/index.html.

18. US Department of Education, "Race to the Top—Early Learning Challenge," http://www2.ed.gov/programs/racetothetop-earlylearningchallenge/index.html; "Five More

States Secure Race to the Top-Early Learning Challenge Grants," December 12, 2012, Press Release.

19. US Department of Education, "Race to the Top District," http://www2.ed.gov/programs/racetothetop-district/index.html; "Nearly 900 Intents to Apply Submitted For $400 Million Race to the Top-District Competition to Implement Local Reforms," August 31, 2012, Press Release;"61 Finalists Announced for Race to the Top District Competition," November 29, 2012, Press Release; Michele McNeil, "Arne Duncan Sketches Out 'Long Haul' Agenda, *Education Week*, December 4, 2012; US Department of Education, "Department of Education Awards $200 Million to Seven States to Advance K–12 Reform," December 23, 2011, Press Release.

20. See, for example, "Dissenting Views of Hon. John N. Erlenborn, John W. Wydler, Clarence J. Brown, Paul N. McCloskey, Jr., Dan Quayle, Robert S. Walker, Arlan Stangeland, and John E. (Jack) Cunningham," in Department of Education Organization Act, Mr. Brooks, from the Committee on Government Operations, submitted the following Report together with Additional and Dissenting Views (to accompany H.R. 13778), August 25, 1978, in *Legislative History of Public Law 96-88, Department of Education Organization Act Part 1 and Part 2*, 96th Congress, 2nd Session, Committee Print, US Congress, Washington, DC, Senate Committee on Government Operations, 1980, 1057. See also the remarks of Sen. Schmitt, September 28, 1978 (for legislative day of September 26, 1978), 303; the remarks of Brookings Institution Senior Fellow David W. Breneman quoted in "Dissenting Views of Hon. John N. Erlenborn, Hon. Benjamin S. Rosenthal, Hon. Peter H. Kostmayer, Hon. John H. Wydler, Hon. Clarence J. Brown, Hon. Paul N. McCloskey, Hon. Thomas N. Kindness, Hon. Robert S. Walker, Hon. Arlan Stangeland, Hon. M. Caldwell Butler, Hon. Jim Jeffries, Hon. Olympia Snowe, and Hon. Wayne Grisham," May 14, 1979, 1176–1177.

21. Sam Dillon and Tamer Lewin, "Education Chief Vies to Expand U.S. Role as Partner on Local Schools, *New York Times*, May 3, 2010.

22. Public Law 111-152, Title II of the Health Care and Education Reconciliation Act of 2010; Thomas D. Snyder and Sally A. Dillow, *Digest of Education Statistics, 2011*, June 2012, Institute of Education Sciences, US Department of Education, 551.

23. Vicki Alger, "Student Loans and College Affordability," Independent Women's Forum Policy Focus, August 7, 2012; Neil McCluskey, "SAFRA Stinks," *Forbes.com*, August 10, 2009, http://www.forbes.com/2009/08/10/education-loans-tuition-financial-aid-opinions-colleges-safra.html.

24. Common Core State Standards Initiative, http://www.corestandards.org/.

25. Lindsey M. Burke, "States Must Reject National Education Standards While There Is Still Time," Heritage Foundation Backgrounder, April 16, 2012.

26. Common Core State Standards Initiative, "About the Standards," http://www.corestandards.org/about-the-standards.

27. Alyson Klein, "To Duncan, Incentives a Priority," *Education Week*, January 30, 2009.

28. US Department of Education, "Secretary Arne Duncan Speaks at the 91st Annual Meeting of the American Council on Education," February 9, 2009, News Release.

29. National Governors Association, "Forty-Nine States and Territories Join Common Core Standards Initiative," June 1, 2009, Press Release.

30. "Excerpts from Secretary Arne Duncan's Remarks at the National Press Club," *Homeroom* (blog), US Department of Education, June 1, 2009, http://www.ed.gov/blog/2009/06/excepts-from-secretary-arne-duncan%E2%80%99s-remarks-at-the-national-press-club/; National Governors Association, "Forty-Nine States and Territories Join Common Core Standards Initiative," June 1, 2009, Press Release.

31. Arne Duncan, "Partners for Success: Secretary Arne Duncan's Remarks to the National Association of State Boards of Education," October 16, 2009, News Release. See also Sam Dillon and Tamar Lewin, "Education Chief Vies to Expand U.S. Role as Partner on Local Schools," *New York Times*, May 3, 2010.

32. "Overview Information; Race to the Top Fund; Notice Inviting Applications for New Awards for Fiscal Year (FY) 2010," *Federal Register*, Vol. 74, No. 221 (November 18, 2009), 59, 836–59, 872. See especially p. 59, 838.

33. Ibid., 59, 688–69, 834. See especially p. 59, 733.

34. Quotation from US Department of Education, *A Blueprint for Reform: The Reauthorization of the Elementary and Secondary Education Act*, March 2010, 3, http://www2.ed.gov/policy/elsec/leg/blueprint/index.html.

35. Robert S. Eitel and Kent D. Talbert, "The Road to a National Curriculum: The Legal Aspects of the Common Core Standards, Race to the Top, and Conditional Waivers," The Federalist Society, February 16, 2012, http://www.fed-soc.org/publications/detail/the-road-to-a-national-curriculum-the-legal-aspects-of-the-common-core-standards-race-to-the-top-and-conditional-waivers.

36. National Council of State Legislatures, Common Core State Standards Adopting States, updated October 19, 2012, https://sites.google.com/site/ncslccssupdate/home/ccss-adopting-states.

37. Lance Izumi, *Obama's Education Takeover* (New York: Encounter Books, 2012).

38. Andrew C. Porter, "In Common Core, Little to Cheer About," *Education Week*, August 9, 2011. See also Andrew Porter, Jennifer McMaken, Jun Hwang, and Rui Yang, "Common Core Standards: The New U.S. Intended Curriculum," *Educational Researcher*, Vol. 40, No. 3 (April 2011): 103–116.

39. Ze'ev Wurman and W. Stephen Wilson, "The Common Core Math Standards," *Education Next*, Vol. 12, No. 3 (Summer 2012): 46–47.

40. Lance Izumi, *Obama's Education Takeover* (New York: Encounter Books, 2012), 16.

41. "Testimony on the CCSSI Core Standards and the new draft TX math standards," R. James Milgram, Professor of Mathematics Emeritus, Stanford University, May 2011, http://coehp.uark.edu/colleague/9864.php.

42. Sandra Stotsky, "Equalizing Mediocrity," *New York Times*, April 28, 2009.

43. Ze'ev Wurman and Sandra Stotsky, *Why Race to the Middle? First-Class State Standards Are Better than Third-Class National Standards*, Pioneer Institute for Public Policy Research, White Paper No. 52, February 23, 2010, 17.

44. Sandra Stotsky, "National Academic Standards: The First Test—More Complex than Simple English," *New York Times*, September 22, 2009.

45. Common Core State Standards Initiative, Common Core State Standards for English Language Arts & Literacy in History/ Social Studies, Science, and Technical Subjects: Appendix B: Text Exemplars and Sample Performance Tasks, 181 and 183. For reactions to this release, see Lyndsey Layton, "Common Core Sparks War over Words," *Washington Post*, December 2, 2012; Ezra Kline, "Wonkbook: Should

High Schoolers Be Reading Executive Order 13423?," *Washington Post*, December 3, 2012; Stanley Kurtz, "Obamacore: The White House Takes the Schools," *National Review Online*, December 3, 2012, http://www.nationalreview.com/corner/334645/ obamacore-white-house-takes-schools-stanley-kurtz; Stanley Kurtz, "Obama and Your Child's Mind," *National Review Online*, December 5, 2012, http://www .nationalreview.com/corner/334878/obama-and-your-childs-mind-stanley-kurtz; Rachel Sheffield, "National Education Standards Trade Literature for Reading Government Documents," December 15, 2012, *The Daily Signal* (blog), The Heritage Foundation, http://blog.heritage.org/2012/12/15/national-education-standards-trade -literature-for-reading-government-documents/; Lindsey Burke, "Why All the Cool Kids Are Reading Executive Order 13423," *FoxNews.com*, December 27, 2012, http:// www.foxnews.com/opinion/2012/12/27/why-all-cool-kids-are-reading-executive -order-13423/.

46. Ze'ev Wurman and W. Stephen Wilson, "The Common Core Math Standards," *Education Next*, Vol. 12, No. 3 (Summer 2012): 46, 49–50.

47. Marc Tucker, "The Feds' Education Power Grab," *Los Angeles Times*, January 24, 2013.

48. Quotation from US Department of Education, *A Blueprint for Reform: The Reauthorization of the Elementary and Secondary Education Act*, March 2010, 2 and 3; cf. US Department of Education, "Obama Administration's Education Reform Plan Emphasizes Flexibility, Resources and Accountability for Results," March 15, 2010, Press Release.

49. US Department of Education, "Obama Administration's Education Reform Plan Emphasizes Flexibility, Resources and Accountability for Results," March 15, 2010, Press Release.

50. US Department of Education, *A Blueprint for Reform: The Reauthorization of the Elementary and Secondary Education Act*, March 2010, 39.

51. Section 9401 of the Elementary and Secondary Education Act of 1965. See Secretary Arne Duncan, "Letter to Chief State School Officers from Secretary Duncan," September 23, 2011, http://www2.ed.gov/policy/gen/guid/secletter/110923.html; "The U.S. Department of Education's Report to Congress on Waivers Granted Under Section 9401 of the Elementary and Secondary Education Act," April 2007, http:// www2.ed.gov/nclb/freedom/local/flexibility/waiverletters/2007waiverrpt.doc. Duncan also cited the precedent set by his predecessors under the George W. Bush administration for initiating this race to the waiver. See US Department of Education, "Obama Administration Sets High Bar for Flexibility from No Child Left Behind in Order to Advance Equity and Support Reform," September 23, 2011, Press Release; ESEA Flexibility: Overview, http://www.ed.gov/esea/flexibility.

52. US Department of Education, "Duncan Says 82 Percent of America's Schools Could 'Fail' Under NCLB This Year," March 9, 2011, Press Release; Valerie Strauss, "Was Arne Duncan Right on AYP?" *Washington Post* Answer Sheet Blog, March 31, 2011, http://www.washingtonpost.com/blogs/answer-sheet/post/was-arne-duncan-right -on-ayp/2011/03/31/AFX3TXBC_blog.html; Alexandra Usher, "AYP Results for 2010–11," Center on Education Policy, December 15, 2011, 2.

53. Michele McNeil, "Duncan: 82 Percent of Schools Could Be 'Failing' This Year," *Education Week*, March 9, 2011, http://blogs.edweek.org/edweek/campaign-k-12/2011/03/

duncan_82_of_schools_could_be.html; Michele McNeil, "Duncan's 82% NCLB Failure Prediction Way Off Base, New Data Show," *Education Week*, December 15, 2011; Nick Anderson, "Most Schools Could Face 'Failing' Label under No Child Left Behind, Duncan Says," *Washington Post*, March 10, 2011.

54. Quoted in Nick Anderson, "Most Schools Could Face 'Failing' Label under No Child Left Behind, Duncan Says," *Washington Post*, March 10, 2011.

55. Alexandra Usher, "AYP Results for 2010-11," Center on Education Policy, December 15, 2011, 2,3, and 4; Michele McNeil, "Duncan's 82% NCLB Failure Prediction Way Off Base, New Data Show," *Education Week*, December 15, 2011.

56. See US Department of Education, "Obama Administration Plans NCLB 'Flexibility' Package Tied to Reform If Congress Does Not Act Soon on Reauthorization," June 13, 2011, Press Release

57. Congressmen John Kline and Duncan Hunter, "Letter to Secretary Duncan from Reps. Kline and Hunter Voicing Concern about Conditional Waivers," June 23, 2011.

58. *Real Relief for Schools: Accomplishing Effective Flexibility*, Report from Education and Workforce Committee Democrats, US House of Representatives, July 2011, 10.

59. Congressional Research Service Memorandum from Emily Barbour, Jody Feder, and Rebecca Skinner to the Majority Committee Staff of the House Committee on Education and the Workforce, *Secretary of Education's Waiver Authority with Respect to Title I-A Provisions Included in the Elementary and Secondary Education Act*, June 28, 2011, 6–7.

60. US Department of Education, "Letter to Congressman Kline from Secretary Duncan in response to June 23 letter," July 6, 2011.

61. The White House, Office of the Press Secretary, "Press Briefing by Press Secretary Jay Carney, Domestic Policy Council Director Melody Barnes, and Secretary of Education Arne Duncan, 8/8/2011," August 8, 2011, Press Briefing.

62. Quoted in Ben Wolfgang, "Duncan: No Link between Cheating, NCLB," *Washington Times*, August 24, 2011.

63. Arne Duncan, "Providing Our Schools Relief from No Child Left Behind," *Homeroom* (blog), US Department of Education, August 8, 2011, http://www.ed.gov/blog/2011/08/providing-our-schools-relief-from-no-child-left-behind/; cf. Cameron Brenchley, "Top 5 Questions About NCLB Flexibility," *Homeroom* (blog), US Department of Education, August 8, 2011, http://www.ed.gov/blog/2011/08/top-5-questions-about-nclb-flexibility/.

64. "Obama Administration Presses Forward with Backdoor Education Reform Agenda," Alert from the US House of Representatives Committee on Education and the Workforce, August 19, 2011. See also Lindsey Burke, "No Child Left Behind by Executive Overreach," *National Review Online*, August 19, 2011, http://www.nationalreview.com/articles/275015/no-child-left-behind-executive-overreach-lindsey-burke#; Rep. John Kline, "Schools Need More Reform, Less Federal Control," *Washington Examiner*, September 22, 2011.

65. "Letter to Secretary Duncan from Senator Rubio Regarding Waivers," US Senate, September 12, 2011; Alyson Klein, "GOP Senators Introduce Own ESEA Renewal Bills," *Education Week*, September 14, 2011; S.B. 1568, State Innovation Pilot Act of 2011, http://www.govtrack.us/congress/bills/112/s1568

66. "Remarks by the President on No Child Left Behind Flexibility," White House Office of the Press Secretary, September 23, 2011.

67. Section 9401 of the Elementary and Secondary Education Act of 1965. See Secretary Arne Duncan, "Letter to Chief State School Officers from Secretary Duncan," September 23, 2011; "The U.S. Department of Education's Report to Congress on Waivers Granted Under Section 9401 of the Elementary and Secondary Education Act," April 2007.

68. US Department of Education, "Obama Administration Sets High Bar for Flexibility from No Child Left Behind in Order to Advance Equity and Support Reform," September 23, 2011, Press Release; "ESEA Flexibility: Overview," http://www.ed.gov/esea/flexibility; "Remarks by the President on No Child Left Behind Flexibility," White House Office of the Press Secretary, September 23, 2011, Press Release.

69. US Department of Education, "ESEA Flexibility," updated June 7, 2012, originally issued September 23, 2011, 4.

70. Senator Mike Enzi, "Statement from Senator Enzi, Ranking Member of the Senate Health, Education, Labor and Pensions Committee," US Senate, "September 23, 2011.

71. Quoted in Michele McNeil, "House Committee to Hold Hearings on New ESEA," *Education Week*, February 24, 2010,; cf. Motoko Rich, "Loopholes Seen at Schools in Obama Get-Tough Policy," *New York Times*, October 5, 2012.

72. "Obama Administration Ignores Education Reform Efforts in House, Presses Forward with Backdoor Education Agenda," Alert from the US House of Representatives Committee on Education and the Workforce, September 29, 2011; cf. Lindsey Burke, "Rewriting No Child Left Behind with Waivers and Conditions," *Washington Examiner*, September 28, 2011; the remarks of Jack Jennings, president of the Center on Education Policy, in Michele McNeil, "House Committee to Hold Hearings on New ESEA," *Education Week*, February 24, 2010. See also the Center on Education Policy, NCLB/ESEA Waiver Watch website, updated February 17, 2015, http://www.cep-dc.org/index.cfm?DocumentSubTopicID=48.

73. Thomas D. Snyder and Sally A. Dillow, *Digest of Education Statistics, 2011*, June 2012, Institute of Education Sciences, US Department of Education, 551.

74. US Department of Education, "ESEA Flexibility," http://www.ed.gov/esea/flexibility; Michele McNeil, "Arne Duncan Sketches Out 'Long Haul' Agenda, *Education Week*, December 4, 2012; Lindsey Burke, "No Child Left Behind Waivers: Regulatory Purgatory," February 11, 2013, *The Daily Signal* (blog), The Heritage Foundation, http://blog.heritage.org/2013/02/11/no-child-left-behind-waivers-regulatory-purgatory/. See also Center on Education Policy, NCLB/ESEA Waiver Watch, updated February 17, 2015, http://www.cep-dc.org/index.cfm?DocumentSubTopicID=48; See "U.S. Senate Committee on Health, Education, Labor, and Pensions, No Child Left Behind: Early Lessons from State Flexibility Waivers, February 7, 2013, Testimony of Secretary of Education Arne Duncan."

75. Quoted in "School's Out: The Failure of No Child Left Behind," *Cato Policy Report*, November/December 2007.

76. Quoted in ibid.

77. Lydia Saad, "Americans Support Federal Involvement in Education," Gallup Politics, September 8, 2010; Frank Newport, "Americans Doubt Effectiveness of 'No Child Left Behind'," Gallup Politics, August 19, 2009.

78. Lydia Saad, "Americans Support Federal Involvement in Education," Gallup Politics, September 8, 2010.

Chapter 6

1. Author's calculations based on Table 388 of *Digest of Education Statistics 2010*, National Center for Education Statistics, Institute of Education Sciences, US Department of Education.

2. Less than 1 percent of this amount, $659 million (0.72 percent) was spent on research and statistics. See US Department of Education, *Digest of Education Statistics 2011*, Table 388.

3. US Department of Education, "2013 Education Budget: What It Means for You," *Homeroom* (blog), February 13, 2012, http://www.ed.gov/blog/2012/02/2013 -education-budget-what-it-means-for-you/; Detail: US Department of Education, "U.S. Department of Education 2013 Budget Continues Investments to Strengthen Workforce and Rebuild American Economy," February 13, 2012, Press Release; Lindsey Burke and Rachel Sheffield, "Obama's Education Budget Chooses to Fund Failure," Heritage Foundation Education Notebook, March 26, 2012; "President's FY 2013 Budget Request for the U.S. Department of Education," http://www2.ed.gov/ about/overview/budget/budget13/index.html.

4. Lindsey Burke and Rachel Sheffield, "Obama's 2013 Education Budget and Blueprint: A Costly Expansion of Federal Control, Heritage Foundation Backgrounder," April 12, 2012. See also Lindsey Burke, "President Obama's Education Budget Buster," April 2, 2012, http://blog.heritage.org/2012/04/02/president-obamas-education -budget-buster/.

5. US Census Bureau, "Federal Gov't Finances & Employment: Federal Civilian Employment" part of *The 2012 Statistical Abstract: The National Data Book*, Table 499.

6. Gross obligations include annual expenditures for personnel compensation and benefits, contractual services and supplies, and grants and fixed charges. Thus, they include program, operations, and maintenance costs. See *Object Class Analysis*, part of *Budget of the United States Government, Fiscal Year 2012*, March 24, 2011.

7. "No Child Left Behind," *Education Week*, updated September 19, 2011. Historical figures are from *Digest of Education Statistics*, US Department of Education, National Center for Education Statistics, various years. Tables accessed: "Appropriations for Title I and selected other programs under the No Child Left Behind Act of 2001, by program and state or jurisdiction."

8. See Public Law print of PL 107-110, the No Child Left Behind Act of 2001. See Subpart 1 — Basic Program Requirements, SEC. 1111. STATE PLANS (b)(2) (F) Timeline. See also, US Department of Education, "No Child Left Behind: Elementary and Secondary Education Act (ESEA)," http://www2.ed.gov/nclb/landing.jhtml.

9. Government Accountability Office, "Education Finance: Extent of Federal Funding in State Education Agencies," GAO/HEHS-95-3, October 14, 1994, 2, 5, and 11–12, and Appendix I. See also the remarks of Rep. Scott Garrett (R-NJ) in "School's Out: The Failure of No Child Left Behind," Cato Policy Report, November/December 2007; Dan Lips and Evan Feinberg, "The Administrative Burden of No Child Left Behind," The Heritage Foundation, March 23, 2007.

10. Government Accountability Office, "Education Finance: Extent of Federal Funding in State Education Agencies," GAO/HEHS-95-3, October 14, 1994, 11 and Appendix III, 28 ff.

11. US Department of Education, "Supporting Statement for Paperwork Reduction Act Submission of Additions to Regulations for Title I, Part A, Grants to Local Education Agencies," n.d., 8; cf. "Supporting Statement for Paperwork Reduction Act Submission of Additions to Regulations for Title I, Part A, Grants to Local Education Agencies," April 17, 2008; Neal McCluskey, "Downsizing the Federal Government: K–12 Education Subsidies," Cato Institute, May 2009.

12. *Federal Register*, Vol. 71, No. 202 (October 19, 2006): 61,730; cf. US Department of Education, "Supporting Statement for Paperwork Reduction Act Submission of Additions to Regulations for Title I, Part A, Grants to Local Education Agencies," n.d., 8, April 17, 2008; Jennifer A. Marshall, testimony before the Education Subcommittee on Early Childhood, Elementary, and Secondary Education, Committee on Education and the Workforce, United States House of Representatives, March 15, 2011, 2.

13. Neal McCluskey, "Downsizing the Federal Government: K–12 Education Subsidies," May 2009.

14. US Department of Education, "Supporting Statement for Paperwork Reduction Act Submission of Additions to Regulations for Title I, Part A, Grants to Local Education Agencies," n.d., 8; cf. "Supporting Statement for Paperwork Reduction Act Submission of Additions to Regulations for Title I, Part A, Grants to Local Education Agencies," April 17, 2008.

15. "Kline Statement: Hearing on Education Regulations," Committee on Education and the Workforce, March 1, 2011, Press Release; "Education Regulations: Weighing the Burden on Schools and Students," Committee on Education and the Workforce, March 1, 2011; Lindsey Burke, "Reducing the Federal Footprint on Education and Empowering State and Local Leaders," Heritage Foundation Backgrounder, June 2, 2011.

16. Lindsey Burke, "Reducing the Federal Footprint on Education and Empowering State and Local Leaders," Heritage Foundation Backgrounder, June 2, 2011, 3.

17. Ibid.

18. Nancy Kober and Diane Stark Rentner, "After the Stimulus Money Ends: The Status of State K–12 Education Funding and Reforms," Center on Education Policy, February 7, 2012, 13.

19. "Hunter Statement: Hearing on Education Regulations: Burying Schools in Paperwork," Education and the Workforce Committee, US House of Representatives, March 15, 2011, Press Release.

20. Author's tally based on US Department of Education, "Significant Guidance Documents," December 20, 2012 [document is misdated. It should read January 20, 2012].

21. GAO, *Follow-up on 2011 Report: Status of Actions Taken to Reduce Duplication, Overlap, and Fragmentation, Save Tax Dollars, and Enhance Revenue,* February 2012, 53.

22. See, for example, Raegen Miller and Robin Lake, "Federal Barriers to Innovation," the Center on Reinventing Public Education, November 2012.

23. The Department of Education Organization Act, October 17, 1979, in *Legislative History of Public Law 96-88,* 96th Congress, 2nd Session, Committee Print, US Congress, Washington, DC, Senate Committee on Government Operations, 1980, 2–31.

24. See remarks of Sen. Harrison Schmitt (R-NM) in the *Congressional Record*, September 18, 1978, pp. S. 16441, 16453-54, and April 26, 1979, S. 4787-88.

25. See remarks of Sen. William Cohen (R-ME) in "Minority Views of Mr. Cohen," part of Department of Education Organization Act of 1979, Report of the Committee on Governmental Affairs, US Senate, to Accompany S. 210 to Establish a Department of Education Together with Additional and Minority Views, March 27 (legislative day February 22), 1979, in *Legislative History of Public Law 96-88, Department of Education Organization Act Part 1 and Part 2*, 96th Congress, 2nd Session, Committee Print, U.S. Congress, Washington, DC, Senate Committee on Government Operations, 1980, p. 615; and Remarks of Sen. Cohen in the *Congressional Record, Proceedings and Debates of the 96th Congress, First Session*, Vol. 125, No. 44, April 5, 1979, part of *Legislative History of Public Law 96-88, Department of Education Organization Act Part 1 and Part 2*, 96th Congress, 2nd Session, Committee Print, US Congress, Washington, DC, Senate Committee on Government Operations, 1980, pp. 698-99.

26. US Census Bureau, Table 556. Federal Civilian Employment, by Branch, Agency, and Area, 1980 to 1999; and US Census Bureau, Table 499. Federal Civilian Employment by Branch and Agency: 1990 to 2010 from Statistical Abstract of the United States: 2012.

27. US Department of Education Coordinating Structure, updated July 3, 2014.

28. US Department of Education, "The Federal Role in Education," updated February 13, 2012.

29. Unless otherwise noted, Department of Education obligations figures used in this section come from respective fiscal years' *Object Class Analysis*, part of *Budget of the United States Government,* Government Printing Office's Federal Digital System (FDsys).

30. Author's average based on 1994–2010 data from the US Department of Labor, Bureau of Labor Statistics, Consumer Price Index, All Urban Consumers, US City Average, 1913–2012.

31. See "Detail of Full-Time Equivalent Employment" in US Department of Education, "Department of Education Salaries and Expenses Overview," for fiscal years 2008 through 2012. See also US Office of Personnel Management, "2012 Pay Tables for Executive and Senior Level Employees."

32. Government Accountability Office, Report to the Ranking Member, Committee on Education and the Workforce, House of Representatives. *Improved Oversight and Controls Could Help Education Better Respond to Evolving Priorities*, February 2011, 11, 24–27.

33. Ibid., 41–42.

34. US Department of Education, *Digest of Education Statistics 2011*, Table 388.

35. Author's percentages based on current 2010 figures from Table 388 of the *Digest of Education Statistics, 2011*. Explanatory notes are from Figure 20 of "Federal Education Programs for Education and Related Activities," Chapter 4 of Thomas D. Snyder and Sally A. Dillow, *Digest of Education Statistics 2010*, National Center for Education Statistics, Institute of Education Sciences, US Department of Education, April 5, 2011, 546.

36. Author's calculations based on Tables 3 and 388 of *Digest of Education Statistics 2010*, National Center for Education Statistics, Institute of Education Sciences, US Department of Education.

37. Author's percentage refers only to elementary, secondary, and postsecondary spending. Excluded are Department of Education outlays for other education programs as well as research and statistics.

38. "Purpose of the Legislation" part of Department of Education Organization Act of 1978 (S. 991), Mr. Ribicoff, from the Committee on Governmental Affairs, submitting the following Report together with Additional Views (To accompany S. 991), August 9 (legislative day May 17), 1978, in *Legislative History of Public Law 96-88, Department of Education Organization Act Part 1 and Part 2*, 96th Congress, 2nd Session, Committee Print, US Congress, Washington, DC, Senate Committee on Government Operations, 1980, 64–65, and 68.

39. Author's review of the *CFDA's* Historical Index: Archived programs revealed 245 archived or deleted programs and six programs incorporated into existing programs.

40. "Minority Views of Mr. Cohen," part of Department of Education Organization Act of 1979, Report of the Committee on Governmental Affairs, US Senate, to Accompany S. 210 to Establish a Department of Education Together with Additional and Minority Views, March 27 (legislative day February 22), 1979, in *Legislative History of Public Law 96-88, Department of Education Organization Act Part 1 and Part 2*, 96th Congress, 2nd Session, Committee Print, US Congress, Washington, DC, Senate Committee on Government Operations, 1980, 614. Remarks of Sen. Cohen in the *Congressional Record, Proceedings and Debates of the 96th Congress, First Session*, Vol. 125, No. 44, April 5, 1979, part of Legislative History, 698–99.

41. "Additional Views of Hon. L. H. Fountain" in Department of Education Organization Act, Mr. Brooks, from the Committee on Government Operations, submitted the following Report together with Separate, Additional, Supplementary, and Dissenting Views (to accompany H.R. 2444), May 14, 1979, in *Legislative History of Public Law 96-88, Department of Education Organization Act Part 1 and Part 2*, 96th Congress, 2nd Session, Committee Print, US Congress, Washington, DC, Senate Committee on Government Operations, 1980, 1150 and 1152.

42. This amount excludes off-budget education support that is not tied to appropriations and non-federal funds generated by federal legislation, such as private loans, grants, and aid. See Table 385 in *Digest of Education Statistics 2011*, National Center for Education Statistics, Institute of Education Sciences, US Department of Education.

43. US Government Accountability Office, *Federal Education Funding: Overview and Early Childhood Education Programs*, GAO-10-51, January 2010, 4, 7, and 9.

44. US Government Accountability Office, *Opportunities to Reduce Potential Duplication in Government Programs, Save Tax Dollars, and Enhance Revenue*, GAO-11-318SP, March 1, 2011.

45. Ibid., 144 and 146.

46. Ibid., 205.

47. Ibid., 205–206.

48. House Education and the Workforce Committee, "Kline Discusses Waste in Federal Education Programs 'On the Record with Greta Van Susteren'," September 1, 2011, Press Release.

49. Government Accountability Office, Report to the Ranking Member, Committee on Education and the Workforce, House of Representatives. *Improved Oversight and Controls Could Help Education Better Respond to Evolving Priorities*, February 2011, 9.

50. Ibid., 10.
51. Ibid., 9.
52. Ibid., 40–42.
53. Unpublished data from "Appropriations for Programs Authorized by the Elementary and Secondary Education Act, 1966–2012," available upon request from the US Department of Education, Office of Planning, Evaluation and Policy Development (OPEPD)/Budget Service. Figures presented have been inflation-adjusted by author.
54. "Statement of Hon. Shirley Chisholm, A Representative in Congress from the State of New York," August 1, 1978, in "Establishing a Department of Education," Hearings Before a Subcommittee of the Committee on Government Operations, House of Representatives, 95th Congress, Second Session, on H.R. 13343, To Establish a Department of Education and for Other Purposes, July 17, 20, 31; August 1 and 2, 1978, 385; cf. Testimony of Rep. Shirley Chisholm (D-NY), quoted in "Dissenting Views of Hon. John N. Erlenborn, John W. Wydler, Clarence J. Brown, Paul N. McCloskey, Jr., Dan Quayle, Robert S. Walker, Arlan Stangeland, and John E. (Jack) Cunningham ," in Department of Education Organization Act, Mr. Brooks, from the Committee on Government Operations, submitted the following Report together with Additional and Dissenting Views (to accompany H.R. 13778), August 25, 1978, in *Legislative History of Public Law 96-88, Department of Education Organization Act Part 1 and Part 2*, 96th Congress, 2nd Session, Committee Print, US Congress, Washington, DC, Senate Committee on Government Operations, 1980, 1050.
55. US Department of Education, Long-Term Trends in Student Science Performance, Setember 1998, http://nces.ed.gov/pubs98/web/98465.asp; Interpreting NAEP Science Results, http://nces.ed.gov/nationsreportcard/science/interpret-results.asp.
56. J.R. Campbell, C.M. Hombo, and J. Mazzeo, *NAEP 1999 Trends in Academic Progress: Three Decades of Student Performance,* US Department of Education. Office of Educational Research and Improvement. National Center for Education Statistics, August 2000, 17–19; US Department of Education, "What Are the Differences Between Long-Term Trend NAEP and Main NAEP," updated June 25, 2013, http://nces.ed.gov/nationsreportcard/about/ltt_main_diff.asp.
57. US Department of Education, What Are the Differences Between Long-Term Trend NAEP and Main NAEP, updated June 25, 2013, http://nces.ed.gov/nationsreportcard/about/ltt_main_diff.asp.
58. J.R. Campbell, C.M. Hombo, and J. Mazzeo, *NAEP 1999 Trends in Academic Progress: Three Decades of Student Performance*, August 24, 2000, 17–19. See also US Department of Education, Reading Performance-Level Descriptions, last updated June 25, 2013, http://nces.ed.gov/nationsreportcard/ltt/reading-descriptions.asp; Mathematics Performance-Level Descriptions, last updated June 25, 2013, http://nces.ed.gov/nationsreportcard/ltt/math-descriptions.asp; The NAEP Long-Term Trend Performance Levels, last updated June 25, 2013, http://nces.ed.gov/nationsreportcard/ltt/performance-levels.asp. Recent NAEP science results indicate less than 2 percent of American students score at advanced NAEP science levels across grades. See "Statement by U.S. Secretary of Education Arne Duncan on the Release of the NAEP Science Report Card," January 25, 2011, Press Release; US Department of Education, National Assessment of Educational Progress, http://nces.ed.gov/nationsreportcard/

science/; Sarah D. Sparks, "Most 8th Graders Fall Short on NAEP Science Test," *Education Week*, May 10, 2012. Those results are not included because long-term NAEP and main NAEP assessments are not comparable. See S. Department of Education, More About the NAEP Long-Term Trend Assessment, http://nces.ed.gov/nations reportcard/ltt/moreabout.asp; NAEP Overview, http://nces.ed.gov/nationsreportcard/about/; What Are the Differences Between Long-Term Trend NAEP and Main NAEP, http://nces.ed.gov/nationsreportcard/about/ltt_main_diff.asp. "SD and ELL students are included using the same participation guidelines and with the same accommodations (as needed) in main NAEP," http://nces.ed.gov/nationsreportcard/about/ltt_main_diff.asp; Permitted NAEP Accommodations Tables, http://nces.ed.gov/nationsreportcard/about/inclusion.asp#accom_table.

59. Bobby D. Rampey, Gloria S. Dion, and Patricia L. Donahue, *The Nation's Report Card: Trends in Academic Progress in Reading and Mathematics 2008*, National Center for Education Statistics, Institute of Education Sciences, US Department of Education, April 2009, 2 and 51. See also US Department of Education, Inclusion of Special-Needs Students, http://nces.ed.gov/nationsreportcard/about/inclusion.asp. Even so, NCES notes, "Comparisons of the 2008 results to the 2004 original or previous trend results should be interpreted with caution, bearing in mind the differences in assessment accommodations and changes to assessment procedures." National Center for Education Statistics, Interpreting NAEP Long-Term Trend Results: Cautions in Interpretations, http://nces.ed.gov/nationsreportcard/ltt/interpreting_results.asp.

60. For exclusion rates, see Bobby D. Rampey, Gloria S. Dion, and Patricia L. Donahue, *The Nation's Report Card: Trends in Academic Progress in Reading and Mathematics 2008*, National Center for Education Statistics, Institute of Education Sciences, US Department of Education, April 2009, 55; J.R. Campbell, C.M. Hombo, and J. Mazzeo, *NAEP 1999 Trends in Academic Progress: Three Decades of Student Performance*, August 24, 2000, 90.

61. US Department of Education, Frequently Asked Questions, "Is Participation in NAEP Voluntary?" Last updated November 28, 2012, http://nces.ed.gov/nationsreportcard/faq.asp.

62. Paul E. Peterson, "Little Gain in Student Achievement," Chapter 2 of *Our Schools and Our Future...Are We Still at Risk*, ed. Paul E. Peterson (Stanford: Hoover Institution Press, 2003), 47–49.

63. US Department of Education, What Are the Differences Between Long-Term Trend NAEP and Main NAEP, http://nces.ed.gov/nationsreportcard/about/ltt_main_diff.asp; What Does the NAEP Mathematics Assessment Measure, http://nces.ed.gov/nationsreportcard/mathematics/whatmeasure.asp.

64. US Department of Education, What Does the NAEP Reading Assessment Measure, http://nces.ed.gov/nationsreportcard/reading/whatmeasure.asp; Comparison of the 1992–2007 and 2009 Frameworks, http://nces.ed.gov/nationsreportcard/reading/whatmeasure.asp#sec5.

65. US Department of Education, The NAEP Reading Achievement Levels by Grade, http://nces.ed.gov/nationsreportcard/reading/achieveall.asp.

66. Ibid.

67. Author's percentages based on total elementary and secondary education spending from the US Department of Education, *Digest of Education Statistics 2012*, Table 423; unpublished US Department of Education, Budget Service, ESEA program spending data provided to the author.

Chapter 7

1. Paul E. Peterson, "Little Gain in Student Achievement," Chapter 2 of *Our Schools and Our Future...Are We Still at Risk*, ed. Paul E. Peterson (Stanford: Hoover Institution Press, 2003), 60.

2. Arthur W. Forshay, Robert L. Thorndike, Fernand Hotyat, Douglas A. Pidgeon, and David A. Walker, *Educational Achievements of Thirteen-Year-Olds in Twelve Countries: Results of an International Research Project, 1959–1961*, Hamburg: UNESCO Institute for Education, 1962.

3. Ibid., 26.

4. Benjamin S. Bloom, *Cross-National Study of Educational Attainment: Stage I of the IEA. Investigation in Six Subject Areas. Final Report,* Vol. 1, February 1969, Chicago Univ., Ill.; International Project for the Evaluation of Educational Achievement, Hamburg, West Germany, 1–2.

5. IEA, First International Mathematics Study, http://www.iea.nl/fims.html; First International Science Study, http://www.iea.nl/fiss.html.

6. National Center for Education Statistics, International Activities Program, http://nces.ed.gov/surveys/international/table-library.asp; IEA, TIMSS 1995, http://www.iea.nl/timss_1995.html. Throughout the 1980s IEA conducted Second International Mathematics Study (SIMS), http://www.iea.nl/sims.html, and Second International Science Study, http://www.iea.nl/siss.html.

7. IEA, Brief History, http://www.iea.nl/brief_history.html; Paul E. Peterson, "Little Gain in Student Achievement," Chapter 2 of *Our Schools and Our Future...Are We Still at Risk*, Paul E. Peterson, ed. (Stanford: Hoover Institution Press, 2003): 60, 62.

8. National Center for Education Statistics, Program for International Student Assessment, http://nces.ed.gov/surveys/pisa/; Peterson, "Little Gain in Student Achievement," 60, 62.

9. IEA, Brief History, http://www.iea.nl/brief_history.html; National Center for Education Statistics, Progress in International Reading Literacy Study, http://nces.ed.gov/surveys/pirls/.

10. On the limitations of the various international assessments conducted through the early 1990s, see Elliott A. Medrich and Jeanne E. Griffith, *International Mathematics and Science Assessment: What Have We Learned?*, National Center for Education Statistics, US Department of Education, January 1992.

11. See, for example, "Criticisms of International Assessments: Fact or Fiction?" summary, based on a document written by Jim Hull, policy analyst, Center for Public Education, September 12, 2006, http://www.centerforpubliceducation.org/Main-Menu/Evaluating-performance/A-guide-to-international-assessments-At-a-glance/Criticisms-of-international-assessments-Fact-or-fiction.html.

12. Tom Loveless, *The 2010 Brown Center Report on American Education: How Well are American Students Learning?*, The Brown Center on Education Policy at the Brookings Institution, February 7, 2011, 11; National Center for Education Statistics, "Frequently Asked Questions, U.S. Participation: What international assessments does the United States participate in, and what do they measure," http://nces.ed.gov/surveys/international/faqs.asp.

13. For example, the PISA mathematics framework was revised in 2003, making it impossible to compare mathematics scores from prior PISA assessments. See n. 2 from Table A-5 in Stephen Provasnik, Patrick Gonzales, and David Miller, *U.S. Performance Across International Assessments of Student Achievement: Special Supplement to The Condition of Education 2009*, National Center for Education Statistics, Institute of Education Sciences, US Department of Education, August 2009, 59; National Center for Education Statistics, Frequently Asked Questions, Reported Results: Can you compare scores from one study to another, http://nces.ed.gov/surveys/international/faqs.asp.

14. National Center for Education Statistics, "About NAEP and International Assessments," http://nces.ed.gov/nationsreportcard/about/international.asp; "How Results Are Reported," http://nces.ed.gov/nationsreportcard/about/nathowreport.asp.

15. "Indicators of Risk" in *A Nation at Risk: The Imperative for Educational Reform. A Report to the Nation and the Secretary of Education United States Department of Education*, National Commission on Excellence in Education, April 1983, 11.

16. *Digest of Education Statistics 2014*, Table 235.10; Figure 6.7 in Chapter 6.

17. *OECD Eaducation at a Glance: Indicators 2014*, OECD Publishing, Table B1.1a, 215. Amounts are in 2011 US dollars, the latest data available as of this writing.

18. Eric A. Hanushek and Ludger Woessmann, *The High Cost of Low Educational Performance — The Long-Run Economic Impact of Improving PISA Outcomes*, Indicators and Analysis Division of the OECD Directorate for Education, 2010.

19. Eric A. Hanushek and Ludger Woessmann, *The High Cost of Low Educational Performance — The Long-Run Economic Impact of Improving PISA Outcomes*, Indicators and Analysis Division of the OECD Directorate for Education, 2010, see Figures 1, 2, and 4 on pp. 6–8, and pp. 9, 22, 25; Eric A. Hanushek, "Feeling Too Good About Our Schools," *Education Next*, January 18, 2011.

20. Jay P. Greene and Greg Forster, *The Teachability Index: Can Disadvantaged Students Learn?*, Education Working Paper No. 6, Manhattan Institute, September 2004.

21. OECD, *PISA 2012 Results: Excellence Through Equity: Giving Every Student the Chance to Succeed* (Volume II), Figure II.2.4, 41 and Figure II.3.6, 76, OECD Publishing, 2013.

22. OECD, *PISA 2012 Results: Excellence Through Equity: Giving Every Student the Chance to Succeed* (Volume II), note to Figure II.2.4, 41, OECD Publishing, 2013. Students are first identified as being in the bottom quarter of socio-economic levels and achieving scores in the top quarter level in reading. Their actual performance is then compared to their predicted performance based on results from students of similar socio-economic backgrounds across countries.

23. See, for example, Michael O'Brien, "Obama: Students Should Have Longer School Year in Order to Compete," *The Hill*, September 27, 2010; Seema Mehta, "Schwarzenegger Proposes 5 Fewer School Days," *Los Angeles Times*, January 8, 2009.

24. Eric A. Hanushek and Ludger Woessmann, *The High Cost of Low Educational Performance—The Long-Run Economic Impact of Improving PISA Outcomes*, Indicators and Analysis Division of the OECD Directorate for Education, 2010, 6 and 25.

25. The following results based on 2012 data substantiate author's previous findings based on an unpublished analysis prepared for the California Governor's Office, "The Effect of School Year Length on Student Performance," January 12, 2008. The results are presented in Vicki Murray (Alger), "Kids Need More School Choice," *Human Events*, January 21, 2009; Republished as "California School Days," *Investor's Business Daily*, January 21, 2009.

26. OECD, *Education Indicators at a Glance 2014*, Table D4.1, 485, OECD Publishing.

27. Ludger Woessmann, Elke Ludemann, Gabriela Schutz, and Martin R. West, *School Accountability, Autonomy, Choice, and the Level of Student Achievement: International Evidence from PISA 2003*, OECD Education Working Papers, No. 13, December 21, 2007.

28. Jaap Dronkers and Peter Robert, "School Choice in the Light of the Effectiveness Differences of Various Types of Public and Private Schools in 19 OECD Countries," *Journal of School Choice*, Vol. 2, No. 3 (2008): 260–301. See also "Private Schools: Who Benefits? PISA in Focus. No. 7," OECD Publishing, August 2011.

29. Ludger Woessmann, "Why Students in Some Countries Do Better: International Evidence on the Importance of Education Policy, Education Matters," *Education Next*, Vol. 1, No. 2 (Summer 2001): 67–74. Quotation from p. 74.

30. See Chapter 5 of OECD, *PISA 2006: Science Competencies for Tomorrow's World: Volume 1: Analysis*, PISA, OECD Publishing, December 2007, 213–281.

31. OECD, *Public and Private Schools: How Management and Funding Relate to Their Socio-Economic Profile*, OECD Publishing, April 20, 2012.

32. Gabriela Schutz, Martin R. West, Ludger Woessmann, *School Accountability, Autonomy, Choice, and the Equity of Student Achievement: International Evidence from PISA 2003*, OECD Education Working Papers, No. 14, December 21, 2007, 34–35.

33. Eric A. Hanushek, Paul E. Peterson, and Ludger Woessmann, *U.S. Math Performance in Global Perspective: How Well Does Each State Do at Producing High-Achieving Students?*, Program on Education Policy and Governance, Report 10–19, Harvard University, November 2010.

34. Paul E. Peterson, Ludger Woessmann, Eric A. Hanushek, and Carlos X. Lastra-Anadon, "Globally Challenged: Are U.S. Students Ready to Compete? The Latest on Each State's International Standing in Math and Reading," *Education Next*, Vol. 11, No. 4 (Summer 2011): 51–59. Quotations are from pp. 51 and 59.

35. OECD, *Education at a Glance 2010: OECD Indicators*, Annex 3, Indicator D5: School Choice, 419 and 422; cf. Table D5.6, available online. See also OECD, *PISA Results 2009: What Makes a School Successful? Resources, Policies and Practices*, Vol. 4, OECD Publishing, December 7, 2010, 72.

36. *PISA Results 2009: What Makes A School Successful?*, 42.

37. Ibid., Table IV.3.8a, 222.

38. Ibid., Table IV.38.a, 222.

39. This does not mean that vouchers or tax credits are universally available in these countries. In some countries, vouchers or tax credits are available in education systems, but only a limited proportion of students use them. See *PISA Results 2009: What Makes a School Successful?*, Figure IV.3.4, 73; 86, n. 6. See also OECD, *Education at a Glance 2010: OECD Indicators*, 421–22, and Table D5.1, 428.

40. OECD, *Education at a Glance 2010: OECD Indicators*, Annex 3, Indicator D5, School Choice, Table D5.1, 428; cf. 11–20. See also OECD, *Education at a Glance 2010*, Annex 3, Table D5.3, 20–24.

41. For all OECD countries with vouchers and tax credits, see *Education at a Glance 2010: OECD Indicators*, 419, and Table D5.3, 430; *PISA Results 2009:* Figure IV.3.7, 219. See also Kit-Ho Chanel Fung and Chi-Chung Lam, "Empowering Parents' Choice of Schools: The Rhetoric and Reality of How Hong Kong Kindergarten Parents Choose Schools Under the Voucher Scheme," *Current Issues in Education*, 14(1), 1–47.

42. *Education at a Glance 2010: OECD Indicators*, 423.

43. Ibid., Table D.5.3, 430. For school type definitions, see pp. 426–27. See also OECD *Education at a Glance 2010*, Annex 3, 20–24.

44. Ibid., 423.

45. Ibid., 424.

46. Combined average PISA reading, science, and math scores are author's average based on *PISA Results 2009: What Students Know and Can Do*, Figure I.3.b, 155. Competition percentages are from *PISA Results 2009: What Makes a School Successful*, Table IV.3.8.a, 222. The percentages of students who attend schools where principals and/or teachers have considerable responsibility for resource allocation as well as curricula and assessments are the author's based on *PISA Results 2009: What Makes a School Successful*, Figures IV.3.3 a and b, 70–71. Resource allocation consists of six sub-categories: autonomy to hire teachers, fire teachers, establish teachers' starting salaries, determine their salary increases, formulate school budgets, and decide budget allocations within the school. Autonomy over curricula and assessments consists of four sub-categories: establishing assessment polices, choosing textbooks, determining course content, and deciding which courses are offered. The author determined the overall percentage of students attending schools where principals/teachers have considerable responsibility for resource allocation based on a 0 to 100 point scale for each of the six resource allocation sub-categories, where each point represents one percentage point, for a total of 600 possible points. The author used the same method for autonomy over curricula and assessment, with four sub-categories and a total of 400 possible points. Information on whether countries offer vouchers or tax credits to attend public, government dependent private, or independent private schools at the elementary or secondary levels is from *PISA Results 2009: What Makes a School Successful*, Figure IV.3.4 and Table IV.3.7, 73 and 219; OECD, *Education at a Glance 2010: OECD Indicators*, Table D5.3, 430; *Education at a Glance 2010*, Annex 3, 20–24.

47. OECD, *Public and Private Schools: How Management and Funding Relate to Their Socio-economic Economic Profile*, OECD Publishing 2012, 20–22; Figure 1.3, 21; Table B 1.4, 78.

48. *PISA Results 2009: What Makes A School Successful?*, 42.

49. OECD, *Education Indicators at a Glance 2007*, OECD Publishing, 392–394.

Chapter 8

1. Andrew J. Coulson, "Markets vs. Monopolies in Education: A Global Review of the Evidence," Cato Institute, Policy Analysis No. 620, September 10, 2008, 3.

2. Ina V.S. Mullis, Michael O. Martin, Chad A. Minnich, Gabrielle M. Stanco, Alka Arora, Victoria M.S. Centurino, and Courtney E. Castle, eds. *TIMSS 2011 Encyclopedia: Education Policy and Curriculum in Mathematics and Science*, Vol. 1, TIMSS & PIRLS International Study Center, Lynch School of Education, Boston College, September 14, 2012, 107; National Center on Education and the Economy (NCEE), Center on International Benchmarking, "Australia," http://www.ncee.org/programs-affiliates/center-on-international-education-benchmarking/top-performing-countries/australia-overview/.

3. *TIMSS 2011 Encyclopedia, Vol. 1,* 107 and 114–15.

4. NCEE, "Australia."

5. *TIMSS 2011 Encyclopedia, Vol. 1,* 107–108 and 110.

6. Ibid.

7. Ibid., 110.

8. Ibid., 112–13.

9. NCEE, "Australia."

10. *TIMSS 2011 Encyclopedia,* Vol. 1, 115–16.

11. *TIMSS 2011 Encyclopedia,* Vol. 1, 116; NCEE, "Australia."

12. Organisation for Economic Co-operation and Development (OECD), *PISA Results 2009: What Makes a School Successful? Resources, Policies and Practices,* Vol. 4, OECD Publishing, December 7, 2010, Figure IV.3.3b, 71.

13. Ibid.

14. Ibid., Table IV.3.8a, 222.

15. OECD, *Lessons from PISA for the United States: Strong Performers and Successful Reformers in Education,* OECD Publishing, 2011, 47; *PISA Results 2009: What Makes a School Successful?,* Figure IV.3.9, 224–25.

16. Rosemary Cahill and Jan Gray, "Funding And Secondary School Choice in Australia: A Historical Consideration," *Australian Journal of Teacher Education,* Vol. 35 (1 February 2010), 122.

17. Ibid., 134.

18. *TIMSS 2011 Encyclopedia,* 108.

19. Australian Bureau of Statistics, updated February 2, 2012.

20. *PISA Results 2009: What Makes a School Successful?,* Figure IV.3.9, 225.

21. *TIMSS 2011 Encyclopedia,* Vol. 1, 164–65.

22. Ibid.

23. Ibid., 173.

24. OECD, *Education at a Glance 2010,* Annex 3, Indicator D5: School Choice, Table D5. School Choice, 27.

25. Ibid., 30.

26. Ibid.

27. *TIMSS 2011 Encyclopedia,* Vol. 1, 173–74. See also OECD, *Education at a Glance 2010: OECD Indicators,* OECD Publishing, 421–22, and Table D5.4, 431.

28. *PISA Results 2009: What Makes a School Successful?,* Figure IV.3.3b, 71.

29. *TIMSS 2011 Encyclopedia,* Vol. 1, 164.

30. *PISA Results 2009: What Makes A School Successful?,* 41

31. OECD, *Education at a Glance 2010,* Annex 3, Indicator D5: School Choice, Table D5. School Choice, 10, 11, 36, 40, 45, and 53.

32. *PISA Results 2009: What Makes A School Successful?*, Table IV.3.8a, 222.

33. Ibid., Figure IV.3.7, 219; OECD, *Education at a Glance 2010*, 421–22, and Table D5.3, 430. See also OECD, *Education at a Glance 2010*, Annex 3, Indicator D5: School Choice, 2081 and 82.

34. Ibid., Table D5.4, 31.

35. *Angloinfo*, "Brussels: The School System," http://brussels.angloinfo.com/information/family/schooling-education/school-system/.

36. OECD, *Education at a Glance 2010*, Annex 3, Indicator D5: School Choice, 17 and 59.

37. NCEE, "Canada," http://www.ncee.org/programs-affiliates/center-on-international-education-benchmarking/top-performing-countries/canada-overview/

38. "From Basket Case to World Beater," Chapter 3 of Brian Lee Crowley, Jason Clemens, and Niels Veldhuis, *The Canadian Century: Moving Out of America's Shadow* (Toronto: Key Porter, May 1, 2010), 84–113.

39. *TIMSS 2011 Encyclopedia*, Vol. 1, 77.

40. Lance Izumi and Jason Clemens, "Learning form Canada's Schools," *Washington Times*, February 23, 2010.

41. *PISA Results 2009: What Makes A School Successful?*, Table IV.3.8.a, 222.

42. Marvin Olasky, "Canada's Experience Shows School Choice Works," *Townhall.com*, July 30, 2002.

43. Ibid.

44. Claudia R. Hepburn, "Public Funding of School Choice in Canada: A Case Study," Chapter 1 of *What America Can Learn from School Choice in Other Countries*, eds. David Salisbury and James Tooley (Washington, DC: Cato Institute, 2005), 9.

45. Ibid., 10.

46. Ibid., 11 and 13.

47. Ibid., 18 and 19.

48. Ibid., 19.

49. Ibid.

50. Olasky, "Canada's Experience Shows School Choice Works."

51. Hepburn, "Public Funding of School Choice in Canada," 20.

52. *PISA Results 2009: What Makes a School Successful?* Figure IV.3.9, 225.

53. *TIMSS 2011 Encyclopedia*, Vol. 1, 207.

54. *TIMSS 2011 Encyclopedia*, Vol. 1, 28 and 207.

55. OECD, *Education at a Glance 2010: OECD Indicators*, 424–25 and Table D5.4, 431.

56. *TIMSS 2011 Encyclopedia*, Vol. 1, 207–208.

57. Shen-Keng Yang, "Dilemmas of Education Reform in Taiwan: Internationalization or Localization?," Paper presented at the Annual Meeting of the Comparative and International Education Society, Washington, DC, March 2011, 8. See also pp. 12 and 15.

58. OECD, *Education at a Glance 2010: OECD Indicators*, 424–25 and Table D5.4, 431.

59. *TIMSS 2011 Encyclopedia*, Vol. 1, pp. 215–16.

60. *PISA Results 2009: What Makes a School Successful?*, Figure IV.3.3b, 71.

61. OECD, *Education at a Glance 2010*, Annex 3, Indicator D5: School Choice, 61, 62, 63, and 64.

62. *PISA Results 2009: What Makes a School Successful?*, Table IV.3.8a, 222.

63. Ibid., Figure IV.3.7, 219; *Education at a Glance 2010: OECD Indicators*, 421–22, and Table D5.3, 430; *Education at a Glance 2010*, Annex 3, Indicator D5: School Choice, 22.

64. *PISA Results 2009: What Makes a School Successful?*, Figure IV.3.7, 219.

65. *Lessons from PISA for the United States*, 47; *PISA Results 2009: What Makes a School Successful?*, Figure IV.3.9, 224–25.

66. *TIMSS 2011 Encyclopedia*,Vol. 1, 313. See also OECD, *Education at a Glance 2010*, Annex 3, Indicator D5: School Choice, 10.

67. *TIMSS 2011 Encyclopedia*, Vol. 1, 314.

68. Ibid., 322.

69. Ibid., 324.

70. Ibid., 331. See also OECD, *Education at a Glance 2010: OECD Indicators*, 424–25 and Table D5.4, 431.

71. *PISA Results 2009: What Makes a School Successful?*, Figure IV.3.3b, 71.

72. OECD, *Education at a Glance 2010*, Annex 3, Indicator D5: School Choice, 10.

73. Ibid., 48, 49, 50, and 57.

74. Ibid., 53.

75. Ibid., 53–54.

76. *PISA Results 2009: What Makes A School Successful?*, Table IV.3.8.a, 222.

77. OECD, *Education at a Glance 2010*, Annex 3, Indicator D5: School Choice, 21.

78. *PISA Results 2009: What Makes a School Successful?*, Figure IV.3.7, 219; OECD *Education at a Glance 2010: OECD Indicators*, 421–22, and Table D5.3, 430.

79. *Lessons from PISA for the United States*, 105; *TIMSS 2011 Encyclopedia*, Vol. 1, 367–68.

80. NCEE, "Hong Kong," http://www.ncee.org/programs-affiliates/center-on -international-education-benchmarking/top-performing-countries/hong-kong -overview/.

81. OECD, *Education at a Glance 2010*, Annex 3, Indicator D5: School Choice, 31 and 45.

82. *TIMSS 2011 Encyclopedia*, Vol. 1, 368.

83. OECD, *Education at a Glance 2010,* Annex 3, Indicator D5: School Choice, 61.

84. Ibid., 50 and 52.

85. *PISA Results 2009: What Makes a School Successful?*, Figure IV.3.3b, 71.

86. Ibid., 222.

87. Kit-Ho Chanel Fung and Chi-Chung Lam, "Empowering Parents' Choice of Schools: The Rhetoric and Reality of How Hong Kong Kindergarten Parents Choose Schools Under the Voucher Scheme," *Current Issues in Education*, 14(1), 1–47; OECD, *Education at a Glance 2010*, Annex 3, Indicator D5: School Choice, 71, 73, 75, and 77.

88. *Lessons from PISA for the United States*, 100.

89. Ina V.S. Mullis, Michael O. Martin, John F. Olsen, Debra R. Berger, Dana Milne, Gabrielle M. Stanco, eds. *TIMSS 2007 Encyclopedia: A Guide to Math and Science Education Around the World*, Vol. 1, TIMSS & PIRLS International Study Center, Lynch School of Education, Boston College, December 9, 2008, 228.

90. *TIMSS 2011 Encyclopedia*,Vol. 1, 368–69.

91. Ibid.

92. Ibid.; OECD, *Education at a Glance 2010,* Annex 3, Indicator D5: School Choice,55.

93. Ibid., 56.

94. *Lessons from PISA for the United States*, 47; *PISA Results 2009: What Makes a School Successful?*, 73, and Figure IV.3.9, 224–25.

95. *Education in Hungary: Past, Present, and Future*, Department for EU Relations, Ministry of Education and Culture, Hungary, 2008, 12 and 19.

96. Ibid., 13.

97. *The System of Education in Hungary*, prepared by the Ministry of National Resources of Hungary in cooperation with the Hungarian Eurydice Unit, August 2012, 5.

98. *Education in Hungary: Past, Present, and Future*, 13 and 24; *The System of Education in Hungary*, 14 and 40; OECD, *Education at a Glance 2010*, Annex 3, Indicator D5: School Choice, 28.

99. *TIMSS 2011 Encyclopedia*, 392.

100. OECD, *Education at a Glance 2010: OECD Indicators*, 421–22, and Table D5.4, 431.

101. *PISA Results 2009: What Makes a School Successful?*, Table IV.3.8a, 222.

102. *Education in Hungary: Past, Present, and Future*, 13; *The System of Education in Hungary*, 5.

103. *Education in Hungary: Past, Present, and Future*, 20; *TIMSS 2011 Encyclopedia,* 381.

104. OECD, *Education at a Glance 2010*, Annex 3, Indicator D5: School Choice, 46.

105. *TIMSS 2011 Encyclopedia*, Vol. 1, 421.

106. OECD, *Education at a Glance 2010*, Annex 3, Indicator D5: School Choice, 28; *Education at a Glance 2010: OECD Indicators*, 42425 and Table D5.4, 431.

107. OECD, *Education at a Glance 2010*, Annex 3, Indicator D5: School Choice, 30; *TIMSS 2011 Encyclopedia*, Vol. 1, 435–36.

108. OECD, *Education at a Glance 2010*, Annex 3, Indicator D5: School Choice, 29.

109. *PISA Results 2009: What Makes a School Successful?*, Figure IV.3.3b, 71.

110. Ibid., Table IV.3.8a, 222.

111. *TIMSS 2011 Encyclopedia*, Vol. 1, 421–22.

112. OECD, *Education at a Glance 2010*, Annex 3, Indicator D5: School Choice, 45.

113. *Lessons from PISA for the United States*, 47; *PISA Results 2009: What Makes a School Successful?*, 73, and Figure IV.3.9, 224–25.

114. *Lessons from PISA for the United States*, 148–49.

115. Ibid., 141–42.

116. Ibid., 146.

117. Ibid.

118. *PISA Results 2009*, Figure IV.3.3b, 71.

119. Ibid., Table IV.3.8a, 222.

120. Ibid., Figure IV.3.9, 225.

121. Ibid., Table IV.3.7, 221; OECD, *Education at a Glance 2010*, Annex 3, Indicator D5: School Choice, 21–22.

122. *TIMSS 2011 Encyclopedia*, 469.

123. *Lessons from PISA for the United States*, 144.

124. Minako Sato, "Juku Boom: Cram Schools Cash In on Failure of Public Schools," *The Japan Times*, July 28, 2005.

125. Coulson, *Market Education*, 226.

126. *PISA Results 2009: What Makes A School Successful?*, Table IV.3.7, 221.

127. OECD, *Education at a Glance 2010*, Annex 3, Indicator D5: School Choice, 59, 61, and 62.

128. *Lessons from PISA for the United States*, 47; *PISA Results 2009*, 73, and Figure IV.3.9, 224–25.

129. *TIMSS 2011 Encyclopedia*, Vol. 1, 509.

130. NCEE, "South Korea," http://www.ncee.org/programs-affiliates/center-on
-international-education-benchmarking/top-performing-countries/south-korea
-overview/.

131. *TIMSS 2011 Encyclopedia*, Vol. 1, 509.

132. NCEE, "South Korea."

133. *Lessons from PISA for the United States*, 44; *PISA Results 2009: What Makes a School
Successful?*, Figure IV.3.3b, 71.

134. *Lessons from PISA for the United States*, 47; *PISA Results 2009: What Makes a School
Successful?*, 73, and Figure IV.3.9, 224–25.

135. *PISA Results 2009: What Makes a School Successful?*, Figure IV.3.7, 219; OECD, *Education at a Glance 2010: OECD Indicators*, 419, and Table D5.3, 430.

136. *Lessons from PISA for the United States*, 47; *PISA Results 2009*, Figure IV.3.9, 225.

137. AnnaMarie L. Sheldon, "Macao," *Education Encyclopedia*, http://education.state
university.com/pages/890/Macau.html.

138. "Education in Macao," Macao Government Information Bureau, June 2012, 1.

139. OECD, *Education at a Glance 2010*, Annex 3, Indicator D5: School Choice,39.
See also Education and Youth Affairs Bureau (DSEJ), "Chapter 1. Formal Education
in Figures 2011/2012," part of the *General Survey of Education in Figures*.

140. "Is Macau's Education System Changing?," *Macau Daily Times*, October 17, 2012.
See also CHOU Kwok Ping, "State, Market Force, and National Identity in Hong
Kong and Macao," EAI (East Asia Institute) Background Brief No. 469, August 20,
2009; Tang Kwok-Chun and Mark Bray, "Colonial Models and the Evolution of
Education Systems: Centralization and Decentralization in Hong Kong and Macau,"
World Bank Group, 2000; James Borton, "Macau's Commitment to Education,"
The Washington Times, October 25, 1999.

141. Bob Adamson and Li Sui Pang, "Primary and Secondary Schooling," in *Education
and Society in Hong Kong and Macao: Comparative Perspectives on Continuity and
Change*, 2nd ed., eds. Mark Bray and Ramsey Koo (Dordrecht, Netherlands: Springer/
Comparative Education Research Center, University of Hong Kong, 2005), 40.

142. OECD, *Education at a Glance 2010*, Annex 3, Indicator D5: School Choice, 29 and 31.

143. *PISA Results 2009: What Makes a School Successful?*, Figure IV.3.3b, 71.

144. Ibid., Table IV.3.8a, 222.

145. Ibid., Figure IV.3.7, p. 219; OECD, *Education at a Glance 2010: OECD Indicators*,
419, and Table D5.3, 430; "Education in Macao," Macao Government Information
Bureau, June 2012, 1.

146. *Lessons from PISA for the United States*, 47; *PISA Results 2009: What Makes a School
Successful?*, 73, and Figure IV.3.9, 224–25.

147. *TIMSS 2011 Encyclopedia*, Vol. 2, 619.

148. Ibid., 619–20.

149. OECD, *Education at a Glance 2010: OECD Indicators*, 424–25 and Table D5.4, 431–32;
NCEE, "The Netherlands," http://www.ncee.org/programs-affiliates/center-on
-international-education-benchmarking/top-performing-countries/netherlands
-overview/

150. NCEE, "The Netherlands."

151. OECD, *Education at a Glance 2010*, Annex 3, Indicator D5: School Choice, 46, 54.

152. *TIMSS 2011 Encyclopedia*, Vol. 2, 619.

153. NCEE, "The Netherlands."

154. European Commission, Education, Audiovisual & Culture Executive Agency, *Organisation of the Education System in the Netherlands, 2008/09*, Dutch Eurydice Unit, 13.

155. NCEE, "The Netherlands."

156. *PISA Results 2009: What Makes a School Successful?*, Figure IV.3.3b, 71.

157. European Commission, *Organisation of the Education System in the Netherlands, 2008/09*, 24, 72, 105, and 152.

158. *TIMSS 2011 Encyclopedia*, Vol. 2, 619. See also OECD, *Education at a Glance 2010*, Annex 3, Indicator 5: School Choice, 66; the Dutch Inspectorate of Education, http://www.onderwijsinspectie.nl/english.

159. OECD, *Education at a Glance 2010*, Annex 3, Indicator D5: School Choice, 13.

160. NCEE, "The Netherlands"; OECD, *Education at a Glance 2010*, Annex 3, Indicator D5: School Choice, 38. Parental choice at the lower secondary level, however, is affected by students' primary school performance and the advice of teachers given that schools are differentiated.

161. *PISA Results 2009: What Makes a School Successful?*, Table IV.3.8a, 222.

162. *PISA Results 2009: What Makes a School Successful?*, Figure IV.3.7, 219; *Education at a Glance 2010: OECD Indicators*, 419, and Table D5.3, 430; *Lessons from PISA for the United States*, 47; *PISA Results 2009: What Makes a School Successful?*, 73, and Figure IV.3.9, 224–25.

163. OECD, *Education at a Glance 2010*, Annex 3, Indicator D5: School Choice, 17 and 58; Dutch Inspectorate of Education.

164. Dutch Inspectorate of Education.

165. NCEE, "New Zealand," http://www.ncee.org/programs-affiliates/center-on-international-education-benchmarking/top-performing-countries/new-zealand-overview/.

166. *TIMSS 2011 Encyclopedia*, Vol. 2, 631–32.

167. *Education at a Glance 2010: OECD Indicators*, 424–25 and Table D5.4, 431–32.

168. *TIMSS 2011 Encyclopedia*, Vol. 2, 635.

169. Ibid., 636; New Zealand Ministry of Education, National Standards, http://www.minedu.govt.nz/theMinistry/Consultation/NationalStandards.aspx.

170. *TIMSS 2011 Encyclopedia*, Vol. 2, 645–46; OECD, *Education at a Glance 2010*, Annex 3, Indicator D5: School Choice, 30.

171. *TIMSS 2011 Encyclopedia*, Vol. 2, 632.

172. *PISA Results 2009: What Makes a School Successful?*, Figure IV.3.3b, 71.

173. There may, however, be space restrictions which then require a lottery to determine which students are admitted. See OECD, *Education at a Glance 2010*, Annex 3, Indicator D5: School Choice, 46–47, and 49.

174. *Lessons from PISA for the United States*, 47; *PISA Results 2009: What Makes a School Successful?*, 73 and Figure IV.3.9, 224–25. See also OECD, *Education at a Glance 2010*, Annex 3, Indicator D5: School Choice, 60.

175. *PISA Results 2009: What Makes a School Successful?*, Figure IV.3.7, 219 and Table IV.3.8a, 222; OECD, *Education at a Glance 2010*, Annex 3, Indicator D5: School Choice, 21–22. See also Organisation for Economic Co-operation and Development (OECD), *Education at a Glance 2010: OECD Indicators*, 419, and Table D5.3, 430.

176. *Lessons from PISA for the United States*, 162.

177. *TIMSS 2011 Encyclopedia*, Vol. 2, 801; NCEE, "Singapore," http://www.ncee.org/programs-affiliates/center-on-international-education-benchmarking/top-performing-countries/singapore-overview/; *Lessons from PISA for the United States,* 164.

178. *Lessons from PISA for the United States,* 170–72.

179. Winston Hodge, "Basic Education Curriculum Revisited: A Look at the Current Content and Reform," Training and Development Division, Ministry of Education Singapore, 2010, 1; Singapore Ministry of Education, Desired Outcomes of Education, http://www.moe.gov.sg/education/desired-outcomes/.

180. *Lessons from PISA for the United States,* 170–72.

181. Hodge, "Basic Education Curriculum Revisited," 4.

182. *TIMSS 2011 Encyclopedia,*Vol. 2, 803.

183. *Lessons from PISA for the United States,* 163 and 173.

184. *PISA Results 2009: What Makes a School Successful?,* Figure IV.3.3b, 71.

185. *Lessons from PISA for the United States,* 47; *PISA Results 2009: What Makes a School Successful?,* 73, and Figure IV.3.9, 224–25.

186. Singapore Ministry of Education, Desired Outcomes of Education; the Council for Private Education, Singapore, https://www.cpe.gov.sg/.

187. *PISA Results 2009: What Makes a School Successful?,* Table IV.3.8a, 222.

188. Matthew J. Brouillette, "The 1850s and Beyond," 4–10, quotation from p. 5.

189. Quoted in Sheldon Richman, *Separating School & State: How to Liberate America's Families* (Fairfax, VA: The Future of Freedom Foundation, 1994), 11.

Chapter 9

1. US Department of Education, "Overview of the U.S. Department of Education," Office of Communications and Outreach, September 2010.

2. See the remarks of Neil McCluskey in "School's Out: The Failure of No Child Left Behind," *Cato Policy Report,* November/December 2007.

3. This estimate reflects $14.1 billion in salaries, benefits, contractual services, supplies, and other overhead costs minus the $192 million in base salaries and awards: $14.1 billion - $192 million = $13.9 billion. The US Department of Education reported $14.1 billion in salaries, benefits, contractual services, supplies, and other overhead costs. See Office of Management and Budget, *Budget of the U.S. Government,* Federal Credit Supplement: Object Class Analysis, March 24, 2011, Table 1, pp. 4 and 11. The $192 million in base salaries and awards for the 1,818 employees come from the US Office of Personnel Management, FedScope, December 2010. Base salary and award data are compiled by the *Asbury Park Press,* DataUniverse for Federal Employees 2011. Programs and corresponding annual funding are from the *Catalog of Federal Domestic Assistance,* accessed February 23, 2013.

4. The US Department of Education obligations represent 2.6 percent of all federal branches' obligations based on 2010 data from the OMB, *Budget of the U.S. Government,* Object Class Analysis, Fiscal Year 2012, Table 1, pp. 1 and 4.

5. US Department of Education Coordinating Structure, updated October 22, 2012. The number of federal employees by office is from the US Office of Personnel Management, FedScope, December 2010. Base salary and award data are compiled by the *Asbury Park Press,* DataUniverse for Federal Employees 2011. Programs and

corresponding annual funding are from the *Catalog of Federal Domestic Assistance,* accessed February 23, 2013. Unless otherwise noted, throughout this chapter base salaries and awards figures, as well as program funding and the number of employees all come from these sources.

6. Neal McCluskey, *Feds in the Classroom: How Big Government Corrupts, Cripples, and Compromises American Education* (New York: Rowman & Littlefield, 2007), 189–90.

7. GAO, *2013 Annual Report: Actions Needed to Reduce Fragmentation, Overlap, and Duplication and Achieve Other Financial Benefits,* April 9, 2013, Figure 4, p. 19.

Chapter 10

1. "Additional Views of Hon. L. H. Fountain" in Department of Education Organization Act, Mr. Brooks, from the Committee on Government Operations, submitted the following Report together with Separate, Additional, Supplementary, and Dissenting Views (to accompany H.R. 2444), May 14, 1979, in *Legislative History of Public Law 96-88, Department of Education Organization Act Part 1 and Part 2,* 96th Congress, 2nd Session, Committee Print, US Congress, Washington, DC, Senate Committee on Government Operations, 1980, 1150 and 1152.

2. Based on a review of 96 programs. See Office of Management and Budget, Department of Education Programs, ExpectMore.gov. Unless otherwise noted, all individual program ratings and reviews come from this resource.

3. "Additional Views of Hon. L. H. Fountain," May 14, 1979, in *Legislative History of Public Law 96-88,* 1151.

4. Unless otherwise noted, all descriptions and statements are taken from the respective management office, program, and White House initiative websites listed by the US Department of Education Pricipal Office Functional Statements website, http://www2.ed.gov/about/offices/list/om/fs_po/index.html.

5. US Department of Health and Human Services, Office of Head Start, http://www.acf.hhs.gov/programs/ohs.

6. US Department of Health and Human Services, Head Start Program Fact Sheet Fiscal Year 2011.

7. US Department of Health and Human Services, *Third Grade Follow-up to the Head Start Impact Study: Final Report,* December 21, 2012, xvii, 92, and 147; *Head Start Impact Study: Final Report,* January 15, 2010, 3-51 and 9-3 and 9-4.

8. Vicki Alger, "Obama's Underperforming Preschool Plan," *Washington Examiner,* February 27, 2013.

9. Joy Pullmann, "Race to the Top: Year One," Heartland Institute, January 24, 2012; "Meander to the Top: Federal Competition for School Reform Isn't Delivering," *Chicago Tribune,* January 08, 2012.

10. For more on TEACH grants, see Emilie Deans, "Examining the Data: Where Do Federal TEACH Grants Go?," New America Foundation, January 20, 2011.

11. *Scaling Teach for America: Growing the Talent Force Working to Ensure All Our Nation's Students Have Access to a Quality Education,* submitted to the U.S Department of Education Office of Innovation and Improvement, May 11, 2010, 7, 30, and 39.

12. National Comprehensive Center for Teacher Quality, Teacher Recruitment and Retention State Policy Database.

13. US Department of Veterans Affairs, http://www.va.gov/.

14. Neal McCluskey, "I'll Take 'Whatever Evidence I Like' for Hundreds of Billions, Alex," *Cato at Liberty* (blog), Cato Institute, February 17, 2011.

15. Patrick J. Howard, *The Department's Management of the Federal Real Property Assistance Program*, Final Audit Report by the US Department of Education, Office of the Inspector General to Winona H. Varnon, Principal Deputy Assistant Secretary, Office of Management, US Department of Education, October 23, 2012, 3.

16. Education Commission of the States, Open Enrollment Database, "Intradistrict or Interdistrict? Mandatory or Voluntary School District Participation?," last updated September 2011.

17. Mark Lerner, "President Obama Kills D.C. Voucher Program and Washington Scholarship Fund," *Washington Examiner*, December 10, 2009; "President Obama Closes the Washington Scholarship Fund," *Washington Examiner*, July 6, 2010.

18. See Chester E. Finn, Jr., Andrew J. Rotherham, Charles R. Hokanson, Jr., eds., *Rethinking Special Education for a New Century*, Thomas B. Fordham Institute, May 2001. See especially, Patrick J. Wolf and Bryan C. Hassel, "Effectiveness and Accountability (Part 1): The Compliance Model," 52–75; G. Reid Lyon, et al., "Rethinking Learning Disabilities," 259–88; Bryan C. Hassel and Patrick J. Wolf, "Effectiveness and Accountability (Part 2): Alternatives to the Compliance Model," 309–34. See also Jay P. Greene and Greg Forster, "Effects of Funding Incentives on Special Education Enrollment," Manhattan Institute Civic Report No. 32, December 2002.

19. In addition to the OMB's assessment, see *Longitudinal Study of the Vocational Rehabilitation (VR) Services Program, Third Final Report: The Context of VR Services*, Prepared for the US Department of Education, Office of Special Education and Rehabilitative Services by Becky J. Hayward and Holly Schmidt-Davis, Research Triangle Institute, September 2005.

20. Neal McCluskey, "No Federal Failure Left Behind—The Feds Should Get Out of America's Schools," *National Review Online*, July 12, 2004; Marvin H. Kosters and Brent D. Mast, *Closing the Education Achievement Gap: Is Title I Working?*, (Washington, DC: AEI Press, 2001).

21. Milbrey Wallin McLaughlin, *Evaluation and Reform: The Elementary and Secondary Education Act of 1965, Title I*, RAND, January 1974; Michele Stillwell-Parvensky, "Reforming Title I: Closing the Academic Achievement Gap for Disadvantaged Students," Harvard Kennedy School conducted for the Children's Defense Fund, April 2011.

22. Government Accountability Office (GAO), *K–12 Education: Selected States and School Districts Cited Numerous Federal Requirements As Burdensome, While Recognizing Some Benefits*, Washington, DC, June 27, 2012; GAO, *Disadvantaged Students: School Districts Have Used Title I Funds Primarily to Support Instruction*, Washington, DC, July 15, 2011.

23. GAO, *2013 Annual Report: Actions Needed to Reduce Fragmentation, Overlap, and Duplication and Achieve Other Financial Benefits*, Washington, DC, April 9, 2013, Figure 4, p. 19.

24. GAO, "Opportunities to Reduce Fragmentation, Overlap, and Potential Duplication in Federal Teacher Quality and Employment and Training Programs," April 6, 2011.

25. GAO, *2013 Annual Report: Actions Needed*, 245.

26. GAO, *Education of Military Dependent Students: Better Information Needed to Assess Student Performance*, Washington, DC, March 1, 2011; *Education: Assessment of the Impact Aid Program*, Washington, DC, October 15, 1976.

27. GAO, *2013 Annual Report: Actions Needed*, 128–30 and 266.

28. See, for example, Neal McCluskey, "Our Greedy Colleges," *Cato at Liberty* (blog), Cato Institute, June 15, 2012; "How Much Ivory Does This Tower Need? What We Spend on, and Get from, Higher Education," Cato Institute, Policy Analysis No. 686, October 27, 2011; Neal McCluskey, "From the Ed Stats Truth Squad," *Cato at Liberty* (blog), Cato Institute, January 31, 2008.

29. FinAid, Pell Grant Historical Figures, http://www.finaid.org/educators/pellgrant .phtml.

30. US Department of Education, *2009–2010 Federal Pell Grant End-of-Year Report*, Office of Postsecondary Education, Table 22.

31. Chris Edwards and Neal McCluskey, "Higher Education Subsidies," Downsizing the Federal Government, Cato Institute, May 2009.

32. OMB, High-Error Programs, PaymentAccuracy.gov.

33. US Department of Education, *FY 2012 Agency Financial Report*, Washington, DC, 2012, 119–20 and 125–26; cf. "Erroneous Pell Grant Payments in 2011 Total $1 Billion," *Inside Higher Ed*, November 16, 2011; US Department of Education, Office of Inspector General, *FY 2013 Management Challenges*, Washington, DC, January 2013, 1, 5–6.

34. US Department of Education, Office of Inspector General, *FY 2012 Management Challenges*, Washington, DC, October 2011, 1–2, 21–22.

35. Quoted in Michael C. Moynihan, "We Don't Need No Education: Obama Wants to Make College Grants into an Entitlement. Bad Idea," Reason Foundation, June 5, 2009, *Reason.com*.

36. US Chamber of Commerce, *Leaders and Laggards, 2012*, Institute for a Competitive Workforce, Washington, DC, June 2012, 15–16.

37. US Department of Education, Federal Work Study Program, http://www2.ed.gov/ programs/fws/index.html; US Department of Labor, Changes in Basic Minimum Wage in Non-Farm Employment under State Law: Selected Years: 1968 to 2013, revised December 2014.

38. Michael Brostek and George A. Scott, *Multiple Higher Education Tax Incentives Create Opportunities for Taxpayers to Make Costly Mistakes*, GAO Testimony Before the Subcommittee on Select Revenue Measures, Committee on Ways and Means, House of Representatives, May 1, 2008, 4 and 21.

39. College Board, *Trends in Financial Aid 2010*, Figure 2A, 11.

40. Shahien Nasiripour, "Obama Student Loan Policy Reaping $51 Billion Profit," *Huffington Post*, May 14, 2013.

41. *Digest of Education Statistics 2011*, 544.

42. GAO, *2013 Annual Report: Actions Needed*, Figure 4, p. 19.

43. GAO, *Multiple Employment and Training Programs: Providing Information on Co-locating Services and Consolidating Administrative Structures Could Promote Efficiencies*, January 13, 2011, 6, 10–17, and 39.

44. GAO, *2013 Annual Report: Actions Needed*, 138–39 and 141.

45. Neil S. Seftor, Arif Mamun, and Allen Schirm, *The Impacts of Regular Upward Bound on Postsecondary Outcomes Seven to Nine Years After Scheduled High School Graduation: Final Report*, Mathematica Policy Research, Inc., Prepared for: US Department

of Education, Office of Planning, Evaluation and Policy Development, Policy and Program Studies Service, 2009, xiv–xvi, 34, 41, 45, and 76.

46. Shahien Nasiripour, "Obama Student Loan Policy Reaping $51 Billion Profit," *Huffington Post*, May 14, 2013.

Chapter 11

1. Author's figures based on data from the Friedman Foundation for Educational Choice, as of July 2015.

2. Frank Heller, "Lessons from Maine: Education Vouchers for Students since 1873," Cato Institute Briefing Paper No. 66, September 10, 2001; Libby Sternberg, "Lessons from Vermont: 132-Year-Old Voucher Program Rebuts Critics," Cato Institute Briefing Paper No. 67, September 10, 2001.

3. Milton Friedman, "The Role of Government in Education," in *Economics and the Public Interest*, ed. Robert A. Solo (New Brunswick: Rutgers University Press, 1955), 123–144. Quotation from p. 134. See also, *Capitalism and Freedom* (Chicago: University of Chicago Press, 1962), 99–100.

4. Herbert J. Wahlberg and Joseph L. Bast, *Education and Capitalism: How Overcoming Our Fear of Markets and Economics Can Improve America's Schools* (Stanford: Hoover Institution Press, 2003), xviii.

5. Quoted in David W. Kirkpatrick, "It Began with Adam Smith," *Vermont Education Report*, May 1998.

6. Quoted in ibid.

7. Quoted in ibid.

8. Quoted in ibid.

9. For a partial summary of writings from various voucher proponents see Laura Hersh Salganik, "The Fall and Rise of Education Vouchers," *Teachers College Record*, Vol. 83, No. 2 (1981): 263–283; n. 105, 812–813 of Goodwin Liu and William L. Taylor, "School Choice to Achieve Desegregation," *Fordham Law Review*, Vol. 74, Issue 2 (April 3, 2006); Section 2.3 "Voucher Models" in Ben Jongbloed and Jos Koelman, *Vouchers for Higher Education? — A Survey of the Literature Commissioned by the Hong Kong University Grants Committee*, Center for Higher Education Policy Studies, University of Twente Enschede (Netherlands), June 2000; and n. 3 of Judith Areen and Christopher Jencks, "Education Vouchers: A Proposal for Diversity and Choice," *Teachers College Record*, Vol. 72, No. 3 (1971): 327–336.

10. Virgil C. Blum, *Freedom of Choice in Education* (New York: The Macmillan Company, 1958), 36. See also Joseph L. Bast and David Harmer versus Douglas Dewey, "Vouchers and Educational Freedom: A Debate," Cato Institute, Policy Analysis No. 269, March 12, 1997; "Introduction" in Joseph L. Bast and Herbert J. Walberg, *Education and Capitalism* (Stanford, CA: Stanford University, Hoover Institution Press, 2003).

11. Kirkpatrick, "It Began with Adam Smith." Forty years later, a 2006 US Chamber of Commerce national survey found that nearly seven out of 10 businesses support some kind of voucher program to improve education. See US Department of Commerce, "Education Reform — Insight into the Business Community's Views About the U.S. Education System," Statistics and Research Center, November 2006.

12. Joel Klein, *U.S. Education Reform and National Security*, Task Force Report, Council on Foreign Relations, Washington, DC, March 2012, 58.

13. Ibid., 5 and 45.

14. "School Reform's Establishment Turn," *Wall Street Journal*, Review and Outlook, March 19, 2012.

15. Quoted in Kirkpatrick, "It Began with Adam Smith."

16. Martin Morse Wooster, *Angry Classrooms, Vacant Minds* (San Francisco, CA: Pacific Research Institute for Public Policy, 1994), 106; cf. "California, The Self-Determination in Education Act, 1968," in *Parents, Teachers, and Children* (San Francisco: Institute for Contemporary Studies, 1977).

17. Wooster, *Angry Classrooms, Vacant Minds*, 160–161.

18. Quoted in David W. Kirkpatrick, "How Many Recommendations Are Needed?," The Blum Center for Parental Freedom in Education, August 1997.

19. See Salganik, "The Fall and Rise of Education Vouchers"; Judith Areen and Christopher Jencks, "Education Vouchers: A Proposal for Diversity and Choice," *Teachers College Record*, Vol. 72, No. 3, (1971): 327–336.

20. Areen and Jencks, "Education Vouchers: A Proposal for Diversity and Choice."

21. Quoted in David W. Kirkpatrick, "How Many Recommendations Are Needed?," The Blum Center for Parental Freedom in Education, August 1997.

22. Quoted in Kirkpatrick, "It Began with Adam Smith."

23. Kirkpatrick, "How Many Recommendations Are Needed?"

24. Quoted in Jongbloed and Koelman, *Vouchers for Higher Education?*, 14.

25. Quoted in Salganik, "The Fall and Rise of Education Vouchers," 272.

26. Kirkpatrick, "It Began with Adam Smith."

27. Judith Areen and Christopher Jencks, "Education Vouchers: A Proposal for Diversity and Choice," *Teachers College Record*, Volume 72, Number 3, 1971, 327–336.

28. David W. Kirkpatrick, "Emergence of the Voucher Controversy," *The Vermont Education Report*, July 26, 2004, Vol. 4, No. 27.

29. Jongbloed and Koelman, *Vouchers for Higher Education?*

30. "Reagan's 1971 State of the State Message," *California Journal*, January 12, 1971, 15; cf. Bruce Keppel, "Riles Rips Reagan on Vouchers," *Modesto Bee*, January 21, 1971.

31. Kirkpatrick, "It Began with Adam Smith"; see also Dwight R. Lee, "The Political Economy of Educational Vouchers," The Foundation for Economic Education, *The Freeman*, Vol. 36, No. 7 (July 1986); Judith Kimball Taylor, "Educational Vouchers: Addressing The Establishment Clause Issue", *Pacific Law Journal* Vol. 11 (July 1980): 1063.

32. Jim Warren, "Alum Rock Voucher Project," *Educational Researcher*, Vol. 5, No. 3 (March 1976): 13–15.

33. See Kirkpatrick, "It Began with Adam Smith"; Jongbloed and Koelman, *Vouchers for Higher Education?*; Salganik, "The Fall and Rise of Education Vouchers"; Herbert J. Walberg and Joseph A. Bast, "School Choice: The Essential Reform," in *Cato Journal*, Vol. 13, No.1 (Spring/Summer 1993): 103–104.

34. Quoted in Kirkpatrick, "It Began with Adam Smith."

35. Quoted in ibid.

36. Office of Education, *Inside-out: The Final Report and Recommendations of the Teachers National Field Task Force on the Improvement and Reform of American Education*, National Center for Improvement of Educational Systems, Washington, DC, May 1974, 40.

37. *Serrano v. Priest*, Supreme Court of Ca., December 30, 1976, As Modified, February 1, 1977, *Pacific Reporter,* 2nd Series, Vol. 557, p. 2d, St. Paul, MN: West Pub. Co., 1977, 929–970. Cited in Kirkpatrick, "It Began with Adam Smith"; "A Foolish Constituency," Blum Center for Parental Freedom in Education, November 1997.

38. "School Choice as Family Policy: John E. Coons," interview with George A. Clowes, *School Reform News*, Heartland Institute, February 1, 2002.

39. Kirkpatrick, "How Many Recommendations Are Needed?"

40. Ibid.

41. Ibid.

42. "Reagan Directs E. D. To Develop Model Voucher Bill for States," *Education Week*, February 3, 1988.

43. Lawrence J. McAndrews, "Late and Never: Ronald Reagan and Tuition Tax Credits," *Journal of Church and State* 42 (2000): 467–83. Quotation from p. 475.

44. Erica Toliver, "D.C. Opportunity Scholarship Program Awards New Scholarships to Nearly 300 K–12 Students for the 2012–13 School Year," *DC Children and Youth Investment Trust Corporation*, August 2, 2012, Press Release.

45. Former Mayor Anthony Williams, then D.C. City Council Member and Education Committee Chair Kevin P. Chavous, and then President of the D.C. Board of Education, Peggy Cooper Cafritz, worked with the Bush administration to implement the funding plan. See "Statement of Anthony A. Williams, Former Mayor of Washington D.C. and Chairman of D.C. Children First before the Committee on Homeland Security and Governmental Affairs," United States Senate, Hearing on the D.C. Opportunity Scholarship Program, May 13, 2009.

46. Anthony A. Williams and Kevin P. Chavous, "Education, By Any Means," *Washington Post*, April 14, 2009.

47. Emma Brown, "Private-school Vouchers Go to about 300 D.C. Students," *Washington Post*, August 4, 2012.

48. Patrick Wolf, Babette Gutmann, Michael Puma, Brian Kisida, Lou Rizzo, Nada Eissa, and Matthew Carr, *Evaluation of the DC Opportunity Scholarship Program: Final Report* (NCEE 2010-4018), National Center for Education Evaluation and Regional Assistance, Institute of Education Sciences, US Department of Education, June 2010; Jason Riley, "The Evidence is In: School Vouchers Work," *Wall Street Journal*, May 3, 2011.

49. http://www.dcscholarships.org/elements/file/OSP/DC%20OSP%20Parental%20 Satisfaction%20and%20Program%20Fact%20Sheet%20(revised%202012_05_17) .pdf; Vicki E. Alger, "ED's 'What Works' Division Validates Voucher Program the 'Fund Whatever Works' Obama Administration Killed," *IWF blog*, Independent Women's Forum, February 24, 2010.

50. Children and Youth Investment Trust Corporation, "Parental Satisfaction and Program Fact Sheet: D.C. Opportunity Scholarship Program 2011–12," revised May 17, 2012.

51. Rachel Sheffield, "D.C. Public Schools Spend Almost $30,000 Per Student," *The Daily Signal* (blog), The Heritage Foundation, July 25, 2012.

52. Andrew J. Coulson, "Dems Want Vouchers Dead. Hope Someone Else Pulls the Plug," *Cato at Liberty* (blog), Cato Institute, February 24, 2009.

53. "D.C. Council Wants Vouchers," *Wall Street Journal*, Review and Outlook, July 14, 2009; Vicki Murray (Alger) and Evelyn B. Stacey, *Down but Not Out in D.C.:*

Bi-Partisan, Bi-Cameral Efforts to Continue the Opportunity Scholarship Program, Independent Women's Forum Policy Brief # 25, August 13, 2009.

54. "Presumed Dead," *Washington Post*, April 11, 2009.

55. "Who Will Step Up to Save D.C.'s Opportunity Scholarship Program?," *Washington Post*, July 10, 2009; "D.C. Council Wants Vouchers," *Wall Street Journal*.

56. Malcolm Glenn and Michelle Gininger, *School Choice Now: The Year of School Choice: School Choice Year Book 2011–12* (Washington, DC: Alliance for School Choice, 2012), 18.

57. Ibid., 7, 18.

58. "D.C. Children Need the Administration's Help to Get a Quality Education," Editorial Board, *Washington Post*, May 22, 2012.

59. Rachel Sheffield, "Obama Continues to Deny D.C. Children Educational Opportunity," *The Daily Signal* (blog), The Heritage Foundation, May 24, 2012.

60. "D.C. Children Need the Administration's Help."

61. Lindsey Burke, "Boehner and Lieberman (Once Again) Save the D.C. Opportunity Scholarship Program," *The Corner* (blog), National Review, June 18, 2012.

62. Ibid.

63. Tom Howell, Jr., "Vouchers Available to 1,788 D.C. Students," *Washington Times*, August 3, 2012.

64. Remarks of Sen. Moynihan, "Millbrook's 50th Anniversary and Federal Aid to Education," October 20, 1981, in the *Congressional Record, Proceedings and Debates of the 97th Congress, First Session*, Vol. 127, Part 18, pp. S. 24566–68. Retrieved from Congressional Record Archive, October 20, 1981.

65. Lawrence J. McAndrews, "Late and Never: Ronald Reagan and Tuition Tax Credits," *Journal of Church and State* 42 (2000): 467–83. Quotation from p. 467.

66. Robert Packwood, "Tuition Tax Credits: Pro and Con," *Deseret News*, April 22, 1978; Fact Sheet: Roth-Ribicoff-Packwood-Moynihan Tuition Tax Relief Act of 1978, Carnegie Mellon Digital Collections Library; Muskie Senate Congressional Record, August 14, 1978, p, 25852, http://abacus.bates.edu/muskie-archives/ajcr/1978/Tuition%20Tax.shtml; "S.2142, Tuition Tax Credit Act," 95th Congress (1977–1978), Library of Congress, THOMAS.

67. McAndrews, "Late and Never: Ronald Reagan and Tuition Tax Credits," 467.

68. Ibid.

69. Jean Rosenblatt and Hoyt Gimlin, "Tuition Tax Credits: Renewed Legislative Struggle, Timing for Vote Turns Unexpectedly Bad," *CQ Researcher*, August 14, 1981, from Editorial research reports 1981 (Vol. 2). Washington, DC: CQ Press. Retrieved from http://library.cqpress.com/cqresearcher/cqresrre1981081400.

70. McAndrews, "Late and Never: Ronald Reagan and Tuition Tax Credits," 468–69.

71. Ibid., 470–71.

72. Ibid. See also Ronald Reagan, "Address Before a Joint Session of the Congress on the State of the Union," January 25, 1983 and "Message to the Congress Transmitting the Fiscal Year 1984 Budget," January 31, 1983; S.528, the Educational Opportunity and Equity Act of 1983, http://www.govtrack.us/congress/bills/98/s528.

73. McAndrews, "Late and Never: Ronald Reagan and Tuition Tax Credits," 471–72.

74. Ibid., 477–80.

75. Ibid., 473.

76. Ibid., 472–74; Senate Vote #355 in 1983, http://www.govtrack.us/congress/votes/98-1983/s355.

77. The other Democrats voting against S. 991 were Robert B. Morgan (D-NC) and William Proxmire (D-WI). Sen. Harry F. Byrd, Jr. (I-VA) also voted against the bill. See the *Congressional Record, Proceedings of the 95th Congress, Second Session*, Vol. 124, No. 154, September 28, 1978 (for legislative day of September 26, 1978), in *Legislative History of Public Law 96-88, Department of Education Organization Act Part 1 and Part 2*, 96th Congress, 2nd Session, Committee Print, US Congress, Washington, DC, Senate Committee on Government Operations, 1980, 382–83.

78. Remarks of Sen. Baker in the *Congressional Record, Proceedings of the 95th Congress, Second Session*, Vol. 124, No. 154, September 28, 1978 (for legislative day of September 26, 1978), in *Legislative History of Public Law 96-88, Department of Education Organization Act Part 1 and Part 2*, 96th Congress, 2nd Session, Committee Print, US Congress, Washington, DC, Senate Committee on Government Operations, 1980, 379.

79. Quoted in Jean Rosenblatt and Hoyt Gimlin, "Tuition Tax Credits: Renewed Legislative Struggle, Timing for Vote Turns Unexpectedly Bad," *CQ Researcher*, August 14, 1981, from Editorial research reports 1981 (Vol. 2). Washington, DC: CQ Press. Retrieved from http://library.cqpress.com/cqresearcher/cqresrre1981081400.

80. McAndrews, "Late and Never: Ronald Reagan and Tuition Tax Credits," 474.

81. Ibid., 474–75. See also Ronald Reagan, "Address Before a Joint Session of the Congress on the State of the Union," February 6, 1985. "Message to the Congress on America's Agenda for the Future," February 6, 1986.

82. Ronald Reagan, "America's Economic Bill of Rights," July 3, 1987.

83. Remarks of Sen. Moynihan, "Millbrook's 50th Anniversary and Federal Aid to Education," October 20, 1981, in the *Congressional Record, Proceedings and Debates of the 97th Congress, First Session*, Vol. 127, Part 18, S. 24566–68. Retrieved from Congressional Record Archive, October 20, 1981, http://archive.org/details/congressional rec127gunit.

84. Author's tally based on data from the Friedman Foundation for Educational Choice.

85. Friedman Foundation for Educational Choice, *The ABCs of School Choice, 2015 Edition*.

86. Ibid.

87. Ibid.

88. Ibid.

89. Ibid.

90. Adam B. Schaeffer, "The Public Education Tax Credit," Cato Institute, Policy Analysis No. 605, December 5, 2007.

91. A.R.S. § 43-1089 (1997). See William Howell and Mindy Spencer, *School Choice Without Vouchers Expanding Education Options Through Tax Benefits*, Pioneer Institute White Paper, No. 41, October 2007. See also Carrie Lips Lukas, "The Arizona Scholarship Tax Credit: Providing Choice for Arizona Taxpayers and Students," Goldwater Institute Policy Report No. 186, December 11, 2003; Carrie Lips and Jennifer Jacoby, "The Arizona Scholarship Tax Credit: Giving Parents Choices, Saving Taxpayers Money," Cato Institute, Policy Analysis No. 414, September 17, 2001; Michele S. Moses, "The Arizona Education Tax Credit and Hidden Considerations of Justice," *Education Policy Analysis Archives*, Vol. 8, No. 37, January 1, 2000; Dan Laitsch, "School Choice and Privatization Efforts in the States: A Legislative Survey," American Association of Colleges of Teacher Education Issue Paper, October 1998.

92. Author's tally based on data from the Friedman Foundation for Educational Choice.

93. *Arizona Christian School Tuition Organization v. Winn* USSC Decision, 3, available through the Institute for Justice, http://www.ij.org/images/pdf_folder/school_choice/arizona/usss_winn_decision.pdf; Vicki Alger, "The *New York Times* Needs a School Choice Reality Check," *Townhall.com*, June 5, 2012; Vicki E. Murray (Alger), *An Analysis of Arizona Individual Income Tax-credit Scholarship Recipients' Family Income, 2009–10 School Year*, Program on Education Policy and Governance, Harvard University 10-18, October 2010.

94. Progressive Policy Institute, *21st Century Schools Project Bulletin*, Vol. 5, No. 13, June 28, 2005; Ted Kolderie, "Ray Budde and the Origins of the 'Charter Concept'," *Education Evolving*, Vol. 1, No. 6, July 3, 2005; Gloria Negri, "Ray Budde; Coined Phrase 'Charter Schools'," *Boston Globe*, June 21, 2005. Budde eventually published his paper in 1989, at a time when the country was still coming to terms with the findings of *A Nation at Risk* published in April 1983. See *Education by Charter: Restructuring Schools and School Districts*. Andover, MA: The Regional Laboratory for Educational Improvement of the Northeast Islands.

95. Quoted in Vicki Murray (Alger), *Empowering Teachers With Choice: How a Diversified Education System Benefits Teachers, Students, and America*, Independent Women's Forum, Position Paper No. 605, July 2007, 22.

96. Vicki E. Murray (Alger), "State's Rules Stifle Charter Schools, Threaten Success," *Arizona Republic*, November 6, 2006.

97. National Alliance for Public Charter Schools, Public Charter Schools Dashboard, 2013–2014.

98. Ibid., 2009–10.

99. The number of districts converting schools within their boundaries to charter schools, however, has increased nationwide from 8.6 percent in 2009–10 to 10.6 percent in 2012–13. In Arizona, for example, a growing number of districts have been converting their schools to charter schools to take advantage of the additional $1,000 in per-pupil funding the state awards to charter schools to help offset the prohibition against local overrides. Thus district-sponsored conversion charter schools bring in additional funds and districts retain their taxing authority. National Alliance for Public Charter Schools Dashboard, 2009–10 through 2012–13; Amy B. Wang, "Districts Convert Schools to Charters for More Money," *Arizona Republic*, June 30, 2013.

100. Patrick J. Wolf, "The Research Facts about Parental School Choice," February 2010, 5, available at Voucher Research Summaries, University of Arkansas, School Choice Demonstration Project.

101. Ibid.

102. Ibid.

103. Ibid.

104. Paul E. Peterson and William G. Howell, "The Latest Results from the New York City Voucher Experiment," Multidisciplinary Program in Inequality & Social Policy, John F. Kennedy School of Government, Harvard University, November 3, 2003; William G. Howell and Paul E. Peterson, "Voucher Research Controversy," *Education Next*, Vol. 4, No. 2 (Spring 2004): 73–78; Howell and Peterson, "Randomized Trials in New York City; Dayton, Ohio; Washington, DC" and Appendix E in

The Education Gap (Washington, DC: Brookings Institution: 2006 revised edition). See also Jay P. Greene, *Education Myths: What Special Interest Groups Want You to Believe About Our Schools—And Why It Isn't So* (New York: Rowman & Littlefield Publishers, 2006), 153; Greg Forster, *A Win-Win Solution: The Empirical Evidence on School Choice, Third Edition*, Friedman Foundation for Educational Choice, April 17, 2013, 7–8; Matthew Chingos and Paul E. Peterson, "Experimentally Estimated Impacts of School Vouchers on College Enrollment and Degree Attainment," *Journal of Public Economics*, Vol. 122 (February 2015): 1–12.

105. Clive R. Belfield and Henry M. Levin, "The Effects of Competition on Educational Outcomes: A Review of the US Evidence," National Center for the Study of Privatization of Education, Teachers College, Columbia University, March 2002. See p. 2 of pdf version for quotation, and Table 1, p. 47 of pdf version.

106. Susan Aud, "Education by the Numbers: The Fiscal Effect of School Choice Programs. 1990–2006," Friedman Foundation for Educational Choice, *School Choice Issues in Depth*, April 2007; Jeff Spalding, The Voucher Audit: Do Publicly Funded Private School Choice Programs Save Money? Friedman Foundation for Educational Choice, September 2014.

107. John Watson et al., *Keeping Pace with K–12 Online Learning: A Review of State-level Policy and Practice*, Evergreen Education Group, November 2009, 5, 46, 52, 54.

108. Ibid., 46.

109. *Education Week*, "Nebraska — State Technology Report 2009," A Special State-Focused Supplement to *Technology Counts 2009*," 6.

110. John Watson et al., *Keeping Pace with K–12 Digital Learning: An Annual Review of Policy and Practice*, Evergreen Education Group, 2014, 28.

111. John Watson et al., *Keeping Pace with K–12 Online Learning: An Annual Review of Policy and Practice*, Evergreen Education Group, 2011, 9, 12, 14, 28.

112. John Watson and Bruce Gemin, "Promising Practices in Online Learning," iNACOL, 12; cf. "The Student-Centered Funding Act," American Legislative Exchange Model Legislation, January 2010, www.alec.org.

113. Michael S. Holstead, Terry E. Spradlin, and Jonathan A. Plucker, "Promises and Pitfalls of Virtual Education in the United States and Indiana," Indiana University Center for Evaluation and Policy Education Policy Brief, Vol. 6, No. 6 (Spring 2008): 8.

114. Ibid.

115. Ibid.

116. Watson and Gemin, "Promising Practices in Online Learning," 11.

117. *Florida's Race to the Top Application of Initial Funding*, submitted to the US Department of Education June 1, 2010, 245. On the pitfalls of funding virtual schools based on "seat time," see Watson and Gemin, "Promising Practices in Online Learning," 11.

118. US Department of Education, *Transforming American Education: Learning Powered by Technology, National Education Technology Plan Draft*, Office of Educational Technology, Washington, DC, March 5, 2010, x and xi.

119. Quoted in Watson and Gemin, "Promising Practices in Online Learning," 11.

120. Quoted in Katie Ash, "Sustaining Funding Seen as Challenge for Online Ed," *Education Week*, April 23, 2010.

121. Ash, "Sustaining Funding Seen as Challenge for Online Ed."

122. Watson, *Keeping Pace with K–12 Online Learning*, 2011, 62.

123. Susan Patrick, "How Online Learning Can Increase Opportunities for Students," presentation at the American Legislative Exchange Council Education Task Force, 2009; "How to Introduce, Sustain, and Expand K–12 Online Learning Opportunities in Your State," January 21, 2010, Webinar presentation hosted by the American Legislative Exchange Council and iNACOL; "Online Teaching and Learning: Digital Directions Live Chat," moderated by Michelle Davis, *Education Week*, September 26, 2008.

124. Southern Regional Education Board, "Cost Guidelines for State Virtual Schools: Development, Implementation, and Sustainability," August 2006. See also Cathy Cavanaugh, "Online Course Funding: the Influence of Resources on Practices," in Watson et al., *Keeping Pace with K–12 Online Learning: A Review of State-level Policy and Practice*, Evergreen Education Group, November 2009, 40.

125. Patrick, "How to Introduce, Sustain, and Expand K–12 Online Learning Opportunities in Your State"; Gov. Bob Wise, "The Online Learning Imperative: A Solution to Three Looming Crises in Education," Alliance for Excellent Education, February 2010, 6–7.

126. Anthony G. Picciano and Jeff Seaman, *K–12 Online Learning; A 2008 Follow-up of the Survey of U.S. District Administrators*, The Sloan Consortium, January 2009, 5–6.

127. Wise, "The Online Learning Imperative," 8.

128. Virtual schools contend with participation and truancy issues by having specified student communications requirements. In Wisconsin, for example, parents of students who do not respond to assignments or directives from instructional staff within five school days are notified by the virtual school. If students fail to participate three times a semester, they may be transferred to another school or program. See Watson and Gemin, "Promising Practices in Online Learning," 12.

129. Watson and Gemin, "Promising Practices in Online Learning," 4; Patrick, "How Online Learning Can Increase Opportunities for Students."

130. "Creating Our Future: Students Speak Up About their Vision for 21st Century Learning—Speak Up 2009: National Findings K–12 Students and Parents, Project Tomorrow," March 2010, 16.

131. "Creating Our Future: Students Speak Up About their Vision for 21st Century Learning," 25.

132. Watson et al., *Keeping Pace with K–12 Online Learning*, 2011, 156.

133. Barbara Means, Yukie Toyama, Robert Murphy, Marianne Bakia, and Karla Jones, *Evidence-Based Practices in Online Learning: A Meta-Analysis and Review of Online Learning Studies*, US Department of Education Office of Planning, Evaluation, and Policy Development, Policy and Program Studies Service, May 2009. See also William R. Thomas, "Overcoming Doubts About Online Learning," Southern Regional Education Board, November 2009, 2–3 and Rosina Smith, Tom Clark, and Robert L. Blomeyer, *A Synthesis of New Research on K–12 Online Learning*, North Central Regional Education Laboratory/Learning Point Associates, November 2005, 17–18; cf. International Association for K–12 Online Learning (iNACOL), "Fast Facts About Online Learning," n.d., 3.

134. Thomas, "Overcoming Doubts About Online Learning;" cf. Means, et al., *Evidence-Based Practices in Online Learning*; Ohio Alliance for Public Charter Schools, "E-schools Show Superior Results," July 2009; *KidsOhio.org*, "Ohio's 8 Large Urban

Districts and Charter Schools Rank Higher on Educational Progress Than on Absolute Test Scores," June 9, 2009; Katherine Mackey, "Wichita Public Schools' Learning Centers: Creating a New Educational Model to Serve Dropouts and At-risk Students," Innosight Institute [now the Chritensen Institute], March 2010; Leland Anderson, "Alpine Online Case study: A Utah School District's Move into K–8 Online Education," Innosight Institute [now the Chritensen Institute] Case Study, August 28, 2009.

135. See the remarks of Susan Patrick in "Breaking Away From Tradition: E-Education Expands Opportunities for Raising Achievement," *Education Week* Webinar moderated by Kevin Bushweller, 19 and 21.

136. iNACOL, Online Learning in the Race to the Top Finalists' Round 2 Applications web site; cf. Ian Quille, "iNACOL Analyzes E-Learning in RTT," *Digital Education* (blog), *Education Week*, August 27, 2010.

137. Watson, *Keeping Pace with K–12 Online Learning*, 106.

138. For quotation, see iNACOL, Online Learning in the Race to the Top Finalists' Round 2 Applications web site.

139. Ibid.; Quille, "iNACOL Analyzes E-Learning in RTT."

140. David Feith, "The Empire Strikes Back," *Wall Street Journal*, March 3, 2011; Parent Revolution, "Our History," http://parentrevolution.org/content/our-history.

141. Vicki Murray (Alger), "Lessons for California from National School Choice Week," *San Francisco Examiner*, January 11, 2011; "Lynch Mob or Seekers of School Equity?," *The Swarm* (blog), *Sacramento Bee*, January 6, 2010.

142. Education Commission of the States, "Vouchers"; cf. Vicki Murray (Alger), "Georgia Joins School Voucher States," *Orange County Register*, May 23, 2007.

143. A.B. 1625, sponsored by Assembly member Anthony Pescetti (R-11).

144. A.B. 349, sponsored by Assembly member Ray Haynes (R-66). See also "Voucher Proposed for Compton District," *School Reform News*, Heartland Institute, May 1, 2003; People for the American Way, "Fighting Vouchers: PFAW in the State Trenches" website at: http://www.pfaw.org/pfaw/general/default.aspx?oid=14988.

145. Joel Rubin, "Locke Principal Rips LAUSD," *Los Angeles Times*, May 4, 2007; Vicki E. Murray (Alger), "Tear Down the Walls Trapping Students in 'Filthy Rich,' Failing Schools," Pacific Research Institute Capital Ideas, Vol. 12, No. 20, May 16, 2007.

146. "Unlocked," Reason TV, Hosted by Drew Carey, February 18, 2008, beginning at 2.25 minutes, http://reason.com/reasontv/2008/02/18/unlocked

147. Troy Senik, "The Worst Union in America," *City Journal*, Vol. 22, No. 2 (Spring 2012).

148. Parent Revolution, Our History, http://parentrevolution.org/content/our-history; Our Track Record, http://parentrevolution.org/content/our-track-record.

149. Vicki Alger, "70 Percent of U.S. Voters Support Parent Trigger Laws," *School Reform News*, Heartland Institute, September 11, 2012; National Conference on State Legislatures, "Parent Trigger Laws in the States," http://www.ncsl.org/issues-research/educ/state-parent-trigger-laws.aspx.

150. Alger, "70 Percent of U.S. Voters Support Parent Trigger Laws," Heartland Institute, September 11, 2012.

151. Malcolm Glenn and Michelle Gininger, "School Choice Now: The Year of School Choice: School Choice Year Book 2011–12" (Washington D.C.: Alliance for School Choice, 2012), 12.

152. The Friedman Foundation for Educational Choice, *2012 ABCs of School Choice: Rising Tide*, 16.

153. "Superior Court Upholds Education Savings Accounts," Goldwater Institute Press Release, January 26, 2012; "*Niehaus v. Huppenthal*," Goldwater Institute, November 21, 2011; "Arizona Governor Signs Education Savings Account Expansion Bill," *Goldwater Institute*, May 15, 2012.

154. Institute for Justice, "*Niehaus v. Huppenthal*."

155. Friedman Foundation for Educational Choice.

156. Michael Chartier, "Everything You Need to Know About Nevada's Universal ESA Bill," Friedman Foundation Blog, updated June 2, 2015.

157. John E. Chubb and Terry Moe, *Politics, Markets, and America's Schools* (Washington, DC: Brookings Institution, 1990), 3.

158. Herbert J. Walberg and Joseph L. Bast, *Education and Capitalism: How Overcoming Our Fear of Markets Can Improve America's Schools* (Stanford, Calif.: Hoover Institution Press, 2003), xxiii.

159. Author's tally based on data from the Friedman Foundation for Educational Choice.

160. National Alliance for Public Charter Schools, Public Charter Schools Dashboard.

161. American Federation for Children, Facts, April 2013.

162. Author's tally based on data from the Friedman Foundation for Educational Choice.

163. National Alliance for Public Charter Schools, Dashboard.

164. Vicki Alger, *The Vital Need for Virtual Schools in Nebraska*, The Platte Institute for Economic Research, June 2011; "International and National Overview," in Lance Izumi and Vicki (Murray) Alger, *Short Circuited: The Challenges Facing the Online Learning Revolution in California* (San Francisco: Pacific Research Institute, 2010), 19–65.

165. "Fast Facts About Online Learning," iNACOL, February 2012, 1.

166. Quoted in Coulson, *Market Education*, 83. See also Neal McCluskey, "As American as Bavarian Pie."

167. Quoted in Christopher J. Klicka, "Decisions of the United States Supreme Court Upholding Parental Rights as 'Fundamental'," Home School Legal Defense Association, Issue Analysis, October 27, 2003.

Chapter 12

1. Quoted by Sen. Hayakawa in the *Congressional Record, Proceedings of the 95th Congress, Second Session*, Vol. 124, No. 154, September 28, 1978 (for legislative day of September 26, 1978), in *Legislative History of Public Law 96-88, Department of Education Organization Act Part 1 and Part 2*, 96th Congress, 2nd Session, Committee Print, U.S. Congress, Washington, DC, Senate Committee on Government Operations, 1980, 361.

2. Two-year college revenue totals just under $13,000 per student. Author's summary based on *Digest of Education Statistics 2011*, Table 366, http://nces.ed.gov/programs/digest/d11/tables/dt11_366.asp.

3. Milton Friedman, "The Role of Government in Education," *Economics and the Public Interest*, ed. Robert A. Solo (New Brunswick: Rutgers University Press, 1955): 123–144. See also, *Capitalism and Freedom* (Chicago: University of Chicago Press,1962), 99–100.

4. Summarized in Vicki Murray (Alger), *Cash for College: Bringing Free Market Reform to Higher Education*, Goldwater Institute Policy Report No. 208, March 14, 2006, 17, http://goldwaterinstitute.org/sites/default/files/Cash%20for%20College.pdf.

5. Ben Jongbloed and Jos Koelman, *Vouchers for Higher Education? — A Survey of the Literature Commissioned by the Hong Kong University Grants Committee*, Center for Higher Education Policy Studies, June 2000, 14, http://doc.utwente.nl/7824/1/engartoovouchers.pdf.

6. September 12, 2003, interview with Richard Vedder. See *Going Broke by Degree: Why College Costs Too Much* (Washington, DC: AEI Press, 2004), 127.

7. Pamela Ebert Flattau, Jerome Bracken, Richard Van Atta, Ayeh Bandeh-Ahmadi, Rodolfo de la Cruz, and Kay Sullivan, *The National Defense Education Act of 1958: Selected Outcomes*, IDA, Science & Technology Policy Institute, March 2006, II-1 through II-5, https://www.ida.org/upload/stpi/pdfs/ida-d-3306.pdf.

8. For a brief history, see US Department of Education, *FY 2012 Annual Report for Federal Student Aid, November 16, 2012, 4*.

9. H.R. 2669: College Cost Reduction and Access Act, http://www.govtrack.us/congress/bills/110/hr2669; and Summary, Library of Congress, http://www.govtrack.us/congress/bills/110/hr2669#summary/libraryofcongress; and College Cost Reduction and Access Act, Open Congress, http://www.opencongress.org/wiki/College_Cost_Reduction_Act_of_2007.

10. Vicki Alger, "College Loans and Student Affordability," Independent Women's Forum Policy Focus, August 2012, http://c1355372.cdn.cloudfiles.rackspacecloud.com/f7d75689-b7e7-4bf4-a9d5-9f2b03c4c7a9/Newsletter%20August%202012%20Proof%203.pdf; and H.R. 4348 (112th): MAP-21, http://www.govtrack.us/congress/bills/112/hr4348#overview.

11. See Chris Edwards and Neal McCluskey, "Higher Education Subsidies," Downsizing the Federal Government, Cato Institute, May 2009, http://www.downsizinggovernment.org/education/higher-education-subsidies.

12. Ibid.

13. "Statement of John P. Higgins, Jr., Inspector General Department of Education Before the House Committee on Government Reform," United States House of Representatives, May 26, 2005, 2, https://www2.ed.gov/about/offices/list/oig/auditrpts/stmt052005.pdf.

14. Quoted in Amit R. Paley, "Education Secretary Defends Loans Record," *Washington Post*, May 11, 2007, http://www.washingtonpost.com/wp-dyn/content/article/2007/05/10/AR2007051002031.html.

15. Chris Edwards and Neal McCluskey, "Higher Education Subsidies," Downsizing the Federal Government, Cato Institute, May 2009, http://www.downsizinggovernment.org/education/higher-education-subsidies.

16. Paley, "Education Secretary Defends Loans Record."

17. GAO, Federal Family Education Loan Program: Increased Department of Education Oversight of Lender and School Activities Needed to Help Ensure Program Compliance, July 31, 2007, http://www.gao.gov/assets/270/265014.pdf; cf. "Student borrowers unprotected: GAO says federal education agency has no watchdog system," New York Times News Service, August 2, 2007, http://articles.baltimoresun.com/2007-08-02/news/0708020158_1_gao-report-student-borrowers-lenders; and *FinAid*,

Illegal Inducements and Preferred Lender Lists: US Department of Education Regulations, http://www.finaid.org/educators/illegalinducements.phtml.

18. Doug Lederman, "Education Department, on the Case," *Inside Higher Ed*, July 10, 2007, http://www.insidehighered.com/news/2007/07/10/nasfaa; and Stephen Burd, "More Scare Tactics from the Student Loan Industry and Friends," *Higher Ed Watch*, July 28, 2009, http://www.newamerica.net/blog/higher-ed-watch/2009/more-scare-tactics-student-loan-industry-and-friends-13549.

19. Doug Lederman, "Education Department, on the Case," *Inside Higher Ed*, July 10, 2007, http://www.insidehighered.com/news/2007/07/10/nasfaa.

20. GAO, *Federal Family Education Loan Program: Increased Department of Education Oversight of Lender and School Activities Needed to Help Ensure Program Compliance*, July 31, 2007, 1, 8, 13, 20–21, 26–27, and 30–31, http://www.gao.gov/assets/270/265014.pdf.

21. Janice C. Eberly, "Comment on 'Guaranteed versus Direct Lending: The Case of Student Loans'" by Deborah Lucas and Damien Moore, National Bureau of Economic Research Conference held February 8–9, 2007. Subsequently included in *Measuring and Managing Federal Financial Risk*, ed. Deborah Lucas (Chicago: University of Chicago Press, February 2010), 205–11. See pp. 209–10, http://www.nber.org/chapters/c3076.

22. See, for example, Penny Starr, "Education Secretary Denies Govt Takeover of Student Loan Programs Will Hurt Private Sector, Cause Job Loss," *CNSNews.com*, March 25, 2010, http://cnsnews.com/news/article/education-secretary-denies-govt-takeover-student-loan-programs-will-hurt-private-sector; Arne Duncan, "Banks Don't Belong in the Student Loan Business," *Wall Street Journal*, December 17, 2009, http://online.wsj.com/article/SB10001424052748703514404574588751838773352.html; and Neal McCluskey, "SAFRA Stinks," *Forbes.com*, August 10, 2009, http://www.forbes.com/2009/08/10/education-loans-tuition-financial-aid-opinions-colleges-safra.html.

23. US Department of Education, First Official Three-Year Student Loan Default Rates Published, September 28, 2012, http://www.ed.gov/news/press-releases/first-official-three-year-student-loan-default-rates-published.

24. "Testimony of Inspector General Kathleen S. Tighe U.S. Department of Education Office of Inspector General before the Subcommittee on Labor, Health and Human Services, Education, and Related Agencies Committee on Appropriations," U.S. House of Representatives March, 19, 2013, 4, https://www2.ed.gov/about/offices/list/oig/auditrpts/testimony03192013.pdf.

25. "Testimony of Inspector General Kathleen S. Tighe U.S. Department of Education Office of Inspector General before the Subcommittee on Labor, Health and Human Services, Education, and Related Agencies Committee on Appropriations," US House of Representatives March, 19, 2013, 2, https://www2.ed.gov/about/offices/list/oig/auditrpts/testimony03192013.pdf.

26. Shahien Nasiripour, "http://www.huffingtonpost.com/users/login/Obama Student Loan Policy Reaping $51 Billion Profit," *Huffington Post*, May 14, 2013, http://www.huffingtonpost.com/2013/05/14/obama-student-loans-policy-profit_n_3276428.html; and "Student Loan Rates Boost Government Profit As Debt Damps Economy," *Huffington Post*, April 9, 2013, http://www.huffingtonpost.com/2013/04/09/student-loan-rates-debt-economy_n_3048216.html.

27. See Vicki Alger, "College Loans and Student Affordability," Independent Women's Forum Policy Focus, August 2012, http://c1355372.cdn.cloudfiles.rackspacecloud .com/f7d75689-b7e7-4bf4-a9d5-9f2b03c4c7a9/Newsletter%20August%202012%20 Proof%203.pdf.

28. *FinAid*, Tuition Inflation, http://www.finaid.org/savings/tuition-inflation.phtml.

29. Robert E. Martin and Andrew Gillen, "How College Pricing Undermines Financial Aid," Center for College Affordability and Productivity, March 2011, http://center forcollegeaffordability.org/research/studies/college-pricing-and-financial-aid.

30. Brian Kelly, "Is a College Education Worth the Price?" *U.S. News & World Report*, August 17, 2010, http://www.usnews.com/opinion/blogs/editors-note/2010/08/17/ is-a-college-education-worth-the-price.

31. "Helping Students, Not Lenders," *New York Times* Editorial Board, March 3, 2009, http://www.nytimes.com/2009/03/04/opinion/04wed3.html.

32. *Digest of Education Statistics 2011*, Table 198, http://nces.ed.gov/programs/digest/d11/ tables/dt11_198.asp.

33. American Student Assistance, Student Loan Debt Statistics, http://www.asa.org/ policy/resources/stats/; and Project on Student Debt, "Risky Private Student Lending on the Rise Again," December 22, 2011, http://www.ticas.org/files/pub//Private _Student_Lending_on_the_Rise.pdf.

34. John Bridgeland, Jessica Milano, and Elyse Rosenblum, *Across the Great Divide: Perspectives of CEOs and College Presidents on America's Higher Education and Skills Gap*, Institute for a Competitive Workforce, US Chamber of Commerce, March 2011, 4 and 7, http://icw.uschamber.com/sites/default/files/Great%20Divide%20Final%20 Report%20.pdf.

35. US Department of Education, "Statement of U.S. Secretary of Education Arne Duncan—FY 2014 Budget Request Senate Appropriations Subcommittee on Labor, Health and Human Services, Education, and Other Related Agencies," April 17, 2013, http://www.ed.gov/news/speeches/statement-us-secretary-education-arne -duncanfy-2014-budget-request.

36. Robert Samuelson, "It's Time to Drop the College-for-All Crusade," *Washington Post*, May 27, 2012, http://articles.washingtonpost.com/2012-05-27/opinions/35456501_1 _college-students-josipa-roksa-private-colleges-and-universities.

37. Richard Vedder, "Ditch…the College-for-All Crusade," *Chronicle of Higher Education*, June 6, 2012, http://chronicle.com/blogs/innovations/ditch-the-college-for-all -crusade/32661.

38. New America Foundation, Federal Pell Grant Program, Federal Education Budget Project, http://febp.newamerica.net/background-analysis/federal-pell-grant-program.

39. US Department of Education, Federal Pell Grant Program, http://www2.ed.gov/ programs/fpg/index.html.

40. David Jesse, "Colleges Chase Pell Grant Scammers," *USA Today*, February 16, 2013, http://www.usatoday.com/story/news/nation/2013/02/16/colleges-chase-pell-grant -scammers/1925013/.

41. Andrew J. Rotherham, "How to Fix Pell Grants," *Time*, May 24, 2012, http://ideas .time.com/2012/05/24/how-to-fix-pell-grants/?xid=newsletter-ideas.

42. Neal McCluskey, "Pell Grants Best at Buying Votes," Cato Institute, August 12, 2011, http://www.cato.org/blog/pell-grants-best-buying-votes

43. Ibid.
44. Katy Hopkins, "Universities That Claim to Meet Full Financial Need," *U.S. News & World Report*, February 11, 2013, http://www.usnews.com/education/best-colleges/ paying-for-college/articles/2013/02/11/universities-that-claim-to-meet-full-financial -need; and "12 Tuition Free Colleges," *U.S. News & World Report*, http://www.usnews .com/education/best-colleges/paying-for-college/slideshows/12-tuition-free-colleges.

Conclusion

1. Remarks made on June 8, 1866, contained in the *Congressional Globe, 1st Session, 39th Congress* (Washington, DC: John C. Rives) part of *A Century of Lawmaking for a New Nation: U.S. Congressional Documents and Debates, 1774–1875*, 3048.
2. "Dissenting Views of Hon. Peter H. Kostmayer" in Department of Education Organization Act, Mr. Brooks, from the Committee on Government Operations, submitted the following Report together with Separate, Additional, Supplementary, and Dissenting Views (to accompany H.R. 2444), May 14, 1979, in *Legislative History of Public Law 96-88,* Department of Education Organization Act Part 1 and Part 2, 96th Congress, 2nd Session, Committee Print, US Congress, Washington, DC, Senate Committee on Government Operations, 1980, 1168.
3. *Congressional Record*, September 24, 1979, p. 25826.
4. "Reagan Calls Department of Education 'Bureaucratic Boondoggle'," NBC News, New York, NY: NBC Universal, May 4, 1980, NBC Learns archives.
5. Remarks of Sen. Nunn in the *Congressional Record, Proceedings and Debates of the 96th Congress, First Session*, Vol. 125, No. 44, April 5, 1979, 704.
6. Remarks of Sen. Moynihan in the *Congressional Record, Proceedings and Debates of the 96th Congress, First Session*, April 26, 1979, 784–85.
7. "Dissenting Views of Hon. John N. Erlenborn, Hon. Benjamin S. Rosenthal, Hon. Peter H. Kostmayer, Hon. John H. Wydler, Hon. Clarence J. Brown, Hon. Paul N. McCloskey, Hon. Thomas N. Kindness, Hon. Robert S. Walker, Hon. Arlan Stange-land, Hon. M. Caldwell Butler, Hon. Jim Jeffries, Hon. Olympia Snowe, and Hon. Wayne Grisham" in Department of Education Organization Act, Mr. Brooks, from the Committee on Government Operations, May 14, 1979, in *Legislative History of Public Law 96-88*, 1173.
8. Remarks of Rep. Bob Michel in the *Congressional Record, Proceedings and Debates of the 96th Congress, First Session*, September 27, 1979, 1809.
9. Quoted in David W. Kirkpatrick, "It Began with Adam Smith," *Vermont Education Report*, May 1998.
10. Barry Goldwater, "Some Notes on Education," in *Conscience of a Conservative*, ed. CC Goldwater, (Princeton, NJ: Princeton University Press, 2007), 80.

References

Archives

Annals of the Congress

Bartelby.com, Inaugural Addresses of the Presidents of the United States

California Journal

Congressional Globe

Federal Reserve Archival System for Economic Research (FRASER) [started in 2004 as a data preservation and accessibility project of the Federal Reserve Bank of St. Louis; maintains the Budget of the United States Government from 1923 forward]

Journals of the Continental Congress

Kevin R. Kosar, Federal Education Policy History website, https://federaleducation policy.wordpress.com Library of Congress

National Archives

New York State Archives, States' Impact on Federal Education Policy (SIFEPP), New York State Education Department, Office of Cultural Education

Ronald Reagan Presidential Library

University of California, Santa Barbara, American Presidency Project (Gerhard Peters and John T. Woolley)

University of Virginia, Miller Center Presidential Speech Archive

U.S. Office of Management and Budget (OMB), ExpectMore.gov

Books/Chapters

Adamson, Bob and Li Sui Pang, "Primary and Secondary Schooling." In *Education and Society in Hong Kong and Macao: Comparative Perspectives on Continuity and Change*, 2nd ed., edited by Mark Bray and Ramsey Koo, 35–59. Dordrecht, The Netherlands: Springer/Comparative Education Research Center, University of Hong Kong, 2005.

Adolphus, Frederick Packard, *The Daily Public School in the United States*. Philadelphia: J. B. Lippincott & Co., 1866.

Alger, Vicki E. (née Murray), "International and National Overview." In Lance Izumi and Vicki (née Murray) Alger, *Short Circuited: The Challenges Facing the Online Learning Revolution in California*. San Francisco: Pacific Research Institute, 2010.

Annis, James Lee, *Howard Baker: Conciliator in an Age of Crisis*. Knoxville: Univ. of Tennessee Press, 2007.

Blum, Virgil C., *Freedom of Choice in Education*. New York: The Macmillan Company, 1958.

Blumenfeld, Samuel L., *Is Public Education Necessary?* Old Greenwich, CT: Devin-Adair, 1981.

Canes-Wrone, Brandice, *Who Leads Whom? Presidents, Policy, and the Public*. Chicago: Univ. of Chicago Press, 2006.

Carter, James G., *Essays Upon Popular Education Containing a Particular Examination of the Schools of Massachusetts and an Outline of an Institution for the Education of Teachers*. Boston: Bowles & Dearborn, 1826.

Chubb, John E. and Terry Moe, *Politics, Markets, and America's Schools*. Washington, DC: Brookings Institution, 1990.

Collins, Craig, "The Politics of Education," in *National Education Association: 1857 – 2007: 150 Years of Advancing Great Public Schools*. Washington, DC: NEA, 2007.

Coons, John E., William H. Clune III, and Stephen D. Sugarman, *Private Wealth and Public Education*. Cambridge, MA: Belknap Press of Harvard Univ. Press, 1970.

Coulson, Andrew J., *Market Education: The Unknown History*. New Brunswick, NJ: Social Philosophy and Policy Center and Transaction Publishers, 1999.

Cousin, M. Victor, *Report on the Condition of Public Instruction in Germany, and particularly Prussia*. Translated by Sarah Austin. London: Effingham Wilson, Royal Exchange, 1834.

Crowley, Brian Lee, Jason Clemens, and Niels Veldhuis, *The Canadian Century: Moving Out of America's Shadow*. Toronto: Key Porter, May 1, 2010.

Cubberley, Ellwood P., *Public Education in the United States: A Study and Interpretation of American Educational History*. New York: Houghton Mifflin Co., 1919.

Dain, Floyd R., *Education in the Wilderness*. Lansing, MI: Michigan Historical Society, 1968.

Dewey, John, *Democracy and Education: An Introduction to the Philosophy of Education*. New York: Macmillan, 1916.

———, *Freedom and Culture*. New York: G. P. Putnam's Sons, 1939.

———, *Human Nature and Conduct: An Introduction to Social Psychology*. New York: Henry Holt, 1922.

———, *My Pedagogic Creed*. New York: E.L. Kellogg & Company, 1897.

Dexter, Edwin Grant, *A History of Education in the United States*. London: Macmillan & Co., LTD., 1904.

Eberling, Eric R., "Massachusetts Education Laws of 1642, 1647, and 1648." In *Historical Dictionary of American Education*, edited by Richard J. Altenbaugh. Westport, CT: Greenwood Press, 1999.

Edmondson III, Henry T., *John Dewey & Decline of American Education: How Patron Saint of Schools Has Corrupted Teaching and Learning*. Wilmington, DE: ISI Books, 2006.

Friedman, Milton, *Capitalism and Freedom*. Chicago: University of Chicago Press, 1962.

———, "The Role of Government in Education." In *Economics and the Public Interest*, edited by Robert A. Solo. New Brunswick: Rutgers University Press, 1955.

Goldwater, Barry, *Conscience of a Conservative*. Shepherdsville, KY: Victor Publishing Company, 1960.

Greene, Jay P., Greg Forster, and Marcus A. Winters, *Education Myths: What Special Interest Groups Want You to Believe About Our Schools—And Why It Isn't So*. New York: Rowman & Littlefield Publishers, 2006.

Gutek, Gerald L., *An Historical Introduction to American Education*, 2nd ed. Prospect Heights, IL: Waveland Press, Inc., 1991.

Hamilton, Alexander, James Madison, and John Jay, *The Federalist Papers*. Edited by Clinton Rossiter. New York: Mentor Books, 1999.

Heffernan, Robert V., *Cabinetmakers: Story of the Three-Year Battle to Establish the U.S. Department of Education*. Lincoln, NE: iUniverse, 2001.

Hepburn, Claudia R., "Public Funding of School Choice in Canada: A Case Study." In *What America Can Learn from School Choice in Other Countries*, edited by David Salisbury and James Tooley. Washington, DC: Cato Institute, 2005.

Hinsdale, B.A., comp., *U.S. Office of Education, Documents Illustrative of American Educational History*, 53d Cong., 2d sess., 1892–93, 2 vols. Washington, DC: Government Printing Office, 1895, Library of American Civilization 10588.

Hinsdale, Burke Aaron, *President Garfield and Education*. Boston: Osgood & Co., 1881.

Izumi, Lance, *Obama's Education Takeover*. New York: Encounter Books, 2012.

Jeynes, William H., *American Educational History: School, Society, and the Common Good*. Thousand Oaks, CA: Sage Publications, 2007.

Kosters, Marvin H. and Brent D. Mast, Closing the Education Achievement Gap: Is Title I Working? Washington, DC: AEI Press, 2001.

Kursh, Harry, *The United States Office of Education*. Philadelphia: Chilton Company, 1965.

Labaree, David F., "An Uneasy Relationship: The History of Teacher Education in the University." In Handbook of Research on Teacher Education: Enduring

Issues in Changing Contexts, edited by Marilyn Cochran-Smith, Sharon Feiman Nemser, D. John McIntyre, and Kelly E. Demer, 3rd ed. New York: Routledge/Taylor & Francis Group and the Association of Teacher Educators, 2008.

Madison, James, *Notes of Debates in the Federal Convention of 1787 Reported by James Madison*. New York: Norton, 1966.

McCluskey, Neal, *Feds in the Classroom: How Big Government Corrupts, Cripples, and Compromises American Education*. Lanham, MD: Rowman & Littlefield, 2007.

McGuinn, Patrick J., *No Child Left Behind and the Transformation of Federal Education Policy, 1965–2005*. Lawrence, KS: Univ. of Kansas Press, 2006.

Menand, Louis, *The Metaphysical Club: A Story of Ideas in America*. New York: Macmillan, 2001.

Mulhern, James, *A History of Education: A Social Interpretation*. 2nd ed. New York: Ronald Press Co, 1959.

National Education Association, *National Education Association: 1857–2007: 150 Years of Advancing Great Public Schools*. Washington, DC: NEA, 2007.

Paine, Thomas, *The Rights of Man*. 1791, New York: Penguin

Perkinson, Henry J., *The Imperfect Panacea: American Faith in Education*, 4th ed. New York: McGraw-Hill, 1995.

Peterson, Paul E., "Little Gain in Student Achievement." Chap. 2 of *Our Schools and Our Future…Are We Still at Risk*, edited by Paul E. Peterson. Stanford: Hoover Institution Press, 2003.

———— and William G. Howell, eds., *The Education Gap: Vouchers and Urban Schools*, Revised Edition. Washington, DC: Brookings Institution, 2006.

Poulson, Barry W., "Education and the Family During the Industrial Revolution," in *The American Family and the State*, edited by Joseph R. Peden and Fred R. Glahe. San Francisco: Pacific Research Institute, 1986.

Ravitch, Diane, *Left Back: A Century of Battles Over School Reform*. New York: Simon & Schuster, 2000.

Richardson, James D., ed., *Compilation of the Messages and Papers of the Presidents, 1789–1897*, 10 vols. Washington, DC: Government Printing Office, 1896.

Richman, Sheldon, *Separating School & State: How to Liberate America's Families*. Fairfax, VA: The Future of Freedom Foundation, 1994.

Rothbard, Murray, "Education: Free and Compulsory," reproduced by the Ludwig von Mises Institute, September 9, 2006, http://mises.org/daily/2226.

Ryan, James E., "The Tenth Amendment and Other Paper Tigers: The Legal Boundaries of Education Governance." In *Who's In Charge Here? The Tangled Web of School Governance and Policy*, edited by Noel Epstein. Denver: Education Commission of the States; and Washington, DC: Brookings Institution Press, 2004.

Seybolt, Robert, *Sources and Studies in American Colonial Education: The Private School*. New York: Arno Press, 1925.

Smith, Adam, *An Inquiry Into the Nature and Causes of the Wealth of Nations*, Edwin Cannan, ed. Chicago: Univ. of Chicago Press, 1976.

Smith, Theodore C., *The Life and Letters of James Abram Garfield*, 2 vols. New Haven: Yale Univ. Press, 1925, Library of American Civilization 23799–800.

Stahura, Barbara, "The NEA and the U.S. Department of Education." In *National Education Association: 1857 – 2007: 150 Years of Advancing Great Public Schools*. Washington, DC: NEA, 2007, 86–91.

U.S. Congress, Executive Documents of the House of Representatives for the Second Session of the Fifty-Third Congress 1893–94. Washington, DC: Government Printing Office, 1895.

————, Legislative History of Public Law 96-88, Department of Education Organization Act. Part 1 and Part 2. 96th Congress, 2d Session. Committee Print. Washington, DC: Senate Committee on Government Operations, 1980.

Wahlberg, Herbert J. and Joseph L. Bast, *Education and Capitalism: How Overcoming Our Fear of Markets and Economics Can Improve America's Schools*. Stanford: Hoover Institution Press, 2003.

West, Allan M. *The National Education Association: The Power Base for Education*. New York: The Free Press, 1980.

Wooster, Martin Morse, *Angry Classrooms, Vacant Minds*. San Francisco: Pacific Research Institute for Public Policy, 1994.

Journal Articles

Areen, Judith and Christopher Jencks, "Education Vouchers: A Proposal for Diversity and Choice," *Teachers College Record*, Vol. 7, No. 3 (February 1971): 327–36.

Belfield, Clive R. and Henry M. Levin, "The Effects of Competition on Educational Outcomes: A Review of the U.S. Evidence," *Review of Educational Research*, Vol. 72, No. 2 (March 2002): 279–341.

Bell, Terrel H., "Education Policy Development in the Reagan Administration," *Phi Delta Kappan*, Vol. 67, No. 7 (March 1986): 487–93.

————, "One Decade after *A Nation at Risk*," *Phi Delta Kappan*, Vol. 74, No. 8 (April 1993): 592–97.

Brown, Donald R., "Jonathan Baldwin Turner and the Land-Grant Idea," *Journal of the Illinois State Historical Society (1908–1984)*, Vol. 55, No. 4 (Winter 1962): 370–84.

Cahill, Rosemary and Jan Gray, "Funding and Secondary School Choice in Australia: A Historical Consideration," *Australian Journal of Teacher Education*, Vol. 35, No. 1 (February 2010): 121–38.

Dronkers, Jaap and Peter Robert, "School Choice in the Light of the Effectiveness Differences of Various Types of Public and Private Schools in 19 OECD Countries," *Journal of School Choice*, Vol. 2, No. 3 (2008): 260–301.

Everhart, Robert B., "From Universalism to Usurpation: An Essay on the Antecedents to Compulsory School Attendance Legislation," *Review of Educational Research*, Vol. 47, No. 3 (Summer 1977): 499–530.

Fuller, Bruce, Joseph Wright, Kathryn Gesicki, and Erin Kang, "Gauging Growth: How to Judge No Child Left Behind?," *Educational Researcher*, Vol. 36, No. 5 (June 2007): 268–78.

Fung, Kit-Ho Chanel and Chi-Chung Lam, "Empowering Parents' Choice of Schools: The Rhetoric and Reality of How Hong Kong Kindergarten Parents Choose Schools Under the Voucher Scheme," *Current Issues in Education*, Vol. 14, No. 1 (2011): 1–47.

Garfield, James A., "Education—A National Interest: Speech of James A. Garfield of Ohio in the House of Representatives, June 8, 1866, on a Bill 'To Establish a National Bureau of Education,' Reported by the Select Committee on the Memorial of the National Association of School Superintendents," in *The American Journal of Education*, Vol. 1 [Entire Series Vol. XVI I], No. 1 (September 1867): 49–63.

Greene, Samuel S., "Educational Duties of the Hour," Introductory Discourse before the National Teachers' Association at Harrisburg, Penn., in August 1865 in *The American Journal of Education*, Vol. 16, No. 42 [New Series No. 17] (March 1866): 229–43.

Greer, Collin, review of *Private Wealth and Public Education*, by John E. Coons, William H. Chine III and Stephen D. Sugarman (Cambridge: Harvard University Press, 1970) in *Teachers College Record*, Vol. 72, No. 3 (February 1971): 449–51.

Holcomb, Sabrina, "Answering the Call: A History of the National Education Association, Part I," *NEA Today*, January 21, 2006, http://www.nea.org/home/11547.htm.

———, "Answering the Call: A History of the National Education Association, Part II," *NEA Today*, February 21, 2006, http://www.nea.orghome/12172.htm.

———, "Answering the Call: A History of the National Education Association, Part III," *NEA Today*, March 21, 2006, http://www.nea.org/home/12241.htm.

———, "Answering the Call: A History of the National Education Association, Part IV," *NEA Today*, April 25, 2006, http://www.nea.org/home/12372.htm.

Howell, William G. and Paul E. Peterson, "Voucher Research Controversy," *Education Next*, Vol. 4, No. 2 (Spring 2004): 73–78.

Kahlenberg, Richard D., "Philosopher or King? The Ideas and Strategy of Legendary AFT Leader Albert Shanker," *Education Next*, Vol. 3, No. 3 (Summer 2003): 34–39. This is the abridged version of "Albert Shanker's Legacy," January 4, 2003, http://media.hoover.org/sites/default/files/documents/ednext20033unabridged_kahlenberg.pdf.

Liu, Goodwin and William L. Taylor, "School Choice to Achieve Desegregation," *Fordham Law Review*, Vol. 74, Iss. 2 (April 3, 2006): 791–823.

McAndrews, Lawrence J., "Late and Never: Ronald Reagan and Tuition Tax Credits," *Journal of Church and State*, Vol. 42, Iss. 3 (2000): 467–83.

Munich, John R. and Rocco E. Testani, "NEA Sues over NCLB," *Education Next*, Vol. 5, No. 4 (Fall 2005): 10.

Peterson, Paul E., Ludger Woessmann, Eric A. Hanushek, and Carlos X. Lastra-Anadon, "Globally Challenged: Are U.S. Students Ready to Compete? The Latest on Each State's International Standing in Math and Reading," *Education Next*, Vol. 11, No. 4 (Summer 2011): 51–59.

Porter, Andrew, Jennifer McMaken, Jun Hwang, and Rui Yang, "Common Core Standards: The New U.S. Intended Curriculum," *Educational Researcher*, Vol. 40, No. 3 (April 2011): 103–16.

Rickoff, Andrew Jackson, "National Bureau of Education," Address delivered before the National Teachers' Association, August 18, 1864 [should be 1865], in *The American Journal of Education*, Vol. 16, No. 43 [New Series No. 18] (June 1866): 299–310.

Salganik, Laura Hersh, "The Fall and Rise of Education Vouchers," *Teachers College Record*, Vol. 83, No. 2 (Winter 1981): 263–83.

Savage, David C., "Education of a New Department," *Educational Leadership*, Vol. 38, Iss. 2 (November 1980): 117–19.

Smarick, Andy, "Toothless Reform," *Education Next*, Vol. 10, No. 2 (Spring 2010): 15–22.

Spoehr, Luther, "Where Did NCLB Come From?," review of *See Government Grow: Education Politics from Johnson to Reagan*, by Gareth Davies (Lawrence: University of Kansas Press, 2007) in *Education Next*, Vol. 8, No. 4 (Fall 2008): 80–81.

Stallings, D. T., "A Brief History of the U.S. Department of Education, 1979–2002," *Phi Delta Kappan*, Vol. 83, No. 9 (May 2002): 677–683.

Stevens, David, "President Carter, the Congress, and NEA: Creating the Department of Education," *Political Science Quarterly*, Vol. 98, No. 4 (Winter 1983–84): 641–63.

Swan, William D., "Immigration," *The Massachusetts Teacher*, Vol. 4, No. 10 (October 1851): 1–5.

Taylor, Judith Kimball, "Educational Vouchers: Addressing the Establishment Clause Issue", *Pacific Law Journal*, Vol. 11 (1979–1980): 1061–83.

Walberg, Herbert J. and Joseph A. Bast, "School Choice: The Essential Reform," in *Cato Journal*, Vol. 13, No.1 (Spring/Summer 1993): 101–21.

Warren, Jim, "Alum Rock Voucher Project," Educational Researcher, Vol. 5, No. 3 (March 1976): 13–15.

West, Martin and Ludger Woessmann, "Crowd Control: Does Reducing Class Size Work?," *Education Next*, Vol. 3, No. 3 (Summer 2003): 56–62.

White, E.E., "National Bureau of Education," Read before the National Association of School Superintendents in Washington, DC, on February 7, 1866, in

The American Journal of Education, Vol. 16, No. 42 [New Series No. 17] (March 1866): 177–86.

White, S.H., "National Bureau of Education," Read before the National Teachers' Association, n.d., in *The American Journal of Teacher Education*, Vol. 15, No. 38 [New Series No. 13] (March 1865): 180–84.

Woessmann, Ludger, "Why Students in Some Countries Do Better: International Evidence on the Importance of Education Policy, Education Matters," *Education Next*, Vol. 1, No. 2 (Summer 2001): 67–74.

Wurman, Ze'ev and W. Stephen Wilson, "The Common Core Math Standards," *Education Next*, Vol. 12, No. 3 (Summer 2012): 45–50.

Policy/Evaluation Reports

Adkins, Deborah, G. Gage Kingsbury, Michael Dahlin, and John Cronin, *The Proficiency Illusion*, Fordham Institute, October 4, 2007.

Alger, Vicki E., *Student Loans and College Affordability*, Independent Women's Forum Policy Focus, August 7, 2012.

_____, *The Vital Need for Virtual Schools in Nebraska,* The Platte Institute for Economic Research, June 2011.

_____ (née Murray) and Evelyn B. Stacey, *Down but Not Out in D.C.: Bi-Partisan, Bi-Cameral Efforts to Continue the Opportunity Scholarship Program*, Independent Women's Forum Policy Brief # 25, August 13, 2009.

Anderson, Leland, *Alpine Online Case Study: A Utah School District's Move into K–8 Online Education*, Innosight Institute [now the Clayton Christenson Institute], August 28, 2009.

Aud, Susan, *Education by the Numbers: The Fiscal Effect of School Choice Programs. 1990–2006*, Friedman Foundation for Educational Choice, *School Choice Issues in Depth*, April 2007.

Bast, Joseph L. and David Harmer versus Douglas Dewey, *Vouchers and Educational Freedom: A Debate*, Cato Institute, Policy Analysis No. 269, March 12, 1997.

Berman, Paul and Milbrey Wallin McLaughlin, *Federal Programs Supporting Educational Change, Vol. III: Implementing and Sustaining Innovations*, Prepared for the U.S. Office of Education, Department of Health, Education and Welfare, RAND Corporation, May 1978.

Brouillette, Matthew J., *Parental Choice in Michigan: A Primer for Freedom in Education; A Guide for Exercising Parents' Rights and Responsibilities to Direct the Education of Their Children*, Mackinac Center for Public Policy, 1999.

Budde, Ray, *Education by Charter: Restructuring Schools and School Districts*. Andover, MA: The Regional Laboratory for Educational Improvement of the Northeast Islands, 1989.

Burke, Lindsey M., "Reducing the Federal Footprint on Education and Empowering State and Local Leaders," Heritage Foundation Backgrounder, June 2, 2011.

————, "States Must Reject National Education Standards While There Is Still Time," *Heritage Foundation Backgrounder*, April 16, 2012.

Burke, Lindsey M. and Rachel Sheffield, "Obama's 2013 Education Budget and Blueprint: A Costly Expansion of Federal Control," *Heritage Foundation Backgrounder*, April 12, 2012.

————, "Obama's Education Budget Chooses to Fund Failure," Heritage Foundation, *Education Notebook*, March 26, 2012.

Coulson, Andrew J., Markets vs. Monopolies in Education: A Global Review of the Evidence, Cato Institute, Policy Analysis No. 620, September 10, 2008.

————, "School's Out: The Failure of No Child Left Behind," *Cato Policy Report*, November/December 2007.

Deans, Emilie, "Examining the Data: Where do Federal TEACH Grants Go?," New America Foundation, January 20, 2011.

Eitel, Robert S. and Kent D. Talbert, "The Road to a National Curriculum: The Legal Aspects of the Common Core Standards, Race to the Top, and Conditional Waivers," The Federalist Society, Engage Vol. 13, No. 1, March 2012 (online February 16, 2012).

Finn, Chester E., Jr., Andrew J. Rotherham, and Charles R. Hokanson, Jr., eds., *Rethinking Special Education for a New Century*, Washington, DC: Thomas B. Fordham Institute, May 2001.

Fisher, Jennifer L., "A Hermeneutics Approach to Studying Agenda-setting: The Postwar Education Agenda (1945–1998)," PhD diss., University of West Virginia, 2000.

Flattua, Pamela Ebert et al., *National Defense Education Act of 1958: Selected Outcomes*, IDA, Science and Technology Policy Institute, March 2006.

Forgione, Pascal D., Jr., *Achievement in the United States: Progress Since* A Nation at Risk, Center for Education Reform and Empower America, April 3, 1998.

Forster, Greg, *A Win-Win Solution: The Empirical Evidence on School Choice, Third Edition*, Friedman Foundation for Educational Choice, April 17, 2013.

Foshay, A.W., R.L. Thorndike, F. Hotyat, D.A. Pidgeon, and D.A. Walker, *Educational Achievements of Thirteen-Year-Olds in Twelve Countries: Results of an International Research Project, 1959–1961*, Hamburg: UNESCO Institute for Education, 1962.

Friedman Foundation for Educational Choice, *2012 ABCs of School Choice: Rising Tide*.

Glenn, Malcolm and Michelle Gininger, *School Choice Now: The Year of School Choice: School Choice Year Book 2011–12*, Alliance for School Choice, 2012.

Greene, Jay P. and Greg Forster, *The Teachability Index: Can Disadvantaged Students Learn?*, Education Working Paper No. 6, Manhattan Institute, September 2004.

Heller, Frank, "Lessons from Maine: Education Vouchers for Students since 1873," Cato Institute Briefing Paper No. 66, September 10, 2001.

Hickok, Eugene and Matthew Ladner, "Reauthorization of No Child Left Behind: Federal Management or Citizen Ownership of K–12 Education?," *Heritage Foundation Backgrounder*, June 27, 2007.

High, Jack, "DOE: Mixing Politics and Education," *Cato Institute Policy Report*, Vol. 2, No. 3, March 1980.

Holstead, Michael S., Terry E. Spradlin, and Jonathan A. Plucker, "Promises and Pitfalls of Virtual Education in the United States and Indiana," Indiana University Center for Evaluation and Policy Education Policy Brief, Vol. 6, No. 6, Spring 2008.

Howell, William and Mindy Spencer, *School Choice Without Vouchers: Expanding Education Options Through Tax Benefits*, Pioneer Institute White Paper, No. 41, October 2007.

Jongbloed, Ben and Jos Koelman, *Vouchers for Higher Education? A Survey of the Literature*, Commissioned by the Hong Kong University Grants Committee, Center for Higher Education Policy Studies, University of Twente Enschede (The Netherlands), June 2000.

Kafer, Krista, "Wasting Education Dollars: The Women's Educational Equity Act," Heritage Foundation Backgrounder, October 11, 2001.

Kober, Nancy and Diane Stark Rentner, "After the Stimulus Money Ends: The Status of State K–12 Education Funding and Reforms," Center for Education Policy, February 7, 2012.

Laitsch, Dan, "School Choice and Privatization Efforts in the States: A Legislative Survey," American Association of Colleges of Teacher Education, Issue Paper, October 1998.

Lee, Dwight R., "The Political Economy of Educational Vouchers," The Foundation for Economic Education, *The Freeman*, Vol. 36, No. 7, July 1986.

Lee, Jaekyung, *Tracking Achievement Gaps and Assessing the Impact of NCLB on the Gaps: An In-depth Look into National and State Reading and Math Outcome Trends*, The Civil Rights Project at Harvard University, June 2006.

Lips, Carrie and Jennifer Jacoby, "The Arizona Scholarship Tax Credit: Giving Parents Choices, Saving Taxpayers Money," Cato Institute Policy Analysis No. 414, September 17, 2001.

Loveless, Tom, *The 2010 Brown Center Report on American Education: How Well Are American Students Learning?*, Brown Center on Education Policy, Brookings Institution, February 7, 2011.

————, *The Peculiar Politics of No Child Left Behind*, Brown Center on Education Policy, Brookings Institution, August 2006.

Lukas, Carrie Lips, "The Arizona Scholarship Tax Credit: Providing Choice for Arizona Taxpayers and Students," Goldwater Institute Policy Report No. 186, December 11, 2003.

Mackey, Katherine, "Wichita Public Schools' Learning Centers: Creating a New Educational Model to Serve Dropouts and At-Risk Students," Innosight Institute [now the Clayton Christenson Institute], March 2010.

Martin, Ruby and Phyllis McClure, *Title I of ESEA: Is It Helping Poor Children? Revised second edition,* Washington Research Project of the Southern Center for Studies in Public Policy and AACP Legal Defense and Education Fund, December 1969.

McCluskey, Neal, "As American as Bavarian Pie," Cato Policy Report, July/August 2008, Vol. 30, No. 4.

————, "How Much Ivory Does This Tower Need? What We Spend on, and Get from, Higher Education," Cato Institute Policy Analysis No. 686, October 27, 2011.

————, "Why We Fight How Public Schools Cause Social Conflict," Cato Institute, Policy Analysis No. 587, January 23, 2007.

McCluskey, Neal and Chris Edwards, "Higher Education Subsidies," Downsizing the Federal Government, Cato Institute, May 2009.

McGraw, Onalee, ed. "Reagan Revolution Stalled in Education Department," *Education Update*, Vol. 6, No. 2, The Heritage Foundation, April 1982.

McLaughlin, Donald H., *Title I, 1965–1975: Synthesis of the Findings of Federal Studies*, American Institutes for Research, July 1977.

McLaughlin, Milbrey Wallin, *Evaluation and Reform: The Elementary and Secondary Education Act of 1965, Title I*, RAND, January 1974.

Miller, Raegen and Robin Lake, "Federal Barriers to Innovation," Center on Reinventing Public Education (CRPE), November 2012.

Morgan, Kerry L., "The Constitution and Federal Jurisdiction in American Education," Lonang Institute, 1985, rev. 2006.

Moses, Michele S., "The Arizona Education Tax Credit and Hidden Considerations of Justice," *Education Policy Analysis Archives*, Vol. 8, No. 37, January 1, 2000.

Picciano, Anthony G. and Jeff Seaman, *K–12 Online Learning; A 2008 Follow-up of the Survey of U.S. District Administrators*, The Sloan Consortium, January 2009.

Ping, Chou Kwok, "State, Market Force, and National Identity in Hong Kong and Macao," EAI (East Asia Institute), Background Brief No. 469, August 20, 2009.

Richman, Sheldon L., "The Sad Legacy of Ronald Reagan," *The Free Market*, Vol. VI, No. 10, Mises Institute, October 1988, http://mises.org/freemarket_detail .aspx?control=488

Schaeffer, Adam B., "The Public Education Tax Credit," Cato Institute Policy Analysis No. 605, December 5, 2007.

Shulman, Carol Herrnstadt, *Compliance with Federal Regulations: At What Cost?*, American Association for Higher Education-ERIC/Higher Education Research Report No. 6, 1978.

Smith, Rosina, Tom Clark, and Robert L. Blomeyer, *A Synthesis of New Research on K–12 Online Learning*, North Central Regional Education Laboratory/Learning Point Associates, November 2005.

Sternberg, Libby, "Lessons from Vermont: 132-Year-Old Voucher Program Rebuts Critics," Cato Institute Briefing Paper No. 67, September 10, 2001.

Stillwell-Parvensky, Michele, "Reforming Title I: Closing the Academic Achievement Gap for Disadvantaged Students," Harvard Kennedy School conducted for the Children's Defense Fund, April 2011.

Tang, Kwok-Chun and Mark Bray, "Colonial Models and the Evolution of Education Systems: Centralization and Decentralization in Hong Kong and Macau," World Bank Group, 2000.

Thomas, William R., "Overcoming Doubts About Online Learning," Southern Regional Education Board (SREB), November 2009.

Usher, Alexandra, "AYP Results for 2010–11," Center on Education Policy, December 15, 2011.

————, "AYP Results for 2010–11 — November 2012 Update," Center for Education Policy, November 1, 2012.

Watson, John et al., *Keeping Pace with K–12 Online Learning: An Annual Review of Policy and Practice*, Evergreen Education Group, 2011.

————, *Keeping Pace with K–12 Online Learning: A Review of State-Level Policy and Practice*, Evergreen Education Group, November 2009.

Wurman, Ze'ev and Sandra Stotsky, *Why Race to the Middle? First-Class State Standards Are Better than Third-Class National Standards*, Pioneer Institute for Public Policy Research, White Paper No. 52, February 23, 2010.

Xiang, Yun, Michael Dahlin, John Cronin, and Donna McCahon, *The Accountability Illusion*, The Thomas B. Fordham Institute and the Northwest Evaluation Association, February 19, 2009.

Yang, Shen-Keng, "Dilemmas of Education Reform in Taiwan: Internationalization or Localization?," Paper presented at the Annual Meeting of the Comparative and International Education Society, Washington, DC, March 2011.

Government/Statistical Reports

Alger, Vicki E. (née Murray), *An Analysis of Arizona Individual Income Tax-credit Scholarship Recipients' Family Income, 2009–10 School Year*, Program on Education Policy and Governance, Harvard University 10–18, October 2010.

Barbour, Emily, Jody Feder, and Rebecca Skinner, *Secretary of Education's Waiver Authority with Respect to Title I-A Provisions Included in the Elementary and Secondary Education Act*, Congressional Research Service (CRS) Memorandum to the Majority Committee Staff of the House Committee on Education and the Workforce, June 28, 2011.

Baum, Sandy, Kathleen Payea, and Diane Cardenas-Elliott, *Trends in Student Aid 2010*, The College Board, 2010.

Bloom, Benjamin S., *Cross-National Study of Educational Attainment: Stage I of the IEA. Investigation in Six Subject Areas. Final Report,* Vol. I, February 1969, Chicago Univ., Ill.; International Project for the Evaluation of Educational Achievement, Hamburg, West Germany, sponsored by the Office of Education, Department of Health Education and Welfare (DHEW), Washington, DC: Bureau of Research, February 1969.

Campbell, J.R., C.M. Hombo, and J. Mazzeo, *NAEP 1999 Trends in Academic Progress: Three Decades of Student Performance* (NCES 2000469), Washington, DC: U.S. Department of Education. Office of Educational Research and Improvement. National Center for Education Statistics, 2000.

Hanushek, Eric. A., Paul E. Peterson, and Ludger Woessmann, *U.S. Math Performance in Global Perspective: How Well Does Each State Do at Producing High-Achieving Students?*, Program on Education Policy and Governance, Report 10-19, Harvard University, November 2010.

Hanushek, Eric. A and Ludger Woessmann, *The High Cost of Low Educational Performance—The Long-Run Economic Impact of Improving PISA Outcomes*, Indicators and Analysis Division of the Organisation for Economic Co-operation and Development, OECD Directorate for Education, OECD Publishing, 2010.

Howard, Patrick J., *The Department's Management of the Federal Real Property Assistance Program*, Final Audit Report by the U.S. Department of Education, Office of the Inspector General to Winona H. Varnon, Principal Deputy Assistant Secretary, Office of Management, U.S. Department of Education, October 23, 2012.

Klein, Joel, *U.S. Education Reform and National Security*, Task Force Report, Council on Foreign Relations, Washington, DC, March 1, 2012.

Medrich, Elliott A. and Jeanne E. Griffith, *International Mathematics and Science Assessment: What Have We Learned?* (NCES 92-011), Washington, DC: U.S. Department of Education, Office of Educational Research and Improvement, January 1992.

Miller, Hon. George et al., *Real Relief for Schools: Accomplishing Effective Flexibility*, Report from the Education and Workforce Committee Democrats, U.S. House of Representatives, July 2011.

Mullis, Ina V.S., Michael O. Martin, Chad A. Minnich, Gabrielle M. Stanco, Alka Arora, Victoria M.S. Centurino, and Courtney E. Castle, eds. *TIMSS 2011 En-*

cyclopedia: Education Policy and Curriculum in Mathematics and Science, Vol. I, TIMSS & PIRLS International Study Center, Lynch School of Education, Boston College, September 14, 2012.

National Association of State Budget Officers (NASBO), *State Expenditure Fund Report, 2010: Examining Fiscal 2009–2011 State Spending*, December 2011.

National Center for Education Statistics (NCES), *Digest of Education Statistics* (Washington, DC: Institute of Education Sciences, U.S. Department of Education, various years).

National Commission on Excellence in Education, *A Nation at Risk: The Imperative for Educational Reform*, A Report to the Nation and the Secretary of Education, United States Department of Education, April 26, 1983.

Puma, Mike, Stephen Bell, Ronna Cook, Camilla Heid, Pam Broene, Frank Jenkins, Andrew Mashburn, and Jason Downer, *Third Grade Follow-up to the Head Start Impact Study Final Report*, OPRE Report # 2012-45, Washington, DC: Office of Planning, Research and Evaluation, Administration for Children and Families, U.S. Department of Health and Human Services (HHS), 2012.

Organisation for Economic Co-operation and Development (OECD), *Education Indicators at a Glance*, OECD Publishing, various years.

————, *PISA Results 2009: Overcoming Social Background: Equity in Learning Opportunities and Outcomes*, Vol. II, OECD Publishing, December 7, 2010.

————, "Private Schools: Who Benefits? PISA in Focus. No. 7," OECD Publishing, August 2011.

————, Programme for International Student Assessment (PISA), *PISA Results 2009: What Makes a School Successful? Resources, Policies and Practices*, Vol. IV, OECD Publishing, July 12, 2010.

————, Programme for International Student Assessment (PISA), *PISA Results 2009: What Students Know and Can Do: Student Performance in Reading, Mathematics and Science*, Vol. I, OECD Publishing, December 7, 2010,

————, *Public and Private Schools: How Management and Funding Relate to Their Socio-Economic Profile*, OECD Publishing, April 20, 2012.

Peterson, Paul E. and William G. Howell, "The Latest Results from the New York City Voucher Experiment," Multidisciplinary Program in Inequality & Social Policy, John F. Kennedy School of Government, Harvard University, November 3, 2003.

Rampey, Bobby D., Gloria S. Dion, and Patricia L. Donahue, *The Nation's Report Card: Trends in Academic Progress in Reading and Mathematics 2008* (NCES 2009–479), Washington, DC: National Center for Education Statistics, Institute of Education Sciences, U.S. Department of Education, April 2009.

Seftor, Neil S., Arif Mamun, and Allen Schirm, *The Impacts of Regular Upward Bound on Postsecondary Outcomes Seven to Nine Years After Scheduled High School*

Graduation: Final Report, Mathematica Policy Research, Inc., Prepared for: U.S. Department of Education, Office of Planning, Evaluation and Policy Development, Policy and Program Studies Service, 2009.

U.S. Advisory Commission on Intergovernmental Relations, *Federal Regulation of State & Local Governments: The Mixed Record of the 1980s*. Washington, DC: DIANE Publishing Company, 1993.

U.S. Census Bureau (Census), *The 2012 Statistical Abstract: The National Data Book*.

U.S. Department of Commerce, *Education Reform — Insight into the Business Community's Views About the U.S. Education System*, November 2006.

U.S. Department of Education (ED), 2009–2010 Federal Pell Grant End-of-Year Report. Washington, DC: Office of Postsecondary Education, 2011.

———, *A Blueprint for Reform: The Reauthorization of the Elementary and Secondary Education Act*, March 2010.

———, *A Nation Accountable: Twenty-Five Years After A Nation at Risk*, April 2008.

———, Office of Educational Research and Improvement (OERI), *A Study of Charter Schools*, various years.

———, Office of Inspector General (OIG), *Management Challenges*, various years.

U.S. Department of Health and Human Services (HHS), Administration for Children and Families, *Head Start Impact Study: Final Report*. Washington, DC, January 15, 2010.

U.S. Department of Homeland Security (DHS), *The 2013 Yearbook of Immigration Statistics*.

U.S. Department of Labor, Bureau of Labor Statistics (BLS), Consumer Price Index, various years.

U.S. Government Accountability Office (GAO), *Department of Education: Improved Oversight and Controls Could Help Education Better Respond to Evolving Priorities* (GAO-11-194), Report to the Ranking Member, Committee on Education and the Workforce, House of Representatives, February 10, 2011.

———, *Disadvantaged Students: School Districts Have Used Title I Funds Primarily to Support Instruction* (GAO-11-595), July 15, 2011.

———, *Education: Assessment of the Impact Aid Program: Office of Health, Education, and Welfare* (HRD 76-116), October 15, 1976.

———, *Education Finance: Extent of Federal Funding in State Education Agencies* (GAO/HEHS-95-3), October 14, 1994.

———, *Education of Military Dependent Students: Better Information Needed to Assess Student Performance* (GAO-11-231), March 1, 2011.

———, *Federal Education Funding: Overview and Early Childhood Education Programs*, GAO-10-51, January 27, 2010.

_____, *Follow-up on 2011 Report: Status of Actions Taken to Reduce Duplication, Overlap, and Fragmentation, Save Tax Dollars, and Enhance Revenue* (GAO-12-453SP), February 2012.

_____, *Funding Retained Teachers, but Education Could More Consistently Communicate Stabilization Monitoring Issues* (GAO-11-804), September 22, 2011.

_____, *K–12 Education: Selected States and School Districts Cited Numerous Federal Requirements as Burdensome, While Recognizing Some Benefits* (GAO-12-672), June 27, 2012.

_____, *Opportunities to Reduce Potential Duplication in Government Programs, Save Tax Dollars, and Enhance Revenue*, GAO-11-318SP, March 1, 2011.

_____, *Race to the Top: Reform Efforts Are Under Way and Information Sharing Could Be Improved* (GAO-11-658), June 30, 2011.

_____, *States' and Localities' Current and Planned Uses of Funds While Facing Fiscal Stresses* (GAO-09-829), July 8, 2009.

_____, *2013 Annual Report: Actions Needed to Reduce Fragmentation, Overlap, and Duplication and Achieve Other Financial Benefits* (GAO-13-279SP), April 9, 2013.

Woessmann, Ludger, Elke Ludemann, Gabriela Schutz, and Martin R. West, *School Accountability, Autonomy, Choice, and the Level of Student Achievement: International Evidence from PISA 2003*, OECD Education Working Papers, No. 13, December 21, 2007.

Wolf, Patrick, Babette Gutmann, Michael Puma, Brian Kisida, Lou Rizzo, Nada Eissa, and Matthew Carr, *Evaluation of the DC Opportunity Scholarship Program: Final Report* (NCEE 2010-4018), Washington, DC: National Center for Education Evaluation and Regional Assistance, Institute of Education Sciences, U.S. Department of Education, June 2010.

Online Articles/Blogs

Alger, Vicki, "ED's 'What Works' Division Validates Voucher Program the 'Fund Whatever Works' Obama Administration Killed," Independent Women's Forum, *Inkwell Blog*, February 24, 2010, http://iwf.org/blog/2430475/ED's-%22What -Works%22-Division-Validates-Voucher-Program-the-%22Fund-Whatever-Works %22-Obama-Administration-Killed.

_____ (née Murray), "Georgia Joins School Voucher States," *Orange County Register*, May 23, 2007, online at http://www.ocregister.com/ocregister/opinion/ nationalcolumns/article_1703264.php.

_____ (née Murray), "Kids Need More School Choice," *Human Events*, January 21, 2009, http://humanevents.com/2009/01/21/kids-need-more-school-choice/ (republished as "California School Days," *Investor's Business Daily*, January 21, 2009, http://news.investors.com/article/459153/200901211837/california-school -days.htm?p=full.

———— (née Murray), "Lessons for California from National School Choice Week," *San Francisco Examiner,* January 11, 2011, http://www.sfexaminer.com/opinion/op-eds/2011/01/lessons-california-national-school-choice-week.

————, "The *New York Times* Needs a School Choice Reality Check," *Townhall.com,* June 5, 2012, http://townhall.com/columnists/vickialger/2012/06/05/the_new_york_times_needs_a_school_choice_reality_check.

Baker, Bruce, "Potential Abuses of the Parent Trigger???," *School Finance 101,* December 7, 2010, http://schoolfinance101.wordpress.com/2010/12/07/potential-abuses-of-the-parent-trigger/.

Brenchley, Cameron, "Top 5 Questions About NCLB Flexibility," *Homeroom* (blog), U.S. Department of Education, August 8, 2011, http://www.ed.gov/blog/2011/08/top-5-questions-about-nclb-flexibility/.

Burke, Lindsey, "Boehner and Lieberman (Once Again) Save the D.C. Opportunity Scholarship Program," *The Heritage Foundation,* June 19, 2012, http://www.heritage.org/research/commentary/2012/06/boehner-and-lieberman-once-again-save-the-dc-opportunity-scholarship-program.

————, "No Child Left Behind by Executive Overreach," *National Review Online,* August 19, 2011, http://www.nationalreview.com/articles/275015/no-child-left-behind-executive-overreach-lindsey-burke#.

————, "No Child Left Behind Waivers: Regulatory Purgatory," *The Daily Signal* (blog), The Heritage Foundation, February 11, 2013, http://blog.heritage.org/2013/02/11/no-child-left-behind-waivers-regulatory-purgatory/.

————, "Why All the Cool Kids Are Reading Executive Order 13423," *FoxNews.com,* December 27, 2012, http://www.foxnews.com/opinion/2012/12/27/why-all-cool-kids-are-reading-executive-order-13423/.

Constable, Anne, Douglas Brew, and Maureen Dowd, "A Course in Politics," *Time,* June 20, 1983, http://www.time.com/time/magazine/article/0,9171,926033,00.html.

Coulson, Andrew J., "Dems Want Vouchers Dead. Hope Someone Else Pulls the Plug," *Cato at Liberty* (blog), Cato Institute, February 24, 2009, http://www.cato-at-liberty.org/dems-want-dc-vouchers-dead-hope-someone-else-pulls-plug/.

Duncan, Arne, "Providing Our Schools Relief from No Child Left Behind," *Homeroom* (blog), U.S. Department of Education, August 8, 2011, http://www.ed.gov/blog/2011/08/providing-our-schools-relief-from-no-child-left-behind/.

Edwards, Chris, "Department of Education: Timeline of Growth," Cato Institute, Downsizing the Federal Government, http://www.downsizinggovernment.org/education/timeline-growth.

FoxNews.com, "Teachers Union Still Plans NCLB Lawsuit," June 27, 2004, http://www.foxnews.com/story/0,2933,123858,00.html.

Gryphon, Marie, "Utah Stands Up for the Children," *Reason* Online, May 6, 2005, http://www.cato.org/publications/commentary/utah-stands-children.

Kirkpatrick, David W., "Emergence of the Voucher Controversy," *The Vermont Education Report*, July 26, 2004, Vol. 4, No. 27, http://www.schoolreport.com/vbe/nlet/07_26_04.htm.

———, "How Many Recommendations Are Needed?," The Blum Center for Parental Freedom in Education, On School Choice No. 25, August 1997, http://www.schoolreport.com/schoolreport/newsletters/Blum_8_97.htm.

———, "It Began with Adam Smith," 1998, http://www.schoolreport.com/schoolreport/articles/itbeganwithadamsmith_5_98.htm.

Kolderie, Ted, "Ray Budde and the origins of the 'Charter Concept'," *Education Evolving*, Vol. 1, No. 6, July 3, 2005, http://www.educationevolving.org/newsletters/vol-1-no-6.

Kurtz, Stanley, "Obama and Your Child's Mind," *National Review Online*, December 5, 2012, http://www.nationalreview.com/corner/334878/obama-and-your-childs-mind-stanley-kurtz.

———, "Obamacore: The White House Takes the Schools," *National Review Online*, December 3, 2012, http://www.nationalreview.com/corner/334645/obamacore-white-house-takes-schools-stanley-kurtz.

Lips, Dan and Evan Feinberg, "The Administrative Burden of No Child Left Behind," Heritage Foundation WebMemo #1406, March 23, 2007, http://www.heritage.org/research/reports/2007/03/the-administrative-burden-of-no-child-left-behind#_ftn4.

Lopez, Pia, "Lynch Mob or Seekers of School Equity?," *The Swarm* (blog), *Sacramento Bee*, January 6, 2010, http://blogs.sacbee.com/the_swarm/2010/01/lynch-mob-or-seekers-of-school.html.

McCluskey, Neal, "From the Ed Stats Truth Squad," *Cato at Liberty Blog*, January 31, 2008, http://www.cato.org/blog/ed-stats-truth-squad.

———, "I'll Take 'Whatever Evidence I Like' for Hundreds of Billions, Alex," *Cato at Liberty* (blog), Cato Institute, February 17, 2011, http://www.cato.org/blog/ill-take-whatever-evidence-i-hundreds-billions-alex.

———, "K–12 Education Subsidies," Downsizing the Federal Government, Cato Institute, May 2009, http://www.downsizinggovernment.org/education/k-12-education-subsidies.

———, "No Federal Failure Left Behind: The Feds Should Get Out of America's Schools," *National Review Online*, July 12, 2004, http://www.cato.org/publications/commentary/no-federal-failure-left-behind.

———, "Our Greedy Colleges," *Cato at Liberty* (blog), Cato Institute, June 15, 2012, http://www.cato.org/blog/our-greedy-colleges.

———, "SAFRA Stinks," *Forbes.com*, August 10, 2009, http://www.forbes.com/2009/08/10/education-loans-tuition-financial-aid-opinions-colleges-safra.html.

Moynihan, Michael C., "We Don't Need No Education: Obama Wants to Make College Grants into an Entitlement. Bad Idea," Reason Foundation, *Reason .com*, June 5, 2009, http://reason.com/archives/2009/06/05/we-dont-need-no -education.

National Association of State Boards of Education EDU Weblog, "AASA [American Association of School Administrators] Supports NEA NCLB Lawsuit," April 4, 2006, http://nasbe.blogspot.com/2006/04/aasa-supports-nea-nclb-lawsuit.html.

Olasky, Marvin, "Canada's Experience Shows School Choice Works," *Townhall .com*, July 30, 2002, http://townhall.com/columnists/marvinolasky/2002/07/30/ canadas_experience_shows_that_school_choice_works

Ramirez, Eddy, "Connecticut's NCLB Lawsuit Is Dismissed," *U.S. News & World Report*, April 29, 2008, http://www.usnews.com/education/blogs/on-education/ 2008/04/29/connecticuts-nclb-lawsuit-is-dismissed.

Schaeffer, Adam B., "Great Leadership + Thoughtful Policy = Huge Victory for Educational Freedom," *Cato at Liberty* (blog), Cato Institute, June 27, 2012, http:// www.cato.org/blog/great-leadership-thoughtful-policy-huge-victory-educational -freedom.

Seaborg, Glenn T., "Part 1: *A Nation at Risk* Revisited," August 1991, http://www2 .lbl.gov/Publications/Seaborg/risk.htm.

Senik, Troy, "The Worst Union in America," *City Journal*, Vol. 22, No. 2 (Spring 2012), http://www.city-journal.org/2012/22_2_california-teachers-association .html.

Sheffield, Rachel, "D.C. Public Schools Spend Almost $30,000 Per Student," *The Daily Signal* (blog), *The Heritage Foundation*, July 25, 2012, http://blog.heritage.org/2012/ 07/25/d-c-public-schools-spend-almost-30000-per-student/.

———, "National Education Standards Trade Literature for Reading Government Documents," *The Daily Signal* (blog), *The Heritage Foundation*, December 15, 2012, http://blog.heritage.org/2012/12/15/national-education-standards -trade-literature-for-reading-government-documents/.

———, "Obama Continues to Deny D.C. Children Educational Opportunity," *The Daily Signal* (blog), *The Heritage Foundation,* May 24, 2012, http://blog .heritage.org/2012/05/24/obama-continues-to-deny-d-c-children-educational -opportunity/.

Testimony

Alger, Vicki (née Murray), "Testimony submitted to the California Assembly Education Committee - AB-2739 Student Proficiency Transfers (struggling students transfers)," April 10, 2008.

Graduation: Final Report, Mathematica Policy Research, Inc., Prepared for: U.S. Department of Education, Office of Planning, Evaluation and Policy Development, Policy and Program Studies Service, 2009.

U.S. Advisory Commission on Intergovernmental Relations, *Federal Regulation of State & Local Governments: The Mixed Record of the 1980s.* Washington, DC: DIANE Publishing Company, 1993.

U.S. Census Bureau (Census), *The 2012 Statistical Abstract: The National Data Book.*

U.S. Department of Commerce, *Education Reform — Insight into the Business Community's Views About the U.S. Education System*, November 2006.

U.S. Department of Education (ED), 2009–2010 Federal Pell Grant End-of-Year Report. Washington, DC: Office of Postsecondary Education, 2011.

————, *A Blueprint for Reform: The Reauthorization of the Elementary and Secondary Education Act*, March 2010.

————, *A Nation Accountable: Twenty-Five Years After A Nation at Risk*, April 2008.

————, Office of Educational Research and Improvement (OERI), *A Study of Charter Schools*, various years.

————, Office of Inspector General (OIG), *Management Challenges*, various years.

U.S. Department of Health and Human Services (HHS), Administration for Children and Families, *Head Start Impact Study: Final Report*. Washington, DC, January 15, 2010.

U.S. Department of Homeland Security (DHS), *The 2013 Yearbook of Immigration Statistics.*

U.S. Department of Labor, Bureau of Labor Statistics (BLS), Consumer Price Index, various years.

U.S. Government Accountability Office (GAO), *2013 Annual Report: Actions Needed to Reduce Fragmentation, Overlap, and Duplication and Achieve Other Financial Benefits* (GAO-13-279SP), April 9, 2013.

————, *K–12 Education: Selected States and School Districts Cited Numerous Federal Requirements as Burdensome, While Recognizing Some Benefits* (GAO-12-672), June 27, 2012.

————, *Follow-up on 2011 Report: Status of Actions Taken to Reduce Duplication, Overlap, and Fragmentation, Save Tax Dollars, and Enhance Revenue* (GAO-12-453SP), February 2012.

————, *Funding Retained Teachers, but Education Could More Consistently Communicate Stabilization Monitoring Issues* (GAO-11-804), September 22, 2011.

————, *Disadvantaged Students: School Districts Have Used Title I Funds Primarily to Support Instruction* (GAO-11-595), July 15, 2011.

————, *Race to the Top: Reform Efforts Are Under Way and Information Sharing Could Be Improved* (GAO-11-658), June 30, 2011.

mentary and Secondary Education Act (Title I); and Individuals with Disabilities Education Act (IDEA), Part B. The result of those programs was to save or create jobs and advance education reforms] An act to make technical corrections to the Higher Education Act of 1965, and for other purposes (P.L. 111-39) [July 1, 2009] [included Race to the Top (RTT)].

Augustus F. Hawkins-Robert T. Stafford Elementary and Secondary School Improvement Amendments of 1988 (P.L. 100-297) [April 28, 1988].

Department of Education Act (14 Stat. 434) [March 2, 1867].

Department of Education Act (P.L. 96-88) [October 17, 1979].

Education Consolidation and Improvement Act of 1981 (Part of P.L. 97-35, The Omnibus Budget Reconciliation Act of 1981) [August 13, 1981].

Education for All Handicapped Children Act (P.L. 94-142) [November 30, 1975].

Education Jobs Fund (P.L. 111-226) [August 10, 2010].

Elementary and Secondary Education Act (ESEA) of 1965 (P.L. 89-10) [April 11, 1965].

Elementary and Secondary Education Amendments of 1967 (P.L. 90-247) [January 2, 1968].

Elementary & Secondary Education Amendment of 1974 (P.L. 93-380) [August 21, 1974].

Elementary and Secondary Education Amendments of 1977(P.L. 95-112) [June 2, 1977].

Elementary and Secondary Education Amendments of 1984 (P.L. 98-511) [October 19, 1984].

Goals 2000: Educate America Act (P.L. 103- 227) [March 31, 1994].

Health Care and Education Reconciliation Act of 2010 (P.L. 111-152) [March 30, 2010] [included the Student Aid and Fiscal Responsibility Act (SAFRA)].

Improving America's Schools Act of 1994 [ESEA Reauthorization] (P.L. 103-382; 108 Stat. 3518) [October 20, 1994].

Montgomery GI Bill—Active Duty (P.L. 98-525) [October 19, 1984].

Montgomery GI Bill—Selected Reserve (P.L. 98-525) [October 19, 1984].

Morrill Act of 1862 (7 U.S.C. § 301 et seq.) [July 2, 1862].

National Defense Education Act of 1958 (P.L. 85-864) [September 2, 1958].

National School Lunch Act (P.L. 79-396) [June 4, 1946].

No Child Left Behind Act of 2001 [ESEA Reauthorization] (NCLB; P.L 107-110; 115 Stat. 1425) [January 8, 2002].

Northwest Ordinance (1 Stat. 50) [July 13, 1787].

Servicemen's Readjustment Act [aka GI Bill] (Public Law 78-346) [June 22, 1944].

Smith-Lever Act of 1914 (P.L. 63-95) [May 8, 1914].

Smith-Hughes Act of 1917 [aka the Vocational Education Act of 1917] (P.L. 64-347; 39 Stat. 929) [February 23, 1917].

Judicial Decisions

Arizona Christian School Tuition Organization v. Winn, 536 U.S. 1 (2011)
Mueller v. Allen, 463 U.S. 388 (1983)
Pierce v. Society of Sisters 268 U.S. 510 (1925)
Serrano v. Priest, 5 Cal.3d 584 (1971) (Serrano I)
Serrano v. Priest, 18 Cal.3d 728 (1976) (Serrano II)
Serrano v. Priest, 20 Cal.3d 25 (1977) (Serrano III)
Zelman v. Simmons-Harris, 536 U.S. 639 (2002)

Newspapers/Trade Publications

Associated Press
Bangor Daily News (Maine)
Boston Globe
Chicago Tribune
Chronicle of Higher Education
Deseret News (Salt Lake City, UT)
Education Week
Gettysburg Times
Herald-Journal (Spartanburg, SC)
Huffington Post
Inside Higher Ed
Los Angeles Times
Macau Daily Times

Modesto Bee
New York Times
Pittsburgh Press
Rock Hill Herald
Salt Lake Tribune
Schenectady Gazette
School Library Journal
School Reform News
Wall Street Journal
Washington Examiner
Washington Post
Washington Times
Youngstown Vindicator (Ohio)

Databases

Education Commission of the States (ECS)
Eurydice Network
National Alliance for Public Charter Schools, Public Charter Schools Dashboard
National Assessment of Educational Progress (NAEP), Long-Term Trend NAEP
National Assessment of Educational Progress (NAEP), Main NAEP
National Center on Education and the Economy (NCEE) Center on International
    Benchmarking
National Conference on State Legislatures (NCSL)
PaymentAccuracy.gov
U.S. General Services Administration (GSA), Catalog of Federal Domestic Assistance
    (CFDA).
U.S. Government Publishing Office (GPO), Federal Digital System (FDsys)
U.S. Office of Personnel Management (OPM), FedScope

Index

Note: Page numbers in *italics* indicate a Figure on that page. Page numbers followed by an "*n*" or "*nn*" indicate endnotes; 345*nn*103–104 means page 345, notes 103 and 104.

A

Adams, John, 29–30
adequate yearly progress (AYP) mandates, 104–5, 108, 121, 131
administrative costs of federal mandates, 83, 87, 131–33, *132*, 367*n*41
Affordable Health Care Act (2010), 123
AFL-CIO, 76
AFT. *See* American Federation of Teachers (AFT)
after-school school in Japan, 210
Agricultural College Act (1890), 47–48
agricultural colleges. *See* Morrill Land Grant Acts (1859 and 1862)
Alabama, 14, 301–2
Alaine Leroy Locke Senior High Schools, Watts neighborhood, Los Angeles, 311–12
Allen, Mueller v., 301
Alliance for Excellent Education, 308–9
Alum Rock School District, San Jose, California, 293–94
America 2000 program, 101

American Council on Education, 62
American Federation of Teachers (AFT)
    and federal tuition tax credits, 299
    opposition to DOE establishment, 76–77
    response to *A Nation at Risk* report, 95
    and vouchers, 292, 293
American Institutes for Research, 86
American Recovery and Reinvestment Act
    GAO on effect on education, 146
    Investing in Innovation (i3) Fund, 250
    and Race to the Top, 123
    stabilization aid for states, 111–12, 123
Anderson, Martin, 93
Arizona
    charter schools, 406*n*99
    education savings accounts, 313
    refusal to accept NDEA Title III funding, 79–80
    tuition tax credit scholarship program, 302, 305, 315
    turning down federal funds, 59–60, 79–80
Arizona Christian School Tuition Organization v. Winn, 302

Arkansas, 13

Arkansas Virtual Academy, 308

Arons, Stephen, 292

ARRA (Federal Work-Study Program), 274–75

Arts in Education program, 254–55

assessment, global models

  overview, 330–31

  Australia, 195

  Belgium, 197

  Canada, 199

  Chinese Taipei, 201

  Germany, 203

  Hong Kong, 204

  Hungary, 206

  Ireland, 207–8

  Japan, 209

  Macao, China, 212

  The Netherlands, 213

  New Zealand, 215

  Singapore, 217

assessment of special needs students, 156, 386*n*59

assessment of students. *See also* assessment, global models; global performance; National Assessment of Educational Progress; Program for International Student Assessment (PISA); testing regimes/evaluation mandates

Australia

  overview, 194–96

  immigration rate and PISA scores, 176, *176*

  school autonomy and parental choice, *188–89,* 190

  schools competing for students, 182, *182*

  socioeconomic background and PISA scores, 177, *178*

Austria, 172

autonomy, 390*n*46. *See also* school autonomy, global models

AYP (adequate yearly progress) mandates, 104–5, 108, 121, 131

B

Baker, Bruce, 310

Baker, Howard, 75, 76, 299, 300

Bangor Daily News, 89–90

Banks, Nathaniel P., 42

Barone, Charles, 121

Bast, Joseph L., 288, 314–15

Bayard, James A., 35

Bayh, Birch, 75

Belgium

  overview, 196–98

  government funding and private schools, 190, *191*

  parental choice offerings, global comparison, 183, *184, 186*

  school autonomy and parental choice, *188–89,* 190

Bell, Terrel H., 89–90, 93–94, 97–98

Bielang, Mark, 113

Blaine, James G., 20, 339*n*80

block grants to states, 87–88, 90, 92–93, 98, 222, 333

Blouin, Michael T., 56

blueprints. *See* parental choice blueprint for the future; privatizing the federal role in education

Blumenfeld, Samuel L., 9, 11, 16–17

Blum, Father Virgil C., 289

Boehner, John, 296, 297

Boren, David, 299–300

Boston, Massachusetts, 8, 11, 15–17

Boyer, Ernest, 64

Breneman, David W., 65

Brooks, Charles, 39

Brooks, Jack, 56, 57, 73

Brouillette, Matthew J., 218

Buchanan, James, 25, 32–33, 35–36

Buckalew, Charles R., 46

Budde, Ray, 303

Bureau of Education, Department of
the Interior, 47

Bush, George H.W., 100–101, 331

Bush, George W., 104–9, 331

C

Cabinet of the President
Carter's, 55
and Department of Education,
23–24, 49, 52, 57, 70–74
increase in department in, 51
opposition to Department of
Education post, 64–65, 150, 153
Reagan's, 91

Cafritz, Peggy Cooper, 403*n*45

California
Alaine Leroy Locke Senior High
Schools, Watts neighborhood,
Los Angeles, 311–12
Alum Rock School District, San
Jose, voucher program, 293–94
California Federation of Teachers,
310
California Teachers Association, 311
parent trigger laws, 310–12
Self-Determination in Education
Act proposal, 290

Calvinism vs. Unitarianism, 15

Canada, 174, *176*, 177, *178*, 198–200

Canham, Erwin D., *191*

Career and Technical Education–Basic
Grants to States program, 277

Carter, James G., 19

Carter, Jimmy

on benefits of DOE, 68
commitment to DOE establishment,
56–57, 63
Department of Education
Organization Act signed by, 52
and ESEA, 85
and NEA, 55, 349*n*23
support for non-segregated private
schools, 298
and uncertainty about DOE bill
passage, 75–76

Catalog of Federal Domestic Assistance,
141–42

Catholic Conference, 76

Catholic immigrants as threat to
Protestants, 18–19, 19–21

centralization
overview, 316
competition vs., 218
DOE consolidation/centralization
for efficiency, 51–52, 141–47,
143–44, 147, 148, 149
as means for streamlining
government, 51, 66–72
for molding children to fit in larger
community, 53
NEA as centralization supporter,
54–55
in Obama era, 120–21
Prussian education model, 18–19
in Singapore, 217

Chamber of Commerce, 289, 401*n*11

Chamber of Commerce, US, 289,
401*n*11

Chapoton, John, 298–99

charter schools
overview, 303–4, 315, 406*n*99
Charter Schools program, 248–49
Credit Enhancement for Charter
School Facilities program, 248–49

and grants, 249
Minnesota as first state with, 101
nationwide increase, 406*n*99
and parent trigger laws, 312
Chavous, Kevin P., 403*n*45
Chicago, City Club of, 294
children
groups that benefit from a national
interest in education, 96
molding into model citizens, 16, 53,
54, 289
as property of the state, 37, 316
See also poor people/children
China. *See* Macao, China
China, Shanghai, *166, 168,* 177, *178*
Chinese Taipei
overview, 200–202
IEA TIMSS results, *167, 169*
parental choice offerings, global
comparison, 183, *184, 186*
school autonomy and parental
choice, *188–89,* 190
schools competing for students,
182, *182*
students' performance levels, 173
Chisholm, Shirley, 150
chronology, USDOE, 1642–2015,
xv–xx, 47–49
Chubb, John, 314, 315
City Club of Chicago, 294
Class Size Reduction program, ESEA,
149
Clay, Clement C., Jr., 29, 33–34, 35,
343*n*54, 343*n*61
Clinton, Bill, 100–101, 102–4, 103, 331
Clohan, William, 299
Clune, William H., III, 290
Cochran, Thad, 75
Cohen, William, 71–72, 142, 149
Coleman, James S., 290

Collamer, Jacob, 31
College Cost Reduction and Access Act
(2007), 319
college remediation rates, 95
Collins, Susan, 296
Colorado Online Learning virtual
school, 306
Columbia University Teachers College
research, 305
Common Core State Standards
Initiative, 15, 111, 114–19, 221, 331
Community Learning Centers program, Twenty-First Century,
244–45
competition among schools
centralization vs. competition, 218
parental choice programs vs. public
schools, 305
performance analysis, global,
179–82, *182,* 190–92, *191*
postsecondary institutions, 318
private schools, 14–15
support for, in United States, 289–90
in United States, 181, *182*
competition for student loans, 272
competitive grant program (Race to the
Top), 15, 112–16, 123, 236–37
compulsory education laws
appealing to the plight of poor
children, 9
for immigrants, 20
in Massachusetts, 8, 15–16, 17
in Prussian system, 18
Congressional Budget Office, 70
Congress of the United States
on amendment allowing land-grants
for education, 30–31, 339*n*80,
340*n*10
on Department of Education (est.
1867), 27–33, 41–46, 345*nn*103–104

ESEA passage, 82, 365*n*14
House Government Operations
  Committee, 73
laws setting aside land for public
  schools, 10–11
national education bureau memorial,
  39–40
on national university, 4–7
Senate Governmental Affairs
  Committee, 58–59, 66, 68, 72, 89
and student loans, 319, 320
Congress on Department of Education
  (est. 1979), 55–77
  Bell's testimony in favor of DOE, 89
  centralization for efficiency theme,
    51–52
  education as national activity
    argument, 63–66
  efficiency, cost savings, and
    accountability argument, 68–72
  House debates, 75, 332
  improving educational quality
    argument, 72–74
  institutionalization of schooling,
    52–55
  management and coordination
    issues, 66–68
  political maneuvers leading to DOE,
    55–57, 332
  supplementing state and local
    governments, 57–62
  vote on, 74–77
Connecticut, 12, 107, 108
Constitutional Convention (1787), 4
Constitution of the United States
  on Congressional power for land
    grants, 25
  on copyright and patent powers, 4, 27
  Education and the Workforce
    Committee hearing, 132–33

education not mentioned in, xxi, 9,
  62, 332–33
failure to act on Obama's policies,
  122–23
ignoring in favor of centralized
  education, 46, 99–100
ignoring in favor of land grants for
  education, 31
Madison on authorizing a national
  university, 5
NCLB passage, 104
and "powers not delegated to the
  United States," xxi
search for land grant for education
  language, 27–28
Spending Clause, 59, 352*n*48
and state-federal relationship, 33–36
constitutions of states, 9, 10–14
Consumer's Education program,
  ESEA, 149
Conyers, John, Jr., 64–65, 67–68, 76
Coons, John E., 290, 294
Coulson, Andrew, 123–24, 193
Council on Foreign Relations, 289–90
Cousin, Victor, 18
Credit Enhancement for Charter
  School Facilities program,
  248–49
Cubberley, Ellwood, 36–37
curriculum
  and charter schools, 101
  Common Core State Standards
    Initiative, 15, 111, 114–19, 221, 331
  dispute over choice of Bible for
    schools, 20–21
  ESEA on control of, 81
  and IASA, 102
  A Nation at Risk report on, 94–95
  prediction of standardized
    curriculum, 61

pre-federal involvement in
  education, 15
rationale for federal involvement in
  education, 96, 106
Reagan's DOE Task Force on, 91
curriculum, global models
  Australia, 194–95
  Belgium, 196
  Canada, 199
  Chinese Taipei, 200–201
  Germany, 202–3
  Hong Kong, 204
  Hungary, 206
  Ireland, 207
  Japan, 209
  Macao, China, 212
  The Netherlands, 213
  New Zealand, 215
  Singapore, 216–17
  South Korea, 210

D
Danforth, John C., 58
Data Systems program, Statewide,
  243
Davis, Garrett, 66
D.C. Children and Youth Investment
  Trust Corporation, 297
D.C. Opportunity Scholarship
  Program, 187, 248, 285, 295–97,
  305, 403*n*45
D.C. School Choice Incentive
  Program, 257
decentralization, 99, 194, 330
decentralization of curriculum, 217
Delaware, 10, 12
Democracy and Education (Dewey),
  53–54
democracy preservation via public
  schools, 18, 36–37

Denmark
  school autonomy and parental
    choice, 187, *188–89,* 190
  socioeconomic background and
    PISA scores, 177, *178*
  teaching hours per school year, 179
Department of Education (DOE)
  chronology, 1642–2015, xv–xx, 47–49
  A Nation at Risk report and updates,
    94–97, 108–9, 169–70, 314
  purpose (*See* Department of
    Education purpose)
  See also Office of the Deputy
    Secretary programs; Office of the
    Secretary programs; Office of
    the Under Secretary programs
Department of Education (est. 1867)
  overview, 23, 24
  as argument against 1979
    Department of Education, 61–62
  centralization as precursor to, 316
  Congressional debates on, 27–33,
    41–46, 345*nn*103–104
  events leading to, xxi–xxiii
  iterations of, 47–49
  National Teachers' Association
    support for, 37–39
  purpose of, 34, 39, 40
  school superintendents' support for,
    39–41
  support for, 23–24
Department of Education (est. 1979)
  overview, 331–32
  as Cabinet agency, 52
  cost and size of, 70, 71–72, 129–31,
    130, 136–39, *137–38*
  dismantling (*See entries beginning
    with* "Department of Education
    dismantling")
  establishment of, xxi

failure of, xxiv

iterations of, 56

National Commission on Excellence in Schools, 93–97

program outlays, 129, 131, *139–41*, 139–42, 381*n*6

purpose of, 57, 129, 130–32

Reagan's DOE Task Force, 90–93, 97, 369*n*59

Reagan's secretary of education supporting federal involvement in education, 89–90, 93–94, 97–98

Reagan's vow to eliminate, 87, 88–89, 92–93, 95, 97, 368*n*43

as sole lender for student loans, 114, 146, *147,* 319–21

and state complaints about NCLB, 108

structure of, 134, *135,* 136, *224–26, 234*

virtual schools analysis, 309

See also Congress on Department of Education (est. 1979)

Department of Education dismantling process, 221–31

overview, 221–23

eliminating duplicate efforts, 229–30

eliminating non-program offices and divisions, 223, 226, *227,* 228

privatizing the federal role, 230

Reagan's downgrading plan, 90–91, 97

reasons for, 221–23

returning autonomy to states, 230

returning funding to taxpayers, 222–23, 228–29, 230–31, 333–34

state-level determination of program preservation, 229

Department of Education dismantling proposal, 233–85

overview, 233, *234,* 235, 284–85, 333

Immediate Office of the Secretary programs, 235–41

Institute of Education Sciences programs, 241–45

Office of Elementary and Secondary Education, 265–71

Office of English Language Acquisition, Language Enhancement and Academic Achievement for Limited English Proficient Students, 264–65

Office of Federal Student Aid, 271–76

Office of Innovation and Improvement, 247–58

Office of Management program, 245–46

Office of Postsecondary Education, 279–84

Office of Special Education and Rehabilitative Services, 258–64

Office of Vocational and Adult Education, 276–79

See also specific offices for additional program information

Department of Education Organization Act (1978), 56, 58, 62, 300, 350*n*30, 405*n*77

Department of Education Organization Act (1979), 52, 56–62, 74–75. *See also* Congress on Department of Education (est. 1979)

Department of Education purpose

1867 version, 34, 39, 40

1979 version, 57, 129, 130–32

consolidation/centralization for efficiency, 51–52, 141–47, *143–44, 147, 148,* 149

education as national activity, 63–66

efficiency, cost savings, and
accountability, 68–72
improving educational quality,
72–74, 150, *151–52, 152–59, 154–55,
158–61,* 161
improving management and
coordination, 66–68, 134, *135,*
136–41, *137–41,* 229–30
institutionalization of schooling,
52–55
supplementing state and local
governments, 57–62, 131–34
Department of Health, Education,
and Welfare (HEW)
DOE vs., 52, 134
Goldwater on state of education
under, 60
Office of Education as part of, 24
regulation impasse, 69
reorganization by Eisenhower, 48
size of, 66
Dewey, John, 51, 52–54
Dingell, Jim, 76
Directed Grants and Awards program,
238
District of Columbia School Choice
Incentive Act (2004), 294
diversity as reason for uniform public
school campaign, 16, 18–19,
20–21
Dixon, James, 46
DOE. *See entries beginning with*
"Department of Education"
Dole, Bob, 103, 299–300
Domenici, Pete, 63
Donnelly, Ignatius, 41–42
Duncan, Arne
overview, 114
and D.C. Opportunity Scholarship
Program, 296–97

and ESEA, 111, 120, 121
on Pell Grant scholarships, 326
on uniform standards/Common
Core initiative, 114–15, 117
and waivers for ESEA mandates, 121,
122, 378n51
Durbin, Dick, 296

E
economic status, impact of immigration and, 175–79, *176, 178,* 388n22
Education Act (Boston, 1789), 11
educational achievement measurement
provisions, 82
Educational Consolidation and
Improvement Act (1982), 87–88
educational freedom in colonial era,
8–9. *See also entries beginning with*
"parental choice"
Educational Opportunity and Equity
Act (1982), 299
Educational Opportunity and Equity
Act (1983), 299
educational spending
Bush, G.H.W., era, 101–2
Congressional support for generous
increases, 103–4
decade from 1950–1960, 49
DOE as containment for, 67
DOE program outlays, 129, 131,
139–41, 139–42, 381n6
duplication of programs, 229–30
Garfield's rationale for, 45
global comparison, spending vs.
results, 164, 171–75, *172, 173*
and NAEP results, 153–55, *154, 155,*
159, 161, *161,* 330, 385n58
postsecondary education, 112, 129,
136, 139–41, *139–41, 147,* 242
and quality of education, 61, 62

See also elimination savings; Government Accountability Office (GAO); Office of Management and Budget (OMB)
educational systems, global models
  Australia, 194
  Belgium, 196
  Canada, 198–99
  Chinese Taipei, 200
  Germany, 202
  Hong Kong, 204
  Hungary, 206
  Ireland, 207
  Japan, 208
  Macao, China, 211–12
  The Netherlands, 213
  New Zealand, 215
  Singapore, 216
  South Korea, 210
Education and Capitalism (Walberg and Bast), 314–15
"Education by Charter" (Budde), 303
"Education Duties of the Hour, The" (Greene), 38–39
education economics, 315
Education for All Handicapped Children Act (1974), 84. *See also* special education
Education Jobs Fund (2010), 123
Education Policy and Governance Program, Harvard University, 181
Education Research, Development and Dissemination program, 241–42
education savings accounts (ESAs), 313–14
educative process, Dewey on, 54
Eisenhower, Dwight D., 48
Eitel, Robert S., 116
Electronic High School, Utah, 309

Elementary and Secondary Education Act of 1965 (ESEA)
  overview, 80, 81–83, 365n6, 365n14
  costs, 84, 86–87, 131–32
  and DOE, 81
  Educational Consolidation and Improvement Act iteration, 87–88
  expansions under Nixon, Ford, and Carter, 84–85
  funding appropriations and NAEP results, 153–55, *154, 155,* 159, 161, *161*
  Hawkins-Stafford Improvements amendments, 98–99
  IASA iteration, 102–3, 104
  and Obama, 111, 112, 120–23
  opinion poll results, 124–25
  and parental choice, 295
  program increases and declines, 146–47, *148,* 149
  in Reagan era, 98
  states' administrative bureaus/costs, 83, 87, 132, 367n41
  studies of impact, 85–86, 105–6
  Title I funds for low-income students redirected by schools, 83, 105, 112–14
  titles list, 82
  waivers for ESEA mandates under Obama, 120–21, 122, 123, 378n51
  See also No Child Left Behind (NCLB)
elimination savings
  overview, 222–23, *227–28,* 397nn3–4
  DOE dismantling by downgrading plan, 90–91, 97
  Immediate Office of the Secretary programs, 240–41
  Institute of Education Sciences programs, 244–45

Office of Elementary and Secondary Education, 269–71
Office of Federal Student Aid, 275–76
Office of Innovation and Improvement, 257–58
Office of Postsecondary Education, 282–84
Office of Special Education and Rehabilitative Services, 261–63
Office of Vocational and Adult Education, 278–79
Empowerment Scholarship Accounts Program (2011, Arizona), 313
English as a second language
and NAEP results, 157–59, *158, 159*
Office of English Language Acquisition, Language Enhancement and Academic Achievement for Limited English Proficient Students, 264–65
Enzi, Mike, 122
ESAs (education savings accounts), 313–14
ESEA. *See* Elementary and Secondary Education Act of 1965 (ESEA)
ESSA (Every Student Succeeds Act of 2015), 111
Estonia, 174
Ethnic Heritage program, ESEA, 149
European countries, 177, *178. See also specific countries*
evaluation mandates. *See* testing regimes/evaluation mandates
Every Student Succeeds Act of 2015 (ESSA), 111
Excellence Commission, 93–98
Exchanges with Historic Whaling and Trading Partners program, ESEA, 149

F
Federal Direct Student Loans program, 123, 272
federal involvement in education
overview, 123–25
direct lending to students, 321–22
imbalance of power, 133–34
lack of constitutional authority, xxi, 9, 46, 62, 99–100, 124, 332–33
on-budget education funding, 142–46, *143, 144, 147, 155*
opponents to, 18th Century, 288–89
pre-1977, 132
and quality of education, 61, 62, 72–74, 150, *151–52,* 152–59, *154–55, 158–61,* 161
under Reagan, 89–90, 93–94, 97–100
See also privatizing the federal role in education; testing regimes/evaluation mandates; *specific laws; entries beginning with* "Department of Education"
federal mandates. *See* testing regimes/evaluation mandates
federal matching grants, 79, 364*n*1
Federal Pell Grant Program, 273–74, 325–28
Federal Perkins Loans, 318–19
Federal Real Property Assistance Program, Office of Management program, 245–46
Federal Real Property Council, US General Services Administration, 246
Federal Supplemental Education Opportunity Grants program, 275
Federal Work-Study Program (ARRA), 274–75
Feinstein, Dianne, 296

Ferraro, Geraldine, 75–76
financial incentives and parental
    choice, 185, *186,* 187, *188–89,*
    189–90, 390*n*46
Finland
    education spending per child, 172
    government funding and private
        schools, 190, *191*
    IEA PIRLS results, *166*
    OECD PISA results, *168*
    school autonomy and parental
        choice, *188–89,* 190
    students' performance levels, 174
    teaching hours per school year, 177
flexibility plan, ESEA, 120–23
Florida, 14, 304–5, 313–14
Florida Educational Society, 14
Florida Virtual School, 307–8
Ford, Gerald, 84
Foreign Language Assistance Program,
    264–65
Forgione, Pascal D., Jr., 108, 109
Foundation for Education Assistance,
    92–93
Fountain, Lawrence
    on DOE authorization, 70, 142,
        233
    DOE program review
        recommendation, 142
    on NEA, 65–66
    on states taking over private schools,
        235
    on weeding out ineffective programs,
        67
Friedman, Milton, 288, 318
Fuller, Bruce, 106
Fund for the Improvement of
    Education, 256
future. *See* parental choice blueprint for
    the future

G
GAO. *See* Government Accountability
    Office (GAO)
Garfield, James A., 39–40, 41, 45
GDP (gross domestic product),
    174–75
Gemin, Butch, 307
General Services Administration's
    Federal Real Property Council,
    246
Georgia, 10, 12
Georgia Virtual School, 309
Gephardt, Richard, 75–76
Germany
    overview, 202–4
    government funding and private
        schools, 190, *191*
    parental choice incentives for
        schools, 185, *186,* 187
    school autonomy and parental
        choice, *188–89,* 190
Gillen, Andrew, 322–23
global models
    overview, 193–94, 330–31
    Australia, 194–96
    Belgium, 196–98
    Canada, 198–200
    Chinese Taipei, 200–202
    Germany, 202–4
    Hong Kong, 204–5
    Hungary, 206–7
    Ireland, 207–8
    Japan, 208–10
    Macao, China, 211–12
    The Netherlands, 213–14, 396*n*160
    New Zealand, 215–16
    Singapore, 216–18
    South Korea, 210–11
    See also Organization for Economic
        Cooperation and Development

(OECD); United States, global comparisons

global performance

overview, xxiv, 163–64

American performance overview, 164–70, *166, 167, 168, 169, 170*

competition among schools and, 179–82, *182,* 190–92, *191*

education spending and performance compared, 164, 171–75, *172, 173*

impact of immigration and economic status, 175–79, *176, 178,* 388*n*22

parental choice and student performance analysis, global, 182–83, *184,* 185, *186,* 187, *188–89,* 189–90, 389*n*39

See also International Association for Evaluation of Education Achievement (IEA); Program for International Student Assessment (PISA)

Goals 2000: The Educate America Act (1993), 102–4, 331

Goldman, Eric F., 82

Goldwater, Barry, xxii, 59–60, 80, 334

Government Accountability Office (GAO)

on administrative and regulatory mandates costs to states, 132

on contractor use and oversight, 138–39

on DOE responsibilities, 146

on federal education programs, 142–45

on Higher Education Institutional Aid program, 280

on number of ESEA programs, 133

on Office of Special Education and Rehabilitative Services programs, 267, 268

on Office of Vocational and Adult Education, 277

on states' use of federal education funds, 113

on student loans, 320–21

See also Office of Management and Budget (OMB)

Governmental Affairs Committee, Senate, 58–59, 66, 68, 72, 89. *See also* Ribicoff, Abraham

government funding and private schools, 190, *191*

Government Operations Committee, House, 73

government schooling. *See* public schools

grants

Adult Education–Basic Grants to States program, 277–78

Career and Technical Education–Basic Grants to States program, 277

and charter schools, 249

Directed Grants and Awards program, 238

Federal Pell Grant Program, 273–74, 325–28

Federal Supplemental Education Opportunity Grants program, 275

grants-in-aid programs, 91

Improving Teacher Quality State Grants program, 266–67

Race to the Top program, 15, 112–16, 123, 236–37

Special Education Grants to States, 259–60

Teacher Quality Partnership Grants program, 251–52
TEACH grants, 239
Title I Grants to Local Educational Agencies, 265–66
Voluntary Public School Choice program, 255–56
Greene, Samuel S., 38–39
Green, James S., 26
Grimes, James W., 46
gross domestic product (GDP), 174–75

H
Hamilton, Alexander, 34
Harvard University, Education Policy and Governance Program, 181
Hatch, Orrin G., 75
Hawkins, Augustus, 98
Hawkins-Stafford Improvements amendments to ESEA, 98–99
Hayakawa, Samuel, 61–62, 70–71, 74, 329
Health Care Act (2010), 123
Hendricks, Thomas, 66
Herndon, Terry, 89
HEW. *See* Department of Health, Education, and Welfare; Department of Health, Education, and Welfare (HEW)
Higgins, John P., Jr., 320
Higher Education Act (1965), 281
Higher Education Act (1972 reauthorization), 326
Higher Education Institutional Aid program, 280
Hill, Mark, 30–31
Hong Kong
overview, 204–5
government funding and private schools, 190, *191*

IEA PIRLS results, *166*
IEA TIMSS results, *167*
immigration rate and PISA scores, 175–77, *176*
school autonomy and parental choice, 187, *188–89,* 190
schools competing for students, 182, *182*
socioeconomic background and PISA scores, 177, *178*
students' performance levels, 173
Hufstedler, Shirley, 89
human capital contracts between businesses and postsecondary students, 325
Humphrey, Hubert, 67
Hungary
overview, 206–7
government funding and private schools, 190, *191*
school autonomy and parental choice, 187, *188–89,* 190
Hunter, Duncan, 121, 133

I
IASA (Improving America's Schools Act of 1994), 102–3, 104
Idaho Digital Learning Academy, 306
IDEA (Individuals with Disabilities Education Act), 84, 112–14, 259, 260
IEA. *See* International Association for Evaluation of Education Achievement (IEA)
Illinois, 24–25, 301–2
Immediate Office of the Secretary programs, 235–41
overview, *234,* 236
Directed Grants and Awards, 238

Education Research, Development and Dissemination, 241–42
elimination savings, 240–41
Institute of Education Sciences, 241–45
Postsecondary Education Scholarships for Veteran's Dependents, 239–40
Race to the Top, 15, 112–16, 123, 237–38
Race to the Top Early Learning Challenge, 114, 236–37
TEACH grants, 239
immigration
Catholic immigrants as threat to Protestantism, 18–19, 19–21
impact of economic status and, 175–79, 176, 178, 388n22
and shift to federal control of education, 3
statistics for late–1800s, 36
Impact Aid program, 267–68
Improving America's Schools Act of 1994 (IASA), 102–3, 104
Improving Teacher Quality State Grants program, 266–67
income taxes, returning to taxpayers, 222–23, 228–29, 230–31, 333–34
Indiana, 301–2
Indiana University, 307
Individuals with Disabilities Education Act (IDEA), 84, 112–14, 259, 260
Inouye, Daniel K., 75
Institute of Education Sciences programs, 241–45
overview, 244
Education Research, Development and Dissemination, 241–42
elimination savings, 244–45

nongovernment agencies' investment in, 230
Research in Special Education program, 242–43
Statewide Data Systems program, 243
Twenty-First Century Community Learning Centers, 243–44
institutionalized schooling, 3, 52–53
interest rates and student loans, 319, 320
International Association for Evaluation of Education Achievement (IEA)
International Mathematics Study and International Science Study, 164–65
pilot study, 164
PIRLS results, 165, 166
reading literacy surveys, 165
TIMSS results, 165, 166, 167, 169, 180, 195
See also global performance
Investing in Innovation (i3) Fund program, 250
Iowa, 301–2
Ireland
overview, 207–8
government funding and private schools, 190, 191
school autonomy and parental choice, 188–89, 190
Izumi, Lance, 118

J
Jackson, Andrew, 30, 31, 343n61
Jackson, Rev. Jesse, 64
Japan
overview, 208–10
OECD PISA results, 168
school autonomy and parental choice, 188–89, 189–90

students' performance levels, 173–74
teaching hours per school year, 177
Jefferson, Thomas, 4, 28–29, 288, 332
Jencks, Christopher, 291
Jennings, Jack, 122–23
Jesuits, 13
Johnson, Lyndon, 81–82, 85
Jongbloed, Ben, 318

K
Kansas virtual schools, 307
Kelly, Brian, 323
Kennedy, Robert, 82, 83, 98
Keppel, Francis "Frank," 81–82
Kilpatrick, William H., 54
Klein, Joel, 289–90
Kline, John, 121, 122, 123, 145–46
Koelman, Jos, 318
Korea
    IEA PIRLS results, *166*
    IEA TIMSS results, *167, 169*
    OECD PISA results, *168*
    school autonomy and parental
        choice, *188–89,* 190
    students' performance levels, 173–74
    teaching hours per school year, 177
Kostmayer, Peter H., 64–65, 74, 329
Kursh, Harry, 26

L
land grants for public schools, 14,
    40–41, 340*n*13. *See also* Morrill
    Land Grant Acts (1859 and 1862)
Land Ordinance (1785), 10
Lee, Jackyung, 106
Levin, Carl, 63, 69
Levin, Henry M., 292
Levitas, Elliott, 73
Lieberman, Joseph, 296, 297
Lincoln, Abraham, xxi–xxii, 26

literacy assessments. *See* Program for
    International Student Assessment
    (PISA)
long-term trend (LTT) NAEP, 150,
    151–52, 153, 156
Louisiana, 13, 301–2
low income. *See* poor people/children
LTT (long-term trend) NAEP, 150,
    151–52, 153, 156
Ludemann, Elke, 179
Luxembourg, 172

M
Macao, China
    overview, 211–12
    immigration rate and PISA scores,
        176, *176*
    Macao Government Information
        Bureau, 211
    parental choice offerings, global
        comparison, 183, *184, 186*
    school autonomy and parental
        choice, 187, *188–89,* 189–90
    schools competing for students, 181,
        182
Madison, James
    on constitutionally limited govern-
        ment, 29–30
    on education in a free society, 4–7
    on federal involvement in education,
        28
    on Spending Clause of the Consti-
        tution, 59, 352*n*48
    on State vs. federal powers, 33–34,
        343*n*54
Magnet Schools Assistance program, 251
Maine, 21
management program, Office of the
    Secretary, 245–46
Mann, Horace, 3, 18–19, 20–21, 52

Martin, Robert E., 322–23
Martin, Ruby, 83
Maryland, 12
Mascaro, Steve, 107–8
Mason, James M., xxi–xxii, 34
Massachusetts, 8, 10, 11–12, 15–17
Massachusetts Education Act (1789), 11
McClure, Phyllis, 83
McCluskey, Neal, 21, 80, 81, 105–6, 327
∴ McKinley Elementary, Compton,
      California, 310
mechanical colleges. *See* Morrill Land
      Grant Acts (1859 and 1862)
Meese, Edwin, III, 93
Metric Education program, ESEA, 149
Mexico, 13–14
Michel, Bob, 74, 332
Michigan Virtual School, 306
Michigan Virtual University, 306
Milgram, James, 117–18
military tactics colleges, 26. *See also*
      Morrill Land Grant Acts
Miller, George, 121–22, 320
Mill, John Stuart, 10, 288–89
Minnesota, 301–2, 303
Mississippi, 14
Mitchill, Samuel L., 5–6
Mobile, Alabama, 14
Moe, Terry, 314, 315
Monroe, James, 29–30
Moorhead, William S., 64
Morrill, Justin S., 23, 25–26, 31–32
Morrill Land Grant Acts (1859 and 1862)
      overview, xxi–xxii, xxiii
      effects of, 26, 341n23
      events leading up to, 24–26, 339n7
      introduction of, 25–26
      Jefferson's proposal compared to, 29
      precedents and the Constitution,
         27–33

See also Department of Education
      (est. 1867)
Morris, Gouverneur, 4
Moulton, Samuel W., 42, 66
Moynihan, Daniel Patrick, 74, 75, 90,
      298, 300–301, 332
Mueller v. Allen, 301

N
NAEP. *See* National Assessment of
      Educational Progress (NAEP)
National Assessment of Educational
      Progress (NAEP)
      educational spending and NAEP
         results, 153–55, *154, 155,* 159, 161, *161,*
         330, 385n58
      LTT (long-term trend) NAEP, 150,
         151–52, 153, *154, 155,* 156
      and National Assessment Governing
         Board, 98
      and NCLB, 106
      reading and math scores, 156–59, *160*
      student subgroup tracking, 156–58,
         158, 159, 160
National Association of School
      Superintendents, 39–41
"National Bureau of Education, A"
      (Rickoff), 38
"National Bureau of Education, A"
      (White), 37–38
National Defense Education Act of
      1958 (NDEA), xxii, 60, 79–80, 81,
      318–19
National Education Association (NEA)
      and Carter, 55, 349n23
      as centralization supporters, 54–55
      and Dewey, 54
      and DOE, 72
      and federal tuition tax credits, 299
      gains from establishment of DOE, 73

influence in Congress, 76
NEA-PAC, 55
and politicization of education, 65
and Reagan's choice for secretary of
    education, 89
and vouchers, 292, 293
vs. NCLB, 107
national education department.
    See entries beginning with
    "Department of Education"
National Education Finance Project,
    291
National Education Goals Panel, 101,
    372n102
national education goals under Bush,
    G.H.W., 100–101
National Governor's Association, 114,
    115
National Governor's Association Task
    Force on Parent Involvement and
    Choice, 294
National Teachers' Association, 37–39
national university proposals, 4–7
Nation at Risk, A (Excellence
    Commission), 94–97, 108–9,
    169–70, 314
Nation's Report Card. *See* National
    Assessment of Educational
    Progress (NAEP)
NCEs (normal curve equivalents),
    98–99
NCLB. *See* No Child Left Behind
    (NCLB)
NDEA (National Defense Education
    Act of 1958), xxii, 60, 79–80, 81,
    318–19
NEA. *See* National Education
    Association (NEA)
NEA-PAC, 55
Netherlands, The

overview, 213–14
government funding and private
    schools, 190, *191*
school autonomy and parental
    choice, 187, *188–89,* 189–90,
    396n160
schools competing for students,
    182, *182*
New American School models, 101
New Hampshire, 10, 12
New Jersey, 12
New York, 12, 337n37
New York Times, 94, 293
New Zealand
    overview, 215–16
    immigration rate and PISA scores,
        176, 177
    parental choice incentives for
        schools, 185, *186*
    parental choice offerings, global
        comparison, 183, *184, 186*
    school autonomy and parental
        choice, 187, *188–89,* 190
Nixon, Richard, 84
No Child Left Behind (NCLB)
    overview, 104, 331
    administrative costs to states,
        131–32
    failure of, 123–24
    NDEA vs., 81
    NEA vs., 107
    public school failure rate, 121
    Unsafe School Choice Option, 105
nongovernment schooling options.
    See parental choice
normal curve equivalents (NCEs),
    98–99
Northwest Ordinance (1787), 10–11
Norway, 172, 183, *184, 186*
Nunn, Sam, 55–56, 69, 332

O

Obama, Barack
  and D.C. Opportunity Scholarship
    Program, 296–97
  on education as America's national
    mission, 113
  and student loans, 123, 322
  tactics for education reform, 120–21
  See also Duncan, Arne
OECD. *See* Organization for Economic Cooperation and Development (OECD)
Office of Economic Opportunity,
  United States, 290–91
Office of Education
  in HEW, 24, *155*
  iterations of, 47–48, 347*nn*126–127
  multiyear studies of ESEA impact,
    85–86, 105–6
  regulatory activities, 69
  size of, 48, 49
Office of Elementary and Secondary
  Education, 265–71
  overview, *234,* 265
  elimination savings, 269–71
  Impact Aid program, 267–68
  Improving Teacher Quality State
    Grants program, 266–67
  increasing responsibilities of, 146
  Title I Grants to Local Educational
    Agencies, 265–66
Office of English Language Acquisition, Language Enhancement
  and Academic Achievement for
  Limited English Proficient
  Students program, *234,* 264–65
Office of Federal Student Aid,
  271–76
  overview, 146, 271, 276
  elimination savings, 275–76

Federal Direct Student Loans
  program, 123, 272
Federal Pell Grant Program, 273–74,
  325–28
Federal Supplemental Education
  Opportunity Grants program,
  275
Federal Work-Study Program
  (ARRA), 274–75
Office of Innovation and Improvement,
  247–58
  overview, *234,* 247–48, 258
  Arts in Education program, 254–55
  Charter Schools program, 248–49
  Credit Enhancement for Charter
    School Facilities program, 248–49
  D.C. School Choice Incentive
    Program, 257
  elimination savings, 257–58
  Fund for the Improvement of
    Education program, 256
  Investing in Innovation (i3) Fund
    program, 250
  Magnet Schools Assistance program,
    251
  Ready-To-Learn Television program,
    254–55
  School Leadership program, 253–54
  Teacher Quality Partnership Grants
    program, 251–52
  Transition to Teaching program,
    252–53
  Voluntary Public School Choice
    program, 255–56
Office of Inspector General audit of
  DOE federal real property inven-
  tory, 246
Office of Management and Budget
  (OMB)
  on DOE, 70, 233, 235

on Education Research, Development and Dissemination program, 242

on Federal Pell Grant Program, 273

on HEW, 69

on Impact Aid program, 267

on Magnet Schools program, 251

on Ready-To-Learn Television program, 254–55

on Research in Special Education program, 242–43

on Special Education Grants to States program, 259–60

on Twenty-First Century Community Learning Centers program, 244

See also Government Accountability Office (GAO)

Office of Management program, Office of the Secretary

overview, *224, 234,* 245

Federal Real Property Assistance Program, 245–46

Office of Postsecondary Education, 279–84

overview, *234,* 279

elimination savings and list of other programs, 282–84

Higher Education Institutional Aid program, 280

TRIO Upward Bound program, 280–82

Office of Special Education and Rehabilitative Services (OSERS), 258–64

overview, *234,* 258–59, 263–64, 268

elimination savings and list of other programs, 261–63

Rehabilitation Services–Vocational Rehabilitation Grants to States, 260–61

Special Education Grants to States, 259–60

Office of the Deputy Secretary programs, 246–71

overview, *224–25, 234, 246, 247*

Arts in Education, 254–55

D.C. School Choice Incentive Program, 257

Foreign Language Assistance Program, 264–65

Fund for the Improvement of Education, 256

Impact Aid, 267–68

Improving Teacher Quality State Grants, 266–67

Investing in Innovation (i3) Fund, 250

Magnet Schools Assistance, 251

Ready-To-Learn Television, 254–55

Rehabilitation Services–Vocational Rehabilitation Grants to States, 260–61

School Leadership, 253–54

Special Education Grants to States, 259–60

Teacher Quality Partnership Grants, 251–52

Title I Grants to Local Educational Agencies, 265–66

Transition to Teaching, 252–53

Voluntary Public School Choice, 255–56

Office of the Deputy Secretary subdivisions

Office of Elementary and Secondary Education, 265–71

Office of English Language Acquisition, Language Enhancement and Academic Achievement for Limited English Proficient Students, 264–65

Office of Innovation and Improvement, 247–58

Office of Special Education and Rehabilitative Services, 258–64

See also specific programs for additional program information

Office of the Secretary programs, 235–46

overview, *224, 234,* 236

Directed Grants and Awards, 238

Education Research, Development and Dissemination, 241–42

elimination savings, 240–41, 244–45

Federal Real Property Assistance Program, 245–46

Postsecondary Education Scholarships for Veteran's Dependents, 239–40

Race to the Top, 15, 112–16, 123, 237–38

Race to the Top Early Learning Challenge, 114, 236–37

Research in Special Education program, 242–43

Statewide Data Systems, 243

TEACH grants, 239

Twenty-First Century Community Learning Centers, 243–44

Office of the Secretary subdivisions

Immediate Office of the Secretary, 235–41

Institute of Education Sciences, 241–45

Office of Management, 245–46

See also specific programs for additional program information

Office of the Under Secretary programs, 271–84

overview, *225–26, 234*

Adult Education–Basic Grants to States, 277–78

Career and Technical Education–Basic Grants to States, 277

Federal Direct Student Loans, 123, 272

Federal Pell Grant Program, 273–74, 325–28

Federal Supplemental Education Opportunity Grants, 275

Federal Work-Study Program (ARRA), 274–75

Higher Education Institutional Aid, 280

TRIO Upward Bound, 280–82

Office of the Under Secretary subdivisions

Office of Federal Student Aid, 271–76

Office of Postsecondary Education, 279–84

Office of Vocational and Adult Education, 276–79

See also specific programs for additional program information

Office of Vocational and Adult Education, 276–79

overview, *234,* 276–77

Adult Education–Basic Grants to States program, 277–78

Career and Technical Education–Basic Grants to States program, 277

elimination savings, 278–79

Ohio, 309–10

OMB. *See* Office of Management and Budget (OMB)

Omnibus Budget Reconciliation Act
(1981), 87
on-budget education funding, 142–46,
143, 144, 147, 155
O'Neill, "Tip," 73
On Liberty (Mill), 10
Organization for Economic
Cooperation and Development
(OECD)
on Belgian schools' autonomy, 197
on Germany, 202, 203
government funding and private
schools, 190, *191*
on Hong Kong, 205
parental choice expansion, 182–83,
184, 186, 389*n*39
on schools competing for students,
180
See also Program for International
Student Assessment (PISA)
OSERS. *See* Office of Special
Education and Rehabilitative
Services (OSERS)
Owen, Robert, 16

P
Packard, Frederick A., 44
Packwood, Robert "Bob," 75, 298
Page, John, 28
Paine, Thomas, 9
parental choice
overview, xxiv, 304–6, 315–16,
334
and Bush, G.W., 104
colonial era and early Republic, 3,
7–16
competition among schools and
performance analysis, global,
179–82, *182,* 190–92, *191*
competitive effects of, 305

financial incentives for schools, 185,
186, 187, *188–89,* 189–90, 390*n*46
global models (*See* parental choice,
global models)
global reduction in, 181
magnet schools, 251
politicians' lack of trust in parents'
ability to educate their children
vs., 3, 16, 23, 54
Reagan on, 91
and student performance analysis,
global, 182–83, *184,* 185, *186,* 187,
188–89, 189–90, 389*n*39
United States Supreme Court ruling
in favor of, 316
See also charter schools; scholarships;
tuition tax credits; voucher system
parental choice blueprint for the future,
287–95
overview, 287
charter schools, 303–4, 406*n*99
D.C. Opportunity Scholarship
Program, 295–97
education savings accounts, 313–14
parent trigger laws, 310–12
predictions of success, 314–16
results without red tape, 304–6
the rise of vouchers, 287–92, 294–95
tuition tax credits, 187, 297–302, 305
virtual schools, 306–10, 315–16
voucher pilot program, 293–94
parental choice, global models
Australia, 195–96
Belgium, 197–98
Canada, 199–200
Chinese Taipei, 201–2
Germany, 203–4
Hong Kong, 205
Hungary, 207
Ireland, 208

Japan, 209–10
Macao, China, 212
The Netherlands, 214, 396*n*160
New Zealand, 216
Singapore, 218
South Korea, 211
Parent Revolution union, California, 312
parent trigger laws, 310–12
Partridge, Alden, 24
Pell, Claiborne, 326
Pell Grant Program, 273–74, 325–28
Pennsylvania, 12, 21
performance contracts of charter schools, 303–4
Perkins, Carl D., 95
Personal Learning Scholarship Account Program, Florida, 313–14
Philadelphia Bible Riots (1844), 21
Pierce, Franklin, 30
Pierce v. Society of Sisters, 316
Pike, Frederick A., 44–45
Pinckney, Charles, 4
PISA. *See* Program for International Student Assessment; Program for International Student Assessment (PISA)
"Plan for an Industrial University for the state of Illinois" (Turner), 24–25
Poland, 177, 185, *186, 188–89,* 190
politicization of education programs, 149
Politics, Markets, and America's Schools (Chubb and Moe), 314, 315
poor people/children
  and compulsory education laws, 9
  and demise of private schools, 15
  as focus of compulsory, public school campaign, 16–17

impact of immigration and economic status, global comparison, 175–79, *176, 178,* 388*n*22
lack of trust in ability to educate their children, 16
and NAEP results, 157–59, *158, 159*
state laws making provisions for, 12, 13
voucher system suggestion for, 9–10
Porter, Andrew C., 116–17
postsecondary education
  administrative costs from federal mandates, 87
  affordability issues, 272–75
  competition among schools, 318
  Congressional debates on national university, 4–7
  federal spending on, 112, 129, 136, 139–41, *139–41, 147,* 242
  human capital contracts between businesses and postsecondary students, 325
  impact of government subsidies, 322–23
  impact of student loan privatization, 324–25
  Postsecondary Education Scholarships for Veteran's Dependents, 239–40, 285
  privatization benefits, 317–18
  virtual schools, 306–7
  See also Office of Postsecondary Education
Poulson, Barry, 14
power-politics period (formalizing progressive theories), xxiii–xxiv
President's Commission on Privatization, 294
Priest, Serrano v., 290, 294
private schools
  overview, xxv

competition among, 14–15
demand for, 14
government funding and private
    schools, 190, *191*
laws on admitting poor children, 13
in Massachusetts, 15–16
parental choice programs competing
    with, 305
and PISA results, 180
privately operated public charter
    schools, 303–4, 406*n*99
religious schools, 8, 12
See also religious schools
Private Wealth and Public Education
    (Coons, Clune, and Sugarman),
    290
privatizing the federal role in educa-
    tion, 317–28
overview, 317–18
nongovernment agencies' interest, 230
Pell Grants, 327–28
Student Direct Loans, 323–25
Program for International Student
    Assessment (PISA)
overview, 175, 193
analysis of competition among
    schools and student performance,
    179–80
common-core standards results, 117
global comparison of OECD PISA
    results, *168*
immigration rate and socioeconomic
    background impact on scores,
    175–79, *176, 178*, 388*n*22
literary assessments, 165
performance increase on PISA
    correlated to GDP increase,
    174–75
and schools that compete for
    students, 190–92

Progress in International Reading
    Literary Study (PIRLS), 165, *166*
Progressive Education Association
    (PEA), 54
progressive pedagogical theories,
    xxiii–xxiv
*Proposal for a Poor Children's Bill of
    Rights, A* (Sizer and Whitten), 290
Protestant support for uniform educa-
    tion, 18–19, 19–21
provisional opt-out laws for NCLB,
    states', 108
Prussian education model, 18–19
public schools
    Boston's first citywide system, 11
    failure rate under NCLB, 121
    indoctrination mission, 20–21, 36–37
    privately operated public charter
        schools, 303–4, 406*n*99
    supporters in 1850s, 20–21
    supporters in early 1800s, 16–20
Pugh, George, E., 30, 35

R
Race to the Top
overview, 112–13, 237
and American Recovery and
    Reinvestment Act, 123
and Common Core State Standards
    Initiative, 15, 111, 114–19, 221
recommendation for dismantling, 238
Race to the Top Early Learning
    Challenge, 114, 236–37
Randall, Samuel J., 43–44, 329
RAND's multiyear study for Office of
    Education, 85, 105–6
Ready-To-Learn Television program,
    254–55
Reagan, Ronald
overview, 331

block grants to states, 87–88, 90, 92–93, 98

Department of Education Task Force, 90–93, 97, 369*n*59

on DOE as bureaucratic boondoggle, 86

DOE dismantling by downgrading plan, 90–91, 97

DOE elimination as goal, 87, 88–89, 92–93, 95, 97, 368*n*43

Excellence Commission, 93–98

on federal intervention in education, 88

federal involvement in eduation, 98–100

President's Commission on Privatization, 294

revitalizing American federalism, 91–92, 94

secretary of education supporting federal involvement in education, 89–90, 93–94, 97–98

and tuition tax credits, 298, 299, 300

and vouchers, 293, 294–95

regulatory burden of federal mandates, 83, 87, 131–33, 132, 367*n*41. *See also* testing regimes/evaluation mandates

Rehabilitation Services–Vocational Rehabilitation Grants to States, 260–61

religious schools, 8, 12. *See also* private schools

reorganization

efficiency as goal, 51, 60–61, 69

Federal Security Agency, 48

for recognizing importance of education, 63

as religion in Washington, refuted, 67–68

Report on the Condition of Public Instruction in Germany (Cousin), 18

Research in Special Education program, 242–43

Rhode Island, 8, 12–13

Ribicoff, Abraham

on debate about Education Department, 52

and DOE Organization Act, 57

on education department proposal, 58, 72

on importance of education, 55

and Senate Governmental Affairs Committee, 58–59, 66, 68, 72, 89

on status of education at federal level, 63–64, 68–69

and tuition tax-credit relief bill, 298

on unified direction for education, 66–67

Rice, Condoleezza, 289–90

Rickoff, Andrew Jackson, 38

Rights of Man, The (Paine), 9

Riley, Richard, 319–20

Roekel, Dennis Van, 107

Rogers, Andrew J., 42–43, 47, 70

Rosenthal, Benjamin S., 64–65, 67–68

Rotherham, Andrew J., xxii, 274

Roth, William, Jr., 58, 69–70, 75, 298

Royer, John, 60–61

Rubio, Marco, 122

Rush, Benjamin, 19

Russian Federation, *166,* 172–73, 174

Ryan, Leo J., 70

S

SAFRA (Student Aid and Fiscal Responsibility Act), 113, 123, 319

Sagues, Holly, 307–8

Samuelson, Robert, 326

San Jose, California, Alum Rock
School District voucher program,
293–94
Sasser, Jim, 70
Saulsbury, Willard, 46
savings. *See* elimination savings
Schmitt, Harrison, 58, 60–61
scholarships
D.C. Opportunity Scholarship
Program, 187, 248, 285, 295–97,
305, 403*n*45
Empowerment Scholarship
Accounts Program (2011,
Arizona), 313
Postsecondary Education
Scholarships for Veteran's
Dependents, 239–40, 285
tuition tax credit scholarships, 187,
302, 305, 315
school autonomy. *See* parental choice
school autonomy, global models
Australia, 195
Belgium, 197
Chinese Taipei, 201
Germany, 203
Hong Kong, 205
Hungary, 206–7
Ireland, 208
Japan, 209
Macao, China, 212
The Netherlands, 213–14
New Zealand, 215–16
and parental choice incentives for
schools, *188–89,* 189
Singapore, 217
South Korea, 211
School Choice Incentive Act (2003), 295
School Leadership program, 253–54
school year extension consideration,
177, 179

Schutz, Gabriela, 179, 180
Science magazine, 49
Seaborg, Glenn T., 97
seat-time requirements, 309–10
Selden, David, 292, 293
Self-Determination in Education Act
proposal (California, 1968), 290
Serrano v. Priest, 290, 294
Seybolt, Robert, 32
Shanghai, China, *166, 168,* 177, *178*
Shanker, Albert, 95, 218, 303
Shen-Keng Yang, 201
Sherman, Roger, 28
Simmons-Harris, Zelman v., 302
Singapore
overview, 216–18
IEA TIMSS results, *167, 169*
parental choice offerings, global
comparison, 183, *184, 186*
school autonomy and parental
choice, *188–89,* 190
schools competing for students,
182, *182*
socioeconomic background and
PISA scores, 177, *178*
students' performance levels, 173
virtual schools, 308
Sizer, Theodore, 290
Smith, Adam, 9, 31–33, 288
Smith-Hughes Act (1917), 47–48,
64*n*1
Smith-Level Act (1914), 47–48
Smith, Samuel Harrison, 19
Society for the Propagation of the
Gospel, 8
Society of Sisters, Pierce v., 316
Souder, Mark, 104–5
South Carolina, 301–2
South Korea, 210–11
Space Race and scientific education, 79

special education
    and assessments, 156, 386*n*59
    and AYP proficiency targets, 104
    Education for All Handicapped
        Children Act (1974), 84
    ESEA funding for, 84
    Individuals with Disabilities
        Education Act (IDEA), 84,
        112–14, 259, 260
    Research in Special Education
        program, 242–43
    Special Education Grants to States,
        259–60
    and Title I recipient schools, 82
    See also Office of Special Education
        and Rehabilitative Services
special interest groups, 65, 76, 93, 118,
    332. *See also* unions for teachers
Spellings, Margaret, 107–8, 109, 320
spending. *See* educational spending
Stafford, Robert, 98
standards, prediction of, 61. *See also*
    global performance; National
    Assessment of Educational Pro-
    gress; Program for International
    Student Assessment (PISA);
    testing regimes/evaluation
    mandates
State Fiscal Stabilization Fund, 112–14
states
    and administrative costs of federal
        mandates, 83, 87, 131–33, 132,
        367*n*41
    and charter schools, 303–4, 406*n*99
    and Common Core initiative, 115,
        116
    constitutions of, 9, 10–14
    crafting individual education
        programs, 223, 226, 228, 229, 230
    as education reform leaders, 101–2

education system remedies that don't
        work for states, 221–22
    federal education funding
        NDEA Title III, 79–80
    federal powers vs., 33–34
    federal requirements for education
        funding, 47–48, 61
    inducements for school system
        maintenance, 39
    need-based financial aid programs,
        328
    provisional opt-out laws for NCLB,
        108
    and Race to the Top funding, 113
    sovereignty and governments of, 33
    Special Education Grants to States,
        259–60
    state-federal relationship, 33–36, 37
    teacher encouragement programs, 239
    and tuition tax credits, 300, 301–2, 305
    virtual schools, 306–10, 315–16
    Vocational Rehabilitation State
        Grants, 260–61
    voucher and tax-credit scholarships,
        187
    See also federal involvement in
        eduation; testing regimes/
        evaluation mandates
States' Impact on Federal Education
    Policy Project, 88, 98–99, 102,
    111–12
Statewide Data Systems program, 243
Stevens, David, 52
Stevens, Ted, 75
Stone, Michael J., 27–28
Stotsky, Sandra, 118–19
Stroufe, Gerald E., 292
student aid
    Federal Work-Study Program
        (ARRA), 274–75

Student Aid and Fiscal Responsibility Act (SAFRA), 113, 123, 319

See also grants; Office of Federal Student Aid; student loans

student loans
DOE as sole lender, 114, 146, *147*, 319–21
DOE profit on, 285, 322
Federal Direct Student Loans program, 123, 272
Federal Perkins Loans, 318–19
funding for, 146
GAO on, 320–21
and interest rates, 319, 320
and Obama, 123
privatizing strategy for Student Direct Loans, 323–25
Student Direct Loans, 318–23
tax-exempt education savings accounts vs., 99

students
and education challenges, 175–79, *176, 178*, 388*n*22
preparing for 21st Century global economy, 181
See also immigration; poor people/children

Sugarman, Stephen D., 290
Swan, William D., 19–20, 338*n*78
Sweden IEA PIRLS results, *166*
Switzerland
educational spending, 172
immigration rate and PISA scores, *176*, 177
parental choice incentives for schools, 185, *186*, 187
socioeconomic background and PISA scores, 177, *178*

T
Taipei, Chinese, 200–202
Talbert, Kent D., 116
Task Force on Parent Involvement and Choice, National Governor's Association, 294
tax credit scholarships, 187, 302, 305, 315
tax credits for tuition, 187, 297–302, 305, 315
taxpayers, returning income taxes to, 222–23, 228–29, 230–31, 333–34
teachers
improving teacher quality, 133, 144–45, 251–52, 266–67
online teachers, 309
opposition to vouchers, 292
Teachers National Field Task Force on the Improvement and Reform of American Education, 294
Transition to Teaching program, 252–53
unions, 292
See also American Federation of Teachers (AFT); National Education Association (NEA)

Teach for America, 230
TEACH grants, 239
testing regimes/evaluation mandates
administrative costs of federal mandates, 83, 87, 131–33, *132*, 367*n*41
AYP mandates, 104–5, 108, 121, 131
Common Core State Standards Initiative, 15, 111, 114–19, 221, 331
for D.C. Opportunity Scholarship Program, 296
inauguration in ESEA, 98–99
international achievement tests, 117
National Education Goals Panel, 101, 372*n*102

NDEA vs. NCLB, 81
science results, 153, 385n58
seat-time requirements, 309–10
state reactions to NCLB mandates, 106–8
waivers for ESEA mandates, 120–21, 122, 123
Texas, 13, 14
Thompson, Frank, Jr., 56
Thurmond, Strom, 75
Time magazine, 97–98
Title I Grants to Local Educational Agencies, 265–66
Title I of ESEA: Is It Helping Poor Children? (Martin and McClure), 83
Transition to Teaching program, 252–53
Trends in International Mathematics and Science Study (TIMSS), 165, 166, *167, 169,* 180, 195
trigger laws, parent, 310–12
TRIO programs, 281
TRIO Upward Bound program, 280–82
Trumbull, Lyman, 45–46
Tucker, Marc, 120
tuition tax credits, 187, 297–302, 305, 315
tuition tax credit scholarships, 187, 302, 305, 315
Tuition Tax Relief Act (1978), 298
Turner, Jonathan Baldwin, 24–25
Twenty-First Century Community Learning Centers program, 244–45

U
uniform education supporters, 16–17, 18–19, 19–21

unions for teachers, 292. *See also* American Federation of Teachers (AFT); National Education Association (NEA)
Unitarian support for private schools, 15–16
United Kingdom
government funding and private schools, 190, *191*
school autonomy and parental choice, 187, *188–89,* 190
United States Department of Education. *See entries beginning with* "Department of Education"
United States, global comparisons
government funding and private schools, 190, *191*
parental choice incentives for schools, 185, *186,* 187
parental choice offerings, global comparison, 183, *184, 186*
PISA results and schools that compete for students, global analysis, 190–92
school autonomy and parental choice, 187, *188–89,* 189
schools competing for students, 181, *182*
teaching hours per school year, 177
United States Supreme Court
Arizona Christian School Tuition Organization v. Winn, on tax-credit scholarship program, 302
limitations on Congress's spending power, 59
Mueller v. Allen, on tuition tax credits, 301
Pierce v. Society of Sisters, on parental choice, 316

Zelman v. Simmons-Harris, on vouchers, 302
universal access, 17–18, 288. *See also* parental choice
Unsafe School Choice Option, 105
Upward Bound Math-Science, 281
US Chamber of Commerce, 289, 401*n*11
USDOE. *See entries beginning with* "Department of Education"
US General Services Administration's Federal Real Property Council, 246
Utah, 107–8, 309

V

Van Roekel, Dennis, 107
Vedder, Richard, 273, 326
Veterans Affairs Department, 240
Veterans Upward Bound, 281
Vietnam, 177, *178*
Virginia, 12
virtual schools, 306–10, 315–16
Voluntary Public School Choice program, 255–56
voucher system
    overview, 287–89, 294–95
    Alum Rock School District pilot program, 293–94
    in America 2000 program, 101
    feasibility study, 291
    in Germany, 204
    global comparison, 185, 187, *188–89,* 389*n*39
    savings from, 305–6
    in states of the United States, 187, 311, 315
    support for, 9–10, 289–92, 401*n*11
    See also D.C. Opportunity Scholarship Program

W

Wahlberg, Herbert J., 288
waivers for ESEA mandates under Obama, 120–21, 122, 123
Walberg, Herbert J., 314–15
Walker, Robert S., 72
Wall Street Journal, 290
War on Poverty, Johnson's, 81–82
Washington, George, 27, 28
Watson, John, 307
Waxman, Henry, 64–65, 67–68
Wealth of Nations, The (Smith), 9, 31–33
Weiss, Ted, 64–65, 67–68, 74
Wells, Frank, 311–12
West, Martin R., 179
White, E. E., 39
Whitefish Bay, Wisconsin, 83
White House Conference on Youth (1971), 291–92
White, S. H., 37–38
Whitten, Philip, 290
Wilde, Richard Henry, 7
Williams, Anthony, 403*n*45
Wilson, W. Stephen, 117
Winn, Arizona Christian School Tuition Organization v., 302
Wisconsin, 301–2
Woessmann, Ludger, 179, 180
Women's Educational Equity program, ESEA, 149
Work-Study Program (ARRA), 274–75
Wurman, Ze'ev, 118–19

Y

Yates, Richard, 46
Young, Julie, 307

Z

Zelman v. Simmons-Harris, 302

About the Author

VICKI E. ALGER is Research Fellow at the Independent Institute. She is also a Senior Fellow at the Fraser Institute, headquartered in Vancouver, British Columbia, and the Independent Women's Forum in Washington, DC. She is president and CEO of Vicki Murray & Associates LLC in Scottsdale, Arizona.

Alger's research focuses on education reforms that promote a competitive education marketplace and increase parents' control over their children's education. She is the author of more than forty education policy studies, co-author of *Lean Together: An Agenda for Smarter Government, Stronger Communities, and More Opportunities for Women*, *Short-Circuited: The Challenges Facing the Online Learning Revolution in California*, and *Not as Good as You Think: Why the Middle Class Needs School Choice*, as well as associate producer of the documentary "Not as Good as You Think: Myth of the Middle Class School."

Alger has advised the US Department of Education on public school choice and higher education reform. She has also advised education policymakers in nearly forty states and England, provided expert testimony before state legislative education committees, and served on two national accountability task forces. Alger's research helped advance four parental-choice voucher and tax-credit scholarship programs in Arizona, as well as the state's first higher education voucher, and she provided expert affidavits as part of the successful legal defense of educational choice programs for low-income, foster-care, and disabled children.

Alger's research also inspired the introduction of the most school choice bills in California history—five in all—and her research was used as part of the successful legal defense by the Institute for Justice of the country's first tax-credit scholarship program in the US Supreme Court (*Arizona Christian School Tuition Organization v. Winn*). Her research and commentary on education policy have been widely published and cited in leading public-policy outlets such as Harvard University's Program on Education Policy and Governance, *Education Week,* and the *Chronicle of Higher Education*, in addition to national news media outlets, including *The Wall Street Journal*, *Investor's Business Daily*, *Forbes*, *Fortune*, *Human Events*, *La Opinión*, *USA Today*, and *US News & World Report*. She has also appeared on the Fox News Channel, local ABC, CBS, NBC, and PBS affiliates, and news radio programs across the country.

Prior to her career in education policy, Alger taught college-level courses in American politics, English composition and rhetoric, and early British literature. She has lectured at numerous American universities, including the US Military Academy, West Point. Alger received her Ph.D. in political philosophy from the Institute of Philosophic Studies at the University of Dallas, where she was an Earhart Foundation Fellow. Alger lives in Arizona with her husband, David.

Independent Institute Studies in Political Economy

THE ACADEMY IN CRISIS | *Ed. by John W. Sommer*

AGAINST LEVIATHAN | *Robert Higgs*

AMERICAN HEALTH CARE | *Ed. by Roger D. Feldman*

ANARCHY AND THE LAW | *Ed. by Edward P. Stringham*

ANTITRUST AND MONOPOLY | *D. T. Armentano*

AQUANOMICS | *Ed. by B. Delworth Gardner & Randy T Simmons*

ARMS, POLITICS, AND THE ECONOMY | *Ed. by Robert Higgs*

A BETTER CHOICE | *John C. Goodman*

BEYOND POLITICS | *Randy T Simmons*

BOOM AND BUST BANKING | *Ed. by David Beckworth*

CALIFORNIA DREAMING | *Lawrence J. McQuillan*

CAN TEACHERS OWN THEIR OWN SCHOOLS? | *Richard K. Vedder*

THE CHALLENGE OF LIBERTY | *Ed. by Robert Higgs & Carl P. Close*

THE CHE GUEVARA MYTH AND THE FUTURE OF LIBERTY | *Alvaro Vargas Llosa*

CHOICE | *Robert P. Murphy*

THE CIVILIAN AND THE MILITARY | *Arthur A. Ekirch, Jr.*

CRISIS AND LEVIATHAN, 25TH ANNIVERSARY EDITION | *Robert Higgs*

CUTTING GREEN TAPE | *Ed. by Richard L. Stroup & Roger E. Meiners*

THE DECLINE OF AMERICAN LIBERALISM | *Arthur A. Ekirch, Jr.*

DELUSIONS OF POWER | *Robert Higgs*

DEPRESSION, WAR, AND COLD WAR | *Robert Higgs*

THE DIVERSITY MYTH | *David O. Sacks & Peter A. Thiel*

DRUG WAR CRIMES | *Jeffrey A. Miron*

ELECTRIC CHOICES | *Ed. by Andrew N. Kleit*

THE EMPIRE HAS NO CLOTHES | *Ivan Eland*

THE ENTERPRISE OF LAW | *Bruce L. Benson*

ENTREPRENEURIAL ECONOMICS | *Ed. by Alexander Tabarrok*

FAILURE | *Vicki E. Alger*

FINANCING FAILURE | *Vern McKinley*

THE FOUNDERS' SECOND AMENDMENT | *Stephen P. Halbrook*

FUTURE | *Ed. by Robert M. Whaples, Christopher J. Coyne, & Michael C. Munger*

GLOBAL CROSSINGS | *Alvaro Vargas Llosa*

GOOD MONEY | *George Selgin*

GUN CONTROL IN THE THIRD REICH | *Stephen P. Halbrook*

HAZARDOUS TO OUR HEALTH? | *Ed. by Robert Higgs*

HOT TALK, COLD SCIENCE | *S. Fred Singer*

HOUSING AMERICA | *Ed. by Randall G. Holcombe & Benjamin Powell*

JUDGE AND JURY | *Eric Helland & Alexander Tabarrok*

LESSONS FROM THE POOR | *Ed. by Alvaro Vargas Llosa*

LIBERTY FOR LATIN AMERICA | *Alvaro Vargas Llosa*

LIBERTY FOR WOMEN | *Ed. by Wendy McElroy*

LIVING ECONOMICS | *Peter J. Boettke*

MAKING POOR NATIONS RICH | *Ed. by Benjamin Powell*

MARKET FAILURE OR SUCCESS | *Ed. by Tyler Cowen & Eric Crampton*

THE MIDAS PARADOX | *Scott Sumner*

MONEY AND THE NATION STATE | *Ed. by Kevin Dowd & Richard H. Timberlake, Jr.*

NATURE UNBOUND | *Randy T Simons, Ryan M. Yonk, and Kenneth J. Sim*

NEITHER LIBERTY NOR SAFETY | *Robert Higgs*

THE NEW HOLY WARS | *Robert H. Nelson*

NO WAR FOR OIL | *Ivan Eland*

OPPOSING THE CRUSADER STATE | *Ed. by Robert Higgs & Carl P. Close*

OUT OF WORK | *Richard K. Vedder & Lowell E. Gallaway*

PARTITIONING FOR PEACE | *Ivan Eland*

PATENT TROLLS | *William J. Watkins, Jr.*

PLOWSHARES AND PORK BARRELS | *E. C. Pasour, Jr. & Randal R. Rucker*

A POVERTY OF REASON | *Wilfred Beckerman*

THE POWER OF HABEAS CORPUS IN AMERICA | *Anthony Gregory*

PRICELESS | *John C. Goodman*

PROPERTY RIGHTS | *Ed. by Bruce L. Benson*

THE PURSUIT OF JUSTICE | *Ed. by Edward J. López*

RACE & LIBERTY IN AMERICA | *Ed. by Jonathan Bean*

RECARVING RUSHMORE | *Ivan Eland*

RECLAIMING THE AMERICAN REVOLUTION | *William J. Watkins, Jr.*

REGULATION AND THE REAGAN ERA | *Ed. by Roger E. Meiners & Bruce Yandle*

RESTORING FREE SPEECH AND LIBERTY ON CAMPUS | *Donald A. Downs*

RESURGENCE OF THE WARFARE STATE | *Robert Higgs*

RE-THINKING GREEN | *Ed. by Robert Higgs & Carl P. Close*

RISKY BUSINESS | *Ed. by Lawrence S. Powell*

SECURING CIVIL RIGHTS | *Stephen P. Halbrook*

STRANGE BREW | *Douglas Glen Whitman*

STREET SMART | *Ed. by Gabriel Roth*

TAKING A STAND | *Robert Higgs*

TAXING CHOICE | *Ed. by William F. Shughart, II*

THE TERRIBLE 10 | *Burton A. Abrams*

THAT EVERY MAN BE ARMED | *Stephen P. Halbrook*

TO SERVE AND PROTECT | *Bruce L. Benson*

VIETNAM RISING | *William Ratliff*

THE VOLUNTARY CITY | *Ed. by David T. Beito, Peter Gordon, & Alexander Tabarrok*

WINNERS, LOSERS & MICROSOFT | *Stan J. Liebowitz & Stephen E. Margolis*

WRITING OFF IDEAS | *Randall G. Holcombe*

For further information:

510-632-1366 • orders@independent.org • http://www.independent.org/publications/books/